D1871669

THE ENCYCLOPAEDIA OF CRICKET

(IN TWO VOLUMES)

Edited by
YOGRAJ THANI

With a Foreword by
Dr. NAROTTAM PURI

VOL. I

GIAN PUBLISHING HOUSE
New Delhi-110002

GIAN PUBLISHING HOUSE
4-C Ansari Road, Daryaganj
New Delhi-110002

All rights reserved with the publishers.

ISBN 81-212-0321-x Set
81-212-0348 Vol.I
81-212-0349-x Vol.II

PRINTED IN INDIA 1991

Published by Mrs. Gayatri Garg for Gian Publishing House, New Delhi-110002.
Printed at Goyal Offset Printers, Delhi.

Compiled by

Lokesh Thani

Statistics by

Vivek Thani
Ekta Gothi
Kishore Sharma

Photographs by

Cricket Yug

Lay-out Artist

Vinod Gola

References

Khel Sahitya Kendra

FOREWORD

History begins, and can only begin, when you have some kind of a written record. Before that all is prehistory no matter what other evidences you can produce, from coins,pottery,living habits, and so on.This does not mean that it is impossible to make a reconstruction of what was going on before history begins: indeed much has to be added to historical written records themselves before true history can be narrated.But, whereas the speculation that any historian has to make has to be complementary to the written record which survives, before the written record begins speculation is on its own.

It is on its own in a relative way:suppose the written record of a town starts many years after the foundation of that town - we do not start thinking that nothing can be said about what happened the day before the first written record.People must have been writing, reading, eating, sleeping, buying, selling, praying,as much before the first surviving written record as after.We can extend back: we can bring in all the other evidences:we can point to ruins discovered far below the present foundations which show that the town existed hundreds of years before the first written record:we can judge from the town's situation how and why the town might have been founded, and with luck, we may find somewhere else another written record which does not,at first sight,refer to this town we are studying.There is an element of doubt : there must always be this element in prehistory.Nevertheless, a careful and imaginative historian may be able to build such an edifice that only a quite fundamental later discovery could over-turn it. That happened with the decipherment of Linear B.

It is doubtful if any such solid edifice can be built about the prehistory of cricket,or even a framework erected on proven foundations.But there is a good deal more evidence available now-a-days than even in the recent past, and a wholly plausible and coherent theory can be put forward even if there are large gaps in it. The soundness of the theory will only be apparent as and when new discoveries are found to tend to confirm it: if they do not,something else will have to be thought up.

The concept of a volume containing the biographies of every notable English cricketer is not a new one.Arthur Haygarth, whilst at Harrow in the 1840s began a search for famous players of the past, a search which was to last a lifetime.Haygarth died in 1903 and his work was continued by F.S.Ashley- Cooper,who devoted the fifteenth and final volume of Haygarth's monumental *Scores and Biographies*. The task of researching and collating biographical material on English cricketers,other than contemporary players, more or less died with Ashley-Cooper, except for certain specialist areas, such as specific clubs or families.

When the Association of Cricket Statisticians was formed in 1973, it was found that a number of members had an interest in reviving the type of biographical research formerly undertaken by Haygarth and Ashley-Cooper, and had in fact been quietly ferreting out details of the cricketers which had eluded their predecessors.The Association was anxious to continue this research ànd to try to direct the footstep of the researchers in order to avoid duplication of effort. It was decided to publish brief biographical details of English first class cricketers on a country by country basis.Before much progress could be made, however it was necessary to solve a problem that had confounded cricket historians and statisticians for fifty years, the compilation of a precise list of English first class matches,for without such a list it was impossible to compose a list of English first class cricketers.Although the modern concept of first class cricket evolved during the 1860 s, it was not until 1947 that a 'first class'match was officially defined.For about 80 years therefore, the decision as to which match to include in the season's first class averages was largely in the hands of sporting press, though since 1890 the MCC had decided which counites could boast first class status.

As with any two volumes of this size the greatest difficulty is knowing what to include and what to leave out, and this applies particularly to biographies. Indeed one wonders whether or not to include any biographies at all,for no matter how many are put in one is certain to be criticised for leaving so and so out.Criticism of these omissions, however, means very little,for, in many cases,the reasons for choosing one player or another are based only on matters of personal opinion. Even then all the outstanding players have been included. This may be pointed out that in compiling these biographies they have been written from a statistician's point of view, and they are largely based on figures of outstanding achievements in the highest class of cricket,i.e.,Tests.However,not all great players have been Test stars, and many others, before and since Test cricket commenced, have been included.

I am certain that this book will have a very successful innings in all cricket playing countries.

Dr. NAROTTAM PURI

INTRODUCTION

The soldiers,sailors, colonial administrators and traders who took cricket from Britain and spread its gospel around the world in the eighteenth century could have had little idea of the immense impact that their game would have on lands as diverse and remote as Australia, New Zealand, India, Sri Lanka, Pakistan, South Africa and the Caribbean.

Well over a century later, cricket is a world game, struggling against many odds but always, in the final analysis, capturing the hearts of those who play and watch it. The problems of the South African controversy, slow over-rates, certain Test captains apparently forgetting about the spectators, and the occasional bouts of loutish behaviour by one or two international players, are all obstacles which cricket has yet to overcome. But in the end, the game will survive all these crises, as it has survived all others.

This book is not primarily concerned with the controversies of the game but look at the origin of cricket in each Test-playing country (including South Africa which has been denied a Test now for over a decade), charts the progress of each Test Player and Test Team, and includes Terms, Laws and Records, etc.

Formation of International Cricket Conference

The techniques, rules and regulations having been established by the Merylebone Cricket Club, the official matches were started between clubs in England. In 1873, the first official County Championship Matches were started. By 1877, England and Australia started touring each other's countries. In March 1877 the first official Test Match was played between England and Australia. In 1909, Imperial Cricket Conference was formulated and cricket became internationally popular. The ICC or Imperial Cricket Conference membership was confined to the British Commonwealth countries only. New Zealand, India and West Indies by virtue of being British Commonwealth countries became the members of I.C.C. in 1926, and Pakistan was granted membership in 1952. Later, in the year 1956 with a view to accommodating the countries outside the Commonwealth, the name Imperial Cricket Conference was changed to International Cricket Conference. Now the associated members of the I.C.C. are - The U.S.A., Denmark, Holland, Hong Kong, New Guinea, East Africa, Gibralter and Panua.

Introduction of Cricket in India

Cricket was introduced in India by the Britishers residing here around the middle of the nineteenth century. However, the game became popular through the efforts of a small affluent community of Parsis,who were economically as well as socially in closer contact with the Britishers. The Parsis, after learning the game started playing frequent matches with Britishers in Bombay.The Parsis then formed several clubs in Bombay - the most popular of them were the Oriental Parsi Club and the Baronet Club. These clubs were formed as early as 1848.

By the year 1886, the Parsis perfected themselves and won several local matches against the Britishers. The same year,the Parsis set on a tour of England under the captaincy of Dr.D.N.Patel.The Indian team went on another tour to England in 1888 under the captaincy of Mr.E.P.Kanga.Though on their first tour Indians did not do well, but on their second tour they left behind a good impression of their cricket potential.

In 1892, Lord Hawke visited Bombay around Christmas time with his strong team of Amateur XI consisting of players like C.F.Vernon, Gibson, A.Hill, Sir Stanley Jackson, Hazeltine, C.G.Wright and others. The Parsi Team played very well and won the match against Lord Hawke's team but unfortunately lost the return match played in the same week by a small margin of only seven runs.

Early History of Cricket in India

On going through the records of the earlier history of cricket in India, it is observed that the first cricket club was established as early as 1872. The Calcutta Cricket Club claims to be a much older club than the Parsi Club of Bombay. The very first official match organised by the officers of the East India Company was played in Calcutta on 18th and 19th of January, 1804 between the old Etonians and the Rest of Calcutta. Richard Walpole, the grandson of the English Prime Minister, Sir Robert Walpole, also played in the match. Another highlight of the match was the first century in India by R. Vansittart.

Gradually several Cricket Clubs were established all over the country not only by the Parsis of Bombay, but also by the Hindus and the Muslims. Most of Indian Nationals began to take interest in the game. Youth in India today is more cricket conscious than ever before. In fact, the youngsters both in the urban and suburban areas and even in remote villages take keen interest in the game which is evident from the crowd of people gathered around a radio to listen to the running commentary of the matches played and people watching the cricket matches telecast by T.V.

Although, we can see the enthusiasm and interest in the game among youth all over the country, yet it is Bombay Presidency which is regarded as the seat of Indian cricket. Even today Bombay is considered the nursery of the Indian cricket and has produced a large number of Test Cricketers. We reckon that the earlier victorious teams consisted of six cricketers from Bombay alone. They are Sunil Gavaskar, Wadekar, Mankad, Engineer, Sardesai and Eknath Solkar.

The credit of prosperity of cricket in Bombay, to a great extent, goes to Lord Harris, the Governor of Bombay from 1890 to 1893. Lord Harris was not only an efficient administrator but also a great cricketer. He often invited leading cricketers of Bombay to play against his team. Lord Harris loved cricket and his own participation in it made the game very popular. He became a respected and a lovable Governor among Indians during those days of British rule, when the Governors were thought of as officials and administrators necessarily aloof from the general Indian elite. Especially due to his attitude on the cricket field, all players began to be regarded as equal regardless of colour.

Lord Harris did a lot to develop the game and it is actually due to his efforts and interest, that Parsi-Presidency contests started in 1892. Both Bombay and Poona Gymkhana Clubs joined together to form a team to play against English cricketers. Every one match was played in Bombay and the return encounter at Poona. These matches were very popular and attracted large number of spectators from 1892 upto 1906.

Among the heroes of the Presidency matches are Colonel K.M.Mistry, stylish left handed batsman and fast bowler; Major R.M.Poore, tall forceful batsman; Colonel Creig of Hampshire, all-rounder; Captain Newnham, M.R.Jardine and many others.

Origin of Cricket

We come across several theories regarding the origin of cricket - yet what we play today is initially known to be played in England. Modern cricket has developed from a crude game which was played as early as the 12th century. Records show that cricket was played in Kent as far back as 1300 A.D. At that time it was a game of shepherds who used to play a game as a pastime while their cattle grazed in the fields.

At the turn of the eighteenth century, this pastime of shepherds was adopted by the affluent class in England and by 1760 a club was founded to standardise the techniques of batting and bowling. The club was called the Hambledon Club. It brought out the rules and regulations of the game. Through the efforts of the Hembledon Club the game started getting popular and by the end of the century, cricket became a very popular sport in England.

The ever-increasing popularity of the game gave birth to the Merylebone Cricket Club with its headquarters at Lord's London. The Merylebone Cricket Club, now more commonly known as the MCC, formulated fresh rules and regulations of cricket in 1835. Up till 1860, only underarm bowling was introduced, with a view to making big changes in the batting techniques. MCC then decided about the surface (or pitch as it is known today) and also about the proper care and preparation of wickets. It has since been the recognized authority on all cricket affairs.

The game was originally played on ordinary English meadow-land, with long uncut grass for the outfield, and only the actual pitch was scythed. Later, light wooden rollers were used on the wicket, sheep were used to keep the grass down to a reasonable height and a boundary line was marked all round the field. These improvements made for much higher scoring, because not only did the ball run over the ground much easier but also the batsmen did not become so tired when it became no longer necessary to run out the 'boundaries'. The next step was the inclusion of a rule which allowed the actual pitch to be brushed, swept and rolled after each innings. Later still, the hand mower made another big improvement, first to the state of the wicket and then to the whole outfield. The scoring was originally done by a 'notcher', who cut a notch in a stick whenever a run was scored. Village cricket in Kent and Sussex was probably the first true home of the game, which steadily grew and developed, in spite of a rather dark period when a considerable amount of gambling and wagering on results took place.

In the early days, it must be remembered, all bowling was underhand, but in 1825 'round arm' bowling was permitted. This means that the ball could be delivered at any angle so long as the hand was not above the elbow. The chief result of this was that bowling became faster but less accurate, and many balls were so erratic that they beat both the wicket-keeper and his assistant, the 'long-stop'.After 1865,when 'over-hand'bowling was legalized, 'lobs' and 'round arm' bowling gradually died out. Most of the players were still classed as either batsmen or bowlers. It was not until the end of the 19th century that the 'all-rounder'began to appear, with a consequent stiffening of the middle of the batting order.

The actual origin of over-arm bowling is uncertain, although a certain John Willes of Sutton Valence is often given the credit for discovering it. It is said that he got the idea from his sister when she bowled-or probably threw-at him in practice. Orthodox bowling at the time was still underhand, and when, in one important match at Lord's, Willes was no-balled for his new action, the story goes that he flew into such a temper that he jumped on his horse, rode out of the ground and never played cricket again. Yet in spite of incidents like that, the bowling arm got gradually higher and higher until no umpire dared to no-ball the bowlers.

While the bats and other accessories have altered greatly during the last hundred years, there has been little change in the actual balls. Except for the finish and the more polished appearance, a modern cricket ball is almost identical to the ones used at the beginning of the 19th century. In fact, in 1811, a Mr. Duke of Penshurst in Kent stated that his family had been making cricket balls for 250 years-crimson leather covers over hemp or hair stuffing - so that takes us back to about 1560. Before that, tennis balls were used for cricket when it was played indoors by both ladies and gentlemen; the poorer folk played it outside in the fields, where the tree 'stumps' would make a handy wicket. This applied particularly in the regions of the Kent and Sussex ports,where the shipbuilders of those days had cut down so many trees.

It is a far cry from those primitive days to our highly organized modern cricket matches.The laws and conditions of play are constantly changing as the years go by, but the spirit of the game remains unchangeable.

YOGRAJ THANI

A

ACB
Australian Cricket Board.

ACU
Association of Cricket Umpires.

AWCC
Australian Women's Cricket Council.

A'BECKETT EDWARD LAMBERT
Australia (born 1907) - A right-handed batsman and medium-fast bowler. He played for Victoria. In his first class career he made, 1,636 runs including 2 centuries and took 105 wickets.

ABDUL QADIR

Test Record - 4 Tests, 143 runs (Av. 20.42), 3 wickets (Av. 105.66) and 4 catches.

ABDUL KADIR
Pakistan (born 1944) - A wicket-keeper and sound right-handed batsman. He played for Karachi. In his first class career he made, 1,523 runs including 1 century and 59 dismissals (46 ct, 13 st).
Test Record - 4 Tests, 272 runs (Av. 34.00) and 1 stumping.

ABDUL QADIR
Pakistan (born 1955) - A stocky leg-spin and googly bowler. A useful right-handed batsman. He scored a century in his second first-class match and has two Test-match fifties to his credit. He plays for Lahore and Habib Bank. In his first class career he made, 2,824 runs including 1 century,took 719 wickets (Av. 21.51).
Test Record - 59 Tests, 967 runs (Av. 15.59),224 wickets (Av. 31.74) and 15 catches.

ABEL ROBERT
England (1857-1936) - A diminutive opening batsman, famous to be afraid of fast bowling, but mastered all types of attack. Useful slow bowler. He played for Surrey. In his first class career he made, 33,124 runs including 74 centuries and took 263 wickets.
Test Record - 13 Tests, 744 runs (Av. 37.20) including 2 centuries, 13 catches.

ABID ALI SYED
India (born 1941) - A right-handed batsman and right-arm medium-fast bowler. Test debut on December 23, 1967 against Australia at the age of 25 years and 104 days. Scores on Test debut were 33 and 33 in the first Test at Adelaide. Performed the best bowling feat on debut for India by capturing 6 wickets for 55 runs. D.R.Doshi joined him for this feat in 1979-80 at Madras. Last Test of the career played against West Indies in December 1974. Scores on last Test appearance were 8 and 4 in the second Test at New Delhi. Age at the time of retirement from Test cricket was 32 years and 96 days. He played for Hyderabad. In his first class career he made, 8,741 runs and took 397 wickets.

Test Record - 29 Tests, 1,018 runs (Av. 20.36), 47 wickets (Av. 42.12) and 33 catches.

ACCOUNT
Open one's account to score the first runs of one's innings.

ACHONG ELLIS EDGAR
West Indies (born 1904) - Of Chinese extraction, 'Puss' Achong was a slow left-arm bowler of immaculate length. He played for Trinidad. In his first class career he made, 503 runs and took 110 wickets.
Test Record - 6 Tests, 81 runs (Av. 8.10), 8 wickets (Av. 47.25) and 6 catches.

ACROSS
Of the ball moving away from the batsman at a considerable angle to the line of the wickets.

ADCOCK NEIL AMWIN TREHARNE
South Africa (born 1931) - He is a right-arm medium-fast bowler with a smooth, rhythmic run. He played for Transvaal and Natal. In his first class career he made, 451 runs and took 405 wickets.
Test Record - 26 Tests, 146 runs (Av. 5.40), 104 wickets (Av. 21.10) and 4 catches.

ADHIKARI HEMCHANDRA RAMCHANDRA
India (born 1919) - A right-handed batsman and right-arm leg-break bowler. Test debut on November 28, 1947 against Australia at the age of 28 years and 106 days. Scores on Test debut were 8 and 13 in the first Test at Brisbane. Last Test of the career played in February 1959 against West Indies. Scores on last appearance in Test were 63 and 40 in the fifth Test at New Delhi. Age at the time of retirement from Test cricket was 39 years and 179 days. First and only century in Test 114 not out scored against the West Indies on November 13,1948 in the first Test at New Delhi at the age of 29 years and 91 days. His partnership of 109 runs with Ghulam Ahmed for the 10th wicket in the first Test against Pakistan at New Delhi in 1952-53 is the highest for 10th wicket for India against any country . Led India in only one Test against the West Indies in the fifth Test at New Delhi in 1958-59 series at the age of 39 years and 172 days and scored 63 and 40 runs. He played for Baroda. In his first class career he made, 8,628 runs including 18 centuries.
Test Record - 21 Tests, 872 runs (Av. 31.12), 3 wickets (Av.27.33) and 8 catches.

AFAQ HUSSAIN
Pakistan (born 1939) - A useful right-arm off-break bowler and batsman. He played for Karachi. In his first class career he made, 1,448 runs including 1 century,took 214 wickets.
Test Record - 2 Tests, 64 runs and 2 catches.

AFTAB BALOCH
Pakistan (born 1953) - A very sound right-handed batsman and occasional off-break bowler. He was an outstanding captain of the National Bank side in the Qaid-e-Azam Trophy. He played for Karachi and Sind. In his first class career he made, 9,166 runs including 20 centuries, took 223 wickets and 137 dismissals.
Test Record - 2 Tests, 97 runs (Av. 48.50).

AFTAB GUL
Pakistan (born 1946) - A stocky, right-handed opening batsman. He played for Lahore. In his first class career he made, 6,129 runs including 11 centuries and took 14 wickets.
Test Record - 6 Tests, 182 runs (Av. 22.75)

AGNEW JONATHAN PHILIP
England (born 1960) - A right-arm fast bowler and tail-end right-handed batsman. He played for Leicestershire. In his first class career he made,1582 runs and took 537 wickets.
Test Record - 3 Tests, 10 runs (Av. 10.00) and 4 wickets (Av. 93.25).

AHANGAMA FRANKLYN SALIYA
Sri Lanka (born 1959) - A right-arm medium-pace bowler and left-handed tail-end batsman. He was

selected for the 1985-86 tour of Pakistan but did not play a Test. He played for Sinhalese. In his first class career he made, 13 runs and took 23 wickets.
Test Record - 3 Tests, 11 runs (Av. 5.50) and 18 wickets (Av. 19.33).

AIR
Give the ball air of a slow bowler to deliver the ball with a relatively high curving trajectory, with the aim of deceiving the batsman as to its line,length, and pace.

AIR-BREAK
Movement of the ball in the air.

AIR-SHOT
A batting stroke in which the bat fails to make contact with the ball.

ALABASTER JOHN CHALONER
New Zealand (born 1930) - A right-arm leg-break bowler and occasionally useful batsman. He played for Otago. In his first class career he made, 2,427 runs and took 500 wickets.
Test Record - 21 Tests, 272 runs (Av. 9.71), 49 wickets (Av. 38.02).

ALCOTT CYRIL FRANCIS WALTER
New Zealand (1896-1973) - A very good all-rounder, a left-handed batsman and left-arm orthodox slow bowler. He played for Auckland. In his first class career he made, 2,514 runs including 5 centuries, and took 220 wickets.
Test Record - 6 Tests, 113 runs (Av. 22.60), 6 Wickets (Av. 90.16) and 3 catches.

ALDERMAN TERENCE MICHAEL
Australia (born 1956) - A right-arm medium-fast bowler with fine control of swing and cut. He was selected for Australia in England in 1981. He plays for Western Australia. In his first class career he made, 773 runs took 579 wickets and 123 catches.
Test Record - 24 Tests, 125 runs (Av.5.95), 86 wickets (Av. 32.16) and 18 catches.

ALEXANDER FRANZ COPELAND MURRAY
West Indies (born 1928) - An aggressive right-handed batsman and sound, sometimes brilliant, wicket-keeper, 'Gerry' Alexander was a Cambridge Blue in 1962 and 1963. He played for Cambridge University and Jamaica. In his first class career he made, 3,238 runs including 1 century, and 256 dismissals.
Test Record - 25 Tests, 961 runs (Av. 30.03) including 1 century, and 90 dismissals (85ct, 5st).

ALEXANDER GEORGE
Australia (1890-1970) - A right handed batsman with powerful wrists and a straight bat with a wide range of strokes. He played for New South Wales. In his first class he made, 8,095 runs including 14 centuries and took 95 wickets.
Test Record - 16 Tests, 592 runs (Av. 26.90) and 12 catches.

ALI INSHAN
West Indies (born 1949) - A small, left-hand back-of-the-hand spinner. He was certainly no failure on his two major tours, but on both tours he played only one Test. He played for Trinidad. In his first class career he made, 1,308 runs and took 324 wickets.
Test Record - 12 Tests, 172 runs (Av. 10.75), 34 wickets (Av. 47.67) and 7 catches.

ALIMUDDIN
Pakistan (born 1930) - A stocky right-handed opening batsman and a magnificent fielder. He played for Karachi. In his first class career he made, 7,276 runs including 14 centuries and took 40 wickets.
Test Record - 25 Tests, 1,091 runs (Av. 25.37) including 2 centuries and 8 catches.

ALL OUT
A cricket team retired because each batsman has been dismissed.

ALL-ROUNDER
A player skilled in both batting and bowling or in both batting and wicket-keeping.

ALLAN DAVID WALTER
West Indies (born 1937) - He came to England as a first-string wicket-keeper in 1963. In his first two Tests against India at Bridgetown and Kingston in 1961-62, he had ten victims and hit 40 not out in the first match. He could be a very useful bastman. He played for Barbados. In his first class career he made, 764 runs and 141 dismissals (117 ct, 24 st.)
Test Record - 5 Tests, 75 runs (Av. 12.50) and 18 dismissals (15ct, 3st).

ALLEN DAVID ARTHUR
England (born 1935) - He could bowl accurately for long spells, turning his off-spinner substantially. He played for Gloucestershire. In his first class career he made, 9,291 runs including 1 century and took 1,209 wickets.
Test Record - 39 Tests, 918 runs (Av. 25.50), 122 wickets (Av. 30.96) and 10 catches.

ALLEN SIR GEORGE OSWALD BROWNING
England (born 1902) - He was born in Australia and had an uncle, R.C.Allen, who played for Australia. A right arm fast bowler and strong batsman. He played for Cambridge University and Middlesex. In his first class career he made, 9,232 runs including 11 centuries and took 785 wickets.
Test Record - 25 Tests, 750 runs (Av.24.19), including 1 century, 81 wickets (Av. 29.37) and 20 catches.

ALLOM MAURICE JAMES CARRICK
England (born 1906) - He was a medium-fast right-arm bowler. In the first ever Test between England and New Zealand at Christchurch, he took 4 wickets in five balls, including the hat-trick. He played for Cambridge University and Surrey. In his first class career he made, 1,953 runs and took 605 wickets.
Test Record - 5 Tests, 14 runs (Av. 14.00) and 14 wickets (Av. 18.92).

ALLOTT PAUL JOHN WALTER
England (born 1956) - A useful right- handed batsman and right-arm fast-medium bowler. A back injury on the 1984-85 tour to India prevented him from playing in any of the Tests. He played for Cheshire and Lancashire. In his first class career he made,2,936 runs and took 578 wickets.
Test Record - 13 Tests, 213 runs (Av.14.20) and 26 wickets (Av. 41.69).

AMAR SINGH LADHA
India (1910-40) - A right-handed batsman and right-arm medium-fast bowler. Younger brother of L. Ramji. Test debut on June 23,1932 against England at the age of 21 years and 201 days. Scores on Test debut were 5 and 51 in the only Test played at Lord's. Last Test of the career played against England in August 1936. Scores on last appearance in Test were 5 and 44 in the third Test at the Oval. Age at the time of retirement from Test cricket was 25 years and 254 days. He played for Western India and Nawanagar. In his first class career he made, 3,241 runs and took 484 wickets.
Test Record - 7 Tests, 292 runs (Av. 22.46), 28 wickets (Av. 30.64) and 3 catches.

AMARNATH LALA
India (born 1911) - A right-handed batsman and right-arm medium-pace bowler. Test debut on December 15, 1933 against England at the age of 21 years and 94 days. Scores on Test debut were 38 and 118 in the first Test at Bombay. Earned the double distinction of being the first Indian to score a Test century and the first among Indians to get hundred on his Test debut on Indian soil on December 17,1933 at the age of 21 years and 96 days. Last Test of the career played in December 1952 against Pakistan. Score on last appearance in Test was 11 in the fifth Test at Calcutta. Age at the time of retirement from Test cricket was 41 years and 94 days. Led India for the first time against Australia in the first Test at Brisbane on November 28,1947 at the age of 36 years and 77 days and scored 22 and 5 runs. Captained Indian team in 15 Tests, out of which won two, lost six and seven were drawn. In his first class career he made, 10,323 runs including 31 centuries and took 457 wickets.
Test Record - 24 Tests, 878 runs (Av. 24.38), 45 wickets (Av. 32.91) and 13 catches.

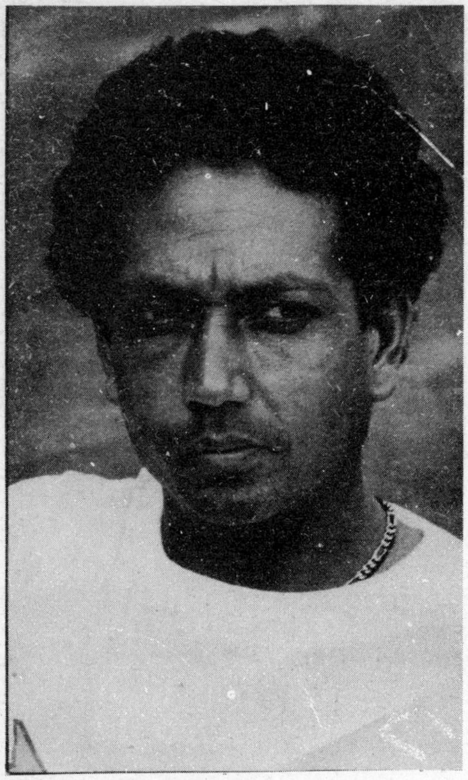

MOHINDER AMARNATH

AMARNATH MOHINDER

India (born 1950)- A right-handed batsman and right-arm medium-pace bowler. With a short, relaxed run-up and good body action, he moves the ball through the air and off the pitch in helpful conditions, and he is an impressively solid orthodox batsman who drives handsomely and hooks bravely. One of the few players to have enjoyed success against the West Indies, fast bowlers of the early 1980s. Son of Lala Amarnath and younger brother of Surinder Amarnath. Test debut on December 26, 1969 against Australia at the age of 18 years and 212 days. Scores on Test debut were 16 not out and 0 in fifth Test at Madras. He played his full part in India's World Cup triumph in 1983, being man-of-the-match in the final at Lord's. He plays for Punjab, Delhi and Durham. In his first class career he made, 14,646 runs including 30 centuries, took 285 wickets and 151 catches.

Test Record - 69 Tests, 4,377 runs (Av. 44.9) including 11 centuries, 32 wickets (Av.55.68) and 47 catches.

AMARNATH SURINDER

India (born 1948) - A left-handed batsman and

SURINDER AMARNATH

right-arm off-break bowler. Test debut on January 24, 1976 against New Zealand at the age of 27 years and 25 days. Scores on Test debut were 124 and 9 in the first Test at Auckland. Emulated his father, Lala Amarnath's feat by scoring a century on Test debut (the first father-son combination in the history of Test cricket to do so) at the age of 27 years and 26 days. Also scored a century in his first appearance in an unofficial Test against Sri Lanka. Last Test of the career played against Pakistan in November 1978. Scores on last appearance in Test were 30 and 14 in the third Test at Karachi. Age at the time of retirement from Test crickt was 29 years and 319 days.In his first class career he made, 8,175 runs including 16 centuries.

Test Record - 10 Tests, 550 runs (Av. 30.55) including 1 century and 1 wicket.

AMERSINGHE MUDALIGE JAYANTHA GAMINI

Sri Lanka (born 1954) - A leg-spinner who came into Test cricket at the age of thirty. He put on a Sri Lanka record tenth-wicket score of 60 with Vinodhan John in the first innings against New Zeal-

and at Kandy in 1983-84. He plays for Bloomfield. In his first class career he made, 60 runs and took 19 wickets.
Test Record - 2 Tests, 54 runs (Av. 18.00), 3 wickets (Av. 50.00) and 3 catches.

AMES LESLIE ETHELBERT GEORGE
England (born 1905)- He was a fine, strongly built, all-round wicket-keeper. He was first choice keeper for England from 1931 until 1938. He was also an orthodox, free-scoring batsman who showed the full face of the bat and was good enough to play for England as a batsman alone. He played for Kent. In his first class career he made, 37,248 runs including 102 centuries and 1,113 dismissals (698ct, 415st).
Test Record - 47 Tests, 2,434 runs (Av.40.56) including 8 centuries, and 97 dismissals (74ct, 23st).

AMIR ELAHI
India (1908-80) - A right-handed batsman and right-arm leg-break googly bowler. Test debut on December 12, 1947 against Australia at the age of 39 years and 101 days. Scores on Test debut were 4 and 13 in the second Test at Sydney. Played in only one Test for India in his career. He was included in the Indian team strictly as a leg-spin bowler but the most interesting aspect of his career is that he did not bowl a single ball in that Test but went in to open India's batting in the Test. Also played for Pakistan in seven Tests from 1952 to 1954. He played for Northern India. In his first class career he made, 2,469 runs and took 501 wickets.
Test Record - For India - 1 Test, 17 runs (Av.8.50) For Pakistan - 5 Tests, 65 runs (Av.10.83) and 7 wickets.

AMISS DENNIS LESLIE
England (born 1943) - The image of Dennis Amiss was one of a loyal and dedicated professional cricketer. He started his career as a middle-order batsman but achieved a new consistency from the moment he began regularly to open the Warwickshire innings. He played for Warwickshire. In his first class career he made, 43,423 runs, including 102 centuries and took 418 catches.
Test Record - 50 Tests, 3612 runs (Av. 46.30) including 11 centuries, and 24 catches.

DENNIS AMISS

ANDERSON ROBERT WICKHAM
New Zealand (born 1948) - A right-handed opening batsman and athletic fielder. Robert Anderson is the son of W.M. Anderson who played in one Test for New Zealand. He played for Canterbury.

In his first class career he made, 1,973 runs including 8 centuries.
Test Record - 12 Tests, 381 runs (Av. 31.75).

ANDREW KEITH VINCENT
England (born 1929) - Played only twice for England. He was a neat, skilful, unobtrusive and very successful wicket-keeper in county cricket. He played for Northamptonshire. In his first class career he made, 4,230 runs and 903 dismissals (721ct, 182st).
Test Record - 2 Tests, 29 runs (Av. 9.66) and 1 dismissal (1ct).

ANDREWS BRYAN
New Zealand (born 1945) - A very useful right arm medium-pace bowler. He played for Canterbury. In his first class career he made, 474 runs and took 198 wickets.
Test Record - 2 Tests, 22 runs (Av. 22.00) and 2 wickets (Av. 77.00).

ANDREWS THOMAS JAMES EDWIN
Australia (1890-1970) - A right-handed with powerful wrists and a straight bat with a wide range of strokes. He played for New South Wales. In his first class career he made, 8,095 runs including 14 centuries and took 95 wickets.
Test Record - 16 Tests, 592 runs (Av. 26.90) and 12 catches.

ANGLE
To deliver the ball in such a way that it either comes into or goes away from the striker at a considerable angle to the line of the wickets.

ANIL DALPAT
Pakistan (born 1963) - A right-handed batsman and a neat and agile wicket-keeper. He played for Karachi. In his first class career he made, 1,340 runs and 278 dismissals.
Test Record - 9 Tests, 167 runs (Av. 15.18) and 25 dismissals (22ct, 3st).

ANURASIRI SANGARANGE DON
Sri Lanka (born 1966) - A left-arm spinner, and a right-handed tail-ender batsman. He plays for Panadura. In his first class career he made, 26 runs and took 13 wickets.
Test Record - 4 Tests, 13 runs (Av.4.33).

ANWAR HUSSIAN
Pakistan (born 1920) - A sound right-handed batsman and fast-medium seam bowler. He played for Karachi. In his first class career he made, 1466 runs and took 34 wickets.
Test Record - 4Tests,42 runs (Av. 7.00), 1 wicket.

APPEAL
Never hesitate to appeal. If you think you have taken a legitimate catch, stumped or run-out a batsman, or if you feel that the person with the bat has put his leg in front of a straight one, do not hesitate to appeal. The umpire will not always uphold your request. Even umpires are not infallible. But if you do not appeal you cannot claim a wicket. Appeal confidently, as though you mean it. Of course, you can't do this if you are in doubt of your appeal. So never be in doubt. If you are certain that the batsman is out, then shout and don't be frightened to let every one know.

APTE ARVIND LAXMANRAO
India (born 1934)- A right-handed opening batsman with an array of brilliant strokes. Younger brother of M.L. Apte. Test debut on July 2, 1959 against England at the age of 24 years and 279 days. Played in only one Test and scored 8 and 7 runs in the third Test at Leeds. He played for Bombay. In his first class career he made, 2,782 runs including 6 centuries.
Test Record - 1 Test, 15 runs (Av. 7.50).

APTE MADHAV LAXMANRAO
India (born 1932) - A right-handed opening batsman and right-arm leg-spin bowler. Test debut on November 13, 1952 against Pakistan at the age of 20 years and 38 days. Scores on Test debut were 30 and 10 not out in the third Test at Bombay. Last Test of the career played against West Indies in March 1953. Scores on last appearance in Test

were 15 and 33 in the fifth Test at Kingston. Age at the time of retirement from Test cricket 30 years and 179 days. First-ever Test century (163 not out) scored against West-Indies in the second innings of the third Test at Port of Spain on February 25, 1953 at the age of 20 years and 139 days. He played for Bombay. In his first class career he made, 3,336 runs including 6 centuries.
Test Record - 7 Tests, 542 runs (Av. 49.27) including one century and 2 catches.

ARCHER KENNETH ALLAN
Australia (born 1928) - A right-handed opening batsman and a good stroke player. He played for Queensland. In his first class career he made, 3,774 runs and took 13 wickets.
Test Record - 5 Tests, 234 runs, (Av. 26.00).

ARCHER RONALD GRAHAM
Australia (born 1933) - A vigorous all-rounder of fine physique. A right-handed hard-hitting batsman and a medium-fast stock bowler. He bowled at the stumps and was often successful with the new ball. He played for the Queensland. In his first class career he made, 3,768 runs and took 255 wickets.
Test Record - 19 Tests, 713 runs, (Av.24.58) including one century, 48 wickets (Av. 27.45) and 20 catches.

ARIF BUTT
Pakistan (born 1944) - A right-arm fast-medium bowler and useful tail-end batsman. He played for Lahore. In his first class career he made, 4,017 runs and took 201 wickets.
Test Record - 3 Tests, 59 runs (Av. 11.80) and 14 wickets (Av. 20.57).

ARM BALL
A ball that goes on with the arm.

ARMITAGE THOMAS
England (1848-1922) - He was a useful right-handed batsman and a round-arm, medium-pace or slow-lob bowler. He played for Yorkshire. In his first class career he made, 1,122 runs and took 119 wickets.
Test Record - 2 Tests, 33 runs (Av. 11.00),no wicket.

ARMSTRONG WARWICK WINDRIDGE
Australia (1879-1947) - A right-handed batsman, he was nonetheless completely assured, certain in defence and confident in attack. As a bowler he took an exceptionally long run for one of his slow pace and would turn his leg-break sharply. He played for Victoria. In his first class career he made, 16,158 runs including 45 centuries, took 832 wickets and 274 catches.
Test Record - 50 Tests, 2,863 runs (Av. 38.68) including 6 centuries, 87 wickets (Av. 33.59) and 44 catches.

ARNOLD EDWARD GEORGE
England (1876-1942)- A long, loose-limbed all-rounder. Ted Arnold was a right-handed batsman, strong in defence and a right-arm bowler above medium-pace. In four consecutive seasons he achieved the double of one thousand runs and one hundred wickets. He played for Devonshire and Worcestershire. In his first class career he made, 15,853 runs including 24 centuries and took 1,069 wickets.
Test Record - 10 Tests, 160 runs (13.33), 31 wickets (25.41) and 8 catches.

ARNOLD GEOFFREY GRAHAM
England (born 1944)- He was an outstanding all-round player. He played for Surrey. In his first class career he made, 3,952 runs,took 1,130 wickets and 122 catches.
Test Record - 34 Tests, 421 runs (Av. 12.02), 115 wickets (Av. 28.29) and 9 catches.

ARUN LAL
India (1955) - A right-handed opener and good close fielder. He has been a consistent scorer in domestic cricket. He plays for Delhi and Bengal. In his first class career he made, 4,126 runs including 10 centuries and 6 wickets.
Test Record - 16 Tests, 729 runs (Av. 26.03) and 13 catches.

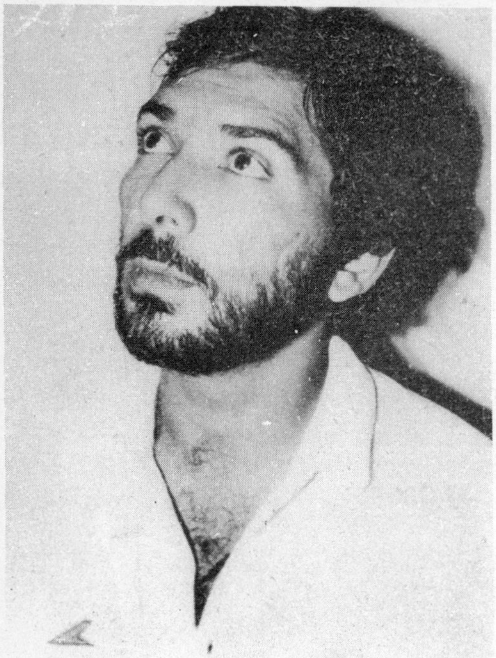

ARUN LAL

ASGAR ALI NYRON

West Indies (born 1922) - A sound right-handed opening batsman and became a professional in the Lancashire League. He played for Trinidad. In his first class career he made, 2,761 runs including 7 centuries, and took 23 wickets.

Test Record - 2 Tests, 62 runs (Av. 15.50).

ASHES

A mythical trophy won by the winner of the England-Australia Test matches series. The title is regularly contested in Test series played in both countries,and changes hands only if the current holders lose a rubber. The name of the title originates from a mock obituary published shortly after England's first-ever defeat by Australia on English soil, when magnificent bowling by Spofforth (who took 14 for 90) carried Australia to dramatic 7 run victory.

ASHRAF ALI

Pakistan (born 1958) - A right-handed batsman with considerable flair. Ashraf Ali came to national prominence in 1980-81 and his highest score in that season was 137 and he was chosen to tour Australia. He played for Lahore. In his first class career he made, 4,296 runs including 2 centuries 249 dismissals (197ct, 52st).

Test Record - 5 Tests, 206 runs (Av. 103.00) and 11 dismissals (9ct, 2st).

ASIF IQBAL RAZVI

Pakistan (born 1943) - An exciting stroke-playing right-handed batsman. His second Test century against England came at Edgbaston in 1971, 104 not out. He played for Karachi. In his first class career he made, 23,375 runs including 45 centuries,took 291 wickets and 304 catches.

Test Record - 52 Tests, 3,308 runs (Av. 39.85) including 11 centuries, 51 wickets (Av. 28.03) and 32 catches.

ASIF IQBAL

ASIF MASOOD

Pakistan (born 1946) - He was a right-arm fast-medium bowler. He started his run with an eccentric double-chassis. He played for Lahore. In his first class career he made, 635 runs and took 305 wickets.

Test Record - 16 Tests, 93 runs (Av. 10.33), 38 wickets (Av. 41.26) and 5 catches.

The attacking strokes

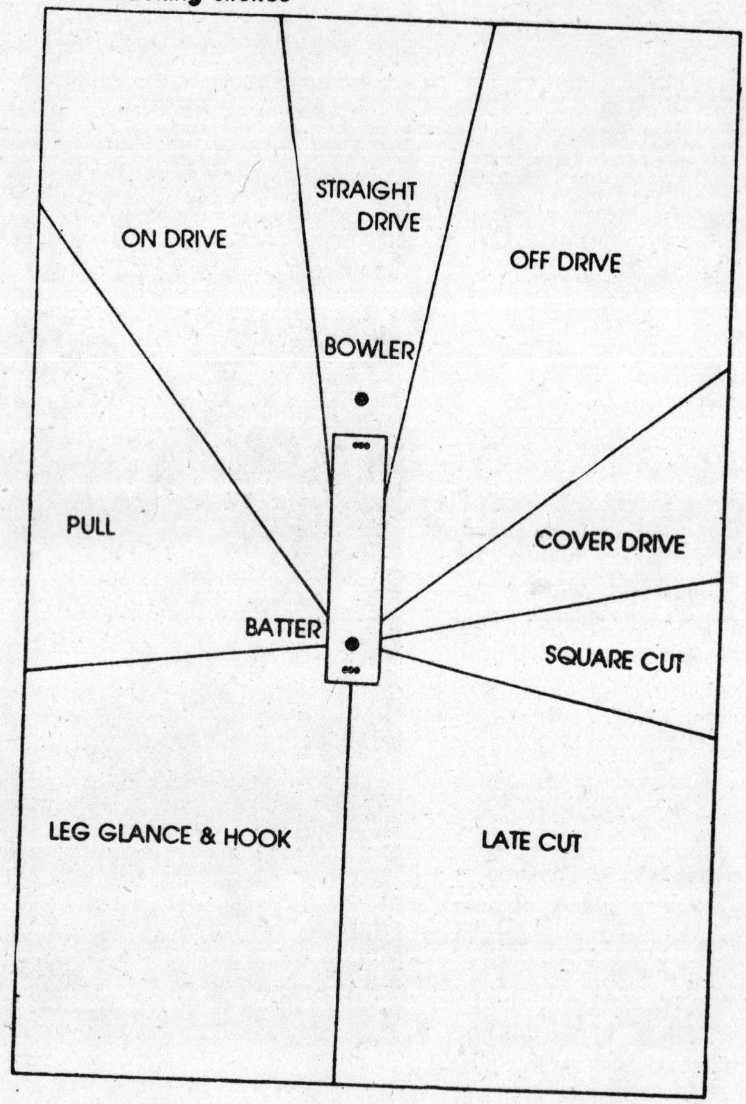

ASTILL WILLIAM EWART

England (1888-1948)- He was an orthodox right-handed batsman and off-spin bowler. He played for Leicestershire. In his first class career he made, 22,731 runs,took 2,432 wickets and 464 catches.

Test Record - 9 Tests, 190 runs (Av. 12.66), 25 wickets (34.24) and 7 catches.

ATHEY CHARLES WILLIAM JEFFREY

England (born 1957)- A right-handed batsman and useful medium-pace bowler. After playing with flair in one day international against Australia he was selected for the 1980 centenary Test. He plays for Yorkshire. In his first class career he made 13,458 runs, including 28 centuries,took 37 wickets and 259 dismissals (257ct, 2st).

Test Record - 17 Tests,722 runs (Av.24.89) and 10 catches.

ATKINSON DENIS ST EVAL

West Indies (born 1926) - A sound right-handed batsman and medium-pace bowler. He captained the West Indies in three Tests against Australia in 1954-55 in the absence of Jeff Stollmeyer through injury, losing two of them. He played for Barbados and Trinidad. In his first class career he made, 2,812 runs and took 200 wickets.

Test Record - 22 Tests, 922 runs (Av. 31.79) including 1 century and 47 wickets (Av. 35.04).

ATKINSON ERICST EVAL

West Indies (born 1925) - A right-handed batsman and medium-fast bowler. He played for Barbados. In his first class career he made, 696 runs and took 61 wickets.

Test Record - 8 Tests, 126 runs (Av. 15.75), 25 wickets (Av. 23.56) and 2 catches.

ATTACKING FIELD

Any arrangement of fielders that is primarily intended to get batsmen out rather than to prevent them from scoring runs.

ATTEWELL WILLIAM

England (1861-1927) - A right-arm medium pace bowler. He was also a useful late-order batsman and a good fielder at cover-point. He took 100 wickets in a season 10 times. He became an umpire after retirement. He played for Nottinghamshire. In his first class career he made, 8,086 runs including 1 century, and took 1949 wickets.

Test Record - 10 Tests, 150 runs (Av. 16.66), 27 wickets (Av. 23.18) and 9 catches.

AUSTIN RICHARD ARKWRIGHT

West Indies (born 1954) - A sound right-handed batsman and medium-pace bowler. He was the outstanding batsman in the 1977-78 Shell Shield season, starting the season as Jamaica's opening batsman. He played for Jamaica. In his first class career he made, 2,097 runs including 4 centuries, and took 73 wickets.

Test Record - 2 Tests, 22 runs (Av. 11.00).

ARSHAD AYUB

AYUB ARSHAD

India (born 1958) - A right-arm off spinner and right-handed batsman. He got a Test cap after a long struggle at the age of 29 against West Indies. He plays for Hyderabad. In his first class career he made, 2,833 runs including 6 centuries, and took 135 wickets.

Test Record - 11 Tests, 246 runs (Av.18.92), 41 wickets (Av.27.75) and 2 catches.

AZAD KIRTI

India (born 1959) - A right-handed batsman and right-arm off-break bowler. Test debut on Febru-

MOHAMMED AZHARUDDIN

ary 21, 1981 against New Zealand at the age of 22 years and 49 days. Scores on Test debut were 20 and 16 in the first Test at Wellington. After a successful time in India's World Cup-winning team in England in 1983 he played two Tests at home against West Indies the following season, with little reward, and one against Pakistan. He plays for Delhi. In his first class career he made, 4,774 runs including 13 centuries and took 163 wickets.

Test Record - 7 Tests, 135 runs (Av. 11.25), 3 wickets (Av. 124.33) and 3 catches.

AZHARUDDIN MOHAMMED

India (born 1963) - A right-handed batsman and medium-pace bowler. Seldom has any cricketer made quite so glittering a start in his Test career as the slim, humble, smiling genius who forced his way into the Indian team to play against England at Calcutta in December 1984. He scored 110, followed this with 48 and 105 at Madras and completed his part in the series with scores of 122 and 54 not out at Kanpur. No one else has hit hundreds in each of his first three Tests. Also a brilliant fielder, he held his place in a strong Indian batting side despite a relatively unsuccessful tour of Australia in 1985-86. He plays for Hyderabad. In his first class career he made, 4,338 runs including 16 centuries.

Test Record - 30 Tests, 1,912 runs (Av. 46.53) including 6 centuries, 24 catches.

B

BACCHUS SHEIKH FAOUD AHUMUL
West Indies (born 1954) - A right-handed opening or middle-order batsman and superb cover fielder. He was outstanding on the tour of India in 1978-79 finishing second in the Test averages with 472 runs (Av. 47.20). On a batsman's paradise at Kanpur he hit 250 in 512 minutes. He played for Guyana. In his first class career he made, 5,874 runs including 8 centuries, and took 9 wickets.
Test Record - 19 Tests, 782 runs (Av.26.06) including 1 century, and 17 catches.

BACHER DR. ARON (ALI)
South Africa (born 1942) - He was mainly a back-foot player, very strong on the leg-side. He was a brilliant fielder and a competent second-string 'keeper'. He played for Transvaal. In his first class career he made, 7,889 runs including 18 centuries, 110 catches and one stumping.
Test Record - 12 Tests, 679 runs (Av. 32.33) and 10 catches.

BACK
Striking or attempting to strike the ball from a position relatively close to the wicket, with most of the weight of the body thrown on to the Back Foot.

BACK DEFENCE
In this, a batsman puts his weight on the right foot, which has been drawn back towards the stumps. The front foot is kept just touching the ground to keep one's balance with a firm left wrist and left elbow upright. The bat should be slightly inclined to the ground when it meets the ball. When you play back you have a space of four feet between the wicket and batting crease and you can use a great deal of that in taking the backward pace.

Back Defence

Being careful that you don't go so far back that you hit the stumps or bump into them while playing a stroke.

BACK SPIN
A reverse spin imparted to the ball, causing it to lose pace significantly after pitching, with little or no lateral deviation.

BACK UP
Of the non-striker to begin to move down the wicket as the bowler delivers the ball in order to optimise the chances of taking a run should the striker hit the ball.

BACK DEFENSIVE SHOT
The alternative to the forward defensive shot is the back defensive. The shot is played to a ball pitching on a length, but not quite so far up as to allow the batsman to deal with it safely forward at its pitch. In this case one steps back giving a little more time to see the ball off the pitch and enabling one to play more easily. The first movement is back with the right foot, placing it approximately half-way to the stumps and behind the spot on which the ball pitched. All the weight is taken on the back foot, the front just

Back Defensive Short

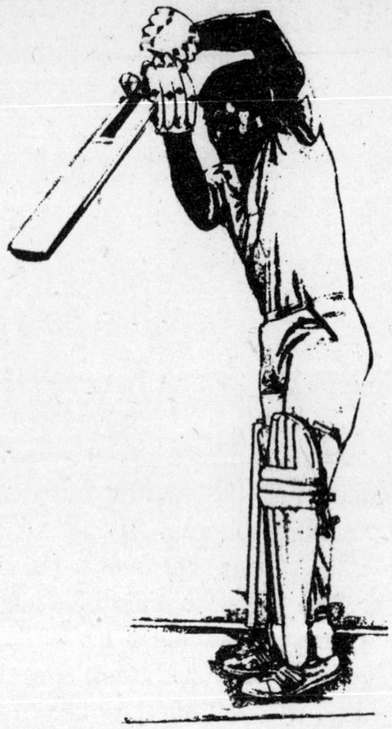

Back-Foot Cover Drive

touching the ground to keep one's balance. The body is tilted slightly forward over the right leg which is placed parallel to the popping crease. With a firm left wrist and left elbow upright, the bat is brought through just past the right leg. The bat should be slightly inclined to the ground when it meets the ball. The right-hand grip loosens to finger-tip grip, similar to the right hand in the forward shot. The main points to watch are: to step back behind the pitch of the ball, providing the ball pitches in line with the wickets; if the ball pitches outside the off stump the right foot should cover the off stump and go no farther; when the ball pitches outside the leg stump,the right foot steps back into the wicket turning the body to allow the face of the bat to meet the ball.

BACK-FOOT COVER DRIVE

The back-foot cover drive is played to hit a ball bouncing short of a length and wide on the off side of the wicket, through the cover area without risk of dismissal. To hit a back-foot cover drive move as if you were hitting the back-foot drive, except that the movements of your back foot, head and eyes will be more towards the off side. The movement of your front foot to the rear foot will bring that foot and the front shoulder to the off side of the rear foot and shoulder. The front shoulder, elbow and side point towards cover in the execution of the stroke.

BACK-FOOT ON-DRIVE

The back-foot on-drive is played in order to hit a short delivery bouncing on or outside the line of leg stump through the area between mid-wicket and the bowler without risk of dismissal. For the back-foot on-drive follow the movements of the back-foot drive, except that your back foot should move back nearer leg stump and your front shoulder, elbow and hip fall away to the leg side and point in the direction of the stroke.

BACK-FOOT STRAIGHT DRIVE

The back-foot straight drive is played in order to hit a short, straight ball back past the bowler without risk of dismissal. To hit the back-foot straight drive, follow the movements of the back-foot drive, except that your back foot, head and eyes move towards middle stump and your front shoulder should point straight back towards the bowler.

BACK-SPINNER

A ball delivered with back spin, like the top-spinner, it is very likely to cause a mistimed stroke.

BACKLIFT

With eyes glued on the ball in the bowler's hand,

Backlift

the batsman's first movement is to pick the bat up as the bowler's arm is coming over to deliver the ball. Keeping head and body still, he pushes the bat straight back in line with the middle stump by the left arm bending at the elbow and keeping the right arm fairly close to the side. The face of the bat will open towards point. Do not pick the bat up too high until you are sure of the shot you have to play. If it is a bad ball you will then have time to pick the bat up a little higher. With practice you will find that the bat will be picked up according to the ball to be played. A very good method of practising the pick-up is to take your stance as close as possible to a wall and then pick the bat up without the bat touching the wall.

BADCOCK CLAYVEL LINDSAY

Australia (1914-1982) - 'Jack' Badcock played for Tasmania at fifteen. He could drive magnificently on either side of the wicket, and his square-cut was so hard and clean that cover point had little chance of getting a hand to it. The second youngest Australian to play first class cricket. He played for South Australia and Tasmania. In his first class career he made, 7,371 runs including 27 centuries.

Test Record - 7 Tests, 160 runs (Av. 14.54) including 1 century.

BADCOCK FREDERICK THEODORE

New Zealand (1898-1982) - Born in India, died in Australia, and lived a part of his childhood in England. He was a dashing right-handed batsman and a medium-pace bowler, devoted many years to playing and coaching in New Zealand. He played for Wellington. In his first class career he made, 2,385 runs and took 221 wickets.

Test Record - 7 Tests, 137 runs (Av. 19.57) and 16 wickets (Av. 38.12).

BAICHAN LEONARD

West Indies (born 1946) - A left-handed opening batsman. He was unfortunately injured in a car accident and missed several matches. He played for Guyana. In his first class career he made, 4,569 runs including 13 centuries.

Test Record - 3 Tests, 184 runs (Av. 46.00) including 1 century.

BAIG ABBAS ALI

India (born 1939) - A right-handed batsman and right-arm leg-spin bowler. Test debut on July 23, 1959 against England at the age of 20 years and 124 days. Scores on Test debut were 26 and 112 in the fourth Test at Manchester. Became the fourth Indian batsman to score a century on his Test debut and the second to earn distinction against England on July 28, 1959 at the age of 20 years and 129 days. Last Test of the career played against West Indies in January 1967. Scores on last appearance in Test were 4 and 6 in the second Test at Calcutta. Age at the time of retirement from Test cricket was 27 years and 287 days. He played for Hyderabad, Oxford University and Somerset. In his first class career he made, 12,567 runs including 21 centuries.

Test Record - 10 Tests, 428 runs (Av. 23.77) including 1 century and 6 catches.

BAILS

The cylindrical wooden stumps (each 28 in. - 71.12 cm. - high) are set up at the centre of the bowling crease at both ends of the pitch in two groups of three, called the wickets, and surmounted by two bails (each 4(3/8) in. - 11.1 cm. long) which rest in grooves cut in the tops of the stumps and project no more than 1/2 in. (1.27 cm.).

BAILEY TREVOR EDWARD
England (born 1923) - A right-arm, medium-fast bowler, brilliant fielder and a sound batsman. He played for Nottinghamshire. In his first class career he made, 28,642 runs including 28 centuries, took 2,172 wickets and 425 catches.
Test Record - 61 Tests, 2,290 runs (Av. 29.74) including 1 century, 132 wickets (Av. 29.21) and 32 catches.

BAKEAWLL ALFRED HARRY
England (1908-1983) - A right-handed batsman and a useful fielder. He played for Northamptonshire. In his first class career he made, 14,570 runs including 32 centuries and 267 catches.
Test Record - 6 Tests, 409 runs (Av. 45.44) and 3 catches.

BALASKAS XENOPHON CONSTANTINE
South Africa (born 1910) - A right-arm slow leg-spin bowler and was a very useful lower-order batsman. He played for Border, Transvaal, and North-Eastern Transvaal. In his first class career he made, 2,696 runs including 6 centuries, and 276 wickets.
Test Record - 9 Tests, 174 runs (Av. 14.50) including 1 century, and 22 wickets (Av. 36.63).

BALL
Although the primitive cricket ball was made of anything that would roll or tie into spherical shape, by the middle of the eighteenth century it was bound in red-dyed leather and was required to weigh between 5 to 6 oz. (142 to 170 g.). There was then already a flourishing industry in the manufacture of cricket balls in West Kent. Now the ball is formed of a cork and twine core and a red leather outer casing. It must weigh between 5(1/2) and 5(3/4) oz. (156 - 163 g.), and between 8(13/16) and 9 in. (22.38 - 22.86 cm.) in circumference. Its seam can be employed by the bowler to make the ball 'break' or swing.

BANERJEE SAROBINDU NATH SHUTE
India (1913-1980) - A right-handed batsman and right-arm medium-fast bowler. Test debut on February 4, 1949 against West Indies at the age of 35 years and 121 days. Played in only one Test and scored 5 and 8 runs in the fifth Test at Bombay. He played for Bengal and Bihar. In his first class career he made, 3,671 runs including 5 centuries, and took 381 wickets.
Test Record - 1 Test, 13 runs (Av. 6.50) and 5 wickets (Av. 25.49).

BANERJEE SUDANGSU ABINASH MONTU
India (born 1919) - A right-handed batsman and right-arm medium pace bowler. Test debut on December 31, 1948 against West Indies at the age of 29 years and 60 days. Played in only one Test scoring 'duck' in the third Test at Calcutta. Took a wicket (that of D. Atkinson) with his fifth ball in Test cricket. In his first class career he made, 237 runs and took 92 wickets.
Test Record - 1 Test, 0 run and 5 wickets (Av. 36.20

BANNERMAN ALEXANDER CHALMERS
Australia (1854-1924) - He made many large scores and was invaluable as a partner for bigger hitters. In the field, he was superb at mid-off fast, safe and untiring. He played for New South Wales. In his first class career he made, 7,816 runs including 4 centuries and took 22 wickets.
Test Record - 28 Tests, 1,108 runs (Av. 23.08), 4 wickets (Av. 40.75) and 21 catches.

BANNERMAN CHARLES
Australia (1851-1930) - He was fine, upstanding and polished batsman. He was also a first-rate versatile field. He played for New South Wales. In his first class career he made, 1,687 runs including 1 century.
Test Record - 3 Tests, 239 runs (Av. 59.75) including 1 century.

BAPTISTE ELDINE ASHWORTH ELDERFIELD
West Indies (born 1960) - A relatively slimly built right-handed all-rounder batsman. He played for Leeward Islands and Kent. In his first class career he made, 3,725 runs including 3 centuries, and took 268 wickets.

ELDINE BAPTISTE

Test Record - 9 Tests, 224 runs (Av. 24.88), 15 wickets (Av. 32.40), and 2 catches.

BAQA JILANI MOHAMMAD

India (1911-1941) - A right-handed batsman and right-arm medium-fast bowler. Test debut on August 15, 1936 against England at the age of 25 years and 26 days. Scores on Test debut were 4 not out and 12 in the third Test at the Oval. Played in only one Test. Died on July 2, 1941 at the age of 29 years and 343 days. He played for Northern India. In his first class career he made, 896 runs including 1 century and took 81 wickets.

Test Record - 1 Test, 16 runs.

BARBER ROBERT WILLIAM

England (born 1935) - A left-handed opening batsman, talented leg-break bowler and an excellent fielder in the leg-trap. He played for Lancashire and Warwickshire. In his first class career he made, 17,571 runs including 17 centuries, took 549 wickets and 209 catches.

Test Record - 28 Tests, 1,495 runs (Av. 35.59) including 1 century, 42 wickets and 21 catches.

BARBER WILFRED

England (1901-1968) - He was a text-book right-handed batsman and was a first-rate outfield. He played for Yorkshire. In his first class career he made, 16,402 runs including 29 centuries, and took 16 wickets.

Test Record - 2 Tests, 83 runs (Av. 20.75).

BARDSLEY WARREN

Australia (1882-1954) - A stylish left-handed opening batsman and was a fine outfield. He played for New South Wales. In his first class career he made, 17,025 runs including 53 centuries, and 123 catches.

Test Record - 41 Tests, 2,469 runs (Av. 40.47) including 6 centuries, and 12 catches.

BARLOW EDGAR JOHN

South Africa (born 1940) - A right-handed opening batsman with a solid defence and a right-handed medium-pace bowler who could make the ball swing prodigiously. He was his usual dynamic self-doing hat-trick and taking four wickets in five balls against England at Headingley in 1970 playing for Rest of the World. He played for Transvaal and Derbyshire. In his first class career he made, 18,212 runs including 43 centuries, took 571 wickets and 335 catches.

Test Record - 30 Tests, 2,516 runs (Av. 45.74) including 6 centuries, 40 wickets (Av. 34.05) and 35 catches.

BARLOW GRAHAM DEREK

England (born 1950) - He was an important member of the Middlesex side which won the championship five times between 1977 and 1985, taking up the role of opening batsman following Mike Brearley's retirement. He played for Middlesex. In his first class career he made, 12,387 runs including 26 centuries, took 3 wickets and 136 catches.

Test Record - 3 Tests, 17 runs (Av. 4.25).

BARLOW RICHARD GORTON

England (1851-1919) - A right-handed batsman and was also a left-arm, medium-pace bowler. On retirement he became a much respected Test match umpire. He played for Lancashire. In his

first class career he made, 10,732 runs including 4 centuries, and took 805 wickets.
Test Record - 17 Tests, 591 runs (Av. 22.73), 34 wickets (Av. 22.55) and 14 catches.

BARNES SIDNEY GEORGE
Australia (1916-1973) - He shared a world-record partnership for the fifth wicket of 405 with Don Bradman in the second Test at Sydney against England in 1946-47, each man making 234. He played for New South Wales. In his first class career he made, 8,333 runs including 26 centuries, and took 57 wickets.
Test Record - 13 Tests, 1,072 runs (Av. 63.05) including 3 centuries, 4 wickets (Av. 54.50) and 14 catches.

BARNES SYDNEY FRANCIS
England (1873-1967) - He was a right-arm, medium-fast bowler. He played for Warwickshire and Lancashire. In his first class career he made, 1,573 runs and took 719 wickets.
Test Record - 27 Tests, 242 runs (Av. 8.06), 189 wickets (Av. 16.43) and 12 catches.

BARNES WILLIAM
England (1851-1899) - A right-handed batsman and a medium-pace bowler. On retiring from the game he became, perhaps appropriately landlord of an inn. He played for Nottinghamshire. In his first class career he made, 15,425 runs including 23 centuries, and took 903 wickets.
Test Record - 21 Tests, 725 runs (Av. 23.38) including 1 century, 51 wickets (Av. 15.54) and 19 catches.

BARNETT BENJAMIN ARTHUR
Australia (1908-1979) - He was a wicket-keeper and steady left-handed batsman. He played for Victoria and Buckinghamshire. In his first class career he made, 5,531 runs including 4 centuries, 358 dismissals (216ct, 142st).
Test Record - 4 Tests, 195 runs (Av. 27.85) and 5 dismissals (3ct, 2st).

BARNETT CHARLES JOHN
England (born 1910) - An opening right-handed batsman of vigour and imagination, especially adept at driving and square-cutting. He played for Gloucestershire. In his first class career he made, 25,389 runs including 48 centuries, took 394 wickets and 318 catches.
Test Record - 20 Tests, 1,098 runs (Av. 35.41) including 2 centuries and 14 catches.

BARRATT FREDERICK
England (1894-1947) -'Fred' Barratt was a burly coal-miner turned right-arm fast bowler. He played for Nottinghamshire. In his first class career he made, 6,445 runs including 2 centuries, took 1,224 wickets.
Test Record - 5 Tests, 28 runs (Av. 9.33) and 5 wickets (Av. 47.00) and 2 catches.

BARRETT ARTHUR GEORGE
West Indies (born 1944) - A good and accurate if relatively straightforward right-arm leg-break bowler. He toured India and Pakistan in 1974-75 and at home played against India in 1970-71. He played for Jamaica. In his first class career he made, 1,086 runs including 1 century, and took 169 wickets.
Test Record - 6 Tests, 40 runs (Av. 6.66) and 13 wickets (Av. 46.38).

BARRETT DR. JOHN EDWARD
Australia (1866-1916) - A patient left-handed batsman and a useful medium -pace change -bowler with a high action .He was of eighteen years on his debut for his State against South Australia at Melbourne. He played for Victoria. In his first class career he made, 2,113 runs and took 21 wickets.
Test Record - 2 Tests, 80 runs (Av. 26.66) and 1 catch.

BARRINGTON KENNETH FRANK
England (1930-1981) - He was a useful but underused leg-break and googly bowler and on the 1964-65 tour took 7 for 40 for MCC against Griqualand West at Kimberley. He was also a dependable fielder. He played for Berkshire and Surrey. In his first class career he made, 31,714

***BARRINGTON** with his team*

Bat-Pad

runs including 76 centuries, took 273 wickets and 511 catches.
Test Record - 82 Tests, 6,806 runs (Av. 58.67) including 20 centuries, and 29 wickets (Av. 44.82) and 58 catches.

BARTLETT EDWARD LAWSON

West Indies (1906-1976) - A slightly built right-handed batsman, quick footed, a hard-hitter in front of the wicket and a neat-cutter. He played for Barbados. In his first class career he made, 1,581 runs including 1 century.
Test Record - 5 Tests, 131 runs (Av. 18.71) and 2 catches.

BARTLETT GARY ALEXANDER

New Zealand (born 1941) - A right-arm medium-fast bowler and useful batsman. He performed the hat-trick against Northern Districtsat Hamilton in 1959-60. He played for Central Districts and Canterbury. In his first class career he made, 1,504 runs and took 150 wickets.
Test Record - 10 Tests, 263 runs (Av. 15.47), 24 wickets (Av. 33.00) and 8 catches.

BARTON, PAUL THOMAS

New Zealand (born 1935) - A composed, correct and polished right-handed batsman. He played for Wellington. In his first class career he made, 2,824 runs including 3 centuries.
Test Record - 7 Tests, 285 runs (Av. 20.35) including 1 century.

BAT

The implement used by the batsman to stop or strike the ball was, in early years, similar in shape of a modern hockey stick. It has always been made of wood, but the tendency has been towards decreasing weight. Modern bats weigh between 21b. 4oz. and 2lb. 6oz (1020and 1077g.),but there is no legal restriction. The present shape-straight-sided, with a bulge(known as meat at the back of the bat towards the bottom (toe)-evolved around 1775. The blade is carved from willow; the handle is made from cane reinforced with layers of rubber and bound is twine. A rubber grip usually covers the handle, which extends into the blade of the bat in a V shape (the splice). The permitted maximum dimensions are 38 in. (96.52 cm.) long over-all by 4(1/4)in. (10.80cm.)wide.

BAT-PAD

Relating to a close leg-side fielding position in front of the wicket, where a fielder is stationed in order to snap up catches from balls coming off the edge of the striker's bat and deflected by his pads.

BATES WILLIAM

England (1855-1900) - A right-handed batsman and a first-rate slow, round-arm bowler, commanding both a high degree of spin and an immaculate length. He played for Yorkshire. In his first class career he made, 10,214 runs including 10 centuries, and took 860 wickets.
Test Record - 15 Tests, 656 runs (Av. 27.33), 50 wickets (Av. 16.42) and 9 catches.

BATSMAN

The player who scores runs for his team.

BATTING

It is often observed that both players and the spectators are fascinated by the quality of batting. Batting is liked by everybody and often people remember the number of runs scored by a batsman rather than the number of wickets captured by a bowler. Moreover, the feeling of lone hero being watched by thousands of spectators, holding their breath in great suspense and thrill gives a batsman great satisfaction and pleasure. Batting also represents challenge, where the batsman is completely alone surrounded by a great defiance of eleven players around him who are asking for his blood and are making every effort to dismiss him in the shortest possible time.

BATTING AVERAGE

The average number of runs scored by a cricketer per number of times out.

BATTING SIDE
Each member of the batting side takes a turn to bat. There are always two batsmen on the pitch. One of them faces the bowler and tries to hit the ball. In cricket, there are no foul lines. The ball can be hit in any direction, including behind you. Batsmen can run once,twice, thrice, or more times per hit,and scores can get quite high. Batsmen stay out on the pitch for as long as they can.

BCCI
Board of Control for Cricket in India.

BCCP
Board of Control for Cricket in Pakistan.

BCCSL
Board of Control for Cricket in Sri Lanka.

BEAMER
A usual intimidatory delivery of the ball in cricket that passes or hits the batsman at above waist height before it bounces.

BEAN GEORGE
England (1864-1923) - He was a fast-scoring right-handed batsman, especially on dry wickets and also a useful medium-pace bowler. At the time of his death, he was the senior member of MCC's ground staff. He played for Nottinghamshire. In his first class career he made, 8,634 runs including 9 centuries, took 260 wickets and 145 catches.
Test Record - 3 Tests, 92 runs (Av. 18.40).

BEARD DONALD DEREK
New Zealand (1920-1982) - A right-arm medium-pace bowler and a flamboyant hitter. He became principal at Te Aroha College. He played for Wellington. In his first class career he made, 2,166 runs and took 281 wickets.
Test Record - 4 Tests, 101 runs (Av. 20.20), 9 wickets (Av. 33.55).

BEAT
To break through a batsman's defence, though without necessarily dismissing him.

BEAUMONT ROLLAND
South Africa (1884-1958) - A right-handed batsman and right-arm medium-fast bowler. He played for Transvaal. In his first class career he made, 1,086 runs including 1 century.
Test Record - 5 Tests, 70 runs (Av. 7.77) and 2 catches.

BEDI BISHEN SINGH GIAN SINGH
India (born 1946) - A left-arm slow spin bowler and right-handed batsman. Test debut on December 31, 1966 against the West Indies at the age of 20 years and 96 days. Scores on Test debut were 5 and 0 in the second Test at Calcutta. Last Test of the career played against England in August-September 1979. Score on last appearance in Test was 1 in the fourth Test at the Oval. Age at the time of retirement from Test cricket was 32 years and 355 days. He captured maximum of 266 wickets for India. He is the first among Indian bowlers to reach 200-wicket mark. At one time he was the only bowler in the world of Test cricket to capture over 50 wickets against all cricket playing countries except South Africa (against

BISHEN SINGH BEDI

whom he has not played) and Pakistan. In his first class career he made, 3,564 runs, and took 1,547 wickets.
Test Record - 67 Tests, 656 runs (Av. 8.98), 266 wickets (Av. 28.71) and 26 catches.

BEDSER ALEC VICTOR
England (born 1918) - He was a talented county all-rounder. He began his illustrious Test career with 11 wickets from each of his first two Tests against India in 1946. He was a truly great medium-fast bowler and his batting was wooden but straight, and often useful, especially in the role of night watchman. He played for Surrey. In his first class career he made, 5,735 runs, including 1 century, took 1,924 wickets and 289 catches.
Test Record - 51 Tests, 714 runs (Av. 12.75), 236 wicket (Av. 24.89) and 26 catches.

BEGBIE DENIS WARBURTON
South Africa (born 1914) - A quick-scoring but rather inconsistent batsman and change-bowler. He played for Transvaal. In his first class career he made, 2,727 runs including 6 centuries and took 88 wickets.
Test Record - 5 Tests, 138 runs (Av. 19.71) and 2 catches.

BELL ALEXANDER JOHN
South Africa (1906-1985) - A right-arm medium-fast bowler. He played for Western Province and Rhodesia. In his first class career he made, 333 runs and took 228 wickets.
Test Record - 16 Tests, 69 runs (Av. 6.27), 48 wickets (Av. 32.64) and 6 catches.

BELL WILLIAM
New Zealand (born 1931) - A right-arm and leg-break bowler. He played for Canterbury. In his first class career he made, 170 runs and 44 wickets.
Test Record - 2 Tests, 21 runs and 2 wickets (Av. 117.50).

BENAUD JOHN
Australia (born 1944) - A right-handed batsman. In his second Test, against Pakistan at Melbourne in 1972-73 he hit 142 runs after learning that the selectors had left him out of the third Test. He played for New South Wales. In his first class career he made, 2,888 runs including 4 centuries.
Test Record - 3 Tests, 223 runs (Av. 44.60) including 1 century.

BENAUD RICHARD
Australia (born 1930) - A forcing right-handed batsman. His drives powerfully hit with a follow-through, were often lofted. He bowled the leg-break, the googly, the top-spinner and his speciality, the 'flipper'. He was awarded the OBE for his services to Australian cricket. A journalistalso and has written several cricket books. He played for New South Wales. In his first class career he made, 11,719 runs including 23 centuries, took 945 wickets and 255 catches.
Test Record - 63 Tests, 2,201 runs (Av. 24.45) including 3 centuries, 248 wickets (Av. 27.03) and 65 catches.

BENEFIT
Benefits were formerly awarded to players who were on the verge of retirement after a long career with their country, and the bulk of the money they received came their own choosing the benefit match.

BENNETT MURRAY JOHN
Australia (born 1956) - A bespectacled slow left-arm bowler and useful lower-order right-handed batsman. He played for New South Wales. In his first class career he made, 1,214, runs and took 144 wickets.
Test Record - 3 Tests, 71 runs (Av. 23.66), 6 wickets (Av. 54.16) and 5 catches.

BENSON AND HEDGES CUP
Established in 1972, the competition is restricted to twenty teams.
Cup Final Results (Winners)
1972 Leicestershire
1973 Kent
1974 Surrey
1975 Leicestershire

1976 Kent
1977 Gloucestershire
1978 Kent
1979 Essex
1980 Northamptonshire
1981 Somerset
1982 Somerset
1983 Middlesex
1984 Lancashire
1985 Leicestershire
1986 Middlesex
1987 Yorkshire
1988 Hampshire
1989 Nottinghamshire

BENSON RICHARD MARK
England (born 1958) - A solid left-handed opening batsman of a little under medium height. He played for Kent. In his first class career he made, 7,802 runs and including 17 centuries and took 4 wickets.
Test Record - 1 Test, 51 runs (Av. 25.50).

BERRY ROBERT
England (born 1926) - A left-arm, spin bowler from the Lancashire and Cheshire League. He was a deep field with a good arm. He played for Lancahsire and Worcestershire. In his first class career he made, 1463 runs and took 703 wickets.
Test Record - 2 Tests, 6 runs (Av. 3.00), 9 wickets (Av. 25.33) and 2 catches.

BEST CARLISLE ALONZA
West Indies (born 1959) - A right-hander who sometimes opens and a useful occasional off-spin bowler. On his first Test appearance at Sabina Park against England in 1985-86 he got off the mark in Test cricket with a hook for six. He played for Barbados. In his first class career he made, 2301 runs including 5 centuries and took 3 wickets.
Test Record - 3 Tests, 78 runs (Av. 26.00) and 4 catches.

BHANDARI PARKASH
India (born 1935) - A right-handed batsman and right-arm off-break bowler. Test debut on February 26, 1955 against Pakistan at the age of 19 years and 87 days. Score on Test debut was 19 in the fifth Test at Karachi. Last Test of the career played against Australia in November 1956. Scores on last appearance in Test were 17 and 2 in the third Test at Calcutta. Age at the time of retirement from Test cricket was 20 years and 339 days. In his first class career he made, 2,453 runs including 4 centuries, and took 122 wickets.
Test Record - 3 Tests, 77 runs (Av. 19.25) and 1 catch.

BILBY GRAHAME PAUL
New Zealand (born 1941) - A competent right-handed opening batsman. He played for Wellington. In his first class career he made, 2936 runs including 3 centuries.
Test Record - 2 Tests, 55 runs (Av. 13.75) and 3 catches.

BINKS JAMES GRAHAM
England (born 1935) - He was a highly skilled but often underrated wicket-keeper, the Bob Taylor of his day. He was normally a useful lower-order batsman, with his county. He played for Yorkshire and Lincolnshire. In his first class career he made, 6910 runs and 1071 dismissals (895ct, 176st).
Test Record - 2 Tests, 91 runs (Av. 22.75) and 8 catches.

BINNS ALFRED PHILLIP
West Indies (born 1929) - A right-handed batsman and wicket-keeper. He played for Jamaica. In his first class career he made, 1446 runs including 4 centuries and 65 dismissals.
Test Record - 5 Tests, 64 runs (Av. 9.14) and 17 dismissals (14ct, 3st).

BINNY ROGER
India (born 1955) - A right-handed batsman and right-arm medium-fast bowler. Test debut on November 21, 1979 against Pakistan at the age of 24 years and 122 days. Score on Test debut was 46 in the first Test at Bangalore. He plays for Karnataka. In his first class career he made, 5,093 runs and including 10 centuries, and took 172 wickets.

ROGER BINNY

Test Record - 27 Tests, 830 runs (Av. 23.05), 47 wickets (Av. 32.63) and 11 catches.

BIRD MORICE CARLOS

England (1888-1933) - He was a fine, forcing, right-handed batsman, and a good medium-pace bowler. He played for Lancashire and Surrey. In his first class career he made, 6,920 runs and 149 wickets.

Test Record - 10 Tests, 280 runs (Av. 18.66), 8 wickets (Av. 15.00) and 5 catches.

BIRKENSHAW JACK

England (born 1940) - He was a safe slip field, but his main strength lay in bowling, an orthodox, right-arm, slow, off-break bowler. He had a light-footed, springy approach and a high action combining accuracy with subtle variations of flight and spin. He played for Yorkshire. In his first class career he made, 12,780 runs including 4 centuries, took 1,073 wickets and 318 catches.

Test Record - 5 Tests, 148 runs (Av. 21.14), 13 wickets (Av. 36.07) and 3 catches.

BIRKETT LIONEL SYDNEY

West Indies (born 1905) - A right-handed batsman and a useful medium-pace change-bowler. He was the vice-captain of the first team to Australia in 1930-31. He played for Barbados. In his first class career he made, 1,295 runs including 3 centuries.

Test Record - 4 Tests, 136 runs (Av. 17.00) and 4 catches.

BISSET SIR MURRAY

South Africa (1876-1931) - A quick scoring right-handed batsman. His highest was 184 against Derbyshire in 1901. Also reserve wicket-keeper, he would stand right up to the fiery pace of the fast bowling. He played for Western Province. In his first class career he made, 1,436 runs including 2 centurics and 64 dismissals

Test Record - 3 Tests, 103 runs (Av. 25.75) and 3 dismissals (2ct, 1st).

BISSITT GEORGE FINLAY

South Africa (1905-1965) - A right-arm fast bowler who could be devastating. He played for Griqualand West. In his first class career he made, 294 runs and took 67 wickets.

Test Record - 4 Tests, 38 runs (Av. 19.00) and 25 wickets (Av. 18.76).

BLACKHAM JOHN MCCARTHY

Australia (1854-1932) - He was very useful right-handed batsman and wicket-keeper. He played for Victoria. In his first class career he made, 6,395 runs including 1 century and 451 dismissals.

Test Record - 35 Tests, 800 runs (Av. 15.68) and 60 dismissals (36ct, 24st).

BLACKIE DONALD DEARNESS

Australia (1882-1955) - He was a vintage right-arm off-spin bowler, starting his run near mid-off. He played for Victoria. In his first class career he made, 548 runs and took 211 wickets.

Test Record - 3 Tests, 24 runs (Av. 8.00), 14 wickets (Av. 31.71) and 2 catches.

BLAIR ROBERT WILLIAM

New Zealand (born 1932) - A right-arm medium-fast bowler and occasionally useful late-order batsman. He played for Wellington. In his first class career he made, 1,672 runs and took 546

wickets.
Test Record - 19 Tests, 189 runs (Av. 6.75), 43 wickets (Av. 35.23) and 5 catches.

BLANCKENBERG JAMES MANUEL
South Africa (born 1893 presumed dead) - He was a right-arm medium-pace bowler who could bowl for hours on end to a perfect length. He played for Natal and Western Province. In his first class career he made, 2,232 runs including 1 century and took 293 wickets.
Test Record - 18 Tests, 455 runs (Av. 19.78), 60 wickets (Av. 30.28) and 9 catches.

BLAND KENNETH COLIN
South Africa (born 1938) - He was a crowd-puller, as a right-handed forcing batsman. He played for Rhodesia and Eastern Province. In his first class career he made, 7,208 runs including 13 centuries and took 43 wickets.
Test Record - 21 Tests, 1,669 runs (Av. 49.08) including 3 centuries, 2 wickets (Av. 62.50) and 10 catches.

BLIGH HON. IVO FRANCIS WALTER
England (1859-1927) - A tall man, he was a right-handed batsman with a fine drive. He captained the team to Australia in 1882-83. He played for Cambridge University and Kent. In his first class career he made, 2,642 runs including 2 centuries.
Test Record - 4 Tests, 62 runs (Av. 10.33) and 7 catches.

BLOCKHOLE
The mark or indentation in the pitch made by a batsman when "taking block" and serving to fix his position in relation to the wickets and to guide him in assessing the ball's line of flight.

BLUNT ROGER CHARLES
New Zealand (1900-1966) - He was a very useful right-arm leg-break bowler who developed into a fine, stylish and adaptable batsman. He played for Canterbury. In his first class career he made, 7,953 runs including 15 centuries and took 214 wickets.
Test Record - 9 Tests, 330 runs (Av. 27.50), 12 wickets (Av. 39.33) and 5 catches.

BLYTHE COLIN
England (1879-1917) - He was one of the greatest slow left-arm bowlers. He played for Kent. In his first class career he made, 4,455 runs, took 2,506 wickets and 189 catches.
Test Record - 19 Tests, 183 runs (Av. 9.63), 100 wickets (Av. 18.63) and 6 catches.

BOARD
Scoreboard.

BOARD JOHN HENRY
England (1867-1924) - A fearless and untiring wicket-keeper. He played for Hawkes Bay and Gloucestershire. In his first class career he made, 15,674 runs including 9 centuries and 1,206 dismissals.
Test Record - 6 Tests, 108 runs (Av. 10.80) and 11 dismissals (8ct, 3st).

BODYLINE
Intimidatory fast bowling in cricket aimed persistently at the batsman's body and directed especially towards the leg side.

BOLUS JOHN BRAIN
England (born 1934) - He was an occasional left-arm medium-pace bowler. He was a skilful and powerful stroke-player. He played for Yorkshire. In his first class career he made, 25,598 runs including 39 centuries took 24 wickets and 201 catches.
Test Record - 7 Tests, 496 runs (Av. 41.33) and 2 catches.

BONNOR GEORGE JOHN
Australia (1855-1912) - He was a hitter with extraordinary power. He toured England in 1880, 1882, 1884, 1886 and 1888. He played for Victoria. In his first class career he made, 4,820 runs including 5 centuries and took 12 wickets.
Test Record - 17 Tests, 512 runs (Av. 17.06) in-

cluding 1 century, 2 wickets (Av. 42.00) and 16 catches.

BOOCK STEPHEN LEWIS
New Zealand (born 1951) - He was a slow left-arm orthodox spin bowler with excellent control and considerable power of spin. He played for Otago. In his first class career he made, 870 runs and took 476 wickets.
Test Record - 26 Tests, 192 runs (Av. 6.62), 65 wickets (Av. 32.33) and 13 catches.

BOON DAVID CLARENCE
Australia (born 1960) - A somewhat dour charac-

DAVID BOON

ter, Tasmania's David Boon can be more extrava gant with the bat, particularly in one-day hybrid. Combining with Geoff Marsh, Boon has become one of the most consistent opening batsmen in world cricket. He plays for Tasmania. In his first class career he made, 6,428 runs including 19 centuries, and 3 wickets.
Test Record - 42 Tests, 2,852 runs (Av.40.74) including 7 centuries.

BRIAN BOOTH

BOOTH BRIAN CHARLES
Australia (born 1933) - A very slim right-handed batsman with a great gift of timing, and he was a stroke-player. He played for New South Wales. In his first class career he made, 11,265 runs including 26 centuries, took 16 wickets and 119 catches.
Test Record - 29 Tests, 1,773 runs (Av. 42.21) including 5 centuries, 3 wickets and 17 catches.

BOOTH MAJOR WILLIAM
England (1886-1916) - He was tall, good-looking and a fine punishing, right-handed batsman and fast-medium bowler. He played for Yorkshire. In his first class career he made, 4,754 runs including 1 century and took 603 wickets.
Test Record - 2 Tests, 46 runs (Av. 23.00) and 7 wickets (Av. 18.57).

BORDE CHANDERKANT GULABRAO
India (born 1934) - A right-handed batsman and right-arm leg-break bowler. Test debut on November 29, 1958 against West Indies at the age of 24 years and 127 days. Score on Test debut was 7 in the first Test at Bombay. Last Test of the career played against Australia in November 1969. Scores

on last appearance in Test were 2 and 18 in the first Test at Bombay. Age at the time of retirement from Test cricket was 35 years and 108 days. First-ever Test century (109) scored on February 7, 1959 against West Indies in the fifth Test at Delhi at the age of 24 years and 194 days. Led India in one Test only against Australia in the first Test at Adelaide in 1967-68 at the age of 33 years and 152 days scoring 69 and 12 runs. His unbeaten knock of 177 in the fourth Test against Pakistan at Madras in 1960-61 is the highest score for a batsman at No. 6 in the batting order for India. He played for Maharashtra and Baroda. In his first class career he made, 12,821 runs, including 30 centuries and took 331 wickets.
Test Record - 55 Tests, 3,061 runs (Av. 35.59) including 5 centuries, 52 wickets (Av. 46.48) and 37 catches.

BORDER ALLAN ROBERT
Australia (born 1955) - Allan Border was, by his own admission, a slow starter in the field of cricketing ambitions. While his contemporaries werebeginningto emerge on the interstate scene, young Border was opting for the more idyllic playground of sun, sand and surf. But when things happened to him, they happened fast. He was a tentative NSW Sheffield Shield hopeful when the World Series Cricket phenomenon propelled him into the international arena. A few years later, he found himself captain of Queensland, his adopted State. Then the dramatic resignation of Kim Hughes threw him into the Australian captaincy. The slow starter has now done it all. As a regular member of the Australian team for almost a decade. A stocky left-handed batsman, specialist slip fielder and steady slow left-arm orthodox spin bowler. He plays for New South Wales. In his first class career he made, 17,748 runs including 51 centuries and 205 catches.
Test Record - 102 Tests, 7,831 runs (Av. 52.55) including 23 centuries and 113 catches.

ALLAN BORDER

BOSANQUET BERNARD JAMES TINDAL
England (1877-1936) - Over 6 feet in height, he was a fine, upstanding, right-handed batsman, and also a medium-fast bowler. He played for Oxford University. In his first class career he made, 11,696 runs including 21 centuries, took 629 wickets and 191 catches.
Test Record - 7 Tests, 147 runs (Av. 13.36), 25 wickets (Av. 24.16) and 9 catches.

BOTHAM IAN TERENCE
England (born 1955) - Ian Botham is the most exciting player in world cricket, a colourful and often controversial figure with a massive talent and a public image to match it. He was already a larger-than-life character in the county game when he first played for England in 1977, and at once the records began to tumble - 5 wickets in an innings in his first Test, 100 wickets and 1000 runs in only 21 Tests, 200 wickets and 2000 runs in fewer Tests (42) than anyone in history and in the shortest time (4 years 126 days). In 1985 he hit more sixes than anyone has ever done in one season. The other side of the coin is that he has a conviction for possessing drugs, has found himself in court on an assault charge, has had public

IAN BOTHAM

clashes with his employers, Somerset CCC, and has had a personal manager who sought to promote him as a Hollywood film star. He played for Somerset and now plays for Worcestershire. In his first class career he made, 15,750 runs including 33 centuries and took 1,012 wickets.

Test Record - 94 Tests, 5,057 runs (Av. 34.87), 373 wickets (Av. 27.86) and 109 catches.

BOTTOM EDGE

The edge of the bat closer to the ground, either at the bottom of the blade or on the lower side of a bat held horizontally.

BOUNCER

A ball that is bowled short so that it bounces often to chest or head height usually to intimidate the batsman. The bumper is analogous to baseball's brushback and sometimes to the beanball.

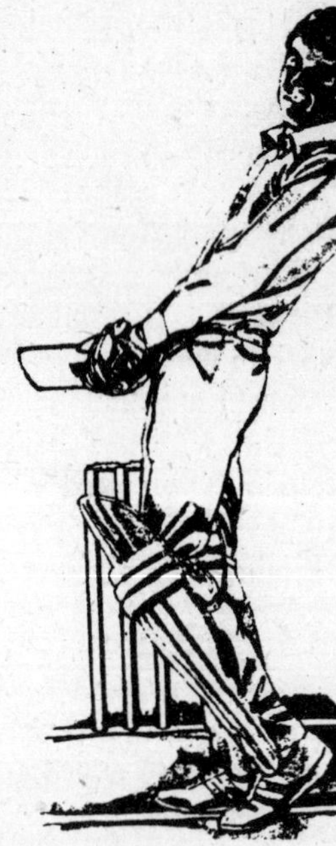

Avoiding Action

BOUNDARY

An award of usually 4 runs to a batsman who hits a ball beyond the boundary of the playing field. If the ball crosses the boundary of the fly, the batsman is automatically awarded 6 runs.

BOWDEN MONTAGUE PARKER

England (1865-1892) - He was a right-handed batsman and wicket-keeper. He played for Surrey. In his first class career he made, 2,316 runs including 3 centuries and 72 dismissals.

Test Record - 2 Tests, 25 runs (Av. 12.50) and 1 catch.

BOWES WILLIAM ERIC

England (born 1908) - He could make the ball kick and would bowl a few bumpers to test out a batsman's nerve and technique. He played for Yorkshire. In his first class career he made, 1,529 runs and took 1,638 wickets.

Test Record - 15 Tests, 28 runs (Av. 4.66), 68 wickets (Av. 22.33) and 2 catches.

BOWL
To propel a cricket ball at the far wicket with an overhand motion while keeping the arm straight. The bowler is permitted to bend his wrist but he must not throw the ball by allowing his elbow top bend. In the very early days of cricket, it was customary to bowl the ball with an underhand motion. Gradually players began to move the arm higher and higher in bowling the ball until today the delivery is straight overdistinction between has remained and the distinction between thorwing the ball and bowling it is a matter of keeping the elbow straight during the delivery.

BOWLED
A batsman out when a bowler ball is not hit but knocks the bails from the defended wicket.

BOWLER
A member of the fielding side who bowls the ball to the batsman. Also a cricketer who specializes in bowling rather than batting or fielding.

BOWLEY EDWARD HENRY
England (1890-1974) - He was one of the finest back foot, right-handed batsman of his time and a useful change-bowler. He played for Auckland and Sussex. In his first class career he made, 28,378 runs including 52 centuries took 741 wickets and 373 catches.

Test Record - 5 Tests, 252 runs (Av. 36.00) including 1 century and 2 catches.

BOWLING
Bowling is the hardest work in cricket. Bowling doesn't mean simply running to the wicket and letting the ball go down to the batsman with any length and any direction. The real bowling is a combination of length, direction, and ability to bowl the ball with an intended length and direction. But all this will come out after tremendous practise. For all bowlers the first, and by far the most important, aim must be to attain this. There are four essential things:-

(i) A right attitude of mind;
(ii) A proper grip of the ball;
(iii) A rhythmical run up and
(iv) A basically correct action.

BOWLING ARM
As your front arm moves away from the body after the rock-back of the trunk, so does your bowling arm. Initially it is extended and close to the front arm high on the leading side of the body before moving downwards and backwards in a circular movement alongside your chest. It is fully extended and straight behind the body when the front elbow is tucked into your hip where it stabilies. This sudden lowering of the leading elbow drages the bowling arm over quickly, high and straight alongside your head. The ball is released in this position, For slower bowlers the point of release is generally just before the bowling arm reaches the vertical position. For faster bowlers the release occurs just after the bowling arm has passed the vertical point. It is important to ensure that the shoulders are throughout in the delivery swing and rotate vertically towards the batter. If you are a fast bowler, keep your hand behind the ball at the moment of release. Lay your wrist back before flicking it through behind the ball towards the batter.

BOWLING CREASE
Either of 2 paralled lines 8(1/2) feet long and 66

feet apart on which the wickets are centered and behind which the bowler must keep his rear foot in bowling the ball.

BOWLING TECHNIQUE

Bowling is a profound skill with many facets. A good bowler relies on two basic qualities to restrict the batsman's run-scoring, while he employs any of some seven technical resources to achieve his dismissal. The two primary requisites are direction and length. In the case of direction-sometimes called 'line'- the ball must be directed so accurately on the line of the wicket or slightly to a selected side of it that the batsman cannot hit it freely or to areas free of fieldsmen. A ball of 'good length' is one which pitches at such a point that the batsman cannot use either of the two kinds of batting stroke-forward or back-with command. Length depends upon the batsman and the pace of the bowling. A tall batsman can hit on that half-volley a ball which a shorter man would have to play as of good length. Again, a good-length ball from a slow bowler will pitch substantially nearer the batsman than one from a fast bowler. In effect, a good-length ball is not sufficiently full-pitched to be driven nor short enough to be cut or hooked.

BOYCE KEITH DAVID

West Indies (born 1943) - He was an exciting all-rounder. He adored hitting sixes and was a master in limited-overs cricket. He played for Barbados and Essex. In his first class career he made 8,800 runs including 4 centuries, took 852 wickets and 215 catches.

Test Record - 21 Tests, 657 runs (Av. 24.33), 60 wickets (Av. 30.01) and 5 catches.

BOYCOTT GEOFFREY

England (born 1940) - A right-handed batsman and medium-pace bowler. No cricketer has stirred the emotions of supporters, administrators and fellow players more than Geoff Boycott. This dedicated, but self-centred opening batsman developed his talent to its limit after winning his England place against Australia in 1964 and quickly established himself as a player of Test quality.He played for Yorkshire. In his first

GEOFFREY BOYCOTT

class career he made, 48,426 runs including 151 centuries, took 45 wickets and 264 catches.

Test Record - 108 Tests, 8,114 runs (Av. 47.72),including 22 centuries,7 wickets (Av. 54.57) and 33 catches.

BOYLE HENRY FREDERICK

Australia (1847-1907) - A right-handed overarm bowler. He was one of the most daring of fieldsmen at short-mid-on. He played for Victoria. In his first class career he made, 1,711 runs including one century, took 370 wickets and 125 catches.

Test Record - 12 Tests, 153 runs (Av. 12.75), 32 wickets (Av. 20.03) and 10 catches.

BRACEWELL BRENDON PAUL

New Zealand (born 1959) - A right-arm fast bowler. He played for Otago. In his first class career he made, 692 runs and took 136 wickets.

Test Record - 6 Tests, 24 runs (Av. 2.40), 14 wickets (Av. 41.78) and one catch.

BRACEWELL JOHN GARRY

New Zealand (born 1958) - John is a tall, quick-ish off-break bowler with a high action and a useful, hard-hitting, right-handed batsman. He played for Otago and Auckland. In his first class career he made, 2,741 runs including 3 centuries, and took 346 wickets.

Test Record - 20 Tests, 441 runs (Av. 20.04), 58 wickets (Av. 29.86) and 16 catches.

BRADBURN WYNNE PENNELL

New Zealand (born 1939) - A sound right-handed batsman and slow-medium change in-swing bowler. He played for Northern Districts. In his first class career he made, 2,077 runs including one century and took 19 wickets.

Test Record - 2 Tests, 62 runs, (Av. 15.50).

BRADLEY WALTER MORRIS

England (1875-1944) - A right-arm bowler and right-handed batsman. He played for Kent. In his first class career he made, 906 runs and took 624 wickets.

Test Record - 2 Tests, 23 runs (Av. 23.00) and 6 wickets (Av. 38.83).

DON BRADMAN

BRADMAN SIR DONALD GEORGE

Australia (born 1908) - Bradman remains the only great batsman in history who was never really out of form. He destroyed all bowlers who challenged him at State and Test levels for more than 20 years. Then, right in his early 40s, he finally gave away his bat and gloves and was knighted for his services to the game. No player has ever approached this remarkable individual's relentless dedication and almost unnatural talent when it came to run scoring. It may, indeed, be sufficient merely to record the fact that he ended with the incredible Test average of 99.94. He played for New South Wales. In his first class career he made, 28,067 runs including 117 centuries, took 36 wickets and 131 catches.

Test Record - 52 Tests, 6,996 runs (Av.99.94) including 29 centuries, 2 wickets (Av. 36.00) and 32 catches.

BRANN WILLIAM HENRY

South Africa (1899-1953) - A right-handed batsman. He played for Eastern Province. In his first class career he made, 1,045 runs.

Test Record - 3 Tests, 71 runs (Av. 14.20) and 2 catches.

BRAUND LEONARD CHARLES

England (1875-1955) - He was one of the greatest all-rounder. An aggressive right-handed batsman with powerful strokes on the leg. He played for Surrey. In his first class career he made, 17,801 runs including 25 centuries, took 1,113 wickets and 508 catches.

Test Record - 23 Tests, 987 runs (Av. 25.97) including 3 centuries, 47 wickets (Av. 38.51) and 39 catches.

BREARLEY JOHN MICHAEL

England (born 1942) - A solid right-handed opening batsman. He had the ability to stroke the ball effortlessly in his more felicitous moods, almost an ideal captain. He played for Cambridge University and Middlesex. In his first class career he made, 25,185 runs including 45 centuries took 3 wickets and 418 catches.

Test Record - 39 Tests, 1,442 runs (Av.22.88) and 52 catches.

BREARLEY WALTER
England (1876-1937) - A right-arm fast bowler. He played for Lancashire. In his first class career he made, 849 runs and took 845 wickets.
Test Record - 4 Tests, 21 runs (Av.7.00) and 17 wickets (Av. 21.11).

BRENNAN DONALD VINCENT
England (1920-1985) - A wicket-keeper and right-handed batsman. He played for Yorkshire. In his first class career he made, 1,937 runs and 434 dismissals.
Test Record - 2 Tests, 16 runs (Av. 8.00) and 1 stumping.

BRIGGS JOHN
England (1862-1902) - He was an aggressive right-handed batsman and left-arm slow bowler. He made his debut at sixteen in 1885, and hit his highest score, 186 against Surrey. He played for Lancashire. In his first class career he made, 14,092 runs including 10 centuries, took 2,221 wickets and 223 catches.
Test Record - 33 Tests, 815 runs (Av. 18.11), 118 wickets (Av. 17.74) and 12 catches.

BRIGHT RAYMOND JAMES
Australia (born 1954) - Left-arm spin bowler. He played World Series Cricket between 1977-79 and was appointed captain of Victoria in 1983. In his first class career he made, 3,946 runs including 2 centuries and took 428 wickets.
Test Record - 22 Tests, 407 runs (Av. 14.13), 45 wickets (Av. 41.97) and 11 catches.

BRISCOE ARTHUR WELLESLEY
South Africa (1911-1941) - A right-handed batsman. He played for Transvaal. In his first class career he made, 2,189 runs including 6 centuries. He was killed in action during the Abyssinian campaign.
Test Record - 2 Tests, 33 runs (Av.11.00) and 1 catch.

BROAD BRIAN CHRISTOPHER
England (born 1957) - A left-handed opening batsman and occasional right-arm medium-pace bowler. He was selected to make his Test debut against the West Indies at Lord's in 1984. He played for Gloucestershire, Nottinghamshire and Orange Free State. In his first class career he made, 10,297 runs including 18 centuries.
Test Record - 23 Tests, 1579 runs, (Av.41.55) and 8 catches.

BROCKWELL WILLIAM
England (1865-1935) - A brilliant right-handed batsman and useful medium-pace bowler. He played for Surrey. In his first class career he made, 13,285 runs including 22 centuries.
Test Record - 7 Tests, 202 runs (Av. 16.83), 5 wickets (Av. 61.80) and 6 catches.

BROMFIELD HENRY DUDLEY
South Africa (born 1932) - A competent right-arm off-spin bowler. He played for Western Province. In his first class career he made, 374 runs and took 205 wickets.
Test Record - 9 Tests, 59 runs (Av.11.80), 17 wickets (Av. 35.23) and 13 catches.

BROMLEY DAVENPORT HUGH RICHARD
England (1870-1954) - He was a medium-fast left-arm bowler and a useful batsman. He played for Cambridge University. In his first class career he made, 1,540 runs and 123 wickets.
Test Record - 4 Tests, 128 runs, (Av. 21.33) and 4 wickets (Av. 24.50).

BROMLEY ERNEST HARVEY
Australia (1912-1967) - A left-handed batsman and superb fielder. He played for Victoria. In his first class career he made, 2,055 runs including 3 centuries and took 39 wickets.
Test Record - 2 Tests, 38 runs (Av. 9.50) and 2 catches.

BROWN DAVID JOHN
England (born 1942) - A right-arm medium-fast bowler. He played for Warwickshire. In his first class career he made, 4,110 runs and 1,165 wickets

and 157 catches.
Test Record - 26 Tests, 342 runs (Av. 11.79), 79 wickets (Av. 28.31) and 7 catches.

BROWN FREDERICK RICHARD
England (born 1910) - He was a hard-hitting right-handed batsman and leg-spin googly bowler. He played for Cambridge University, Surrey and Northamptonshire. In his first class career he made, 13,325 runs including 22 centuries, took 1,221 wickets and 212 catches.
Test Record - 22 Tests, 734 runs (Av. 25.31), 45 wickets (Av. 31.06) and 22 catches.

BROWN WILLIAM ALFRED
Australia (born 1912) - A right-handed opening batsman and an excellent fielder. He played for Queensland. In his first-class career he made, 13,838 runs including 39 centuries and 110 catches.
Test Record - 22 Tests, 1,592 runs (Av. 46.82) including 4 centuries and 14 catches.

BROWNE CYRIL
West Indies (1890-1964) - A right-handed hard-hitting batsman and medium-pace leg-break bowler. Brown was the first black West Indian to be elected to honorary life membership of MCC. He played for Barbados and British Guiana. In his first class career he made, 2,077 runs and took 278 wickets.
Test Record - 4 Tests, 176 runs (Av. 25.14), 6 wickets (Av. 48.00) and one catch.

BRUCE WILLIAM
Australia (born 1864-1925) - A left-arm,medium-pace bowler and left-handed opening batsman. He played for Victoria. In his first class career he made, 5,732 runs and took 143 wickets.
Test Record - 14 Tests, 702 runs (Av. 29.25), 12 wickets (Av. 36.66) and 12 catches.

BUCKENHAM CLAUDE PERCIVCAL
England (1876-1937) - He bowled very fast with a good high delivery and a hard-hitting batsman. He played for Essex. In his first-class career he made, 5,666 runs and took 1,152 wickets.
Test Record - 4 Tests, 43 runs (Av.6.14), 21 wickets (Av. 28.23) and 2 catches.

BUMP
To rise steeply off the wicket after pitching typically as a result of some irregularity in the surface steeple.

BURGE PETER JOHN PARNELL
Australia (born 1932) - An attractive right-handed batsman. He represented Australia for the first time at Sydney in the fifth Test against England in 1954-55. He played for Queensland. In his first class career he made, 14,640 runs including 38 centuries and 170 dismissals.
Test Record - 42 Tests, 2,290 runs (Av. 38.16) including 4 centuries and 23 catches.

BURGESS MARK GORDON
New Zealand (born 1944) - A right-handed batsman. In 1979, he led New Zealand into the semi-final of the Prudential World Cup. He played for Auckland. In his first class career he made, 10,281 runs including 20 centuries, took 30 wickets and 151 catches.
Test Record - 50 Tests, 2,684 runs (Av.31.20) including 5 centuries and 34 catches.

BURKE JAMES WALLACE
Australia (1930-1979) - He was a right-handed batsman with a sound defence and a good fielder at point. He played for New South Wales. In his first class career he made, 7,563 runs including 21 centuries and took 101 wickets.
Test Record - 24 Tests, 1,280 runs (Av. 34.59) including 3 centuries and 8 wickets (Av. 28.75).

BURKE SYDNEY FRANK
South Africa (born 1934) - A right-arm medium-fast bowler. He played for Orange Free State. In his first class career he made, 2,334 runs including 1 century and took 241 wickets.
Test Record - 2 Tests, 42 runs (Av. 14.00) and 11 wickets (Av. 23.36).

BURN EDWIN JAMES KENNETH

Australia (1862-1956) - An attractive right-handed batsman whose game was built on attack. He played for Wellington and Tasmania. In his first class career he made, 1,750 runs including 2 centuries and took 14 wickets.

Test Record - 2 Tests, 41 runs (Av. 10.25).

BURTT THOMAS BROWNING

New Zealand (born 1915) - A left-arm slow bowler and a left-handed batsman. He played for Canterbury. In his first class career he made, 1,631 runs and took 408 wickets.

Test Record - 10 Tests, 252 runs (Av.21.00), 33 wickets (Av. 35.45) and 2 catches.

BUTCHER ROLAND ORLANDO

England (born 1953) - A stocky, fair-handed right-handed batsman.He played with modest success for Barbados in 1974-75. In his first class career he made, 10,043 runs including 14 centuries and 245 dismissals.

Test Record - 3 Tests, 71 runs (Av. 14.20) and 3 catches.

BUTT HARRY RIGDEN

England (1965-1928) - A right-handed batsman and wicket-keeper. He played for Sussex. In his first class career he made, 7,313 runs and 1,262 dismissals.

Test Record - 3 Tests, 22 runs (Av. 7.33) and 2 dismissals (1 ct, 1 st).

BYE

A run scored from a ball other than a wide or no-ball, that passes the wicket without touching either the striker or his bat. Any runs accruing in this way are credited to the batting side as byes, under extras.

BYNOE MICHAEL ROBIN

West Indies (born 1941)- A stylish right-handed opening batsman and left-arm medium-pace bowler. He toured India and Pakistan in 1958-59. He played for Barbados. In his first class career he made, 1,572 runs including 6 centuries.

Test Record - 4 Tests, 111 runs (Av. 18.50) and 4 catches.

C

C & B

Used in the score book, following the name of a batsman and preceding the name of a bowler, to indicate that the batsman has been dismissed by a catch taken by the bowler of the ball.

CAIRNS BERNARD LANCE

New Zealand (born 1949) - A right-arm medium-pace bowler and equally valuable as a late-order batsman. His fastest century recorded in New Zealand in 52 minutes off 45 balls, playing for Otago against Wellington scored 110 out of 170. He played for Central Districts. In his first class career he made, 4,143 runs including one century.
Test Record - 43 Tests, 928 runs (Av. 16.28), 130 wickets (Av. 32.91) and 30 catches.

CALCUTTA

Founded in 1792. The cricket ground known as Eden Garden is now the oldest in the world on which Test Matches are played. The first Test Match on the ground was played in 1933-34 between India and England. Capacity of this ground is over 80,000.

CALL

1. From the point of view of batsman it may be his 'yes' 'no' 'wait' while the bowler throws the ball or his call to the second batsman after the first runs have been taken.
2. It may be call from Umpire declaring the ball wide or no-ball.

CALLAWAY SYDNEY THOMAS

Australia (1868-1923) - A splendid batsman when in form and a medium-fast bowler with a good length. He played for New South Wales. In his first class career he made, 1,747 runs and took 321 wickets.
Test Record - 3 Tests, 87 runs (Av. 17.40) and 6 wickets (Av. 23.66).

CALTHORPE HON. FREDERICK SOMERSET GOUCH

England (1892-1935) - He was an attractive right-handed batsman and a medium-pace bowler. He founded the Cricketer's Golf Society. He played for Cambridge University and Sussex. In his first class career he made, 12,596 runs including 13 centuries and took 782 wickets.
Test Record - 4 Tests, 129 runs (Av. 18.42), 1 wicket (Av. 91.00) and 2 catches.

CAMACHO GEORGE STEPHEN

West Indies (born 1945) - A very sound right-handed opening batsman. He became Secretary of the West Indies Cricket Board. He played for Guyana. In his first class career he made, 4,019 runs including 7 centuries.
Test Record - 11 Tests, 640 runs (Av. 29.09) and 4 catches.

CAMBRIDGE UNIVERSITY

Cambridge University C.C. owes much for its early progress to the Rev. A. R. Ward, who was son of William Ward, the man who saved Lord's from the builders in 1825. The first recorded match by Cambridge University was played against Eton in 1754 and the annual match against Oxford began in 1827.

CAMBRIDGESHIRE

Founded in 1891 though was in existence before 1849. First appeared in the Minor Counties Championship in 1898.

CAMERON FRANCIS JAMES

West Indies (born 1923) - A right-handed batsman and off-break bowler. He played for Jamaica. In his first class career he made, 551 runs and took 29 wickets.
Test Record - 5 Tests, 151 runs (Av. 25.16) and 3 wickets (Av. 92.66).

CAMERON FRANCIS JAMES

New Zealand (born 1932) - A wily right-arm medium-fast bowler. He played for Otago. In his first class career he made, 993 runs and took 447 wickets.
Test Record - 19 Tests, 116 runs (Av. 11.60) and 61 wickets (Av. 30.31).

CAMERON HORACE BRAKENRIDGE

South Africa (1905-1935) - A high ranking wicket-keeper and batsman. He was a fast-scoring and right-handed batsman. He played for Transvaal. In his first class career he made, 5,396 runs including 11 centuries and 224 dismissals.
Test Record - 26 Tests, 1,239 runs (Av. 30.21) and 51 dismissals (39ct, 12st).

CAMERON JOHN HENSLEY

West Indies (born 1914) - A right-handed batsman, reliable fielder and off-break bowler. He played for Cambridge University and Jamaica. In his first class career he made, 2,772 runs including 4 centuries and 184 wickets.
Test Record - 2 Tests, 6 runs (Av. 2.00) and 3 wickets (Av. 29.33).

CAMPBELL THOMAS

South Africa (1882-1924) - A competent wicket-keeper though of small account as a batsman. He played for Transvaal. In his first class career he made, 371 runs and 51 dismissals.
Test Record - 5 Tests, 90 runs (Av. 15.00) and 8 dismissals (7ct, 1st).

CANADA

British Army officers introduced cricket in Canada at the end of the 18th Century and although it has never achieved the popularity of a national game, it has always had a keen following around Montreal and Toronto. In 1844 Canada and the United States met in their first international. This was over 30 years before the famed England v Australia series began and historians believe the contest is the oldest international sporting fixture in the world. By the time Canada became a nation in 1867, the game was so popular that it was declared the national sport of the country by the first Prime Minister, Sir John A. MacDonald and his cabinet. The Australian team to tour Canada was the 1878 side led by W.L. Murdoch. In 1935 the first tour to England by a Colts side was successfully carried out and repeated in 1937 and 1939.
Canada entered the first ICC Trophy Competition for associate members of ICC and lost the final to Sri Lanka. In preparation for the third ICC Trophy Competition which was held again in England in 1986, Canada toured Jamaica for the first time in 1984 gaining valuable experience.

CANTERBURY, KENT

This is one of the most picturesque of English county grounds. It was laid out in 1847. The first important match was played between Kent v England.

CAPTAIN

Any team's performance depends on a qualified leader. It is said that cricket is a 'game of chance' between teams of same standard but that team wins whose captain is qualified and capable of executing a flexible, well planned policy. The captain's first decision whether to bat or bowl upon winning the toss, depends upon the wicket. A captain should know the batting strength of the opposition against the bowling team attack. In most cases the captain should decide to bat, to put runs on the board and thus create a psychological hurdle for the side batting second.
It is true that the captain's decision is final, but to keep up the team spirit and faith of the senior players he should consult his colleagues.
A captain is the image of his team. Thus at the time of crisis he should keep his team's spirit and in between he should praise the player giving good performance.
As a tactician, the captain's first decision is whether to bat or bowl upon winning the toss. For this he should have thorough knowledge of the wicket. If the opposition team bats first and puts on a huge total, then too the captain will be blamed. Thus a good captain is he, who keeps his nerves cool and capable of executing a flexible, well-planned policy aimed at winning a match in an ethical manner.
The captain's task is not easy. Specific instructions must be given to individual. A great part of

the captain's responsibility on the field lies in consultation with the bowler and at times with other players, such as the wicket keeper, before placing the field. It is very important for the captain to place his top batsmen and or bowlers while fielding in such a position that they do not have to run too much, or get exhausted.

The captain must be aware of the psychological make-up of the team: who will best stand up to crisis and pressures? Bowlers who are tired must be rested.

The captain of the side must know when certain types of bowlers are ineffective - under certain conditions and against certain types of batsmen - and change them accordingly. A good skipper appreciates when to take the new ball, when to attack for quick runs, when to pressurise a batsman newly arrived at the crease, and when to slow down the opposition's scoring rate. Judgement is needed to know when to enforce the follow-on and when to instruct batters to consolidate the team's position.

It may become obvious that the opposition is attacking in a certain way, and that his tactics has to be countered. A restrictive opposition bowling and fielding policy, with a declaration approaching, may call for adventurousness on the part of the batsman. Aggression from the opposition batsman or an inclination to go for quick singles demands a knowledge of sensible field changes to increase the batting risks and prevent the flow of runs.

A captain has to decide in a very critical position. For instance, declaring an innings. An innings is declared in three circumstances:

1. When a team has made too many runs.
2. When a match is becoming very slow and the viewers become 'bored' then the captain takes decision of declaring the innings to make a match interesting.
3. When the captain realises that the wicket is taking turn and the opposition team can be bowled out easily.

A captain commands respect by being a good example of on-field alertness, sportsmanship, self-discipline, playing ability and by bringing out the best talents of the side. He must be a competitive, thoughtful and impartial leader.

CAREW GEORGE MCDONALD

West Indies (1910-1974) - A right-handed batsman. He played for Barbados. In his first class career he made, 2,131 runs including 3 centuries and took 13 wickets.

Test Record - 4 Tests, 170 runs (Av. 28.33) including 1 century and 1 catch.

CAREW MICHAEL CONRAD

West Indies (born 1937) - A left-handed opening batsman and a useful right-arm leg-break bowler. He later became a Test selector. He played for Trinidad. In his first class career he made, 7,810 runs including 13 centuries and took 108 wickets.

Test Record - 19 Tests, 1,127 runs (Av. 34.15) including 1 century, 8 wickets (Av. 54.62) and 13 catches.

CARKEEK WILLIAM

Australia (1878-1937) - A left-handed batsman and a useful wicket-keeper. He played for Victoria. In his first class career he made, 1,388 runs and 159 dismissals.

Test Record - 6 Tests, 16 runs (Av. 5.33) and 6 dismissals (6ct).

CARLSON PHILIP HENRY

Australia (born 1951) - A useful medium-pace bowler, swing bowler and gifted batsman. He played for Queensland. In his first class career he made, 4,167 runs including 5 centuries and took 126 wicket.

Test Record - 2 Tests, 23 runs (Av. 5.75), 2 wickets (Av. 49.50) and 2 catches.

CARLSTEIN PETER RUDOLPH

South Africa (born 1938) - A fine fielder, right-handed batsman. He played for Orange Free State. In his first class career he made, 7,554 runs including 9 centuries.

Test Record - 8 Tests, 190 runs (Av. 14.61) and 3 catches.

CARPET

The ground.

CARRYING BAT

This term is used when a batsman is not out at the end of an innings and more particularly when one of the two opening batsmen is not out when all the ten wickets have fallen. W.G. Grace and C.J.B. Wood each batted through a completed innings no less than 17 times in their careers. This is a record.

CARR ARTHUR WILLIAM

England (1893-1963) - A fine right-handed attacking batsman, a splendid fielder and a strong and inspiring - if provocative - captain. He played for Nottinghamshire. In his first class career he made, 21,051 runs including 45 centuries, took 31 wickets, 393 catches and 1 stumping.

Test Record - 11 Tests, 237 runs (Av. 19.75) and 3 catches.

CARR DONALD BRYCE

England (born 1926) - A right-handed batsman and a very good hooker. He was also an erratic unorthodox slow left-arm bowler. His son John is an outstanding batsman and off-break bowler. He played for Oxford University and Derbyshire. In his first class career he made, 19,257 runs including 24 centuries, took 328 wickets and 501 catches.

Test Record - 2 Tests, 135 runs (Av. 33.75) and 2 wickets (Av. 70.00).

CARTER CLAUDE PAGET

South Africa (1881-1952) - He was a left-arm slow bowler and also a hard-hitting batsman. He played for Natal. In his first class career he made, 1,333 runs and took 366 wickets.

Test Record - 10 Tests, 181 runs (Av. 18.10), 28 wickets (Av. 24.78) and 2 catches.

CARTER HANSON

Australia (1878-1948) - He was one of the best wicket-keepers and also a useful batsman. He played for New South Wales. In his first class career he made, 2,899 runs including 2 centuries and 273 dismissals.

Test Record - 28 Tests, 873 runs (Av. 22.97) and 65 dismissals (44ct, 21st).

CARTWRIGHT THOMAS WILLIAM

England (born 1935) - He was a medium-pace bowler and also an effective batsman. He played for Warwickshire. In his first class career he made, 13,710 runs including 7 centuries took 1,536 wickets and 332 catches.

Test Record - 5 Tests, 26 runs (Av. 5.20), 15 wickets (Av. 36.26) and 2 catches.

CASTLE

The wicket that a batsman is defending.

CATCH

Catching is another branch of fielding, and is almost entirely a matter of practice. If you are a beginner, practice taking all kinds of catches - snicks, slow high ones, gentle low ones and high drives. Later on, you can do a certain amount of specializing by becoming primarily a slip fielder or a deep fielder.

Hands cupped for catch

Whenever possible, take a catch with the hands about four to five inches away from the chest, allowing the ball to come down, passing your eyes. Keep your eyes all the time on the ball, judge its flight correctly and as the ball meets the hands, the fingers must be closed round it to hold it tight and at the same time the hands should be allowed to sink down on the body so as to receive the ball gently. Care should be taken not to push the hands upwards. If the ball is skied and going too far beyond the position you have occupied, then keep your eyes on the ball and without looking on the ground, turn quickly, simultaneously following straight towards the travelling ball and run as fast as you can, watching the ball throughout. As the ball comes down near your reach stretch your hands fully outwards towards the ball and take the catch in the same running action. The important thing is that while turning and running you should never look down on the ground. Your eyes must be constantly watching the ball. Besides, after turning never take zig-zag course but always follow dead straight the line of the ball. Avoid grabbing or snapping at the ball. Receive it, as explained above.

A golden rule in fielding is to back up at every opportunity. Whenever a bowler or a wicket-keeper or even a fielder is about to stop a ball, it is imperative that the fielder nearby should try to get behind him, in case he misfields the ball.

One very sad mistake generally noticed is to put a man in the wrong position, i.e. , in a place to which he is not accustomed or suited. Good fielding requires speed, good eyesight and quick use of the brain. These requirements vary in different positions. It is useless to put a sprinter as well as a good thrower in the slips, conversely, a person with weak eyes who is slow on his feet and not a good thrower, is not much good for the out field. The fault in this case will not be the fielder's but that of the captain.

It is the duty of each and every cricketer to be able to field in all the required positions with efficiency but there are always some fielders who excel in certain positions.

The slip fielders must bend down properly with the legs comfortably kept apart so that they can get up quickly till it has been played by the batsman. The slips must take positions according to the type of bowlers and the situation of the wicket where the lowest possible catch can be easily taken. Besides, the distance between two slip fielders should be such that they may not clash with each other while taking a catch nor should they allow a ball to pass between them. The other close fielders should also bend down comfortably keeping their eyes on the batsman's bat and expect that each and every ball is coming towards them. They must be so accustomed to the job that they can be able to judge from the batsman's movement of the bat as to the angle as well as the direction the ball is likely to take.

CATTERALL ROBERT HECTOR

South Africa (1900-1961) - He was a right-handed batsman delightfully driving and strong hitting to leg. He was also a fleet-footed and efficient deep field. He played for Natal. In his first class career he made, 5,849 runs including 9 centuries and took 53 wickets.

Test Record - 24 Tests, 1,555 runs (Av. 37.92) including 3 centuries,7 wickets (Av. 23.14) and 12 catches.

CAUGHT

A mode of dismissal in which a batsman is given out if the ball touches his bat or if it touches below the wrist his hand or glove holding the bat, and is subsequently held by a fieldsman before it touches the ground. The catcher must be within the field of play with no part of his body grounded over the boundary line-throughout the act of making the catch. The dismissal is credited to the bowler and is entered in the scorebook as caught. A batsman cannot be out caught off a no-ball. See also CATCH.

CAVE HENRY BUTLER

New Zealand (born 1922) - He was an economical right-arm medium- pace bowler and he was also a late-order batsman and a very good fielder. He played for Wellington. In his first class career he made, 2,187 runs including 2 centuries and took 362 wickets.

Test Record - 19 Tests, 229 runs (Av. 8.80), 34 wickets (Av. 43.12) and 8 catches.

CENTURY

A batsman's score of 100 runs or over, made in a single innings. The first century yet found recorded in the history of cricket is that made by Minshull for the Duke of Dorset's XI against Sevenoaks, in 1769. The first century in a Test match was 165 (retired hurt) by C. Bannerman for Australia v. England, at Melbourne, in 1877. The first man to score two separate hundreds in a single game was W. Lambert. He made 107 and 157 for Sussex v. Epsom, at Lord's in 1817. The first man to score a century in each innings of a Test match was W. Bardsley. He made 136 and 130 for Australia v. England, at the Oval, in Aug.1909.

CHALLENGE CUP

Decided by the MCC on a knock-out basis between county clubs at Lord's in January, 1873. Only one match was played in this competition in June 1873 when Kent beat Sussex by 52 runs, at Lords.

CHALLENOR GEORGE

West Indies (1888-1947) - He was an opening batsman and off-side player of perfect timing. He played for Barbados. In his first class career he made, 5,822 runs including 15 centuries and took 54 wickets.

Test Record - 3 Tests, 101 runs (Av. 16.83).

CHANCELESS

Made without any opportunity for dismissal being given.

CHANDRASEKHAR BHAGWAT SUBRAHMANYA

India (born 1945) - A right-handed batsman and right-arm unorthodox leg-break and googly bowler. Test debut on January 21,1964, against England at the age of 18 years and 243 days. Score on Test debut was 0 in the second Test at Bombay. Last Test of the career played against England in July 1979. Remained unbeaten without scoring a run in both the innings of the 1st Test at Edgbaston on his last appearance in Test. Age at the time of retirement from Test cricket was 34 years and 55 days. Holds the world record of scoring highest number of 39 zeros in his 58 appearances in Tests which include 11 "pairs of spectacles". One of the "pairs" was a "king pair", when he was claimed by the very first ball in both the innings. Shares along with L.R. Gibbs of the West Indies, the world record of being unbeaten on a maximum of 39 occasions. While Gibbs was not out 39 times in his 80 innings, Chandra remained not out 39 times out of his 58 Test appearances. He took five or more wickets in an innings on 16 occasions for India, which is a record for India. His haul of 35 wickets in the five-Test series against England in India in 1972-73 constitutes a record of most wickets in a series for India. He has performed the rare feat of capturing 50 or more wickets in a calendar year when he bagged 52 wickets conceding 1,458 runs at an average of 28.04 in 11 Tests in the year 1976. Among those bowlers who have taken over 100 wickets in Tests, he is the only bowler who has scored less runs as a batsman than the wickets he has taken. He claimed his 100th Test wicket in his 22nd Test appearance having D.L. Amiss caught at the wicket for 8 in the 2nd innings of the third Test against England at Madras on January 14th, 1973. He played for Mysore. In his first class career he made 600 runs and took 1,063 wickets.

Test Record- 58 Tests, 167 runs, 242 wickets (Av.29.74) and 25 catches.

BHAGWAT CHANDRASEKHAR

CHANGE-BOWLER

A bowler typically not a specialist whose principal function is to relieve bowlers or to enable a front-line bowler to change ends.

CHAPMAN ARTHUR PERCY FRANK

England (1900-1961) - He was a left-handed batsman, off-drives and leg-side strokes player. He

played for Cambridge University and Kent. In his first class career he made, 16,309 runs including 27 centuries, took 22 wickets and 356 catches.
Test Record - 26 Tests, 925 runs (Av. 28.90) including 1 century and 32 catches.

CHAPMAN HORACE WILLIAM

South Africa (1890-1941) - A useful right-handed and googly bowler. He played for Natal. In his first class career he made, 587 runs and took 30 wickets.
Test Record - 2 Tests, 39 runs (Av. 13.00) and 1 catch.

CHAPPELL GREGORY STEPHEN

Australia (born 1948) - Greg Chappell is the most gifted of the modern Australian batsman. A

GREG CHAPPELL

right-handed batsman and right-arm medium-pace bowler. He is a brilliant slip fielder and a medium-pace bowler able to swing the ball. In 1975 Ian handed the Australian captaincy to Greg, who celebrated with 123 and 109 not out at Brisbane and by going on to win a series against the West Indies 5-1. He announced his retirement in 1977, to play World Series for Kerry Packer, but he returned, although he has tended to pick his series to suit the business commitments which have made him one of the richest cricketers. He captained his country in 48 Tests. He played for South Australia and Somerset. In his first class cricket he made, 24,535 runs including 74 centuries, took 291 wickets and 376 catches.
Test Record - 87 Tests, 7,110 runs (Av. 53.86) including 24 centuries, 47 wickets (Av. 40.70) and 122 catches.

CHAPPELL IAN MICHAEL

Australia (born 1943) - A right-handed batsman both gritty and attractive, a brilliant slip fielder and useful leg-spin bowler. With Greg he shares a record unlikely to be equalled, Both scored centuries in each innings of the first Test against New Zealand at wellington in 1973-74. Both acted as player and adviser, in World Series Cricket. He returned to Test cricket when WSC was disbanded but the controversies continued to follow him. He played for South Australia. In his first class careerhe made, 19,680 runs including 59 centuries and took 176 wickets.
Test Record - 75 Tests, 5,345 runs (Av. 42.42) including 14 centuries, 20 wickets (Av. 65.80) and 105 catches.

CHAPPELL TREVOR MARTIN

Australia (born 1952)- Trevor is the third of the Chappell brothers and that is a difficult act to follow ! He did have his moment of international glory when used as a makeshift opener for the 1983 World Cup. A right-handed batsman and right-arm medium-paced bowler. He played for South Australia. In his first class career he made, 7,641 runs including 8 centuries and took 75 wickets.
Test Record - 3 Tests, 79 runs (Av. 15.80) and 2 catches.

CHAPPLE MURRAY ERNEST

New Zealand ((born 1930) - A steady, strokemaking right-handed batsman and a left-arm change slow bowler, He became involved in the national administration of the game and has managed New Zealand touring teams. He played for Canterbury. In his first class career he made, 5,344 runs including 4 centuries and took 142 wickets.
Test Record - 14 Tests, 497 runs (Av. 19.11).

CHARLTON DR PERCIE CHATOR

Australia (1867-1954) - He was a batsman and fast-medium bowler. He played for New South Wales. In his first class career he made, 648 runs and took 97 wickets.
Test Record - 2 Tests, 29 runs (Av. 7.25) and 3 wickets (Av. 8.00).

CHARLWOOD HENRY RUPERT JAMES

England (1846-1888) - He was the most useful and the most dashing batsman. He played for Sussex. In his first class career he made, 7,095 runs including 4 centuries.
Test Record - 2 Tests, 63 runs (Av. 15.75).

CHATFIELD EWEN JOHN

New Zealand (born 1951)- A right-arm medium-fast bowler. He took 5 for 95 against England at Leeds in 1983. He played for Wellington. In his first class career he made, 941 runs and took 591 wickets.
Test Record - 43 Test, 180 runs (Av. 8.57), 123 wickets (Av. 32.15) and 16 catches.

CHAUHAN CHETANDRA PRATAP SINGH

India (born 1947) - A right-handed opening batsman and right-arm off-break bowler. Test debut on September 19,1969 against New Zealand at the age of 22 years and 148 days. Scores on Test debut were 18 and 34 in the first test at Bombay. He partnered with S.M. Gavaskar to open India's innings in 60 innings of 36 Tests, which is a world record of opening the innings by the same pair on most occasions. He has made the highest aggregate for India of as many as 2084 runs in 40 Tests, without the aid of a century. His highest score being 97 against Australia at Adelaide in January 1981. He played for Delhi and Maharashtra. In his first class career he made, 11,143 runs including 21 centuries, took 51 wickets and 190 catches.
Test Record - 40 Tests, 2,084 runs (Av. 31.57), 2 wickets (Av. 53.00) and 38 catches.

CHEETHAM JOHN ERSKINE

South Africa (1920-1980) - A cheerful sportsman, respected captain and very capable batsman. He played for Western Province. In his first class career he made, 5,697 runs including 8 centuries.
Test Record - 24 Tests, 883 runs (Av. 23.86) and 13 catches.

CHIPPERFIELD ARTHUR GORDON

Australia (born 1905) - He was a solid batsman, busy and competent, essentially a front-foot player. He was also a slow spin bowler. He played for New South Wales. In his first class career he made, 4,295 runs including 9 centuries and took 65 wickets.
Test Record - 14 Tests, 552 runs (Av. 32.47) including 1 century, 5 wickets (Av. 87.40) and 15 catches.

CHOP

A form of cut, usually played to a ball that keeps unexpectedly low, in which the bat is held horizontally and brought sharply down on the ball just after it has passed the batsman.

CHOWDHURY NIRODE RANJAN

India (1923-1979) - A right-handed batsman and right-arm medium-fast and off-break bowler. Test debut on Jan. 27, 1949 against West Indies at the age of 25 years and 244 days. Scores on Test debut were 3 and 0 in the fourth Test at Madras. Last Test of the career played against England in November 1951 but did not bat in the first Test at New Delhi. Age at the time of retirement from Test cricket was 28 years and 164 days. He played for Bengal. In his first class career he made, 424 runs and took 200 wickets.
Test Record - 2 Tests, 3 runs (Av. 3.00).

CHRISTCHURCH

Christchurch, the ground having been opened in 1881-82 when Canterbury played the English touring team. The Test Match which was played there against England in 1929 was the first such game staged on New Zealand soil.

CHRISTIANI ROBERT JULLIAN

West Indies (born 1920) - A right-handed

batsman and an occasional off-break bowler, a brilliant close field and a reserve wicket-keeper. He played for British Guiana. In his first class career he made, 5,103 runs including 12 centuries, took 18 wickets and 109 dismissals.
Test Record - 22 Tests, 896 runs (Av. 26.35) including 1 century, 3 wickets (Av. 36.00), 21 dismissals (19ct, 2st).

CHRISTY JAMES ALEXANDER JOSEPH
South Africa (1904-1971) - A powerful right-handed batsman and accomplished player of fast bowling. He played for Transvaal and Queensland. In his first class career he made, 3,670 runs including 11 centuries and took 32 wickets.
Test Record - 10 Tests,618 runs (Av. 34.33) including 1 century, 2 wickets (Av. 46.00) and 3 catches.

CHUBB GEOFFREY WALTER ASHTON
South Africa (1911-1982) - A right-arm medium-pace bowler. He served two terms as President of the South African Cricket Association. He played for Border. In his first class career he made, 835 runs and took 160 wickets.
Test Record - 5 Tests, 63 runs (Av. 10.50) and 21 wickets (Av. 27.47).

CHUCKER
A bowler whose action is regarded as 'unfair' in that it approximates to throwing rather than bowling.

CLARK EDWARD WINCHESTER
England (1902-1982) - He was left-arm fast bowler and right-handed batsman. He played for Northamptonshire and Cambridgeshire. In his first class career he made, 1,971 runs and took 1,208 wickets.
Test Record - 8 Tests, 36 runs (Av. 9.00) and 32 wickets (Av. 28.09).

CLARK WAYNE MAXWELL
Australia (born 1953) - A strong medium-fast right-arm swing bowler. He played for Western Australia. In his first class career he made, 764 runs and took 223 wickets.
Test Record - 10 Tests, 98 runs (Av. 5.76) 43 wickets (Av. 28.75) and 6 catches.

CLARKE DR. CARLOS BERTRAM
West Indies (born 1918) - He was a right-arm slow leg-break bowler, a very hard-hitter and a brilliant and versatile fielder. He played for Barbados. In his first class career he made, 1,292 runs and took 333 wickets.
Test Record - 3 Tests, 3 runs (Av. 1.00) and 6 wickets (Av. 43.50).

CLARKE SYLVESTER THEOPHILUS
West Indies (born 1954) - A former carpenter and a genuinely fast bowler, who has played a prominent part in the West Indies speed attack. His best bowling 7 for 53 against Warwickshire at Oval. In his first class career he made, 2,712 runs including 1 century, took 761 wickets and 113 catches.
Test Record - 11 Tests, 172 runs (Av. 15.63), 42 wickets (Av. 27.88) and 2 catches.

CLEAN BOWL
To bowl a batsman out with a ball that knocks his wicket down without first touching his bat or body.

CLOSE DENNIS BRIAN
England (born 1931) - He was a gifted left-handed batsman, and right-arm medium-pace bowler also offspin bowler and a quite fearless close fielder. He played for Yorkshire and Somerset. In his first class career he made, 34,994 runs including 52 centuries took 1,171 wickets and 814 dismissals.
Test Record - 22 Tests, 887 runs (Av. 25.34), 18 wickets (Av. 29.55) and 24 catches.

CLOSURE
The voluntary closing of an innings; declaration.

CLUB CRICKET CONFERENCE
It was founded in 1915 at a meeting called by Mr.E.A.C. Thompson at the request of a number of clubs. The Club Cricket Conference is an organisation of clubs set up to control and safe-

guard amateur cricket on strictly non-competitive lines in the old amateur tradition. In recent years the Conference has been honoured by H.R.H. the Duke of Edinburgh becoming its Patron.

COEN STANLEY KEPPEL

South Africa (1902-1967) - He was a right-handed batsman. He played for Transvaal and Border. In his first class career he made, 2,808 runs including 6 centuries and took 22 wickets.

Test Record - 2 Tests, 101 runs (Av. 50.50).

COLAH SORABJI HORMASJI M.

India (1902-1950) - A right-handed batsman and right-arm medium pace bowler. Test debut on June 25, 1932 against England at the age of 29 years and 273 days. Scores on Test debut were 22 and 4 in the only Test played at Lord's. He played for Western India. In his first class career he made, 3,374 runs including 5 centuries.

Test Record - 2 Tests, 69 runs (Av. 17.25) and 2 catches.

COLDWELL LEONARD JOHN

England (born 1933) - A medium-fast, right-arm in-swing bowler. He played for Devon and Worcestershire. In his first class career he made, 1,474 runs and took 1,076 wickets.

Test Record - 7 Tests, 9 runs (Av. 4.50) and 22 wickets (Av. 27.72).

COLLEY DAVID JOHN

Australia (born 1947) - A right-arm fast-medium bowler and a more than useful late order batsman. He played for New South Wales. In his first class career he made, 2,374 runs including 1 century and took 236 wickets.

Test Record - 3 Tests, 84 runs (Av. 21.00), 6 wickets (Av. 52.00) and 1 catch.

COLLINGE RICHARD OWEN

New Zealand (born 1946) - A left-arm medium-fast bowler and a right-handed tail-end batsman. He played for Central Districts and Wellington. In his first class career he made, 1,848 runs and took 524 wickets.

Test Record - 35 Tests, 533 runs (Av. 14.40), 116 wickets (Av. 29.25) and 10 catches.

COLLINS HERBERT LESLIE

Australia (1889-1959) - He was a right-handed batsman and a slow left-arm bowler. He played for New South Wales. In his first class career he made, 9,924 runs including 32 centuries, took 181 wickets and 115 catches.

Test Record - 19 Tests, 1,352 runs (Av. 45.06) including 4 centuries, 4 wickets (Av. 63.00) and 13 catches.

COLOMBO

In 1879 the Colombo Academy (now the Royal College) played for the first time against St.Thomas's College. It was formed in 1832.

COMMAILLE JOHN MCILLWAIN MOORE

South Africa (1883-1956) - He was a right-handed opening batsman. He played for Western Province. In his first class career he made, 5,026 runs including 9 centuries.

Test Record - 12 Tests, 355 runs (Av. 16.90) and 1 catch.

COMPTON DENIS CHARLES SCOTT

England (born 1918) - He was a dazzling right-handed batsman, left-arm unorthodox spin bowler. Denis Compton first turned out for Middlesex against Sussex at Lord's in 1936, as a slow bowler batting at number eleven. Soon he was moving up the order and he made over 1000 runs in his first season. On his Test debut against New Zealand at Oval in 1937 he hit 65. He played for Middlesex. In his first class career he made, 38,942 runs including 123 centuries, took 622 wickets and 415 catches.

Test Record - 78 Tests, 5,807 runs (Av. 50.06) including 17 centuries, 25 wickets (Av. 56.40) and 49 catches.

CONEY JEREMY VERNON

New Zealand (born 1952) - A right-handed bats-

man and medium-pace bowler. He topped country's batting in 1983 World Cup with 197 runs (Av. 49.35) besides picking up nine wickets. He played for Wellington. In his first class career he made, 7,528 runs including 8 centuries, took 108 wickets and 183 catches.
Test Record - 52 Tests, 2,668 runs (Av. 37.57) including 3 centuries, 27 wickets (Av. 35.77) and 64 catches.

CONNOLLY ALAN NORMAN
Australia (born 1939) - A right-arm fast-medium bowler. No one has taken more wickets for Victoria than his 330 in 83 Matches. In his first class career he made, 1,073 runs and took 676 wickets.
Test Record - 29 Tests, 260 runs (Av. 10.40), 102 wickets (Av. 29.22) and 17 catches.

CONSTANTINE SIR LEARIE NICHOLAS
West Indies (1902-1971) - He was great all-rounder, right-handed hitter with powerful drives. As a bowler he used every variation of medium-pace, with an occasional fast ball. He played for Trinidad and Barbados. In his first class career he made, 4,451 runs including 5 centuries, took 424 wickets and 133 catches.
Test Record - 18 Tests, 635 runs (Av. 19.24), 58 wickets (Av. 30.10) and 28 catches.

CONTRACTOR NARIMAN JAMSHEDJI
India (born 1934) - A left-handed opening batsman and right-arm medium-pace bowler. Test debut on Dec. 2nd, 1955 against New Zealand at the age of 21 years and 265 days. Score on Test debut was 16 in the second Test at Bombay. Last Test of the career played against West Indies in March 1962. Scores on last appearance in Test were 1 and 9 in the second Test at Kingston. Age at the time of retirement from Test cricket was 28 years and 5 days. First-ever Test century scored on Jan.1st, 1960 against Australia in the third Test at Bombay at the age of 25 years and 295 days. Led India for the first time against Pakistan in the first Test at New Delhi on Dec.2nd, 1960 at the age of 26 years and 266 days, scoring 62 runs. Captained India in 12 Tests out of which won two, lost two and eight were drawn. Made a sensational debut in Ranji Trophy championship for Gujarat against Baroda, scoring a century in each innings of the match 102 not out and 152 emulating the feat of great Australian batsman Arthur Morris. He played for Gujarat and Railways. In his first class career he made, 8,611 runs including 22 centuries and took 26 wickets.
Test Record - 31 Tests, 1,611 runs (Av.31.58) including 1 century and 18 catches.

COOCH-BEHAR TROPHY WINNERS

1945-46 Sind
1946-47 Sind
1947-48 Not played
1948-49 Saurashtra
1949-50 Bombay
1950-51 Final not played
1951-52 National Academy
1952-53 West Zone
1953-54 West Zone
1954-55 West Zone
1955-56 West Zone
1956-57 West Zone
1957-58 West Zone
1958-59 West Zone
1959-60 West Zone
1960-61 South Zone
1961-62 Not held
1962-63 West Zone
1963-64 West Zone
1964-65 North Zone
1965-66 West Zone
1966-67 West Zone
1967-68 North Zone
1968-69 East Zone
1969-70 South Zone
1970-71 Not Held
1971-72 East Zone
1972-73 South Zone
1973-74 East Zone
1974-75 South Zone
1975-76 West Zone
1976-77 West Zone
1977-78 North Zone
1978-79 North Zone
1979-80 North Zone
West Zone (joint winners)
1980-81 Not held

1981-82 North Zone
1982-83 Central Zone
1983-84 West Zone
1984-85 East Zone
1985-86 North Zone
1986-87 West Zone
1987-88 South Zone
1988-89 North Zone

COOK GEOFFREY

England (born 1951) - A right-handed batsman and slow left-arm bowler. He toured India, Sri Lanka, Australia and New Zealand . He played for Northamptonshire. In his first class cricket career he made, 21,497 runs including 34 centuries.

Test Record - 7 Tests, 203 runs (Av. 15.61).

COOK NICHOLAS

England (born 1956) - An accurate slow left-arm spin bowler. He made steady progress in taking more than 350 wickets since his county debut in 1978. He took 5 for 35 on Test debut against New Zealand at Lord's in 1983. He played for Leicestershire. In his first class career he made, 1,874 runs and took 555 wickets.

Test Record - 9 Tests, 101 runs (Av. 7.21), 40 wickets (Av. 30.30) and 5 catches.

COOPER WILLIAM HENRY

Australia (1849-1939) - He was a right-arm, slow, leg break bowler, He was successively captain of his State, a State selector and Vice-President of Victoria Cricket Association. He played for Victoria. In his first class career he made, 247 runs and took 73 wickets.

Test Record - 2 Tests, 13 runs (Av. 6.50), 9 wickets (Av. 25.11) and 1 catch.

COPE GEOFFREY ALAN

England (born 1947) - He was off-spin bowler, determined tail-end batsman and sound fielder. He played for Yorkshire and Leicestershire. In his first class carrier he made 2,383 runs and took 686 wickets.

Test Record- 3 Tests, 40 runs (Av. 13.33), 8 wickets (Av. 34.62) and 1 catch.

COPSON WILLIAM HENRY

England (1908-1971) - He was a fast-medium pace bowler. In his first match at Lord's in 1939 he captured 5 for 85 and 4 for 67, and England won handsomely. He became an umpire after his retirement. He played for Derbyshire. In his first class career he made, 1,711 runs and took 1,094 wickets.

Test Record - 3 Tests, 6 runs (Av. 6.00), 15 wickets (Av. 19.80) and 1 catch.

CORLING GRAHAME EDWARD

Australia (born 1941) - An opening right-arm fast-medium bowler. He played for New South Wales. In his first class career he made, 484 runs, took 173 wickets and 11 catches.

Test Record - 5 Tests, 5 runs (Av. 1.66) and 12 wickets (Av. 37.25).

CORNFORD WALTER LATTER

England (1900-1964) - He was one of the best wicket-keepers and useful late: -order right-handed batsman. He played for Sussex. In his first class career he made, 6,554 runs and 1,000 dismissals (656ct, 344st).

Test Record - 4 Tests, 36 runs (Av. 9.00) and 8 dismissals (5ct, 3st).

CORNWALL

Founded in 1894 and joined the Minor Counties Championship in 1904.

COSIER GARY JOHN

Australia (born 1953)- A right-handed batsman and also a very useful slow-medium bowler. He played for Victoria. In his first class career he made, 5,005 runs including 7 centuries and took 77 wickets.

Test Record - 18 Tests, 897 runs (Av. 28.93) including 2 centuries, 5 wickets (Av. 68.20) and 14 catches.

COTTAM ROBERT MICHAEL HENRY

England (born 1944) - A tall, right-arm medium-fast bower. He is now the NCA's chief coach in the West Country. He played for Hampshire and

Northamptonshire. In his first class career he made, 1,286 runs and took 1,010 wickets.
Test Record - 4 Tests, 27 runs (Av. 6.75), 14 wickets (Av. 23.35) and 2 catches.

COTTER ALBERT

Australia (1883-1917) - He was a right-handed batsman and fearsome medium-fast bowler. Tibby was killed in action by a sniper at Beer-sheba while serving in the Australian Light Horse. He played for New South Wales. In his first class career he made, 2,484 runs and took 442 wickets.
Test Record - 21 Tests, 457 runs (Av. 13.05), 89 wickets (Av. 28.64) and 8 catches.

COUNTY CHAMPIONSHIP

The first known 'county' cricket match took place in 1709 between Kent and Surrey. The number of such 'county'matches had steadily increased throughout the 1730s, attracting gradually increasing interest in the Press. The clubs included in the first official championship season of 1890 in the order of finishing Surrey, Lancashire, Kent and Yorkshire (tied), Nottinghamshire, Gloucestershire, Middlesex, and Sussex. Since then Somerset were added in 1891, Essex, Derbyshire, Leicestershire, Warwickshire and Hampshire in 1895, Worcestershire in 1899, Northamptonshire in 1905, and Glamorgan in 1921. All these clubs are regularly playing in County Championship.

REGULATIONS FOR BRITANNIC ASSURANCE CHAMPIONSHIP

1. Scoring of Points

(a) For a win, sixteen points, plus any points scored in the first innings.

(b) In a tie, each side to score eight points, plus any points scored in the first innings.

(c) If the scores are equal in a drawn match, the side batting in the fourth innings to score eight points, plus any points scored in the first innings.

(d) First Innings points (awarded only for performances in the first 100 overs of each first innings and retained whatever the result of the match).

(i) A maximum of four batting points to be available as under :
150 to 199 runs - 1 point: 200 to 249 runs:- 2 points; 250 to 299 runs- 3 points; 300 runs of over - 4 points.

(ii) A maximum of four bowling points to be taken as under :
3 to 4 wickets taken - 1 point; 5 to 6 wickets taken - 2 points; 7 to 8 wickets taken - 3 points; 9 to 10 wickets taken - 4 points.

(e) If play starts when fewer than eight hours' playing time remains and a one innings match is played, no first innings points shall be scored. The side winning on the one innings to score twelve points.

(f) The side which has the highest aggregate of points gained at the end of the season shall be the Champion County. Should any sides in the Championship taken be equal on points the side with most wins will have priority.

2. Hours of play

1st.2nd [3rd] days... 11.00 a.m. to 6.30 p.m. or after 110 overs, whichever is the later.
(For Sunday play, the home county may decide to play from 12 noon to 7.30 p.m.)
Final day............ 11.00 a.m. to 6.00 p.m or after 102 overs, whichever is the later.

(a) If play is suspended (including any interval between innings) the minimum number of overs to be bowled in a day to be reduced by one over for each 3(1/2) minutes or part thereof of such sus-pension or suspensions in aggregate.

(b) If at 5.00 p.m. on the final day, nineteen overs or fewer remain to be bowled, the umpires shall indicate that play shall continue until a minimum, of a further twenty overs has been bowled, or until 6.00 p.m. whichever is the later. Play may cease on the final day at any time between 5.30 p.m. and 6.00 p.m. by mutual agreement of the captains. Should an innings end between 4.50 p.m. and 5.0 p.m. the time at the end of the ten-minute interval shall replace 5.00 p.m.

(c) The captains may agree or, in the event of disagreement, the umpires may decide to play 30 minutes (or minimum ten overs) extra time at the end of the first and/or second day's play (and /or the third day of four) if, in their opinion, it would bring about a definite result on that day. In the event of the possibility of a finish disappearing before the full period has expired, the whole period must be played out. Any time so claimed does not affect the timing for cessation of play on the final day.

(d) If an innings ends during the course of an over, that part shall count as a full over so far as the minimum number of overs per day is concerned.

(e) If play is suspended for the day in the middle of an over, that over must be completed next day in addition to the minimum overs required that day.

Intervals

Lunch: 1.15 p.m. to 1.55 p.m. (1st,2nd [3rd] days), 2.15 p.m. to 2.55 p.m. on Sunday when play commences at 12 noon.
1.00 p.m. to 1.40 p.m. (final day)
Tea: 4.10 p.m. to 4.30 p.m. (1st,2nd [3rd] days), 5.10 p.m. to 5.30 p.m. on Sunday when play commences at 12 noon, or when 40 overs remain to be bowled, whichever is the later. 3.40 p.m. to 4.00 p.m. (final day), or when 40 overs remain to be bowled, whichever is the later.

3. **Substitutes**

A substitute shall be allowed as of right in the event of a cricketer currently playing in a Championship match being required to join the England team for a Test match (or one-day international). Such substitutes may be permitted to bat or bowl in that match, subject to the approval of the TCCB. The player who is substituted may not take further part in the match, even though he might not be required by England. If batting at the time, the player substituted shall be retired "not out" and his substitute may be permitted to bat subject to the approval of the TCCB.
The opposing captain shall have no right of objection to any player acting as substitute in the field, nor as to where he shall field. However, no substitute may act as wicket-keeper.
No substitute may take the field until the player for whom he is to substitute has been absent from the field for five consecutive complete overs.

4. New ball

The captain of the fielding side shall have the choice of taking the new ball after 100 overs have been bowled with the old one.

5. **Covering of Pitches and Bowler's Run-up**

The whole pitch shall be covered:

(a) The night before a match and, if neces sary, until the first ball is bowled.

(b) On each night of a match and, if neces sary, throughout Sunday. In the event of play being suspended because of bad light or rain, during the hours of play.The bowler's run-up shall be covered to a dis tance of at least ten yards, with a width of four yards.

6. **Declaration**

Law 14 will apply, but, in addition, a captain may also forfeit his first innings, subject to the provisions set out in Law 14.2. If, owing to weather conditions, the match has not started when fewer than eight hours of playing time remain, the first innings of each side shall automatically be forfeited and a one-innings match played.

CHAMPION COUNTY SINCE 1864

1864 Surrey
1865 Nottinghamshire
1866 Middlesex
1867 Yorkshire
1868 Nottinghamshire
1869 Nottinghamshire
Yorkshire (joint winners)
1870 Yorkshire
1871 Nottinghamshire
1872 Nottinghamshire
1873 Gloucestershire
Nottinghamshire (joint winners)
1874 Gloucestershire
1875 Nottinghamshire
1876 Gloucestershire
1877 Gloucestershire
1878 Undecided
1879 Nottinghamshire
Lancashire (joint winners)
1880 Nottinghamshire
1881 Lancashire
1882 Nottinghamshire
Lancashire (joint winners)
1883 Nottinghamshire
1884 Nottinghamshire

Year	Winner
1885	Nottinghamshire
1886	Nottinghamshire
1887	Surrey
1888	Surrey
1889	Surrey
	Lancashire
	Nottinghamshire (joint winners)
1890	Surrey
1891	Surrey
1892	Surrey
1893	Yorkshire
1894	Surrey
1895	Surrey
1896	Yorkshire
1897	Lancashire
1898	Yorkshire
1899	Surrey
1900	Yorkshire
1901	Yorkshire
1902	Yorkshire
1903	Middlesex
1904	Lancashire
1905	Yorkshire
1906	Kent
1907	Nottinghamshire
1908	Yorkshire
1909	Kent
1910	Kent
1911	Warwickshire
1912	Yorkshire
1913	Kent
1914	Surrey
1915	No match
1916	No match
1917	No match
1918	No match
1919	Yorkshire
1920	Middlesex
1921	Middlesex
1922	Yorkshire
1923	Yorkshire
1924	Yorkshire
1925	Yorkshire
1926	Lancashire
1927	Lancashire
1928	Lancashire
1929	Nottinghamshire
1930	Lancashire
1931	Yorkshire
1932	Yorkshire
1933	Yorkshire
1934	Lancashire
1935	Yorkshire
1936	Derbyshire
1937	Yorkshire
1938	Yorkshire
1939	Yorkshire
1940	No match
1941	No match
1942	No match
1943	No match
1944	No match
1945	No match
1946	Yorkshire
1947	Middlesex
1948	Glamorgan
1949	Middlesex
	Yorkshire (joint winners)
1950	Lancashire
	Surrey (joint winner)
1951	Warwickshire
1952	Surrey
1953	Surrey
1954	Surrey
1955	Surrey
1956	Surrey
1957	Surrey
1958	Surrey
1959	Yorkshire
1960	Yorkshire
1961	Hampshire
1962	Yorkshire
1963	Yorkshire
1964	Worcestershire
1965	Worcestershire
1966	Yorkshire
1967	Yorkshire
1968	Yorkshire
1969	Glamorgan
1970	Kent
1971	Surrey
1972	Warwickshire
1973	Hampshire
1974	Worcestershire
1975	Leicestershire
1976	Middlesex
1977	Middlesex
	Kent
1978	Kent
1979	Essex
1980	Middlesex

CHRIS COWDREY

1981	Nottinghamshire
1982	Middlesex
1983	Essex
1984	Essex
1985	Middlesex
1986	Essex
1987	Nottinghamshire
1988	Worcestershire
1989	Worcestershire

COVER

Off side fielding position between point and mid-off but deeper. 'Extra-cover' is a position between cover and mid-off. 'Deep extra-cover' is out on the boundary behind extra cover.

COVER DRIVE

Cover drive is played for a delivery which bounces

Cover-Drive

within reach or arrives on the full toss wide of the stumps on the off side. The first movements of the cover drive are identical to those of the front-foot drive, but the movement of the front foot, head and eyes, and the front shoulder, elbow and knee will be more towards the cover position, and the ball will be struck far squarer, towards cover. The toe of your front foot should point towards cover point. This shot can be risky since the direction of the stroke is across the line of the ball in an off-side direction.

COVER-POINT

This is one of the key positions on the field, because with a steady bowler keeping the ball on or outside the off stump, a very large percentage of the batsman's strokes will send the ball in the direction. Cover-point should take up his position 20 to 35 yards from the bat according to the class of cricket, and he should be the type of fieldsman who can pounce swiftly on the ball, pick it up with either hand and return it smartly to the wicket-keeper. If you happen to possess an ambidextrous player on your side, cover is probably the place for him, as he will save valuable time if he has not to transfer the ball from one hand to the other before his return to the keeper. Cover must also be a brilliant catch, as drives which have been slightly mistimed will hurtle through the air at him to left or right, high or low. Like many off-side fielders, he must remember that a driven ball will tend to swing towards or away from his left hand, and many of his catches will be spinning vigorously

COWANS NORMAN GEORGE

England (born 1961) - He was a right-arm medium-fast bowler. He took 5 for 28 and 5 for 34 in consecutive matches in 1982. He played for Middlesex. In his first class career he made, 1,041 runs and took 381 wickets.

Test Record - 19 Tests, 175 runs (Av. 7.95) and 51 wickets (Av. 39.27).

COWDREY CHRISTOPHER STUART

England (born 1957) - A useful medium-pace bowler. He played for Kent. In his first class career he made, 8,326 runs and took 124 wickets.

Test Record - 6 Tests, 101 runs (Av. 14.42), 4 wickets (Av. 77.25) and 5 catches.

COWDREY MICHAEL COLIN

England (born 1932) - He was an attacking batsman and flightily leg-spinner. His first Test century was a saving 102 out of an innings of 191 at

Melbourne 1954-55, and he made 3 other centuries against Australia. He played for Oxford University and Kent. In his first class career he made, 42,719 runs including 107 centuries, took 65 wickets and 638 catches.
Test Record - 114 Tests, 7,624 runs (Av. 44.06) including 22 centuries and 120 catches.

COWIE JOHN
New Zealand (born 1912) - A well-built right-arm fast bowler, nicknamed (The Bull). His best analysis was 6 for 3 against Ireland at Dublin in 1937. He played for Auckland. In his first class career he made, 762 runs and took 359 wickets.
Test Record - 9 Tests, 90 runs (Av. 10.00), 45 wickets (Av. 21.53) and 3 catches.

COWPER ROBERT MASKEW
Australia (born 1940) - He was a well-built left-handed batsman and a useful off-spin bowler. He acted as adviser to Kerry Packer during his first negotiations with the Australian Cricket Board. He played for Victoria and Western Australia. In his first class career he made, 10,595 runs including 26 centuries and took 183 wickets.
Test Record - 27 Tests, 2,061 runs (Av. 46.84) including 5 centuries, 36 wickets (Av. 31.63) and 21 catches.

COX JOSEPH LOVELL
South Africa (1886-1971) - He was a right-arm fast-medium pace bowler, indifferent batsman and fielder. He played for Natal. In his first class career he made, 357 runs and took 120 wickets.
Test Record - 3 Tests, 17 runs (Av. 3.40) and 4 wickets (Av. 61.25).

CRAIG IAN DAVID
Australia (born 1935) - He was Australia's youngest player in Test cricket. He played for New South Wales. In his first class career he made, 7,328 runs including 15 centuries.
Test Record - 11 Tests, 358 runs (Av. 19.88) and 2 catches.

CRANSTON KENNETH
England (born 1917) - A forcing right-handed batsman and fast-medium opening bowler. He played for Lancashire. In his first class career he made, 3,099 runs including 3 centuries and took 178 wickets.
Test Record - 8 Tests, 209 runs (Av. 14.92), 18 wickets (Av. 25.61) and 3 catches.

CRAPP JOHN FREDERICK
England (1912 - 1981) - He was an extremely sound left-handed batsman and a brilliant slip fielder. On retirement he became a highly respected umpire. He played for Gloucestershire. In his first class career he made, 23,615 runs including 38 centuries and 383 catches.
Test Record - 7 Tests, 319 runs (Av. 29.00) and 7 catches.

CRAWFORD JOHN NEVILLE
England (1986 - 1963) - A right-handed batsman and a medium-pace bowler. He played first-class cricket for only 4 full seasons, twice achieving the double of 1,000 runs and 100 wickets, the first time under the age of 20. As a bowler his pace varied from medium to really quick. He ran to deliver in easy swinging strides. He played for Surrey. In his first class career he made, 9,488 runs including 15 centuries and took 815 wickets.
Test Record - 12 Tests, 469 runs (Av. 22.33), 39 wickets (Av. 29.48) and 13 catches.

CRAWFORD WILLIAM PATRICK ANTHONY
Australia (born 1933) - A right-arm medium-fast bowler and right-handed batsman. He played for New South Wales. In his first class career he made, 424 runs and took 110 wickets.
Test Record - 4 Tests, 53 runs (Av. 17.66), 7 wickets (Av. 15.28) and 1 catch.

CREASE
Originally, there was no stipulation as to the length of the bowling crease. The first limit was made in 1774 - 3 feet long on either side of the wicket. This was increased to 6 feet 7 inches in about 1821, and to 6 feet 8 inches about 5 years

later. The present length of the crease is 8 feet 8 inches. The 'return creases' are short lines at each end of the bowling crease and at right angles to it. The 'popping crease' is a line parallel to the bowling crease and 4 feet in front of it, being the forward limit of the batsman's ground.

CRESSWELL GEORGE FENWICK

New Zealand (1915-1966) - A right-arm medium-pace leg-theory bowler and left-handed batsman. He played for Wellington and Central Districts. In his first class career he took 124 wickets.

Test Record - 3 Tests, 14 runs (Av. 7.00) and 13 wickets (Av. 22.46).

CRICKETRESS

A woman who plays cricket.

CRISP ROBERT JAMES

South Africa (born 1911) - A right-arm medium pace bowler and right-handed batsman. He played for Rhodesia and Western Province. In his first class career he made, 888 runs and claimed 276 wickets.

Test Record - 9 Tests, 123 runs (Av. 10.25) and 20 wickets (Av. 37.25).

CROFT COLIN EVERTON HUNTE

West Indies (born 1953) - A right-arm medium-fast bowler. He was one of the biggest names to join the rebel West Indies team in South Africa in 1983. He also played for Kerry Packer. He played for Guyana and Lancashire. In his first class career he made, 865 runs and took 428 wickets.

Test Record - 27 Tests, 158 runs (Av. 10.53), 125 wickets (Av 23.30) and 8 catches.

CROMB IAN BURNS

New Zealand (1905-1984) - He was a right-arm fast-medium bowler and a useful late-order batsman. He played for Canterbury. In his first class career he made, 3,950 runs including 3 centuries and took 222 wickets.

Test Record - 5 Tests, 123 runs (Av. 20.50), 8 wickets (Av. 55.25) and 1 catch.

CROSS BAT

Playing this stroke, the bat moves across the line of flight of the ball rather than straight down it

CROWE JEFFREY JOHN

New Zealand (born 1958) - Jeff Crowe developed his obvious natural talent in Australia

JEFF CROWE

before returning home to work for a finance company and to claim a Test place in 1983 against Sri Lanka. A right-handed batsman. He played for Auckland. In his first class career he made, 9,436 runs including 15 centuries.

Test Record - 37 Tests, 1,536 runs (Av. 26.48), including 3 centuries and 40 catches.

CROWE MARTIN DAVID

New Zealand (born 1962) - Martin Crowe has a copy-book technique and impressed, without scoring heavily on the 1983 tour to England. Picked to play for New Zealand at only 19, against Australia. He plays for Auckland. In his first class career he made, 11,008 runs including 28 centuries.

Test Record - 44 Tests, 3,035 runs (Av. 45.29) including 10 centuries, 13 wickets (Av. 46.69) and 46 catches.

CUNIS ROBERT SMITH

New Zealand (born 1941) - A right-arm fast-medium bowler and right-handed batsman. He played for Auckland. In his first class career he made, 1,849 runs including 1 century and took 386 wickets.

Test Record - 20 Tests, 295 runs (Av. 12.82), 51 wickets (Av. 37.00) and 1 catch.

CURNOW SYDNEY HARRY

South Africa (1907-1986) - A right-handed impressive batsman. He played for Transvaal. In his first class career he made, 3,409 runs including 9 centuries.

Test Record - 7 Tests, 168 runs (Av. 12.00) and 5 catches.

CURRIE CUP WINNERS (SOUTH AFRICA)

1889-90	Transvaal
1890-91	Griqualand West
1892-93	Western Province
1893-94	Western Province
1894-95	Transvaal
1895-96	Not held
1896-97	Western Province
1897-98	Western Province
1898-99	Not held
1899-1900	Not held
1900-01	Not held
1901-02	Not held
1902-03	Transvaal
1903-04	Transvaal
1904-05	Transvaal
1905-06	Not held
1906-07	Transvaal
1907-08	Not held
1908-09	Western Province
1909-10	Not held
1910-11	Natal
1911-12	Not held
1912-13	Natal
1913-14	Not held
1914-15	Not held
1915-16	Not held
1916-17	Npt held
1917-18	Not held
1918-19	Not held
1919-20	Not held
1920-21	Western Province
1921-22	Transvaal/Natal/W.Prov.(Tied)
1922-23	Not held
1923-24	Transvaal
1924-25	Not held
1925-26	Transvaal
1926-27	Transvaal
1927-28	Not held
1928-29	Not held
1929-30	Transvaal
1930-31	Not held
1931-32	Western Province
1932-33	Not held
1933-34	Natal
1934-35	Transvaal
1935-36	Not held
1936-37	Natal
1937-38	Natal/Transvaal (Tied)
1938-39	Not held
1939-40	Not held
1940-41	Not held
1941-42	Not held
1942-43	Not held
1943-44	Not held
1944-45	Not held
1945-46	Not held
1946-47	Not held
1947-48	Natal
1948-49	Not held
1949-50	Not held
1950-51	Transvaal
1951-52	Natal
1952-53	Western Province
1953-54	Not held
1954-55	Natal
1955-56	western Province
1956-57	Not held
1957-58	Not held
1958-59	Transvaal
1959-60	Natal
1960-61	Natal
1961-62	Not held
1962-63	Natal
1963-64	Natal
1964-65	Not held
1965-66	Natal/Transvaal (Tied)
1966-67	Natal
1967-68	Natal
1968-69	Transvaal
1969-70	Transvaal/W.Province (Tied)
1970-71	Transvaal
1971-72	Transvaal

1972-73	Not held
1973-74	Natal
1974-75	Western Province
1975-76	Natal
1976-77	Natal
1977-78	Western Province
1978-79	Transvaal
1979-80	Transvaal
1980-81	Natal
1981-82	Western Province
1982-83	Transvaal
1983-84	Transvaal
1984-85	Transvaal
1985-86	Western Province
1986-87	Transvaal
1987-88	Transvaal
1988-89	Eastern Province

CUT

A cut is typically played attacking shot to a fast ball pitching rather short of a length outside the off stump.

Cut

CUTTELL WILLIS ROBERT

England (1864-1929) - A right-handed batsman and a slow-bowler of good length. He played for Yorkshire and Lancashire. In his first class career he made, 5,938 runs including 5 centuries and took 791 wickets.

Test Record - 2 Tests, 65 runs (Av. 16.25), 6 wickets (Av. 12.16) and 2 catches.

D

D'ARCY JOHN WILLIAM

New Zealand (born 1936) - He was a right-handed opening batsman of tremendous determination and concentration. He played for Wellington and Otago. In his first class career he made, 2,109 runs.

Test Record - 5 Tests, 136 runs (Av. 13.60).

D'OLIVEIRA BASIL LEWIS

England (born 1931) - He was a right-handed batsman and medium- pace bowler. He was awarded the OBE in 1969 for his services to cricket. He is now county coach and one player whose progress he has carefully charted is his son Damian, now established in the Worcestershire side. In his first class career he made, 18,919 runs including 43 centuries, took 548 wickets and 211 catches.

Test Record - 44 Tests, 2,484 runs (Av. 40.06) including 5 centuries, 47 wickets (Av. 39.55) and 29 catches.

D'SOUZA ANTAO

Pakistan (born 1939) - A very useful right-handed medium-fast bowler sometimes bowled slower off-break and a tail-end batsman. He played for Karachi. In his first class career he made, 815 runs and took 190 wickets.

Test Record - 6 Tests, 76 runs (Av. 38.00), 17 wickets (Av. 43.82) and 3 catches.

DA COSTA OSCAR C.

West Indies (1907-1936) - A very talented all-rounder and a reliable right-handed batsman, useful medium pace bowler and versatile fielder. He played for Jamaica. In his first class career he made, 1,563 runs including 1 century and took 44 wickets.

Test Record - 5 Tests, 153 runs (Av. 19.12) and 3 wickets (Av. 58.33) and 3 catches.

DALTON ERIC LONDESBROUGH

South Africa (1906-1981) - He was a determined and hard-hitting right-handed batsman and useful change bowler. He played for Natal. In his first class career he made, 5,333 runs including 13 catches and took 139 wickets.

Test Record - 15 Tests, 698 runs (Av. 31.72) including 2 centuries, 12 wickets (Av. 40.83) and 5 catches.

DANGER AREA

That part of the pitch which according to the laws, must be protected from damage by the bowlers.

DANIEL WAYNE WENDELL

West Indies (born 1956) - He was a right-handed strong fast bowler. He played for Barbados and Middlesex. In his first class career he made, 1,520 runs and took 833 wickets.

Test Record - 10 Tests, 46 runs (Av. 6.57), 36 wickets (Av. 25.27) and 4 catches.

DARLING HON. JOSEPH

Australia (1870-1946) - He was a great left-handed batsman. He played for South Australia. In his first class career he made, 10,635 runs including 19 centuries and took 148 catches.

Test Record - 34 Tests, 1,657 runs (Av. 28.56) including 3 centuries and 27 catches.

DARLING LEONARD STUART

Australia (born 1909) - He was a left-handed batsman. He remembered for his superb catches on the leg-side. He played for Victoria. In his first class career he made, 5,780 runs including 16 centuries and took 32 wickets.

Test Record - 12 Tests, 474 runs (Av. 27.88) and 8 catches.

DARLING WARRICK MAXWELL

Australia (born 1957) - A right-handed opening batsman and brilliant cover fielder and also a brilliant hooker and cover drivers. He played for South Australia. In his first class career he made, 5,721 runs including 10 centuries.

Test Record - 14 Tests, 697 runs (Av. 26.80) and 5 catches.

DAVIDSON ALAN KEITH

Australia (born 1929) - He was a left-handed all-rounder of the highest class. He had power in his attacking strokes. He was once President of the New South Wales Cricket Association. He played for New South Wales. In his first class career he made, 6,804 runs including 9 centuries took 672 wickets and 168 catches.
Test Record - 44Tests 1,328 runs (Av. 24.59), 186 wickets (Av. 20.53) and 42 catches.

DAVIES ERIC QUAIL

South Africa (1909-1976) - A right-arm out-swinger fast bowler. He played for Eastern Province, Transvaal and North-Eastern Transvaal. In his first class career he made, 64 runs and took 47 wickets.
Test Record - 5 Tests, 9 runs (Av. 1.80) and 7 wickets (Av. 68.71).

DAVIS BRYAN ALAN

West Indies (born 1940) - A sound leg-break bowler and an excellent close-in fielder. He played for Trinidad and Glamorgan. In his first class career he made, 6,231 runs including 5 centuries.
Test Record - 4 Tests, 245 runs (Av. 30.62) and 1 catch.

DAVIS CHARLES ALAN

West Indies (born 1944) - A sound slow right-handed batsman and useful medium-pace bowler. He played for Trinidad. In his first class career he made, 5,538 runs including 14 centuries and took 63 wickets.
Test Record - 15 Tests, 1,301 runs (Av. 54.20) including 4 centuries, 2 wickets (Av. 165.00) and 4 catches.

DAVIS IAN CHARLES

Australia (born 1953) - He was slightly built, neat, right-handed opening or middle-order batsman. He played for New South Wales and Queensland. In his first class career he made, 4,609 runs including 8 centuries.
Test Record - 15 Tests, 692 runs (Av. 26.61) including 1 century and 9 catches.

IAN DAVIS

DAVIS WINSTON WALTER

West Indies (born 1958) - He was a right-arm fast bowler. He plays for Windward Islands, Glamorgan and Tasmania. In his first class career he made, 1,237 runs and took 392 wickets.

Test Record - 11 Tests, 157 runs (Av. 19.62) 32 wickets (Av. 33.81) and 7 catches.

DAWSON EDWARD WILLIAM

England (1904-1979) - A very sound right-handed batsman. He played for Cambridge University and Leicestershire. In his first class career he made, 12,597 runs including 14 centuries.

Test Record - 5 Tests, 175 runs (Av. 19.44).

DAWSON OSCAR CHARLES

South Africa (born 1919) - He was a right-handed batsman and also a medium-pace, out-swing bowler. He played for Natal and Border. In his first class career he made, 3,804 runs including 6 centuries and took 123 wickets.

Test Record - 9 Tests, 293 runs (Av. 20.92), 10 wickets (Av. 57.80) and 10 catches.

DE ALWIS RONALD GUY

Sri Lanka (born 1959) - A wicket-keeper and a useful lower middle-order right-handed batsman. He plays for Sinhalese. In his first class career he made, 401 runs and 38 dismissals.

Test Record - 10 Tests, 144 runs (Av. 8.47) and 21 dismissals (19ct, 2st).

DE COURCY JAMES HARRY

Australia (born 1927) - He was attacking right-handed batsman. He played for New South Wales. In his first class career he made, 3,778 runs including 6 centuries.

Test Record - 3 Tests, 81 runs (Av. 16.20) and 3 catches.

DE MEL ASANTHA LAKDASA FRANCIS

Sri Lanka (born 1959) - A right-handed medium-fast bowler and a good out-swinger. He plays for Sinhalese. In his first class career he made, 1733 runs including 4 century and 191 wickets.

Test Record - 17 Tests, 326 runs (Av. 14.17), 59 wickets (Av. 36.94) and 9 catches.

DE SILVA ELLEWELAKANKANANGE ASOKA RANJIT

Sri Lanka (born 1956) - A left-handed tail-ender leg-spin bowler. He played for Colombo. In his first class career he made, 988 runs and took 78 wickets.

Test Record - 5 Tests, 72 runs (Av. 14.40) and 2 wickets. (206.50).

DE SILVA GINIGALGODANGE RAMBA AJITH

Sri Lanka (born 1952) - He was a very steady, orthodox slow left-arm bowler and useful late-order left-handed batsman. He played for Bloomfield. In his first class career he made, 695 runs and took 287 wickets.

Test Record - 4 Tests, 41 runs (Av. 8.20) and 7 wickets (Av. 55.00).

DE SILVA PINNADUWAGE ARAVINDA

Sri Lanka (born 1965) - A tall right-handed batsman and loves cut and hook strokes. He plays for Nondescripts. In his first class career he made, 2,766 runs including 5 centuries and took 3 wicket.

Test Record - 15 Tests, 660 runs (Av. 25.38) including 2 centuries and 8 catches.

DEAD

When a batsman is out or if the ball gets lost, or it becomes lodged in the clothing of either the batsman or the umpires and secondly when a member of the fielding side wilfully obstructs a batsman in running or incommodes the striker by any noise or action while he is receiving a ball.

DEAD BAT

When the batsman plays defensively, either in making a forward blocking stroke with no back-lift, or holds loosely in a backward defensive position.

DEAN HARRY

England (1884-1957) - He was a left-arm fast medium or slow spin bowler. He played for Cheshire and Lancashire. In his first class career he made, 2,448 runs and took 1,301 wickets.

Test Record - 3 Tests, 10 runs (Av. 5.00), 11 wickets (Av. 13.90) and 2 catches.

DEANE HUBERT GOUVAINE

South Africa (1895-1939) - He was an attractive fast-scoring right-handed batsman and a brilliant fielder at cover. He played for Natal and Transvaal. In his first class career he made, 3,795 runs including 6 centuries.

Test Record - 17 Tests, 628 runs (Av. 25.12) and 8 catches.

DECLARATION

Second innings may be forfeited by a captain, provided the decision to do so is notified to the opposing, captain and umpires in sufficient time to allow seven minutes rolling of the pitch.

Irrespective of its duration, the captain of the batting side may declare an innings closed at any time during a match.

DEEP

The area of the ground that is relatively far from the wicket; the outfield.

DEFENCE

When playing a defensive shot, the bat should be near the body and the left hand should always have control over the bat.

The forward defensive stroke is played to a ball of perfect length, varying of course with the speed of the bowler. First movement for the batsman concerns the feet. The left leg should be placed as near the line of flight as possible, leaving enough space for the bat to come alongside the leg. With the left hand in control of the bat, the ball, if edged, will not carry to the slips or short-legs.

The back defensive short is made from a ball just short of good length, and is made by drawing the right foot back six to nine inches, and bringing the left foot to the right, keeping the bat perfectly straight. This shot, after years of practice, can be made into a great scoring stroke, especially on an easy-paced wicket.

The most beautiful strokes in cricket are those played to the off-drives, whether straight past mid-off or wider through the covers and cuts, especially the late cut which is so rarely seen in modern cricket. The young batsman should do everything he can to learn these strokes as soon as possible, for unless he acquires them early he will find them difficult to learn later on.

DEFENSIVE FIELD

Fielding is the most important department of cricket. Defensive fielding is primarily intended to prevent the batsmen from scoring runs rather than to get them out. A defensive field may either be forced upon the fielding side, if the batsmen are able to dominate the bowling and disperse the close fielder, or it may be deployed by the fielding captain for good tactical reasons.

DEFREITAS PHILIP ANTHONY JASON

England (born 1966) - A right-handed batsman

DEFREITAS

and right-arm fast-medium bowler. Under the guiding hand of Botham, the West Indies-born 'Daffy'DeFreitas blossomed as a Test and limited-overs international all rounder of note during the 1986-87 England tour of Australia. He plays for Leicestershire. In his first class career he made, 4,334 runs, and took 997 wickets.
Test Record - 4 Tests, 77 runs (Av.19.25), 9 wickets (Av.49.56) and 1 catch.

DELIVERY
The manner in which a bowler delivers the ball; a bowler's action.

DEMPSTER ERIC WILLIAM
New Zealand (born 1925) - A competent left-handed batsman and slow bowler. He played for Wellington. In his first class career he made, 1,592 runs including 1 century and took 102 wickets.
Test Record - 5 Tests, 106 runs (Av. 17.66), 2 wickets (Av. 109.50) and 1 catch.

DEMPSTER CHARLES STEWART
New Zealand (1903-1974) - As an opening batsman Dempster was one of the finest New Zealand ever produced, and a brilliant fielder. He captained the country for three seasons, and then handed over to M. St. Packe. He played for Leicestershire and Wellington. In his first class career he made, 12,145 runs including 36 centuries.
Test Record - 10 Tests, 723 runs (Av. 65.72) including 2 centuries and 2 catches.

DENNESS MICHAEL HENRY
England (born 1940) - A right-handed attacking batsman. He was 18 when he came down from Scotland to take his chance with Kent. He played a useful part at an exciting time in the country's history, both as player and youthful manager. He played for Scotland, Kent and Essex. In his first class carrer he made, 25,886 runs including 33 centuries and 411 catches.
Test Record - 28 Tests, 1,669 runs (Av. 39.69) including 4 centuries and 28 catches.

DENTON DAVID
England (1874-1950) - He was a right-handed batsman. He played for Yorkshire. In his first class career he made, 36,440 runs including 69 centuries took 34 wickets 353 catches and 1 stumping.
Test Record - 11 Tests, 424 runs (Av. 20.19) including 1 century and 8 catches.

DEODHAR TROPHY TOURNAMENT
Instituted in 1973-74. It is the limited- overs competition in India.

The winners have been as follows:

YEAR	VENUE	WINNER-RUNNER-UP
1973-74	Bombay	South-West
1974-75	Hyderabad	South-West
1975-76	Madras	West-South
1976-77	Calcutta	Central-South
1977-78	Pune	North-West
1978-79	Delhi	South-North
1979-80	Delhi	West-North
1980-81	Madras	South-West
1981-82	Chandigarh	South-Central
1982-83	Cuttack	West-North
1983-84	Sholapur	West-North
1984-85	Vijyawadada	West-North
1985-86	Madras & Hyderabad	West-North
1986-87	Delhi	North-West
1987-88	Faridabad	North-West
1988-89	Kanpur	North-South

DEPEIAZA CYRIL CLAIRMONTE
West Indies (born 1927) - A useful wicket-keeper. He played for Barbados. In his first class career he made, 623 runs including 1 century and 40 dismissals.
Test Record - 5 Tests, 187 runs (Av. 31.16) including 1 century and 11 dismissals (7ct, 4st).

DERBYSHIRE
Foundation of present club : November 1870
First first-class match: Lancashire v Derbyshire (Old Trafford) May 26,27 (1981)
Present principal ground: County Ground, Notting-

ham Road, Derby
County Champion: 1936
Highest team total :645 v Hampshire (Derby) 1898
Lowest team total: 16 v Nottingamshire (Trent Bridge) 1879
Highest individual innings: 274 G.Davidson v Lancashire
(Old Trafford) 1896
Highest wicket partnership: 349 (2nd) Trent Bridge)1947

DESAI RAMAKANT BHIKAJI

India (born 1939) - A right-handed batsman and a right-arm medium-fast bowler. Test debut on February 6, 1959 against West Indies at the age of 19 years and 224 days. Scores on Test debut were 2 not out and 5 in the fifth Test at New Delhi. Last Test of the career he played, against Australia in December-January 1968. Scores on last appearance in Test were 13 not out and 14 in the second Test at Madras. Age at the time of retirement from Test cricket was 28 years and 194 days. His 85 in the first Test against Pakistan at Bombay in 1960-61 is the highest score for a batsman at No.10 in the batting order for India and his partnership of 149 runs with P.G. Joshi for the 9th wicket in the same Test is the highest for the 9th wicket for India against any country. He played for Bombay. In his first class career he made, 2,384 runs including 1 century and took 467 wickets .
Test Record - 28 Tests, 418 runs (Av. 13.48), 74 wickets (Av. 37.31) and 9 catches.

DESILVA DANDENIYAGE SOMACHANDRA

Sri Lanka (born 1944) - He was a right-arm leg-spin bowler and a useful right-handed batsman. He captained Sri Lanka in Mendis's absence for two Tests. He plays for Moratuwa, Lincolnshire and Shorpshire. In his first class career he made, 1,735 runs and took 238 wickets.
Test Record - 12 Tests, 406 runs (Av. 21.36), 37 wickets (Av. 36.40) and 5 catches.

DEWDNEY DAVID THOMAS

West Indies (born 1933) - A tall well-developed right-arm fast bowler. He played for Jamaica. In his first class career he made, 171 runs and took 92 wickets.
Test Record - 9 Tests, 17 runs (Av. 2.42) and 21 wickets (Av. 38.42).

DEWES JOHN GORDON

England (born 1926) - A left-handed batsman and a fine outfielder. He played for Cambridge University and Middlesex. In his first class career he made, 8,564 runs including 18 centuries.
Test Record - 5 Tests, 121 runs (Av. 12.10).

DEXTER EDWARD RALPH

England (born 1935) - A right-handed batsman often demonstrating that the best answer to great bowling is attack. He was also a useful medium-pace bowler. Though handicapped by injury, he was an effective partnership-breaker. He was a fine cover-point and an athletic fielder anywhere. He played for Cambridge University and Sussex. In his first class career he made, 21,150 runs including 51 centuries and took 419 wickets and 230 catches.
Test Record - 62 Tests, 4,502 runs (Av. 47.89) including 9 centuries, 66 wickets (Av. 34.93) and 29 catches.

DIAS ROY LUKE

Sri Lanka (born 1952) - A silm elegant and exceptionally gifted right-handed batsman, a fine cover-point fielder, and occasional right-arm medium-pace bowler. He played for Sinhalese. In his first class career he made, 3,652 runs including 5 centuries and took 1 wicket.
Test Record - 20 Tests, 1,285 runs (Av. 36.71) including 3 centuries, and 6 catches.

DICK ARTHUR EDWARD

New Zealand (born 1936) - An outstanding wicket-keeper and competent right-handed batsman. He played for Otago and Wellington. In his first class career he made, 2,315 runs including 1 century and 169 dismissals.
Test Record - 17 Tests, 370 runs (Av. 14.23) and 51 dismissals (47ct, 4st).

DILAWAR HUSSAIN DR.

India (1907-1967) - A right-handed batsman and wicket-keeper. Test debut on January 5, 1933 against England at the age of 25 years and 287 days. Scores on Test debut were 59 and 57 in the second Test at Calcutta. Last Test of the career played against England in Australia in 1936. Scores on last appearance in Test were 35 and 54 in the third Test at the Oval. Age at the time of retirement form Test cricket was 29 years and 150 days. He played for Central India. In his first class career he made, 2,261 runs including 4 centuries, and 98 dismissals.

Test Record - 3 Tests, 254 runs (Av. 42.33) and 7 dismissals (6ct, 1st).

DIRECT ATTACK

A fast short-pitched bowling aimed at the batsman; bodyline.

DISMISS

To cause a batsman to be out. There are a number of ways in which a batsman may be dismissed: by hitting the wicket with a bowled ball, by catching a hit ball in the air, or by breaking a wicket that a batsman is running to before he reaches the crease.

DISMISSAL

Involved in the taking of a wicket,as by catching the ball.

DIVECHA RAMES

India (born 1923) - A right-handed batsman and a right-arm medium-fast and off-break bowler. Test debut on December 30, 1951 against England at the age of 24 years and 72 days. Score on Test debut was 26 in the third Test at Calcutta. Last Test of the career played against Pakistan in November 1952 but did not bat (the fourth Test at Madras). Age at the time of retirement from Test cricket was 25 years and 44 days. He played for Bombay. In his first class career he made, 1,423 runs and took 217 wickets.

Test Record - 5 Tests, 60 runs (Av. 12.00), 11 wickets (Av. 32.81) and 5 catches.

DOLLERY HORACE EDGAR

England (born 1914) - A right-handed batsman and useful deputy wicket-keeper. He played for Bershire and Warwickshire. In his first class career he made, 24,413 runs including 50 centuries, 291 catches and 13 stumpings.

Test Record - 4 Tests, 72 runs (Av. 10.28)

DONNAN HENRY

Australia (1864-1956) - He was a right-handed batsman. He was brother-in-law of Syd Gregory. He played for New South Wales. In his first class career he made, 4,262 runs including 6 centuries.

Test Record - 5 Tests, 75 runs (Av. 8.33) and 1 catch.

DONNELLY MARTIN PETERSON

New Zealand (born 1917) - He was the best left-handed batsman in the world and he was equally valubale at cover-point, gully or in the leg-trap. In his youth Donnelly had toured England with the New Zealand in 1937. He played for Taranaki, Wellington, Canterbury, Oxford University, Middlessex and Warwickshire. In his first class career he made, 9,250 runs including 23 centuries and took 43 wickets.

Test Record - 7 Tests, 582 runs (Av. 52.90) including 1 century and 7 catches.

DOOLAND BRUCE

Australia (1923-1980) - A tall right-arm leg-break and googly bowler. He performed the first post-war hat-trick. He played for South Australia and Nottinghamshire. In his first class career he made, 7,141 runs including 4 centuries and took 1,016 wickets and 180 catches.

Test Record - 3 Tests, 76 runs (Av. 19.00), 9 wickets (Av. 46.55) and 3 catches.

DOSHI DILIP RAZAKLAL

India (born 1947) - A left-arm slow spin bowler and left-handed batsman. Test debut on September 12,1979 against Australia at the age of 31 years and 260 days. Score on Test debut was 3 in the first Test at Madras. Shares with S.Abid Ali the best bowling feat for India on Test debut (6 for 103 in the first innings of the Test). He played

DILIP DOSHI

for Bengal. In his first class career he made 1,442 runs and took 898 wickets.

Test Record - 33 Tests, 129 runs (Av. 4.60), 114 wickets (Av. 30.71) and 10 catches.

DOUBLE

The 'double' is a term applied usually to the feat of scoring 1,000 runs and taking 100 wickets in first-class cricket in an English season.

DOUBLE CENTRUY

When a batsman scores 200 runs or over in a single innings.

DOUBLE FIGURES

When a batsman scores ten or more runs in a single innings.

DOUGLAS JOHN WILLIAM HENRY TYLER

England (1882-1930) - He was a right-handed batsman and occasionally revealed his hitting powers. He was also a change left-arm bowler. He played for Essex. In his first class career he made, 24,531 runs including 26 centuries, took 1,894 wickets and 330 catches.

Test Record - 23 Tests, 962 runs (Av. 29.15) including 1 century 45 wickets (Av. 33.02) and 9 catches.

DOWLING GRAHAM THORNE

New Zealand (born 1937) - A lean athletic, right-handed batsman. He is one of the most successful of New Zealand Test Captains. He led his country for 4 of its Test victories. His batting was based on a sound defence. He played for Canterbury. In his first class career he made, 9,399 runs including 16 centuries.

Test Record - 39 Tests, 2,306 runs (Av. 31.16) including 3 centuries and 23 catches.

DOWNTON PAUL

England (born 1957) - A wicket-keeper and right-handed batsman. He got his England chance in 1981, by which time he had moved to Middlesex,

PAUL DOWNTON

OFF/ON DRIVES

Batsmen play front foot drives to balls that are bowled to a full length. The illustrations show the off or cover drive and the finish of the on-drive

The backlift is high. The head and front shoulder lead on to the line of the ball.

Contact! The ball is struck with the full face of the bat. The weight is on the front foot – there is no pivot on the back foot.

A full follow through with good balance.

A short stride helps the batsman maintain his balance for the finish of the on-drive.

and was dropped after four Tests. He plays for Kent and Middlesex. In his first class career he made, 5,189 runs including 3 centuries, and 544 dismissals.
Test Record - 27 Tests, 701 runs (Av. 19.47) and 66 dismissals (61ct, 5st).

DRAPER RONALD GEORGE

South Africa (born 1926) - A wicket-keeper but primarily a fast-scoring right-handed opening batsman. He played for Eastern Province and Griqualand West. In his first class career he made, 3,290 runs including 11 centuries and 42 dismissals.
Test Record - 2 Tests, 25 runs (Av. 8.33).

DRAW

An unfinished cricket match that ends without either side winning; that is, in the case of a two-innings match, without one side dismissing the other side twice and scoring a higher total of runs.

DRESS

Cricketers wear white or cream shirts and trousers, white pullovers with or without long sleeves. Depending on the conditions, shoes with spikes or rubber soles are worn. Because the ball is hard and moves very fast, cricket injuries are not uncommon. In recent years, first class cricketers have started wearing protective helmets with visors while batting. Helmets are also worn by fielders in positions close to the bat. The fielders may not wear gloves. A batsman's body needs good protective padding. Leg pads are strapped to his legs, and heavy batting gloves cover his hands. Inside his trousers he wears a metal or plastic box, and pads on his thighs. Wicket-keepers wear similar protective clothing, but they have special heavy leather gloves for catching the ball.

DRINKS INTERVAL

A break of not more than five minutes during a session of play in which drinks are brought on to the field for the players.

DRIVE

A stroke made with the left foot (for a right-handed batsman) brought forward and the bat swinging downward,sending the ball back to-

SRIKKANTH & CHANDRASEKHAR in Drinks Interval

wards the bowler (a straight drive), to mid-off (an off-drive) on mid-on (an on drive), towards cover (a cover drive) or sometime towards point (square drive).

DROP
To drop a ball hit in the air by a particular batsman.

DRUCE NORMAN FRANK
England (1875-1954) - A right-handed batsman. He played for Cambridge University and Surrey. In his first class career he made, 3,526 runs including 9 centuries.

Test Record - 5 Tests, 252 runs (Av. 28.00) and 5 catches.

DUCK
A situation in which a batsman is retired without having scored a single run.

DUCKWORTH CHRISTOPHER ANTHONY
South Africa (born 1933) - He was second-string wicket-keeper and also a capable batsman. He played for Natal and Rhodesia. In his first class career he made, 2,572 runs including 3 centuries and 104 dismissals.

Test Record - 2 Tests, 28 runs (Av. 7.00) and 3 catches.

DUCKWORTH GEORGE
England (1901-1966) - He was the county's regular wicket-keeper until 1937. Also he was wicket-keeper for England in 24 Test matches. In his most prosperous season 1928 he caught 77 and stumped 30 a record. He played for Lancashire. In his first class career he made, 4,945 runs and 1,090 dismissals.

Test Record - 24 Tests, 234 runs (Av. 14.62) and 60 dismissals (45ct, 15st).

DUFF REGINALD ALEXANDER
Australia (1878-1911) - He was a very punishing right-handed batsman. He played for New South Wales. In his first class career he made, 6,589 runs including 10 centuries and 14 wickets.

Test Record - 22 Tests, 1,317 runs (Av. 35.59) including 2 centuries 4 wickets (Av. 21.25) and 14 catches.

DUJON PETER JEFFREY
West Indies (born 1956) - A natural cricketer, a graceful orthodox right-handed batsman and

JEFFREY DUJON

acrobatic wicket-keeper. He is a cool-headed cricketer. Dujon played his first two Tests as a specialist batsman. He plays for Jamaica. In his first class career he made, 5,439 runs including 13 centuries took 1 wicket, and 236 dismissals.

Test Record - 64 Tests, 2,885 runs (Av. 36.06) including 5 centuries and 208 dismissals (203ct, 5st).

DULEEPSINHJI KUMAR SHRI
England (1905-1959) - A right-handed batsman, occasional leg-break bowler and fine silp fielder. After his retirement, he played one or two gentle matches in India, became Indian High Commissioner in Australia; and later, at home, Chairman of the All India Council for Sports where he campaigned keenly for young cricketers. Two years after his death, a domestic inter-zonal tournament

in India named 'The DuleepTrophy' was instituted as tribute to him. He played for Cambridge University. In his first class career he made 15,485 runs including 50 centuries, took 28 wickets and 243 catches.
Test Record - 12 Tests, 995 runs (Av. 58.52) including 3 centuries and 10 catches.

DULEEP TROPHY CHAMPIONSHIP

In September 1961, the Board of Control for Cricket in India Established the Zonal Tournament for the Duleep Trophy.

WINNERS

Year	Winner	Venue
1961-62	West Zone	Bombay
1962-63	West Zone	Calcutta
1963-64	West Zone-South Zone (Jt. Winners)	Delhi
1964-65	West Zone	Bombay
1965-66	South Zone	Madras
1966-67	South Zone	Bombay
1967-68	South Zone	Bombay
1968-69	West Zone	Hyderabad
1969-70	West Zone	Ahmedabad
1970-71	South Zone	Bombay
1971-72	Central Zone	Bangalore
1972-73	West Zone	Bombay
1973-74	North Zone	Bombay
1974-75	South Zone	Hyderabad
1975-76	South Zone	Madras
1976-77	West Zone	Baroda
1977-78	West Zone	Bombay
1978-79	North Zone	Delhi
1979-80	North Zone	Bombay
1980-81	West Zone	Calcutta
1981-82	West Zone	Bombay
1982-83	North Zone	Bombay
1983-84	North Zone	Cuttack
1984-85	South Zone	Delhi
1985-86	West Zone	Bangalore
1986-87	South Zone	Bombay
1987-88	North Zone	Bhilai
1988-89	North Zone-West Zone (Jt. Winners)	Delhi

DUMBRILL RICHARD

South Africa (born 1938) - A genuine all-rounder, right-handed batsman and a medium-pace bowler. He played for Natal. In his first class career he made, 1,761 runs and took 132 wickets.
Test Record - 5 Tests, 153 runs (Av. 15.30) and 9 wickets (Av. 37.33) and 3 catches.

DUNNING JOHN ANGUS

New Zealand (1903-1971) - A right-arm medium-pace bowler. He played for Oxford University and Otago. In his first class career he made, 1,057 runs and 228 wickets.
Test Record - 4 Tests, 38 runs (Av. 7.60), 5 wickets (Av. 98.60) and 2 catches.

DURANI SALIM AZIZ

India (born 1934) - A left-handed batsman and left-arm slow spin bowler. Test debut on January 1, 1960 against Australia at the age of 25 years and 21 days. Score on Test debut was 18 in the third Test at Bombay. Last Test of the career played against England in February 1973. Scores on last appearance in Test were 73 and 37 in the fifth Test at Bombay. Age at the time of retirement from Test cricket was 38 years 60 days. First-ever Test century (104) scored on April 7, 1962 against West Indies at the age of 27 years and 116 days in the fourth Test at Port-of-Spain. He played for Gujarat and Rajasthan. In his first class career he made, 8,545 runs including 14 centuries and took 484 wickets.
Test Record - 29 Tests, 1,202 runs (Av. 25.04) including 1 century, 75 wickets (Av.35.42) and 14 catches.

DYER DENNIS VICTOR

England (born 1914) - A right-handed opening batsman. He played for Natal. In his first class career he made, 1,725 runs including 3 centuries.
Test Record - 3 Tests, 96 runs (Av. 16.00).

DYMOCK GEOFFREY

Australia (born 1945) - A medium-fast left-arm opening bowler. He took seven wickets in his first Test Match at Adelaide. He played for Queensland. In his first class career he made, 1,518 runs

including 1 century and took 425 wickets.
Test Record - 21 Tests, 236 runs (Av. 9.44), 78 wickets (Av. 27.18) and 1 catch.

DYSON JOHN
Australia (born 1954) - A right-handed opening batsman. He had his first chance at Test level during the days of Kerry Packer, in 1977. He played for New South Wales. In his first class career he made, 8,514 runs including 15 centuries.
Test Record - 30 Tests, 1,359 runs (Av. 26.64) including 2 centuries and 10 catches.

E

E S C A
It stands for English Schoolboys' Cricket Association. It was founded in 1948.

EADY CHARLES JOHN
Australia (1870-1945) - He was a powerful pace bowler. He played for Tasmania. In his first class career he made, 1,490 runs including 3 centuries and took 135 wickets.
Test Record - 2 Tests, 20 runs (Av. 6.66) and 7 wickets (Av. 16.00).

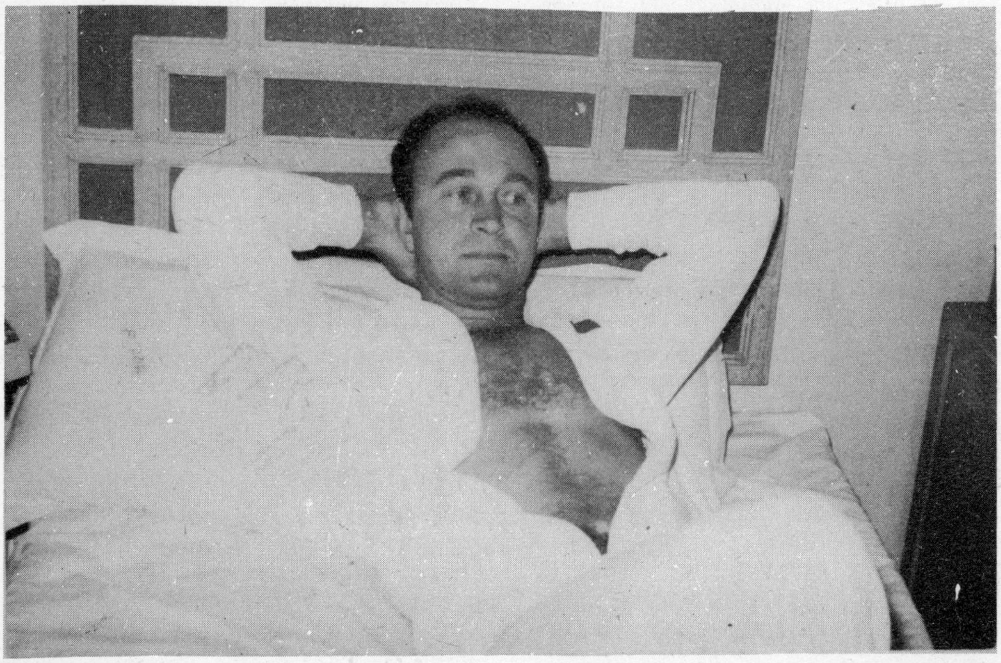

PHILIPPE EDMONDS

EASY-PACED
Slowness of pace and evenness of bounce which provides conditions more favourable to batting than to bowling.

EDGAR BRUCE ADRIAN
New Zealand (born 1956) - A left-handed batsman. He played for Wellington. In his first class career he made, 8,754 runs including 17 centuries and took 1 wicket.
Test Record - 39 Tests, 1,958 runs (Av. 30.59) including 3 centuries and 14 catches.

EDGE
A ball is deflected from top, bottom, inside or outside the blade of the bat rather than hitting it cleanly.

EDMONDS PHILIPPE HENRI
England (born 1951) - A tall, strongly built, richly gifted cricketer is an orthodox slow left-arm spinner, hard-hitting middle-order batsman and a brilliant all-rounder fielder. He played for Cambridge University and Middlesex. In his first class career he made, 7,347 runs including 3 centuries and 1,185 wickets.
Test Record - 41 Tests, 765 runs (Av. 17.79), 106 wickets (Av. 33.16) and 37 catches.

EDRICH JOHN HUGH

England (born 1937) - He was a left-handed batsman. He was not a natural athlete, being a virtual non-bowler and possessed of no more than a modest throwing arm. He played for Norfolk and Surrey. In his first class career he made, 39,790 runs including 103 centuries and took 311 catches.
Test Record - 77 Tests, 5,138 runs (Av. 43.54) and 43 catches.

EDRICH WILLIAM JOHN

England (1916-1986) - He was a right-handed batsman whose favourite shots were the pulled cover drive the hook and the late cut. His fast bowling was explosive and tearaway. He played for Norfolk and Middlesex. In his first class career he made, 36,965 runs including 86 centuries , and took 479 wickets and 527 catches.
Test Record - 39 Tests, 2,440 runs (Av. 40.00) including 6 centuries, 41 wickets (Av. 41.29) and 39 catches.

EDWARDS GRAHAM NEIL

New Zealand (born 1955) - A short heavily built wicket-keeper, very hard-hitting right-handed batsman and natural comic, 'Jock'. He played for Central Districts. In his first class career he made, 4,589 runs including 5 centuries and 142 dismissals.
Test Record - 8 Tests, 377 runs (Av. 25.13) and 7 dismissals (7ct).

EDWARDS RICHARD MARTIN

West Indies (born 1940) - A strong and lively right-arm fast-medium bowler. He played for Barbados. In his first class career he made, 389 runs and took 78 wickets.
Test Record - 5 Tests, 65 runs (Av. 9.28) and 18 wickets (Av. 34.77).

EDWARDS ROSS

Australia (born 1942) - He was a sound and steady middle-order right-handed batsman and a superb cover fielder, swift as a hawk to swoop on the ball. He played for Western Australia and New South Wales. In his first class career he made, 7,345 runs including 14 centuries and took 107 catches.
Test Record - 20 Tests, 1,171 runs (Av. 40.37) including 2 centuries and 7 catches.

EDWARDS WALTER JOHN

Australia (born 1950) - He was an attractive left-handed opening batsman. He played for Western Australia. In his first class career he made, 1,381 runs including 2 centuries.
Test Record - 3 Tests, 68 runs (Av. 11.33).

EHTESHAM-UD-DIN

Pakistan (born 1950) - A right-arm medium-pace bowler poorly built, but with a good action. He played for Lahore. In his first class career he made, 1.063 runs and took 506 wickets.
Test Record - 5 Tests, 2 runs (Av. 1.00) 16 wickets (Av. 23.43) and 2 catches.

ELGIE MICHAEL KELSEY

South Africa (born 1933) - A very good right-handed batsman and useful change slow left-arm bowler. He played for Natal. In his first class career he made, 1,834 runs including 3 centuries and took 10 wickets.
Test Record - 3 Tests, 75 runs (Av. 12.50) and 4 catches.

ELLIOTT HARRY

England (1891-1976) - He was a good wicket-keeper. He played for Derbyshire. In his first class career he made, 7,580 runs and 1,211 dismissals.
Test Record - 4 Tests, 61 runs (Av. 15.25) and 11 dismissals (8ct, 3st).

ELLISON RICHARD MARK

England (born 1959) - He was a right-arm swing bowler and a powerful left-handed middle-order batsman. He played for Kent and Tasmania. In his first class career he made, 2,805 runs including 1 century and took 247 wickets.
Test Record - 11 Tests, 202 runs (Av. 13.46), 35 wickets (Av. 29.94) and 2 catches.

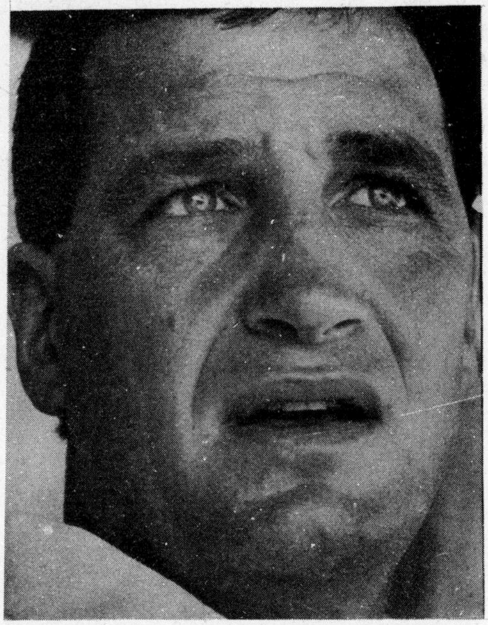

JOHN EMBUREY

EMBUREY JOHN ERNEST

England (born 1952) - A tall off-spinner with a classical high action causing awkward bounce. He played for Middlesex and Western Province. In his first class career he made, 6,744 runs including 3 centuries, took 1,066 wickets and 293 catches.

Test Record - 57 Tests, 1,409 runs (Av. 21.89), 130 wickets (Av. 30.61) and 33 catches.

EMERGENCY

When a player not belonging to a team but brought in to replace a regular member.

EMERY RAYMOND WILLIAM GEORGE

New Zealand (1915-1982) - A competent right-handed opening batsman and occasional medium-pace bowler. He played for Auckland and Canterbury. In his first class career he made, 1,177 runs including 3 centuries and took 22 wickets.

Test Record - 2 Tests, 46 runs (Av. 11.50) and 2 wickets (Av. 26.00).

EMERY SIDNEY HAND

Australia (1886-1967) - A right-arm googly bowler of lively medium-pace. He played for New South Wales. In his first class career he made, 1,192 runs and took 183 wickets.

Test Record - 4 Tests, 6 runs (Av. 3.00), 5 wickets (Av. 49.80) and 2 catches.

EMMETT THOMAS

England (1841-1904) - He was a left-arm medium-fast bowler having a round-arm action, who could pitch on the leg-stump and hit the off. He played for Yorkshire. In his first class career he made, 8,734 runs including 1 century and took 1,582 wickets.

Test Record - 7 Tests, 160 runs (Av. 13.33) 9 wickets (Av. 31.55) and 9 catches.

END

The wicket defended by a particular batsman. (To score a run the batsmen must exchange ends).

ENDEAN WILLIAM RUSSELL

South Africa (born 1924) - A fine batsman and all-round fielder with very quick reflexes. He was also the best of the outstanding fielding side, holding 29 catches on the tour. He played for Transvaal. In his first class career he made, 7,577 runs including 15 centuries and 171 dismissals.

Test Record - 28 Tests, 1,630 runs (Av. 33.95) including 3 centuries and 41 catches.

ENGINEER FAROKH MANEKSHA

India (born 1938)- A right-handed batsman and wicket-keeper. Test debut on December 1, 1961 against England at the age of 23 years and 277 days. Score on Test debut was 33 in the second Test at Kanpur. Last Test of the career played against West Indies in January 1975. Scores on last appearance in Test were 0 and 0 in the fifth Test at Bombay. Age at the time of retirement from Test cricket was 36 years and 334 days. First-ever Test century scored on January 13, 1967 against West Indies in the third Test at Madras at the age of 28 years and 319 days. His 90 in the first Test against New Zealand at Madras in 1964-65 is the highest score for a batsman at No.9 in the batting order for India. His partnership of 143 runs with R.G. Nadkarni for the 8th wicket in the same Test is also the highest for 8th wicket for

FAROKH ENGINEER

India against any country. He played for Bombay. In his first class career he made, 13,436 runs including 13 centuries and 824 dismissals.
Test Record - 46 Tests, 2,611 runs (Av.31.08) including 2 centuries and 82 dismissals (66ct, 16st).

EQUIPMENT
The bat and ball are the two most important items of equipment. The bat, made of white willow, is flat on the face and rounded at the back. Its handle is of cane, bound in twine, and covered by a rubber sleeve. Bats vary in weight, according to the preference of the batsman. The ball has a cork and twine come and a cover of red leather. The heavy seam that joins the leather is very important, because bowlers use it to make the ball swing in the air and bounce in different directions.

ESSEX
Foundation of Present Club: January 14,1876
First First class Match : Essex v Leicestershire May 14,15,16,(1894)
Present Principal Ground: County Ground, New Writtle Strert, Chelmsford
County Champions: 1979,1983 and 1985
JPL Champions : 1981,1984 and 1985
Benson & Hedges Cup Champions : 1979
Highest Team Total : 692 v Somerset (Taunton)1895
Lowest Team Total: 30 v Yorkshire 1901
Highest Individual Innings: 343* P.A.Perrin v Derbyshire 1904

EVANS EDWIN
Australia (1849-1921) - He was a very accurate right-arm spin bowler with a high action. He played for New South Wales. In his first class career he made, 1,016 runs and took 203 wickets.
Test Record - 6 Tests, 82 runs (Av. 10.25), 7 wickets (Av. 47.42) and 5 catches.

EVANS THOMAS GODFREY
England (born 1920) - An irrepressible extrovert and outstanding wicket-keeper of his day. He made nonsense of the convention that wicket-keeper should be sound rather than showy. He played for Kent. In his first class career he made, 14,882 runs including 7 centuries and 1,060 dismissals.
Test Record - 91 Tests, 2,439 runs (Av. 20.49) including 2 centuries and 219 dismissals (173ct, 46st).

EVEN TIME
A scoring rate of one run per minute.

EXPENSIVE
Relatively high number of runs per over.

EXPRESS
It is regarded as a very fast delivery.

F

FACE

It is that portion of the blade of the bat with which the ball is usually struck.

FAG

A fielder who is not a full member of the team but whose function is simply to retrieve balls in the deep field.

FAGG ARTHUR EDWARD

England (1915-1977) - A very sound right-handed opening batsman. He strokes all round the wickets, being a fine hooker. He played for Kent. In his first class career he made, 27,291 runs including 58 centuries, 421 catches and 5 stumpings.

Test Record - 5 Tests, 150 runs (Av. 18.75) and 5 catches.

FAIRFAX ALAN GEORGE

Australia (1906-1955) - He was a sound right-handed stroke-player who used his long reach extremely well. He was also a lively fast-medium bowler. He played for New South Wales. In his first class career he made, 1,910 runs including 1 century and took 134 wickets.

Test Record - 10 Tests, 410 runs (Av. 51.25) 21 wickets (Av. 30.71) and 15 catches.

FALL

When a bowler dismisses a batsman by taking his wicket.

FANE FREDERICK LUTHER

England (1875-1960) - A fine attractive right-handed batsman with front-foot style. Fane was a familiar feature on Essex ground and he was an opening batsman of his team. He played for Oxford University. In his first class career he made, 18,548 runs including 25 centuries and 181 catches.

Test Record - 14 Tests, 682 runs (Av. 26.33) including 1 century, and 6 catches.

FARM

It is an attempt to take singles of the last ball of each over to ensure that a weaker batting partner is not exposed to the bowling.

FARNES KENNETH

England (1911-1941) - He was a right-arm pace bowler. He played for Cambridge University. In his first class career he made, 1,182 runs and took 690 wickets.

Test Record - 15 Tests, 58 runs (Av. 4.83), 60 wickets (Av. 28.65) and 1 catch.

FARRER WILLIAM STEPHEN

South Africa (born 1936) - A hard hitting right-handed batsman. He played for Border. In his first class career he made, 4,815 runs including 12 centuries.

Test Record - 6 Tests, 221 runs (Av. 27.62) and 2 catches.

FARRIMOND WILLIAM

England (1903-1979) - A second-string wicket-keeper. He played for Lancashire. In his first class career he made, 2,908 runs and 333 dismissals.

Test Record - 4 Tests, 116 runs (Av. 16.57) and 7 dismissals (5ct, 2st).

FAST

To a fast bowler, all that has been said about the easy rhythmical delivery is of the first importance, for a fast bowler's worst enemy is fatigue, and one does not want to develop a tiring, unrhythmical action which is only effective for three or four overs. A fast bowler must make his run exact and automatic. A fast bowler's usual methods of getting a batsman out are:

1. Hitting the wicket. This is usually done by an off-break, by a yorker or by sheer speed.
2. Making the batsman touch the ball into the

hands of the wicket-keeper, silps or gully. This kind of ball is an out-swinger, pitching on or near the off-stump so as to make the batsman reach out to play it and then swinging away to wards the off.

3. By bowling 'leg theory'. This means bowling at the leg stump and pitching an occasional ball.

FAULKNER MAJOR GEORGE AUBREY
South Africa (1881-1930) - A right-handed batsman. He also used a well-concealed and swift, yorker. He played for Transvaal. In his first class career he made, 6,392 runs including 13 centuries, and took 449 wickets.
Test Record - 25 Tests, 1,754 runs (Av. 40.79) including 4 centuries, 82 wickets (Av. 26.58) and 20 catches.

FAVELL LESLIE ERNEST
Australia (born 1929) - A stocky hard-hitting right-handed opening batsman. He played for South Australia. In his first class career he made, 12,379 runs including 27 centuries and 110 catches.
Test Record - 19 Tests, 757 runs (Av. 27.03) including 1 century and 9 catches.

FAZAL MAHMOOD
Pakistan (born 1927) - A right-arm fast-medium pace bowler. He was also a hard-hitting lower-order batsman and a very good fielder. He played for Lahore. In his first class career he made, 2,602 runs including 1 century and took 460 wickets.
Test Record - 34 Tests, 620 runs (Av. 14.09), 139 wickets (Av. 24.70) and 11 catches.

FEED
Bowling in such a way to induce a batsman to score and to play stroke but towards especially placed fielder.

FELLOWS-SMITH JONATHAN PAYAN
South Africa (born 1932) - A right-handed batsman. As a stock bowler he could be waspish and he also bowled leg-spin. He played for Oxford University and Transvaal. In his first class career he made, 3,419 runs including 5 centuries and took 149 wickets
Test Record - 4 Tests, 166 runs (Av. 27.66) and 2 catches.

FENDER PERCY GEORGE HERBERT
England (1892-1985) - A right-handed batsman and he was also a slow leg-break bowler. He played for Sussex and Surrey. In his first class career he made, 19,034 runs including 21 centuries, took 1,894 wickets and 599 catches.
Test Record - 13 Tests, 380 runs (Av. 19.00), 29 wickets (Av. 40.86) and 14 catches.

FERGUSON WILFRED
West Indies (1917-1961) - A right-handed well-pitched leg-breaks and a hard-hitting late-order batsman. He played for Trinidad. In his first class career he made, 1,225 runs and took 165 wickets.
Test Record - 8 Tests, 200 runs (Av. 28.58), 34 wickets (Av. 34.26) and 11 catches.

FERNANDES MARIUS PACHACO
West Indies (1898-1981) - A right-handed batsman and strokes all round the wicket, and a safe catcher. He played for British Guiana. In his first class career he made, 2,087 runs including 4 centuries.
Test Record - 2 Tests, 49 runs (Av. 12.25).

FERRIS JOHN JAMES
Australia (1867-1900) - A left-arm medium-pace bowler. He played for New South Wales, South Australia and Gloucestershire. In his first class career he made, 4,264 runs including 1 century and took 813 wickets.
Test Record (Australia) - 8 Tests, 98 runs (Av. 8.16), 48 wickets (Av. 14.25) and 4 catches. (England): - 1 Test, 16 runs (Av. 16.00) and 13 wickets (Av. 7.00).

FIELD
A generally oval or rectangular field with no specific dimensions. A representative British cricket field may be 200 yards long and 120 yards wide. Near the centre of the field is a firm closely-

FIELDING POSITION

Field placements

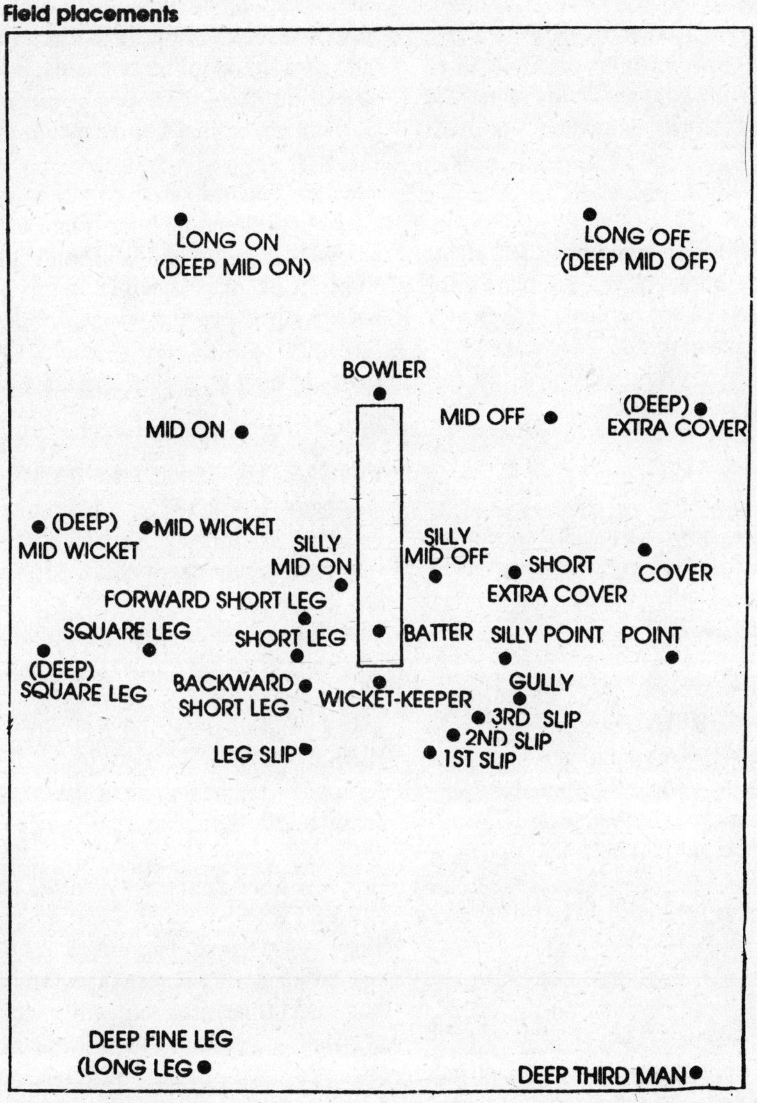

cut strip 22 yards long and 10 feet wide (the pitch) at each end of which is erected a wicket. On the ground through each wicket is an 8-foot-8-inch line (the bowling crease) and 4 feet in front of and parallel to each bowling crease is a popping crease of unlimited length but usually marked no longer than 10 feet. All 4 lines are parallel. Extending back at right angles from the ends of each bowling crease is a return crease. The return crease and the bowling crease mark the area in which the bowler must have his rear foot when delivering the ball; the popping crease marks the forward edge of the batsman's ground.

FIELDER ARTHUR

England (1877-1949) - He could bowl fast right-arm, off-cutters and out swingers. He played for Kent. In his first class career he made, 2,290 runs including 1 century and took 1,277 wickets.

Test Record - 6 Tests, 78 runs (Av. 11.14), 26 wickets (Av. 27.34) and 4 catches.

FIGURES

It is the summary of a bowler's performance in an innings or a match, showing wickets taken against runs scored. It also includes the number of overs and maidens bowled.

FINDLAY THADDEUS MICHAEL

West Indies (born 1943) - A genial and intelligent man competent both as a wicket-keeper and right-handed batsman. He played for Windward Island. In his first class career he made, 2,927 runs and 252 dismissals.

Test Record - 10 Tests, 212 runs (Av. 16.30) and 21 dismissals (19ct, 2st).

FINE

Passing through a fielding position in cricket behind the batsman and near an extension of the line between the wickets.

FINE - LEG

A fielding position to the rear of the batsman and just on the leg side.

FINGER-SPIN

A ball after pitching from leg (a leg break), or from the off (an off break), or it may make haste off the pitch (a top-spinner). Broadly speaking, there are two ways of producing these breaks. One is by means of the fingers, clicking them as we sometimes do in order to attract the attention of a dog; this is known as 'finger-spin'. The other way is by changing the position of the hand as the ball leaves it, thus rolling the ball out and making it spin in a certain direction; this is called 'rolled spin'. On the whole, finger spin is used by slow bowlers and rolled spin by medium-paced and fast bowlers.

The way in which a bowler grips the ball is particularly important for spin. First and foremost, a bowler does not hold the ball in his hand. It is all fingers, and the principle is to get as much friction between the fingers and the ball as possible, so as to start it spinning at the same time as it is being propelled forward.

FINGLETON JOHN HENRY WEBB

Australia (1908-1981) - A right-handed opening batsman. He played for New South Wales. In his first class career he made, 6,816 runs and including 22 centuries.

Test Record - 18 Tests, 1,189 runs (Av. 42.46) including 5 centuries and 13 catches.

FIRST CHANGE

A bowler replacing one of the two opening bowlers in a side's attack.

FIRST CLASS

Since 1947, a first-class match has been defined as one arranged for three days minimum between two teams of 11 players each, with each team allowed two innings. Each of the two teams should be regarded as of first-class standard by the relevant body controlling cricket in the country in which the match was played.

The Cricket 'averages' published in newspapers and other periodicals are usually compiled from performances in first-class matches only, unless stated otherwise. This means that players' performances in one-day internationals, the Sunday League, the Nat West Trophy and Benson &

Hedges Cup are not included in the 'first-class' averages.

Prior to 1947, the press generally decided which matches qualified as 'first-class', and provided the teams were playing two innings a side and involved 'first-class' cricketers, the press included matches arranged for two days matches involving 12 players on each side and in the second half of the 19th century some matches in which 11 players opposed 12,13,14 or 15 opponents.

The concept of having 'first-class' matches evolved around the middle of the 19th century and by the time overarm bowling was legalised in 1864 'first class' cricket was established and definitive 'averages' and records could be compiled from such matches.

FIRST CLASS RECORDS, BATTING RECORDS, HIGHEST INDIVIDUAL SCORES

499	Hanif Mohammad	Karachi v Bahawalpur	1958-59
452*	D.G.Bradman	NSW v Queensland	1929-30
443*	B.B.Nimbalkar	Maharashtra v Kathiawar	1948-49
437	W.H.Ponsford	Victoria v Queensland	1927-28
429	W.H.Ponsford	Victoria v Tasmania	1922-23
428	Aftab Baloch	Sind v Baluchistan	1973-74
424	A.C.MacLaren	Lancashire v Somerset...........	1985
405*	G.A.Hick	Worcestershire v Somerset	1988
385	B.Sutcliffe	Otago v Canterbury	1952-53
383	C.W.Gregory	NSW v Queensland	1906-07
369	D.G.Bradman	South Australia v Tasmania	1935-36
365	C.Hill	South Australia v NSW	1900-01
365*	G.S.Sobers	West Indies v Pakistan	1957-58
364	L.Hutton	England v Australia	1938
359*	V.M.Merchant	Bombay v Maharashtra...........	1943-44
359	R.B. Simpson	NSW v Queensland	1963-64
357*	R.Abel	Surrey v Somerset	1899
357	D.G.Bradman	South Australia v Victoria	1935-36
356	B.A. Richards	South Australia v W.Australia	1970-71
355	B. Sutcliffe	Otago v Auckland	1949-50
352	W.H. Ponsford	Victoria v NSW	1926-27
350	Rashid Israr	Habib Bank v National Bank ..	1976-77

TWO DOUBLE HUNDREDS IN A MATCH

A.E.Fagg....... .... 244 ...... 202* .... Kent v Essex 1938

HUNDREDS AND DOUBLE HUNDREDS IN A MATCH

Player	1st	2nd	Match	Year
C.B.Fry	125	229	Sussex v Surrey	1900
W.W.Armstrong	157*	245	Victoria v South Australia	1920
H.T.W.Hardinge	207	102*	Kent v Surrey	1921
C.P.Mead	113	224	Hampshire v Sussex	1921
Duleepsinhji	115	246	Sussex v Kent	1929
D.G.Bradman	124	225	Woodfull's XI v Ryder' XI	1929
B.Sutcliffe	243	100*	New Zealanders v Essex	1949
M.R.Hallam	210*	157	Leicester v Glamorgan	1959
M.R.Hallam	203*	143*	Leicestershire v Sussex	1961
Hanumants	109	213*	Rajasthan v Bombay	1966
Salah-ud-Din	256	102*	Karachi v East Pakistan	1968
K.D.Walters	242	103	Australia v West Indies	1968
S.M.Gavaskar	124	220	India v West Indies	1970
L.G.Rowe	214	100*	West Indies v New Zealand	1971
G.S.Chappell	247*	133	Australia v New Zealand	1973
L.Baichan	216*	102	Berbice v Demerara	1973
Zaheer Abbas	216*	156*	Gloucestershire v Surrey	1976
Zaheer Abbas	230*	104*	Gloucestershire v Kent	1976
Zaheer Abbas	205*	108	Gloucestershire v Sussex	1977
Saadat Ali	141	222	Income Tax v Multan	1977
Talat Ali	140*	104	PIA v Punjab	1978
Shafiq Ahmed	129	217*	National Bank v MCB	1978
Randall	209	146	Nottinghamshire v Middlesex	1979
Zaheer Abbas	215*	150*	Gloucestershire v Somerset	1981
Qasim Omar	210*	110	MCB v Lahore	1982
A.Kallicharan	200*	117*	Warwickshire v Northamptonshire	1984

MOST HUNDREDS IN A CAREER

	Hundreds Total	Abroad
J.B.Hobbs	197	22
E.H.Hendren	170	19
W.R.Hammond	167	33
C.P.Mead	153	8
G.Boycott	151	27
H.Sutcliffe	149	14
F.E.Woolley	145	10
L.Hutton	129	24
W.G.Grace	126	01
D.C.S.Compton	123	31
T.W.Graveney	122	31
D.G.Bradman	117	41

35,000 RUNS IN A CAREER

	R	I	NO	HL	100s
J.B.Hobbs	61,237	1,315	106	316*	197
F.E.Woolley	58,969	1,532	85	305	145
E.H.Hendren	57,611	1,300	166	301*	170
C.P.Mead	55,061	1,340	185	280*	153
W.G.Grace	54,896	1,493	105	344	126
W.R.Hammond	50,551	1,005	104	336*	167
H.Sutcliffe	50,138	1,088	123	313	149
G.Boycott	48,426	1,014	162	261*	151
T.W.Graveney	47,793	1,223	158	258	122
T.W.Hayward	43,551	1,138	96	315*	104
D Amiss	43,423	1,139	126	262*	102
M.C.Cowdrey	42,719	1,130	134	307	107
A.Sandham	41,284	1,000	79	325	107
L.Hutton	40,140	814	91	364	129
M.J.K.Smith	39,832	1,091	139	204	69
W.Rhodes	39,802	1,528	237	267*	58
J.H.Edrich	39,790	979	104	310*	103
R.E.S.Wyatt	39,405	1,141	157	232	85
D.C.S.Compton	38,942	839	88	300	123
E.Tyldesley	38,874	961	106	256*	102
J.T.Tyldesley	37,897	994	62	295*	86
K.W.R.Fletcher	37,665	1,167	170	228*	63
J.W.Hearne	37,252	1,025	116	285*	96
L.E.G.Ames	37,248	951	95	295	102
D.Kenyon	37,002	1,159	59	259	74
W.J.Edrich	36,965	964	92	267*	86
J.M.Parks	36,673	1,227	172	205*	51
D.Denton	36,479	1,163	70	221	69
G.H.Hirst	36,323	1,215	151	341	60
A.Jones	36,049	1,168	72	204*	56
W.G.Quaife	36,012	1,203	185	255*	72
R.E.Marshall	35,725	1,053	59	228*	68
G.Gunn	35,208	1,068	82	220	62

FASTEST HUNDREDS

Minutes

35	P.G.H.Fender	(113*)	Surrey v Northamptonshire	1920
35	S.J.O'Shaughnessy	(105)	Lancashire v Leicestershire	1983
37	C.M.Old	(107)	Yorkshire v Warwickshire	1977
40	G.L.Jessop	(101)	Gloucestershire v Yorkshire	1897

RAVI SHASTRI

FASTEST DOUBLE CENTURIES

Minutes

113 .... R.J. Shastri .... (200*) .... Bombay v Baroda 1984-85
120 .... G.L.Jessop .... (286) .... Gloucestershire v Sussex......................... 1903

FASTEST TRIPLE CENTURIES

Minutes

181 .... D.C.S.Compton ...... (300) .... MCC v N.E.Transvaal at Benoni 1948-49
205 .... C.G.Macartney........ (345) .... Australians v Nottinghamshire at Nottingham 1921
205 .... F.E.Woolley .... (305*) .. MCC v Tasmania at Hobart 1911-12

MOST RUNS SCORED OFF ONE OVER

36 ...... G.S.Sobers off M.A.Nash,Nottinghamshire v Glamorgan at Swansea (six 6s) 1968
36 ...... R.J.Shastri off Tilak Raj, Bombay v Baroda at Bombay (six 6s)............... 1984-85
34 ...... E.B.Alletson off E.H.Killick,Nottinghamshire v Sussex at Hove
(46604446;including two no balls) 1911
34 ...... F.C.Hayes off M.A.Nash, Lancashire v Glamorgan at Swanse (646666) 1977

MOST SIXES IN AN INNINGS

15 ...... J.R.Reid .... (296) .. Wellington v N.Districts at Wellington................... 1962-63
13 ...... Majid Khan .... (147*) Pakistan v Glamorgan at Swansea 1967
13 ...... C.G.Greenidge .... (273*) D.H.Robins'XI v Pakistan at Eastbourne 1974
13 ...... C.G.Greenidge .... (259) .. Hampshire v Sussex at Southampton 1975
13 ...... G.W.Humpage .... (254) .. Warwickshire v Lancashire at Southport 1982
13 ...... R.J.Shastri .... (200*) Bombay v Baroda at Bombay 1984-85

MOST BOUNDARIES IN AN INNINGS

68 ...... P.A. Perrin .... (343*) Essex v Derbyshire at Chesterfield 1904
65 ...... A.C.MacLaren .... (424) .. Lancashire v Somerset at Taunton 1895
64 ...... Hanif Mohammad .. (499) .. Karachi v Bhawalpur at Karachi............................. 1958-59
57 ...... J.H.Edrich .... (310*) England v New Zealand at Leeds 1965
55 ...... C.W.Gregory .... (383) NSW v Queensland at Brisbane 1906-07

54 ...... G.H.Hirst .... (341) Yorkshire v Leicestershire at Leicester 1905
53 ...... A.W.Nourse .... (304*) Natal v Transvaal at Johannesburg
53 ...... K.R.Rutherford ...... (317) New Zealand v D. B Close XI at Scarborough 1986
51 ...... C.G. Macartney ...... (345) Australia v Nottinghamshire at Nottingham 1921

HIGHEST PARTNERSHIPS

577 .... V.S.Hazare (288) and Gul Mahomed (319),
fourth wicket, Baroda v Holker at Baroda 1946-47

574* .. F.M.M.Worrell (255*) and C.L. Walcott (314*),
fourth wicket, Barbados v Trinidad at Port of Spain 1945-46

561 .... Waheed Mirza (324) and Mansoor Akhtar (224*),
first wicket, Karachi Whites v Quetta at Karachi 1976-77

555 .... P.Holmes (224*)and H.Sutcliffe (313),
first wicket, Yorkshire v Essex at Leyton 1932

554 .... J.T.Brown (300) and J.Tunnicliffe (243),
first wicket,Yorkshire v Derbyshire at Chesterfield 1898

502* .. F.M.M. Worrell (308*) and J.D.C.Goddard (218*),
fourth wicket,Barbados v Trinidad at Bridgetown 1943-44

MOST WICKETS IN A MATCH

9-90 .... J.C.Laker........................ England v Australia at Manchester
17-48 .... C.Blythe .... Kent v Northamptonshire at Northampton
17-50 .... C.T.B. Turner .... Australia v England XI at Hastings
17-54 .... W.P.Howell..................... Australia v Western Province at Cape Town
17-56 .... C.W.L.Parker .... Gloucestershire v Essex at Gloucester
17-67 .... A.P.Freeman .... Kent v Sussex at Hove
17-89 .... W.G.Grace .... Gloucestershire v Nottinghamshire at Cheltenham
17-89 .... F.C.L.Matthews.............. Nottinghamshire v Northants at Nottingham
17-91 .... H.Dean .... Lancashire v Yorkshire at Liverpool
17-91 .... H.Verity .... Yorkshire v Essex at Leyton
17-92 .... A.P.Freeman .... Kent v Warwickshire at Folkestone
17-103 .... W.Mycroft .... Derbyshire v Hampshire at Southampton
17-106 .... G.R.Cox .... Sussex v Warwickshire at Horsham
17-106 .... T.W.Goddard .... Gloucestershire v Kent at Bristol
17-119 .... W.Mead .... Essex v Hampshire at Southampton
17-137 .... W.Brearley .... Lancashire v Somerset at Manchester
17-159 .... S.F.Barnes...................... England v South Africa at Johannesburg
17-201 .... G.Giffen .... South Australia v Victoria at Adelaide
17-212 .... J.C.Clay .... Glamorgan v Worcestershire at Swansea

SEVENTEEN OR MORE WICKETS IN A DAY

17-48 .... C.Blythe .... Kent v Northamptonshire at Northampton
17-91 .... H.Verity .... Yorkshire v Essex at Leyton
17-106 .... T.W.Goddard .... Gloucestershire v Kent at Bristol

HAT - TRICKS

Double Hat-Trick

A.Shaw	Nottinghamshire v Gloucestershire at Nottingham	1884
T.J.Matthews	Australia v South Africa at Manchester	1912
C.W.L.Parker	Gloucestershire v Middlesex at Bristol	1924
R.O.Jenkins	Worcestershire v Surrey at Worcester	1949
J.S.Rao	Services v Northern Punjab at Amritsar	1963-64
Amin Lakhani	Combined XI v Indians at Multan	1978-79

Most Hat-Tricks

Seven times: D.V.P.Wright.
Six times: T.W.Goddard, C.W.L.Parker.
Five times: S.Haigh,V.W.C.Jupp,A.E.G,Rhodes,F.A.Tarrant.
Four times: R.G.Barlow,J.T.Hearne,J.C.Laker, G.A.R.Lock,G.G.Macaulay, T.J. Matthews, M.J.Procter.T.Richardson, F.R.Spofforth, F.S.Truman.

250 WICKETS IN A SEASON

	Season	O	M	R	W	Av.
A.P.Freeman	1928	1,976.1	423	5489	304	18.05
A.P.Freeman	1933	2,039	651	4549	298	15.26
T.Richardson	1895+	1,690.1	463	4170	290	14.37
C.T.B.Turner	1888+	4,227.2	1,127	3307	283	11.68
A.P.Freeman	1931	1,618	360	4307	276	15.60
A.P.Freeman	1930	1,914.3	472	4632	275	16.84
T.Richardson	1897+	1,603.4	495	3945	273	14.45
A.P.Freeman	1929	1,670.5	381	4879	267	18.27
W.Rhodes	1900	1,553	455	3606	261	13.81

2,500 WICKETS IN A CAREER

	Career	W	R	Avge
W.Rhodes	1898-1930	4,187	69,993	16.71
A.P.Freeman	1914-36	3,776	69,577	18.42
C.W.L.Parker	1903-35	3,278	63,817	19.46
J.T.Hearne	1888-1923	3,061	54,352	17.75
T.W.Goddard	1922-52	2,979	59,116	19.84
W.G.Grace	1865-1908	2,876	51,545	17.92
A.S.Kennedy	1907-36	2,874	61,034	21.23
D.Shackleton	1948-69	2,857	53,303	18.65
G.A.R.Lock	1946-70	2,844	54,709	19.23
F.J.Titmus	1949-82	2,830	63,313	22.37
M.W.Tate	1912-37	2,784	50,571	18.16
G.H.Hirst	1891-1829	2,739	51,282	18.72
C.Blythe	1899-1914	2,506	42,136	16.81

2,000 RUNS AND 100 WICKETS

	Season	R	W
W.G.Grace	1873	2,139	106
W.G.Grace	1876	2,622	129
C.L.Townsend	1899	2,440	101
G.L.Jessop	1900	2,210	104
G.H.Hirst	1904	2,501	132
G.H.Hirst	1905	2,266	110
W.Rhodes	1909	2,094	141
W.Rhodes	1911	2,261	117
F.A.Tarrant	1911	2,030	111
J.W.Hearne	1913	2,036	124
J.W.Hearne	1914	2,116	123
F.E.Woolley	1914	2,272	125
J.W.Hearne	1920	2,148	142
V.W.C.Jupp	1921	2,169	121
F.E. Woolley	1921	2,101	167
F.E.Woolley	1922	2,022	163
F.E.Woolley	1923	2,091	101
L.F.Townsend	1933	2,268	100
D.E.Davies	1937	2,012	103
James Langridge	1937	2,082	101
T.E.Bailey	1959	2,011	100

1,000 RUNS AND 200 WICKETS

	Season	R	W
A.E.Trott	1899	1,175	239
A.E.Trott	1900	1,337	211
A.S.Kennedy	1922	1,129	205
M.W.Tate	1923	1,168	219
M.W.Tate	1924	1,419	205
M.W.Tate	1925	1,290	228

WICKET-KEEPING RECORDS

MOST DISMISSALS IN AN INNINGS

8(all ct)	A.T.W.Grout	Queensland v Western Australia	1959-60
8(all ct)	D.E.East	Essex v Somerset	1985
7(4ct,3st)	E.J.Smith	Warwickshire v Derbyshire	1926
7(6ct,1st)	W.Farrimond	Lancashire v Kent	1930
7(all ct)	W.F.F.Price	Middlesex v Yorkshire	1937
7(3ct,4st)	D.Tallon	Queensland v Victoria	1938-39
7(all ct)	R.A.Saggers	New South Wales v Combined XI	1940-41
7(1st,6st)	H.Yarnold	Worcestershire v Scotland	1951
7(4ct,3st)	J.Brown	Scotland v Ireland	1957
7(6ct,1st)	N.Kirsten	Border v Rhodesia	1959-60
7(all ct)	M.S.Smith	Natal v Border	1959-60
7(all ct)	K.V.Andrew	Northamptonshire v Lancashire	1962
7(all ct)	A.Long	Surrey v Sussex	1964
7(all ct)	R.M.Schofield	Central Districts v Wellington	1964-65
7(all ct)	R.W.Taylor	Derbyshire v Glamorgan	1966
7(6ct,1st)	H.B.Taber	New South Wales v South Australia	1968-69
7(6ct,1st)	E.W.Jones	Glamorgan v Cambridge University	1970
7(6ct,1st)	S.Benjamin	Central Zone v North Zone	1973-74
7(all ct)	R.W.Taylor	Derbyshire v Yorkshire	1975
7(6ct,1st)	Shahid Israr	Karachi Whites v Quetta	1976-77
7(4ct,3st)	Wassim Bari	PIA v Sind	1977-78
7(all ct)	J.A.Maclean	Queensland v Victoria	1977-78
7(5ct,2st)	Taslim Arif	National Bank v Punjab	1978-79
7(all ct)	Wassim Bari	Pakistan v New Zealand	1978-79
7(all ct)	R.W.Taylor	England v India	1979-80
7(all ct)	D.L.Bairstow	Yorkshire v Derbyshire	1982
7(6ct,1st)	R.B.Phillips	Queensland v New Zealanders	1982-83
7(3ct,4st)	Basood Iqbal	Habib Bank v Lahore	1982-83
7(3ct,4st)	Arif ud din	United Bank v PACO	1983-84
7(6ct,1st)	R.J.East	OFS v Western Province B	1984-85
7(all ct)	B.A.Young	Northern Districts v Canterbury	1986-87

TEAM RECORDS

HIGHEST TOTALS

1,107	Victoria v New South Wales	1926-27
1,059	Victoria v Tasmania	1922-23
951-7 dec.	Sind v Baluchistan	1973-74
918	New South Wales v South Australia	1988-89
912-6 dec.	Tamil Nadu v Goa	1900-01
912-8 dec.	Holker v Mysore	1945-46
910-6 dec.	Railways v Dera Ismail Khan	1964-65
903-7 dec.	England v Australia	1938

LOWEST TOTALS

12	Oxford University v MCC and Ground	1877
12	Northamptonshire v Gloucestershire	1907
13	Auckland v Canterbury	1877-78
13	Nottinghamshire v Yorkshire	1901
14	Surrey v Essex	1983
15	MCC v Surrey	1839
15	Victoria v MCC	1903=04
15	Northamptonshire v Yorkshire	1908
15	Hampshire v Warwickshire	1922
	(Following on, Hampshire scored 521 and won by 155 runs.)	
16	MCC and Ground v Surrey	1872
16	Derbyshire v Nottinghamshire	1879
16	Surrey v Nottinghamshire	1880
16	Warwickshire v Kent	1913
16	Trinidad v Barbados	1942-43
16	Border v Natal	1959-60

LOWEST TOTAL IN A MATCH

34	(16 and 18)	Border v Natal	1959-60
42	(27 and 15)	Northamptonshire v Yorkshire	1908

HIGHEST MATCH AGGREGATES

2,376 for 38 wickets	Maharashtra v Bombay	1948-49
2,078 for 40 wickets	Bombay v Holkar	1944-45
1,981 for 35 wickets	England v South Africa	1938-39
1,929 for 39 wickets	New South Wales v South Australia	1925-26

LARGEST VICTORIES

Inns and 851 runs:	Railways (910-6 dec.) v Dera Ismail Khan	1964-65
Inns and 666 runs:	Victoria (1,059) v Tasmania	1922-23
Inns and 656 runs:	Victoria (1,107) v New South Wales	1926-27
Inns and 605 runs:	New South Wales (918) v South Australia..........	1900-01

LARGEST VICTORIES BY RUNS MARGIN

685 runs:	New South Wales (235 and 76-8 dec.) v Queensland	1929-30
675 runs:........	England (521 and 342-8 dec.) v Australia	1928-29
638 runs:	New South Wales (304 and 770) v South Australia	1920-21
625 runs:..........	Sargodha (376 and 416) v Lahore Municipal Corporation..	1978-79
609 runs:	Muslim Commercial Bank (575 and 282-0 dec.) v WAPDA	1977-78

FIRST SLIP

An off-side fielding position behind the batsman's wicket, between the wicket-keeper and the gully. First slip should stand sufficiently wide of the wicket-keeper to ensure a clear view of batsman and bowler in case the wicket-keeper moves across to take the ball on the off-side. He must watch the ball from the bowler's hand and concentrate on every delivery.

FISHLOCK LAURENCE BARNARD

England (1907-1986) - A left-handed strokemaker with a style quite free from fuss. He played for Surrey. In his first class career he made, 25,376 runs including 57 centuries, took 11 wickets and 216 catches.

Test Record - 4 Tests, 47 runs (Av. 11.75) and 1 catch.

FIVER

A ball hit over the boundary without bouncing, which, under regulations in force in Australia during the first few years of the present century, carried an allowance of five runs.

FLASH

This is playing a ball passing outside the off stump with a quick, involuntary movement of the bat, usually withdrawing the bat again hastily in an attempt to avoid making contact with the ball.

FLAT

It is some sort of dead ball characterised by a low, straight trajectory rather than a high 'looping' arc.

FLAT BAT

A bat held with his full face to the ball.

FLAVELL JOHN ALFRED

England (born 1929) - He was one of the fastest right-arm bowlers in England. He played for Worcestershire. In his first class career he made, 2,032 runs and took 1,529 wickets.

Test Record - 4 Tests, 31 runs (Av. 7.75) and 7 wickets (Av. 52.42).

FLEETWOOD-SMITH LESLIE O'BRIEN

Australia (1910-1971) - A left-arm back-of-the-hand spin bowler. He played for Victoria. In his

first class career he made, 617 runs and took 597 wickets.
Test Record - 10 Tests, 54 runs (Av. 9.00) and 42 wickets (Av. 37.38).

FLETCHER KEITH WILLIAM ROBERT
England (born 1944) - He was a right-handed batsman and had a gift of perfect timing. He was occasional leg-spin bowler and a fine all-round fielder for Essex. He played for Essex. In his first class career he made, 37,665 runs including 63 centuries 51 wickets and 631 catches.
Test Record - 59 Tests, 3,272 runs (Av. 39.90) including 7 centuries 2 wickets (Av. 96.50) and 54 catches.

FLIGHT
To bowl a ball in such a way as to cause it to drop suddenly or to carry a little beyond the point at which the batsman expects it to bounce.

FLIPPER
It is a typically produced slow ball mainly with the tips of the first and third fingers and squeezing or 'flipping' it out so that it emerges from the back or side of the hand with an extra helping of top spin on it. If successfully executed it will hurry through without deviation, gaining pace as it pitches and keeping low. The flipper has been described as 'the most arcane and esoteric ball in cricket'.

FLOATER
A slow delivery of a cricket ball that rises after it leaves the bowler's hand before dropping towards the batsman.

FLOWERS WILFRED
England (1856-1926) - He was a right-handed batsman and a steady off-break bowler. He played for Nottinghamshire. In his first class career he made, 12,891 runs including 9 centuries, took 1,187 wickets and 216 catches.
Test Record - 8 Tests, 256 runs (Av. 18.14) 14 wickets (Av. 21.14) and 3 catches.

FLY-SLIP
An off-side fielding position behind the slips and somewhat shorter than third man. Fly-slip is used for trapping a batsman who is inclined to slice the ball over the heads of the slips.

FOLLOW ON
In a match in which teams are allowed two innings each, when the side that bats second are dismissed cheaply and have a large deficit on the first innings, they can be asked to take their second innings immediately. The team which batted first reserves the right to bat again. When a team continues their second innings directly after their first in this way, the team 'follows on'.
The first law governing this was published in 1835, when the follow-on was compulsory if a side were 100 or more runs behind.
As the law now stands the follow-on regulation is optional and the amount of runs required as the difference between the sides depends on the number of days arranged for the match: for a five-day match it is 200 runs; three-or four-day match 150; two-day 100 and one-day 75.

FOLLOW THROUGH
In the follow-through the front arm resumes its movement downwards and back behind the body, absorbing the impetus of the bowling arm. The bowling arm comes over and across the front of the body, finishing alongside and outside the front knee.

FOOTHOLD
A roughened area on the pitch offering a secure grip for a player's foot, especially for a batsman or bowler.

FOOTWORK
Style of the batsman moving his feet while playing. This especially contributes to effective strokeplay.

FORCING SHOT
It is an aggressive stroke played off the back foot

to a ball pitching rather short of a length and typically just outside off stump (or leg stump), in which the bat is swung downwards and forwards from a full backlift, sending the ball into the area between cover and mid-off or between mid-wicket and mid-on.

FORTHERGILL ARNOLD JAMES
England (1854-1932) - A medium-pace left-arm bowler and hard-hitting batsman. He played for Northumberland and Somerset. In his first class career he made, 843 runs and took 119 wickets.
Test Record - 2 Tests, 33 runs (Av. 16.50) and 8 wickets (Av. 11.25).

FORWARD
Moving, tending or leading towards the position in front or occupying a fielding position in cricket in front of the batsman's wicket.

FORWARD-CUT
A batting stroke in which the front foot is brought forward and somewhat across towards the off, and the ball, typically a short-pitched delivery well outside the off stump, is struck with a horizontal bat into the area between point and cover.

FOSTER FRANK ROWBOTHAM
England (1889-1958) - He was a right-handed batsman and also a left-arm medium-fast bowler with short runs and beautifully easy action. He played for Warwickshire. In his first class career he made, 6,540 runs including 7 centuries and took 724 wickets and 118 catches.
Test Record - 11 Tests, 330 runs (Av. 23.57), 45 wickets (Av. 20.57) and 11 catches.

FOSTER MAURICE LINTON CHURCHILL
West Indies (born 1943) - A right-handed batsman and a useful off-break bowler. He played for Jamaica. In his first class career he made, 6,731 runs including 17 centuries and took 132 wickets.
Test Record - 14 Tests, 580 runs (Av. 30.52) including 1 century, 9 wickets (Av. 66.66) and 3 catches.

FOSTER NEIL ALAN
England (born 1962) - A right-arm fast-medium pace bowler. He is tall and slim having a classical bowling action. He plays for Essex. In his first class career he made, 1,764 runs and took 391 wickets.
Test Record - 25 Tests, 342 runs (Av. 10.68), 76 wickets (Av. 31.26) and 6 catches.

FOSTER REGINALD ERSKINE
England (1878-1914) - He was a right-handed batsman. He played for Oxford University and Worcestershire. In his first class career he made, 9,076 runs including 22 centuries 25 wickets and 175 catches.
Test Record - 8 Tests, 602 runs (Av. 46.30) including 1 century and 13 catches.

FOUR
A shot in cricket that crosses the boundary after having hit the ground inside it and that automatically results in four runs. This may result from a bye or wide ball.

FOWLER GRAEME
England (born 1957) - A neat, jaunty left-handed opening batsman, a fine athlete, a very useful wicket-keeper and also a fine all-rounder fielder. He played for Lancashire. In his first class career he made, 10,166 runs including 24 centuries and took 5 wickets.
Test Record - 21 Tests, 1,307 runs (Av. 35.52) including 3 centuries and 10 catches.

FRANCIS BRUCE COLLIN
Australia (born 1948) - A right-handed opening batsman. He played for New South Wales. In his first class career he made, 6,183 runs including 13 centuries.
Test Record - 3 Tests, 52 runs (Av. 10.40) and 1 catch.

FRANCIS GEORGE NATHANIEL
West Indies (1897-1942) - He was right-handed fast bowler. He played for Barbados. In his first class career he made, 874 runs and took 223 wick-

ets.
Test Record - 10 Tests, 81 runs (Av. 5.78) and 23 wickets (Av. 33.17).

FULLER EDWARD RUSSELL HENRY
South Africa (born 1931) - He was a right-arm fast-medium pace bowler. He played for Western Province. In his first class career he made, 1,062 runs and took 190 wickets.
Test Record - 7 Tests, 64 runs (Av. 8.00), 22 wickets (Av. 30.36) and 3 catches.

FRANCOIS CYRIL MATTHEW
South Africa (1897-1944) - A hard-hitting right-handed batsman and fast-medium pace bowler. He played for Griqualand West . In his first class career he made, 1,232 runs and took 101 wickets.
Test Record - 5 Tests, 252 runs (Av. 31.50) 6 wickets (Av. 37.50) and 5 catches.

FRANKLIN TREVOR JOHN
New Zealand (born 1962) - An exceptionally tall right-handed batsman of sound techniques. He plays for Auckland. In his first class career he made, 5,793 runs including 11 centuries and took 4 wickets.
Test Record - 8 Tests, 220 runs (Av.15.00) and 4 catches.

FREDERICKS ROY CLINTON
West Indies (born 1942) - He was a tough left-handed opening batsman of high class who hit the ball exceptionally hard. He played for Guyana and Glamorgan. In his first class career he made, 16,834 runs including 40 centuries, took 75 wickets and 177 catches.
Test Record - 59 Tests, 4,334 runs (Av. 42.49) including 8 centuries, 7 wickets (Av. 78.28) and 62 catches.

FREEMAN ALFRED PERCY
England (1888-1965) - He was a right-arm leg-break, mixed with a skilfully disguised googly and a top spinner. He played for Kent. In his first class career he made, 4,913 runs, took 3,776 wickets, 249 catches and 1 stumping.
Test Record - 12 Tests, 154 runs (Av. 14.00), 66 wickets (Av. 25.86) and 4 catches.

FREEMAN DOUGLAS LINFORD
New Zealand (born 1914) - A right-arm googly bowler. He played for Nelson and Wellington. In his first class career he made, 28 runs and took 14 wickets.
Test Record - 2 Tests, 2 runs (Av. 1.00).

FREEMAN ERIC WALTER
Australia (born 1944) - A right-arm fast-medium pace bowler, hard-hitting batsman and excellent fielder. He played for South Australia. In his first class career he made, 2,244 runs including 1 century and took 241 wickets.
Test Record - 11 Tests, 345 runs (Av. 19.16), 34 wickets (Av. 33.17) and 5 catches.

FRONT FOOT
The foot that automatically comes forward from the stumps when a batsman is standing at the crease; the left foot in the case of a right-handed batsman or the right-foot in the case of a left-handed batsman.

FRY CHARLES BURGESS
England (1872-1956) - He was pre-eminently a back-foot player, had a powerful straight drive but scored mainly on the leg-side and he had a cast-iron defence. He played for Oxford University. In his first class career he made, 30,886 runs including 94 centuries. took 165 wickets and 218 catches.
Test Record - 26 Tests, 1,223 runs (Av. 32.18) including 2 centuries and 17 catches.

FULL TOSS
A throw, especially a bowled ball in cricket. that has not hit the ground by the time it arrives at the point at which it was aimed. It reaches the batsman about the height of his knees. It is, therefore, generally regarded as a bad delivery.

FULLERTON GEORGE MURRAY

South Africa (born 1922) - A right-handed batsman. He played for Transvaal. In his first class career he made, 2,768 runs including 3 centuries and 82 dismissals.

Test Record - 7 Tests, 325 runs (Av. 25.00) and 12 dismissals (10ct, 2st).

FUNSTON KENNETH JAMES

South Africa (1925) - A right-handed batsman. He was a magnificent outfield. He played for North-Eastern Province, Transvaal, and Orange Free State. In his first class career he made, 4,164 runs including 5 centuries.

Test Record - 18 Tests, 824 runs (Av. 25.75) and 7 catches.

G

GADKARI CHANDRASEKHAR VAMAN
India (born 1928) - A right-handed batsman and right-arm medium pace bowler. Test debut on January 21, 1953 against West Indies at the age of 24 years and 348 days. Scores on Test debut were 7 and 11 not out in the first Test at Port of Spain. Last Test of the career played in February 1955 against Pakistan. Scores on last appearance in Test was 15 in the fourth Test at Peshawar. Age at the time of retirement from Test cricket was 27 years and 12 days. He played for Maharashtra. In his first class career he made, 3,024 runs including 7 centuries, and took 48 wickets.
Test Record - 6 Tests, 129 runs (Av. 21.50) and 6 catches.

GAEKWAD ANSHUMAN DATTAJIRAO
India (born 1952) - A right-handed batsman and right-arm off break bowler. Son of India's ex-captain, D.K. Gaekwad. Test debut on December 27, 1974 against West Indies at the age of 22 years and 94 days. Scores on Test debut were 36 and 4 in the third Test at Calcutta. Last Test of the career played against West Indies in February 1979. Score on last appearance in Test was 102 in the sixth Test at Kanpur. Age at the time of retirement from Test cricket was 26 years and 133 days. He played for Baroda. In his first class career he made, 10,296 runs including 28 centuries, and took 115 wickets.
Test Record - 40 Tests, 1,985 runs (Av. 30.07) including 2 centuries and 15 catches.

GAEKWAD DATTAJIRAO KRISHNARAO
India (born 1928) - A right-handed batsman and right-arm leg-break bowler. Father of A.D.Gaekwad. Test debut on June 5, 1952 against England at the age of 23 years and 218 days. Scores on Test debut were 9 and 0 in the first Test at Leeds. Last Test of the career played against Pakistan in January 1961. Scores on last appearance in Test was 9 in the fourth Test at Madras. Age at the time of retirement from Test cricket was 32 years and 82 days. Led India for the first time against England in the first Test at Nottingham on June 4, 1959, at the age of 30 years and 217 days, scoring 33 and 31 runs. Captained Indian team in four Tests (all against England) which India lost in 1959. He played for Baroda. In his first class career he made, 5,783 runs including 17 centuries, and took 24 wickets.
Test Record - 11 Tests, 350 runs (Av. 18.42) and 5 catches.

GAMSY DENNIS
South Africa (born 1940) - An outstanding wicket-keeper. He played for Natal. In his first class career he made, 3,106 runs including 2 centuries, and 311 dismissals.
Test Record - 2 Tests, 39 runs (Av. 19.50) and 5 catches.

GANDOTRA ASHOK
India (born 1948) - A left-handed batsman and left-arm slow spin bowler. Test debut on October 15, 1969 against New Zealand at the age of 20 years and 322 days. Scores on Test debut were 18 and 15 in the third Test at Hyderabad. Last Test of the career played against Australia in November 1969. Scores on last appearance in Test were 13 and 8 in the second Test at Kanpur. Age at the time of retirement from Test cricket was 20 years and 356 days. He played for Delhi. In his first class career he made, 2,121 runs including 2 centuries and took 23 wickets.
Test Record - 2 Tests, 54 runs (Av. 13.50) and 1 catch.

GANNON JOHN BRIAN
Australia (born 1947) - A fast-medium paced left-arm bowler and athletic fielder. He played for Western Australia. In his first class career he made, 141 runs and took 117 wickets.
Test Record - 3 Tests, 3 runs (Av. 3.00), 11 wickets (Av. 32.82) and 3 catches.

GARNER JOEL

West Indies (born 1952) - A strongly built as well as very tall, is not only a fast bowler but also

JOEL GARNER

swings and cuts the ball, to present batsman with very exceptional problems. He plays for Barbados. In his first class career he made, 2,802 runs including 1 century, took 837 wickets and 122 catches.

Test Record - 58 Tests, 672 runs (Av. 12.44), 259 wickets (Av. 20.97) and 42 catches.

GARRETT THOMAS WILLIAM

Australia (1858-1943) - A good right-arm medium-pace fast bowler and a useful hard-hitter. He played for New South Wales. In his first class career he made, 3,673 runs including 2 centuries and took 445 wickets.

Test Record - 19 Tests, 339 runs (Av. 12.55), 36 wickets (Av. 26.94) and 7 catches.

GASKIN BERKELEY BERTRAM MCGARRELL

West Indies (1908-1979) - A steady right-arm medium-pace bowler. He played for British Guiana. In his first class career he made, 782 runs and took 138 wickets.

Test Record - 2 Tests, 17 runs (Av. 5.66), 2 wickets (Av. 79.00) and 1 catch.

GATTING MICHAEL WILLIAM

England (born 1957) - A cheerful Londoner, short but very solidly built. He is a tenacious, hard-hitting, right-handed batsman, useful medium-pace bowler and a good all-round fielder. He plays for Middlesex. In his first class career he made, 17,126 runs including 47 centuries, 129 wickets and 272 catches.

Test Record - 67 Tests, 3,848 runs (Av. 38.09) including 9 centuries, 4 wickets (Av. 79.25) and 51 catches.

GAUNT RONALD ARTHUR

Australia (born 1934) - A right-arm fast-medium pace bowler, and a useful left-handed batsman. He played for Western Australia and Victoria. In his first class career he made, 616 runs and took 266 wickets.

Test Record - 3 Tests, 6 runs (Av. 3.00), 7 wickets (Av. 44.28) and 1 catch.

GAVASKAR SUNIL MANOHAR

India (born 1949) - A right-handed opening batsman and right-arm medium-pace and leg-break bowler. He has been acclaimed as one of the best opening batsman in the world and compared to Sir Don Bradman of Australia for his batting technique, concentration and ability to punch any class of bowling at will. Test debut on March 6, 1971 against West Indies at the age of 21 years and 237 days. Scores on Test debut were 65 and 67 not out in the second Test at the Port-of-Spain. Playing for his country for the first time and on his maiden tour, Gavaskar earned several rare distinctions. On the tour he scored 1240 runs (Av. 145.08). Gavaskar's achievement is even more because he had not played until the tour was three weeks old. He missed the two opening matches (the first Test and the match against Guyana). It was in the Tests that he reached peak form. He is the only Indian cricketer to score 700 runs or more in a Test series and also the first and only among his countrymen to score a century and

SUNIL GAVASKAR

a double-century in the same Test. Gavaskar's aggregate of 774 runs is the highest against the West Indies by any player, eclipsing Pasty Hendren's total of 693 (Av. 115.50) in 1930. Another record toppled by him was that, he is the only opening batsman and the youngest-ever Test cricketer in world to have crossed the 750 runs mark in a Test series. The only player to come near the target was Herbert Sutcliffe of England who made 734 runs (Av. 81.55) against Australia in 1926. Gavaskar scored a century 124 and a double century 220 in the fifth Test to become the 21st batsman to score two separate hundreds in a Test. The only other Indian to achieve this distinction is Vijay Hazare who performed the feat against Australia at Adelaide in 1947-48. Gavaskar is, however, the second batsman in cricket history to score a century and a double-century in the same Test. He shares this distinction with K.D. Walters of Australia (against the West Indies at Sydney in 1968-69), L.G.Rowe of the West Indies (against New Zealand at Kingston in 1972) and G.S.Chappell of Australia (against New Zealand at Wellington in 1974). He became the second batsman in Test history when he scored three hundreds in successive innings twice (117 not out in the fourth Test at Bridgetown and 124 and 220 in the fifth Test at Port of Spain against West Indies in 1971. He repeated this feat by scoring 111 and 137 at Karachi against Pakistan in 1978 and 205 against West Indies at Bombay in 1978-79). Just as his 774 runs in a series made in 1971 against West Indies in West Indies is a record of most runs in a series outside India, his 732 runs in six-Test series against West Indies in India in 1978-79 is also the highest score in a series for India against any Test side in India. He is the only player in the world to hit up two separate centuries in a Test three times (124 and 220 in the fifth Test against West Indies at Port-of-Spain in 1971: 111 and 137 in the third Test against Pakistan at Karachi in 1978 and 107 and 182 not out in the third Test against West Indies at Calcutta in 1978-79). Herbert Sutcliffe of England, Greg Chappell of Australia, George Headley and Clyde Walcott of West Indies had scored hundreds in both innings twice. He completed the first 1,000 runs of his career in his 21st innings of the 11th Test on the opening day of the Kanpur Test against England in 1972-73 the fastest 1000 by an Indian. His 2,000 runs in 23rd Test against West Indies at Port-of-Spain in 1975-76. He earned the unique honour of becoming the first player of the four Test playing countries in Asia and Africa (India, Pakistan, New Zealand and South Africa) to cross 4,000 run mark in a Test career on December 29, 1978, when his score reached 49 on the opening day of the third Test against West Indies at Calcutta in 1978-79, and a further landmark of 5,000 runs on September 20, 1979 against Australia at Bangalore (in his 95th innings of 52nd Test). His 10,122 runs are the highest aggregate in Test history. He celebrated his 50th Test appearance for India, in the fourth Test at the Oval against England in 1979, by one of the most distinguished knocks of 221 runs. Earned the distinction of winning a Test in his very first Test on appointment as captain (first Test against New Zealand at Auckland in 1975-76). Gavaskar has scored a century against and in every Test playing country except South Africa. His first eight centuries out of a total of 34, were scored abroad and only his ninth one was made in India. No batsman has ever scored more than six centuries against West Indies since their entry in Test cricket arena in 1928, but, Gavaskar distinguishes himself by scoring as many as 13 centuries against West Indies and with

SUNIL GAVASKAR

this he has secured the fourth rank among the batsmen who have scored most centuries against one single country. The other three are Don Bradman of Australia (19 centuries against England). Jack Hobbs of England (12 centuries against Australia) and Gary Sobers of West Indies (10 centuries against England). Gavaskar figures in 100 run partnerships for India on more occasions than any other Indian batsman. He has opened both batting and bowling in a Test for India on four occasions. Also has emulated the feat of Don Bradman of Australia and Vijay Hazare of India, of scoring four consecutive hundreds in four Tests at one place. Bradman made hundred at Leeds in his every appearance there in 1930, 1934, 1938 and 1948 and Vijay Hazare scored centuries at Bombay 134 not out and 122 against West Indies in the second and fifth Test in 1948-49, 155 against England in 1951-52 and 146 not out against Pakistan in 1952-53 while Gavaskar also scored centuries in Bombay. He made 119 against New Zealand in 1977-76, 108 against England in the same season, 205 against West Indies in 1978-79 and 123 against Australia in 1979-80. Gavaskar has led India in 47 Tests . He has won 9 Tests for India lost 8 and remaining 30 were drawn. Joined the distinguished company of Test captains who had won the toss in all the matches in a series before him when he won the toss in all the three Tests against New Zealand in 1981. He played for Bombay and Somerset. In his first class career he made 25,834 runs including 81 centuries, took 22 wickets and 293 catches.
Test Record - 125 Tests, 10,122 runs (Av. 51.12) including 34 centuries, 1 wicket and 108 catches.

GEARY GEORGE
England (1893-1981) - He was a right-arm, fast-medium pace bowler with a high action and unwavering accuracy. He was also off-spinner. He played for Leicestershire. In his first class career he made, 13,504 runs including 8 centuries, took 2,063 wickets and 451 catches.
Test Record - 14 Tests, 249 runs (Av. 15.56), 46 wickets (Av. 29.41) and 13 catches.

GEDYA SYDNEY GRAHAM
New Zealand (born 1929) - A competent right-handed opening batsman. He played for Auckland. In his first class career he made, 2,388 runs including 3 centuries.
Test Record - 4 Tests, 193 runs (Av. 24.12).

GEHRS DONALD RAEBURN ALGERNON
Australia (1880-1953) - He was an attractive right-handed batsman, who could hook superbly against any type of bowler. He played for South Australia. In his first class career he made, 4,377 runs including 13 centuries.
Test Record - 6 Tests, 221 runs (Av. 20.09) and 6 catches.

GHAVRI KARSAN DEVJIBHAI
India (born 1951)- A left-handed batsman and left-arm fast medium and slow spin bowler. Test debut

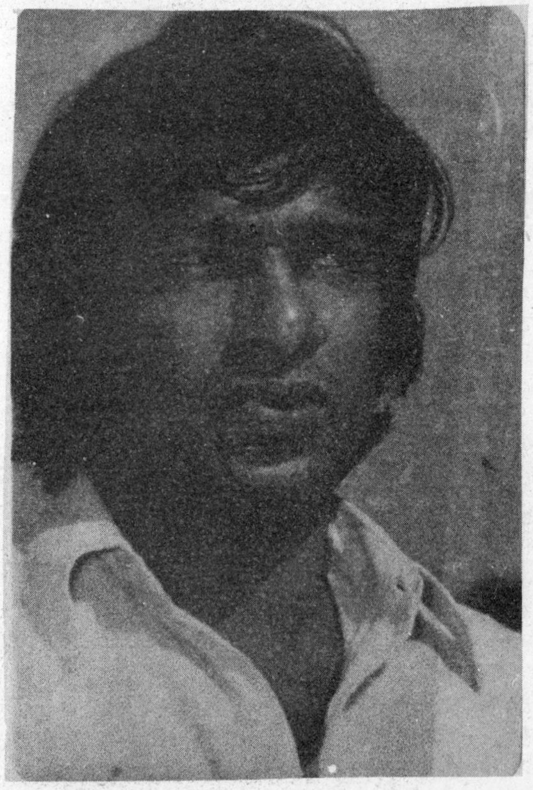

KARSAN GHAVRI

on December 27,1974 against West Indies at the age of 23 years and 270 days. Scores on Test debut were 3 and 27 in the third Test at Calcutta. Joined the select band of bowlers who have taken 100 or more Test wickets, when he claimed the wicket of Rodney Marsh caught by Binny for 12 in the first innings of the 1st Test against Australia at

Sydney on January 4,1981. He played for Saurashtra. In his first class career he made, 4,500 runs including 1 century and took 452 wickets.
Test Record - 39 Tests, 913 runs (Av. 21.23), 109 wickets (Av. 33.54) and 16 catches.

GHAZALI MOHAMMED EBRAHIM ZAINUDDIN
Pakistan (born 1924) - A forcing right-handed batsman, useful leg-break bowler and an excellent fielder. He played for Services. In his first class career he made, 1,569 runs including 2 centuries and took 62 wickets.
Test Record - 2 Tests, 32 runs (Av. 8.00).

GHORADE JAYA SINGH MAN SINGH
India (1930-1978) - A right-handed batsman and right-arm leg-break bowler. Test debut on February 19, 1953 against West Indies at the age of 22 years and 137 days. Scores on Test debut were 35 and 0 in the third Test at Port-of-Spain. Last Test of the career played against England in August 1959. Scores on last appearance in Test were 5 and 24 in the fifth Test at the Oval. Age at the time of retirement from Test cricket was 28 years and 322 days. He played for Baroda and Maharashtra. In his first class career he made, 2,631 runs including 2 centuries and took 114 wickets.
Test Record - 8 Tests, 229 runs (Av. 15.26) and 4 catches.

GULAM AHMED
India (born 1922) - A right-handed batsman and right-arm off-break bowler. Test debut on December 31, 1948 against West Indies at the age of 26 years and 177 days. Score on Test debut were 0 in the third Test at Calcutta. Last Test of the career played against West Indies in December-January 1959. Scores on last appearance in Test were 4 and 0 in the third Test at Calcutta. Age at the time of retirement from Test cricket was 36 years and 180 days. Led India for the first time against New Zealand in the first Test at Hyderabad in 1955-56. He played for Hyderabad. In his first class career he made, 1,341 runs and took 407 wickets.
Test Record - 22 Tests, 192 runs (Av. 8.72), 68 wickets (Av. 30.17) and 11 catches.

GIBB PAUL ANTHONY
England (1913-1977) - He was a right-handed batsman and also a very useful wicket-keeper. He played for Cambridge University. In his first class career he made, 12,520 runs including 19 centuries and 544 dismissals.
Test Record - 8 Tests, 581 runs (Av. 44.69) including 2 centuries, 4 dismissals (3ct, 1st).

GIBBS LANCELOT RICHARD
West Indies (born 1934) - A right-arm off-spinner with long fingers which gave him exceptional spin and bounces. He played for Guyana, South Australia and Warwickshire. In his first class career he made, 1,729 runs, took 1,024 wickets and 203 catches.
Test Record - 79 Tests, 488 runs (Av. 6.97), 309 wickets (Av. 29.09) and 52 catches.

GIFFEN GEORGE
Australia (1859-1927) - He was highly gifted all-rounder. A determined attacking right-handed batsman and slow-medium pace bowler of great accuracy. He played for South Australia. In his first class career he made, 11,758 runs including 18 centuries, took 1,023 wickets and 195 catches.
Test Record - 31 Tests, 1,238 runs (Av. 23.25) including 1 century, 103 wickets (Av. 27.09) and 24 catches.

GIFFORD NORMAN
England (born 1940) - He was a beautiful leg-arm spin bowler. He is also a determined and resourceful left-handed tail-ender. He played for Worcestershire and Warwickshire. In his first class career he made, 6,812 runs, took 2,001 wickets and 316 catches.
Test Record - 15 Tests, 179 runs (Av. 16.27), 33 wickets (Av. 31.09) and 8 catches.

GILBERT DAVID ROBERT
Australia (born 1960) - A well-built right-arm fast bowler with the ability to move the ball off the seam. He played for New South Wales. In his first class career he made, 267 runs and took 149 wickets.

Test Record - 7 Tests, 56 runs (Av. 8.00) and 15 wickets (Av. 48.26).

GILCHRIST ROY

West Indies (born 1934) - He was a fast-medium pace bowler. He was sent home in disgrace from 1958-59 of India tour for bowling fast 'beamers' (full tosses around the batsman's head) and other misdemeanours. He played for Jamaica. In his first class career he made, 255 runs and took 167 wickets.

Test Record - 13 Tests, 60 runs (Av. 5.45), 57 wickets (Av. 26.68) and 4 catches.

GILLETTE CUP (SOUTH AFRICA)

Limited overs competition in South Africa

	Winners
1969-70	Western Province
1970-71	Western Province
1971-72	Eastern Province
1972-73	Western Province
1973-74	Transvaal
1974-75	Natal
1975-76	Eastern Province
1976-77	Natal

After this Gillette Cup competition was replaced by Datsun Shield.

Datsun Shield

1977-78	Rhodesia
1978-79	Transvaal
1979-80	Transvaal
1980-81	Transvaal
1981-82	Western Province
1982-83	Transvaal
1983-84	Transvaal
1984-85	Transvaal

GILLETTE CUP (WEST INDIES)

Sponsored by Gillette for the first two seasons. The competition is played on a zonal basis with three teams in each zone.

Cup Final Results
Gillette Cup (Winners)

1975-76	Barbados
1976-77	Barbados

After this Gillette Cup competition was replaced by Geddes Grant/Harrison Line Trophy.

	Winners
1977-78	Jamaica
1978-79	Trinidad
1979-80	Guyana
1980-81	Trinidad
1981-82	Leeward Islands
1982-83	Guyana
1983-84	Jamaica
1984-85	Guyana
1985-86	Guyana
1986-87	Jamaica
1987-88	Barbados

GILLETTE CUP (ENGLAND)

This competition was held form 1963 to 1980 and then was replaced by Nat West Bank Trophy.

	Winners
1963	Sussex
1964	Sussex
1965	Yorkshire
1966	Warwickshire
1967	Kent
1968	Warwickshire
1969	Yorkshire
1970	Lancashire
1971	Lancashire
1972	Lancashire
1973	Gloucestershire
1974	Kent
1975	Lancashire
1976	Northamptonshire
1977	Middlesex
1978	Sussex
1979	Somerset
1980	Middlesex

After this Gillette Cup competition was replaced by Nat West Bank Trophy.

	Winners
1981 ..	Derbyshire
1982 ..	Surrey
1983 ..	Somerset
1984 ..	Middlesex
1985 ..	Essex
1986 ..	Sussex
1987 ..	Nottinghamshire
1988 ..	Middlesex

GILLIGAN ARTHUR EDWARD ROBERT

England (1894-1976) - A right-arm fast bowler, accurate and always bowling on the stumps. He played for Cambridge University. In his first class career he made, 9,140 runs including 12 centuries and took 868 wickets.

Test Record - 11 Tests, 209 runs (Av. 16.07), 36 wickets (Av. 29.05) and 3 catches.

GILMOUR GARY JOHN

Australia (born 1951) - He was a left-handed all-rounder and a fast-medium over-the-wicket bowler. He played for New South Wales. In his first class career he made, 3,126 runs including 5 centuries and took 233 wickets.

Test Record - 15 Tests, 483 runs (Av. 23.00) including 1 century, 54 wickets (Av. 26.03) and 8 catches.

GIMBLETT HAROLD

England (1914-1978) - A right-hander, he cut, drove, pulled and hooked in a manner which gave him fame overnight. He played for Somerset. In his first class career he made, 23,007 runs including 50 centuries and took 41 wickets.

Test Record - 3 Tests, 129 runs (Av. 32.25) and 1 catch.

GLADWIN CLIFFORD

England (born 1916) - He was a right-arm in-dipping seam bowler, and a tail-end batsman. He played for Derbyshire. In his first class career he made, 6,238 runs including 1 century and took 1,653 wickets.

Test Record - 8 Tests, 170 runs (Av. 28.33), 15 wickets (Av. 38.06) and 2 catches.

GLAMORGAN

Foundation of Present Club : July 5, 1888 in Cardiff

First first class Match : Glamorgan v Sussex, May 18,19,20,1921

Present Principal Ground : Sophia Gardens, Cardiff and St. Helen's, Swansea.

County Champions : 1948 and 1969

Nat West Trophy : losing finalists in 1977

Highest Team Total: 587 for 7 dec. v Derbys, in 1951

Lowest Team Total: 22 v Lancs, (Liverpool) 1924

Highest Individual Innings: 287* D.E.Davies v Glos, 1939

GLEESON JOHN WILLIAM

Australia (born 1938) - A right-arm spin bowler. He is short and sinewy with the weather-beaten face of a jockey. He played for New South Wales. In his first class career he made, 1,095 runs and took 430 wickets.

Test Record - 29 Tests, 395 runs (Av. 10.39), 93 wickets (Av. 36.20) and 17 catches.

GLOUCESTERSHIRE

Foundation of Present Club : Established in 1863

First first class Match: Gloucestershire v Surrey (Bristol) June 2,3,4 (1870)

Present Principal Ground: County Ground ,Nevil Road, Bristol

Benson & Hedges Cup: Winners in 1977

Nat West Trophy: Winners in 1973

Highest Team Total : 653 for 6 dec v Glamorgan (Bristol) 1928

Lowest Team Total: 17 v Australians (Cheltenham)1896

Best Innings Analysis : 10-40 E.G.Dennett v Essex (Bristol)

Highest Individual Innings: 318* W.G.Grace v Yorkshire in 1876

GLOVE

Deflection of the ball from one's batting gloves often presenting the fielding side with a catch.

GODDARD JOHN DOUGLAS CLAUDE

West Indies (born 1919) - He was a vigilant and

determined left-handed batsman and a right-arm medium-pace in-swinging or off-break bowler. He played for Barbados. In his first class career he made, 3,769 runs including 5 centuries and took 146 wickets.
Test Record - 27 Tests, 859 (Av. 30.67) 33 wickets (Av. 31.81) and 22 catches.

LARRY GOMES

GODDARD THOMAS WILLIAM JOHN
England (1900-1966) - He was a right-arm fast bowler. He played for Gloucestershire. In his first class career he made, 5,224 runs and took 2,979 wickets.
Test Record - 8 Tests, 13 runs (Av. 6.50) 22 wickets (Av. 26.72) and 3 catches.

GODDARD TREVOR LESLIE
South Africa (born 1931) - A left-handed opening batsman and bowler, an excellent close-to-the-wicket fielder. He was an all-rounder. He captained South Africa in 13 Tests. He played for Natal and Northern-Eastern Transvaal. In his first class career he made, 11,279 runs including 26 centuries, took 534 wickets and 174 catches.
Test Record - 41 Tests, 2,516 runs (Av. 34.46) including 1 century, 123 wickets (Av. 26.22) and 48 catches.

GRAHAM GOOCH

GOMES LARRY ANGELO
West Indies (born 1953) - A silm, shy, artistic cricketer. A left-handed batsman, a good fielder and a useful right-arm bowler who switched from medium pace to slow-off-break. His brother, Sheldon Gomes has also played for Trinidad. He played for Trinidad and Middlesex. In his first class career he made, 12,353 runs including 31 centuries and took 101 wickets.
Test Record - 54 Tests, 3,032 runs (Av. 42.70) including 9 centuries, 13 wickets (Av. 66.69) and 17 catches.

GOMEZ GERALD ETHRIDGE
West Indies (born 1919) - A dependable middle-order right-handed batsman, and an energetic fast-medium swing bowler. He was a active administrator on the West Indies Cricket Board of Control for many years. He played for Trinidad. In

his first class career he made, 6,764 runs including 14 centuries and took 200 wickets.

Test Record - 29 Tests, 1,243 runs (Av. 30.31) including 1 century, 58 wickets (Av. 27.41) and 18 catches.

GOOCH GRAHAM ALAN

England (born 1953) - A big, dark fresh-faced man. He was a right-handed opening batsman who loves to attack and hits the ball immensely hard, especially excelling in the drive and hook and a useful medium-pace seam bowler and a fine fielder anywhere. He played for Essex and Western Province. In his first class career he made, 22,835 runs including 57 centuries, took 179 wickets and 329 catches.

Test Record - 68 Tests, 4,541 runs (Av. 38.15) including 8 centuries, 13 wickets (Av. 42.30) and 69 catches.

GOOGLE

A ball which is bowled by a right-handed bowler and released with the same wrist action as a leg-break but which spins like an off break upon striking the ground.

GOOGLER

Googly bowler.

GOONASEKERA YOHAN

Sri Lanka (born 1957) -A right-handed batsman and outstanding fielder. He plays for Nondescripts. In his first class career he made, 429 runs and took one wicket.

Test Record - 2 Tests, 48 runs (Av. 12.00) and 6 catches.

GOONATILIEKE HETTIARACHIGE MAHES

Sri Lanka (born 1952) - An accomplished wicket-keeper polished and swift, and a solid right-handed batsman. He plays for Kandy. In his first class career he made, 430 runs and 54 dismissals.

Test Record - 5 Tests, 177 runs (Av. 22.12) and 13 dismissals (10ct, 3st).

GOPALAN MORAPPARKAM JOYSAM

India (born 1909) - A right-handed batsman and right-arm fast- medium bowler. Test debut on January 5, 1933 against England at the age of 23 years and 210 days. Played in only one Test scoring 11 not out and 7 runs in the second Test at Calcutta. He played for Madras. In his first class career he made, 2,916 runs including 1 century and took 194 wickets.

Test Record - 1 Test, 18 runs (Av. 18.00), 1 wicket and 1 catch.

GOPALAN TROPHY

Winners

1952-53	Ceylon won by 95 runs (Madras)
1953-54	Ceylon won by an innings and 108 runs (Colombo)
1955-56	Ceylon won by an innings and 14 runs (Madras)
1956-57	Ceylon won by 5 wickets (Colombo)
1957-58	Madras won by 2 wickets (Madras)
1958-59	Drawn (Colombo)
1959-60	Madras won by 8 wickets (Madras)
1960-61	Ceylon won by 169 runs (Colombo)
1961-62	Ceylon won by an innings and 66 runs (Madras)
1962-63	Not held
1963-64	Ceylon won by 6 wickets (Colombo)

1965-66	Madras won by first innings lead (Colombo)
1966-67	Madras won by first innings lead (Madras)
1967-68	Ceylon won by 105 runs (Colombo)
1968-69	Ceylon won by first innings lead (Madras)
1969-70	Ceylon won by first innings lead (Colombo)
1970-71	Tamil Nadu won by first innings lead (Madras)
1971-72	Tamil Nadu won by one innings and 9 runs (Colombo)
1972-73	Tamil Nadu won by 3 runs (Madras)
1973-74	Sri Lanka won by first innings lead (Colombo)
1974-75	Tamil Nadu won by an innings and 73 runs (Salem)
1975-76	Sri Lanka won by 22 runs (Colombo)
1976-77	Sri Lanka won by first innings lead (Madras)
1977-78	Not held
1978-79	Not held
1979-80	Not held
1980-81	Sri Lanka won by first innings lead (Salem)
1982-83	Sri Lanka won by first innings lead (Colombo)
Since 1983-84	this Trophy has not been held.

GOPINATH COIMBATARAO DORAIKANNU

India (born 1930) - A right-handed batsman and right-arm off-break bowler. Test debut on December 14, 1951 against England at the age of 21 years and 283 days. Scores on Test debut were 50 and 42 in the Test at Bombay. Last Test of the career played against Australia in January 1960. Scores on last appearance in Test were 39 and 0 in the fifth Test at Calcutta. Age at the time of retirement from Test cricket was 29 years and 327 days. He played for Madras.In his first class career he made, 4,260 runs including 9 centuries and 14 wickets.

Test Record - 8 Tests, 242 runs (Av. 22.00) and 2 catches.

GORDON NORMAN

South Africa (born 1911) - He was a right-handed bowler. He played for Transvaal. In his first class career he made, 109 runs and took 126 wickets.

Test Record - 5 Tests, 8 runs (Av. 2.00), 20 wickets (Av. 40.35) and 1 catch.

GOVER ALFRED RICHARD

England (born 1908) - A right-arm fast bowler. He played for Surrey. In his first class career he made, 2,312 runs, 1,555 wickets and 171 catches.

Test Record - 4 Tests, 2 runs, 8 wickets (Av. 44.87).

DAVID GOWER

GOWER DAVID IVON

England (born 1957) - A left-handed batsman of rare brilliance and a superb fielder. He became

vice captain in 1982. He was a useful wicket-keeper. He played for Leicestershire. In his first class career he made, 18,597 runs including 41 centuries, took 4 wickets and 201 dismissals.
Test Record - 100 Tests, 7,000 runs (Av. 44.02) including 14 centuries and 68 catches.

GRACE DR WILLIAM GILBERT
England (1848-1915) - He was a tall, broad, bearded figure. He was instantly recognized wherever the game was played. He was a right-handed batsman and his batting was based on a correct technique. He played for London County. In his first class career he made, 54,896 runs including 126 centuries, took 2,876 wickets and 872 catches.
Test Record - 22 Tests, 1,098 runs (Av. 32.39) including 2 centuries, 9 wickets (Av. 26.22) and 39 catches.

GRAHAM HENRY
Australia (1870-1911) - A splendid right-handed hitter with plenty of dash and vigour. He played for Victoria, South Island and Otago. In his first class career he made, 5,054 runs including 7 centuries.
Test Record - 6 Tests, 301 runs (Av. 31.10) including 2 centuries and 3 catches.

GRAHAM ROBERT
South Africa (1877-1946) - An all-rounder. He played for Western Province. In his first class career he made, 260 runs and took 61 wickets.
Test Record - 2 Tests, 6 runs (Av. 1.50), 3 wickets (Av. 42.33) and 2 catches.

GRANT GEORGE COPELAND
West Indies (1907-1978) - A good right-handed batsman and a brilliant field in the gully where he brought off some amazing catches. He played for Cambridge University. In his first class career he made, 3,831 runs including 4 centuries and took 19 wickets.
Test Record - 12 Tests, 413 runs (Av. 25.81) and 10 catches.

GRANT ROLPH STEWART
West Indies (1909-1977) - He was a superb fielder, especially at short-leg and a very useful right-handed batsman. He played for Cambridge University. In his first class career he made, 1,883 runs including 1 century and took 79 wickets.
Test Record - 7 Tests, 220 runs (Av. 22.00), 11 wickets (Av. 32.09) and 13 catches.

GRASS
To drop a catch.

GRAVENEY THOMAS WILLIAM
England (born 1927) - He was a stylish right-handed batsman with a complete array of elegant

THOMAS WILLIAM GRAVENEY

strokes played mainly off the front foot. He was also a good slip and occasionally useful leg-break bowler. He played for Gloucestershire. In his first class career he made, 47,793 runs including 122 centuries, took 80 wickets and 547 catches, 1 stumping.
Test Record - 79 Tests, 4,882 runs (Av. 44.38) including 11 centuries and 80 catches.

GRAY EVAN JOHN
New Zealand (born 1954) - A steady left-arm orthodox slow bowler and competent right-handed batsman. He played for Wellington. In his first class career he made, 4,123 runs including 6 centuries and took 323 wickets.
Test Record - 8 Tests, 208 runs (Av. 17.33), 14 wickets (Av. 44.07) and 4 catches.

GREEN
A wicket with more covering of grass that retains morning moisture which helps in the movement of the ball off the pitch.

GREENHOUGH THOMAS
England (born 1931) - He was a right-handed leg-break bowler. He played for Lancashire. In his first class career he made, 1,913 runs and took 751 wickets.
Test Record - 4 Tests, 4 runs (Av. 1.33), 16 wickets (Av. 22.31) and 1 catch.

GREENIDGE ALVIN TALBERT
West Indies (born 1956) - A right-handed batsman. He played for Barbados. In his first class career he made, 2,323 runs including 4 centuries and took 5 wickets.
Test Record - 6 Tests, 222 runs (Av. 22.00) and 5 catches.

GREENIDGE CUTHBERT GORDON
West Indies (born 1951) - A compact, strong right-handed opening batsman with a marvellous temperament. His driving in the air between cover and mid-wicket is his special glory. He plays for Barbados and Hampshire. In his first class career he made, 33,103 runs including 81 centuries, took 19 wickets and 464 catches.
Test Record - 96 Tests, 6,826 runs (Av. 46.12) including 17 centuries and 90 catches.

GREENIDGE GEOFFREY ALAN
West Indies (born 1948) - A sound, right-handed opening batsman and occasional leg-break bowler. He played for Barbados and Sussex. In his first class career he made, 9,112 runs including 12 centuries and took 13 wickets.
Test Record - 5 Tests, 209 runs (Av. 29.85), and 3 catches.

GREENWOOD ANDREW
England (1847-1889) - He was a plucky, sound batsman and a brilliant outfield. He played for Yorkshire. In his first class career he made, 4,307 runs including 1 century.
Test Record - 2 Tests, 77 runs (Av. 19.25) and 2 catches.

GREGORY DAVID WILLIAM
Australia (1845-1919) - He was a batsman. He played for New South Wales. In his first class career he made, 889 runs and took 29 wickets.
Test Record - 3 Tests, 60 runs (Av. 20.00).

GREGORY JOHN MORRISON
Australia (1895-1973) - A good all-rounder, a left-handed batsman and a useful right-arm fast bowler. He bowled a good out-swinger with the new ball. He was a superb slip fielder. He played for New South Wales. In his first class career he made, 5,661 runs including 13 centuries, took 504 wickets and 195 catches.
Test Record - 24 Tests, 1,146 runs (Av. 36.96) including 2 centuries, 85 wickets (Av. 31.15) and 37 catches.

GREGORY ROSS GERALD
Australia (1916-1942) - A very quick-footed right-handed batsman. He could produce brilliant front-of-the wicket forcing strokes. He played for Victoria. In his first class career he made, 1,874 runs including 1 century and took 50 wickets.
Test Record - 2 Tests, 153 (Av. 51.00) and 1 catch.

GREGORY SYDNEY EDWARD
Australia (1870-1929) - He was a right-handed batsman having a keen eye and strong wrists. He was particularly strong on the off-side and was also brilliant at cover-point . He played for New South Wales. In his first class career he made, 15,192 runs including 25 centuries and 174 catches.

Test Record - 58 Tests, 2,282 runs (Av. 24.53) including 4
centuries and 25 catches.

GREIG ANTHONY WILLIAM

England (born 1946) - He was a right-handed batsman and his batting was based on the front foot, his particular glories were the off-drives and the lofted straightdrives. He was normally a medium-fast bowler unpredictable but able to swing the ball a great deal and to get steep bounce. He was a slip fielder, the safest and also the most brilliant of his era. He played for Border, Eastern Province and Sussex. In his first class career he made, 16,660 runs including 26 centuries, took 856 wickets and 345 catches.

Test Record - 58 Tests, 3,599 runs (Av. 40.43) including 8 centuries, 141 wickets (Av. 32.20) and 87 catches.

GREIG IAN ALEXANDER

England (born 1955) - He was a strong and capable right-handed all-round cricketer and a medium-fast bowler with a good action. He played for Cambridge University, Sussex, Border, and Griqualand West. In his first class career he made, 4,003 runs including 4 centuries and took 30 wickets.

Test Record - 2 Tests, 26 runs (Av. 6.50) and 4 wickets (Av. 28.50).

GRIEVESON RONALD EUSTACE

South Africa (born 1909) - He was a splendid wicket-keeper and batsman. He played for Transvaal. In his first class career he made, 1,130 runs including 1 century and 36 dismissals (25ct, 11st).

Test Record - 2 Tests, 114 runs (57.00) and 10 dismissals (7 ct, 3 st).

GRIFFIN GEOFFREY MERTON

South Africa (born 1939) - A fast bowler. He became the first touring player to be no-balled for throwing in England in 1960. He was no-balled 11 times. He played for Natal and Rhodesia. In his first class career he made, 892 runs and took 108 wickets.

Test Record - 2 Tests, 25 runs (Av. 6.25) and 8 wickets (Av. 24.00).

GRIFFITH CHARLES CHRISTOPHER

West Indies (born 1938) - He was a right-arm spinner. He once filled a gap for his new club side as a fast bowler and, after taking seven wickets for one run with his new mode of attack, seldom looked back. He played for Barbados. In his first class career he made, 1,502 runs and took 332 wickets.

Test Record - 28 Tests, 530 runs (Av. 16.56), 94 wickets (Av 28.54) and 16 catches.

GRIFFITH HERMAN CLARENCE

West Indies (1893-1980) - He was a fast bowler who also bowled brisk medium-fast out-swingers and off-break, cleverly changing pace and maintaining a good length. He played for Barbados. In his first class career he made, 1,214 runs and took 259 wickets.

Test Record - 13 Tests, 91 runs (Av. 5.05), 44 wickets (Av. 28.25) and 4 catches.

GRIFFITH STEWART CATHIE

England (born 1914) - He was one of the best wicket-keepers and a right-handed opening batsman. Appointed captain and secretary of Sussex. He toured the West Indies with MCC, in 1948-49 as player and assistant-manager. He played for Cambridge University. In his first class career he made, 4,846 runs including 3 centuries, and 413 dismissals.

Test Record - 3 Tests, 157 runs (Av. 31.40) including 1 century and 5 dismissals (5ct).

GRIMMETT CLARENCE VICTOR

Australia (1891-1980) - He was a leg-break bowler, exceptionally accurate with googly but a wicket dipping top-spinner. He played for Victoria, South Australia and Wellington. In his first class career he made, 4,720 runs, took 424 wickets and 139 catches.

Test Record - 37 Tests, 557 runs (Av. 13.92) and 216 wickets (Av. 24.21) and 17 catches.

GROUND

The playing field.

GROUND FIELDING

Ground fielding is the most important department of cricket, and every player ought to make a close study of this branch of the game. Whether in the deep or close in the fielder must be ready to make the fastest possible move to any ball that comes his way. For those fielding deep at cover, mid-off and mid-on, the main task is to stop ground shots and save runs and if they are already moving as the ball is bowled, they will be all the better equipped to do so. One can easily tell the trained fielder by noting whether he is walking in as the bowler runs. Close fielders, of course, crouch motionless, ready for a ball coming head-high or at their toes. They should also be on their toes, too, with weight evenly divided so that they can move either way.

GROUNDSMAN

A person who maintains the ground and prepares wickets for matches.

GROUT ARTHUR THEODORE WALLACE

Australia (1927-1968) - He was a very good wicket-keeper. He was also a good enough right-handed batsman to open for his State. He played for Queensland. In his first class career he made, 5,168 runs including 4 centuries and 587 dismissals.

Test Record - 51 Tests, 890 runs (Av. 15.08), and 187 dismissals (163ct, 24st).

GUARD

The position adopted by the batsman in which the bat is held upright in front of the wicket. Batsman takes guard after arriving at the crease so that when he takes up stance and places his bat in the position indicated by the umpire.

GUARD GHULAM MUSTAFA

India (1925-1978)- A left-handed batsman and left-arm medium fast bowler. Test debut on November 28, 1958 against West Indies at the age of 32 years and 346 days. Score on Test debut was 4 in the first Test at Bombay. Last Test of the career played against Australia in January 1960. Score on last appearance in Test was 7 in the third Test at Bombay. Age at the time of retirement from Test cricket was 34 years and 25 days. He played for Bombay and Gujarat. In his first class career he made, 238 runs and took 124 wickets.

Test Record - 2 Tests, 11 runs (Av. 5.50), 3 wickets (Av. 60.66) and 2 catches.

GUHA SUBROTO

India (born 1946) - A right-handed batsman and right-arm medium- fast bowler. Test debut on June 8, 1967 against England at the age of 21 years and 127 days. Scores on Test debut were 4 and 1 in the first Test at Leeds. Last Test of the career played against Australia in December 1969. Scores on last appearance in Test were 4 and 1 not out in the fourth Test at Calcutta. Age at the time of retirement from Test cricket was 23 years and 317 days. He played for Bengal. In his first class career he made, 1,067 runs and took 299 wickets.

Test Record - 4 Tests, 17 runs (Av. 3.40), 3 wickets (Av. 103.00) and 2 catches.

GUILLENSIMPSON CHAIRMONTE

West Indies (born 1924) - A very competent wicket-keeper and a useful right-handed batsman. He played for Trinidad and Canterbury. In his first class career he made, 2,672 runs including 3 centuries, and 134 dismissals.

Test Record - (West Indies - 5) - 104 runs (Av. 26.00) and 11 dismissals (9ct, 2st). (New Zealand - 3) - 98 runs (Av. 16.33) and 5 dismissals (4ct, 1st).

GUL MAHOMED

India (born 1921)- A left-handed batsman and left-arm bowler. Also played for Pakistan in one Test in 1956-57. Test debut on June 22,1946 against England at the age of 24 years and 247 days. Scores on Test debut were 1 and 9 in the first Test at Lord's. Last Test of the career played against Pakistan in October 1952. Scores on last appearance in Test were 0 and 2 in the second Test at Lucknow. Age at the time of retirement

from Test cricket was 31 years and 11 days. He played for Baroda, Hyderabad and Punjab. In his first class career he made, 5,600 runs including 12 centuries and took 107 wickets.
Test Record - (India) - 8 Tests, 166 runs (Av. 11.06), 2 wickets and 3 catches. (Pakistan) - 1 Test, 39 runs (Av. 39.00).

GULLY
The area of the field on the off side somewhat between point and third man and slightly to the rear of the striker's wicket.

GUNN GEORGE
England (1879-1958) - He was a right-handed opening batsman and unorthodox such as cutting a ball square from the leg-stump or walking out to the fastest bowling. He played for Nottinghamshire. In his first class career he made, 35,208 runs including 62 centuries, took 66 wickets and 472 catches.
Test Record - 15 Tests, 1,120 runs (Av. 40.00) including 2 centuries and 15 catches.

GUNN JOHN RICHMOND
England (1876-1963) - A hard-working all-rounder, John Gunn was a left-handed batsman and a slow medium pace bowler. He played for Nottinghamshire. In his first class career he made, 24,557 runs including 40 centuries, took 1,243 wickets and 239 catches.
Test Record - 6 Tests, 85 runs (Av. 10.62), 18 wickets (Av. 21.50) and 3 catches.

GUNN WILLIAM
England (1858-1921) - A right-handed batsman and a useful slow, round arm bowler. He played for Nottinghamshire. In his first class career he made, 25,840 runs including 49 centuries, took 76 wickets and 325 catches.
Test Record - 11 Tests, 392 runs (Av. 21.77) including 1 century.

GUPTE BALKRISHNA PANDHARINATH
India (born 1934) - A right-handed batsman and right-arm leg-break bowler. Younger brother of S.P.Gupte. Test debut on January 13,1961 against Pakistan at the age of 26 years and 134 days. Score on Test debut were 17 not out in the fourth Test at Madras. Last Test of the career played against New Zealand in March 1965. Score on last appearance in Test was 3 not out in the second Test at Calcutta. Age at the time of retirement from Test cricket was 30 years and 189 days. He played for Bombay. In his first class career he made, 587 runs and took 414 wickets.
Test Record - 3 Tests, 28 runs (Av. 28.00) and 3 wickets.

GUPTE SUBHAS PANDHARINATH
India (born 1929)- A right-handed batsman and right-arm leg-break and googly bowler. Elder brother of B.P.Gupte. Test debut on December 30,1951 against England at the age of 22 years and 19 days. Score on Test debut was 0 in the third Test at Calcutta. Last Test of the career played against England in December 1961. Score on last appearance in Test was 0 in the third Test at New Delhi. Age at the time of retirement from Test cricket was 32 years and 7 days. Shares with Jasu M.Patel and Kapil Dev the record of best bowling performance in an innings for India - 9 for 102 in the second Test against West Indies at Kanpur in 1958-59. He played for Bombay. In his first class career he made, 761 runs and 530 wickets.
Test Record - 36 Tests, 183 runs (Av. 6.31), 149 wickets (Av. 29.55) and 14 catches.

GURUSINHA ASANKA PRADEEP
Sri Lanka (born 1966) - A tall but compact left-handed batsman and a competent wicket-keeper. He plays for Sinhalese. In his first class career he made, 878 runs including 6 centuries.
Test Record - 7 Tests, 351 runs (Av. 35.10) including 1 century and 3 catch.

GUY JOHN WILLIAM
New Zealand (born 1934) - A flat-footed left-handed batsman of very sound defence and concentration. He played for Central Districts. In his first class career he made, 3,923 runs including 3 centuries.
Test Record - 12 Tests, 440 runs (Av. 20.95) including 1 century and 2 catches.

H

HACKER
A hard-hitting batsman batting in the lower order.

HADLEE DAYLE ROBERT
New Zealand (born 1948) - He was a right-arm fast-medium pace bowler, he became a fine swing bowler and a very useful fielder. He played for Canterbury. In his first class career he made, 1,810 runs and took 327 wickets.
Test Record - 26 Tests, 530 runs (Av. 14.32), 71 wickets (Av. 33.64) and 8 catches.

HADLEE SIR RICHARD JOHN
New Zealand (born 1951) - A fast-bowler, all-rounder famous for his superb control of pace, swing and cut. He is one of the great bowlers of any era or nationality and he is also a capable fielder and a dynamic, hard-hitting, left-handed batsman. though like most fast bowlers uncomfortable when tasting his own medicine. He plays for Canterbury. In his first class career he made, 9,989 runs including 12 centuries, took 1,341 wickets and 171 catches.
Test Record - 79 Tests, 2,884 runs (Av. 26.70) including 2 centuries, 396 wickets (Av. 22.22) and 37 catches.

HADLEE WALTER ARNOLD
New Zealand (born 1915) - He was a tall and right-handed batsman who frequently opened the batting. He played for Canterbury and Otago. In his first class career he made, 7,421 runs including 1 century.
Test Record - 11 Tests, 543 runs (Av. 30.16) including 1 century and 6 catches.

HAIG NIGEL ESME
England (1887-1966) - He was a right-arm medium pace bowler and also a dangerous forcing batsman with strong wrists, whose upper-cut shocked the purists, and a fielder of feline prowess. He played for Middlesex. In his first class career he made, 15,224 runs including 12 centuries, took 1,117 wickets and 221 catches.
Test Record - 5 Tests, 126 runs (Av. 14.00), 13 wickets (Av. 34.46) and 4 catches.

RICHARD HADLEE

HAIGH SCHOFIELD

England (1871-1921) - A right-arm, medium-fast bowler whose off-cutters on sticky wickets would make him practically unplayable. He played for Yorkshire. In his frist class career he made, 11,715 runs including 4 centuries, took 2,012 wickets and 274 catches.

Test Record - 11 Tests, 113 runs (Av. 7.53), 24 wickets (Av. 25.91) and 8 catches.

HALF- CENTURY

A Score between 50 and 99 runs made in a single innings.

HALF-COCK

This is an improvised stroke in which the bat is held quite straight and the ball is allowed to come on to it.

HALF-HIT

Mis -timed shot that sends the ball only a short distance.

HALF-PITCHER

Old name for bouncer, especially used in Australia.

HALF-VOLLEY

A delivery that bounces so close to the batsman that he can hit it just as it leaves the ground without having to stride forward.

HALL ALFRED EWART

South Africa (1896-1964) - He was a left-arm fast-medium bowler. He played for Transvaal and Lancashire. In his first class career he made, 134 runs and took 234 wickets.

Test Record - 7 Tests, 11 runs (Av. 1.83), 40 wickets (Av. 22.15) and 4 catches.

HALL WESLEY WINFIELD

West Indies (born 1937) - A right-arm fast bowler, a muscular six-feet-two-inch man with a classical action and good temper. He played for Barbados, Trinidad and Queensland. In his first class career he made, 2,673 runs including 1 century and took 546 wickets.

Test Record - 48 Tests, 818 runs (Av. 15.73), 192 wickets (Av. 26.38) and 11 catches.

HALLIWELL ERNEST AUSTIN

South Africa (1864-1919) - He was ranked as one of the best wicket-keepers and a useful right-handed batsman. He played for Transvaal and Middlesex. In his first class career he made, 1,702 runs and 112 dismissals.

Test Record - 8 Tests, 188 runs (Av. 12.53) and 11 dismissals (9ct, 2st).

HALLOWS CHARLES

England (1895-1972) - He was tall and silm and stylish left-handed, a useful opening batsman and a fast fielder. He played for Lancashire. In his first class career he made, 20,926 runs including 55 centuries, and took 19 wickets.

Test Record - 2 Tests, 42 runs (Av. 42.00).

HALSE CLIVE GRAY

South Africa (born 1935) - A right-arm fast bowler. He played for Natal. In his first class career he made, 321 runs and took 83 wickets.

Test Record - 3 Tests, 30 runs, 6 wickets (Av. 43.33) and 1 catch.

HAMBLEDON

Hampshire village in England was the headquarters of the leading cricketers prior to the rise of the MCC. A great team Hambledon club was raised in this village.

HAMENCE RONALD ARTHUR

Australia (born 1915) - He was a good outfield and a long-serving, dependable state player, often as opening batsman. He played for South Australia. In his first class career he made, 5,285 runs including 11 centuries.

Test Record - 3 Tests, 81 runs (Av. 27.00) and 1 catch.

HAMMOND JEFFREY ROY

Australia (born 1950) - A right-arm, fast-medium bowler with a good action. He played for South Australia. In his first class career he made, 922 runs and took 184 wickets.

Test Record - 5 Tests, 28 runs (Av. 9.33), 15 wickets (Av. 32.53) and 2 catches.

HAMMOND WALTER REGINALD

England (1903-1965) - He was a brilliant right-handed batsman and also an easy and powerful off stroke-player. He played for Gloucestershire. In his first class career he made, 50,551 runs including 167 centuries, took 732 wickets, 819 catches and 3 stumpings.

Test Record - 85 Tests, 7,249 runs (Av. 58.45) including 22 centuries, 85 wickets (Av. 37.80) and 110 catches.

HAMPSHIRE

Present club formed: 1863, re-organised 1879.
Badge: Tudor rose and crown.
Colours: Blue,gold and white.
First First - Class Match : MCC v Hampshire (Lord's) July 29,30(1861).
Ground: County Cricket Ground, Northlands Road, Southampton SO9 2TY.
Honours:County Champions - 1861,1973
John Player League champions - 1975,1978.
Highest Team Total: 672 for 7 dec v Somerset (Taunton) 1899
Lowest Team Total: 15 v Warwicks. (Edgbaston) 1922
Highest Wicket Partnership : 411 R.M.Poore & E.G.Wynyard in 1899

HAMPSHIRE JOHN HARRY

England (born 1941) - He was a right-handed batsman and a fine fielder and could hit the ball blisteringly hard, notably off the front foot. He played for Yorkshire, Derbyshire and Tasmania. In his first class career he made, 28,059 runs including 43 centuries, took 30 wickets and 446 catches.

Test Record - 8 Tests, 403 runs (Av. 26.86) including 1 century and 9 catches.

HANDLED THE BALL

When a batsman touches the ball with his hand while it is in play, he can be given out. His dismissal is termed as 'Handled Ball'. The wicket is not credited to the bowler. Before 1899 a batsman was given out if he handled a ball which had become lodged in his clothing.

HANDS PHILIP ALBERT MYBURGH

South Africa (1890-1951) - A right-handed batsman noted for his fearless hitting. He was awarded the D.S.O. and M.C. in the First World War. He played for Western Province. In his first class career he made, 2,034 runs including 3 centuries.

Test Record - 7 Tests, 300 runs (Av. 25.00) and 3 catches.

HANG

After pitching,the ball lose pace. It comes to the bat more slowly than expected.

HANIF MOHAMMAD

Pakistan (born 1934) - He was a right-handed opening batsman and also a useful right-arm bowler. His son, Shoaib, is also a Test Player. He played for Bahawalpur and Pakistan International Airlines (PIA). In his first class career he made, 17,059 runs including 55 centuries took 53 wickets, 177 catches and 12 stumpings.

Test Record - 55 Tests, 3,915 runs (Av. 43.98) including 12 centuries, and 40 catches.

HANUMANT SINGH

India (born 1939) - A right-handed batsman with a large repertoire of strokes, a useful leg-break bowler, and a brilliant fielder in the deep. Test debut on February 8, 1964 against England at the age of 24 years and 308 days. Scores on Test debut were 103 and 23 in the fourth Test at New Delhi. Became the fifth Indian cricketer to score a century on Test debut on February 9,1964 at the age of 24 years and 308 days, and the third

batsman to perform the feat against England. Last Test of the career played against New Zealand in September 1969. Scores on last appearance in Test were 1 and 13 in first Test at Bombay. Age at the time of retirement from Test cricket was 30 years and 175 days. His partnership of 193 runs (unfinished) with D.N. Sardesai for the 6th wicket in the third Test against New Zealand at Bombay in 1964-65 is the highest for the 6th wicket for India against New Zealand. Even before donning the Indian cap Hanumant Singh fielded for England (as substitute) against India in second Test at Bombay in 1964. He played for Madhya Pradesh and Rajasthan. In his first class career he made, 12,338 runs including 29 centuries and took 56 wickets.
Test Record - 14 Tests, 686 runs (Av. 31.18) including 1 century and 11 catches.

HARDIKAR MANOHAR SHANKAR

India (born 1936) - A right-handed batsman and right-arm off-break bowler. Test debut on November 28,1958 against West Indies at the age of 22 years and 290 days. Played in two Tests only scoring 0 and 32 not out in the first Test at Bombay and 13 and 11 in the second Test at Kanpur before retiring from Test cricket. Took his only wicket that of R.B.Kanhai of West Indies, with his third delivery in the second Test at Bombay in 1958-59. He also had the mortification of being dismissed by the very first ball he faced in Test cricket on debut. He played for Bombay. In his first class career he made, 3,602 runs including 8 centuries and took 74 wickets.
Test Record - 2 Tests, 56 runs (Av. 18.66), and 3 catches.

HARDSTAFF JOSEPH JUNIOR

England (born 1911) - He was a useful right-handed attacking batsman. He played for Nottinghamshire and Auckland. In his first class career he made, 31,851 runs including 83 centuries and took 36 wickets.
Test Record - 23 Tests, 1,636 runs (Av. 46.74) including 4 centuries, and 9 catches.

HARDSTAFF JOSEPH SENIOR

England (1882-1947) - A brilliant fielder in the deep and a right-handed batsman. He was short but strongly built. He played for Nottinghamshire. In his first class career he made, 17,157 runs including 26 centuries, took 58 wickets, 183 catches and 2 stumpings.
Test Record - 5 Tests, 311 runs (Av. 31.10) and 1 catch.

HARFORD NOEL SHERWIN

New Zealand (1930-1981) - A right-handed batsman and a useful right-arm medium-pace swing bowler. He played for Central Districts and Auckland. In his first class career he made, 3,149 runs including 3 centuries and took 18 wickets.
Test Record - 8 Tests, 229 runs (Av. 15.29).

HARFORD ROY IVAN

New Zealand (born 1936) - A good wicket-keeper and a left-handed batsman. He played for Auckland. In his first class career he made, 143 runs and took 68 wickets.
Test Record - 3 Tests, 7 runs (Av. 2.33) and 11 dismissals (11ct).

HAROON RASHID

HAROON RASHID

Pakistan (born 1953) - He was a powerful right-handed batsman. He played for Karachi, Sind, National Bank, Pakistan International Airways and United Bank. In his first class career he made, 7,500 runs including 15 centuries, took 8 wickets and 126 catches.

Test Record - 23 Tests, 1,217 runs (Av. 34.77) including 3 centuries and 16 catches.

ROGER HARPER

HARPER ROGER ANDREW

West Indies (born 1963) - A right-arm off-spin bowler and a very good fielder . He plays for Guyana and Northamptonshire. In his first class career he made, 3,451 runs including 3 centuries, took 379 wickets and 171 catches.

Test Record - 24 Tests, 532 runs (Av. 19.00), 45 wickets (Av. 27.82) and 35 catches.

HARRIER

A ball that rises very fast off the pitch.

HARRIS 4TH LORD

England (1851-1932) - He was a right-handed batsman and a fast bowler. He played for Oxford University and Kent. In his first class career he made, 9,898 runs including 11 centuries, and took 75 wickets.

Test Record - 4 Tests,145 runs (Av. 29.00) and 2 catches.

HARRIS PARKE GERALD ZINZAN

New Zealand (born 1927) - A right handed batsman and a useful change-bowler. He played for Canterbury. In his first class career he made, 3,122 runs including 5 centuries and took 21 wickets.

Test Record - 9 Tests, 378 runs (Av. 22.23) including 1 century and 6 catches.

HARRIS ROGER MEREDITH

New Zealand (born 1933) - A right-handed opening bastman and a useful medium-pace change bowler. He played for Auckland. In his first class career he made, 3,683 runs including 3 centuries and took 14 wickets.

Test Record - 2 Tests, 31 runs (Av. 10.33).

HARRIS TERENCE ANTHONY

South Africa (born 1916) - A right-handed fast-scoring batsman. He played for Griqualand West and Transvaal. In his first class career he made, 3,208 runs including 6 centuries.

Test Record - 3 Tests, 100 runs (Av. 25.00) and 1 catch.

HARROW BAT

A bat one size down from the full size, used by younger players.

HARROW DRIVE

The batsman deflects the ball off the inside edge of the bat, either through the slips or down towards long leg, when attempting to play a normal off drive, he fails to get properly in line of the ball.

HARTIGAN GERALD PATRICK DESMOND

South Africa (1884-1955) - A right-handed bats-

man and fast-medium bowler. He played for Border. In his first class career he made, 1,544 runs including 3 centuries and took 92 wickets.
Test Record - 5 Tests, 114 runs (Av. 11.40).

HARTIGAN ROGER JOSEPH
Australia (1879-1958) - A right-handed batsman and a brilliant silp fielder. He played for New South Wales and Queensland. In his first class career he made, 1,901 runs including 2 centuries.
Test Record - 2 Tests, 170 runs (Av. 42.50) including 1 century.

HARTLEY COL. JOHN CABORN
England (1874-1963) - A right-arm slow-medium bowler. He played for Oxford University. In his first class career he made, 1,508 runs and took 69 wickets.
Test Record - 2 Tests, 15 runs (Av. 3.75) and 2 catches.

HARVEY ROBERT LYON
South Africa (born 1911) - A right-handed batsman. He played for Natal. In his first class career he made, 1,298 runs including 2 centuries, and took 37 wickets.
Test Record - 2 Tests, 51 runs (Av. 12.75).

NEIL HARVEY

HARVEY ROBERT NEIL
Australia (born 1928) - He was a left-handed batsman, he was continually looking for runs. His footwork was brilliant, but if he was vulnerable anywhere, it was outside the off-stump. He played for Victoria and New South Wales. In his first class career he made, 21,699 runs including 67 centuries and took 30 wickets.
Test Record - 79 Tests, 6,149 runs (Av. 48.42) including 21 centuries, 3 wickets (40.00) and 64 catches.

HASEEB AHSAN
Pakistan (born 1939) - A right-arm off-break bowler. He played for Peshawar and Karachi. In his first class career he made, 244 runs and took 142 wickets.
Test Record - 12 Tests, 61 runs (Av. 6.77), 27 wickets (Av. 49.25) and 1 catch.

HASSETT ARTHUR LINDSAY
Australia (born 1913) - He was a right-handed attacking batsman, and he could hook and cut the short ball and drove the half-volleys but he would also force the good-length ball 'on the up. He played for Victoria. In his first class career he made, 16,890 runs including 59 centuries, took 18 wickets.
Test Record - 43 Tests, 3,073 runs (Av. 46.56) including 10 centuries and 30 catches.

HASTINGS BRIAN FREDERICK
New Zealand (born 1940) - A right-handed batsman, a clip medium-fast bowler, bowling off his legs. He played for Wellington, Central Districts and Canterbury. In his first class career he made, 7,686 runs including 15 centuries, and 112 catches.
Test Record - 31 Tests, 1,510 runs (Av. 30.20) including 4 centuries and 23 catches.

HAT-TRICKS
The dismissal of three wickets with three consecutive balls is known as a hat-trick.

HATHORN CHRISTOPHER MAITLAND
South Africa (1878-1920) - A very sound right-

handed batsman. He played for Transvaal. In his first class career he made, 3,541 runs including 9 centuries.
Test Record - 12 Tests, 325 runs (Av. 17.10) including 1 century, and 5 catches.

HAWKE 7TH LORD
England (1860-1938) - He was a very competent right-handed batsman. He played for Yorkshire. In his first class career he made, 16,506 runs including 13 centuries.
Test Record - 5 Tests, 55 runs (Av. 7.85) and 3 catches.

HAWKE NEIL JAMES NAPIER
Australia (born 1939) - He was a right-arm fast-medium bowler and a useful late-order batsman. He played for Western Australia, South Australia and Tasmania. In his first class career he made, 3,383 runs and took 458 wickets.
Test Record - 27 Tests, 365 runs (Av. 16.59), 91 wickets (Av. 29.41) and 9 catches.

HAYES ERNEST GEORGE
England (1876-1953) - He was a right-handed bastman with a strong drive and fierce pull, a useful leg-break bowler and a brilliant slip. He played tor Surrey and Leicestershire. In his first class career he made, 27,318 runs including 48 centuries, took 597 wickets and 533 catches.
Test Record - 5 Tests, 86 runs (Av. 10.75) and 2 catches.

HAYES FRANK CHARLES
England (born 1946) - He was a right-handed batsman and an athletic cover fielder. He played for Lancashire. In his first class career he made, 13,018 runs including 23 centuries and 176 catches.
Test Record - 9 Tests, 244 runs (Av. 15.25) including 1 century and 7 catches.

HAYES JOHN ARTHUR
New Zealand (born 1927) - A right-arm fast bowler with a glorious action. He played for Auckland and Canterbury. In his first class career he made, 611 runs and took 292 wickets.
Test Record - 15 Tests, 73 runs (Av. 4.86), 30 wickets (Av. 40.56) and 3 catches.

FRANK HAYES

HAYNES DESMOND LEO
West Indies (born 1956) - A right-handed opening batsman. A fine driver, who also hits hard off the back foot, cutting and hooking majestically. He is also a fine fielder anywhere. He was vice-captain of his team, a vibrant character with a broad smile. He plays for Barbados. In his first class career he made, 13,879 runs including 23 centuries, and took 31 wickets.
Test Record - 85 Tests, 5,340 runs (Av. 41.39) including 12 centuries, 1 wicket (Av. 8.00) and 55 catches.

HAYWARD THOMAS WALTER
England (1871-1939) - He was a right-handed batsman with a history in the game. He was medium-pace off-break bowler. He played for Cambridgeshire and Surrey. In his first class career he made, 43,551 runs including 104 centuries, took 481 wickets.
Test Record - 35 Tests, 1,999 runs (Av. 34.46) including 3 centuries and 14 wickets (Av. 36.71) and 19 catches.

HAZARE VIJAY SAMUEL

India (born 1915) - He was a right-handed batsman and right-arm medium - fast bowler. Test debut on June 22, 1946 against England at the age of 31 years and 101 days. Scores on Test debut were 31 and 34 in the first Test at Lord's. Last Test of the career played against West Indies in March-April 1953. Scores on last appearance in Test were 16 and 12 in the fifth Test at Kingston. Age at the time of retirement from Test cricket was 38 years and 23 days. Became the first Indian to score triple century when he made 316 not out for Maharashtra against Baroda in the Ranji Trophy championship in 1939-40. Also the first Indian to score two separate hundreds in the same Test match when he scored 116 and 145 against Australia in the fourth Test at Adelaide in 1947-48 . First ever Test century 116 scored on January 27,1948 at the age of 32 years and 316 days in the fourth Test against Australia at Adelaide. Led India for the first time against England in the first Test at New Delhi on Nov. 2, 1951 at the age of 36 years and 231 days scoring 164 not out. Captained Indian team in 14 Tests, out of which won one, lost five and eight were drawn. He played for Maharashtra and Baroda. In his first class career he made, 18,635 runs including 60 centuries, and took 592 wickets.

Test Record - 30 Tests, 2,192 runs (Av. 47.65) including 7 centuries, 20 wickets (Av. 61.00) and 11 catches.

HAZLITT GERVYS RIGNOLD

Australia (1888-1915) - A very useful batsman and also a right-arm off-break at swerving medium-pace bowler. He played for Victoria and New South Wales. In his first class career he made, 876 runs and took 188 wickets.

Test Record - 9 Tests, 89 runs (Av. 11.12), 23 wickets (Av. 27.08) and 4 catches.

HEADINGLEY

The Headingley Ground at Leeds was opened in 1892. The first Test match was played there in 1899. The largest attendance of 1,58,000 people for a five day match in England was recorded in this ground in 1948

HEADLEY GEORGE ALPHONSO

West Indies (1909-1983) - A compact right-handed batsman and a back foot player. He occasionally bowled enthusiastic and useful leg-break and fielded well anywhere. He played for Jamaica. In his first class career he made, 9,921 runs including 33 centuries and took 51 wickets.

Test Record - 22 Tests, 2,190 runs (Av. 60.83) including 10 centuries and 14 catches.

HEADLEY RONALD GEORGE ALPHONSO

West Indies (born 1939) - He was a left-handed opening batsman with a handsome cover-drive, and a brilliant fielder. He played for Jamaica, Worcestershire and Derbyshire. In his first class career he made, 21,695 runs including 32 centuries, took 12 wickets and 357 catches.

Test Record - 2 Tests, 62 runs (Av. 15.20) and 2 catches.

HEADQUARTERS

Lord's cricket ground is considered . the headquarters of the game.

HEARNE FRANK

England (1858-1949) - He was a right-handed batsman and a useful fast right-arm bowler. He played for Kent and Western Province. In his first class career he made, 4,553 runs including 4 centuries, and took 59 wickets.

Test Record -(England - 2) - 47 runs (Av. 23.50) and 1 catch. (South Africa - 4) - 121 runs (Av. 15.12), 2 wickets (Av. 20.00) and 2 catches.

HEARNE GEORGE ALFRED LAWRENCE

South Africa (1888-1978) - A fast-scoring right-handed opening batsman. He played for Western Province. In his first class career he made, 1,981 runs including 2 centuries and 14 took wickets.

Test Record - 3 Tests, 59 runs (Av. 11.80) and 3 catches.

HEARNE JOHN THOMAS

England (1867-1944) - He was a right-arm medium pace bowler with considerable nip, and his action was perfect with left arm thrust out and left

shoulder pointing towards the batsman. He played for Middlesex. In his first class career he made, 7,205 runs, took 3,061 wickets and 421 catches.
Test Record - 12 Tests, 126 runs (Av. 9.00), 49 wickets (Av. 22.08) and 4 catches.

HEARNE JOHN WILLIAM
England (1891-1965) - A right-handed batsman and a useful leg-break and googly bowler. He played for Middlesex. In his first class career he made, 37,252 runs including 96 centuries, took 1,839 wickets and 349 catches.
Test Record - 24 Tests, 806 runs (Av. 26.00) including 1 century, 30 wickets (Av. 48.73) and 13 catches.

HEINE PETER SAMUEL
South Africa (born 1928) - A right-arm fast bowler. He played for Orange Free State and Transvaal. In his first class career he made, 1,255 runs and took 277 wickets.
Test Record - 14 Tests, 209 runs (Av. 9.95), 58 wickets (Av. 25.08) and 8 catches.

HELMETS
A strong,protective headgear worn by batsman as a protection against fast bowling. Sometimes also worn by fielders in close catching positions. Helmets are usually made of plastic, have webbing of foam padding inside to serve as a cushion, and generally protect the head and ears of the players.

HEMMINGS EDWARD ERNEST
England (born 1949) - A useful right-handed batsman and also a medium-pace bowler but developed his main skill as an off-spinner. He played for Warwickshire and Nottinghamshire. In his first class career he made, 7,694 runs (19.82) including 1 century, took 1,142 wickets and 179 catches.
Test Record - 5 Tests, 198 runs (Av. 22.00), 12 wickets (Av. 46.50) and 4 catches.

HENDREN ELIAS HENRY
England (1889-1962) - He was a right-handed batsman. He played for Middlesex. In his first class career he made, 57,611 runs including 170 centuries, took 47 wickets and 755 catches.
Test Record - 51 Tests, 3,525 runs (Av. 47.63) including 7 centuries and 33 catches.

HENDRICK MICHAEL
England (born 1948) - He was one of the best fast-medium bowlers and a tail-end batsman. He played for Derbyshire and Nottinghamshire. In his first class career he made, 1,601 runs, took 770 wickets and 176 catches.
Test Record - 30 Tests, 128 runs (Av. 6.40), 87 wickets (Av. 25.83) and 25 catches.

HENDRIKS JOHN LESLIE
West Indies (born 1933) - A tall wicket-keeper, slow bowler and a useful right-handed batsman. He played for Jamaica. In his first class career he made, 1,568 runs and 190 dismissals.
Test Record - 20 Tests, 447 runs (Av. 18.62) and 47 dismissals (42ct, 5st).

HENDRY HUNTER SCOTT THOMAS LAURIE
Australia (born 1895) - He was a right-handed batsman who cut and drove and a fast-medium change-bowler and a fine slip fielder. He played for New South Wales and Victoria. In his first class career he made, 6,799 runs including 14 centuries, took 229 wickets and 152 catches.
Test Record - 11 Tests, 335 runs (Av. 20.93) including 1 century, 16 wickets (Av. 40.00) and 10 catches.

HERTFORDSHIRE
The county club was formed in 1876. It captured the title in 1936,1975 and 1983

HESELTINE LT-COL.CHRISTOPHER
England (1869-1944) - A right-handed fast bowler. He played for Cambridge University and Hampshire. In his first class career he made, 1,372 runs and took 165 wickets.
Test Record - 2 Tests, 18 runs (Av. 9.00), 5 wickets (Av. 16.80) and 3 catches.

HIGGS JAMES DONALD

Australia (born 1950) - He was a good leg-spin bowler. He gave the ball a strong flip and had a useful googly. He played for Victoria. In his first class career he made, 384 runs and took 399 wickets.

Test Record - 22 Tests, 111 runs (Av. 5.55), 66 wickets (Av. 31.16) and 3 catches.

HIGGS KENNETH

England (born 1937) - He was a right-arm medium-fast bowler and his short, well-groved approach was the economical launching pad for a strong, thrusting body-action. He played for Lancashire, Leicestershire and Staffordshire. In his first class career he made, 3,648 runs, took 1,536 wickets and 312 catches.

Test Record - 15 Tests, 185 runs (Av. 11.56), 71 wickets (Av. 20.74) and 4 catches.

HILDITCH ANDREW MARK JEFFERSON

Australia (born 1956) - He was a right-handed opening batsman with a thoroughly sound front-foot technique and limitless concentration. He played for New South Wales and South Australia. In his first class career he made, 5,639 runs including 8 centuries.

Test Record - 18 Tests, 1,073 runs (Av. 31.55) including 2 centuries and 13 catches.

HILL ALLEN

England (1854-1910) - He was a right-handed batsman and also a useful right-arm bowler. He played for Yorkshire. In his first class career he made, 2,478 runs and took 745 wickets.

Test Record - 2 Tests, 101 runs (Av. 50.50), 7 wickets (Av. 18.57) and 1 catch.

HILL ARTHUR JAMES LEDGER

England (1871-1950) - He was a right-handed batsman. He played for Cambridge University and Hampshire. In his first class career he made, 10,141 runs including 18 centuries and took 278 wickets.

Test Record - 3 Tests, 251 runs (Av. 62.75) including 1 century, 4 wickets (Av. 2.00) and 1 catch.

HILL CLEMENT

Australia (1877-1945) - He was a left-handed batsman and quick into position to hook or pull and also a fine fielder. He played for South Australia. In his first class career he made, 17,213 runs including 45 centuries.

Test Record - 49 Tests, 3,412 runs (Av. 39.21) including 7 centuries and 33 catches.

HILL JOHN CHARLES

Australia (1923-1974) - An inelegant right-arm leg-break bowler. He played for Victoria. In his first class career he made, 867 runs and took 218 wickets.

Test Record - 3 Tests, 21 runs (Av. 7.00), 8 wickets (Av. 34.12) and 2 catches.

HILTON MALCOLM JAMESON

England (born 1928) - A slow left-arm spinner and also a useful fielder. He played for Lancashire. In his first class career he made, 3,416 runs including 1 century, took 1,006 wickets and 204 catches.

Test Record - 4 Tests, 37 runs (Av. 7.40), 14 wickets (Av. 33.64) and 1 catch.

HINDLEKAR DATTARAM DHARMAJI

India (1909-1949)- A right-handed batsman and wicket-keeper. Test debut on June 27,1936 against England at the age of 27 years and 176 days. Scores on Test debut were 26 and 17 in the first Test at Lord's. Last Test of the career played against England in August 1946. Score on last appearance in Test was 3 in the third Test at the Oval. Age at the time of retirement from Test cricket was 37 years and 229 days. He played for Bombay. In his first class career he made 2,411 runs and 181 dismissals.

Test Record - 4 Tests, 71 runs (Av.14.20) and 3 catches.

HIRST GEORGE HERBERT

England (1871-1954) - He was a left-arm bowler and a useful right-handed batsman. He played for Yorkshire. In his first class career he made, 36,323 runs including 60 centuries, took 2,739 wickets and 550 catches.

Test Record - 24 Tests, 790 runs (Av. 22.57), 59 wickets (Av. 30.00) and 18 catches.

N. HIRWANI

HIRWANI NARENDRA

India (born 1968) - A right-arm leg-spinner. His sparkling record of bowling against West Indies put him in record books. He took 16 wickets in his first Test in Madras. He became man of the Series in Sharjah Cup.

Test Record - 7 Tests, 26 runs (Av. 5.20), 42 wickets (Av. 20.71) and 4 catches.

HIT

To strike and drive the ball with a view to scoring runs.

HIT A SIX

To hit the ball over the boundary on the fly for a score of 6 runs.

HIT BALL TWICE

The batsman can be given out if he hits the ball twice, unless he does so to prevent the ball hitting his wicket.

HIT WICKET

A wicket broken by the batsman while making a stroke with the result that he is out.

HITTER

An attacking batsman.

HOAD EDWARD LISLE GOLDSWORTHY

West Indies (1896-1986) - He was a right-handed batsman and leg-break change-bowler. He played for Barbados. In his first class career he made, 3,518 runs including 8 centuries and took 55 wickets.

Test Record - 4 Tests, 98 runs (Av. 12.25) and 1 catch.

HOBBS ROBIN NICHOLAS STUART

England (born 1942) - He was a good leg-spinner, a cover-fielder and a spirited hitter. He played for Essex, Glamorgan and Suffolk. In his first class career he made, 4,940 runs including 2 centuries, took 1,099 wickets and 294 catches.

Test Record - 7 Tests, 34 runs (Av. 6.80), 12 wickets (Av. 40.08) and 8 catches.

HOBBS SIR JOHN BERRY

England (1882-1963) - He was a right-handed batsman and an occasional bowler. He played for Cambridgeshire and Surrey. In his first class career he made, 61,237 runs including 197 centuries, took 113 wickets and 317 catches.

Test Record - 61 Tests, 5,410 runs (Av. 56.94) including 15 centuries and 17 catches.

HODGES JOHN HENRY

Australia (1856-1933) - A left-arm fast-medium bowler. He played for Victoria. In his first class career he made, 75 runs and took 12 wickets.

Test Record - 2 Tests, 10 runs (Av. 3.33) and 6 wickets (Av. 14.00).

HOGG RODNEY MALCOLM

Australia (born 1951) - He was a right-arm fast-medium bowler and straight in short, electric spells putting all his energy into most deliveries, except when bowling off a shorter run. He played for Victoria and South Australia. In his first class career he made, 1,170 runs and took 356 wickets.

Test Record - 38 Tests, 439 runs (Av. 9.75), 123 wickets (Av. 28.47) and 7 catches.

V. HOLDER

HOLDER VANBURN ALONZA

West Indies (born 1945) - A tall, fast-medium bowler with a good high action after a bandy-legged approach, moving his away-swinger dangerously late and seldom getting the luck he deserved. He played for Barbados, Worcestershire and Orange Free State. In his frist class career he made, 3,393 runs including 1 century, and took 948 wickets.

Test Record - 40 Tests, 682 runs (Av. 14.21), 109 wickets (Av. 33.28) and 16 catches.

HOLDING MICHAEL ANTHONY

West Indies (born 1954) - A right-arm fast bowler. He was being hailed as the fastest bowler in the world at one time. He plays for Jamaica, Lancashire, Derbyshire and Tasmania. In his first class career he made, 3,791 runs and took 797 wickets.

Test Record - 60 Tests, 910 runs (Av. 13.78), 249 wickets (Av. 23.68) and 22 catches.

MICHAEL HOLDING

HOLE GRAEME BLAKE

Australia (born 1931) - A tall right-handed middle-order batsman. He played for New South Wales

and South Austrlia. In his first class career he made, 5, 647 runs including 11 centuries and took 61 wickets.
Test Record - 18 Tests, 789 runs (Av. 25.45), 3 wickets (Av. 42.00) and 21 catches.

HOLE OUT
Dismissal by being caught usually into the deep field.

HOLFORD DAVID ANTHONY JEROME
West Indies (born 1940) - A tall, silm right-arm leg-break bowler and a fine close fielder. He played for Barbados. In his first class career he made, 3,821 runs including 3 centuries, and took 253 wickets.
Test Record - 24 Tests, 768 runs (Av. 22.58), including 1 century, 51 wickets (Av. 39.39) and 18 catches.

HOLLAND ROBERT GEORGE
Australia (born 1946) - A leg-spin bowler. He does not often use the googly his rolling leg-breaks. He played for New South Wales. In his first class career he made, 600 runs and took 291 wickets.
Test Record - 11 Tests, 35 runs (Av. 3.18), 34 wickets (Av. 39.76) and 5 catches..

HOLLIES WILLIAM ERIC
England (1912-1981) - A right-arm, leg-break bowler. He played for Warwickshire and Staffordshire. In his first class career he made, 1,673 runs and took 2,323 wickets.
Test Record - 13 Tests, 37 runs (Av. 5.28), 44 wickets (Av. 30.27) and 2 catches.

HOLMES ERROL REGINALD THOROLD
England (1905-1960) - A tall, right-handed batsman and a useful medium-fast bowler. He played for Oxford University and Surrey. In his first class career he made, 13,598 runs including 24 centuries, and took 283 wickets.
Test Record - 5 Tests, 114 runs (Av. 16.28), 2 wickets (Av. 38.00) and 4 catches.

HOLMES PERCY
England (1886-1971) - An attacking right-handed batsman and a good fielder. He played for Yorkshire. In his first class career he made, 30,574 runs including 67 centuries and 221 catches.
Test Record - 7 Tests, 357 runs (Av. 27.46) and 3 catches.

HOLT JOHN KENNETH JUNIOR
West Indies (born 1923) - A right-handed batsman with strokes all round the wickets. He played for Jamaica. In his first class career he made, 4,256 runs including 9 centuries.
Test Record - 17 Tests, 1,006 runs (Av. 36.75) including 2 centuries and 8 catches.

HOME
The area between the striker's wicket and the popping crease.

HOOK
A cross-batted stroke but differing from the cut in that it is designed to hit the ball to the legside. Also, it is probably the most belligerent shot and in consequence, one of the most risky. At its most effective, the one that will bring you most sixes, or caught on the boundary dismissals. The hook is

Hook

employed against the short-pitched ball coming at some speed - in other words the infamous bouncer - and rising to some height. with not much time to decide, the choice is to duck or go for the hook. And speedy footwork is of the essence. The right foot goes all the way back and to the off stump so that it is outside the line of flight, whereas head and shoulders are in line and facing the bowler. Lift the bat outwards in the direction of third man and then sweep across the chest.

HOOKES DAVID WILLIAM

Australia (born 1955) - A fair-haired, left-handed batsman. He played for South Australia. In his first class career he made, 7,941 runs including 19 centuries and took 31 wickets.

Test Record - 23 Tests, 1,306 runs (Av. 34.36) including 1 century and 12 catches.

HOPKINS ALBERT JOHN YOUNG

Australia (1876-1931) - A right-arm slow-medium bowler with a pronounced swerve and break from the off, and a brilliant fielder. He played for New South Wales. In his first class career he made, 5,563 runs including 8 centuries and took 271 wickets.

Test Record - 20 Tests, 509 runs (Av. 16.42), 26 wickets (Av. 26.76) and 11 catches.

HOPWOOD JOHN LEONARD

England (1903-1985) - He was a right-handed batsman and a left-arm medium-pace bowler. He played for Lancashire. In his first class career he made, 15,548 runs including 27 centuries, took 671 wickets and 198 catches.

Test Record - 2 Tests, 12 runs (Av. 6.00).

HORAN THOMAS PATRICK

Australia (1854-1916) - He was round-arm medium-pace change-bowler. He played for Victoria. In his first class career he made, 4,027 runs including 8 centuries and took 35 wickets.

Test Record - 15 Tests, 471 runs (Av. 18.84), including 1 century, 11 wickets (Av. 13.00) and 6 catches.

HORDERN DR HERBERT VIVIAN

Australia (1884-1938) - A googly bowler of exceptional merit and useful batsman. He played for New South Wales and Philadelphia. In his first class career he made, 721 runs and took 217 wickets.

Test Record - 7 Tests, 254 runs (Av. 23.09), 46 wickets (Av. 23.36) and 6 catches.

HORNBY ALBERT NEILSON

England (1847-1925) - He was a right-handed batsman with an attracting front-foot style and splendid punishing powers. He played for Lancashire. In his first class career he made, 15,763 runs including 15 centuries.

Test Record - 3 Tests, 21 runs (Av. 3.50).

HORNIBROOK PERCIVAL MITCHELL

Australia (1899-1976) - A tall, left-arm slow-medium bowler. He played for Queensland. In his first class career he made, 754 runs and took 279 wickets.

Test Record - 6 Tests, 60 runs (Av. 10.00), 17 wickets (Av. 39.05) and 7 catches

HORTON MARTIN JOHN

England (born 1934) - He was a right-handed opening batsman and also a useful off-break bowler. He played for Worcestershire and Northern Districts. In his first class career he made, 19,944 runs including 23 centuries and took 825 wickets.

Test Record - 2 Tests, 60 runs (Av. 30.00), 2 wickets (Av. 29.50) and 2 catches.

HOUGH KENNETH WILLIAM

New Zealand (born 1928) - A lively right-arm medium-pace bowler. He played for Auckland and Northern Districts. In his first class career he made, 624 runs and took 119 wickets.

Test Record - 2 Tests, 62 runs (Av. 62.00), 6 wickets (Av. 29.16) and 1 catch.

HOW'DAT

Members of the fielding side or spectators demanding that the umpire give a batsman out.

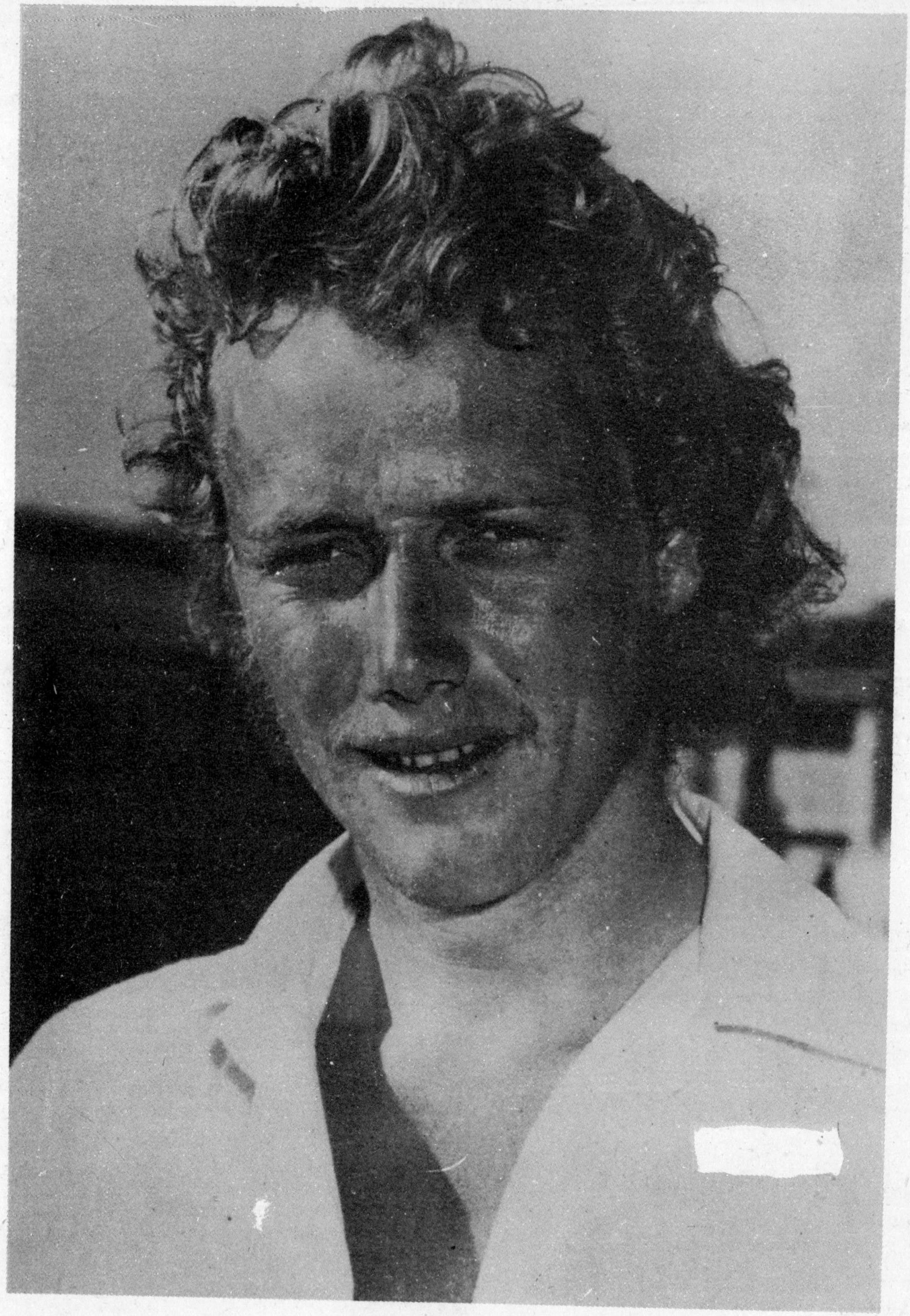

KIMBERLEY HUGHES

HOWARD NEGEL DAVID

England (1925-1979) - He was a right-handed opening batsman. He played for Lancashire. In his first class career he made, 6,152 runs including 3 centuries.

Test Record - 4 Tests, 86 runs (Av. 17.20) and 4 catches.

HOWARTH GEOFFREY PHILIP

New Zealand (born 1951) - A neat right-handed batsman with some flightful offside strokes, a fine fielder anywhere and also a useful off-spin bowler. He played for Northern Districts, Auckland and Surrey. In his first class career he made, 17,294 runs including 32 centuries, took 112 wickets and 229 catches.

Test Record - 47 Tests, 2,531 runs (Av. 32.44) including 6 centuries, 3 wickets (Av. 90.33) and 29 catches.

HOWARTH HEDLEY JOHN

New Zealand (born 1943) - He was an orthodox left-arm spinner who flighted the ball well. He played for Auckland. In his first class career he made, 1,668 runs, took 541 wickets and 138 catches.

Test Record - 30 Tests, 291 runs (Av. 12.12), 86 wickets (Av. 36.95) and 33 catches.

HOWELL HENRY

England (1890-1932) - He was right-arm bowler, nice easy bowling action. He played for Warwickshire. In his first class career he made, 1,679 runs and took 975 wickets.

Test Record - 5 Tests, 15 runs, (Av. 7.50) and 7 wickets (Av. 79.85).

HOWELL WILLIAM PETER

Australia (1869-1940) - Bill Howell spun the ball at medium pace from a strong right hand and also a left-handed batsman. He played for New South Wales. In his first class career he made, 2,228 runs including 1 century, took 520 wickets and 124 catches.

Test Record - 18 Tests, 158 runs (Av. 7.52), 49 wickets (Av. 28.71) and 12 catches.

HOWORTH RICHARD

England (1909-1980) - A left-handed batsman and solid front-foot attacking stroke player. He bowled slow-left-arm, turning the ball from a steady length. He played for Worcestershire. In his first class career he made, 11,479 runs including 4 centuries, and took 1,345 wickets.

Test Record - 5 Tests, 145 runs (Av. 18.12), 19 wickets (Av. 33.42) and 2 catches.

HUGHES KIMBERLEY JOHN

Australia (born 1954) - A fine all-round fielder and a gifted right-handed batsman with a complete array of attractive strokes. A full-blooded stroke-maker, when he commits himself to attack and his defence is solid. He played for Western Australia. In his first class career he made, 11,395 runs including 25 centuries and 135 catches.

Test Record - 70 Tests, 4,415 runs (Av. 37.41) including 9 centuries and 50 catches.

HUMPHRIES JOSEPH

England (1876-1946) - A wicket-keeper was the way he stood up to fast bowlers like Arnold Warren and Bill Bestwick. He played for Derbyshire. In his first class career he made, 5,464 runs and 674 dismissals.

Test Record - 3 Tests, 44 runs (Av. 8.80) and 7 dismissals (7ct).

HUNTE CONRAD CLEOPHAS

West Indies (born 1932) - A right-handed opening batsman. His strength was primarily off his legs, either glancing fine or punching to mid-wicket. He also hooked with power and timed his off-drives perfectly. He was a fine fielder, and occasionally bowled slow-medium cutter. He played for Barbados. In his first class career he made, 8,916 runs including 16 centuries and took 17 wickets.

Test Record - 44 Tests, 3,245 runs (Av. 45.06) including 8 centuries, 2 wickets (Av. 55.00) and 16 catches.

HUNTE ERROL ASHTON CLARIMORE

West Indies (1905-1967) - He was a good opening batsman and useful wicket-keeper. He played

for Trinidad. In his first class career he made, 472 runs and 36 dismissals.
Test Record - 3 Tests, 166 (Av. 33.20) and 5 catches.

HUNTER JOSEPH
England (1855-1891) - He was a good enough wicket-keeper. He played for Yorkshire. In his first class career he made, 1,336 runs and 309 dismissals.
Test Record - 5 Tests, 93 runs (Av. 18.60) and 11 dismissals (8ct, 3st).

HURST ALAN GEORGE
Australia (born 1950) - A tall, right-arm fast-bowler. He played for Victoria. In his first class career he made, 504 runs and took 280 wickets.
Test Record - 12 Tests, 102 runs (Av. 6.00), 43 wickets (Av. 27.91) and 3 catches.

HURWOOD ALEXANDER
Australia (1902-1982) - A tall, right-arm medium-pace bowler. He played for Queensland. In his first class career he made, 575 runs and took 113 wickets.
Test Record - 2 Tests, 5 runs (Av. 2.50), 11wickets (Av. 15.45) and 2 catches.

HUTCHINGS KENNETH LOTHERINGTON
England (1882-1916) - He was right-handed batsman. He played for Kent. In his first class career he made, 10,054 runs including 21 centuries, took 22 wickets and 166 catches.
Test Record - 7 Tests, 341 runs (Av. 28.41) including 1 century, 1 wicket (Av. 81.00) and 9 catches.

HUTTON RICHARD ANTHONY
England (born 1942) - He was a fast-medium bowler in all conditions and a dangerous swinger and cutter of the ball in helpful ones. He played for Cambridge University.. In his first class career he made, 7,561 runs including 5 centuries, took 625 wickets and 216 catches.
Test Record - 5 Tests, 219 runs (Av. 36.50), 9 wickets (Av. 28.55) and 9 catches.

HUTTON SIR LEONARD
England (born 1916) - He was right-handed stocky batsman, a good close fielder and a useful leg-break bowler. He played for Yorkshire. In his first class career he made, 40,140 runs including 129 centuries, took 173 wickets and 387 catches.
Test Record - 79 Tests, 6,971 runs (Av. 56.67) including 19 centuries, 3 wickets (Av. 77.33) and 57 catches.

HYLTON LESLIE GEORGE
West Indies (1905-1955) - A right-arm fast bowler. He played for Jamaica. In his first class career he made, 851 runs and took 120 wickets.
Test Record - 6 Tests, 70 runs (Av. 11.66), 16 wickets (Av. 26.12) and 1 catch.

I

IBRAHIM KHANMOHAMMED CASSUMBHOY

India (born 1919) - A right-handed opening batsman. Test debut on November 10, 1948 against West Indies at the age of 29 years and 284 days. Scores on Test debut were 85 and 44 in the first Test at Delhi. Last Test of the career played against West Indies in February 1949. Scores on last appearance in Test were 4 and 1 in the fifth Test at Bombay. Age at the time of retirement from Test cricket was 30 years and 10 days. He played for Bombay. In his first class career he made, 4,716 runs including 14 centuries.
Test Record - 4 Tests, 169 runs (Av. 21.12).

ICC

International Cricket Conference, recently renamed as International Cricket Council.

ICC TROPHY

This competition has been staged three times, each time in England. Only associate members of ICC take part in this competition.

The results of the finals were:
1979 Sri Lanka beat Canada
1982 Zimbabwe beat Bermuda
1986 Zimbabwe beat Holland

IDDON JOHN

England (1902-1946) - A right-handed hard-hitting batsman and also a slow left-arm bowler. He played for Lancashire. In his first class career he made, 22,681 runs including 46 centuries and took 551 wickets.
Test Record - 5 Tests, 170 runs (Av. 28.33).

IJAZ AHMED

Pakistan (born 1968) - Bats right-hand but a handy left-arm slow bowler too. Pakistan cricket thinks highly of Ijaz, as shown when he played his first Test and limited-overs Internationals aged 18. Is expected to help overcome the void left by the retirement of many classy Pakistan batsmen, by adequately filling an early middle-order batting spot. He plays for Pakistan club team PACO.
In his first class career he made, 14,691 runs including 24 centuries and took 84 wickets.
Test Record - 13 Tests, 457 runs (Av. 28.56) and 13 catches.

IJAZ BUTT

Pakistan (born 1938) - A sound right-handed batsman and wicket-keeper. He played for Rawalpindi. In his first class career he made, 3,842 runs including 7 centuries and 71 dismissals.

IJAZ AHMED

Test Record - 8 Tests, 279 runs (Av. 19.92) and 5 catches.

IJAZ FAQIH

Pakistan (born 1956) - A skilful all-rounder, a right-handed batsman and an off-break bowler. He played for Karachi and Muslim Commercial Bank. In his first class career he made, 4,509 runs including 10 centuries and took 443 wickets.

Test Record - 2 Tests, 63 runs (Av. 15.75) and 1 wickets (Av. 85.00).

IKIN JOHN THOMAS

England (1918-1984) - A left-handed batsman and also a right-arm leg-break and googly bowler. A brilliant and daring fielder in the short-leg area. He played for Lancashire. In his first class career he made, 17,968 runs including 27 centuries, took 339 wickets and 419 catches.

Test Record - 18 Tests, 606 runs (Av. 20.89), 3 wickets (Av. 118.00) and 31 catches.

ILLINGWORTH RAYMOND

England (born 1932) - An all-rounder,he was a right-arm bowler. He played for Yorkshire and Leicestershire. In his first class career he made, 24,134 runs including 22 centuries, took 2,072 wickets and 446 catches.

Test Record - 61 Tests, 1,836 runs (Av. 23.24) including 2 centuries, 122 wickets (Av. 31.20) and 45 catches.

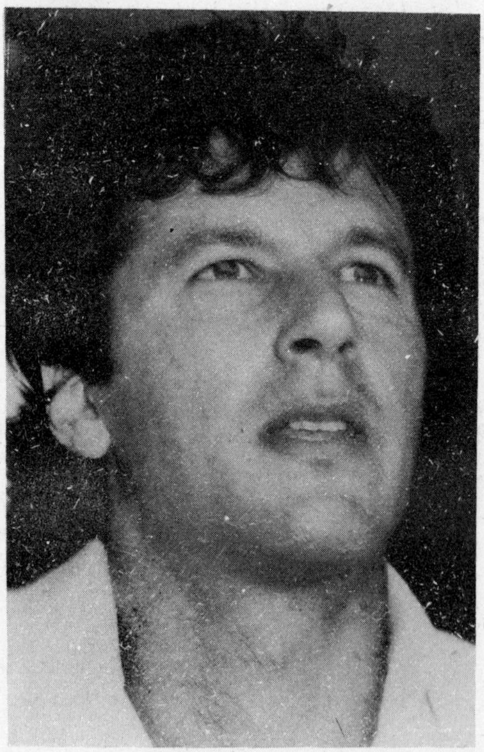

IMRAN KHAN

IMRAN KHAN

Pakistan (born 1952) - An all-rounder. A right-handed batsman who bowls genuinely fast for long periods with a long run up and leaping action. He played for Lahore, Pakistan International Airways, Oxford University, Sussex and New South Wales. In his first class career he made, 15,849 runs including 24 centuries, took 1,182 wickets and 112 catches.

Test Record - 74 Tests, 3000 runs (Av.33.70) including 4 centuries,341 wickets (Av.22.04) and 25 catches.

IMTIAZ AHMED

Pakistan (born 1928) - A right-handed batsman of great fighting qualities and a crowd-puller when in best form. He was one of the best fast bowlers. He played for Northern India and Services. In his first class career he made, 10,383 runs including 22 centuries, and 391 dismissals.

Test Record - 41 Tests, 2,079 runs (Av. 29.28) including 3 centuries and 93 dismissals (77ct, 16st).

IN

The time when a player begins his innings until it ends.

INTIKHAB ALAM

Pakistan (born 1941) - He was a high-class leg-spin and googly bowler and exceptionally hard-hitting right-handed batsman. He played for Karachi and Surrey. In his first class career he made, 14,331 runs including 9 centuries, took 1,571 wickets and 228 catches.

Test Record - 47 Tests, 1,493 runs (Av. 22.28) including 1 century, 125 wickets (Av. 35.93) and 20 catches.

INDIAN TEST UMPIRES

(As on September 1, 1989)

J.W. Hitch, ... (b.7-5-1886, d.7-7-1965), 3 Tests.

F.A. Tarrant, ... (b.11-12-1881, d.29-1-1951), 2 Tests.

J.B. Higgins, ... (b.31-12-1885), 1 Test.

D.K. Naik, ... (b. 1-5-1900, d.25-4-1968), 1 Test.

J.R. Patel, ... (b. 18-4-1914), 9 Tests.

T.A. Ramachandran, ... (b. 12-9-1912, d. 13-4-1951), 1 Test.

P.K. Sinha, ... (b. 26-9-1911), 2 Tests.

B.J. Mohoni, ... (b. 15-4-1901, d. 7-4-1980), 11 Tests.

A.R. Joshi, ... (b. 10-3-1912), 12 Tests.

M.G. Vijayasarathi, ... (b. 11-12-1906, d. 30-6-1979), 13 Tests.

M.M. Naidu, ... (b. 28-10-1911), 1 Test.

N.D. Nagarwala, ... (b. 10-10-1909), 5 Tests.

D.D. Desai, ... (b. 21-10-1916), 3 Tests.

S.K. Ganguly, ... (b. 19-3-1911), 10 Tests.

G. Ayling, ... (b. —), 1 Test.

Mohammad Yunus, ... (b. —), 5 Tests.

H.E. Chowdhary, ... (b. 20-7-1916, d. 1-7-1968), 4 Tests.

N.D. Sane, ... (b. 4-2-1909), 2 Tests.

B. Satyaji Rao, ... (b. 16-10-1920), 17 Tests.

S. Pan, ... (b. 3-1-1919), 9 Tests.

S.K. Raghunatha Rao, ... (b. 10-11-1922), 7 Tests.

Dr. I. Gopalakrishna, ... (b. 15-10-1915, d. 7-8-1981), 7 Tests.

S. Roy, ... (b. 1-2-1917), 6 Tests.

S.V. Kumaraswamy, ... (b. 17-2-1918), 1 Test.

S.K. Banerjee, ... (b. 19-12-1919, d. 1-8-1986), 1 Test.

A.M. Mamsa, ... (b. 15-1-1919), 6 Tests.

M.V. Nagendra, ... (b. 22-3-1933, d. 27-11-1978), 11 Tests.

S. Bhattacharya, ... (b. 1-4-1920), 2 Tests.

V. Rajagopal, ... (b. —), 1 Test.

J. Reuben, ... (b. 21-2-1922), 10 Tests.

M.V. Gothoskar, ... (b. 30-10-1928), 14 Tests.

H.P. Sharma, ... (b. 8-12-1922), 3 Tests.

M.S. Shivshankaraiah, ... (b. 22-5-1927), 3 Tests.

M.I. Mohammad Ghouse, ... (b. 15-3-1931), 8 Tests.

K.B. Ramaswamy, ... (b. 20-2-1929), 8 Tests.

S.N. Hanumantha Rao, ... (b. 4-9-1929), 9 Tests.

Swarup Kishen Rau, ... (b. 13-7-1930), 17 Tests.

P.R. Punjabi, ... (b. 10-6-1928), 7 Tests.

J.D. Ghosh, ... (b. 6-10-1935), 4 Tests.

B. Ganguly, ... (b. 1-8-1931), 5 Tests.

D.N. Dotiwala, ... (b. 30-10-1933), 6 Tests.

S.R. Bose, ... (b. 1-11-1930), 1 Test.

M.G. Subramaniam, ... (b. 5-11-1931), 2 Tests.

P.D. Reporter, ... (b. 24-9-1938), 10 Tests.

V. Vikram Raju, ... (b. 1-1-1934), 2 Tests.

M.Y. Gupte, ... (b. 11-4-1931), 1 Test.

V.K. Ramaswamy, ... (b. 26-4-1946), 10 Tests.

Ram Babu Gupta, ... (b. 17-7-1935), 11 Tests.

Rajen Mehra, ... (b. 23-11-1933), 2 Tests.

S. Ramachandra Rao, ... (b. 16-9-1931), 1 Test.

S.K. Ghosh, ... (b. —), 2 Tests.

SWARUP KISHEN

INDREJITSINHJI KUMAR SHRI

India (born 1937) - A right-handed batsman and a useful wicket-keeper. Test debut on October 2, 1964 against Australia at the age of 27 years and 108 days. Scores on Test debut were 4 and 0 in the first Test at Madras. Last Test of the career played against New Zealand in October 1969. Scores on last appearance in Test were 7 and 12 in the third Test at Hyderabad. Age at the time of retirement from Test cricket was 32 years and 125 days. He played for Madras and Delhi. In his first class career he made, 3,694 runs including 5 centuries, and 210 dismissals

Test Record - 4 Tests, 51 runs (Av. 8.50) and 9 dismissals (6ct, 3st).

INFIELD

Fieldsmen placed beyond the inner catching positions, but usually not more than 30 to 40 metres from the ball,e.g. point, covers, mid-wickets.

INNES ALBERT ROSE

South Africa (1868-1946) - A reliable batsman and a slow left-arm bowler. He played for Transvaal. In his first class career he made, 70 runs and 18 wickets.

Test Record - 2 Tests, 14 runs (Av. 3.50), 5 wickets (Av. 17.80) and 2 catches.

INNER

A delivery from a bowler of any pace, usually from medium to fast, that deviates through the air from off to leg to the batsman. Also, a soft, close-fitting glove worn by a wicket-keeper inside his main glove.

INNINGS

Time spent at batting, either by an individual or a team.

INSOLE DOUGLAS JOHN

England (born 1926) - A powerfully built right-handed batsman, a medium-pace change-bowler and a fine close fine fielder. He played for Essex. In his first class career he made, 25,237 runs including 54 centuries, took 138 wickets and 363 catches and 6 stumpings.

Test Record - 9 Tests, 408 runs (Av. 27.20) including 1 century, and 8 catches.

Grip for the Inswinger

INSWINGER

A delivery from a bowler of any pace, usually from medium to fast, that deviates through the air from off to leg to the batsman.

INTIMIDATION

The use of the fast, short-pitched delivery in an attempt to intimidate the batsman. The hope is that it will claim a wicket by having the batsman caught while fending the ball off his body, while trying to play the hook shot, or by dismissing him in some other way within a few deliveries as a result of the unsettling effect of the intimidation. Umpires are now empowered to take action against intimidating tactic by bowlers. This is a contentious issue pherhaps exacerbated by the recent tactic of loading teams with up to four fast bowlers.

INVERARITY ROBERT JOHN

Australia (born 1944) - A right-handed batsman and a slow left-arm spin bowler. He played for Western Australia and South Australia. In his first class career he made, 11,777 runs including 26 centuries, took 221 wickets and 250 catches.

Test Record - 6 Tests, 174 runs (Av. 17.40), 4 wickets (Av. 23.25) and 4 catches.

IQBAL QASIM MOHAMMAD

Pakistan (born 1953) - An accurate left-arm spin bowler and a fine close fielder. He played for Karachi, Sind and National Bank. In his first class career he made, 1,667 runs, took 677 wickets and 131 catches.

IQBAL QASIM

Test Record - 50 Tests, 551 runs (Av. 13.11), 171 wickets (Av. 28.10) and 41 catches.

IRANI JAHANGIR KHAN

India (born 1923) - A right-handed batsman and a useful wicket-keeper. Test debut on November 28, 1947 against Australia at the age of 24 years and 100 days. Scores on Test debut were 0 and 2 not out in the first Test at Brisbane. Last Test he played against Australia in December 1947. Score on last appearance in Test was 1 not out in the second Test at Sydney. Age at the time of retirement from Test cricket was 24 years and 120 days. He played for Sind. In his first class career he made, 399 runs and 27 dismissals.

Test Record - 2 Tests, 3 runs (Av. 3.00) and 3 dismissals (2ct, 1st).

IRANI CUP MATCH

The Irani Cup Match, associated with the name of the late Mr. Z.R. Irani. The match is played on annual basis between last season's Ranji Trophy champion team and Rest of India.

YEAR	VENUE	WINNERS-RUNNER-UP
1959-60	New Delhi	Bombay-Rest of India
1960-61	No Match	
1961-62	No Match	
1962-63	Bombay	Bombay-Rest of India
1963-64	Anantapur	Bombay-Rest of India
1964-65	*Not held and match shifted to start of the season.*	
1965-66	Madras	Bombay and Rest of India.- -Joint winners as first innings was not completed.
1966-67	Calcutta	Rest of India-Bombay
1967-68	Bombay	Bombay-Rest of India
1968-69	Bombay	Rest of India-Bombay
1969-70	Poona	Bombay-Rest of India
1970-71	Calcutta	Bombay-Rest of India
1971-72	Bombay	Rest of India-Bombay
1972-73	Poona	Bombay-Rest of India
1973-74	Bangalore	Rest of India-Bombay
1974-75	Ahmedabad	Karnataka-Rest of India
1975-76	Nagpur	Bombay-Rest of India
1976-77	Delhi	Bombay-Rest of India
1977-78	Bombay	Rest of India-Bombay
1978-79	Bangalore	Rest of India-Karnataka
1979-80	Jullundur	No Match
1980-81	Delhi	Delhi-Rest of India
1981-82	Indore	Bombay-Rest of India
1982-83	New Delhi	Rest of India-Delhi
1983-84	Rajkot	Karnataka-Rest of India
1984-85	New Delhi	Rest of India-Bombay
1985-86	Nagpur	Bombay-Rest of India
1986-87	Jodhpur	Rest of India-Delhi
1987-88	Hyderabad	Hyderabad-Rest of India
1988-89	Madras	Tamil Nadu-Rest of India

IREDALE FRANCIS ADAMS

Australia (1867-1926) - He was a right-handed batsman. He played for New South Wales. In his first class career he made, 6,794 runs including 12 centuries and took 111 catches.

Test Record - 14 Tests, 807 runs (Av. 36.68) including 2 centuries and 16 catches.

IRONMORGER HERBERT

Australia (1881-1971) - A slow left-arm medium-pace bowler. He played for Victoria. In his first class career he made, 476 runs and took 464 wickets.

Test Record - 14 Tests, 42 runs (Av. 2.62), 74 wickets (Av. 17.97) and 3 catches.

IRONSIDE DAVID ERNEST JAMES

South Africa (born 1925) - A medium-pace bowler and an effective seam bowler. He played for Transvaal. In his first class career he made, 142 runs and took 130 wickets.

Test Record - 3 Tests, 37 runs (Av. 18.50), 15 wickets (Av. 18.33) and 1 catch.

IRVINE BRIAN LEE

South Africa (born 1944) - A left-handed batsman and a fine fielder. He played for Natal, Transvaal and Essex. In his first class career he made, 9,919 runs including 21 centuries and 247 dismissals.

Test Record - 4 Tests, 353 runs (Av. 50.42) including 1 century and 2 catches.

ISRAR ALI

Pakistan (born 1927) - A left-handed batsman and a medium-fast bowler. He played for Multan and Southern Punjab. In his first class career he made, 1,132 runs and took 114 wickets.

Test Record - 4 Tests, 33 runs (Av. 4.71), 6 wickets (Av. 27.50) and 1 catch.

IVERSON JOHN BRIAN

Australia (1915-1973) - A right-handed batsman and also a medium-fast bowler. He played for Victoria. In his first class career he made, 277 runs and took 157 wickets.

Test Record - 5 Tests, 3 runs (Av. 0.75), 21 wickets (Av. 15.23) and 2 catches.

J

JACKMAN ROBIN DAVID
England (born 1945) - He was short, stocky, medium-fast bowler. He played for Surrey, Western Province and Rhodesia. In his first class career he made, 5,681 runs, took 1,402 wickets and 177 catches.
Test Record - 4 Tests, 42 runs (Av. 7.00) and 14 wickets (Av. 31.78).

JACKSON ARCHIBALD
Australia (1909-1933) - He was right-handed batsman and a good outfielder. He played for New South Wales. In his first class career he made, 4,383 runs including 11 centuries.
Test Record - 8 Tests, 474 runs (Av. 47.40) including 1 century, and 7 catches.

JACKSON HERBERT LESLIE
England (born 1921) - A right-arm, medium-fast bowler. He played for Derbyshire. In his first class career he made, 2,083 runs and took 1,733 wickets.
Test Record - 2 Tests, 15 runs (Av. 15.00), 7 wickets (Av. 22.14) and 1 catch.

JACKSON SIR FRANCIS STANLEY
England (1870-1947) - A right-handed batsman and a medium-pace bowler with a model run-up. He played for Cambridge University and Yorkshire. In his first class career he made, 15,824 runs including 31 centuries, and took 770 wickets.
Test Record - 20 Tests, 1,415 runs (Av. 48.79) including 5 centuries, 24 wickets (Av. 33.29) and 10 catches.

JAHANGIR KHAN DR MOHAMMED
India (1910 - 1968) - A right-handed batsman and right-arm fast medium bowler. Father of Majid Jahangir Khan of Pakistan. Test Debut on June 25, 1932 against England at the age of 22 years and 144 days. Scores on Test debut were 1 and 0 in the only Test played at Lord's. Last Test of the career played against England in August 1936. Scores on last appearance in Test were 9 and 1 in the third Test at the Oval. Age at the time of retirement from Test cricket was 26 years and 197 days. He played for Northern India and Cambridge University. In his first class career he made, 3,319 runs including 4 centuries and took 347 wickets.
Test Record - 4 Tests, 39 runs (Av. 5.57), 4 wickets (Av. 63.75) and 4 catches.

JAISIMHA MOTGANHALLI LAKSHMINARSU
India (born 1939)- A right-handed batsman and a right-arm off-break bowler. Test debut on June 18,1959 against England at the age of 20 years and 105 days. Scores on Test debut were 1 and 8 in the second Test at Lord's. Last Test of the career played against West Indies in April 1971. Scores on last appearance in Test were 0 and 23 in the fifth Test at Port-of-Spain. Age at the time of retirement from Test cricket was 32 years and 46 days. First ever Test century 127 scored on December 13,1961 at the age of 22 years and 280 days against England in the third Test at New Delhi. He played for Hyderabad. In his first class career he made, 13,514 runs including 33 centuries, and took 431 wickets.
Test Record - 39 Tests, 2,056 runs (Av.30.68) including 3 centuries and 17 catches.

JALAL-UD-DIN
Pakistan (born 1959) - A right-arm medium-fast bowler. He played for Industrial Development Bank, Public Works Dapartment, Karachi and Allied Bank. In his first class career he made, 653 runs and took 521 wickets.
Test Record - 6 Tests, 3 runs (Av. 3.00) and 11 wickets (Av. 48.81).

JAMES KENNETH CECIL
New Zealand (1904-1976) - He was a good wicketkeeper. He played for Wellington and Northamptonshire. In his first class career he made, 6,413

runs including 7 centuries, and 418 dismissals.
Test Record - 11 Tests, 52 runs (Av.4.72) and 16 dismissals (11ct, 5st).

JAMESON JOHN ALEXANDER
England (born 1941) - He was a right-handed opening batsman and a very fast run scorer. He played for Warwickshire. In his first class career he made, 18,941 runs including 33 centuries, took 89 wickets, 255 catches and 1 stumping.
Test Record - 4 Tests, 214 runs (Av. 26.75).

JARDINE DOUGLAS ROBERT
England (1900-1958) - A right-handed batsman especially strong on the leg side. He played for Oxford University and Surrey. In his first class career he made, 14,848 runs including 35 centuries, took 48 wickets and 188 catches.
Test Record - 22 Tests, 1,296 runs (Av. 48.00) including 1 century and 26 catches.

JARMAN BARRINGTON NOEL
Australia (born 1936) - He was a good wicket-keeper and a good right-handed batsman, vice captain of the Australian Team in 1968. He played for South Australia. In his first class career he made, 5,615 runs including 5 centuries and 560 dismissals.
Test Record - 19 Tests, 400 runs (Av. 14.81) and 54 dismissals (50ct, 4st).

JARVIS ARTHUR HARWOOD
Australia (1860-1933) - A useful wicket-keeper. He played for South Australia. In his first class career he made, 3,161 runs and 198 dismissals.
Test Record - 11 Tests, 303 runs (Av. 16.83) and 18 dismissals (9 ct, 9 st).

JARVIS TERRENCE WAYNE
New Zealand (born 1944) - A ginger-headed, right-handed opening batsman and a fine fielder. He played for Auckland and Canterbury. In his first class career he made, 4,666 runs including 6 centuries and took 102 catches
Test Record - 13 Tests, 625 runs (Av. 29.76) including 1 century and 3 catches.

JAVED BURKI
Pakistan (born 1938) - A right-handed middle-order batsman and an occasional medium-pace bowler. He played for Oxford University and Karachi. In his first class career he made, 9,426 runs including 22 centuries and took 35 wickets.
Test Record - 25 Tests, 1,341 runs (Av. 30.47) including 3 centuries and 7 catches.

JAVED MIANDAD KHAN
Pakistan (born 1957) - A right-handed batsman with full array of strokes and a buccaneering aggression. He is the most glorious cover-driver and square-cutter. He is also a right-arm leg-spin bowler. He played for Karachi, Sind, Habib Bank, Sussex and Glamorgan. In his first class career he made, 32,699 runs including 92 centuries, took 244 wickets, 391 catches and 4 stumpings.
Test Record - 97 Tests, 7,422 runs (Av. 57.09) including 21 centuries, 17 wickets (Av. 40.11), 84 catches and 1 stumping.

JAVED MIANDAD

JEGANATHAN SRIDHARAN
Sri Lanka (born 1951) - A left-handed batsman

and a slow-left-arm spinner. He played for Nondescripts. In his first class career he made, 432 runs and took 47 wickets.
Test Record - 2 Tests, 19 runs (Av. 4.75).

JENKINS ROLAND OLIVER
England (born 1918) - A right-handed batsman and a leg-spin bowler. He played for Worcestershire. In his first class career he made, 10,073 runs including 1 century, took 1,309 wickets and 210 catches.
Test Record - 9 Tests, 198 runs (Av. 18.00), 32 wickets (Av. 34.31) and 4 catches.

JENNER TERENCE JAMES
Australia (born 1944) - He was a right-arm leg-break with a good googly bowler. He played for South Australia. In his first class career he made, 3,580 runs and took 389 wickets.
Test Record - 9 Tests, 208 runs (Av. 23.11), 24 wickets (Av. 31.20) and 5 catches.

JENNINGS CLAUDE BARROWS
Australia (1884-1950) - A right-handed batsman. He played for South Australia and Queensland. In his first class career he made, 2,452 runs including 1 century.
Test Record - 6 Tests, 107 runs (Av. 17.83) and 5 catches.

JESSOP GILBERT LAIRD
England (1874-1955) - He was a right-handed batsman. He was short and compact with great strength about the shoulders. He was also a good fielder. He played for Cambridge University and Gloucestershire. In his first class career he made, 26,698 runs including 53 centuries, took 873 wickets and 453 catches.
Test Record - 18 Tests, 569 runs (Av. 21.88) including 1 century, 10 wickets (Av. 35:40) and 11 catches.

JESSOPIAN
A style of aggressive, big hitting and fast scoring batting.

JERK
To bowl the ball illegally (as by having the arm bent when the ball is released). The act or an instance of jerking the ball.

JOHN VINOTHEN BEDE JEYARAJASINGHAM
Sri Lanka (born 1960) - A right-handed medium-pace bowler. He played for Bloomfield. In his first class career he made, 127 runs and took 72 wickets.
Test Record - 6 Tests, 53 runs (Av. 10.60), 28 wickets (Av. 21.92) and 2 catches.

JOHNSON HOPHIE HORACE HINES
West Indies (born 1910) - A right-arm fast bowler. He played for Jamaica. In his first class career he made, 316 runs and took 68 wickets.
Test Record - 3 Tests, 38 runs (Av. 9.50) and 13 wickets (Av. 18.30).

JOHNSON IAN WILLIAM
Australia (born 1918)_ - A very slow-off-spinner with a teasing flight bowler. He played for Victoria. In his first class career he made, 4,905 runs including 2 centuries, took 619 wickets and 138 catches.
Test Record - 45 Tests, 1,000 runs (Av. 18.51), 109 wickets (Av. 29.19) and 30 catches.

JOHNSTON WILLIAM ARRAS
Australia (born 1922) - A left-arm fast-medium bowler. He played for Victoria. In his first class career he made, 1,129 runs and took 554 wickets.
Test Record - 40 Tests, 273 runs (Av. 11.37), 160 wickets (Av. 23.91) and 16 catches.

JONES ARTHUR OWEN
England (1872-1914) - He was a leg-break bowler and one of the finest all-round fieldsmen ever seen. He played for Cambridge University, and Nottinghamshire. In his first class career he made, 22,955 runs including 34 centuries and took 333 wickets.
Test Record - 12 Tests, 291 runs (Av. 13.85), 3 wickets (Av. 44.33) and 15 catches.

JONES CHARLES M.

West Indies (born 1905)- A competent left-handed batsman and left-arm slow bowler. He played for British Guiana. In his first class career he made, 917 runs and took 24 wickets.

Test Record - 4 Tests, 63 runs (Av. 9.00) and 3 catches.

DEAN JONES

JONES DEAN MERVYN

Australia (born 1961) - A right-handed batsman . He plays for Victoria. In his first class career he made, 7,894 runs including 17 centuries and took 7 wickets.

Test Record - 21 Tests, 1,546 runs (Av.45.47) and 11 catches.

JONES ERNEST

Australia (1869-1943) - A right-arm fast bowler He played for South Australia. In his first class career he made, 2,390 runs and took 641 wickets.

Test Record - 19 Tests, 126 runs (Av. 5.04), 64 wickets (Av. 29.01) and 21 catches.

JONES IVOR JEFFREY

England (born 1941) - A left-arm bowler. He played for Glamorgan. In his first class career he made, 513 runs and took 511 wickets.

Test Record - 15 Tests, 38 runs, (Av. 4.75), 44 wickets (Av. 40.20) and 4 catches.

JONES PRIOR ERSKINE

West Indies (born 1917) - He was a right-arm fast bowler and a slip fielder. He played for Trinidad. In his first class career he made, 775 runs and took 169 wickets.

Test Record - 9 Tests, 47 runs (Av. 5.22), 25 wickets (Av. 30.04) and 4 catches.

JONES SAMUEL PERCY

Australia (1861-1951) - A right-handed batsman, a fast run scorer and a useful change bowler. He played for New South Wales. In his first class career he made, 5,189 runs including 5 centuries and took 55 wickets.

Test Record - 12 Tests, 432 runs (Av. 21.60), 6 wickets (Av. 18.66) and 12 catches.

JOSHI PADMANABH GOVIND

India (born 1926)- A right-handed batsman and wicket-keeper. Test debut on November 2,1951 against England at the age of 25 years and 5 days, played in the first Test at New Delhi but did not bat. Last Test of the career played against Pakistan in December 1960. Score on last appearance in Test was 52 not out in the first Test at Bombay. Age at the time of retirement from Test cricket was 34 years and 41 days. His partnership of 149 runs with R.B.Desai for the 9th wicket in the first Test against Pakistan at Bombay in 1960-61 is the highest for 9th wicket for India against any country. He played for Maharashtra. In his first class career he made, 1,724 runs including 1 century, and 180 dismissals.

Test Record - 12 Tests, 207 runs (Av. 10.89) and 27 dismissals (18ct, 9 st).

JULIEN BERNARD DENIS

West Indies (born 1950) - A left-arm seam bowler and also bowl slow orthodox or unorthodox spin. He played for Trinidad and Kent. In his first class career he made, 5,792 runs including 3 centuries, took 483 wickets (Av. 28.72) and 126 catches.

Test Record - 24 Tests, 866 runs (Av. 30.92) including 2 centuries, 50 wickets (Av. 37.36) and 14 catches.

JUMADEEN RAPHICK RASIF
West Indies (born 1948) - A left-arm orthodox bowler. He played for Trinidad. In his first class career he made, 604 runs and took 347 wickets.
Test Record - 12 Tests, 84 runs (Av. 21.00), 29 wickets (Av. 39.34) and 4 catches.

JUPP HENRY
England (1841-1889) - He was a right-handed batsman. He played for Surrey. In his first class career he made, 15,319 runs including 12 centuries, 229 catches and 19 stumpings.
Test Record - 2 Tests, 68 runs (Av. 17.00) and 2 catches.

JUPP VALLANCE WILLIAM CRISP
England (1891-1960) - A right-handed batsman and slow-medium off-break bowler. He played for Sussex. In his first class career he made, 23,278 runs including 30 centuries, took 1,658 wickets.
Test Record - 8 Tests, 208 runs (Av. 17.33), 28 wickets (Av. 22.00) and 5 catches.

K

KALLICHARAN ALVIN ISAAC

West Indies (born 1949) - A brilliant left-handed batsman, fine fielder with a deceptively strong throw from the deep, and an occasional slow right-arm off-break bowler. He is a determined competitor with a full armoury of strokes and immaculate timing whether driving, hooking, cutting or glancing. He played for Guyana, Warwickshire, Queensland, Transvaal and Orange Free State. In his first class career he made, 30,775 runs including 83 centuries, took 77 wickets and 299 catches.

Test Record - 66 Tests, 4,399 runs (Av. 44.43) including 12 centuries, 4 wickets (Av. 39.50) and 51 catches.

ALVIN KALLICHARAN

KALUPERUMA LALITH WASANTHA

Sri Lanka (born 1949) - A right-arm off-break bowler, gritty late-order right-handed batsman and good close fielder. He played for Bloomfield. In his first class career he made, 1,023 runs and took 129 wickets.

Test Record - 2 Tests, 12 runs (Av. 4.00) and 2 catches.

KALUPERUMA SANATH MOHAN SILVA

Sri Lanka (born 1961) - A right-handed middle-order batsman. He played for Bloomfield. In his first class career he made, 513 runs including 1 century and took 6 wickets.

Test Record - 3 Tests, 82 runs (Av. 13.66), 2 wickets (Av. 31.00) and 6 catches.

KANHAI ROHAN BABULAL

West Indies (born 1935) - A small, right-handed batsman. He became a more reliable player as his experience grew. He played for Guyana, Trinidad, Warwickshire, Western Australia and Tasmania. In his first class career he made, 28,639 runs including 83 centuries, took 18 wickets, 315 catches and 7 stumpings.

Test Record - 79 Tests, 6,227 runs (Av. 47.53) including 15 centuries and 50 catches.

KANITKAR HEMANT SHAMSUNDER

India (born 1942)- A right-handed batsman and wicket-keeper. Test debut on November 22, 1974 against West Indies at the age of 31 years and 344 days. Scores on Test debut were 65 and 18 in the first Test at Bangalore. Last Test of the career played against the West Indies in December 1974. Scores on last appearance in Test were 8 and 20 in the second Test at New Delhi. Age at the time of retirement from Test cricket was 32 years and 7 days. He played for Maharashtra. In his first class career he made 5,007 runs including 13 centuries and 87 dismissals.

Test Record- 2 Tests, 111 runs (Av. 27.75)

KANPUR

The Oxford Authentics played a match here against Northern India in 1902-03. Green Park Kanpur (The Mody Stadium) was accorded Test status during 1951-52. The pitch is heavily weighed in the batsman's favour.

KAPIL DEV NIKHANJ

India (born 1959) - A right-handed batsman and right-arm fast medium bowler. Test debut on October 16, 1978 against Pakistan at the age of 19 years and 280 days. Score on Test debut was 8 in the first Test at Faisalabad in Pakistan. Became the youngest batsman from India to hit a century. He was 20 years and 21 days old when he made 126 not out on January 27, 1979 in the fifth test against West Indies at New Delhi. Holds the Indian record of capturing most wickets in a calendar year. He dismissed 74 batsmen in 17 Tests in the year 1979 (11 West Indians in three Tests; 16 Englishmen in four Tests; 28 Australians in six Tests and 19 Pakistanis in four Tests). He had also scored 619 runs in the same period. He completed the all-rounders "double " of 1000 runs and 100 wickets in 25 Tests. In achieving this feat at the age of 21 years, he became the youngest all-rounder in the world to perform the "double". Kapil Dev is the second Indian all-rounder to do so after M.H. (Vinoo) Mankad. The unique feature of his achievement is that he completed the "double in the one and the same Test i.e. sixth Test against Pakistan at Calcutta in 1979-80. That he completed the "double" in the shortest period of one year and 108 days which is also a world record. He is an all-round cricketer of charismatic brilliance, who has been one of the great players of world cricket in the 1980s. The best fast bowler produced by India for many years. He is one of the four players who have taken 300 wickets and 4,000 runs. He plays for Haryana. In his first class career he made 10,800 runs including 16 centuries and took 815 wickets.

Test Record - 99 Tests, 4,087 runs (Av. 31.19) including 6 centuries, 347 wickets (Av. 29.02) and 53 catches.

KAPIL DEV

KARACHI

The National Stadium in Karachi has been the venue of Test Matches since 1954-55. Earlier the pitches were of matting but in 1960 grass wickets were introduced.

KARDAR ABDUL HAFEEZ

India (born 1925)- A left-handed batsman. Test debut on June 22, 1946 against England at the age of 21 years and 155 days. Scores on Test debut were 43 and 0 in the first Test at Lord's. Also played for Pakistan in 23 Test matches from 1952 to 1958. Last Test for India played against England in August 1946. Score on last appearance in Test was 1 in the third Test at the Oval. He played for Northern India, Oxford University and Warwickshire. In his first class career he made 6,814 runs including 8 centuries, took 344 wickets and 108 catches.

Test Record - India - 3 Tests, 80 runs (Av. 16.00) and 1 catch

Pakistan -23 Tests, 847 runs (Av. 24.91) and 21 wickets.

KEEPER

Wicket keeper

KEETON WILLIAM WALTER

England (1905-1980) - He was a right-handed

opening batsman. He played for Nottinghamshire. In his first class career he made, 24,276 runs including 54 centuries.
Test Record - 2 Tests, 57 runs (Av. 14.25).

KEITH HEADLEY JAMES
South Africa (born 1927) - A forceful left-handed batsman, strong in square-cutting and driving, and part of the powerful line-up. He played for Natal. In his first class career he made, 3,203 runs including 8 centuries and took 79 wickets.
Test Record - 8 Tests, 318 runs (Av. 21.20), and 9 catches.

KELLEWAY CHARLES
Australia (1889-1944) - A very sound right-handed batsman and also a medium-fast bowler. He played for New South Wales. In his first class career he made, 6,389 runs including 15 centuries, took 339 wickets and 103 catches.
Test Record - 26 Tests, 1,422 runs (Av. 37.42) including 3 centuries, 52 wickets (Av. 32.36) and 24 catches.

KELLY JAMES JOSEPH
Australia (1867-1938) - An outstanding wicket-keeper, and a right-handed batsman. He played for New South Wales. In his first class career he made, 4,108 runs including 3 centuries, and 355 dismissals.
Test Record - 36 Tests, 664 runs (Av. 17.02) and 63 dismissals (43ct, 20st).

KENDALL THOMAS
Australia (1851-1924) - A left-arm slow bowler, he bowled orthodox left-arm spin with considerable flight and command of length. He played for Victoria and Tasmania. In his first class career he made, 141 runs and took 40 wickets.
Test Record - 2 Tests, 39 runs (Av. 13.00), 14 wickets (15.35) and 2 catches.

KENNEDY ALEXANDER STUART
England (1891-1959) - He was a right-handed batsman and right-arm medium-fast bowler. He played for Hampshire. In his first class career he made, 16,586 runs including 10 centuries, took 2,874 wickets and 523 catches.
Test Record - 5 Tests, 93 runs (Av. 15.50), 31 wickets (Av. 19.32) and 5 catches.

KENNY RAMNATH BHAURA
India (1930 - 1985) A right-handed batsman. Test debut on December 31, 1958 against West Indies at the age of 28 years and 92 days. Scores on Test debut were 16 and 0 in the third Test at Calcutta. Last Test of the career played against Australia in January 1960. Scores on last appearance in Test were 7 and 69 in the fifth Test at Calcutta. Age at the time of retirement from Test cricket was 30 years and 90 days. He played for Bombay. In his first class career he made, 3,079 runs including 11 centuries and took 15 wickets.
Test Record - 5 Tests, 245 runs (Av. 27.22) and 1 catch.

KENT
Foundation of Present Club: August 6,1842 in Canterbury
Present Principal Ground: St Lawrence Ground, Canterbury
First First-class Match: Kent was one of the first 'great' cricketing counties and was ranked as 'first-class' when such a definition was originally created.
County Champions : 1906,1909,1910,1913,1970,1977,1978
JPL Champions: 1972,1973,1976
Benson & Hedges Cup Winners : 1973,1976, 1978
Highest Team Total: 803 for 4 dec v Essex in 1934
Lowest Team Total: 18 v Sussex in 1867
Highest Individual Innings: 332 W.H.Ashdown v Essex in 1934

KENT MARTIN FRANCIS
Australia (born 1959) - A right-handed batsman. He played for Queensland. In his first class career he made, 3,567 runs including 7 centuries.
Test Record - 3 Tests, 171 runs (Av. 28.50) and 6 catches.

KENTISH ESMOND SEYMOUR MAURICE
West Indies (born 1916) - A right-arm fast-bowler.

He played for Jamaica and Oxford University. In his first class career he made, 109 runs and took 78 wickets.
Test Record - 2 Tests, 1 run (Av. 1.00), 8 wickets (Av. 22.25) and 1 catch.

KENYON DONALD
England (born 1924) - A right-handed opening batsman. He played for Worcestershire. In his first class career he made, 37,002 runs including 74 centuries, and 327 catches.
Test Record - 8 Tests, 192 runs (Av. 12.80) and 5 catches.

KERR JOHN LAMBERT
New Zealand (born 1910) - A right-handed batsman and also a fine fielder. He played for Canterbury. In his first class career he made, 4,289 runs including 8 centuries.
Test Record - 7 Tests, 212 runs (Av. 19.27) and 4 catches.

KERR ROBERT BYERS
Australia (born 1961) - A right-handed batsman of high quality. He played for Queensland. In his first class career he made, 3,727 runs including 12 centuries.
Test Record - 2 Tests, 31 runs (Av. 7.75) and 1 catch.

KHALID WAZIR
Pakistan (born 1936) - A useful hard-hitting right-handed batsman, medium-pace change-bowler and good fielder. He played for Karachi. In his first class career he made, 271 runs and took 14 wickets.
Test Record - 2 Tests, 14 runs (Av. 7.00).

KHAN MOHAMMAD
Pakistan (born 1928) - A medium-fast bowler, and a right-handed batsman. He played for Bahawalpur and Somerset. In his first class career he made, 524 runs and took 212 wickets.
Test Record - 13 Tests, 100 runs (Av. 10.00), 54 wickets (Av. 23.92) and 4 catches.

KICK
Rising of the ball steeply and unexpectedly high of the pitch.

KILLICK REV.EDGAR THOMAS
England (1907-1953) - A graceful right-handed stroke-player. He played for Cambridge University and Middlesex. In his first class career he made, 5,730 runs including 15 centuries.
Test Record - 2 Tests, 81 runs (Av. 20.25) and 2 catches.

KILNER ROY
England (1890-1928) - He was a left-handed batsman, and a useful slow bowler. His spin and accuracy made him at times unplayable. He played for Yorkshire. In his first class career he made, 14,442 runs including 17 centuries, took 991 wickets.
Test Record - 9 Tests, 233 runs (Av. 33.28), 24 wickets (Av. 30.58) and 6 catches.

KING COLLIS LLEWELLYN
West Indies (born 1951) - A right-handed batsman and also a useful medium pace bowler. He played for Barbados, Glamorgan and Natal. In his first class career he made, 6,620 runs including 14 centuries, and took 125 wickets.
Test Record - 4 Tests, 211 runs (Av. 35.16), 2 wickets (Av. 56.50) and 3 catches.

KING FRANK MC DONALD
West Indies (born 1926) - A right-arm fast bowler. He possessed much stamina and bowled a considerable number of bumpers but only in his first series. He played for Barbados. In his first class career he made, 237 runs and took 90 wickets.
Test Record - 14 Tests, 116 runs (Av. 8.28), 29 wickets (Av. 39.96) and 5 catches.

KING LESTER ANTHONY
West Indies (born 1939) - A right-arm medium-fast bowler. He played for Jamaica and Bengal. In his first class career he made, 1,404 runs and took 142 wickets.

Test Record - 2 Tests, 41 runs (Av. 10.25), 9 wickets (Av. 17.11) and 2 catches.

KING PAIR

Fail to score runs in either innings of a match by a batsman in cricket involving dismissal of batsman on the first ball in each innings.

KIPPAX ALAN FALCONER

Australia (1897-1972) - He was a right-handed batsman, orthodox in his stroke-play but never dull or boring. He played for New South Wales. In his first class career he made, 12,762 runs including 43 centuries and took 21 wickets.
Test Record - 22 Tests, 1,192 runs (Av. 36.12) including 2 centuries and 13 catches.

KIRMANI SYED MUJTABA HUSSAIN

India (born 1949)- A right-handed batsman and wicket-keeper. Test debut on January 24, 1976 against New Zealand at the age of 26 years and 26 days. Score on Test debut was 14 in the first Test at Auckland. Scored the first-ever Test century (101 not out) on November 4, 1979 against Australia in the sixth Test at Bombay at the age of 29 years and 305 days. He has captured most victims behind the stumps in an innings for India when he caught five and stumped one batsman in the second Test against New Zealand at Christchurch in 1975-76 which is a record for India. Shares with N.S.Tamhane the record of most dismissals behind the stumps in a match for India. His 19 dismissals (17 catches and 2 stumpings) in the six-Test series against Pakistan in India in 1979-80 constitute a record for India of capturing most victims in a series by a wicket-keeper. Kirmani shares this record too with N.S.Tamhane. He is the first and only wicket-keeper from India to dismiss 100 victims behind the stumps. His 100 victims (77 by catches and 23 stumpings) are the highest for India. He has also scored over 1000 runs earlier. Thus with 1675 runs and 118 victims (92 catches and 26 stumpings), he becomes the sole cricketer from India to achieve the wicket-keeper's "double". He accomplished the "double" in his 42nd Test. He has also scored the highest number of runs as a "night-watchman" for India when he came to bat at No.5 on the 1st

SYED KIRMANI

evening of the sixth Test against Australia at Bombay in 1979-80 and went to score an unbeaten 101 to become the highest scorer as a night-watchman for India. He scored a century after playing most Tests for India (34 Tests). He played for Mysore (Karnataka). In his first class career he made, 6,953 runs including 4 centuries and 414 dismissals.
Test Record - 88 Tests, 2,759 runs (Av. 27.04) including 2 centuries and 198 dismissals.

KISCHENCHAND GOGUMAL

India (born 1925)- A right-handed batsman. Test debut on November 28, 1947 against Australia at the age of 22 years and 224 days. Scores on Test debut were 1 and 0 in the first Test at Adelaide. Last Test of the career played against Pakistan in October 1952. Scores on last appearance in Test were 0 and 20 in the second Test at Lucknow. Age at the time of retirement from Test cricket was 27 years and 192 days. He played for Delhi, Sind, Gujarat, and Baroda. In his first class career he made, 6,983 runs including 14 centuries and took 37 wickets.
Test Record - 5 Tests, 89 runs (Av. 8.90) and 1 catch.

KLINE LINDSAY FRANCIS

Australia (born 1934) - A left-arm off-break and googly bowler and a dogged tail-end batsman. He played for Victoria. In his first class career he made, 567 runs and took 276 wickets.

Test Record - 13 Tests, 58 runs (Av. 8.28), 34 wickets (Av. 22.82) and 9 catches.

KNIGHT ALBERT ERNEST

England (1872-1946) - He was a very good hard-wicket player. A right-handed batsman and also with a favourite square-drive. He played for Leicestershire. In his first class career he made, 19,357 runs including 34 centuries.

Test Record - 3 Tests, 81 runs (Av. 16.20) and 1 catch.

KNIGHT BARRY ROLFE

England (born 1938) - A right-arm medium-fast bowler, right-handed batsman and an excellent fielder. He played for Essex and Leicestershire. In his first class career he made, 13,336 runs including 12 centuries, took 1,089 wickets and 260 catches.

Test Record - 29 Tests, 812 runs (Av. 26.19) including 2 centuries, 70 wickets (Av. 31.75) and 14 catches.

KNIGHT DONALD JOHN

England (1894-1960) - He was a right-handed opening batsman, and also short-leg fielder. He played for Oxford University and Surrey. In his first class career he made, 6,231 runs including 13 centuries.

Test Record - 2 Tests, 54 runs (Av. 13.50) and 1 catch.

KNOTT ALAN PHILIP ERIC

England (born 1946) - A brilliant wicket-keeper, a right-handed batsman and an ever better player of fast bowlers. He played for Kent. In his first class career he made, 18,105 runs including 17 centuries, took 2 wickets and 1,344 dismissals.

Test Record - 95 Tests, 4,389 runs (Av. 32.75) including 5 centuries and 269 dismissals (250ct, 19st).

KNOX NEVILLE ALEXANDER

England (1884-1935) - He was a right-handed batsman and also bowled with great pace with a sharp break-back. He played for Surrey. In his first class career he made, 831 runs and took 411 wickets.

Test Record - 2 Tests, 24 runs (Av. 8.00) and 3 wickets (Av. 35.00).

KOOKABNURA BALL

A hard type of cricket ball mostly used in Australia,tending to retain its shine longer on hard wickets.

KOTZE JOHANNES JACOBUS

South Africa (1879-1931) - He was a right-arm fast bowler. He could make the ball move even on the hardest pitches. He played for Western Province and Transvaal. In his first class career he made, 688 runs and took 348 wickets.

Test Record - 3 Tests, 2 runs (Av. 0.40), 6 wickets (Av. 40.50) and 3 catches.

KRIPAL SINGH AMRITSAR GOVIND SINGH

India (born 1933)- A right-handed batsman and right-arm off-break bowler. Elder brother of A.G. Milkha Singh. Test debut on November 19, 1955 against New Zealand at the age of 22 years and 103 days. Score on Test debut was 100 not out in the first Test at Hyderabad, thus became the third Indian batsman to score century on Test debut. Last Test of the career played against Australia in October 1964. Scores on last appearance in Test were 0 and 0 in the first Test at Madras. Age at the time of retirement from Test cricket was 31 years and 61 days. He played for Madras. In his first class career he made 4,947 runs including 10 centuries and took 177 wickets.

Test Record - 14 Tests, 422 runs (Av. 28.13) including 1 century, 10 wickets (Av. 58.40) and 4 catches.

KRISHNAMURTHY POLLAMANI

India (born 1947) - A right-handed batsman and wicket keeper. Test debut on February 18, 1971 against West Indies at the age of 23 years and 216 days. Score on Test debut was 10 in the first Test

at Kingston. Last Test of the career played against West Indies in April 1971. Scores on last appearance in Test were 20 and 2 in the fifth Test at Port of Spain. Age at the time of retirement from Test cricket was 23 years and 277 days. He played for Hyderabad. In his first class career he made 1,559 runs and 218 dismissals.
Test Record - 5 Tests, 33 runs (Av. 5.50) and 8 dismissals.

KULKARNI UMESH NARAYAN
India (born 1942) - A left-handed batsman and left-arm medium fast bowler. Test debut on December 23, 1967 against Australia at the age of 25 years and 286 days. Scores on Test debut were 0 and 2 in the first Test at Adelaide. Last Test of the career played against New Zealand in February 1968. Scores on last appearance in Test were 0 not out and 1 not out in the second Test at Christchurch. Age at the time of retirement from Test cricket was 25 years and 350 days. He played for Bombay. In his first class career he made 158 runs and took 40 wickets.
Test Record - 4 Tests, 13 runs (Av. 4.33) and 5 wickets.

KUMAR VAMAN VISHWANATH
India (born 1935)- A right-handed batsman and right-arm leg-break and googly bowler. Test debut on February 8, 1961 against Pakistan at the age of 25 years and 220 days. Score on Test debut was 6 in the fifth Test at New Delhi. Took a wicket, that of Imtiaz Ahmed of Pakistan with his sixth ball in Test cricket on debut. Last Test of the career played against England in November 1961. Score on last appearance in Test was 0 in the first Test at Bombay. Age at the time of retirement from Test cricket was 26 years and 140 days. He played for Madras. In his first class career he made 673 runs and took 599 wickets.
Test Record - 2 Tests, 6 runs (Av. 3.00) and 7 wickets (Av. 20.05).

KUNDERAN BUDHISAGAR KRISHNAPPA
India (born 1939)-A right- handed batsman and wicket-keeper. Test debut on January 1, 1960 against Australia at the age of 20 years and 90 days. Scores on Test debut were 19 and 2 in the third Test at Bombay. Last Test of the career played against England in July 1967. Scores on last appearance in Test were 2 and 33 in the third Test at Birmingham. Opened India's innings with another wicket-keeper F.M.Engineer in the third Test against England at Birmingham in 1967, which is very rare in Test cricket. Also had the additional distinction of opening rare bowling when he shared the new ball with V. Subramanyam in the same Test. First-ever Test century 192 scored on January 10,1964 against England in the first Test at Madras at the age of 24 years and 98 days. Age at the time of retirement from Test cricket was 27 years and 283 days. His 192 in the first Test against England at Madras in 1964 is the highest score for a wicket-keeper batsman for India. As a wicket-keeper batsman, he is the second cricketer, after D.T.Lindsay of South Africa (606 runs in five-Test series against Australia in South Africa in 1966-67) to cross the 500 run mark in a series - 525 runs against England in India in 1964-a record for an Indian wicket-keeper batsman. He played for Railways and Mysore. In his first class career he made, 5,708 runs including 12 centuries and 251 dismissals.
Test Record - 18 Tests, 981 runs (Av. 32.70) including 2 centuries and 30 dismissals.

L

LAHORE

Pakistan. First at the Gymkhana ground and then at the Gaddafi Stadium there have been some excellent turf wickets in Lahore, capable of holding 50,000 people. First Test match Pakistan v India (Jun. 29, 1955).

LAIRD BRUCE MALCOLM

Australia (born 1950) - A right-handed opening batsman. He played for Western Australia. In his first class career he made, 6,085 runs including 8 centuries.

Test Record - 21 Tests, 1,341 runs (Av. 35.28) and 16 catches.

LAKER JAMES CHARLES

England (1922-1986) - He was the best of all off-spinners, sharp spin with great accuracy, flight and the intelligence to think batsman out. He was a useful sturdy tail-end batsman and a reliable catcher. He played for Surrey and Essex. In his first class career he made, 7,304 runs including 2 centuries, took 1,944 wickets and 270 catches.

Test Record - 46 Tests, 676 runs (Av. 14.08), 193 wickets (Av. 21.24) and 12 catches.

LALL SINGH

India (born 1909)- A right-handed batsman and right-arm bowler. Test debut on June 25, 1932 against England at the age of 22 years and 189 days. Played in only Test at Lord's scoring 15 and 29 runs. He played for Punjab. In his first class career he made, 1,059 runs including 1 century.

Test Record - 1 Test, 44 runs (Av. 22.00) and 1 catch.

LAMB ALLAN JOSEPH

England (born 1954) - A right-handed batsman with a simple method and a desire to take the initiative from bowlers whenever possible. He played for Western Province and Northamptonshire. In his first class careeer he made, 21,764 runs including 51 centuries, took 7 wickets (Av. 22.69) and 253 catches.

Test Record - 56 Tests, 2,969 runs (Av. 33.35) including 8 centuries, 1 wicket (Av. 23.00) and 53 catches.

ALLAN LAMB

LANCASHIRE

Present club formed: 1864.
Badge: Red rose. Colours: red, green and blue.
Ground: Old Trafford, Manchester, M 16 0PX.
Honours: County Champions - 1879 (Jointly with Nottinghamshire), 1881,1882,1889, (Jointly with Nottinghamshire and Surrey) 1897,1904,

1926,1927,1928,1930,1934,1950.
JPL Champions: 1969 and 1970
Highest Team Total: 801 v Somerset (Taunton) 1895
Lowest Team Total: 25 v Derbyshire (Old Trefford) 1871

LANCE HERBERT ROY
South Africa (born 1940) - He was a right-handed stroke-player and a useful change medium-fast bowler. He played for North-Eastern Transvaal and Transvaal. In his first class career he made, 5,336 runs including 11 centuries, took 167 wickets and 101 catches.
Test Record - 13 Tests, 591 runs (Av. 28.14), 12 wickets (Av. 39.91) and 7 catches.

LANGLEY GILBERT ROCHE ANDREWS
Australia (born 1919) - He was one of the best wicket-keepers and a right-handed batsman. He played for South Australia. In his first class career he made, 3,226 runs including 4 centuries, and 369 dismissals.
Test Record - 26 Tests, 374 runs (Av. 14.96) and 98 dismissals (83 ct, 15 st).

LANGRIDGE JAMES
England (1906-1966) - He was a left-arm bowler with flight, accuracy and spin. He played for Sussex and Auckland. In his first class career he made, 31,716 runs including 42 centuries, and took 1,530 wickets.
Test Record - 8 Tests, 242 runs (Av. 26.88), 19 wickets (Av. 21.73) and 6 catches.

LANGTON ARTHUR BEAUMONT CHUDLEIGH
South Africa (1912-1942) - He was a left-arm medium-pace bowler. He always needed careful watching for hit, break or change of speed. He played for Transvaal. In his first class career he made, 1,218 runs and took 193 wickets.
Test Record - 15 Tests, 298 runs (Av. 15.68), 40 wickets (Av. 45.67) and 8 catches.

LAP
A half -sweep half-drive that is lofted over the on-side infield in front of square leg.

LARKINS WAYNE
England (born 1953) - A right-handed opening batsman, a fine fielder and occasional medium-pace swing bowler. He played for Northamptonshire, Western Province and Eastern Province. In his first class career he made, 16,878 runs including 37 centuries, took 39 wickets and 161 catches.
Test Record - 6 Tests, 176 runs (Av. 16.00) and 3 catches.

LARTER JOHN DAVID FREDERICK
England (born 1940) - He was a medium-fast bowler. He played for Northamptonshire. In his first class career he made, 639 runs and took 666 wickets.
Test Record - 10 Tests, 16 runs (Av. 3.20), 37 wickets (Av. 25.43) and 5 catches.

LARWOOD HAROLD
England (born 1904) - A right-arm medium-fast bowler and a useful but underrated hard-hitting batsman. He played for Nottinghamshire. In his first class career he made, 7,290 runs including 3 centuries, took 1,427 wickets and 204 catches.
Test Record - 21 Tests, 485 runs (Av. 19.40), 78 wickets (Av. 28.35) and 15 catches.

LASHLEY PATRICK DOUGLAS
West Indies (born 1937) - A left-handed batsman, an occasional medium-pace bowler and an excellent fielder. He played for Barbados. In his first class career he made, 4,932 runs including 8 centuries and took 27 wickets.
Test Record - 4 Tests, 159 runs (Av. 22.71), and 4 catches.

LATE CUT
The only stroke on the off-side of the wicket now remaining for us to consider is the late cut. The stroke is usually attempted and considered safe against medium and fast medium bowling, when

the ball is pitched a little short of a good length, is well wide of the off- stump, and coming straight through or moving away to the off-side and bouncing no higher than the stumps. It should never be attempted when the ball is coming in towards the stumps from the off-side. It is a particularly dangerous stroke to play against fast bowling and balls rising abnormally high. The margin for error is so small and the reward rarely exceeds one run as the fieldsman at deep third man is generally situated close to the boundary. It is a splendid tactical stroke off a slow bowler who attacks the off and middle stumps and spins the ball away to slips. Often a batsman who is strong at driving this type of bowling, is thwarted by the opposing captain placing an outer circle of defence.

LATE ORDER
Tail-ender batsman.

LAUGHLIN TREVOR JOHN
Australia (born 1951) - A hard-hitting left-handed batsman, a steady medium-pace right-arm bowler, and a useful close fielder. He played for Victoria. In his first class career he made, 2,770 runs including 1 century, and took 99 wickets.
Test Record - 3 Tests, 87 runs (Av. 17.40), 6 wickets (Av. 43.66) and 3 catches.

LAVER FRANK
Australia (1869-1919) - A medium-pace bowler. He had an excellent command on length and a deceptive flight. He played for Victoria. In his first class career he made, 5,431 runs including 6 centuries, took 404 wickets and 148 catches.
Test Record - 15 Tests, 196 runs (Av. 11.52), 37 wickets (Av. 26.05) and 8 catches.

LAWRENCE GODFREY BERNARD
South Africa (born 1932) - A right-arm opening medium-fast bowler and also a useful batsman. He played for Natal and Rhodesia. In his first class career he made, 1,079 runs and took 342 wickets.
Test Record - 5 Tests, 141 runs (Av. 17.62), 28 wickets (Av. 18.28) and 2 catches.

LAWRY WILLIAM MORRIS
Australia (born 1937) - A left-handed opening batsman with a short back-lift and scoring greedily on the on-side. He was a very fine player of fast bowling and hooked with authority. He was also a fast outfielder with a good arm. His opposing bowlers will recall his broad, straight bat and his

BILL LAWRY

endless patience. He played for Victoria. In his first class career he made, 18,734 runs including 50 centuries and 121 catches.
Test Record - 67 Tests, 5,234 runs (Av. 47.15) including 13 centuries and 30 catches.

LAWS OF CRICKET

LAW 1.

THE PLAYERS - A match is played between eleven players on each of two sides. One of the players on each side shall be captain. In the event of the captain not being available at anytime, a deputy shall act in his place.

Before the toss for innings, players shall be nominated by the captain. They may not be changed

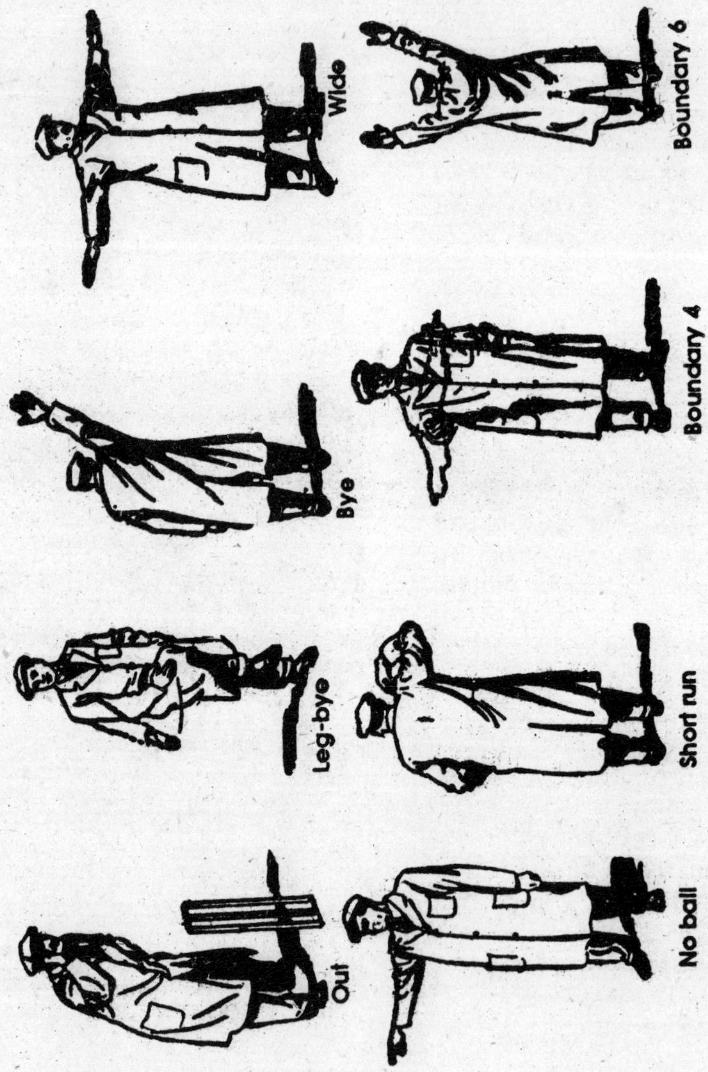
Wide
Bye
Leg-bye
Out
Boundary 6
Boundary 4
Short run
No ball

thereafter without the consent of the opposing captain.

LAW 2.

SUBSTITUTES AND RUNNERS: BATSMAN OR FIELDSMAN LEAVING THE FIELD: BATSMAN RETIRING: BATSMAN COMMENCING INNINGS

Substitutes shall be allowed to the field for any player who, is, incapacitated by illness or injury during the match. The consent of the opposing captain is to be obtained for the use of such substitute if any player is prevented from fielding for any other reason.

RICK Mc COSKER

The opposing captain has no right of objection to any player acting as substitute in the field, nor as to where he is to field, although he can object to the substitute acting as a wicket-keeper.

A substitute shall not be allowed to bat or bowl.

A player is entitled to bat, bowl or field even though a substitute has acted for him.

A runner is allowed for a batsman who, during the match, is incapacitated by injury or illness. The player acting as runner shall be a member of the batting team and shall, if possible, have already batted in that innings.

The acting runner for an injured batsman shall wear batting gloves and pads if the injured batsman is so equipped.

The injured batsman (when not a striker) shall stand where he does not interfere the play. Should he bring himself into the game, then he shall suffer the penalties that any transgression of the Law demands.

Without the consent of the umpire, no fieldsman shall leave the field or return during a session of play. If a substitute is required for a fieldsman, the consent of umpire is also required, when his side returns to the field after an interval. If a member of a fielding side leaves the field or fails to return after an interval and is absent from the field for over fifteen minutes, he shall not be permitted to bowl after his return until he has been on the field for at least the length of time for which he was absent.

Having previously notified the umpire at the bowler's end, a batsman may leave the field or retire at any time owing to illness, injury or other unavoidable cause. He can resume his innings at the fall of a wicket, which for the purposes of this Law shall include the retirement of another batsman.

If he leaves the field or retires for any other reason, he may resume his innings with the consent of the opposing captain.

When a batsman leaving the field is unable to return owing to illness, injury or other unavoidable cause, his innings to be recorded as 'retired, not out'. Otherwise it is to be recored as 'retired, out'.

LAW 3.

THE UMPIRES - Before the toss of the, innings, two umpires shall be appointed, one for each end, to control the game with absolute impartiality as deemed by the Laws.

No umpire be changed during the course of a match without the consent of both the captains.

CLUB XI
BOWLING FIGURES

1st Innings

Bowler	Overs	Maidens	Wkts.	Runs Against
2nd Innings				
Total				

RESULT

	Opposing XI	Club XI
1st Innings		
2nd Innings		
Extras		
Total		

MATCH DETAILS

Ground ______ Date ______

Opposing XI ______ Competition ______

CLUB XI

Batting Order	1st Inn. Runs	How Out	2nd Inn. Runs	How Out
TOTAL				

The umipres shall agree with both captains on any special conditions affecting the match, before the toss of the innings.

The umpires shall satisfy themselves before the start of the match that the wickets are properly pitched.

The umpires shall agree between themselves and inform both the captains before the start of the match on the watch or clock to be followed during the match.

The umpires shall ensure before and during the match that the conduct of the game and the implements used are strictly in accordance with the Laws.

The umpires shall be the sole judges of fair and unfair play.

The umpires shall be the sole judges of the fitness of the ground, weather and light for play.

(a) However, before deciding to suspend play, or not to start or resume play after an interval/ stoppage, the umpires shall establish whether both the captains (the batsmen at the wicket may deputise for their captain) wish to commence in the prevailing conditions: if so, their wishes shall be met.

(b) In addition, if during the play the umpires decide that the light is unfit, only the batting side shall have the option of continuing play. After agreeing to continue in unfit light, the captain of the batting side (or a batsman at the wicket) may appeal against the light for their opinion if the light has deteriorated since the agreement to continue was made.

The umpires may decide to suspend or abandon play in exceptional circumstances, other than those of weather, ground, or light. Before such decision, the umpires shall establish, if the circumstances allow, whether both captains (the batsmen at the wicket may deputise for their captain) wish to continue in the prevailing conditions. If so, their wishes shall be met.

The umpires shall stand from where they can see best any act upon which their decision may be required.

Subject to this over-riding consideration, the umpire at the bowler's end shall stand where he does not interfere with either the bowler's run-up or the striker's view.

The umpire at the striker's end may elect to stand on the off instead of leg side of the pitch, provided he informs the captain of the fielding side and the striker.

The umpires shall change ends after each side has had one innings.

The umpire shall determine all disputes, and if they disagree the actual state of things shall continue.

LAW 4.

THE SCORERS - The scorers appointed for the purpose shall record all the runs. Where there are two scorers they shall frequently check to ensure that the score sheet tally.

All instructions and signals given to the scorers shall be accepted and immediately acknowledged by them.

LAW 5.

THE BALL - The ball shall weigh not less than 5(1/2) ounces /155.9g and not more than 5(3/4) ounces/163g. It shall measure not less than 8(13/16) inches /22.4cm and not more than 9 inches /22.9cm in circumference.

All balls shall be approved by the umpires and the captains before the start of the match.

Either captain may demand a new ball at the start of each innings, subject to agreement to the contrary having been made before the toss.

The captain of the fielding side may demand a new ball after the prescribed number of overs has been bowled with the old one, in a match of three or more days'duration. The governing body of the cricket in the country concerned shall be not less than 75 six-ball overs (55 eight-ball overs).

In the event of a ball during the course of play

being lost or in the opinion of the umpires, becoming unfit for play, the umpires shall allow it to be replaced by one that in their opinion has had a similar amount of wear. If a ball is to be replaced,the umpires shall inform the batsman.

LAW 6.

THE BAT - The overall bat shall not be more than 38 inches /96.5cm in length; the blade of the bat shall be made of wood and shall not exceed 4(1/4)inches/10.8cm at the widest part.

LAW 7.

THE PITCH - The pitch is the area between bowling creases. It shall measure 5ft/ 1.52m in width on either side of a line joining the centre of the middle stumps of the wickets - see Law 8 (The Wickets).

Before the toss for innings, the executive of the ground shall be responsible for the selection and preparation of the pitch; thereafter the umpires shall control its use and maintenance.

The pitch shall not be changed during a match unless it becomes unfit for play, and that too with the consent of both captains.

The following shall apply in the event of non-turf pitch:

(a) Length: That of the playing surface to a minimum of 58ft/17.68m.

(b) Width: That of the playing surface to a minimum of 6ft/1.83m.

See Law 10 (Rolling, Mowing, Watering the Pitch & Re-marking of Creases).

LAW 8.

THE WICKETS - The sets of wickets, of 9 inches/22.86cm wide each, and consisting of three wooden stumps with two wooden bails on the top,shall be pitched opposite & parallel to each other at a distance of 22 yards/20.12m. between the centres of the two middle stumps.

The distance between the stumps shall be sufficient to prevent the ball from passing between them. Their tops shall be 28 inches/71.1cm above the ground,and shall be dome shaped except for the bail grooves.

Each bail shall be 4(3/8)inches/11.1cm in length and when in position on the top of the stumps

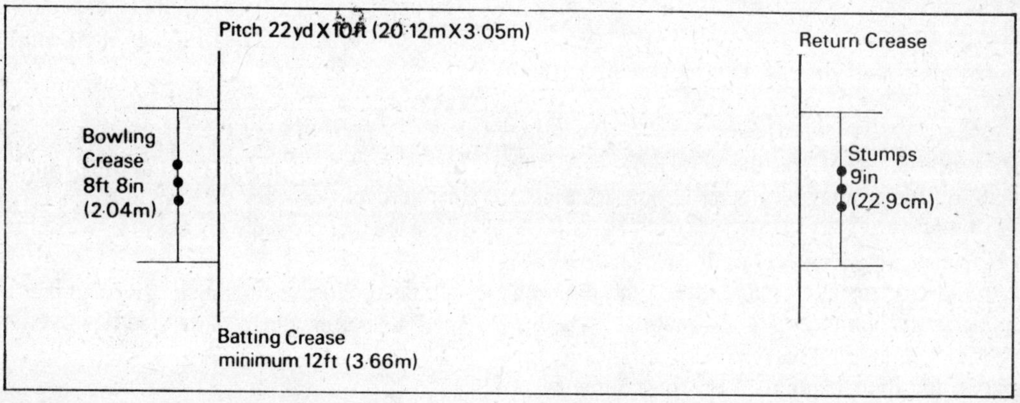

The Pitch

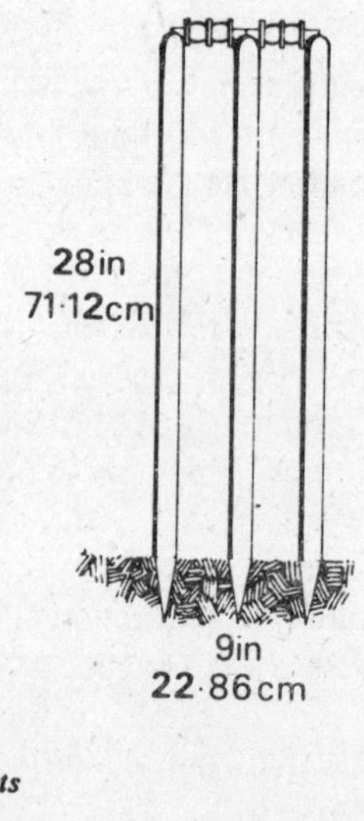

The Wickets

shall not project more than 1/2inch /1.3cm above them.

LAW 9.

***THE BOWLING,POPPING & RETURN* CREASES** - The bowling crease shall be marked in line with the stumps at each end and shall be 8feet 8 inches/2.64m in length, with the stumps in the centre.

The popping crease, i.e.the back edge of the crease marking,shall be in front of the parallel with the bowling crease. It shall have the back edge of the crease marking of 4feet/1.22m from the centre of the stumps and shall extend to a minimum of 6feet/ 1.83m on either side of the line of the wicket. The popping crease shall be considered to be unlimited in length.

The return crease marking of which the inside edge is the crease shall be at each end of the bowling crease and at right angles to it. The return crease shall be marked to a minimum of 4feet /1.22m behind the wicket and shall be considered to be unlimited in length. A forward extension shall be marked to the popping crease.

LAW 10.

ROLLING,SWEEPING,MOWING, WATERING THE PITCH & RE-MARKING OF CREASE - The pitch may be rolled during the match at the request of the captain of the batting side, for not more than seven minutes before the start of each innings, other than the first innings of the match, and before the start of each day's play. If the start is delayed after the toss and before the first innings of the match, the captain of the batting side shall have the right to have the pitch rolled for not more than seven minutes.

The pitch shall not otherwise be rolled during match. The seven minutes' rolling permitted before the start of a day's play shall take place not earlier than half an hour before the start of play. The captain of the batting side may delay such rolling until ten minutes before the start of play, should he so desire.
If an innings is declared closed by a captain in less than fifteen minutes of resumption of play, and the other captain is thereby prevented from exercising his option of seven minutes'rolling or if he is so prevented for any other reason, the time for rolling shall be taken out of the normal playing time.

The necessary sweeping of the pitch during the match shall be done so that the seven minutes allowed for rolling the pitch, provided for in above, is not affected.

(a) Responsibilities of Ground Authority and of Umpires: All mowings which are carried out before the toss for innings shall be the responsibility of the ground authority. Thereafter, they shall be carried out under the supervision of the umpires. See Law 7 (Selection & Preparation). (b) Initial Mowing - The pitch shall be mown before play begins on the day the match is scheduled to start,or in the case of a delayed start on the day the match is expected to start.See 3(a) above (Responsibilities of Ground Authority & of Umpires)- (c) Subsequent Mowing in a Match of Two or More Days'- In a match of two or more days'. duration, the pitch shall be mown daily before play begins.
Should this mowing not take place because of weather conditions, rest day or other reasons the pitch shall be mown on the first day on which the match is resumed. (d) Mowing of the Outfields in Match of Two or More Days' In order to ensure that the conditions are as similar as possible for both sides, the outfield shall normally be mown before the commencement of play on each day of the match, if ground and weather conditions allow. See Note (b) to this Law.

The pitch shall not be watered during a match. Whenever possible, the creases shall be re-marked.

In wet weather, the umpires shall ensure that the holes made by the bowlers and batsmen are cleaned out and dried whenever necessary to facilitate play. In matches of two or more days' duration, the umpires shall allow, if necessary, the returfing of foot-holes made by the bowler in his delivery stride, or the use of quick setting fillings for the same purpose, before the start of each day's play.

During the play, the umpires shall allow the batsman to beat the pitch with bat and to the fielders to secure footholds by using sawdust, provided no damage is caused to the pitch and Law 42 (unfair play) is not contravened.

LAW 11.

COVERING THE PITCH - Complete covering of the pitch shall be allowed before the start of a match.

Pitch shall not be completely covered during a match unless prior arrangement or regulations provide this.

LAW 12.

INNINGS - Not later than fifteen minutes before the time schedule to start the match, the captains shall toss for the choice of innings on the field of play. Or before the time agreed upon for play to start.

The toss winner shall notify his decision to bat or field not later than ten minutes before the time schedule. The decision shall not thereafter be altered.

Each side shall take their innings alternatively in a two innings match except in the case provided in Law 13.

According to an agreement reached before the start of play, a match shall be of one or two innings.

LAW 13.

THE FOLLOW-ON - In case no play takes place on the first day of a match of two or more days', below shall apply in accordance with the number of days' play remaining from the actual start of the match.

In a two innings match the side which leads by 200 runs and bats first in a match of five days or more, by 150 runs in a three day or four day match, by 100 runs in a two day match or by 75 runs in a one day match, shall have the option of requiring the other side to follow their innings.

LAW 14.

DECLARATIONS - Second innings may be forfeited by a captain, provided the decision to do so is notified to the opposing captain and umpires in sufficient time to allow seven minutes rolling of the pitch.

Irrespective of its duration, the captain of the batting side may declare an innings closed at any time during a match.

LAW 15.

START OF PLAY - There shall not be any practice on the pitch atanytime on any day of the match.

The umpire at the bowler's end shall call "play" at the start of each innings and of each day's play, and on the resumption of play after any interval or interruption.

After play has resumed no bowler shall have a trial run-up,except at the fall of a wicket when an umpire may allow such a trial run-up if he is satisfied that it will not cause any waste of time.

LAW 16.

INTERVALS - If an innings ends or there is a stoppage caused by weather or bad light within ten minutes of the agreed time for the lunch or interval, the interval shall be taken immediately.

The time remaining in the session of play shall be added to the agreed length of the interval but no extra allowance shall be made for the ten minute interval between innings.

If an innings is stopped due to weather or bad light within thirty minutes of the agreed time for the tea interval, the interval shall be taken immediately.

The interval shall be of an agreed length and, if possible, shall include the ten minute interval between innings.

The umpires shall allow such intervals as have been agreed upon for meals, and ten minutes between each innings.

If at the agreed time for the tea interval, nine wickets are down, play shall continue for a period not exceeding thirty minutes or until the innings is concluded.

LAW 17.

CESSATION OF PLAY - After the call of

"time", the umpires shall remove the bails from both the wickets.

"Time" call shall be given by the umpire at the bowler's end on the cessation of play before any interval or interruption at the end of each day's play, and at the conclusion of the match. See Law 27 (Appeals).

The last over before an interval or the close of play shall be started, provided the umpire after walking at his normal pace, has arrived at the position behind the stumps at the bowler's end before time has been reached.

Last over before an interval or at the close of play shall be completed unless a batsman is out or retires during that over within two minutes of the interval or the close of play or unless the players have occasion to leave the field.

At the close of play, an over in progress on the final day of a match shall be completed at the request of either captain, even if a wicket falls after time has been reached.

If, during the last over, the players have occasion to leave the field, the umpires shall call "time" and there shall be no resumption of play and the match shall be at an end.

According to the agreed hours of play the umpires shall indicate when one hour of play time of the match remains. The next over after that shall be the first of a minimum of 20 six ball overs, provided a result is not reached earlier or there is no interval or interruption of play.

If, at the commencement of the last hour of the match, there is an interval or interruption of play or if during the last hour,there is an interval between innings or an interruption of play, the minimum number of overs to be bowled on the resumption of play shall be reduced in proportion to the duration within the last hour of the match of any such interval or interruption.

LAW 18.

SCORING - If the striker is caught, no run shall be scored.

If a batsman is run out, the run which was being attempted shall not be scored. If however, an injured striker himself is run out, no runs shall be scored.

The score shall be reckoned by runs . A run is scored:

(a) So often as the batsmen, after a hit or at any time while the ball is in play, shall have crossed ground and made good their from end to end.

(b) When a boundary is scored.

(c) When penalty runs are awarded.

When a batsman is out obstructing a field, any run completed before the obstruction occur shall be scored unless such obstruction prevents a catch being made, in which case no runs shall be scored.

If the ball is in play and the batsmen have crossed in running neither shall return to the wicket he has left, even though a short run has been called or no run has been scored as in the case of a catch. Batsmen, however, shall return to the wickets they originally left in the cases of a boundary and of any disallowance of runs and of an injured batsman being himself, runout.

Under Law 20 (Lost Ball), 24 (No ball),25 (Wide ball), 41.1 (Feilding the Ball) and for boundary allowances under Law 19 (Boundaries), runs shall be scored for penalties.

LAW 19.

BOUNDARIES - The umpires shall agree with both captains on the boundary of the playing area before the toss of innings. The boundary shall be marked by a white line,. a rope laid on the ground, or a fence. If flags or posts only are used to mark a boundary, the imaginary line joining such points shall be regarded as the boundary.

A boundary shall be scored and signalled by the umpire at the bowler's end whenever, in his opinion:

(a) A ball in play touches or crosses the boundary marked.

(b) A fieldsman with ball in hand touches or grounds any part of his person on or over a boundary line.

An overthrow resulting in a boundary or from the wilful act of the fieldsman,any runs already completed and the allowance shall be added to the score. The run in progress shall count provided that the batsman has crossed at the instant of the throw or act.

LAW 20.

LOST BALL - If in a play a ball cannot be found or recovered, any fieldsman may call "lost ball" when 6 runs shall be added to the score; but if more than six have been run before"lost ball" is called, as many runs as have been completed shall be scored. The run in progress shall count provided that the batsmen have crossed at the instant of the call of "lost ball".

The runs shall be added to the score of the striker if the ball has been struck, but otherwise to the score of byes, leg-byes, no balls or wides as the case may be.

LAW 21.

THE RESULT - One innings matches, unless played out as below, shall be decided on the first innings.

If the captains agree to continue the play after completion of one innings of each side in accordance with Law 12 and a result is not achieved on the second, the first innings, result shall stand.

A side which has scored a total of runs in excess of that scored by the opposing side in its two completed innings shall be the winner.

When the scores are equal at the conclusion of play, but only if the side batting last has completed its innings, the result of a match shall be a 'tie'.

LAW 22.

THE OVER - When agreed numbers of balls have been bowled, and as the ball becomes dead or when it becomes clear to the umpire at the bowlers' end that both the fielding side and the batsmen at the wicket have ceased to regard the ball as in play, the umpire shall call "over" before leaving the wicket.

According to agreement before the match, the ball shall be bowled from each wicket alternately in overs of either six or eight balls.

Neither a no-ball nor a wide ball shall be reckoned as one of over.

Miscounting the number of balls by umpire the over as counted by the umpire shall stand.

A bowler shall be allowed to change ends as often as desired, provided only that he does not bowl two overs consecutively in an innings.

The batsman at the bowler's end shall normally stand on the opposite side of the wicket to that from which the ball is being delivered, unless request to do otherwise is granted by the umpire.

In case, a bowler is incapacitated while running up to bowl the first ball of an over, or is incapacitated or suspended during an over, the umpire shall call and signal'dead ball' and another bowler shall be allowed to bowl or complete the over from the same end provided only that he shall not bowl two overs,or part thereof, consecutively in one innings.

LAW 23.

DEAD BALL- When:

(a) A serious injury to a player or umpire occurs.

(b) He intervenes in a case of unfair play.

(c) The bowler drops the ball accidently before the delivery or the ball does not leave his hand.

(d) For an adequate reason, the striker is not ready to receive the ball and makes no attempt to play it.

(e) He leaves his normal position for consultation.

(f) Before the delivery, one or both bails fall from the striker's wicket.

A ball ceases to be dead when the bowler starts his run-up or bowling action.

When the umpire has called "no-ball"or "wide", the ball is not dead.

LAW 24.

NO-BALL - The umpire shall indicate "no-ball"if he is not satisfied that in the delivery stride:

(a) Some part of the front foot whether grounded or raised was behind the popping crease.

(b) The bowler's back foot has landed within and not touching the return crease or its forward extension.

For a delivery to be fair the ball must be bowled and not thrown (see not 'a'above). If either umpire is not entirely satisfied fairness of a delivery in this respect, he shall call and signal "no ball".

The bowler's intention to bowl round the wicket

No - Ball

or over the wicket shall be indicated to the striker by the umpire.

Failure on the part of the bowler to indicate in advance a change in his mode of delivery is unfair and the umpire shall call and signal "no ball".

The Umpire shall.call & signal "no ball", if the bowler, before delivering the ball,throws it at the striker's end in an attempt to run him out.

If a bowler before delivering the ball, throws it at the striker's end in an attempt to run him out.

A no ball may be hit by a striker and runs resulting shall be added to his score. Runs made otherwise from a no-ball shall be scored no-balls.

If the ball does not leave the bowler's hand for any reason the umpire shall revoke the call "no-ball".

In case of a no-ball, a penalty of 1 run shall be scored if no runs are made otherwise.

LAW 25.

WIDE-BALL - If the bowler bowls the ball so wide of the wicket or so high over that in the opinion of the umpire,it passes out of the reach of the striker.

The umpire shall not adjudge a ball as being wide if :

(a) The striker moves and thus brings the ball within his reach.

(b) By moving from his guard position, causes the ball to pass out of his reach.

If in the opinion of the umpire, a ball delivered comes to rest in front of the line of the striker's wicket, "wide" shall not be called. Without interference from the fielding side, a striker has the right to make one attempt to hit the ball. If the fielding side interfere, the umpire shall replace the ball where it came to rest and shall order the fieldsmen to resume the places they occupied in the field before the ball was delivered.
The umpire shall call and signal "dead ball" as soon as it is clear that the striker does not intend to hit the ball, or after the striker has made an unsuc-

cessful attempt to hit the ball.

If a batsman be given out off a wide, the penalty for bowling it shall stand unless runs are otherwise made.

All runs resulting from a wide ball which is not a no ball shall be considered wide balls, or if no runs are made 1 run shall be scored.

If Law 35 (Hit wicket), or Law 39 (Stumped) are surpassed, the striker shall be out from a wide ball. Either batsman shall be run out if he breaks Law 33 (Handled the ball) or Law 37 (Obstructing the Field).

The umpire shall revoke the call if the striker hits a ball which has been called "wide".

A penalty of 1 run for a wide shall be scored if no runs are made otherwise.

LAW 26.

BYE AND LEG BYE **-** If a ball not called "wide" or "no ball", is unintentionally deflected by the striker's dress or person, except a hand holding the bat, and any runs are obtained, the umpire shall signal "leg-bye" and the run or runs so scored shall be credited as such to the batting side.

Such leg-byes shall be scored only if the striker has :

(a) Attempted to play the ball with his bat.

(b) Tried to avoid being hit by the ball.

If a ball that has not been called "wide" or "no ball" passes the striker without touching his bat or person, and any runs are scored, the umpire shall signal"bye" and the run or runs shall be credited as such to the batting side.

If a deflection by the striker's person results, other than in
(a) above & (b) above, the umpire shall call and signal "dead ball" as soon as 1 run has been completed or when it is clear that a run is not being attempted, or the ball has reached the boundary. On the call and signal of "dead ball" the batsmen shall return to their original ends and no runs shall be allowed.

LAW 27.

APPEALS **-** Unless appealed by the other side which shall be done prior to the bowler beginning his run-up or bowling action to deliver the next ball, the umpires shall not give a batsman out. Under Law 23 (e) the ball becomes dead, the ball is dead on "over" being called; this does not, however, invalidate an appeal made prior to the first ball of the following over provided "time" has not been called - see Law 17 (Call of Time). The umpire's decision is final. He may alter his decision, provided that such alteration is made promptly.

The umpire shall intervene if satisfied that a batsman has left his wicket under a misapprehension that he has been dismissed but having not been given out.

The captain of the fielding side shall seek permission (in exceptional cases) of the umpire to withdraw an appeal provided the outgoing batsman has not left the playing area. If this is allowed, the umpire shall cancel his decision.

An umpire may consult another umpire on a point of fact which the latter may have been in a better position to judge and shall then give his decision. If, after consultation there is still doubt remaining the decision shall be in favour of the batsman.

LAW 28.

THE WICKET IS DOWN **-** If it has been agreed to dispense with the bails in accordance with Law 8 (a) Dispensing with Bails, owing to the strength of the wind, the decision as to when the wicket is down is one for the umpire to decide on the facts before them. In such circumstances and if the umpires so decide, the wicket shall be held to be down even though a stump has not been struck out of the ground.

It shall be sufficient for the purpose of putting the wicket down to remove the remaining bail, if one bail is off, or to strike or pull any of the three stumps out of the ground in many of the ways.

If all stumps are out of the ground, the fielding side shall be allowed to put back one or more stumps in order to have an opportunity to putting the wicket down.

LAW 29.

BATSMAN OUT OF HIS GROUND - Unless some part of his bat in his hand or of his person is grounded behind the line of the popping crease the batsman shall be considered to be out of his ground.

LAW 30.

BOWLED - The striker shall be out 'Bowled' if:

(a) He breaks his wicket by hitting or kicking the ball on to it before the completion of a stroke, or as a result of attempting to guard his wicket.

(b) His wicket is bowled down, even if the ball first touches his bat or person.

LAW 31.

TIMED OUT - If a batsman wilfully takes more than two minutes to come in, he shall be out 'Time out'- the two minutes being timed from the moment a wicket falls until the new batsman steps on the field of play.

The time taken by the umpires to investigate the cause of the delay shall be added at the normal close of play.

LAW 32.

CAUGHT - The striker shall be caught out if the ball touches his bat or if it touches below the wrist of his hand or glove, holding the bat, and is subsequently held by a fieldsman before it touches the ground.

LAW 33.

HANDLED THE BALL- Either of the batsman shall be out 'Handled the Ball'on appeal, if he wilfully touches the ball while in play with the hand not holding the bat unless he does so with the consent of the opposite side.

LAW 34.

HIT THE BALL TWICE - If, after the ball is struck or is stopped by any part of his person, he wilfully strikes it again with his bat or person except for the sole purpose of guarding his wicket, the striker on appeal, shall be out ' Hit the Ball Twice' this he may do with his bat or any part of his person other than his hands, but see Law 37. For the purpose of this law, a hand holding the bat shall be regarded as part of the bat.

No runs except those resulting from an overthrow or penalty-see Law 41 - shall be scored from a ball lawfully struck twice.

Under this law the striker shall be out if, without the consent of the opposite side, he uses his bat or person to return the ball to any of the fielding side.

LAW 35.

HIT WICKET - The striker shall be out "Hit Wicket" if,

Hit Wicket

(a) He hits down his wicket lawfully making a second stroke for the purpose of guarding his wicket within the provisions of Law 34 (Out Hit the Ball Twice).

(b) With any part of his person, dress, or equipment as a result of any action taken by him in preparing to receive a delivery, or in setting off for his first run, immediately after playing, or playing at the ball, his wicket is broken.

LAW 36.

LEG BEFORE WICKET- The striker shall be out LBW in the circumstance set below:

(a) Striker attempting to Play the Ball.

The striker shall be out LBW if he first intercepts with any part of his person, dress or equipment, a fair ball which would have hit the wicket and which has not previously touched his bat or a hand holding the bat, provided :

(i) The point of impact is in a straight line between wicket and wicket, even if above the level of bails.

(ii) The ball pitched in a straight line between wicket and wicket or on the off side of the striker's wicket, or in the case of a ball intercepted full pitch would have pitched in a straight line between wicket and wicket.

(b) Striker Making No Attempt to play the Ball.
The striker shall be given out LBW if the ball is intercepted outside the line of the off stump if, in the opinion of the umpire, he has made no genuine attempt to play the ball with his bat, but has intercepted the ball and if the circumstances set out in (a) above apply.

LAW 37.

RUN OUT - On appeal, either batsman shall be given out obstructing the field if he wilfully obstructs the opposite side by work or action.

On appeal, the striker shall be given out should he wilfully obstructs a fielder and prevent a catch being made.

This shall apply even though the striker causes the obstruction in lawfully guarding his wicket under the provisions of Law 34. See Law 34 (Out Hit the Ball Twice).

LAW 38.

RUN OUT - Either batsman shall be given out "Run Out" if during running of at any time while the ball is in play-except in the case of Law 39 (Stumped)- he is out of his ground and his wicket is put down by the opposite side. If, however, a batsman in running make good his ground he shall not be out run out if he subsequently leaves

GOWER Run Out

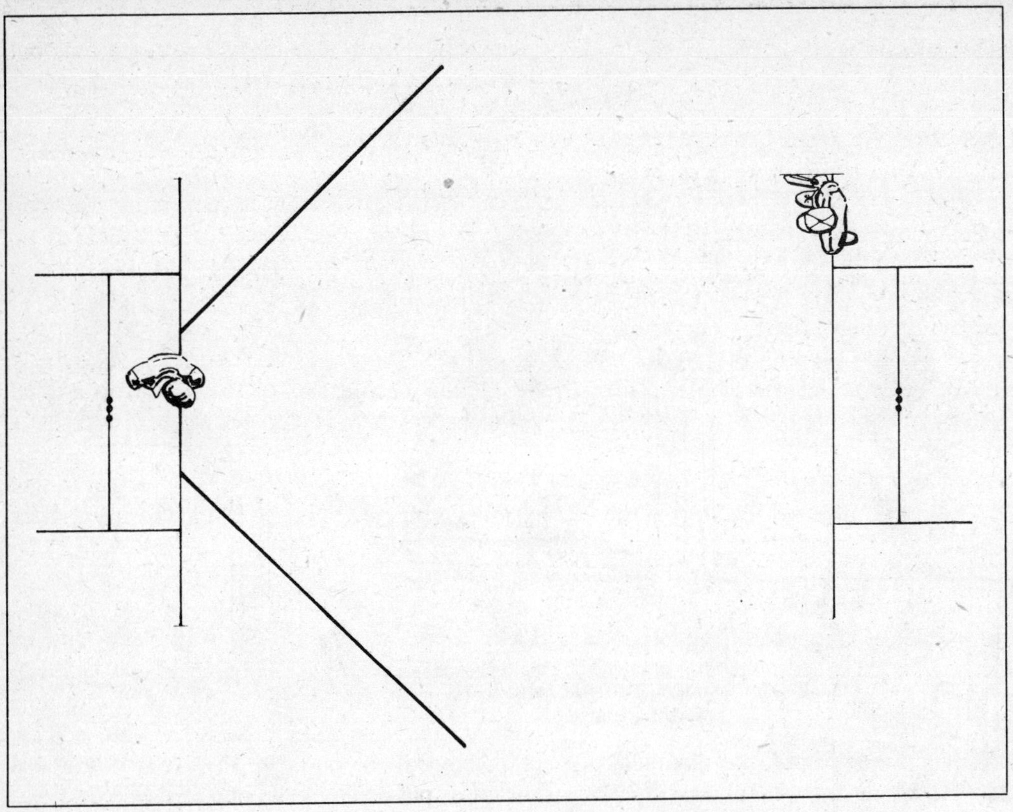

Calling and running . The striking batsman decides if runs are possible only for balls travelling in his line of vision.

his ground, in order to avoid injury, and the wicket is put down.

In the event of a batsman being run out only that run which is being attempted shall not be scored if, however, an injured striker himself is run out, no runs shall be scored. See Law 27 (Transgression of the Laws by an Injured Batsman or Runner).

He who runs for the wicket which is put down shall be out, if the batsmen have crossed in running. If they have not crossed, he who has left the wicket which is put down shall be out. If a batsman remains in his ground or returns to his ground and the other batsman joins him there, the latter shall be out if his wicket is put down.

LAW 39.

STUMPED - If in receiving the ball, not being a no-ball, he is out of his ground otherwise than in attempting a run and the wicket is put down by the wicket-keeper without the inter-

Stumped

TAKING ON THE LEG SIDE

There are two methods. As you'll see, the difference lies in the footwork.

In the first method the keeper adopts a sideways scissors movement with the weight on the right foot.

The left foot takes another step but the weight is kept on the right foot.

The weight is transferred to the inside leg. The ball is taken to the stumps by the right hand.

In the second method the movement is again sideways, but this time the right foot crosses behind the left foot as it moves across.

The left foot takes another step and the ball is taken outside the left leg.

The right hand takes the ball to the stumps.

vention of another fieldsman the striker shall be out stumped.

LAW 40.

THE WICKET-KEEPER - The Wicket-keeper shall remain wholly behind the wicket until a ball delivered by the bowler touches the bat or person of the striker, or passes the wicket, or until the striker attempts a run.

In the event of the wicket-keeper contravening this Law, the umpire at the striker's end shall call and signal "no-ball" at the instant of delivery or as soon as possible thereafter.

In case the wicket-keeper interferes with the striker's right to play the ball and to guard his wicket, the striker shall not be out except under Laws 33 (Handled the Ball), Law 34 (Hit the Ball Twice), Law 37 (Run Out).

LAW 41.

THE FIELDSMAN - Not more than two fieldsmen shall be behind the popping crease at the instant of the bowler's delivery. In the event of infringement by the fielding side, the umpire at the striker's end shall call and signal "no ball".

A fieldsman is entitled to stop the ball with any part of his person, but if he intentionally stops it otherwise,5 runs will be added to the run or runs already scored. If no runs have been scored, 5 penalty runs shall be awarded. The run in progress shall count provided that the batsmen have crossed at the act. If the ball has been struck, the penalty shall be added to the score of the striker, else to the score of byes, leg-byes, no-balls or wides as the case may be.

LAW 42.

UNFAIR PLAY - The captains are responsible at all times for ensuring that play is conducted within the spirit of the game as well as within the Laws. The umpires are the sole judges of fair and unfair play.

(This is easily the most important and far-reaching Law, concerning, as it does, the spirit in which the game is played and involving such difficult and often hard to assess subjects as lifting the seam of the ball, polishing the ball with an artificial substance, obstruction of the batsman in running, excessive bowling of short-pitched balls, time wasting, bowlers following through on to the and the players' general conduct. Where possible, the Laws include notes which provide guidelines to umpires.)

LAWSON GEOFFREY FRANCIS

Australia (born 1957) - A tall, silm, right-arm medium-fast bowler and hard-hitting batsman. He played for New South Wales and Lancashire. In his first class career he made, 1,869 runs and took 423 wickets.

Test Record - 38 Tests, 756 runs (Av. 15.12), 148 wickets (Av. 30.52) and 8 catches.

LEADBERATER EDRIC

England (born 1927) - A right-arm leg-break

1	wicketkeeper	15	long off
2	first slip	16	fine leg
3	second slip	17	short leg
4	third slip	18	short square leg
5	fourth slip	19	silly mid-on
6	gully	20	square leg
7	third man	21	deep square leg
8	silly point	22	deep fine leg
9	point	23	mid-wicket
10	cover point	24	mid-on
11	extra cover	25	long-on
12	deep extra cover	26	short square leg
13	silly mid-off	27	mid-fine leg
14	mid-off	28	the umpires

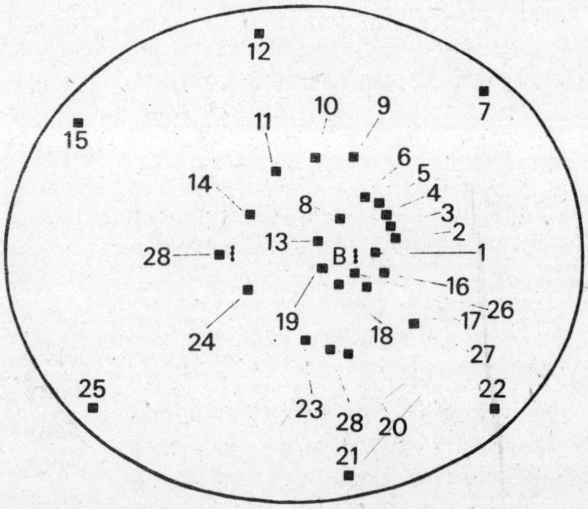

Field Placements

bowler and also a very useful batsman. He played for Yorkshire and Warwickshire. In his first class career he made, 1,548 runs including 1 century and took 289 wickets.
Test Record - 2 Tests, 40 runs (Av. 20.00), 2 wickets (Av. 109.00) and 3 catches.

LEDING ARM
The bowler's non bowling arm.

LEE PHILIP KEITH
Australia (1904-1980) - He was a right-arm off-spin bowler. He played for South Australia. In his first class career he made, 1,669 runs including 2 centuries and took 152 wickets.
Test Record - 2 Tests, 57 runs (Av. 19.00), 5 wickets (Av. 42.40) and 1 catch.

LEES WALTER SCOTT
England (1875-1924) - He was right-arm medium-pace bowler and also a useful batsman. He played for Surrey. In his first class career he made, 7,642 runs including 2 centuries and took 1,402 wickets.
Test Record - 5 Tests, 66 runs (Av. 11.00), 26 wickets (Av. 17.96) and 2 catches.

LEES WARREN KENNETH
New Zealand (born 1952) - He was a wicket-keeper and a right-handed batsman. He played for Otago. In his first class career he made, 4,435 runs including 4 centuries, took 2 wickets and 306 dismissals.
Test Reocrd - 21 Tests, 778 runs (Av. 23.57) including 1 century, and 59 dismissals (52ct, 7st).

LEG
That half of the field divided by the continuous line from centre stump that is behind the batsman when he takes his stance.

LEG BEFORE WICKET
(Usually abbreviated to 'l.b.w.') when a ball which has pitched on the line of the stumps, or outside the line of the off stump (i.e. the stump furthest from the batsman - the others are 'middle' and 'leg'), and without contact with the bat, would, in the opinion of the umpire, have hit the wicket had it not been stopped - voluntarily or involuntarily, the point of contact being between wicket and wicket by any part of the batsman's body or clothing except his hand (holding the bat). If he deliberately pads away a ball outside the off stump, even though the contact is made outside the line of the stumps, it is out (provided, as always, that the ball would have hit the wicket).

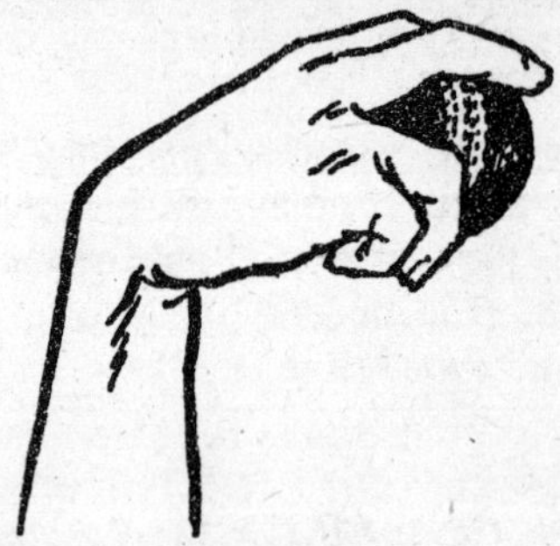

Grip for the Leg Break

LEG BREAK
A delivery form a pace bowler that deviates from leg to off upon landing on the wickets. (See also CUTTERS).

LEG-BYE
A run that is scored when the ball is deflected off any part of the batsman's body except his hands allowing the batsmen to exchange places. A run cannot be scored if the batsman deliberately kicks the ball away.

Grip for the Leg Cutter

LEG-CUTTER
Similar to the inswinger, but with the second finger wedged alongside the seam which points in the same direction as the inswinger. Everything

must be just right at the instant of delivery when the second finger pulls the seam down in an anti-clockwise direction. The thumb helps by twisting the ball as it is released. Like the inswinger, the bowler has the feeling of pushing the ball down the leg-side. In fact, the bowler should look to pitch the leg-cutter on or just outside the off-stump.

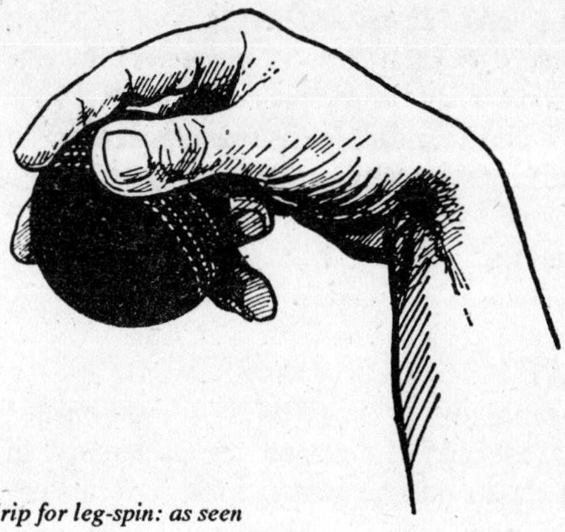

Grip for leg-spin: as seen by batsman

Leg glance off the back foot

Grip for leg-spin: as seen from behind the bowler

LEG GLANCE
In batting, to deflect the ball off the angled face of the bat away behind square leg.

LEG GUARD
Padded covering worn by batsmen to protect their legs.

LEG SIDE
Anything on the leg side of the field. Also, a batsman who scores strongly on that side of the wicket is known as a 'leg-side' player.

LEG SLIP
A fielding position just behind and to the leg side of the wicketkeeper comparable to the slip position on the off side.

LEG-SPIN
The ball is spun off the inside of the top joint of the third finger. You should forward, and keep the leverage same as in turning a door knob from right to left. The palm of your hand must be kept facing the batsman as long as possible, if turned over too soon, top spin or googly and not leg spin will result. These can be more valuable variants to leg spin. In bowling leg spin, you keep your arm as straight as you can. A bent arm makes accuracy of length and direction much more difficult.

LEG THEORY
See BODYLINE.

LEG TRAP
A bowling attack set on the legs of a batsman with a strong catching cordon in front of and behind square leg.

LEGALL RALPH ARCHIBALD

West Indies (born 1926) - A competent wicket-keeper and a right-handed batsman. He played for Barbados and Trinidad. In his first class career he made, 485 runs and 42 dismissals.

Test Record - 4 Tests, 50 runs (Av. 10.00) and 9 dismissals (8ct, 1st).

LEGGAT JOHN GORDON

New Zealand (1926-1973) - A right-handed opening batsman. He played for Canterbury. In his first class career he made, 3,550 runs including 7 centuries.

Test Record - 9 Tests, 351 runs (Av. 21.93).

LEGGE GEOFFREY BEVINGTON

England (1903-1940) - He was a right-handed batsman. He played for Oxford University and Kent. In his first class career he made, 4,955 runs including 7 centuries, took 8 wickets and 118 catches.

Test Record - 5 Tests, 299 runs (Av. 49.83) including 1 century and 1 catch.

LEICESTERSHIRE

Present club formed: 1879.

Badge: A running fox, coloured gold, on a green background.

Colours: Scarlet and dark green.

County Ground: Grace Road, Leicester, LE2 8 AD.

Honours:County Champions - 1975

John Player League Champions - 1974,1977

Benson & Hedges Cup-winners - 1972,1975

LENGTH

The distance between the stumps and the place where the ball lands when bowled by the bowler.

LESLIE CHARLES FREDERICK HENRY

England (1861-1921) - A right-handed batsman and an all-rounder. He played for Oxford University, Middlesex and Shropshire. In his first class career he made, 1,860 runs including 4 centuries, and took 8 wickets.

Test Record - 4 Tests, 106 runs (Av. 15.14), 4 wickets (Av. 11.00) and 1 catch.

LEVER JOHN KENNETH

England (born 1949) - A fast-medium left-arm bowler and brilliant outfielder. He played for Essex and Natal. In his first class career he made, 3,411 runs, and took 1633 wickets.

Test Record - 21 Tests, 306 runs (Av.11.76), 73 wickets (Av.62.73) and 11 catches.

PETER LEVER

LEVER PETER

England (born 1940) - A right-arm medium-fast bowler and a right-handed batsman. He played for Lancashire and Tasmania. In his first class career he made, 3,554 runs, took 786 wickets and 106 catches.

Test Record - 17 Tests, 350 runs (Av. 21.87), 41 wickets (Av. 36.80) and 11 catches.

LEVESON GOWER

England (1873-1954) - He was a right-handed batsman and revelled in the cut and as a slow-medium-pace bowler. He played for Oxford University and Surrey. In his first class career he made, 7,638 runs including 4 centuries, and took 46 wickets.

DENNIS LILLEE

Test Record - 3 Tests, 95 runs (Av. 23.75) and 1 catch.

LEWIS ANTHONY ROBERT

England (born 1938) - He was a right-handed batsman and an occasional leg-break bowler. He played for Cambridge University and Glamorgan. In his first class career he made, 20,495 runs including 30 centuries and took 6 wickets.

Test Record - 9 Tests, 457 runs (Av. 32.64) including 1 century.

LEWIS DESMOND MICHAEL

West Indies (born 1946) - A right-handed batsman and wicket-keeper of high potential. He played for Jamaica. In his first class career he made, 1,623 runs and 78 dismissals.

Test Record - 3 Tests, 259 runs (Av. 86.33) and 8 dismissals (8ct).

LEYLAND MORRIS

England (1900-1967) - He was a left-handed batsman and also a right-arm spin bowler. He

played for Yorkshire. In his first class career he made, 33,660 runs including 80 centuries, and took 466 wickets.
Test Record - 41 Tests, 2,764 runs (Av. 46.06) including 9 centuries, 6 wickets (Av. 97.50) and 13 catches.

LIAQAT ALI KHAN
Pakistan (born 1955) - A left-arm medium-pace seam bowler. He played for Karachi, Habib Bank and Sind. In his first class career he made, 708 runs, took 468 wickets.
Test Record - 5 Tests, 28 runs (Av. 7.00), 6 wickets (Av. 59.83) and 1 catch.

LIGHT
The degree of visibility affecting the fitness of conditions for play to continue without the batsman being too inconvenienced.See action on the laws.

LILLEE DENNIS KEITH
Australia (born 1949) - A glorious action was at the heart of his success. He was a right-arm medium-fast bowler and a useful tailend right-handed batsman who played very straight. He had always courted controversy, but he was unquestionably one of the greatest bowlers in Test history. He played for Western Australia. In his first class career he made, 2,220 runs and took 845 wickets.
Test Record - 70 Tests, 905 runs (Av. 13.71), 355 wickets (Av. 23.92) and 23 catches.

LILLEY ARTHUR FREDERICK AUGUSTUS
England (1866-1929) - He was a wicket-keeper and a right-handed batsman. He played for Warwickshire. In his first class career he made, 15,597 runs including 16 centuries, 41 wickets and 899 dismissals.
Test Record - 35 Tests, 903 runs (Av. 20.52) and 92 dismissals (70ct, 22st).

LILLYWHITE JAMES JUNIOR
England (1842-1929) - A left-arm slow bowler with a high and exceptionally accurate delivery. He was also a left-handed batsman. He played for Sussex. In his first class career he made, 3,643 runs and took 1,140 wickets.
Test Record - 2 Tests, 16 runs (Av. 8.00), 8 wickets (Av. 15.75) and 1 catch.

LINDSAY DENIS THOMSON
South Africa (born 1939) - A brilliant wicket-keeper and a right-handed attacking stroke-player. He played for North-Eastern Transvaal and Transvaal. In his first class career he made, 7,174 runs including 12 centuries, and 334 dismissals.
Test Record - 19 Tests, 1,130 runs (Av. 37.66) including 3 centuries, and 59 dismissals (57ct, 2st).

LINDSAY JOHN DIXON
South Africa (born 1909) - A brilliant wicket-keeper. He played for North-Eastern Transvaal and Transvaal. In his first class career he made, 346 runs and 55 dismissals.
Test Record - 3 Tests, 21 runs (Av. 7.00), and 5 dismissals (4ct, 1st).

LINDWALL RAYMOND RUSSELL
Australia (born 1921) - He was a right-arm swing bowler. He had a genuine pace, a great variety of swing and speed and good control. He played for New South Wales. In his first class career he made, 5,042 runs including 5 centuries, took 794 wickets and 123 catches.
Test Record - 61 Tests, 1,502 runs (Av. 21.15) including 2 centuries, 228 wickets (Av. 23.03) and 26 catches.

LING WILLIAM VICTOR STONE
South Africa (1891-1960) - A right-arm googly bowler and a very useful batsman. He played for Griqualand West. In his first class career he made, 2,618 runs including 3 centuries and took 72 wickets.
Test Record - 6 Tests, 168 runs (Av. 16.80) and 1 catch.

LISSETTE ALAN FISHER
New Zealand (1919-1973) - He was a left-arm

slow bowler. He played for Waikato, Auckland and Northern Districts. In his first class career he made, 476 runs and took 116 wickets.
Test Record - 2 Tests, 2 runs (Av. 1.00), 3 wickets (Av. 41.33) and 1 catch.

LLEWELLYN CHARLES BENNETT
South Africa (1876-1964) - He was a left-handed forcing batsman, a left-arm slow to medium-paced bowler and a fine fielder. He played for Natal and Hampshire. In his first class career he made, 11,425 runs including 18 centuries, took 1,013 wickets and 200 catches.
Test Record - 15 Tests, 544 runs (Av. 20.14), 48 wickets (Av. 29.60) and 7 catches.

LLOYD CLIVE HUBERT
West Indies (born 1944) - A tall and commanding left-handed batsman and useful right-arm medium-paced bowler. His action, however, signified the importance of Lloyd's calm captaincy. Although he had a relatively simple task in the field, manipulating a succession of fit, hostile and accurate fast bowlers, he pointed to the results when criticised for the tactical use of slow over-rates and frequent bouncers. He played for Guyana and Lancashire. In his first class career he made, 31,232 runs including 79 centuries, took 114 wickets and 377 catches.
Test Record - 110 Tests, 7,515 runs (Av. 46.67) including 19 centuries, 10 wickets (Av. 62.20) and 90 catches.

CLIVE LLOYD

LLOYD DAVID
England (born 1947) - He was an under-used, slow, left-arm orthodox spinner, a brilliant close fielder and a left-handed batsman. He played for Lancashire and Cumberland. In his first class career he made, 19,269 runs including 38 centuries, took 237 wickets and 334 catches.
Test Record - 9 Tests, 552 runs (Av. 42.46) including 1 century and 11 catches.

LOCK GRAHAM ANTHONY RICHARD
England (born 1929) - He was an orthodox slow left-arm spinner possessed of aggression seldom found in the fastest of bowlers. He played for Surrey, Leicestershire and Western Australia. In his first class career he made, 10,342 runs, took 2,844 wickets and 830 catches.
Test Record - 49 Tests, 742 runs (Av. 13.74), 174 wickets (Av. 25.58) and 59 catches.

LOCKWOOD WILLIAM HENRY
England (1868-1932) - A right-handed batsman and a great bowler. He played for Nottinghamshire and Surrey. In his first class career he made, 10,673 runs including 15 centuries and took 1,376 wickets.
Test Record - 12 Tests, 231 runs (Av. 17.76), 43 wickets (*Av*. 20.55) and 4 catches.

LOFT
Hit a ball high in the air.

LOFTED
A ball hit high in the air, usually clearing the infield.

LOGIE AUGUSTINE LAWRENCE
West Indies (born 1960) - A right-handed batsman. He played for Trinidad. In his first class career he made, 3,516 runs including 9 centuries and took 3 wickets.
Test Record - 37 Tests, 1,707 runs (Av. 34.14) including 2 centuries and 41 catches.

LOGIE

LOHMANN GEORGE ALFRED
England (1865-1901) - He was a right-handed quick-footed, match winning batsman, a useful fielder and a graceful medium pace bowler. He played for Surrey and Western Province. In his first class career he made, 7,247 runs including 3 centuries, took 1,841 wickets, and 336 catches.
Test Record - 18 Tests, 213 runs (Av. 8.87), 112 wickets (Av. 10.75) and 28 catches.

LOLLY
A simple catch.

LONG HANDLE
An aggressive style of batting, when batsman playing attacking strokes to grip the bat closer to the top of the handle.

LONG HOP
A short-pitched delivery, usually from a slow or slow-medium paced bowler, that can be easily despatched with a cross-bat stroke to either side of the wicket.

LONG LEG
A fielding position deep on the leg side behind the striker's wicket.

LONG-OFF and LONG-ON
It has already been stated that third man often fields in the deep for alternative overs, so his ability to run, pick up and throw will come in very useful. But, whereas third man does not often have the chance of making catches, long-off and long-on must be able to judge high catches perfectly. A slow bowler especially depends on the deep fielders to accept all the chances given them, particularly when he has persevered for a long time to persuade a batsman to risk a high drive. Judging distance so as to be right under the ball as it falls is therefore a key qualification for a deep field; and in that connection, he must resist the natural tendency to run in immediately to meet any high ball which is hit in his direction.
Those, are the main differences between some of the common-to all positions on the cricket field. Yet by far the best method of teaching yourself fielding is not by theory but by practice. Try to field for some time in as many different positions as possible before you make up your mind as to which particular place you prefer and then go and watch an expert. Whenever your captain tells you to stand, see that you remain there; nothing is more irritating to a captain or a bowler than to find his fielders constantly wandering from the position in which he placed them. Above all, show keeness and enthusiasm; the amount of fun

and enjoyment you will obtain from fielding is proportional to the amount of eagerness and zest you put into it.

LONG STOP

Old-fashioned field placing behind the wicketkeeper and close to the boundary. Still used sometimes in junior competition when the wicketkeeper is not very capable.

LORD'S

When Lord's staged its first Test in 1884, the ground, the third found by Thomas Lord for members of the Marylebone Cricket Club, had already been open for 70 years. MCC had bought the freehold-belatedly - in 1866. Though rebuilding has been and will continue to be necessary, the most famous cricket ground in the world has retained its sense of grandeur and remains a superb place to watch cricket. The ground is the headquarters not only of MCC but also of Middlesex, who play most of their home matches here. The Test and County Cricket Board and the National Cricket Association have offices there and, as the secretariat of MCC is also that of the International Cricket Council (I.C.C.), many decisions affecting the whole cricket are taken in the Committee Room where the annual ICC meeting takes place. Concern about the wear and tear on a square little over held as fixtures since the Second World War. Many school and services matches are now played elsewhere, though Oxford and Cambridge, who first played at Lord's in 1827, still meet there, as do Eton and Harrow who met on the original Lord's ground in 1805.

LOST BALL

If the ball is lost, it may be replaced by a ball of similar wear.

LOWSON FRANK ANDERSON

England (1925-1984) - A right-handed batsman. He played for Yorkshire. In his first class career he made, 15,321 runs including 31 centuries, and 191 catches.

Test Record - 7 Tests, 245 runs (Av. 18.84) and 5 catches.

LOXTON SAMUEL JOHN EVERETT

Australia (born 1921) - He was a right-handed batsman and a useful right-arm medium-fast bowler. He played for Victoria. In his first class career he made, 6,249 runs including 13 centuries, and took 232 wickets.

Test Record - 12 Tests, 554 runs (Av. 36.93) including 1 century, 8 wickets (Av. 43.62) and 7 catches.

LUCAS ALFRED PERRY

England (1857-1923) - A classic and defensive batsman. He played for Cambridge University and Middlesex. In his first class career he made, 10,263 runs including 8 centuries and took 155 wickets.

Test Record - 5 Tests, 157 runs (Av. 19.62) and 1 catch.

LUCKHURST BRIAN WILLIAM

England (born 1939) - He was a right-handed opening batsman. He played for Kent. In his first class career he made, 22,313 runs including 49 centuries, took 64 wickets and 391 catches.

Test Record - 21 Tests, 1,298 runs (Av. 36.05) including 4 centuries and 14 catches.

LUNCH INTERVALS

The break in play after the first session when players, umpires and spectators can have lunch.

LYONS JOHN JAMES

Australia (1863-1927) - He was a hard-hitting right-handed opening batsman and also right-arm spin bowler. He played for South Australia. In his first class career he made, 6,792 runs including 11 centuries and 107 catches.

Test Record - 14 Tests, 731 runs (Av. 27.07) including 1 century, 6 wickets (Av. 24.83) and 3 catches.

LYTTELTON RT HON. ALFRED

England (1857-1913) - A right-handed batsman, front-foot batsman in the classical mould and a useful wicket-keeper. He played for Cambridge University and Middlesex. In his first class career he made, 4,434 runs including 7 centuries and 206

dismissals.
Test Record - 4 Tests, 94 runs (Av. 15.66), 4 wickets (Av. 4.75) and 2 dismissals (2ct).

M

MACARTNEY CHARLES GEORGE

Australia (1886-1958) - A great right-handed batsman, a brilliant improviser and an excellent fielder with few equals at mid-off. He played for New South Wales and Otago. In his first class career he made, 15,019 runs including 49 centuries, took 419 wickets and 102 catches.

Test Record - 35 Tests, 2,131 runs (Av. 41.78) including 7 centuries, 45 wickets (Av. 27.55) and 17 catches.

MACAULAY GEORGE GINBSON

Englnd (1897-1940) - A right-arm bowler. He played for Yorkshire. In his first class career he made, 6,212 runs including 3 centuries, took 1,837 wickets and 348 catches.

Test Record - 8 Tests, 112 runs (Av. 18.66), 24 wickets (Av. 27.58) and 5 catches.

MACGIBBON ANTHONY ROY

New Zealand (born 1924) - A right-arm medium-fast bowler with a longish run. He was also a useful late-order batsman and a superb silp fielder. He played for Canterbury. In his first class career he made, 3.611 runs and took 352 wickets.

Test Record - 26 Tests, 814 runs (Av. 19.85), 70 wickets (Av. 30.85) and 13 catches.

MACGREGOR GREGOR

England (1869-1919) - A useful wicket-keeper. He played for Cambridge University and Middlesex. In his first class career he made, 6,381 runs including 3 centuries and 560 dismissals.

Test Record - 8 Tests, 96 runs (Av. 12.00) and 17 dismissals (14ct, 3st).

MACKAY KENNETH DONALD

Australia (1925-1982) - A left-handed batsman and also a useful right-arm medium-pace bowler with a strange, almost furtive approach to the wicket. He played for Queensland. In his first class career he made, 10,823 runs including 23 centuries and took 251 wickets.

Test Record - 37 Tests, 1,507 runs (Av. 33.48), 50 wickets (Av. 34.42) and 16 catches.

MACLAREN ARCHIBALD CAMPBELL

England (1871-1944) - A right-handed batsman, his particular glory being the off-drive and straight drive. He played for Lancashire. In his first class career he made, 22,022 runs including 47 centuries and 411 catches.

Test Record - 35 Tests, 1,931 runs (Av. 33.87) including 5 centuries, and 29 catches.

MACLEAN JOHN ALEXANDER

Australia (born 1946) - A right-handed batsman, particularly good cutter, and a surprisingly agile wicket-keeper. He played for Queensland. In his first class career he made, 3,888 runs including 2 centuries and 385 dismissals.

Test Record - 4 Tests, 79 runs (Av. 11.28) and 18 dismissals (18ct).

MADAN LAL UDHOURAM SHARMA

India (born 1951) - A right-handed batsman and a right-arm medium-fast bowler. Test debut on June 6, 1974 against England at the age of 23 years and 76 days. Scores on Test debut were 2 and 7 in the first Test at Manchester. Last Test of the career played against Australia in December 1977. Scores on last appearance in Test were 43 and 3 in the second Test at Perth. Age at the time of retirement from Test cricket was 26 years and 271 days. He played for Delhi and Punjab. In his first class career he made, 9,373 runs including 20 centuries, took 556 wickets and 127 catches.

Test Record - 39 Tests, 1,042 runs (Av. 22.65), 71 wickets (Av. 40.08) and 15 catches.

MADDOCKS LEONARD VICTOR

Australia (born 1926) - A very useful right-handed batsman and a very competent wicket-keeper. He played for Victoria and Tasmania. In his first class career he made, 4,106 runs including 6 centuries, and 277 dismissals.

Test Record - 7 Tests, 177 runs (Av. 17.70) and 19 dismissals (18ct, 1st).

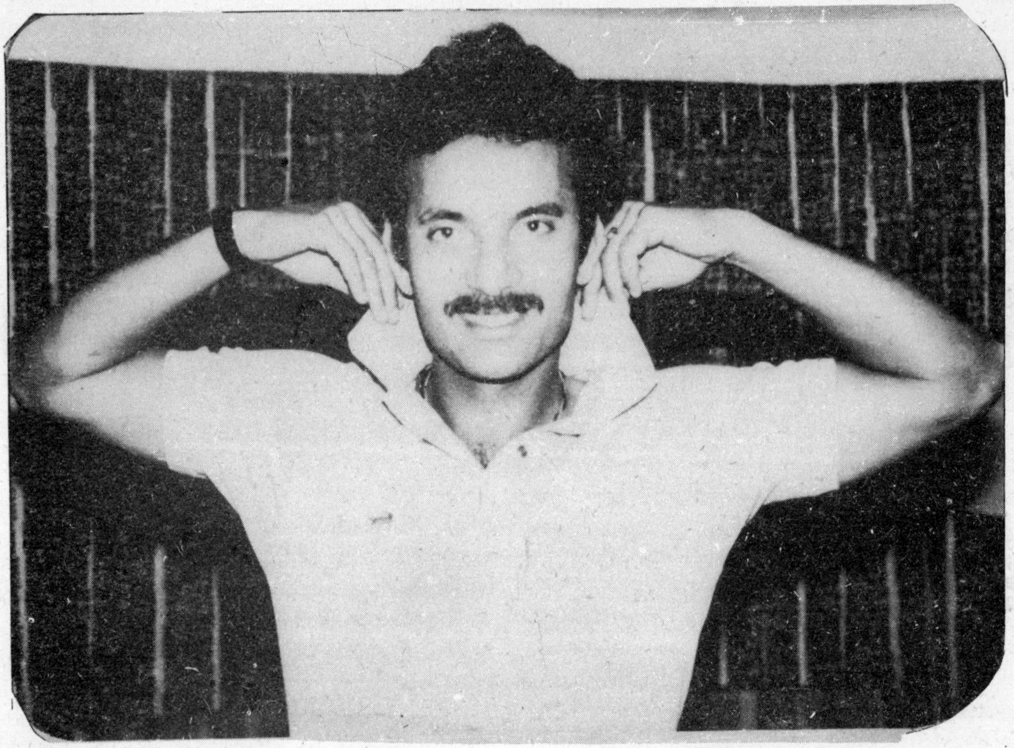

MADAN LAL

MADRAY IVAN SAMUEL

West Indies (born 1934) - A useful all-rounder, a right-handed batsman and a leg-break bowler. He played for British Guiana. In his first class career he made, 73 runs and took 16 wickets.

Test Record - 2 Tests, 3 runs (Av. 1.00) and 2 catches.

MADUGALLE RANJAN SENERATH

Sri Lanka (born 1959) - An effective leg-spin bowler and a right-handed batsman of high quality. He played for Nondescripts. In his first class career he made, 2,369 runs including 2 centuries and took 2 wickets.

Test Record - 21 Tests, 1,029 runs (Av. 29.40) including 1 century and 9 catches.

MAGUIRE JOHN NORMAN

Australia (born 1956) - A tall, right-arm medium-fast pace bowler. He played for Queensland. In his first class career he made, 499 runs and took 194 wickets.

Test Record - 3 Tests, 28 runs (Av. 7.00), 10 wickets (Av. 32.30) and 2 catches.

MAHANAMA ROSHAN SIRIWARDENE

Sri Lanka (born 1966) - A tiny right-handed opening batsman. He played for Bloomfield. In his first class career he made, 433 runs.

Test Record - 3 Tests, 79 runs (Av. 15.80) and 1 catch.

MAHMOOD HUSSAIN

Pakistan (born 1932) - A medium-fast in-swing bowler. He played for Karachi Whites. In his first class career he made, 1,107 runs and took 322 wickets.

Test Record - 27 Tests, 336 runs (Av. 10.18), 68 wickets (Av. 38.64) and 5 catches.

MAIDEN

An over in which no runs are credited to the batsman execpting no balls and wides. No ball and wides affect but byes and leg-byes do not affect maidenhood as the former are debited whereas the latter are not debited to the bowler.

MAILEY ARTHUR ALFRED

Australia (1886-1967) - A right-arm leg-break and googly bowler. He played for New South Wales. In his first class career he made, 1,529 runs, took 779 wickets and 157 catches.

Test Record - 21 Tests, 222 runs (Av. 11.10), 99 wickets (Av. 33.91) and 14 catches.

MAJID JAHANGIR KHAN

Pakistan (born 1946) - A good all-rounder. He was a brilliant attacking right-handed batsman, with a powerful drive, cut and hook. In the later years of his career, he bacame an occasional opener. He was also a fine close fielder and a natural bowler who once opened for Pakistan but later bowled flat, curling off-spinners. He played for Lahore, Pakistan International Airways and Cambridge University. In his first class career he made, 27,444 runs including 73 centuries, took 224 wickets and 410 catches.

Test Record - 63 Tests, 3,931 runs (Av. 38.92) including 8 centuries, 27 wickets (Av. 53.92) and 70 catches.

MAKA EBRAHIM SULEMAN

India (born 1922)- A right-handed batsman and a wicket-keeper. Test debut on November 26, 1952 against Pakistan at the age of 30 years and 263 days. Played in the fourth Test at Madras on debut but did not bat. Last Test of the career played against West Indies in February 1953. Score on last appearance in Test was 2 (retired hurt) in the third Test at Port-of-Spain. Age at the time of retirement from Test cricket was 30 years and 350 days. He played for Bombay. In his first class career he made,607 runs and 85 dismissals.

Test Record - 2 Tests, 2 runs and 3 dismissals (2ct, 1st).

MAKEPEACE JOSEPH WILLIAM HENRY

England (1882-1952) - A right-handed opening batsman. He was also an excellent cover-point fielder. He played for Lancashire. In his first class career he made, 25,799 runs including 43 centuries, took 41 wickets and 183 catches.

Test Record - 4 Tests, 279 runs (Av. 34.87) including 1 century.

MALHOTRA ASHOK OMPRAKASH

India (born 1957) - An adventurous and attractive little right-handed batsman. He played for Haryana and Bengal. In his first class career he made, 10,194 runs including 22 centuries and took 3 wicket.

Test Record - 7 Tests, 226 runs (Av. 25.11) and 2 catches.

MALLETT ASHLEY ALEXANDER

Australia (born 1945) - A right-handed limited batsman, a useful right-arm off-break bowler and also a close fielder. He played for South Australia. In his first class career he made, 2,326 runs, took 693 wickets and 105 catches.

Test Record - 38 Tests, 430 runs (Av. 11.62), 132 wickets (Av. 29.85) and 30 catches.

MAN IN

The call, usually from the captain, to inform his team that a new batsman has arrived at the crease and that they should return to their position in the field.

MANINDER SINGH

MANINDER SINGH HARBANSINGH BILLA

India (born 1956) - A tall, athletic left-arm orthodox spin bowler and a fine fielder. He plays

for Delhi. In his first class career he made, 697 runs and took 347 wickets.
Test Record - 31 Tests, 88 runs (Av.3.82), 79 wickets (Av. 36.43) and 9 catches.

MANJREKAR VIJAY LAXMAN
India (1931-1983) - A right-handed batsman,

VIJAY MANJREKAR

right-arm off-break bowler and an occasional wicket-keeper. Test debut on December 30, 1951 against England at the age of 20 years and 94 days. Score on Test debut was 48 in the third Test at Calcutta. Last Test of the career played against Australia in October 1964. Score on last appearance in Test was 9 in the third Test at Calcutta. First-ever Test century 133 scored on June 5, 1952 against England in the first Test at Leeds at the age of 20 years and 249 days. Age at the time of retirement from Test cricket was 33 years and 27 days. His partnership of 238 runs with P.R.Umrigar for third wicket in the first Test against New Zealand at Hyderabad in 1955-56 is the highest for third wicket for India against New Zealand. His partnership of 222 runs with V.S. Hazare for fourth wicket in the first Test against England at Leeds is the highest for fourth wicket for India against any country. When he scored his 19th run in the first innings of the 2nd Test against Australia at Bombay on October 11, 1964, he completed 3,000 runs in Test career. This was Manjreker's 53rd Test and 88th innings. He played for Bombay, Bengal and Rajasthan. In his first class career he made, 12,832 runs including 38 centuries and took 20 wickets.
Test Record - 55 Tests, 3,208 runs (Av. 39.12) including 7 centuries, 19 catches and 2 stumpings.

MANKAD ASHOK VINOO
India (born 1946) - A right-handed batsman and a right-arm off-break bowler. Eldest son of M.H. (Vinoo) Mankad. Test debut on September 19, 1969 against New Zealand at the age of 22 years and 337 days. Scores on Test debut were 19 not out and 29 in the first Test at Bombay. Last Test of the career played against Australia in January 1978. Score on last appearance in Test was 16 in the fourth Test at Sydney. Age at the time of retirement from Test cricket was 31 years and 90 days. He played for Bombay. In his first class career he made, 13,044 runs including 32 centuries and took 77 wickets.
Test Record - 22 Tests, 991 runs (Av. 25.41) and 12 catches.

MANKAD MULVANTRAI HIMATIAL
India (1917-1978) - A right-handed batsman and a left-arm slow spin bowler. Test debut on June 22, 1946 against England at the age of 29 years and 70 days. Scores on Test debut were 14 and 63 in the first Test at Lord's. Last Test of the career played against West Indies in February 1959. Scores on last appearance in Test were 21 and 0 in the fifth Test at New Delhi. First-ever Test century 116 scored on January 2, 1948 agianst Australia in the third Test at Melbourne at the age of 30 years and 261 days. Age at the time of retirement from Test cricket was 41 years and 297 days. Completed the "double" of an all-rounder in 23 Tests, which is fastest for India. The further "double" of 2,000 runs and 100 wickets was also performed by him in his 39th Test. This feat is also the fastest for India. He was the first Indian bowler who captured 100 wickets in Tests. He has scored the highest number of runs in an innings for India - 231 in the fifth Test against

New Zealand at Madras in 1955-56. With the score of 231 in the aforesaid Test is also the highest score for a batsman at No. 1 in the batting order for India. Holds the Test record with Pankaj Roy, of the highest partnership of 413 runs for the first wicket. Captured over 50 wickets and scored 540 runs in a calendar year in 1952. Also holds a record of bowling most balls in an innings for India (492 balls in the fifth Test against West Indies at Kingston in 1952-53) and also bowling most balls in a Test match (691 balls in the fourth Test against Pakistan at Peshawar in 1954-55). Has conceded most runs for India in an innings. His 228 runs conceded while capturing five wickets in the fifth Test against West Indies at Kingston in 1952-53, is a record for India. Put up one of the best all-round performance of a century and five wickets in the same match. He hit 184 and captured five wickets for 196 runs in 73 overs in the second Test against England at Lord's in 1952 which was virtually between Mankad and England and has eventually been recognised as "Mankad's match". He never enjoyed any settled position in the batting order for India. He is the only batsman who has batted at every number in the batting order right from 1 to11 for India which is also a world record. He played for Western India and Rajasthan. In his first class career he made, 11,558 runs including 26 centuries and took 776 wickets.

Test Record - 44 Tests, 2,109 runs (Av. 31.47) including 5 centuries, 162 wickets (Av. 32.32) and 33 catches.

MANN ANTHONY LONGFORD

Australia (born 1945) - A slow, right-arm leg-break bowler, a useful fine close fielder and a left-handed batsman. He played for Western Australia. In his first class career he made, 2,544 runs including 2 centuries and took 200 wickets.

Test Record - 4 Tests, 189 runs (Av. 23.62) including 1 century, 4 wickets (Av. 79.00) and 2 catches.

MANN FRANCIS GEORGE

England (born 1917) - A superb fielder and a very competent right-handed attacking batsman. He played for Cambridge University and Middlesex. In his first class career he made, 6,530 runs including 7 centuries.

Test Record - 7 Tests, 376 runs (Av. 37.60) including 1 century and 3 catches.

MANN FRANCIS THOMAS

England (1884-1964) - A powerful right-handed batsman. He played for Cambridge University and Middlesex. In his first class career he made, 13,237 runs including 9 centuries and took 176 catches.

Test Record - 5 Tests, 281 runs (Av. 35.12) and 4 catches.

MANN NORMAN BERTRAM FLEETWOOD

South Africa (1920-1955) - A right-arm bowler. He played for Natal and Eastern Province. In his first class career he made, 1,446 runs and took 251 wickets.

Test Record - 19 Tests, 400 runs (Av. 13.33), 58 wickets (Av. 33.10) and 3 catches.

MANSELL PERCY NEVILLE FRANK

South Africa (born 1920) - An all-rounder of high quality. He was a right-handed batsman an inexpensive leg-break bowler and a most reliable silp field. He played for Rhodesia. In his first class career he made, 4,598 runs including 5 centuries, took 299 wickets and 156 catches.

Test Record - 13 Tests, 355 runs (Av. 17.75), 11 wickets (Av. 66.90) and 15 catches.

MANSOOR AKHTAR

Pakistan (born 1956) - A right-handed batsman with a wide range of strokes. He played for Karachi and United Bank. In his first class career he made, 8,681 runs including 13 centuries and took 15 wickets.

Test Record - 18 Tests, 636 runs (Av. 26.50) including 1 century and 7 catches.

MANTRI MADHAV KRISHNAJI

India (born 1921) - A right-handed batsman and wicket-keeper. Test debut on December 14, 1951 against England at the age of 30 years and 113 days. Scores on Test debut were 39 and 7 in the second Test at Bombay. Last Test of the career played against Pakistan in January 1955. Scores on last appearance in Test were 0 and 2 in the first

Test at Dacca (now in Bangladesh). Age at the time of retirement from Test cricket was 33 years and 123 days. He played for Bombay. In his first class career he made, 4,403 runs including 7 centuries, and 193 dismissals.
Test Record - 4 Tests, 67 runs (Av. 9.57) and 9 dismissals (8ct, 1st).

MANZOOR ELAHI

Pakistan (born 1963) - A very strong and promising right-arm medium-pace bowler and a right-handed batsman. He played for Multan and Pakistan Railways. In his first class career he made, 3,783 runs including 6 centuries, and took 87 wickets.
Test Record - 4 Tests, 109 runs (Av. 21.80), 2 wickets (Av.42.00) and 5 catches.

MANZOOR ELAHI

MAQSOOD AHMED

Pakistan (born 1925) - A right-handed batsman, a natural hitter with a good eye. He was also an occasional medium-pace bowler and a fine fielder. He played for Bahawalpur. In his first class career he made, 3,716 runs including 6 centuries and took 120 wickets.
Test Record - 16 Tests, 507 runs (Av. 19.50), 3 wickets (Av. 63.66) and 13 catches.

GEOFFREY MARSH

MALCOLM MARSHALL

MARK

The action of a rugby player marking the ground with his heel and shouting "mark" after catching a ball which has been kicked, knocked, or thrown forward by a member of the opposing team, after which he is awarded a free kick.

MARKS VICTOR JAMES

England (born 1955) - A middle-order batsman and a useful off-break bowler. He played for Oxford University and Somerset. In his first class career he made, 9,861 runs including 5 centuries, took 636 wickets and 111 catches.

Test Record - 6 Tests, 249 runs (Av. 27.66) and 11 wickets (Av. 44.00).

MARSH GEOFFREY ROBERT

Australia (born 1958) - A stocky, correct and determined right-handed batsman, who acquitted himself well. He played for Western Australia. In his first class career he made, 3,378 runs including 9 centuries.

Test Record - 27 Tests, 1,669 runs (Av. 34.77) including 3 centuries and 19 catches.

MARSH RODNEY WILLIAM

Australia (born 1947) - One of the best wicket-keepers and a very useful left-handed batsman. He was an immensely forceful driver, often hitting straight back over the bowler's head, and a ruthless square-cutter of anything short. He could also defend, if necessary. He played for Western Australia. In his first class career he made, 11,067 runs including 12 centuries, and 869 dismissals.

Test Record - 96 Tests, 3,633 runs (Av. 26.51) including 3 centuries, 355 dismissals (343ct, 12st).

MARSHALL ROY EDWIN

West Indies (born 1930) - An attacking and forceful right-handed opening batsman with a variety of strokes, and a useful change-bowler of off-breaks. He played for Barbados. In his first class career he made, 35,725 runs including 68 centuries, took 176 wickets and 293 catches.

Test Record - 4 Tests, 143 runs (Av. 20.42) and 1 catch.

MARSHALL MALCOLM DENZIL

West Indies (born 1958) - A lithe, whipping bowler with electric speed, natural athleticism and rare

determination bowler.He swings and cuts ball sharply and useful right-handed batsman. Once he was considered as the fastest bowler of the world. He was a right-arm bowler. He played for Barbados and Hampshire. In his first class career he made, 7,688 runs including 6 centuries, and took 1,453 wickets.
Test Record - 66 Tests,1438 runs (Av. 18.92),326 wickets (Av. 20.54) and 25 catches.

MARTIN JOHN WESLEY
Australia (born 1931) - He was an unorthodox left-arm off-break and googly bowler, a right-handed batsman and a good fielder. He played for South Australia and New South Wales. In his first class career he made, 3,970 runs including 1 century, took 445 wickets and 114 catches.
Test Record - 8 Tests, 214 runs (Av. 17.83), 17 wickets (Av. 48.94) and 5 catches.

MARX WALDEMAR FREDERICK ERIC
South Africa (1895-1974) - A useful right-arm medium-pace change bowler. He played for Transvaal. In his first class career he made, 656 runs including 2 centuries, and took 13 wickets.
Test Record - 3 Tests,125 runs (Av. 20.83) and 4 wickets (Av. 36.00).

MARYLEBONE CRICKET CLUB

Patron - HER MAJESTY THE QUEEN
President - J.J. WARR
President Designate - FIELD-MARSHAL THE LORD BRAMALL
Treasurer - G.H.G. DOGGART
Chairman of Finance - SIR ANTHONY TUKE
Trustees - D.J.INSOLE, F.G.MANN, SIR OLIVER POPPLEWELL
Life Vice-Presidents - SIR GEORGE ALLEN, F.R.BROWN, S.C. GRIFFITH, C.G.A. PARIS
Secretary - LT-COL. J.R.STEPHENSON
(Lord's Cricket Ground, St. John's Wood, NW8 8QN)
ASSISTANT SECRETARIES - LT-COL. L.G. JAMES (Administration),
M.R.BLOW (Finance), WG-CDR V.J.W.M. LAWRENCE
(Marketing & Personnel)
Curator - S.E.A. GREEN
Ground Administrator - A.W.P.FIEMING

MASON JOHN RICHARD
England (1874-1958) - A right-handed batsman, front-foot player and a fast-medium bowler with a model action and high arm. He played for Kent. In his first class career he made, 17,337 runs including 34 centuries, took 845 wickets and 340 catches.
Test Record - 5 Tests, 129 runs (Av. 12.90), 2 wickets (Av. 74.50) and 3 catches.

MASSIE ROBERT ARNOLD LOCKYER
Austrlia (born 1947) - A right-arm medium-fast bowler, who could swing and cut the ball either way. He played for Western Australia. In his first class career he made, 385 runs and took 179 wickets.
Test Record - 6 Tests, 78 runs (Av. 11.14), 31 wickets (Av. 20.87).

MATHENSON ALEXANDER MALCOLM
New Zealand (born 1906) - A right-arm medium-pace bowler. He played for Auckland. In his first class career he made, 1,844 runs including 1 century, and took 194 wickets.
Test Record - 2 Tests, 7 runs (Av. 7.00), 2 wickets (Av. 68.00) and 2 catches.

MATHIAS WALLIS
Pakistan (born 1935) - An attractive and generally fast-scoring right-handed batsman and occasional medium-pace bowler. He played for Karachi. In his first class career he made, 7,508 runs including 16 centuries, and took 13 wickets.
Test Record - 21 Tests, 783 runs (Av. 23.72) and 22 catches.

MATTHEWS GREGORY RICHARD JOHN
Australia (born 1959) - A right-arm off-spinner, brilliant fielder and correct, left-handed batsman. He played for New south Wales. In his first class career he made, 2,933 runs including 6 centuries and took 112 wickets.
Test Record - 21 Tests,1,031 runs (Av. 30.82)

MEAD CHARLES PHILIP

England (1887-1958) - He was a tall heavily built left-handed batsman. His defence was strong and his strokes were firm and clean. He played for Hampshire and Suffolk. In his first class career he made, 55,061 runs including 153 centuries, took 277 wickets and 668 catches.

Test Record - 17 Tests, 1,185 runs (Av. 49.37) including 4 centuries and 4 catches.

MEALE TREVOR

New Zealand (born 1928) - A tall left-handed opening batsman. He played for Wellington. In his first class career he made, 1,352 runs including 2 centuries.

Test Record - 2 Tests, 21 runs (Av. 5.25).

MEAT

The part of the bat face that is backed by the thickest layer of wood and from which the best power in well-timed strokeplay is available. Usually that section from about a quarter to halfway up the bat from the toe and inwards about an inch from either side (colloquial).

MECKIFF IAN

Australia (born 1935) - A medium-fast left-arm bowler. He played for Victoria. In his first class career he made, 778 runs and took 269 wickets.

Test Record - 18 Tests, 154 runs (Av. 11.84), 45 wickets (Av. 31.62) and 9 catches.

MEDIUM PACE

There are three main classifications of medium-pace which can be mixed, depending upon the bowler's ability. They are swing bowling (in and out swing), seam bowling, wherein the bowler relies on a very precise delivery of the ball to pitch on the vertical seam, and two types of cutter (off and leg), wherein the bowler drags his finger across the ball at delivery, imparting a degree of off or leg spin. The medium-pace bowler who is able to swing a shiny ball almost invariably finds it of greater advantage to bowl against the wind. Like fast bowlers, medium-pace bowlers must also be strong in build with stamina of an athlete. They have to do bowling for a long time till the shine of the ball disappears to usher in the spinners.

Medium Pace Bowling

MEDIUM PACE BOWLERS

Medium-paced bowlers are the patient hard-workers of a team. Their bowling is not as energetic as that of the fast bowler, but for that reason they are expected to continue for much longer periods at a stretch. Also, since their speed through the air is so much slower, it is much easier for the batsman to see the ball; consequently, they have to rely on cunning combined with spin and swerve in order the batsman and make him play that false stroke. There are, however more interesting ways in which a medium-paced bowler may dismiss the batsman, some or all of which may be tried concurrently without even the most experienced and intelligent of bowlers being able to predict which method will actually take the wicket.

MEHRA VIJAY LAXMAN

India (born 1938) - A right-handed batsman and right-arm leg-spin bowler. Test debut on December 2, 1955 against New Zealand at the age of 17 years and 261 days thus becoming the youngest Indian player to make Test debut. Score on Test debut was 10 in the second Test at Bombay. Last Test of the career played against West Indies in April 1962. Scores on last appearance in Test were 8 and 39 in the fifth Test at Kingston. Age at the time of retirement from Test cricket was 24 years and 36 days. He played for Western India and Bombay. In his first class career he made, 5,636 runs including 13 centuries and took 26 wickets.

Test Record - 8 Tests, 329 runs (Av. 25.30) and 1 catch.

MEINTJES DOUGLAS JAMES

South Africa (1890-1979) - A very good all-rounder from a powerful province. He played for Transvaal. In his first class career he made, 1,146 runs and took 91 wickets.

Test Record - 2 Tests, 43 runs (Av. 14.33), 6 wickets (Av. 19.16) and 3 catches.

MELBOURNE

Of all Test matches, the first was played in Melbourne and more than 100 years later the Melbourne Cricket Ground is still the largest in the world. Its already huge capacity was increased (and its surface levelled) to accommodate the Olympic Games of 1956 and now crowd of 120,000 fill it for the Australian Rules Football grand finals. For cricket, the biggest is the 90,800 which watched the Saturday's play in the final Test between Australia and West Indies in 1960-61.The Melbourne Cricket Club moved its grounds to its present site in 1853. The playing area is still vast even by Australian standards but in recent years the square has often been unsatisfactory, possibly because the high stands keep out light and wind. Excavation has brought better pitches in the 1980s. It is a weakness that despite the groves of gum trees which surround the ground and provide an area for car parking facilities, there is no second ground for nets and parctice. But it is a magnificent arena within walking distance of the centre of a city of immense sporting enthusiasm.

MELLE MICHAEL GEORGE

South Africa (born 1930) - A fast right-arm bowler. He played for Transvaal and Western Province. In his first class career he made, 544 runs and took 160 wickets.

Test Record - 7 Tests, 68 runs (Av. 8.50), 26 wickets (Av. 32.73) and 4 catches.

MELVILLE ALAN

South Africa (1910-1983) - A graceful right-handed batsman with a classical upright method. He played for Oxford University, Sussex, Natal and Transvaal. In his first class career he made, 10,598 runs including 25 centuries, took 132 wickets and 156 catches.

Test Record - 11 Tests, 894 runs (Av. 52.58) including 4 centuries, and 8 catches.

MENDIS LOUIS ROHAN DULEEP

Sri Lanka (born 1952) - A right-handed batsman of exceptional talent, a fine fielder, a right-arm medium pace bowler and kept wickets when required. He played for Sinhalese. In his first class career he made, 8,093 runs including 14 centuries and took 1 wicket.

Test Record - 24 Tests, 1,329 runs (Av. 31.64) including 4 centuries and 9 catches.

MENDONCA IVOR LEON

West Indies (born 1934) - A capable wicket-keeper and right-handed batsman. He played for British Guiana. In his first class career he made, 407 runs and 30 dismissals.

Test Record - 2 Tests, 81 runs (Av. 40.50) and 10 dismissals (8 ct, 2 st).

MERCHANT THACKERSEY VIJAY MADHAVJI

India (born 1911) - A right-handed opening batsman and a right-arm medium-fast as well as off-break bowler. Test debut on December 15, 1933 against England at the age of 22 years and 63 days. Scores on Test debut were 23 and 30 in the first Test at Bombay. Last Test of the career played against England in November 1951. Score on last appearance in Test was 154 in the first Test at New Delhi. First-ever Test century 114 scored on July 28, 1936 against England in the second Test at Manchester at the age of 24 years and 286 days. Age at the time of reitirement from Test cricket was 40 years and 25 days. Toured England twice, in 1936 and 1946. During the first tour in 1936 he aggregated 1,745 runs and stood fourth in England averages with 51.32. In the match with Lancashire at Liverpool, he "carried his bat" through both completed innings for 135 and 77, the only Indian to achieve this unique feat, and one of the four anywhere. "Merchant was far and away the outstanding batsman.... No one else was quicker to fine form... but there was never any doubt as to his class. Neat and finished in style, he showed himself in fine exponent of the hook stroke and also got a good proportion of his runs by cutting. It may be added here that Merchant, over and above his batting, was very valuable to the side by his fast and sure work in the field", wrote WISDEN and selected him as one of the "Five Cricketers of the Year". In the 1946 tour, to England he topped the averages again, with 74.55 for his 2,385 runs and was second in English averages after Walter Hammond. WISDEN put it:" No praise could be too high for Merchant who, on any reckoning, must be accounted as one of the world's greatest batsman". With such qualities, one's cricket is bound to be great. His career figures prove the fact. For his 12, 876 runs he averages 72.74, an average second only to that of Sir Don Bradman's 95.14. He made his debut at the age of 18 in the first-class cricket, when he played for the Hindus against the Muslims in Bombay Quadrangular. In this tournament he aggregated 1,965 runs at an average of 109.16. In Ranji Trophy matches his average is 98.35 for 3,639 runs for Bombay. He holds the highest individual record for Bombay with 359 not out, scored against Maharashtra which included bowlers like Phadkar, Sohoni, Jadhav, Vinoo Mankad and Shinde. This feat was performed in 1943-44. During his career Merchant hit up 43 centuries which included 11 double centuries, the most in Indian cricket. In 1941 "he played consecutive innings of 170 not out, 243 not out, 221 and 153 to achieve a new record, for never before has any batsman made four consecutive scores, all over 150". He was conferred Hony. Life Membership by the M.C.C. In his last years with the All-India Council of Sports, he was vice-president. Ths Government of Maharashtra appointed him Sheriff of Bombay. He was Chairman of Indian Selection Committee when India won three successive Test series. He played for Bombay. In his first class career he made, 13,228 runs including 44 centurics and took 65 wickets.

Test Record - 10 Tests, 859 runs (Av. 47.72) including 3 centuries and 7 catches.

MERRI CREEK SOIL

Special clay-based soil form the water course of that name of Victoria. It has been extensively used in wicket preparation in the Eastern States of Australia.

MERRITT WILLIAM EDWARD

New Zealand (1908-1977) - A cheerful and skilful right-arm leg-break and googly bowler of great stamina and a good fielder. He played for Canterbury and Northamptonshire. In his first class career he made, 3,147 runs and took 536 wickets.

Test Record - 6 Tests, 73 runs (Av. 10.42), 12 wickets (Av. 51.41) and 2 catches.

MERRY CYRIL ARTHUR

West Indies (1911-1964) - A brilliant right-handed batsman. He played for Trinidad. In his first class career he made, 1,547 runs including 1 century and took 33 wickets.

Test Record - 2 Tests, 34 runs (Av. 8.50) and 1 catch.

MID OFF

This is an important position in every class of cricket, because it is such a good place for a captain to field. From mid-off, the captain can so easily advise and encourage the bowler. His exact position will vary slightly according to the batsman and the bowler; thus for a defensive batsman mid-off can move up to within about 18 yards of the bat, but for a strong attacking batsman he is usually 25 to 30 yards away. His main job is to stop and hold all the off-drives within his reach. Many balls which are well be hit hard and firmly along the ground in mid-off's direction. If those are mistimed slightly, a possible catch will often result, but it is likely to be a hard catch, hard in the sense that the ball will be travelling fast rather hold it. Consequently many mid-off's are solidly built fellows with large tough hands! Yet they cannot afford to be stolid and inactive because they must be ready to dash in to counter the semi-defensive push stroke which sends the ball slowly in their direction and gives the batsman a quick run if mid-off is a slow starter.

MID-ON

One of the few places on the cricket field where it is possible to 'hide' a poor fielder is mid-on. Like his counter-part, mid-off, the exact position he occupies will vary according to circumstances; but, unlike mid-off, he will have far fewer drives to stop or catches to hold. The reason is simply that it is easier for a batsman to drive a ball on the off side, the balls outside the leg stump being generally placed more squarely in the direction of the umpire or mid-wicket.

MID WICKET

A fielding position on the leg side between square-leg and mid-on, but until the inter-World Wars period mid-wicket was used as a shortened from the mid-wicket on (i.e. mid-on).

MIDDLE

To hit the bowl neatly with the middle of the bat.

MIDDLE ORDER

The batsmen after the openers and before the tail-enders. They are counted from number three or four to number seven or eight. The team generally depends on its stability and strength.

MIDDLESEX

Foundation of Present Club: December 15, 1863 in London.

First First-class Match: Middlesex v Surrey (Lord's), May 20,21 1850.

Present Principal Ground: Lord's, St. John's Wood, London.

County Champions: 1866, 1920, 1921, 1947, 1949, 1976, 1977, 1980, 1982, 1985.

Result in 1985: Won 8, Lost 4, drawn 12.

JPL, Championship: Best Year: Second in 1982

Result in 1985: 12th: won 5, Lost 7, no result 4

Benson and Hedges Cup: Winners in 1983.

Result in 1985: Losing semi-finalists.

Nat West Trophy: Winners in 1977, 1980 and 1984.

Result in 1985: Lost in Second round.

Highest Team Total: 642-3 dec v Hampshire (Southampton) 1923.

Lowest Team Total: 20 v MCC (Lord's) 1864.

MIDFIELD

The middle portion of a field.

MIDNIGHT CRICKET

The Orient Liner Lusitania took a cruise party to Spitzbergen in August 1894 and on 12 August at midnight, by the light of the midnight sun, a cricket was set up on deck.

MIDWINTER WILLIAM EVANS

Australia (1851-1890) - A steady right-handed batsman who could hit hard, a medium-pace bowler and a first-rate outfielder. He played for Gloucestershire and Victoria. In his first class career he made, 4,493 runs including 3 centuries, took 418 wickets and 122 catches.

Test Record - (Australia - 8) : 174 runs (Av. 13.38), 14 wickets (Av. 23.78) and 5 catches. (England - 4) : 95 runs (Av. 13.57), 10 wickets (Av. 27.20) and 5 catches.

MILBURN BARRY DOUGLAS

New Zealand (born 1943) - An energetic and reliable wicket-keeper but moderate right-handed batsman. He played for Otago. In his first class career he made, 705 runs including 1 century, and 173 dismissals.

Test Record - 3 Tests, 8 runs (Av. 8.00) and 8 dismissals (6 ct, 2 st).

MILBURN COLIN

England (born 1941) - A right-handed batsman, sound and straight. He was medium-pace bowler and a reliable forward short-leg field. He played for Durham, Northamptonshire and Western Province. In his first class career he made, 13,262 runs including 23 centuries, took 99 wickets and 226 catches.

Test Record - 9 Tests, 654 runs (Av. 46.71) including 2 centuries and 7 catches.

MILITARY MEDIUM

A medium-pace bowling which is brisk but steady, efficient and reliable.

MILKHA SINGH AMRITSAR GOVIND-SINGH

India (born 1941) - A left-handed batsman. Younger brother of A.G. Kripal Singh. Test debut on January 13, 1960 against Australia at the age of 18 years and 18 days. Scores on Test debut were 16 and 9 in the fourth Test at Madras. Last Test of the career played against England in November 1961. Scores on last appearance in Test were 2 and 12 in the first Test at Bombay. Age at retirement from Test cricket was 19 years and 320 days. He played for Madras. In his first class career he made, 4,324 runs including 8 centuries.

Test Record - 4 Tests, 92 runs (Av. 15.33), and 2 catches.

MILLER GEOFFREY

England (born 1952) - He was a right-arm off-spin bowler, a right-handed batsman and a fine fielder. He played for Derbyshire and Essex. In his first class career he made, 10,670 runs including 2 centuries, took 772 wickets and 243 catches.

Test Record - 34 Tests, 1,213 runs (Av. 25.80), 60 wickets (Av. 30.98) and 17 catches.

MILLER KEITH ROSS

Australia (born 1919) - A right-handed batsman, a delicate late-cutter, but his success as a bowler often depended on his mood. He played for Victoria, New South Wales and Nottinghamshire. In his first class career he made, 14,183 runs including 41 centuries, took 497 wickets and 136 catches.

Test Record - 55 Tests, 2,958 runs (Av. 36.97) including 7 centuries, 170 wickets (Av. 22.97) and 38 catches.

MILLER LAWRENCE SOMERVILLE MARTIN

New Zealand (born 1923) - A tall and likeable left-handed opening batsman and also a good fielder in the deep. He played for Central Districts and Wellington. In his first class career he made, 4,777 runs including 5 centuries.

Test Record - 13 Tests, 346 runs (Av. 13.84) and 1 catch.

MILLIGAN FRANK WILLIAM

England (1870-1900) - He was a right-arm fast bowler. He played for Yorkshire. In his first class career he made, 2,151 runs and took 136 wickets.

Test Record - 2 Tests, 58 runs (Av. 14.50) and 1 catch.

MILLMAN GEOFFREY

England (born 1934) - An accomplished wicket-keeper and a useful, stubborn batsman, who often opened the innings. He played for Bedfordshire and Nottinghamshire. In his first class career he made, 7,770 runs including 3 centuries and 652 dismissals.

Test Record - 6 Tests, 60 runs (Av. 12.00) and 15 dismissals (13ct, 2 st).

MILLS JOHN ERNEST

New Zealand (1905-1972) - A left-handed opening batsman who played with a straight bat, drove

beautifully and cut superbly. He played for Auckland. In his first class career he made, 5,025 runs including 11 centuries.
Test Record - 7 Tests, 241 runs (Av. 26.77) including 1 century and 1 catch.

MILTON CLEMENT ARTHUR
England (born 1928) - A neat and accomplished right-handed opening batsman and a useful medium-pace bowler. He was also a brilliant short-leg, extremely agile, with a very safe pair of hands. He played for Gloucestershire. In his first class career he made, 32,150 runs including 56 centuries, took 79 wickets and 759 catches.
Test Record - 6 Tests, 204 runs (Av. 25.50) including 1 century and 5 catches.

MILTON SIR WILLIAM HENRY
South Africa (1854-1930) - A hard-hitting right-handed batsman with a defence - especially intolerant of loose bowling - and a fine fielder. He played for Western Province. In his first class career he made, 152 runs.
Test Record - 3 Tests, 68 runs (Av. 11.33), 2 wickets (Av. 24.00) and 1 catch.

MINNETT DR ROY BALDWIN
Australia (1888-1955) - A right-handed forward player with a fine, free swing of the bat and a fast-medium bowler with a longish run. He played for New South Wales. In his first class career he made, 2,203 runs including 2 centuries, and took 86 wickets.
Test Record - 9 Tests, 391 runs (Av. 26.06) and 11 wickets (Av. 26.36).

MIRAN BUX
Pakistan (born 1907) - A right-arm off-break bowler. He played for Punjab, Rawalpindi and Services. In his first class career he made, 53 runs and took 48 wickets.
Test Record - 2 Tests, 1 run (Av. 1.00) and 2 wickets (Av . 57.50).

MISCUE
To fail to 'middle' the ball when playing a shot, so that the ball does not go in the direction intended.

MISS
Failure to catch a ball hit by a batsman.

MISSON FRANCIS MICHAEL
Australia (born 1938) - A right-arm medium-fast bowler, and a good fine fielder. He played for New South Wales. In his first class career he made, 1,052 runs and took 177 wickets.
Test Record - 5 Tests, 38 runs (Av. 19.00), 16 wickets (Av. 38.50) and 6 catches.

MITCHELL ARTHUR
England (1902-1976) - A right-handed batsman and a good outfielder. He played for Yorkshire. In his first class career he made, 19,523 runs including 44 centuries, and 462 catches.
Test Record - 6 Tests, 298 runs (Av. 29.80) and 9 catches.

MITCHELL BRUCE
South Africa (born 1909) - He was a right-handed opening batsman. He played for Transvaal. In his first class career he made, 11,395 runs including 30 centuries, took 249 wickets and 229 catches.
Test Record - 42 Tests, 3,471 runs (Av. 48.88) including 8 centuries, 27 wickets (Av. 51.11) and 56 catches.

MITCHELL THOMAS BIGNELL
England (born 1902) - A right-arm leg-break and googly bowler. He played for Derbyshire. In his first class career he made, 2,431 runs, took 1,483 wickets and 132 catches.
Test Record - 5 Tests, 20 runs (Av. 5.00), 8 wickets (Av. 62.25) and 1 catch.

MODI RUSI SHERIYAR
India (born 1924) - A right-handed batsman and right-arm medium-pace bowler. Test debut on June 22, 1946 against England at the age of 21 years and 221 days. Scores on Test debut were 57 not out and 21 in the first Test at Lord's. Last Test of the career played against Pakistan in November 1952. Score on last appearance in Test was 32 in the third Test at Bombay. First-ever Test century 112 scored on December 13, 1948 against West Indies in the second Test at Bombay

at the age of 24 years and 32 days. Age at the time of retirement from Test cricket was 28 years and five days.He played for Bombay. In his first class career he made, 7,509 runs including 20 centuries and took 32 wickets.
Test Record - 10 Tests, 736 runs (Av. 46.00) including 1 century and 3 catches.

MOHSIN KHAN

MOHAMMAD FAROOQ
Pakistan (born 1938) - A right-arm medium-fast bowler. He played for Karachi. In his first class career he made, 173 runs and took 123 wickets.
Test Record - 7 Tests, 85 runs (Av. 17.00), 21 wickets (Av. 32.47).

MOHAMMAD ILYAS
Pakistan (born 1946) - An attacking right-handed opening batsman and a useful leg-break and googly bowler. He played for Pakistan International Airways In his first class career he made, 4,607 runs including 12 centuries and took 53 wickets.
Test Record - 10 Tests, 441 runs (Av. 23.21) including 1 century and 6 catches.

MOHAMMAD MUNAF
Pakistan (born 1935) - A right-arm medium-fast bowler and a useful late-order batsman. He played for Karachi. In his first class career he made, 1,356 runs and took 180 wickets.
Test Record - 4 Tests, 63 runs (Av. 12.60) and 11 wickets (Av. 31.00).

MOHAMMAD NAZIR JUNIOR
Pakistan (born 1946) - A right-arm off-spinner with clever flight and fine control. He played for Pakistan Railways. In his first class career he made, 4,140 runs including 2 centuries and took 783 wickets.
Test Record - 14 Tests, 144 runs (Av. 18.00), 34 wickets (Av. 33.02) and 4 catches.

MOHSIN HASAN KHAN
Pakistan (born 1955) - A right-handed batsman with a wide range of graceful strokes. He played for Pakistan Railways. In his first class career he made, 11,206 runs including 31 centuries, took 14 wickets (Av. 39.00) and 133 catches.
Test Record - 48 Tests, 2,709 runs (Av. 37.10) including 7 centuries and 34 catches.

MOHSIN KAMAL
Pakistan (born 1963) - He has a smooth run-up and fine action. He played for Lahore. In his first class career he made, 243 runs and took 92 wickets.
Test Record - 7 Tests, 31 runs (15.50) 17 wickets (Av. 35.11) and 2 catches.

MOIR ALEXANDER MCKENZIE
New Zealand (born 1919) - A right-arm leg-break and googly bowler and a useful late-order batsman. He played for Otago. In his first class career he made, 2,102 runs and took 368 wickets.
Test Record - 17 Tests, 327 runs (Av. 14.86), 28 wickets (Av. 50.64) and 2 catches.

MOLD ARTHUR WEBB
England (1863-1921) - A great right-arm medium-fast bowler. He played for Northamptonshire and Lancashire. In his first class career he

made, 1,814 runs and took 1,673 wickets.
Test Record - 3 Tests, 0 runs, 7 wickets (Av. 33.42) and 1 catch.

MOLONEY DENIS ANDREW ROBERT
New Zealand (1910-1942) - A right-handed batsman and a useful medium-pace change-bowler. He played for Wellington, Otago and Canterbury. In his first class career he made, 3,219 runs including 2 centuries and took 95 wickets.
Test Record - 3 Tests, 156 runs (Av. 26.00), and 3 catches.

MOON LEONARD JAMES
England (1878-1916) - A right-handed batsman. He played for Cambridge University, and Middlesex. In his first class career he made, 4,223 runs and 88 dismissals.
Test Record - 4 Tests, 182 runs (Av. 22.75) and 4 catches.

MOONEY FRANCIS LEONARD HUGH
New Zealand (born 1921) - A wicket-keeper and a right-handed stroke-maker batsman. He played for Wellington. In his first class career he made, 3,134 runs including 2 centuries and 213 dismissals.
Test Record - 14 Tests, 343 runs (Av. 17.15), and 30 dismissals (22 ct, 8 st).

MORE KIRAN SHANKAR
India (born 1962) - An accomplished wicket-keeper and a right-handed batsman. His highest score is 181 not out against Uttar Pradesh in 1983-84 when he shared a last wicket stand of 143 with V. Patel. He played for Baroda. In his first class career he made, 2,285 runs including 4 centuries and 184 dismissals.
Test Record - 24 Tests, 576 runs (Av.21.33) and 59 dismissals (44 ct.,15 st.)

MORGAN ROSS WINSTON
New Zealand (born 1941) - A sound right-handed batsman and also useful off-spin change-bowler. He played for Auckland. In his first class career he made, 5,940 runs including 8 centuries and took 108 wickets.
Test Record - 20 Tests, 734 runs (Av. 22.24), 5 wickets (Av. 121.80) and 12 catches.

MORKEL DENYS PAUL BECK
South Africa (1906-1980) - A right-handed batsman and a right-arm medium-fast bowler. He played for Western Province. In his first class career he made, 4,494 runs including 8 centuries and took 174 wickets.
Test Record - 16 Tests, 663 runs (Av. 24.55), 18 wickets (Av. 45.61) and 13 catches.

MORLEY FREDERICK
England (1850-1884) - A left-arm medium-fast bowler. He played for Nottinghamshire. In his first class career he made, 1,396 runs and took 1,270 wickets.
Test Record - 4 Tests, 6 runs (Av. 1.50), 16 wickets (Av. 18.50) and 4 catches.

MORONEY JOHN
Australia (born 1917) - A right-handed opening batsman. He played for New South Wales. In his first class career he made, 4,023 runs including 12 centuries.

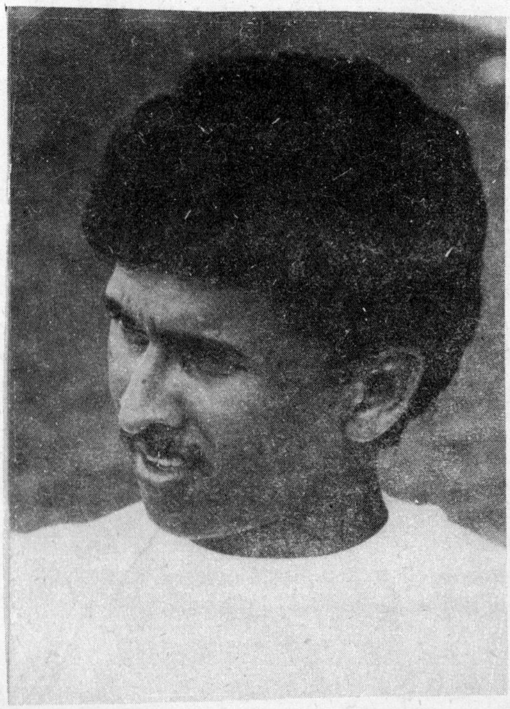
KIRAN MORE

Test Record - 7 Tests, 383 runs (Av. 34.81) including 2 centuries.

MORRIS ARTHUR ROBERT
Australia (born 1922) - He was a left-handed attacking opening batsman who would sometimes move yards down the pitch to break up a length. He played for New South Wales In his first class career he made, 12,614 runs including 46 centuries, and took 12 wickets.
Test Record - 46 Tests, 3,533 runs (Av. 46.48) including 12 centuries, 2 wickets (Av. 25.00) and 15 catches.

MORRISON JOHN FRANCIS MACLEAN
New Zealand (born 1947) - A very careful right-handed batsman, a left-arm spin change-bowler and a reliable fielder. He played for Central Districts. In his first class career he made, 6,142 runs including 7 centuries, took 51 wickets and 133 catches.
Test Record - 17 Tests, 656 runs (Av. 22.62) including 1 century, 2 wickets (Av. 35.50) and 9 catches.

MORTIMORE JOHN BRIAN
England (born 1933) - A right-arm off-break bowler. He played for Gloucestershire. In his first class career he made, 15,891 runs including 4 centuries, took 1,807 wickets and 346 catches.
Test Record - 9 Tests, 243 runs (Av. 24.30), 13 wickets (Av. 56.38) and 3 catches.

MOSES HENRY
Australia (1858-1938) - A left-handed batsman. He played for New South Wales. In his first class career he made, 2,898 runs including 4 centuries.
Test Record - 6 Tests, 198 runs (Av. 19.80) and 1 catch.

MOSS ALAN EDWARD
England (born 1930) - A competent right-arm fast bowler. He played for Middlesex. In his first class career he made, 1,671 runs and took 1,301 wickets.

Test Record - 9 Tests, 61 runs (Av. 10.16), 21 wickets (Av. 29.80) and 1 catch.

MOTZ RICHARD CHARLES
New Zealand (born 1940) - A right-handed fast bowler and a late-order batsman. He played for Canterbury. In his first class career he made, 3,494 runs including 1 century, and took 518 wickets.
Test Record - 32 Tests, 612 runs (Av. 11.54), 100 wickets (Av. 31.48) and 9 catches.

MOVE
To turn the ball sidelong during its flight or after it pitches.

MOW
Description given to a cross-bat, a stroke taken anything but from the copy book.

MOXON MARTYN DOUGLAS
England (born 1960) - A right-handed batsman and also a right-arm medium-pace bowler. He played for Yorkshire and Griqualand West. In his first class career he made, 5,905 runs including 14 centuries and took 17 wickets.
Test Record - 9 Tests, 437 runs (Av.31.21) and 10 catches.

MUDASSAR NAZAR

MUDASSAR NAZAR

Pakistan (born 1956) - A determined right-handed opening batsman, a useful bustling medium-pace bowler and a good close fielder. He played for Lahore, Punjab, Pakistan Universities. In his first class career he made, 13,769 runs including 41 centuries, 138 wickets and 154 catches.

Test Record - 76 Tests,4,114 runs (Av.38.09) including 10 centuries, 66 wickets (Av. 38.36) and 48 catches.

MUDDIAH VENATAPPA MUSANDRA

India (born 1929) - A right-handed batsman and right-arm off-break bowler. Test debut on December 12, 1959 against Australia at the age of 30 years and 184 days. Scores on Test debut were 0 and 0 not out in the first Test at New Delhi. Last Test of the career played against Pakistan in December 1960. Score on last appearance in Test was 11 in the second Test at Kanpur. Age at the time of retirement from Test cricket was 31 years and 193 days. He played for Services. In his first class career he made, 805 runs and took 169 wickets.

Test Record - 2 Tests, 11 runs (Av. 5.50) and 3 wickets (Av. 44.66).

MUNIR MALIK

Pakistan (born 1934) - A big-hearted right-arm medium-fast bowler. He played for Rawalpindi. In his first class career he made, 675 runs and took 197 wickets.

Test Record - 3 Tests, 7 runs (Av. 2.33), 9 wickets (Av. 39.77) and 1 catch.

MURDOCH WILLIAM LLOYD

Australia (1855-1911) - A good wicket-keeper and a right-handed batsman. He had a good style and plenty of strokes. He played for New South Wales and Sussex. In his first class career he made, 16,953 runs including 19 centuries, took 10 wickets, 218 catches and 25 dismissals.

Test Record - (Australia - 18) - 896 runs (Av. 32.00) including 2 centuries and 14 dismissals (13 ct, 1 st). (England - 1) - 12 runs (Av. 12.00) and 1 dismissal (1 st).

MURRAY ANTON RONALD ANDREW

South Africa (born 1922) - A right-handed batsman and also an impressive right-arm slow-medium bowler. He played for Eastern Province. In his first class career he made, 2,685 runs including 4 centuries, and took 188 wickets.

Test Record - 10 Tests, 289 runs (Av. 22.23) including 1 century, 18 wickets (Av. 39.44) and 3 catches.

MURRAY BRUCE ALEXANDER GRENFELL

New Zealand (born 1940) - A tall, calm and right-handed opening batsman with a long reach. He played for Wellington. In his first class career he made, 6,257 runs including 6 centuries and took 30 wickets.

Test Record - 13 Tests, 598 runs (Av. 23.92) and 21 catches.

MURRAY DAVID ANTHONY

West Indies (born 1950) - A right-handed batsman and a useful wicket-keeper. He played for Barbados. In his first class career he made, 4,503 runs including 7 centuries, and 338 dismissals.

Test Record - 19 Tests, 601 runs (Av. 21.46), and 62 dismissals (57 ct, 5 st).

MURRAY DERYCK LANCE

West Indies (born 1943) - A useful batsman and a good wicket-keeper. He played for Trinidad, Cambridge University, Nottinghamshire and Warwickshire. In his first class career he made, 13,289 runs including 10 centuries, and 849 dismissals.

Test Record - 62 Tests, 1,993 runs (Av. 22.90) and 189 dismissals (181ct, 8st).

MUSHTAQ ALI

India (born 1914) - A right-handed batsman and left-arm slow spin bowler. Test debut on December 5, 1933 against England at the age of 18 years and 19 days. Scores on Test debut were 9 and 18 in the second Test at Calcutta. Last Test of the career played against England in February 1952. Score on last appearance in Test was 22 in the fifth Test at Madras. First-ever Test century 112 scored on

July 27, 1936 against England in the second Test at Manchester at the age of 21 years and 220 days, thus stole the honour of registering the first century in Test cricket for India abroad. Age at the time of retirement from Test cricket was 37 years and 51 days. He played for Holkar. In his first class career he made, 13,009 runs including 30 centuries, and took 155 wickets.

Test Record - 11 Tests, 612 runs (Av. 32.31) including 2 centuries, 3 wickets (Av. 67.33) and 7 catches.

MUSHTAQ MOHAMMAD

Pakistan (born 1943) - A stocky right-handed batsman, who could play any stroke with superb timing. His wrists were strong as steel yet flexible as a willow branch. As a leg-break bowler he has been one of the best in the world of a dying breed. He played for Pakistan International Airways and Karachi. In his first class career he made, 31,091 runs including 72 centuries, took 936 wickets and 349 catches.

Test Record - 57 Tests, 3,643 runs (Av. 39.17) including 10 centuries, 79 wickets (Av. 29.24) and 42 catches.

THE ENCYCLOPAEDIA OF CRICKET

(IN TWO VOLUMES)

Edited by

YOGRAJ THANI

With a Foreword by

Dr. NAROTTAM PURI

VOL. II

GIAN PUBLISHING HOUSE

New Delhi-110002

GIAN PUBLISHING HOUSE
4-C Ansari Road, Daryaganj
New Delhi-110002

All rights reserved with the publishers.

ISBN 81-212-0321-x Set
81-212-0349-x

PRINTED IN INDIA 1991

Published by Mrs. Gayatri Garg for Gian Publishing House, New Delhi-110002.
Printed at Goyal Offset Printers, Delhi.

Compiled by

Lokesh Thani

Statistics by

Vivek Thani
Ekta Gothi
Kishore Sharma

Photographs by

Cricket Yug

Lay-out Artist

Vinod Gola

References

Khel Sahitya Kendra

N

NADKARNI RAGHUNATH GANGARAM

India (born 1932) - A left-handed batsman and a left-arm slow spin bowler. Test debut on December 16, 1955 against New Zealand at the age of 23 years and 252 days. Score on Test debut was 68 not out in the third Test at New Delhi. Last Test of the career played against New Zealand in March 1968. Score on last appearance in Test was 21 in the fourth Test at Auckland. Age at the time of retirement from Test cricket was 35 years and 338 days. He played for Maharashtra and Bombay. In his first class career he made, 8,880 runs including 14 centuries and took 500 wickets.

Test Record - 41 Tests, 1,414 runs (Av. 25.70) including 1 century, 88 wickets (Av. 29.07) and 22 catches.

NAIK SUDHIR SAKHARAM

India (born 1946) - A right-handed batsman, Test debut on July 4, 1974 against England at the age of 29 years and 152 days. Scores on Test debut were 4 and 77 in the third Test at Edgbaston. Last Test of the career played against West Indies in December 1975. Scores on last appearance in Test were 0 and 6 in the third Test at Calcutta. Had the humiliation of being dismissed at the very first ball in the aforesaid Test. Age at the time of retirement from Test cricket was 29 years and 330 days. He played for Bombay. In his first class career he made, 4,398 runs including 7 centuries.

Test Record - 3 Tests, 141 runs (Av. 23.50).

NAOOMAL JEOOMAL

India (1904-1980) - A right-handed batsman and a right-arm leg-break bowler. Test debut on June 25, 1932 against England at the age of 28 years and 68 days. Scores on Test debut were 33 and 25 in the only Test played at Lord's. Last Test of the career played against England in February 1933. Score on last appearance in Test was 5 in the third Test at Madras. Age at the time of retirement from Test cricket was 28 years and 294 days. He played for Sind. In his first class career he made, 4,056 runs including 7 centuries and took 102 wickets.

Test Record - 3 Tests, 108 runs (Av. 27.00) and 2 wickets (Av. 34.00).

NASH LAURENCE JOHN

Australia (1910-1986) - He was a right-arm fast bowler and a hard-hitting batsman. He played for Tasmania and Victoria. In his first class career he made, 953 runs including 1 century and took 69 wickets.

Test Record - 2 Tests, 30 runs (Av. 15.00), 10 wickets (Av. 12.60) and 6 catches.

NASIM UL GHANI

Pakistan (born 1941) - A left-handed batsman and also an orthodox slow left-arm bowler. He played for Karachi and Staffordshire. In his first class career he made, 4,490 runs including 7 centuries and took 343 wickets.

Test Record - 29 Tests, 747 runs (Av. 16.60) including 1 century, 52 wickets (Av. 37.67) and 11 catches.

NAT WEST BANK TROPHY AND GILLETTE CUP WINNERS

1963	Sussex beat Worcestershire by 14 runs.
1964	Sussex beat Worcestershire by eight wickets.
1965	Yorkshire beat Surrey by 175 runs.
1966	Warwickshire beat Worcestershire by five wickets.
1967	Kent beat Somerset by 32 runs.
1968	Warwickshire beat Sussex by four wickets
1969	Yorkshire beat Derbyshire by 69 runs.
1970	Lancashire beat Sussex by six wickets.
1971	Lancashire beat Kent by 24 runs.
1972	Lancashire beat Warwickshire by four wickets.
1973	Gloucestershire beat Sussex by 40 runs.
1974	Kent beat Lancashire by four wickets.
1975	Lancashire beat Middlesex by seven wickets.
1976	Northamptonshire beat Lancashire by four wickets.
1977	Middlesex beat Glamorgan by five wick-

ets.
1978 Sussex beat Somerset by five wickets.
1979 Somerset beat Northamptonshire by 45 runs.
1980 Middlesex beat Surrey by seven wickets.
1981 Derbyshire beat Northamptonshire by losing fewer wickets with the scores level.
1982 Surrey beat Warwickshire by nine wickets
1983 Somerset beat Kent by 24 runs.
1984 Middlesex beat Kent by four wickets.
1985 Essex beat Nottinghamshire by 1 run.
1986 Sussex beat Lancashire by seven wickets.
1987 Nottinghamshire beat Northamptonshire by three wickets.
1988 Middlesex beat Worcestershire by three wickets.
1989 Warwickshire beat Middlesex.

NAUSHAD ALI

Pakistan (born 1943) - A sound wicket-keeper and a useful right-handed opening batsman. He played for Karachi. In his first class career he made, 4,136 runs including 8 centuries, and 165 dismissals.

Test Record - 6 Tests, 156 runs (Av. 14.18) and 9 dismissals (9ct).

NAVLE JANARDHAN GNANOBA

India (1902-1979) - A right-handed batsman and a useful wicket-keeper. Test debut on June 25, 1932 against England at the age of 29 years and 198 days. Scores on Test debut were 12 and 13 in the only Test played at Lord's. Last Test of the career played against England in December 1953. Scores on last appearance in Test were 13 and 4 in the first Test at Bombay. Age at the time of retirement from Test cricket was 31 years and 11 days. India's first wicket-keeper and had the honour of facing the first ball for India in Test as an opener in the only Test against England at Lord's in 1932. Also scored the first run for his side. He played for Gwalior. In his first class career he made, 1,958 runs and 135 dismissals.

Test Record - 2 Tests, 42 runs (Av. 10.50) and 1 catch.

NAYAK SUVENDRA VITHAL

India (born 1954) - A stroke-playing right-handed batsman and a medium-pace swing bowler. He played for Bombay. In his first class career he made, 1,541 runs including 2 centuries and took 105 wickets.

Test Record - 2 Tests, 19 runs (Av. 9.50) and 1 catch.

NAYUDU COTTARI SUBHAN

India (born 1914) - A right-handed batsman and a right-arm leg-break and googly bowler. Younger brother of C.K.Nayudu. Test debut on January 5, 1934 against England at the age of 19 years and 258 days. Scores on Test debut were 36 and 15 in the second Test at Calcutta. Last Test of the career played against England in January 1952. Scores on last appearance in Test were 21 and 0 in the fourth Test at Kanpur. Age at the time of reitrement from Test cricket was 37 years and 267 days. He toured England twice, and Australia and Ceylon once. In the famous match against Surrey in England in 1946 he performed the 'hat-trick'. He was the first bowler to capture 40 wickets in Ranji Trophy season of 1942-43 when he gave away less than 13 runs per wicket and took five or more wickets in an innings six times and 10 or more in a match thrice. Against Rajputana he scored 127 runs and took 12 wickets for 56 runs. In the final of 1944-45 against Bombay at Brabourns Stadium he had a marathon spell in history of first-class cricket. He bowled 917 balls (152.5 overs) in the match and in the process captured 11 wickets for 428 runs. He played for Central India and Madhya Pradesh. In his first class career he made, 5,664 runs including 3 centuries and took 636 wickets.

Test Record - 11 Tests, 147 runs (Av. 9.18), 2 wickets (Av. 179.50) and 3 catches.

NAYUDU COL COTTARI KANKAIYA

India (1895-1967) - A right-handed batsman and a right-arm off-break bowler. Elder brother of C.S. Nayudu. Test debut on June 25, 1932 against England at the age of 36 years and 234 days. Scores on Test debut were 40 and 10 in the only Test played at Lord's. Last Test of the career played against England in August 1936. Scores on last appearance in Test were 5 and 81 in the third Test at the Oval. Age at the time of retirement from Test cricket was 40 years and 288

days. Became the first Indian cricketer to be honoured by the Government of India when he was awarded the "Padma Bhushan" for his services to Indian cricket. He played for Madras, Holkar and United Provinces. In his first class career he made, 11,069 runs including 26 centuries and took 402 wickets.
Test Record - 7 Tests, 350 runs (Av. 25.00), 9 wickets (Av. 42.88) and 4 catches.

NAZAR MOHAMMAD
Pakistan (born 1921) - A right - handed batsman and a close fielder. He played for Northern India, Karachi and Sind. In his first class career he made, 2,484 runs including 7 centuries.
Test Record - 5 Tests, 277 runs (Av. 39.57) including 1 century and 7 catches.

NAZIR ALI SYED
India (1906-1975) - A right-handed batsman and a right-arm medium-fast bowler. Younger brother of S.Wazir Ali. Test debut on June 25, 1932 against England at the age of 26 years and 17 days. Scores on Test debut were 13 and 6 in the only Test played at Lord's. Last Test of the career played in February 1933 against England. Scores on last appearance in Test were 3 and 8 in the third Test at Madras. Age at retirement from Test cricket was 26 years and 245 days. He played for Southern Punjab and Sussex. In his first class career he made, 3,379 runs including 7 centuries and took 151 wickets.
Test Record - 2 Tests, 30 runs (Av. 7.50) and 4 wickets (Av. 20.75).

NCA
National Cricket Association: The body with official responsibility for cricket in Britain at all levels except those controlled by the TCCB.

NEL JOHN DESMOND
South Africa (born 1928) - A right-handed opening batsman and a fine player of fast bowling. He played for Western Province. In his first class career he made, 1,839 runs including 4 centuries.
Test Record - 6 Tests, 150 runs (Av. 13.63) and 1 catch.

NELSON
The score of 111 runs superstitiously, considered to be unlucky.

NET
Duration of play in the 'nets' for the purpose of practice.

NETS
General term for a practice wicket area, derived from nets strung up between adjacent wickets to prevent a ball being used in one net endangering those practising in another.

NEW BALL
As suggested, a ball that is brand new or in the very early stages of its use in a game, but more relevant in terms of the taking of a second or third new ball in a long innings. Over the years of competitive cricket, the time when a new ball could be taken has varied significantly. At one stage it was even related to the number of runs scored by the batting side. It now relates to overs bowled, and the minimum figure for a first-class game is 75 six-ball overs.

NEWBERRY CLAUDE
South Africa (1889-1916) - A good fielder. He played for Transvaal. In his first class career he made, 251 runs and took 49 wickets.
Test Record - 4 Tests, 62 runs (Av. 7.75), 11 wickets (Av. 24.36) and 3 catches.

NEWMAN SIR JACK
New Zealand (born 1902) - A left-arm medium-pace bowler. He played for Wellington, Canterbury and Nelson. In his first class career he made, 206 runs and took 69 wickets.
Test Record - 3 Tests, 33 runs (Av. 8.25) and 2 wickets (Av. 127.00).

NEWSON EDWARD SERRURIER
South Africa (born 1910) - A hard-hitting right-arm medium-fast bowler. He played for Transvaal and Rhodesia. In his first class career he made,

553 runs including 1 century and took 60 wickets.
Test Record - 3 Tests, 30 runs (Av. 7.50), 4 wickets (Av. 66.25) and 3 catches.

NIAZ AHMAD
Pakistan (born 1945) - A competent right-arm medium-fast bowler and late-order batsman. He played for East Pakistan. In his first class career he made, 466 runs and took 62 wickets.
Test Record - 2 Tests, 17 runs, 3 wickets (Av. 31.33) and 1 catch.

NICHOLS MORRIS STANLEY
England (1900-1961) - A right-arm bowler and a left-handed batsman. He played for Essex. In his first class career he made, 17,827 runs including 20 centuries, took 1,833 wickets and 332 catches.
Test Record - 14 Tests, 355 runs (Av. 29.58), 41 wickets (Av. 28.09) and 11 catches.

NICHOLSON FRANK
South Africa (1909-1982) - An opening batsman and a wicket-keeper. He played for Griqualand West. In his first class career he made, 2,353 runs including 4 centuries, and 69 dismissals.
Test Record - 4 Tests, 76 runs (Av. 10.85) and 3 dismissals (3ct).

NICOLSON JOHN FAIRLESS WILLIAM
South Africa (1899-1935) - A very competent left-handed batsman. He played for Natal and Oxford University. In his first class career he made, 1,543 runs including 3 centuries.
Test Record - 3 Tests, 179 runs (Av. 35.80).

NIGHT-WATCHMAN
The man sent in up the list from his normal position in the batting order to protect a specialist batsman when a wicket falls in the closing minutes of play.

NIP
An unintentional glance or snick from the bat.

NIPBACKER
A ball that moves sharply in towards the batsman after pitching.

NISSAN SHIELD
The major limited-overs competition in South Africa is played between the leading sides on a knock-out system with 55 overs.

Winners

1969-70	Western Province
1970-71	Western Province
1971-72	Eastern Province
1972-73	Western Province
1973-74	Transvaal
1974-75	Natal
1975-76	Eastern Province
1976-77	Natal
1977-78	Rhodesia
1978-79	Transvaal
1979-80	Transvaal
1980-81	Transvaal
1981-82	Western Province
1982-83	Transvaal
1983-84	Transvaal
1984-85	Transvaal
1985-86	Transvaal
1986-87	Natal
1987-88	Eastern Province

NISSAR MAHOMED
India (1910-1963) - A right-handed batsman and a right-arm medium-fast bowler. Test debut on June 25, 1932 against England at the age of 21 years and 324 days. Scores on Test debut were 1 not out and 0 in the only Test played at Lord's. Earned the honour to bowl the first ball for India in Tests and also to capture the first wicket (Herbert Sutcliffe) for India. Became the first Indian bowler to take five wickets in an innings in a Test on debut when he accounted for five wickets for 93 runs in the first innings of the aforesaid Test. Last Test of the career played against England in August 1936. Scores on last appearance in Test were 14 and 0 in the third Test at the Oval. Age at the time of

retirement from Test cricket was 26 years and 17 days. He played for Southern Punjab. In his first class career he made, 1,027 runs and took 384 wickets.
Test Record - 6 Tests, 55 runs (Av. 6.87), 25 wickets (Av. 28.28) and 2 catches.

NITSCHKE HOLMESDALE CHARLES
Australia (1906-1982) - A useful medium-fast bowler. He played for South Australia. In his first class career he made, 3,320 runs including 9 centuries.
Test Record - 2 Tests, 53 runs (Av. 26.50) and 3 catches.

NO BALL
A delivery which in the judgment of either umpire is unfair or not legal because the ball was thrown or because the bowler did not have one foot behind the bowling crease at the time the ball was released. A no-ball cannot take a wicket, and it does not count as one of the six good deliveries of an over: the batting team automatically credited with a run unless the batsman is able to score more by running. A no-ball is not dead, and the batsman may run on a bye or a wide or the batsman may hit the ball without being out if it is caught. When playing the ball, the batsman will be out on a no-ball if he hits the ball twice, either batsman, when running, can be run out or be out by handling the ball or obstructing the field. Any runs gained as a result of hitting the ball are credited to the batsman's total; runs scored without hitting the ball are extras.

NOBLET GEFFERY
Australia (born 1916) - A right-handed medium-pace bowler. He played for South Australia. In his first class career he made, 975 runs and took 282 wickets.
Test Record - 3 Tests, 22 runs (Av. 7.33), 7 wickets (Av. 26.14) and 1 catch.

NOBLE MONTAGUE ALFRED
Australia (1873-1940) - A right-handed batsman of rare style and execution and a good fielder. He played for New South Wales. In his first class career he made, 13,975 runs including 37 centuries, took 625 wickets and 191 catches.
Test Record - 42 Tests, 1,997 runs (Av. 30.25) including 1 century, 121 wickets (Av. 25.00) and 26 catches.

NON STRIKER
Refers to the batsman standing at the bowler's (or nonstriker's) end of the wicket.

NORFOLK
Largely through the exploits in the first-class game of former Middlesex and England batsman Bill Edrich, Surrey and England's John Edrich and former Lancashire batsman Geoff Edrich, Norfolk has become one of the most familiar names for Minor County cricket. The cricketing Edrich family come from within the county border and Bill Edrich led the side for several seasons. In 1981, captained by P. Sharpe, formerly of Yorkshire and England, they finished runners-up. Their first success came in the first year of the competition when they shared the title with Durham and Worcestershire, winning it again in 1905, 1910, 1913 and 1933.

NOREIGA JACK MOLLISON
West Indies (born 1936) - A right-arm off-break bowler. He played for Trinidad. In his first class career he made, 181 runs and 68 wickets.
Test Record - 4 Tests, 11 runs (Av. 3.66), 17 wickets (Av. 29.00) and 2 catches.

NORTHAMPTONSHIRE
Foundation of Present Club: July 31, 1878 at Ketting.
First First-Class Match: Hampshire v Northants. (Southampton) May 19, 20 1920.
Present Principal Ground: County Ground, Wantage Road,Northampton.
County Championship: Runners-up in 1912, 1957, 1965, 1976.
Result in 1985: 10th; won 5, lost 4,drawn 15.
JPL Championship: Best season : 4th in 1974.
Result in 1985: 5th; won 7, lost 4, tied 1, no result 4.
Benson & Hedges Cup: Winners in 1980.

Result in 1985: Losing quarter-finalists.
Nat West Trophy: Winners in 1976.
Result in 1985: Lost in second round.
Highest Team Total: 557-6 dec v Sussex (Hove) 1914.
Lowest Team Total: 12 v Glos (Gloucester) 1907.

NORTHUMBERLAND

Northumberland have enjoyed two brief periods of near success in their history but have yet to win the championship. The first period was in the mid 1920s when they were forced to settle for second place in successive seasons after losing challenge matches against Berkshire and then Buckinghamshire to decide the outright winner. In the 1950s they twice again finished runners-up.

NOT CRICKET

Phrase applied to a set of circumstances or action taken not acceptable in the code of behaviour of any situation. Derived from the fact that cricket had a strong unwritten code of ethics. The breakdown of that piece of sporting lore in recent years has taken much of the meaning out of the phrase.

NOT OUT

To be undismissed during or after an innings. Also the umpire's negative response to appeal from the fielding side.

NOTTINGHAMSHIRE

Foundation of Present Club: April 1841 in Nottingham.
First First-class Match:Sussex *v*Nottinghamshire (Brighton) August 27, 28, 29, 1835. Prior to 1835, matches of importance were played by the Nottingham Old Club.
Present Principal Club: Trent Bridge. Nottingham.
County Champion: 1865, 1868, 1869, 1871, 1872, 1873, 1875, 1879, 1880, 1882, 1883, 1884, 1885, 1886, 1889, 1907, 1929, 1981.
JPL Championship: Best Season : 2nd in 1984.
B&H Cup: Losing finalists in 1982.
Nat West Trophy: Losing finalists in 1985.
Highest Team Total: 739-7 dec v Leics (Trent Bridge) 1903.
Lowest Team Total: 13 v Yorkshire (Trent Bridge) 1901.

NOURSE ARTHUR DULEY

South Africa (1910-1981) - A right-handed batsman with all the strokes. He seldom went right forward except when moving out to drive the slow bowlers, but off his back foot he hit exceedingly hard, whether hooking, forcing to the off or square-cutting. He played for Natal. In his first class career he made, 12,472 runs including 41 centuries, and 135 catches.
Test Record - 34 Tests, 2,960 runs (Av. 53.81) including 9 centuries and 12 catches.

NOURSE ARTHUR WILLIAM

South Africa (1878-1948) - A left-handed batsman of rocklike stability and nerve. He could score all round the wicket and his swinging left-arm cutters were often useful. He played for Natal, Transvaal and Western Province. In his first class career he made, 14,216 runs including 38 centuries, took 305 wickets and 172 catches.
Test Record - 45 Tests, 2,234 runs (Av. 29.78) including 1 century, 41 wickets (Av. 37.87) and 43 catches.

NUNES ROBERT KARL

West Indies (1894-1958) - A fine left-handed opening batsman with a sound defence and plenty of stroke power. He played for Jamaica. In his first class career he made, 2,695 runs including 6 centuries.
Test Record - 4 Tests, 245 runs (Av. 30.62) and 2 catches.

NUPEN EIULF PETER

South Africa (1902-1977) - A right-arm medium-fast round the wicket bowler. On mat, his off-cutter would nip off quickly and lift sharply and his leg-cutter was more obvious. He played for Transvaal. In his first class career he made, 1,635 runs and took 334 wickets.
Test Record - 17 Tests, 348 runs (Av. 14.50), 50 wickets (Av. 35.76) and 9 catches.

NURSE SEYMOUR MC DONALD

West Indies (born 1933) - A right-handed stroke-playing batsman, a superb driver off the back foot, an occasional off-spin bowler and a specialist

close-to-the-wicket fielder. He played for Barbados. In his first class career he made, 9,489 runs including 26 centuries, and took 12 wickets.
Test Record - 29 Tests, 2,523 runs (Av. 47.60) including 6 centuries and 21 catches.

NYALCHAND SHAH

India (born 1919) - A left-handed batsman and a left-arm slow spin bowler. Test debut on October 23, 1952 against Pakistan at the age of 27 years and 39 days. Scores on Test debut were 6 not out and 1 in the second Test at Lucknow. Played in one Test only. He played for Kathiawar. In his first class career he made, 420 runs and took 235 wickets.
Test Record - 1 Test, 7 runs (Av.3.50) and 3 wickets.

NZCC

New Zealand Cricket Council.

O

O'BRIEN LEO PATRICK JOSEPH
Australia (born 1907) - A small, neat, left-handed opening batsman. He played for Victoria. In his first class career he made, 3,303 runs including 7 centuries.
Test Record - 5 Tests, 211 runs (Av. 26.37) and 3 catches.

O'BRIEN SIR TIMOTHY CAREW BART
England (1861-1948) - A dashing right-handed batsman. He played for Oxford University and Middlesex. In his first class career he made, 11,397 runs including 15 centuries, 172 catches and 2 stumpings.
Test Record - 5 Tests, 59 runs (Av. 7.37) and 4 catches.

O'CONNOR JACK
England (1897-1977) - A right-handed batsman and a good fine hooker. He played for Essex and Buckinghamshire. In his first class career he made, 28,778 runs including 72 centuries, took 557 wickets, 210 catches and 1 stumping.
Test Record - 4 Tests, 153 runs (Av. 21.85) and 2 catches.

O'CONNOR JOHN DENIS ALPHONSUS
Australia (1875-1941) - A right-arm fattish medium pace bowler, with immaculate length, good control and able to make the ball lift and swing towards leg. He played for New South Wales and South Australia. In his first class career he made, 695 runs and took 224 wickets.
Test Record - 4 Tests, 86 runs (Av. 12.28), 13 wickets (26.15) and 3 catches.

O'DONNELL SIMON PATRICK
Australia (born 1963) - A stroke-player and a brisk right-arm seam bowler. He plays for Victoria. In his first class career he made, 2,358 runs including 5 centuries and took 243 wickets.
Test Record - 6 Tests, 206 runs (Av. 29.42), 6 wickets (Av. 84.00) and 4 catches.

O'KEEFFE KERRY JAMES
Australia (born 1949) - A right-arm leg-break bowler and right-handed batsman. He played for New South Wales and Somerset. In his first class career he made, 4,169 runs, took 476 wickets and 112 catches.
Test Reocrd - 24 Tests, 644 runs (Av. 25.76), 53 wickets (38.07) and 15 catches.

O'LINN SYDNEY
South Africa (born 1927) - A left-handed batsman of strong defensive outlook and also a capable deputy wicket-keeper. He played for Western Province and Kent. In his first class career he made, 4,525 runs including 4 centuries and 103 dismissals.
Test Record - 7 Tests, 297 runs (Av. 27.00) and 4 catches.

O'NEILL NORMAN CLIFFORD
Australia (born 1937) - A right-handed stroke-marker batsman and a useful leg-spin bowler. He was also a brilliant cover fielder with a superb throw. He played for New South Wales. In his first class career he made, 13,859 runs including 45 centuries, took 99 wickets and 104 catches.
Test Record - 42 Tests, 2,779 runs (Av. 45.55) including 6 centuries, 17 wickets (Av. 39.23) and 21 catches.

O'REILLEY WILLIAM JOSEPH
Australia (born 1905) - A left-handed batsman. He had no style but could hit tremendously hard. He was also a leg-break bowler. He played for New South Wales. In his first class career he made, 1,655 runs and took 774 wickets.
Test Record - 27 Tests, 410 runs (Av. 12.81), 144 wickets (Av. 22.59) and 7 catches.

O'SULLIVAN DAVID ROBERT
New Zealand (born 1944) - A slow left-handed bowler and often useful right-handed batsman. He

played for Central Districts and Durham. In his first class career he made, 2,174 runs and took 523 wickets.
Test Record - 11 Tests, 158 runs (Av. 9.29), 18 wickets (Av. 67.83) and 2 catches.

OAKMAN ALAN STANLEY MYLES
England (born 1930) - A right-handed batsman, at his best on hard wickets against medium and fast-medium bowling. He played for Sussex. In his first class career he made, 21,800 runs including 22 centuries, took 736 wickets and 594 catches.
Test Record - 2 Tests, 14 runs (Av. 7.00) and 7 catches.

OBSTRUCTING THE FIELD
If either batsman wilfully obstructs a member of the fielding side by sound or action, he may be given out on appeal. The infringement may be caused by either batsman distracting a fieldsman by making a noise or by intervening in some physical manner.
Although a batsman is legally entitled to hit the ball a second time in defence of his wicket, he shall be deemed to have obstructed the field if, in the course of doing so, he balks a fieldsman trying to make a catch. Should either batsman wilfully prevents a ball from being caught, it is the striker who is given out.

OBSTRUCTION
The obstruction of a batsman taking a run. The ball is given out as a dead ball and the runs completed or attempted are credited to the batsman.

OCCUPATION OF THE CREASE
Playing defensively with a view to avoiding dismissal rather than to take runs.

OCHSE ARTHUR EDWARD
South Africa (1870-1918) - A good batsman. He played for Transvaal. In his first class career he made, 231 runs.
Test Record - 2 Tests, 16 runs.

OCHSE ARTHUR LENNOX
South Africa (1899-1949) - A right-arm fast bowler. He played for Eastern Province. In his first class career he made, 564 runs and took 140 wickets.
Test Record - 3 Tests, 11 runs (Av. 3.66), 10 wickets (Av. 36.20) and 1 catch.

OFF
The half of the field, the continuous line from centre stump to centre stump being the divider, in front of the batsman when he takes up his stance.

OFF BREAK
A spin bowler's delivery that deviates from the off to the leg after hitting the pitch.

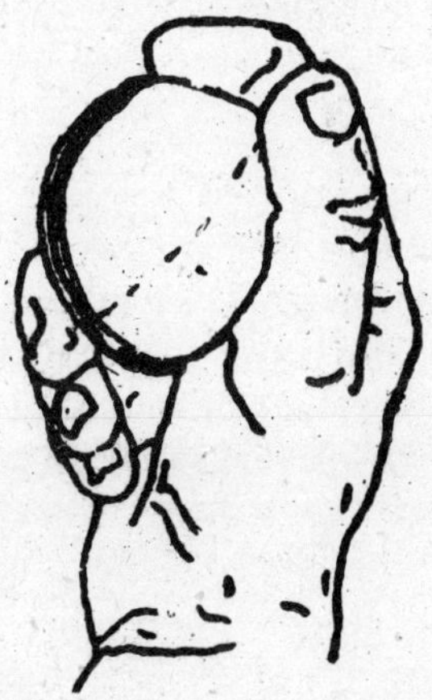

Grip for the Off-Break

OFF CUTTER
A pace bowler's delivery that deviates from the off to the leg after hitting the pitch.

OFF DRIVE
An attacking stroke off the front or back foot when the ball is struck to the mid-off region.

OFF PLAY
Hitting ball on off-side.

OFF SIDE

Anything on the off-side of the field. Also, a batsman who scores strongly on that side of the wicket is often known as an 'off-side' player.

OFF SPIN

The delivery that pitches and turns from the off to the leg, when bowled to a right-handed batsman.

OFFER

To attempt to play a stroke and not to leave in intentionally.

OGILVIE ALAN DAVID

Australia (born 1951) - A right-handed useful batsman. He played for Queensland. In his first class career he made, 3,006 runs including 8 centuries.
Test Record - 5 Tests, 178 runs (Av. 17.80) and 5 catches.

OLD BALL

As suggested, a ball that has been in use for some time in an innings. Often referred to when spinners are in operation or in the period leading up to the availability of a new ball.

CHRIS OLD

OLD CHRISTOPHER MIDDLETON

England (born 1948) - A left-handed batsman, a brilliant fielder and also a right-arm,fast-medium pace bowler. He played for Yorkshire, Northern Transvaal and Warwickshire. In his first class career he made, 7,756 runs including 6 centuries, took 1,070 wickets and 214 catches.
Test Record - 46 Tests, 845 runs (Av. 14.82), 143 wickets (Av. 28.11) and 22 catches.

OLD TRAFFORD

It is not often realised that Old Trafford, where the Manchester Cricket Club built its ground in the 1850s, preceded Lord's as a Test match ground by 11 days in July 1884. With spectators sitting on the grass round a large playing area, it can still accommodate nearly 25,000 and has an adjoining ground for use as a car park as well as for practice facilities.

Conveniently situated beside Warwick Road station in the southern suburbs of Manchester, it has always had a superb outfield, but its pitches have varied between the flawless one on which Bobby Simpson made 311 out of Australia's 656 for eight declared in 1964 (England replied with 611) to the one on undefeatable 19 wickets. It was the scene of a famous match in 1902 when Victor-Trumpoer made a 100 before lunch on the first day and Australia won by three runs.

OLDFIELD WILLIAM ALBERT STANLEY

Australia (1894-1976) - An artistic wicket-keeper and right-handed batsman. He played for New South Wales. In his first class career he made, 6,135 runs including 6 centuries and 661 dismis sals.
Test Record - 54 Tests, 1,427 runs (Av. 22.65) and 130 dismissals (78 ct, 52 st).

ON

That half of the field divided by the continuous line from centre stump to centre stump that is behind the batsman when he takes his stance.

ON DRIVE

As in the OFF-DRIVE, but this time hit to the mid-on region.

ON SIDE
Anything on the on or leg side of the field. Also the 'on-side' player is one who scores predominantly through that side of the field.

ONE DAY CRICKET
A game usually decided on limited-overs in one day, weather permitting. This style of competition, often played on a knockout basis, began cautiously in 1963 with the introduction in English County cricket of the Gillette Cup series and since has spread gradually and almost reached 'plague' proportions. Because of the urgency created by time, innovations have been made by players and captains. In the opinion of many pundits the innovations have not enhanced the first-class game.

RULES OF ONE DAY INTERNATIONAL COMPETITION

Status of Matches

Matches shall not be considered first-class.

Declaration

Declarations may be made at any time.

Restriction on Placement of Fieldsmen

At the instant of delivery, a minimum of four fieldsmen (plus the bowler and wicket-keeper) must be within an arc abounded by two semi-circles centred on each middle stump (each with a radius of 30 yards) and joined by a parallel line on each side of the pitch. In the event of an infringement, the square-leg umpire shall call "No-ball". The fielding circle should be marked by painted white "dots" at five-yard intervals.

Fieldsman Leaving the Field

A player who suffers an injury caused by an external blow (e.g. not a pulled muscle) and has to leave the field for medical attention may bowl immediately on his return.

Substitutes

No substitute may take the field until the player for whom he is to substitute has been absent from the field for a period of five consecutive complete overs.

Mode of Delivery

No bowler may deliver the ball under-arm.

Limitation of Overs by any one Bowler

No bowler may deliver more than one fifth of the allocated overs, except that where the total of overs is not divisible by five, an additional over shall be allowed to the minimum number of bowlers necessary to make up the balance.

Over-rates

All teams are expected to complete the bowling of their overs within an allotted playing time. In the event of their failing to do so, the full quota of overs will be generally completed but the fielding team will be fined when it has failed to bowl in the allotted time. If the innings is limited in advance, the calculations will be revised accordingly.

Wide-ball - Judging a Wide

Umpires are instructed to apply a very strict and consistent interpretation in regard to the Law in order to prevent negative bowling wide of the wicket or over the batsman's head.
The following criteria should be adopted as a guide to umpires:
1. If the ball passes either side of the wicket sufficiently wide to make it virtually impossible for the striker to play a "normal cricket stroke" both from where he is standing and from where he should normally be standing at the crease, the umpire shall call and signal "Wide" ;
2. If the ball passes over head-height of the striker standing upright at the crease, the umpire shall call and signal " Wide".
Note: The above provisions do not apply if the striker makes contact with the ball.

The Bowling of Fast, Short-pitched Balls

A bowler shall be limited to one fast, short-pitched ball per over. If he bowls a second, the umpire shall call and signal **"No-ball"**. If the bowler is no-balled a second time in the innings for the same offence, the bowler shall be warned, and after a further offence he shall be taken off and not allowed to bowl again in the innings.

RULES AND PLAYING CONDITIONS APPLYING ONLY TO THE REFUGE ASSURANCE LEAGUE

Length of Innings

(i). In an uninterrupted match:

(a) Each side shall bat for 40 overs unless all out earlier.

(b) If the side fielding first fails to bowl 40 overs the overs shall be completed and the side batting second shall receive the same number of overs as their opponents.

(c) If the team batting first is all out within two minutes of the scheduled time for the tea interval, the innings of the side batting second shall be limited to the same number of overs as their opponents have received, the overs in which the last wicket falls to count as a complete over.

(ii) In matches where the start is delayed or play is suspended:

(A) The object shall be to rearrange the number of overs so that both teams may receive the same number of overs (minimum 15 each). The calculation of the overs to be bowled shall be based on an average rate of one over per 3(1/2) minutes or part thereof in the time remaining as per the permissible day light conditions of the country when the match is being played.

(B) If the start is delayed by not more than an hour and the match is thereby reduced to no fewer than 31 overs a side, the time of the close of the first innings shall be fixed allowing 3 (1/2) minutes for each over. If the team, fielding first fails to bowl the revised number of overs by the agreed time, the principles set out in (i), c & b shall apply.

(C) Where play is suspended after the match has started on the basis of each team batting for more than twenty overs, the number of overs should be rearranged so that both teams may bat for the same number of overs (minimum of 20 each); the calculation as above.

(D) If, owing to a suspension of play during or immediately prior to the start of the innings of the team batting second, it is not possible for that team to have the opportunity of batting for the same number of overs (minimum, 20 overs) as their opponents, they will bat for a number of overs to be calculated as above. The team batting second shall not bat for a greater number of overs than their opponents unless the latter have been all out in fewer than the agreed number of overs.

(E) If there is insufficient time to provide for a match as above (20 overs minimum), that match shall be void and, conditions permitting, a new match of ten overs each side shall be played provided play begins not later than 5.40 p.m.(5.10 for televised matches) as per rules applicable in England. If there is any suspension of play during the ten-overs minimum that match shall be void and, conditions permitting, a new match of ten overs per side shall be played as described in (e) above.

Over - rates

The allotted playing-time for completing 40 overs is 2 hours 20 minutes.

Limitation of the Bowler's Run-up

The bowler's run-up, including his preliminary approach, shall be limited to 15 yards, to be measured from the wicket.

The Result

(i) Where both sides have had the opportunity to bat for the same number of overs and the scores are level, the result is a tie, no account being taken of the number of wickets which have fallen.

(ii) If, owing to suspension of play, the number of overs in the innings of the side batting second has to be revised their target score which they must exceed to win the match shall be calculated by multiplying the revised number of overs by the average runs per over scored by the side batting first. If the target score involves a fraction, the final scores cannot be equal and the result cannot be a tie.

(iii) If a match is abandoned before the side batting

second has received its allotted number of overs, the result shall be decided on the average run-rate throughout both innings, provided the team batting second has received not less than twenty overs.

(iv) If a result cannot be achieved as above the match shall be declared "No Result".

(v) If the team batting first has been all out without using its full quota of overs, the calculation of the run-rate shall be based on the full quota of overs to which it was entitled.

Scoring of Points

(i) The team winning a match to score four points.
(ii) In a "tie" each team to score two points.
(iii) In a "No Result" match each team to score two points.
(iv) If two or more teams finish with an equal number of points for any of the first four places, their final positions will be decided by:
  (a) The most wins or, if still equal
  (b) The higher run-rate throughout the tournament.

ONE LEG
The position of the bat held by the batsman facing the ball to cover leg stump.

OPENER
Either of the first two batsmen or bowlers of a team in an innings.

ORDER
The order in which the players take their turn to bat.

OUT
To be dismissed when batting. The 1744 Laws state, for example: 'If ye wicket is bowled down its out.'

OUTCRICKET
Outside of the bowling and wicket-keeping, a general term for a team's performance on the field.

OUTER
At first-class cricket venue where spectators must either be members or players to gain entry. The area set aside for the paying public. Usually sited at the opposite or 'outer' end of the ground from the members' area.

OUTFIELD
The part of the playing area out towards the boundary.

OUTING
A period spent in the field.

OUTSWINGER
When bowling to a right-handed batsman, the outstanding bowler should be pitching the ball on the length in line with the off-stump or just outside, attempting to bring the batsman forward.
The grip varies from the basic, in that whilst the seam is vertical on delivery, it is angled towards the slips (First of Second). The inside of the thumb lies against the edge of the seam. At the moment of release, the fingers should be behind the ball with the wrist firm. This action can cause a slow backward rotation of the ball that helps steady the seam for maximum swing towards the slips.

Grip for Outswinger

OVAL ADELAIDE

Without question the most beautiful of all the grounds in Australia and surely among the prettiest in the cricketing world. The Adelaide Oval look out over hectares of parks and gardens to the Adelaide Hill in the distance. Looking down on it from the north-eastern side is the spire of St. Peter's Cathedral, with its friendly, Sunday morning chimes. There is something 'olde worlde' about the corrugated-iron roofs, the brick and timber pavilions, and the ornately dressed scoreboard astride the Oval's 'hill' area at the north-eastern corner.

The land is leased by the South Australia Cricket Association from the Adelaide City Council. The design of its playing area will always make the oval the odd man out, because of the very short boundaries square of the wicket and the extraordinarily long boundaries on the straight hit. The Adelaide Oval was opened in 1873 and hosted its first Test match, against England, captained by Lord Harris in 1884.

That situation lasted only a few years; the red-clay experiment was discarded, and the wickets once more are made with black clay and are more like the earlier Adelaide Oval tracks.

OVER

A series of usually 6 or sometimes 8 balls bowled consecutively by the one bowler from the end of the wicket. During the over the bowler may be bowling to different batsmen. The same bowler is not permitted to bowl successive overs.

OVER RATE

The average rate of oversbowled per hour during period of a match.

OVER THE WICKET

Indicates that the hand with which the bowler, whether right-arm or left-arm, is bowling, is the one nearer the bowler's wicket.

OVERTHROW

A throw at the wicket which is gathered by other members of the fielding side and goes far enough to allow the batsman to take one or more runs. It may go to the boundary, in which case it is four overthrows, and it counts to the batsman if he hit the ball originally. Overthrows can be run even if he has broken the wicket on its course.

OVERTON GUY WILLIAM FITZROY

New Zealand (born 1919) - A right-arm bowler of considerable pace, able to swing the ball both ways. He played for Southland and Otago. In his first class career he made, 137 runs and took 169 wickets.

Test Record - 3 Tests, 8 runs (Av. 1.60), 9 wickets (Av. 28.66) and 1 catch.

OWEN SMITH DR HAROLD GEOFFREY O.

South Africa (born 1909) - A right-handed batsman who drove, cut and hit to leg brilliantly. He bowled slow leg-breaks successfully and fielded with speed and accuracy either at cover-point or in the deep. In his first class career he made, 4,059 runs including 3 centuries and took 319 wickets.

Test Record - 5 Tests, 252 runs (Av. 42.00) and 4 catches.

OXENHAM RONALD KEVEN

Australia (1891-1939) - A right-handed batsman and right-arm medium-pace bowler. He played for Queensland. In his first class career he made, 3,693 runs including 4 centuries, and took 369 wickets.

Test Record - 7 Tests, 151 runs (Av. 15.10), 14 wickets (Av. 37.28) and 4 catches.

Test Record - 14 Tests, 492 runs (Av. 24.60) including 1 century, 5 wickets (Av. 46.20) and 6 catches.

P

PACE
The speed at which a ball is delivered by a bowler.

PAD
The covering worn by batsmen and wicket-keepers on legs to protect their legs, knees and ankles.

PAD PLAY
Thrusting the padded leg at the line of the ball, rather than letting the ball go or offering a stroke. The practice of pad-play was so prevalent among English batsmen when trying to cope with spin bowling that the laws were altered recently to enable a batsman to be given out leg-before-wicket when struck on the pad outside the line of the off stump.

PADGETT DOUGLAS ERNEST VERNON
England (born 1934) - A right-handed batsman. He played for Yorkshire. In his first class career he made, 21,124 runs including 32 centuries and 261 catches.
Test Record - 2 Tests, 51 runs (Av. 12.75).

PADMORE ALBERT LEROY
West Indies (born 1946) - A tall off-spin bowler. He played for Barbados. In his first class career he made, 562 runs and took 193 wickets.
Test Record - 2 Tests, 8 runs (Av. 8.00),1 wicket (Av.135.00)

PAGE MILFORD LAURENSON
New Zealand (born 1902) - A right-handed batsman, a useful slow change-bowler and a reliable slip fielder. He played for Canterbury. In his first class career he made, 5,857 runs including 9 centuries and took 73 wickets.

PAINE GEORGE ALFRED EDWARD
England (1908-1978) - A slow left-arm bowler. He played for Middlesex and Warwickshire. In his first class career he made, 3,430 runs, took 1,021 wickets and 155 catches.
Test Record - 4 Tests, 97 runs (Av. 16.16), 17 wickets (Av. 27.47) and 5 catches.

PAIR
Loose reference to the making of two ducks in a game. Also, two batsmen at the wicket, e.g. the 'opening pair'.

PAIRAUDEAU BRUCE HAMILTON
West Indies (born 1931) - A right-handed opening batsman. He played for British Guiana and Northern Districts. In his first class career he made, 4,930 runs including 11 centuries.
Test Record - 13 Tests, 454 runs (Av. 21.61) including 1 century and 6 catches.

PALAIRET LIONEL CHARLES HAMILTON
England (1870-1933) - A right-handed opening batsman. He played for Oxford University and Somerset. In his first class career he made 15,777 runs including 27 centuries, took 136 wickets and 260 dismissals.
Test Record - 2 Tests, 49 runs (Av. 12.25) and 2 catches.

PALIA PHIROZ EDULJI
India (1910 - 1981) - A left - handed batsman and left-arm slow spin bowler. Test debut on June 25, 1932 against England at the age of 21 years and 290 days. Age at the time of retirement from Test cricket was 25 years and 295 days. He played for Mysore. In his first class career he made, 4,455 runs including 8 centuries, and 204 wickets.
Test Record - 2 Tests, 29 runs (Av. 9.66).

PALMER GEORGE EUGENE
Australia (1860-1910) - A right-arm medium-pace

spin bowler. He played for Victoria and Tasmania. In his first class career he made, 2,728 runs including 1 century, took 594 wickets and 108 catches.
Test Record - 17 Tests, 296 runs (Av. 14.09), 78 wickets (Av. 21.51) and 13 catches.

PARFITT PETER HOWARD
England (born 1936) - A left-handed high class batsman, a useful off-spinner and a superb fielder. He played for Norfolk and Middlesex. In his first class career he made, 26,924 runs including 58 centuries, took 277 wickets and 565 catches.
Test Record - 37 Tests, 1,882 runs (Av. 40.91) including 7 centuries, 12 wickets (Av. 47.83) and 42 catches.

PARKER JOHN MORTON
New Zealand (born 1951) - A right-handed batsman with a short backlift and plenty of pluck. He played for Northern Districts and Worcestershire. In his first class career he made, 11,314 runs including 21 centuries, took 15 wickets and 191 dismissals.
Test Record - 36 Tests, 1,498 runs (Av. 24.55) including 3 centuries and 30 catches.

PARKER NORMAN MURRAY
New Zealand (born 1948) - A right-handed batsman and a good fielder. He played for Otago and Canterbury. In his first class career he made, 2,102 runs including 1 century.
Test Record - 3 Tests, 89 runs (Av. 14.83) and 2 catches.

PARKER RAMNATH DHONDU
India (born 1946) - A right-handed opening batsman. Test debut on December 20, 1972 against England at the age of 26 years and 31 days. He played for Bombay. In his first class career he made, 4,455 runs including 8 centuries and took 1 wicket.
Test Record - 2 Tests, 80 runs (Av. 20.00).

PARKHOUSE WILLIAM GILBERT ANTHONY
England (born 1925) - A sound right-handed batsman and a brilliant slip fielder. He played for Glamorgan. In his first class career he made, 23,508 runs including 32 centuries and 323 catches.
Test Record - 7 Tests, 373 runs (Av. 28.69) and 3 catches.

PARKIN CECIL HARRY
England (1886-1943) - A good off-spin bowler. He played for Durham, Yorkshire and Lancashire. In his first class career he made, 2,456 runs and took 1,048 wickets.
Test Record - 10 Tests, 160 runs (Av. 12.30), 32 wickets (Av. 35.25) and 3 catches.

PARKS JAMES MICHAEL
England (born 1931) - A brilliant right-handed stroke-maker batsman and a good wicket-keeper. He played for Sussex and Somerset. In his first class career he made, 36,673 runs including 51 centuries, took 51 wickets and 1,182 dismissals.
Test Record - 46 Tests, 1,962 runs (Av. 32.16) including 2 centuries, and 114 dismissals (103ct, 11st).

PARRY DEREK RICALDO
West Indies (born 1954) - A right-arm off-spin bowler and a useful right-handed batsman. He played for Leeward Islands and Cambridgeshire. In his first class career he made, 2,552 runs and took 251 wickets.
Test Record - 12 Tests, 381 runs (Av. 22.41), 23 wickets (Av. 40.69) and 4 catches.

PARSANA DHIRAJ DEVSHIBHAI
India (born 1947) - A left-handed batsman and left-arm medium-pace and slow spin bowler. Test debut on January 12, 1979 against West Indies at the age of 31 years and 40 days. He played for Railways and Gujarat. In his first class career he made, 2,943 runs including 2 centuries and took 320 wickets.
Test Record - 2 Tests, 1 run (Av. 0.50) and 1 wicket (Av. 50.00).

PARTNERSHIP
The performance of two batsmen while together during an innings measured in terms of the runs added to the team's total while they are together.

PARTRIDGE JOSEPH TITUS
South Africa (born 1932) - A right-arm seam bowler. He played for Rhodesia. In his first class career he made, 523 runs and took 376 wickets.
Test Record - 11 Tests, 73 runs (Av. 10.42), 44 wickets (Av. 31.20) and 6 catches.

PASCOE LEONARD STEPHEN FORMERLY DURTANOVICH LEN
Australia (born 1950) - A very determined right-arm fast-medium bowler and a good outfielder. He played for New South Wales. In his first class career he made, 502 runs and took 310 wickets.
Test Record - 14 Tests, 106 runs (Av. 10.60), 64 wickets (Av. 26.06) and 2 catches.

PATAUDI NAWAB OF IFTIQAR ALI KHAN
India (1910-1952) - A right-handed stocky-play was based on a patient and correct technique. He played for Oxford University, Worcestershire and Southern Punjab. In his first class career he made, 8,750 runs including 29 centuries and took 15 wickets.
Test Record - (England - 3) - 144 runs (Av. 28.80) including 1 century. (India -3) - 55 runs (Av. 11.00).

PATAUDI NAWAB OF MANSUR ALI KHAN JUNIOR
India (born 1941) - A right-handed batsman and right-arm off-spin bowler. Son of Late Iftiqar Ali Khan Pataudi . Test debut on December 13, 1961 against England at the age of 20 years and 338 days. Age at the time of retirement from Test cricket was 34 years and 24 days. He played for Sussex and Hyderabad. In his first class career he made, 15,425 runs including 33 centuries and took 207 catches .
Test Record - 46 Tests, 2,793 runs (Av. 34.91) including 6 centuries and 27 catches.

PATEL BRIJESH PARSURAM

BRIJESH PATEL

India (born 1952) - A right-handed batsman. Test debut on June 6, 1974 against West Indies at the age of 21 years and 192 days. Age at the time of retirement from Test cricket was 25 years and 28 days. He played for Karnataka. In his first class career he made, 10,704 runs including 32 centuries and took 7 wickets.
Test Record - 21 Tests, 972 runs (Av. 29.45) including 1 century and 17 catches.

PATEL JASUBHAI MOTIBHAI
India (born 1924) - A right-handed batsman and right-arm off-break bowler. Test debut on February 26, 1955 against Pakistan at the age of 20 years and 90 days. Age at the time of retirement from Test cricket was 35 years and 62 days. He played for Gujarat. In his first class career he made, 787 runs including 1 century and took 248 wickets.
Test Record - 7 Tests, 25 runs (Av. 2.77), 29 wickets (Av. 21.96) and 2 catches.

PATIL SANDEEP MADHUSUDAN
India (born 1956) - A right-handed batsman and right-arm medium-pace bowler. Test debut on January 15, 1980 against Pakistan at the age of 23 years and 148 days. He played for Bombay. In his

NAWAB PATAUDI

SANDEEP PATIL

first class career he made, 7,684 runs including 19 centuries and took 71 wickets.
Test Record - 29 Tests, 1,558 runs (Av. 36.93) including 4 centuries, 9 wickets (Av. 26.66) and 12 catches.

PATTERSON BALFOUR PATRICK
West Indies (born 1961) - A right-arm fast-medium opening bowler. He plays for Jamaica and Tasmania. In his first class career he made, 342 runs and took 209 wickets.
Test Record - 17 Tests, 88 runs (Av. 8.80), 59 wickets (Av. 29.81) and 2 catches.

PAYNTER EDWARD
England (1901-1979) - A left-handed batsman . He played for Lancashire. In his first class career he made, 20,075 runs including 45 centuries and took 30 wickets.
Test Record - 20 Tests, 1,540 runs (Av. 59.23) including 4 centuries, and 7 catches.

PEARSE CHARLES ORMEROD CATO
South Africa (1884-1953) - A useful batsman and a change bowler. He played for Natal. In his first class career he made, 973 runs and took 11 wickets.
Test Record - 3 Tests, 55 runs (Av. 9.16), 3 wickets (Av. 35.33) and 1 catch.

PEATE EDMUND
England (1856-1900) - A left-arm slow bowler. He played for Yorkshire. In his first class career he made, 2,327 runs and took 1,076 wickets.
Test Record - 9 Tests, 70 runs (Av. 11.66), 31 wickets (Av. 22.00) and 2 catches.

PEEBLES IAN ALEXANDER ROSS
England (1908-1980) - A leg-spin bowler. He played for Oxford University, Middlesex and Scotland. In his first class career he made, 2,213 runs and took 923 wickets.
Test Record - 13 Tests, 98 runs (Av. 10.88), 45 wickets (Av. 30.91) and 5 catches.

PEEL ROBERT
England (1857-1941) - A left-arm spin bowler. He played for Yorkshire. In his first class career he made, 12,191 runs including 7 centuries, took 1,754 wickets and 203 catches.
Test Record - 20 Tests, 427 runs (Av. 14.72), 102 wickets (Av. 16.81) and 17 catches.

PELLEW CLARENCE EVERARD
Australia (1893-1981) - He was a good batsman. He played for South Australia. In his first class

career he made, 4,536 runs including 9 centuries and took 12 wickets.
Test Reocrd - 10 Tests, 484 runs (Av. 37.23) including 2 centuries and 4 catches.

PENALTIES
Strictly speaking all 'extras' or 'sundries' (i.e. byes, leg-byes, no-balls and wides) are referred to as penalties. However, there are other penalties for illegal play by fieldsmen. The most common occur when a fieldsman wilfully stops the ball illegally, eg, by using his cap, or when the ball hits a helmet lying on the ground. In these circumstances five runs are added to any runs already made off that delivery.

PERKS REGINALD THOMAS DAVID
England (1911-1977) - A right-arm fast-medium pace bowler and useful left-handed batsman. He played for Worcestershire and Hertfordshire and Monmouthshire. In his first class career he made, 8,956 runs, took 2,233 wickets and 244 catches.
Test Record - 2 Tests, 3 runs, 11 wickets (Av. 32.27) and 1 catch.

PERTH
The Western Australia Cricket Association Ground, known as the 'Waca' (pronounced Wacker), is a pleasant relatively open ground seldom required to accommodate more than 15,000. It used to have reputation for providing the fastest and truest pitches in the world but that was not always so in the 1970s.

PERVEZ SAJJAD
Pakistan (born 1942) - A left-arm leg-break bowler, a rather moderate right-handed batsman and a good fielder. He played for Pakistan International Airlines. In his first class career he made, 786 runs and took 493 wickets.
Test Record - 19 Tests, 123 runs (Av. 13.66), 59 wickets (Av. 23.89) and 9 catches.

PETHERICK PETER JAMES
New Zealand (born 1942) - An off-spin bowler. He played for Otago and Wellington. In his first class career he made, 200 runs and took 189 wickets.
Test Record - 6 Tests, 34 runs (Av. 4.85), 16 wickets (Av. 42.93) and 4 catches.

PETRIE ERIC CHARLTON
New Zealand (born 1927) - A neat wicket-keeper. He played for Auckland and Northern Districts. In his first class career he made, 2,788 runs including 2 centuries and 231 dismissals.
Test Record - 14 Tests, 258 runs (Av. 12.90), and 25 dismissals (25 ct).

PHADKAR DATTARAY GAJARAN
India (1925-1985) - A right-handed batsman and a right-arm medium-fast bowler. Test debut on December 12, 1947 against Australia at the age of 22 years. Age at retirement from Test cricket was 33 years and 23 days. He played for Bombay and Railways. In his first class career he made, 5,377 runs including 8 centuries and took 464 wickets.
Test Record - 31 Tests, 1,229 runs (32.34) including 2 centuries, 62 wickets (Av. 36.85) and 21 catches.

PHILIPSON HYLTON
England (1866-1935) - A competent and versatile batsman and an excellent wicket-keeper. He played for Middlesex and Oxford University. In his first class career he made, 1,951 runs including 2 centuries and 149 dismissals.
Test Record - 5 Tests, 63 runs (Av. 9.00) and 11 dismissals (8ct, 3st).

PHILLIP NORBERT
West Indies (born 1949) - A right-arm medium-fast bowler and a hard-hitting right-handed batsman. He played for Windward Islands and Essex. In his first class career he made, 7,013 runs including 1 century, and took 688 wickets.
Test Record - 9 Tests, 297 runs (Av. 29.70), 28 wickets (Av. 37.18) and 5 catches.

PHILLIPS WAYNE BENTLEY
Australia (born 1958) - A left-handed opening batsman. He played for South Australia. In his first class career he made, 5,060 runs including 9

centuries and 118 dismissals.
Test Record - 27 Tests, 1,485 runs (Av. 32.28) including 2 centuries and 52 catches.

PHILPOTT PETER IAN

Australia (born 1934) - A right-arm leg-break bowler and a very useful batsman. He played for New South Wales. In his first class career he made, 2,886 runs including 4 centuries and took 245 wickets.
Test Record - 8 Tests, 93 runs (Av. 10.33), 26 wickets (Av. 38.46) and 5 catches.

PHYSICAL FITNEES

It is of great importance for cricketers to obtain and maintain a high level of physical fitness at first class and club levels. A fast bowler who cannot bowl more than three or four overs at top pace or a batsman who cannot score past the 20s and 30s because of fatigue is simply not realising their potential for the team. Muscular fitness is another important aspect of fitness which allows the muscles to contract with force and power, and ; yet be flexible enough to offer a wide range of motion without incurring injury.
Skill deteriorates, as fatigue develops, when fitness fades, so too does skill, is often said. The bowler loses accuracy and length; the batsman loses timing and placement. Fatigue is particularly noticeable in a bowler at the completion of several overs of fast deliveries. This type of fatigue is rather acute, is associated with shortness of breath, and results in part, from the accumulation of lactic acid in the blood.

Fitness components for cricket
* general endurance
* speed endurance
* speed and agility
* muscle strength and power
* flexibility

General tolerance

Also called 'stamina', 'cardiorespiratory', 'aerobic capacity', 'cardiovascular' tolerance, is the capacity of the heart, lungs and blood. This type of tolerance is particularly needed by fast bowlers and batsmen.

Speed tolerance

It is closely related to general tolerance. It is the capacity to sustain speed over a short distance over a period of time. This incorporates heart and lung fitness with speed of movement. In cricket, players

SHOAIB MOHAMMAD and WASIM AKRAM

have to sprint when running between the wickets, and chasing after the ball in the field, and fast bowlers have to accelerate in their run-up for each delivery throughout the day's play.

Speed and quickness

To perform fast movements speed is the ability. Fast bowlers need fast arm movements, and need to accelerate quickly during their run-up. Agility is related to speed and thus signifies the ability to change body position and direction quickly. Fielders in particular need to be very agile to stop the ball and return to the wicket-keeper.

Power and muscle strength

In cricket strength is important both for the bowlers and batsmen. But for bowlers particularly in muscles of the legs, arms shoulders, hands and truck.

Power allows a player to perform fast movements. It is a combination of strength and speed and is exhibited by top line fast bowlers who bowl at 160 kph (100 mph).

Muscular tolerance

This is the capacity of muscle to exert force repeatedly against some resistance. Bowlers who bowl for long spells and batsmen who bat for over four hours to score a century are displaying sound muscular tolerance in the muscle groups responsible for those movements.

Testing for fitness

Regular fitness testing is an important preparation of Test, State and Club teams. Results from testing can provide the coach with indications of where as individual stands in the various components of fitness. The following are some of the most commonly used tests to measure physical fitness important in cricket, they are easily administered in a field situation and require very little specialized equipment.

PICKETS

Colloquical term for the boundary derived from the fact that the boundary fence at many first-class venues was a picket fence. Hence the term 'ratling the pickets' when a hard-hit stroke races to the boundary.

PILLING RICHARD

England (1855-1891) - A professional wicket-keeper. He played for Lancashire. In his first class career he made, 2,696 runs and 597 dismissals.

Test Record - 8 Tests, 91 runs (Av. 7.58) and 14 dismissals (10 ct, 4 st).

PITCH

A pitch can only be changed during a match if it becomes unfit for play. This must be decided first by the umpires, but only if the captains agree! A different pitch may be used to continue the match.

PITCH UP

To send the ball up on a good length or better.

PITHEY ANTHONY JOHN

South Africa (born 1933) - A right-handed batsman, either as an opener or later in the order. He played for Western Province and Rhodesia. In his first class career he made, 7,073 runs including 13 centuries.

Test Record - 17 Tests, 819 runs (Av. 31.50) including 1 century and 3 catches.

PITHEY DAVID BARTLETT

South Africa (born 1936) - A right-handed forceful batsman and off-break bowler. He played for Natal and Northamptonshire. In his first class career he made, 3,420 runs including 3 centuries, and took 240 wickets.

Test Record - 8 Tests, 138 runs (Av. 12.54), 12 wickets (Av. 48.08) and 6 catches.

PLACE

To hit the ball through the gaps to obtain maximum number of runs.

PLACE WINSTON

England (born 1914) - A very good batsman. He played for Lancashire. In his first class career he made, 15,609 runs including 36 centuries.

Test Record - 3 Tests, 144 runs (Av. 28.80) including 1 century.

PLAY
The call given by the umpire to indicate that the game should begin. Also, the active part of the game is khown as 'play'.

PLAY AT
To try a stroke at a delivery, usually said when a batsman has offered a stroke but missed.

PLAY ON
When a batsman hits or edges the ball and it continues on to break his stumps. Technically, he is out bowled.

PLAYER
A person partaking in a match.

PLAYLE WILLIAM RODGER
New Zealand (born 1938) - A right-handed batsman with a wide range of strokes, and a good fielder. He played for Auckland and Western Australia. In his first class career he made, 2,888 runs including 4 centuries.
Test Record - 8 Tests, 151 runs (Av. 10.06) and 4 catches.

PLUMB
A wicket that is very easy-paced and even-heighted. Normally, one excellent for strokeplay. Also, when a batsman is palpably in front of his stumps when given out leg-before wicket.

PLUNKET SHIELD
This was recognized first class cricket tournament in New Zealand.
The competition was reorganized on a league system for the 1921-22 season. The Plunket Shield was replaced by the Shell Trophy after the 1974-75 season.

PLUNKET SHIELD AND SHELL TROPHY

WINNERS

1921-22 Auckland
1922-23 Canterbury
1923-24 Wellington
1924-25 Otago
1925-26 Wellington
1926-27 Auckland
1927-28 Wellington
1929-30 Wellington
1930-31 Canterbury
1931-32 Wellington
1932-33 Otago
1933-34 Auckland
1934-35 Canterbury
1935-36 Wellington
1936-37 Auckland
1937-38 Auckland
1938-39 Auckland
1939-40 Auckland
1940-45 No competition
1945-46 Canterbury
1946-47 Auckland
1947-48 Otago
1948-49 Canterbury
1949-50 Wellington
1950-51 Otago
1951-52 Canterbury
1952-53 Otago
1953-54 Central Districts
1954-55 Wellington
1955-56 Canterbury
1956-57 Wellington
1957-58 Otago
1958-59 Auckland
1959-60 Canterbury
1960-61 Wellington
1961-62 Wellington
1962-63 Northern Districts
1963-64 Auckland
1964-65 Canterbury
1965-66 Wellington
1966-67 Central Districts
1967-68 Central Districts
1968-69 Auckland
1969-70 Otago
1970-71 Central Districts
1971-72 Otago
1972-73 Wellington
1973-74 Wellington

1974-75 Otago
1975-76 Canterbury
1976-77 Otago
1977-78 Auckland
1978-79 Otago
1979-80 Northern Districts
1980-81 Auckland
1981-82 Wellington
1982-83 Wellington
1983-84 Canterbury
1984-85 Wellington
1985-86 Otago
1986-87 Central Districts
1987-88 Otago

POCOCK PATRICK LAN
England (born 1946) - A right-arm off-spinner bowler. He played for Surrey and Northern Transvaal. In his first class career he made, 4,867 runs, took 1,607 wickets and 185 catches.
Test Record - 25 Tests, 206 runs (Av. 6.24), 67 wickets (Av. 44.41) and 15 catches.

POLLARD RICHARD
England (1912-1985) - A right-arm fast-medium pace bowler. He played for Lancashire. In his first class career he made, 3,505 runs and took 1,119 wickets.
Test Record - 4 Tests, 13 runs (Av. 13.00), 15 wickets (Av. 25.20) and 3 catches.

POLLARD VICTOR
New Zealand (born 1945) - A right-handed attacking batsman, also a useful off-spin bowler and a brilliant fielder. He played for Central Districts and Canterbury. In his first class career he made, 5,314 runs including 6 centuries, and took 224 wickets.
Test Record - 32 Tests, 1,266 runs (Av. 24.34) including 2 centuries and 40 wickets (Av. 46.32) and 19 catches.

POLLOCK PETER MACLEAN
South Africa (born 1941) - A fast-medium bowler, a good fielder and more than useful right-handed batsman. He played for Eastern Province. In his first class career he made, 3,208 runs and took 485 wickets.
Test Record - 28 Tests, 607 runs (Av. 21.67), 116 wickets (Av. 24.18) and 9 catches.

POLLOCK ROBERT GRAEME
South Africa (born 1944) - A left-handed hard hitting batsman and off-spin bowler. He played for Eastern Province and Transvaal. In his first class career he made, 20,484 runs including 62 centuries, took 43 wickets and 246 catches.
Test Record - 23 Tests, 2,256 runs (Av. 60.97) including 7 centuries, 4 wickets (Av. 51.00) and 17 catches.

PONSFORD WILLIAM HAROLD
Australia (born 1900) - An opening right-handed batsman. He played for Victoria. In his first class career he made, 13,819 runs including 47 centuries.
Test Record - 29 Tests, 2,122 runs (Av. 48.22) including 7 centuries and 21 catches.

POOLE CYRIL JOHN
England (born 1932) - A left-handed attacking stroke-maker batsman. He was brilliant in the deep. He played for Nottinghamshire. In his first class career he made, 19,364 runs including 24 centuries, 220 catches and 5 stumpings.
Test Record - 3 Tests, 161 runs (Av. 40.25) and 1 catch.

POORE BRIGADIER GENERAL ROBERT
South Africa (1866-1938) - He was a good batsman. He played for Hampshire and Natal. In his first class career he made, 3,441 runs including 11 centuries.
Test Record - 3 Tests, 76 runs (Av. 12.66) and 3 catches.

POORE MATT BERESFORD
New Zealand (born 1930) - A right-handed batsman and a useful off-spin change-bowler. He played for Canterbury. In his first class career he made, 2,336 runs including 2 centuries and took 68 wickets.
Test Record - 14 Tests, 354 runs (Av. 15.43), 9 wickets (Av. 40.77) and 1 catch.

PORT-OF-SPAIN

It is one of the world's most striking grounds, though the behaviour of mortals has not always matched the graciousness of nature and matches have been marred by riots. The ground has matting pitches long after others in the Caribbean had turned to grass. It was only in the 1950s that turf pitches were introduced with overall success.

POTHECARY JAMES EDWARD

South Africa (born 1933) - A right-arm fast-medium pace bowler. He played for Western Province. In his first class career he made, 1,039 runs and took 143 wickets.
Test Record - 3 Tests, 26 runs (Av. 6.50), 9 wickets (Av. 39.33) and 2 catches.

MANOJ PRABHAKAR

PRABHAKAR MANOJ

India (born 1963) - A right-handed batsman and a right-arm medium-fast bowler. He played for Delhi. In his first class career he made, 3,891 runs including 10 centuries and took 366 wickets.
Test Record - 2 Tests,86 runs (Av.28.66),1 wicket (Av.102.00)

PRASANNA ERAPALLY ANANTHARAO SHRINIVASA

India (born 1940) - A right-handed batsman and a right-arm off-break bowler. Test debut on January 10, 1962 against England at the age of 21 years and 229 days. Age at retirement from Test cricket was 28 years and 159 days. He played for Mysore. In his first class career he made, 2,476 runs and took 957 wickets.
Test Record - 49 Tests, 735 runs (Av. 11.48), 189 wickets (Av. 30.39) and 18 catches.

PRICE JOHN SIDNEY ERNEST

England (born 1937) - A right-arm medium-fast bowler. He played for Middlesex. In his first class career he made, 1,108 runs and took 817 wickets.
Test Record - 15 Tests, 66 runs (Av. 7.33), 40 wickets (Av. 35.02) and 7 catches.

PRIDEAUX ROGER MALCOLM

England (born 1939) - A right-handed opening batsman. He played for Cambridge University, Kent, Northamptonshire, and Orange Free State. In his first class career he made, 25,136 runs including 41 centuries, and 301 catches.
Test Record - 3 Tests, 102 runs (Av. 20.40).

PRINGLE DEREK RAYMOND

England (born 1958) - A hard-hitting right-handed batsman and a right-arm medium-fast bowler with an excellent action. He played for Cambridge University and Essex. In his first class career he made, 5,335 runs including 7 centuries, took 381 wickets and 26 catches.
Test Record - 14 Tests, 413 runs (Av. 18.77), 29 wickets (38.89) and 7 catches.

PROCTER MICHAEL JOHN

South Africa (born 1946) - A left-arm fast bowler. He played for Natal, Western Province, Rhodesia and Gloucestershire. In his first class career he made, 21,904 runs including 48 centuries, took 1,407 wickets and 324 catches.
Test Record - 7 Tests, 226 runs (Av. 25.11), 41 wickets (Av. 15.02) and 4 catches.

PROFESSIONAL
The player who makes the game his profession and not takes it as his pastime.

PROMNITZ HENRY LOUIS ERNEST
South Africa (1904-1983) - A right-arm off-and leg-spin bowler. He played for Border, Griqualand West and Orange Free State. In his first class career he made, 592 runs and took 150 wickets.
Test Record - 2 Tests, 14 runs (Av. 3.50), 8 wickets (Av. 20.12) and 2 catches.

PROTECTOR
Name given to the shield used to protect the genitals.

PRUDENTIAL WORLD CUP
The most ambitious of all sponsored one-day cricket competitions has been Prudential's support of the World Cup. Admittedly, it has to date taken place on only four occasions, in 1975, 1979, 1983 and 1987 yet it has been such an unqualified success that there can be little doubt that it is certain to be a permanent fixture every four years.

WINNERS OF PRUDENTIAL WORLD CUP

1975 WEST INDIES
1979 WEST INDIES
1983 INDIA
1987 AUSTRALIA

PULL
Cross-bat stroke offered at a short-pitched delivery on a line from about middle stump to outside the off stump, the attempt being to hit the ball away for runs on the on side in front of square leg.

PULL OUT
Colloquial term for declaring an innings closed. Also, for a batsman getting into a position to play a stroke and then changing his mind and stoppng the shot

PULLAR GEOFFREY
England (born 1935) - A tall, left-handed batsman. He played for Lancashire and Gloucestershire. In his first class career he made, 21,528 runs including 41 centuries, took 10 wickets and 126 catches.
Test Record - 28 Tests, 1,974 runs (Av. 43.86) including 4 centuries, and 2 catches.

PUNA NAROTAM
New Zealand (born 1929) - A right-arm off-spin bowler, a brilliant fielder and sometimes a useful batsman. He played for Northern Districts. In his first class career he made, 1,305 runs and took 229 wickets.
Test Record - 3 Tests, 31 runs (Av. 15.50), 4 wickets (Av. 60.00) and 1 catch.

PUNJABI PANANMAL HOTCHAND
India (born 1921) - A right-handed opening batsman. Test debut on January 1, 1955 against Pakistan at the age of 23 years and 192 days. Age at the time of retirement from Test cricket was 33 years and 162 days. He played for Gujarat. In his first class career he made, 1,953 runs including 6 centuries.
Test Record - 5 Tests, 164 runs (Av. 16.40) and 5 catches.

PUT IN
Having won the toss, the captain telling the opposition to bat first. In bowling, to toil hard for the team.

PUT ON
Of a bowler, to be brought into the attack; of a pair of batsmen, the runs 'put on' or scored during their partnership.

PUTTING UP THE SHUTTERS
Giving up the chase for a victory target or just trying to play out the remaining time.

Q

QAIFE WILLIAM
England (1872-1951) - A right-handed batsman, a slow leg-break bowler and a fine cover-point fielder. He played for Sussex, and Warwickshire. In his first class career he made, 36,016 runs including 72 centuries, took 931 wickets,346 catches.
Test Record - 7 Tests, 228 runs (Av. 19.00), and 4 catches.

QASIM ALI OMAR
Pakistan (born 1957) - A right-handed batsman. He played for Karachi and Muslim Commercial Bank. In his first class career he made, 6,549 runs including 17 centuries and took 6 wickets.
Test Record - 23 Tests, 1,431 runs (Av. 39.75) including 3 centuries and 15 catches.

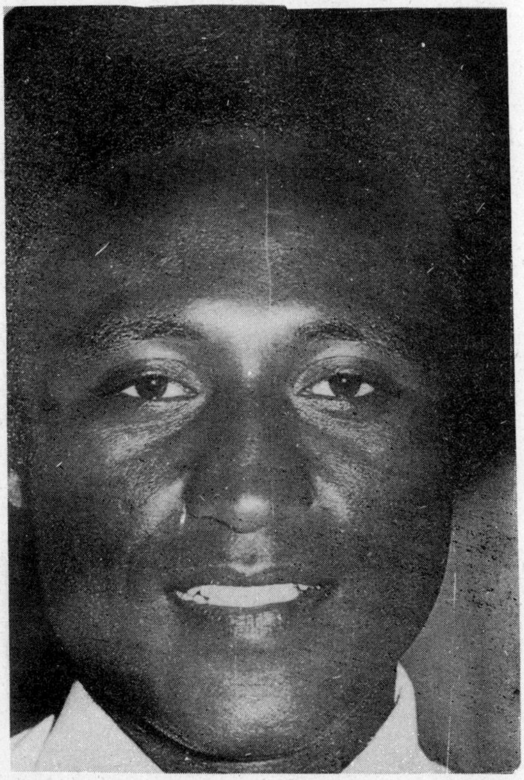

QASIM OMAR

QUAID-E-AZAM TROPHY
Pakistan's principal first-class competition, which was instituted in 1953-54.

WINNERS

1953-54 Bahawalpur
1954-55 Karachi
1955-56 Not held
1956-57 Punjab
1957-58 Bahawalpur
1958-59 Karachi
1959-60 Karachi
1960-61 Not held
1961-62 Karachi Blues
1962-63 Karachi 'A'
1963-64 Karachi Blues
1964-65 Karachi Blues
1965-66 Not held
1966-67 Karachi
1967-68 Not held
1968-69 Lahore
1969-70 P.I.A.
1970-71 Karachi Blues
1971-72 Not held
1972-73 Railways
1973-74 Railways
1974-75 Punjab 'A'
1975-76 National Bank
1976-77 United Bank
1977-78 Habib Bank
1978-79 National Bank
1979-80 P.I.A.
1980-81 United Bank
1981-82 National Bank
1982-83 United Bank
1983-84 National Bank
1984-85 United Bank
1985-86 Karachi
1986-87 National Bank
1987-88 P.I.A.
1988-89 Agricultural Development Bank of Pakistan

QUICK
A fast bowler.

QUILT
A powerful stroker.

QUINN NEVILLE ANTHONY

South Africa (1908-1934) - A left-arm medium-pace bowler. He played for Griqualand West and Transvaal. In his first class career he made, 438 runs and took 186 wickets.

Test Record - 12 Tests, 90 runs (Av. 6.00), 35 wickets (Av. 32.71) and 1 catch.

R

RABONE GEOFFREY OSBOURNE

New Zealand (born 1921) - He was a right-handed batsman, an off-spin bowler and a superb slip fielder. He played for Wellington and Auckland.In his first class career he made, 3,425 runs including 3 centuries and took 173 wickets.
Test Record - 12 Tests, 562 runs (Av. 31.22) including 1 century, 16 wickets (Av. 39.68) and 5 catches.

RACKMANN CARL GRAY

Australia (born 1960) - A tall, right-handed fast bowler. He plays for Queensland. In his first class career he made, 528 runs and took 278 wickets.
Test Record - 5 Tests, 16 runs (Av. 3.20), 23 wickets (Av. 23.43) and 2 catches.

RADFORD NEAL VICTOR

England (born 1957) - A right-arm medium-fast bowler, a good fielder and a useful right-handed batsman. He played for Lancashire and Transvaal. In his first class career he made, 1,763 runs and took 424 wickets.
Test Record - 2 Tests, 13 runs (Av. 6.50) and 3 wickets (Av. 73.00).

RADLEY CLIVE THORNTON

England (born 1944) - He was a right-handed batsman. He played for Middlesex.In his first class career he made, 26,068 runs including 46 centuries,and took 8 wickets and 513 catches.
Test Record - 8 Tests, 481 runs (Av. 48.10) including 2 centuries and 4 catches.

RAJPUT LALCHAND SITARAM

India (born 1961) - A right-handed opening batsman. He played for Bombay. In his first class career he made, 2,989 runs including 6 centuries and took 13 wickets.
Test Record - 2 Tests, 105 runs (Av. 26.25) and 1 catch.

RAMADHIN SONNY

West Indies (born 1930) - A right-arm off-break and leg-break bowler. He first played in the Central Lancashire League in the early 1950s. In his first class career he made, 1,106 runs and took 758 wickets.
Test Record - 43 Tests, 361 runs (Av. 8.20), 158 wickets (Av. 28.98) and 9 catches.

RAMASWAMI COTA

India (born 1896) - A left-handed batsman. Test debut on July 25, 1936 against England at the age of 38 years and 39 days. Scores on Test debut were 40 and 60 in the second Test at Manchester. He played for Madras. In his first class career he made, 2,261 runs including 2 centuries and took 30 wickets.
Test Record - 2 Tests, 170 runs (Av. 56.66).

RAMCHAND GULABRAI SIPAHAHIMALANI

India (born 1927) - A right-handed batsman and a right-arm medium-fast bowler. Test debut on June 5, 1952 against England at the age of 24 years and 309 days. Began his Test career with a "pair of spectacles" when he was dismissed before scoring in both the innings of the first Test at Leeds. Last Test of the career played against Australia in January 1960. Scores on last appearance in Test were 12 and 9 in the fifth Test at Calcutta. Age at the time of retirement from Test cricket was 32 years and 182 days. First-ever Test century (106 not out) scored on January 2, 1956 against New Zealand in the fourth Test at Calcutta at the age of 28 years and 157 days. He played for Sind and Bombay. In his first class career he made, 6,027 runs including 16 centuries and 258 catches.
Test Record - 33 Tests, 1,180 runs (Av. 24.58) including 2 centuries, 41 wickets (Av. 46.34) and 20 catches.

RAMEEZ RAJA

Pakistan (born 1962) - A balanced and gifted right-handed batsman,the brother of all-rounder Wasim Raza.He plays for Lahore.In his first class career he made, 4,623 runs including 11 centuries and took 3 wickets.

RAMEEZ RAJA

Test Record -25 Tests,1156 runs (Av. 30.42) including 2 centuries and 16 catches.

RANASINGHE ANURA NANDANA

Sri Lanka (born 1956) - A right-handed batsman and medium-pace left-arm seamer. He played for Bloomfield. In his first class career he made, 1,253 runs and took 39 wickets.

Test Record - 2 Tests, 88 runs (Av. 22.00), 1 wicket (Av. 69.00)

RANATUNGA ARJUNA

Sri Lanka (born 1963) - A right-arm medium-pace bowler, and right-handed hard-hitting batsman. He played for Sinhalese. In his first class career he made, 2,191 runs including 4 centuries and took 25 wickets.

Test Record - 24 Tests, 1,537 runs (Av. 37.48) including 2 centuries,11 wickets (Av. 55.81),11 catches.

RANDALL DEREK WILLIAM

England (born 1951) - A right-handed batsman and a marvellous fielder. There has never been a keener cover-point and it is difficult to think of any faster ones. Moreover, his throwing has become increasingly accurate. He played for Nottinghamshire. In his first class career he made 21,304 runs including 38 centuries.

Test Record - 47 Tests, 2,470 runs (Av. 33.37) including 7 centuries and 31 catches.

RANGACHARI COMMANDUR

India (born 1916) - A right-handed batsman and right-arm medium-fast bowler. Test debut on January 23, 1948 against Australia at the age of 31 years and 279 days. Scores on Test debut were 0 not out and 0 in the fourth Test at Adelaide. Last Test of the career played against West Indies in December 1948. Score on last appearance in Test was 8 not out in the second Test at Bombay. Age at the time of retirement from Test cricket was 32 years and 240 days. He played for Madras. In his first class career he made, 480 runs and took 200 wickets.

Test Record - 4 Tests, 8 runs (Av. 2.66) and 9 wickets (Av. 54.77).

RANGNEKAR KHANDERAO MORESHWAR

India (1917-1984) - A left-handed batsman. Test debut on November 28, 1947 against Australia at the age of 32 years and 151 days. Scores on Test debut were 1 and 0 in the first Test at Brisbane. Last Test of the career played against Australia in January 1948. Scores on last appearance in Test were 8 and 0 in the fourth Test at Adelaide. Age at the time of retirement from Test cricket was 32 years and 211 days. He played for Bombay, Holkar and Madhya Pradesh. In his first class career he made, 4,602 runs including 15 centuries and took 21 wickets.

Test Record - 3 Tests, 33 runs (Av. 5.50) and 1 catch.

RANJANE VASANT BABURAO

India (born 1937) - A right-handed batsman and a right-arm medium-fast bowler. Test debut on December 12, 1958 against West Indies at the age of 21 years and 321 days. Scores on Test debut were 3 and 12 in the second Test at Kanpur. Last Test of the career played against Australia in

October 1964. Scores on last appearance in Test were 2 and 1 not out in the first Test at Madras. Age at the time of retirement from Test Cricket was 27 years and 256 days. He played for Maharashtra and Railways. In his first class career he made, 698 runs and took 175 wickets.
Test Record - 7 Tests, 40 runs (Av. 6.66), 19 wickets (Av. 34.15) and 1 catch.

RANJI TROPHY

The Indian Cricket Control Board arranged fixtures for the competition for 1934-35 between all the Cricket Associations then affiliated to the Board. The Trophy was organised by dividing India into four zones: North, South, East and West. Each zonal competition was by knock-out with the zonal winners then meeting in two semi-finals and a final. Now the format has changed.There are five zones.Two teams qualify from each to play in theknock-outround.

Ranji Trophy

Ranji Trophy Winners

1934-35 Bombay
1935-36 Bombay
1936-37 Nawanagar
1937-38 Hyderabad
1938-39 Bengal
1939-40 Maharashtra
1940-41 Maharashtra
1941-42 Bombay
1942-43 Baroda
1943-44 Western India
1944-45 Bombay
1945-46 Holkar
1946-47 Bombay
1947-48 Holkar
1948-49 Bombay
1949-50 Baroda
1950-51 Holkar
1951-52 Bombay
1952-53 Holkar
1953-54 Bombay
1954-55 Madras
1955-56 Bombay
1956-57 Bombay
1957-58 Baroda
1958-59 Bombay
1959-60 Bombay
1960-61 Bombay
1961-62 Bombay
1962-63 Bombay
1963-64 Bombay
1964-65 Bombay
1965-66 Bombay
1966-67 Bombay
1967-68 Bombay
1968-69 Bombay
1969-70 Bombay
1970-71 Bombay
1971-72 Bombay
1972-73 Bombay
1973-74 Karnataka
1974-75 Bombay
1975-76 Bombay
1976-77 Bombay
1977-78 Karnataka
1978-79 Delhi
1979-80 Delhi
1980-81 Bombay
1981-82 Delhi
1982-83 Karnataka

1983-84 Bombay
1984-85 Bombay
1985-86 Delhi
1986-87 Hyderabad
1987-88 Tamil Nadu
1988-89 Delhi
1989-90 West Bengal

RANJIT SINHJI KUMAR SHRI
England (1872-1933)- A right-handed batsman, a useful change bowler and a safe catcher in the slips. Ranji came from ancient Rajput stock, and brought eastern magic to the cricket fields of England, America and Australia. He played for Cambridge University and Sussex. In his first class career he made, 24,692 runs including 72 centuries and took 130 wickets.
Test Record - 15 Tests, 989 runs (Av. 44.95) including 2 centuries and 13 catches.

RANSFORD VERNON SEYMOUR
Australia (1885-1958) A very attractive left-handed batsman. He was one of the best outfielders of his day. He played for Victoria. In his first class career he made, 8,268 runs including 25 centuries and took 29 wickets.
Test Record - 20 Tests, 1,211 runs (Av. 37.84) including 1 century.

RASHID KHAN
Pakistan (born 1959) - A tail-end batsman and a medium-fast right-arm bowler. He played for Karachi. In his first class career he made, 1,162 runs and took 250 wickets.
Test Record - 4 Tests, 155 runs (Av. 51.66), 8 wickets (Av. 45.00) and 2 catches.

RATNAYAKE RUMESH JOSEPH
Sri Lanka (born 1964) - A right-arm medium-fast bowler and a right-handed batsman. He plays for Nondescripts. In his first class career he made 1,077 runs and took 91 wickets.
Test Record - 14 Tests, 272 runs (Av. 14.31), 41 wickets (Av. 36.87) and 5 catches.

RATNAYEKE JOSEPH RAVINDRAN
Sri Lanka (born 1960)- A tall right-arm medium-fast bowler and a left-handed batsman. He played for Nondescripts. In his first class career he made 806 runs and took 88 wickets.
Test Record - 20 Tests, 676 runs (Av.23.00),55 wickets (Av.33.27) and 1 catch.

REACH
A batsman's ability to stretch forward from the crease to play a stroke. The taller the player and the longer his legs, the greater his reach and the more difficult for a bowler, especially a spin bowler, to find a good length for him.

READ JOHN MAURICE
England (1859-1929)- A right-handed batsman and a useful medium-fast change bowler. He played for Surrey. In his first class career he made 14,010 runs including 11 centuries, took 73 wickets and 215 catches.
Test Record - 17 Tests, 463 runs (Av.17.14) and 8 catches.

READ WALTER WILLIAM
England (1855-1907) - A right-handed batsman. He played for Surrey. In his first class career he made 22,349 runs including 38 centuries, took 108 wickets and 318 catches.
Test Record - 18 Tests, 720 runs (Av.27.69)including 1 century and 16 catches.

REDPATH IAN RITCHIE
Australia (born 1941)- A right-handed batsman and a brilliant fielder close to the wicket. He played for Victoria. In his first class career he made 14,993 runs including 32 centuries, took 13 wickets and 211 catches.
Test Record - 66 Tests, 4,737 runs (Av.43.45) including 8 centuries and 83 catches.

REDDY BHARAT A.
India (born 1954) - A right-handed batsman and a wicket-keeper. Test debut on July 12, 1979 against England at the age of 24 years and 240 days. Scores on Test debut were 21 and 0 in the

first Test at Manchester. He played for Madras. In his first class career he made, 1,743 runs and 220 dismissals.
Test Record - 4 Tests, 38 runs (Av. 9.50) and 11 dismissals (9ct, 2st).

REFUGE ASSURANCE SUNDAY LEAGUE
Refuge Assurance took over the sponsorship of the John Player Sunday League in the 1987 season. The League was instituted in 1969 and the title winners are as follow:

1969	Lancashire
1970	Lancashire
1971	Worcestershire
1972	Kent
1973	Kent
1974	Leicestershire
1975	Hampshire
1976	Kent
1977	Leicestershire
1978	Hampshire
1979	Somerset
1980	Warwickshire
1981	Essex
1982	Sussex
1983	Yorkshire
1984	Essex
1985	Essex
1986	Hampshire
1987	Worcestershire
1988	Worcestershire
1989	Lancashire

REID BRUCE ANTHONY
Australia (born 1963) - A left-arm fast bowler, six feet eight inches tall. He plays for Western Australia. In his first class career he made 469 runs and took 103 wickets.
Test Record-18 Tests, 75 runs (Av.6.25), 62 wickets (Av.29.61) and 2 catches.

REID JOHN FULTON
New Zealand (born 1958) - A right-handed batsman. He played for Auckland. In his first class career he made, 5,538 runs including 10 centuries, took 6 wickets and 125 dismissals.
Test Record - 19 Tests, 1,296 runs (Av. 46.28) including 6 centuries and 9 catches.

REID JOHN RICHARD
New Zealand (born 1928) - A very strong, sturdily built, a natural forcing right-handed batsman, a powerful driver and a sure hooker and cutter. He was also outstanding medium-fast bowler, turning sometimes to off-cutters. He was also a magnificent fielder. He played for Wellington and Otago. In his first class career he made, 16,128 runs including 39 centuries, took 466 wickets and 7 stumpings .
Test Record - 58 Tests, 3,248 runs (Av. 33.28) including 6 centuries, 85 wickets (Av. 33.41), 43 catches and 1 stumping .

RELF ALBERT EDWARD
England (1874-1937) - A right-arm medium-pace bowler. He played for Norfolk, Sussex and Auckland. In his first class career he made, 22,176 runs

BRUCE REID

including 26 centuries, took 1,897 wickets and 493 catches.
Test Record - 13 Tests, 416 runs (Av. 23.11), 25 wickets (Av. 24.96) and 14 catches.

RENNEBERG DAVID ALEXANDER
Australia (born- 1942) - A right-arm medium-fast bowler. He played for New South Wales. In his first class career he made, 466 runs and took 291 wickets.
Test Record - 8 Tests, 22 runs (Av. 3.66), 23 wickets (Av. 36.08) and 2 catches.

REPLACEMENT BALL
A ball of nearly the same wear as the one being played and is given by the umpires on the latter becoming unfit to play or getting lost before it is due for replacement.

REPORT
A written analysis by the captains of the playing conditions and the standard of the umpiring in a game. Also, a written complaint by one or both of the umpires of the opposing teams about a breach of the code of behaviour.

RESULT
The outcome of the game: win, loss, draw or tie.

RETIRING
A batsman may retire or declare his personal innings closed at any time. In that case he may not resume his innings. However, if through illness or injury a batsman is unable to continue, he may, with the umpires' consent, retire temporarily. In this case, he may resume batting at any future wicket fall in that innings. In the first case, the batsman is considered to be 'out'; in the latter case, if he doesn't resume, the batsman is considered to be 'retired, not out'.

RETURN
Hitting of the ball by the fielder in to either wicket.

RETURN CATCH
A catch made by a bowler off his own bowling.

RETURN CREASE
It is marked at each end of the bowling crease at right angles to it and is extended to join the popping crease and has a minimum length of 4 feet/ 1.22 metres behind the wicket.

RHODES WILFRED
England (1877-1973) - He was a left-arm bowler, a right-handed opening batsman. He played for Yorkshire. In his first class career he made, 39,802 runs including 58 centuries, took 4,187 wickets and 708 catches.
Test Record - 58 Tests, 2,325 runs (Av. 30.19) including 2 centuries, 127 wickets (Av. 26.69) and 60 catches.

RICHARD BARRY ANDERSON
South Africa (born 1945) - A right-handed open-

VIVIAN RICHARDS

ing batsman. He played for Natal, South Australia, Gloucestershire and Hampshire. In his first class career he made, 28,358 runs including 80 centuries, took 77 wickets and 367 catches.
Test Record - 4 Tests, 508 runs (Av. 72.57) including 2 centuries and 3 catches.

RICHARDS ISAAC VIVIAN ALEXANDER
West Indies (born 1952) - An orthodox right-handed batsman with perfect timing and immense power, and a fearless and brilliant hooker. Either close to the wicket or in the covers, he is a fielder of the highest class and also a capable off-spinner who can bowl seam-up, if necessary. He played for Leeward Islands, Somerset and Queensland. In his first class career he made, 28,533 runs including 92 centuries, took 177 wickets and 355 dismissals.
Test Record - 108 Tests, 7,849 runs (Av.51.98) including 24 centuries, 32 wickets (Av.56.56) and 112 catches.

RICHARDSON ARTHUR JOHN
Australia (1888-1973) - A right-handed opening batsman and also a medium-pace off-break bowler. He played for South Australia and Western Australia. In his first class career he made, 5,239 runs including 13 centuries, and took 209 wickets.
Test Record - 9 Tests, 409 runs (Av. 31.00) including 1 century, 12 wickets (Av. 43.41) and 1 catch.

RICHARDSON PETER EDWARD
England (born 1931) - A left-handed opening batsman and also a useful change bowler. He played for Worcestershire and Kent. In his first class career he made, 26,055 runs including 44 centuries, took 11 wickets and 220 catches.
Test Record - 34 Tests, 2,061 runs (Av. 37.47) including 5 centuries, 3 wickets (Av. 16.00) and 6 catches.

RICHARDSON RICHARD BENJAMIN
West Indies (born 1962) - A right-handed batsman. He played for Leeward Islands. In his first class career he made, 5,881 runs including 17 centuries and took 5 wickets.

RICHARD RICHARDSON

Test Record - 45 Tests, 3,320 runs (Av. 48.11) including 10 centuries and 57 catches.

RICHARDSON THOMAS
England (1870-1912) - A right-arm off-break bowler. He played for Surrey and Somerset. In his first class career he made, 3,424 runs and took 2,105 wickets.
Test Record - 14 Tests, 177 runs (Av. 11.06), 88 wickets (Av. 25.22) and 5 catches.

RICKARDS KENNETH ROY
West Indies (born 1923) - A right-handed batsman. He played for Jamaica and Essex. In his first class career he made, 2,065 runs including 2 centuries.
Test Record - 2 Tests, 104 runs (Av. 34.66).

RIDGWAY FREDERICK
England (born 1923) - A medium-fast bowler. He was excellent close fielder and could be useful right-handed lower-order batsman. He played for Kent. In his first class career he made,

4,081 runs, took 1,069 wickets and 233 catches.
Test Record - 5 Tests, 49 runs (Av. 8.16), 7 wickets (Av. 54.14) and 3 catches.

RIGG KEITH EDWARD
Australia (born 1906) - A right-handed batsman. He played for Victoria. In his first class career he made, 5,544 runs including 14 centuries.
Test Record - 8 Tests, 401 runs (Av. 33.41) including 1 century and 5 catches.

RING DOUGLAS THOMAS
Australia (born 1918) - A right-arm leg-break bowler. He played for Victoria. In his first class career he made, 3,418 runs including 1 century and took 451 wickets.
Test Record - 13 Tests, 426 runs (Av. 22.42), 35 wickets (Av. 37.28) and 5 catches.

RITCHIE GREGORY MICHAEL
Australia (born 1960) - A right-handed batsman with flair. He played for Queensland and Buckinghamshire. In his first class career he made, 6,175 runs including 14 centuries and took 3 wickets.
Test Record - 23 Tests, 1,374 runs (Av. 35.23) including 3 centuries and 10 catches.

RIXON STEPHEN JOHN
Australia (born 1954) - A neat and lively wicket-keeper and a useful right-handed batsman. He played for New South Wales. In his first class career he made, 3,984 runs including 6 centuries, and 410 dismissals.
Test Record - 13 Tests, 394 runs (Av. 18.76) and 47 dismissals (42 ct, 5 st).

RIZWAN-UZ-ZAMAN
Pakistan (born 1962) - A right-handed opening batsman with a good temperament and excellent technique. He played for Pakistan International Airlines and Karachi. In his first class career he made, 7,287 runs including 22 centuries and took 67 wickets.
Test Record - 11 Tests, 345 runs (Av. 19.16), 4 wickets (Av. 11.50) and 4 catches.

ROACH CLIFFORD ARCHIBALD
West Indies (born 1904) - A right-handed opening batsman and a brilliant fielder, especially at cover-point. He played for Trinidad. In his first class career he made, 4,851 runs including 5 centuries.
Test Record - 16 Tests, 952 runs (Av. 30.70) including 2 centuries, 2 wickets (Av. 51.50) and 5 catches.

ROBERTS ALBERT WILLIAM
New Zealand (1909-1978) - A right-arm medium-pace bowler, a brilliant silp fielder and an effective batsman. He played for Canterbury and Otago. In his first class career he made, 3,645 runs including 3 centuries and took 167 wickets.
Test Record - 5 Tests, 248 runs (Av. 27.55), 7 wickets (Av. 29.85) and 4 catches.

ANDY ROBERTS

ROBERTS ANDERSON MONTGOMERY EVERTON
West Indies (born 1951) - A right-arm medium-fast bowler, useful right-handed batsman and capable fielder. He played for New South Wales, Leicestershire and Hampshire. In his first class career he made, 3,516 runs and took 889 wickets.

Test Record - 47 Tests, 762 runs (Av. 14.94), 202 wickets (Av. 25.61) and 9 catches.

ROBERTS ANDREW DUNCAN GLENN
New Zealand (born 1947) - A right-handed batsman and a medium-pace bowler. He played for Northern Districts. In his first class career he made, 5,865 runs including 7 centuries and took 84 wickets.
Test Record - 7 Tests, 254 runs (Av. 23.09), 4 wickets (Av. 45.50) and 4 catches.

ROBERTSON JOHN BENJAMIN
South Africa (1906-1986) - A spin bowler. He played for Western Province. In his first class career he made, 450 runs and took 65 wickets.
Test Record - 3 Tests, 51 runs (Av. 10.20), 6 wickets (Av. 53.50) and 2 catches.

ROBERTSON JOHN DAVID BENBOW
England (born 1917) - A right-handed opening batsman and a useful change bowler. He played for Middlesex. In his first class career he made, 31,914 runs including 67 centuries, took 73 wickets and 351 catches.
Test Record - 11 Tests, 881 runs (Av. 46.36) including 2 centuries, 2 wickets (Av. 29.00) and 6 catches.

ROBINS ROBERT WALTER VIVIAN
England (1906-1968) - A right-arm leg-break and googly bowler. He played for Cambridge University and Middlesex. In his first class career he made, 13,884 runs including 11 centuries, took 969 wickets and 220 catches.
Test Record - 19 Tests, 612 runs (Av. 26.60) including 1 century, 64 wickets (Av. 27.46) and 12 catches.

ROBINSON RICHARD DARYL
Australia (born 1948) - An attacking right-handed batsman and useful wicket-keeper. He played for Victoria. In his first class career he made, 4,776 runs including 7 centuries, and 32 9dismissals.
Test Record - 3 Tests, 100 runs (Av. 16.66) and 4 catches.

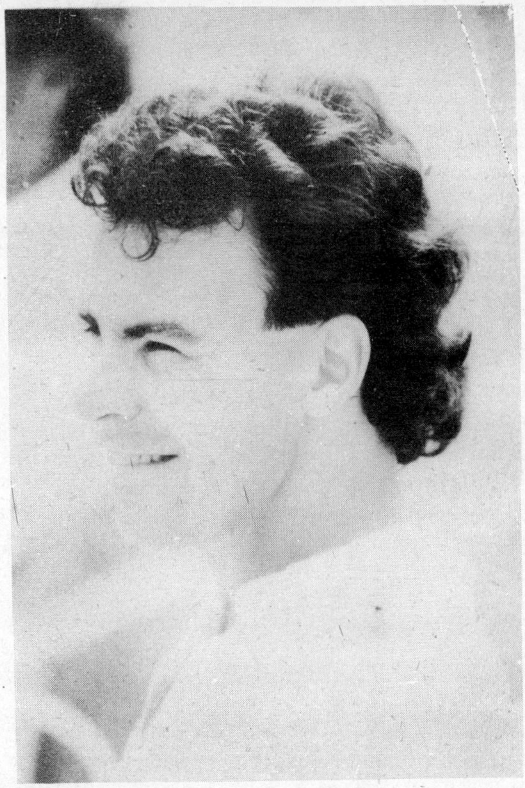

ROBERT ROBINSON

ROBINSON ROBERT TIMOTHY
England (born 1958) - A right-handed batsman and an excellent fielder. He plays for Nottinghamshire. In his first class career he made, 10,354 runs including 22 centuries and took 2 wickets.
Test Record - 16 Tests, 1,052 runs (Av. 42.08) including 3 centuries, and 6 catches.

RODRIGUEZ WILLIAM VINCETE
West Indies (born 1934) - A right-handed batsman and a useful leg-break bowler. He played for Trinidad. In his first class career he made, 2,061 runs including 1 century and took 119 wickets.
Test Record - 5 Tests, 96 runs (Av. 13.71), 7 wickets (Av. 53.42) and 3 catches.

ROLL
To ball (colloquial).

ROLLER
A heavy, cylindrical drum used to prepare and

repair a turf pitch or wicket. These days motorised, but in the old days horse-drawn or hand-pulled.

ROLLING

The act of driving or pulling the roller up and down the turf wicket to smoothen and harden its surface. Can be done under supervision before play and in between innings.

ROOPE GRAHAM RICHARD JAMES

England (born 1946) - A right-handed middle-order batsman. He played for Berkshire, Surrey and Griqualand West. In his first class career he made, 19,116 runs including 26 centuries, took 225 wickets and 604 dismissals.

Test Record - 21 Tests, 860 runs (Av. 30.71) and 35 catches.

ROOT CHARLES FREDERICK

England (1890-1954) - A right-arm leg-break bowler and a master of spin. He was a hard-hitting batsman. He played for Derbyshire and Worcestershire. In his first class career he made, 7,911 runs including 1 century, took 1,512 wickets and 243 catches.

Test Record - 3 Tests, Did not bat, 8 wickets (Av. 24.25) and 1 catch.

RORKE GORDON FREDERICK

Australia (born 1938) - A right-arm medium-fast bowler. He played for New South Wales. In his first class career he made, 248 runs and took 88 wickets.

Test Record - 4 Tests, 9 runs (Av. 4.50), 10 wickets (Av. 20.30) and 1 catch.

ROSE BRIAN CHARLES

England (born 1950) - A left-handed batsman. He played for Somerset. In his first class career he made, 13,176 runs including 25 centuries, took 8 wickets and 123 catches.

Test Record - 9 Tests, 358 runs (Av. 25.57) and 4 catches.

ROUND THE WICKET

The bowler's position in relation to stumps at his end in his act of delivering the ball when he has his back to the stumps. This style is only occasionally used by pace bowlers.

ROUTLEDGE THOMAS WILLIAM

South Africa (1867-1927) - A right-handed batsman and also a change bowler. He played for Transvaal. In his first class career he made, 492 runs.

Test Record - 4 Tests, 72 runs (Av. 9.00) and 2 catches.

ROWAN ATHOL MATTHEW BURCHELL

South Africa (born 1921) - A right-arm slow-medium off-break bowler. He played for Transvaal. In his first class career he made, 1,492 runs including 1 century and took 273 wickets.

Test Record - 15 Tests, 290 runs (Av. 17.05), 54 wickets (Av. 38.59) and 7 catches.

ROWAN ERIC ALFRED BURCHELL

South Africa (born 1909) - A right-handed batsman. He played for Transvaal. In his first class career he made, 11,710 runs including 30 centuries.

Test Record - 26 Tests, 1,965 runs (Av. 43.66) including 3 centuries and 14 catches.

ROWE GEORGE ALEXANDER

South Africa (1874-1959) - A left-arm slow bowler. He played for Western Province. In his first class career he made, 303 runs and took 170 wickets.

Test Record - 5 Tests, 26 runs (Av. 4.33), 15 wickets (Av. 30.40) and 4 catches.

ROWE LAWRENCE GEORGE

West Indies (born 1949) - A right-handed opening batsman . He played for Jamaica and Derbyshire. In his first class career he made, 8,755 runs including 18 centuries, took 2 wickets and 117 catches.

Test Record - 30 Tests, 2,047 runs (Av. 43.55) including 7 centuries and 17 catches.

ROY AMBAR

India (born 1945) - A left-handed batsman. Test debut on October 3, 1969 against New Zealand at the age of 24 years and 149 days. Scores on Test debut were 48 and 2 in the second Test at Nagpur. Last Test of the career played against Australia in December 1969. Scores on last appearance in Test were 18 and 19 in the fourth Test at Calcutta. Age at the time of retirement from Test cricket was 24 years and 222 days. He played for Bengal. In his first class career he made, 7,163 runs including 18 centuries and took 29 wickets.

Test Record - 4 Tests, 91 runs (Av. 13.00).

ROY PANKAJ

India (born 1928) - A right-handed opening batsman and right-arm medium-pace bowler. Test debut on November 2, 1951 against England at the age of 23 years and 151 days. Score on Test debut was 12 in the first Test at New Delhi. Last Test of the career played against Pakistan in December 1960. Score on last appearance in Test was 23 in the first Test at Bombay. Age at the time of retirement from Test cricket was 32 years and 137 days. First-ever Test century 140 scored on December 14, 1951 against England in the second Test at Bombay at the age of 23 years and 194 days. Led India once against England in the second Test at Lord's in June 1959 at the age of 31 years and 17 days which India lost by eight wickets on the third day of the five-day Test. Holds with M.H. (Vinoo) Mankad, the world record of the highest partnership of 413 runs for the first wicket in the fifth Test against New Zealand at Madras in 1955-56. Has been dismissed for a 'duck' 14 times (the largest number of 'ducks' for a recognised Test batsman) in Test career. In 1952, when India played in England, he had five 'ducks' in the series, including four in a row. He is the first Indian to score two centuries in his maiden Test series (against England in 1951-52). He played for Bengal. In his first class career he made, 11,868 runs including 33 centuries and took 21 wickets.

Test Record - 43 Tests, 2,442 runs (Av. 32.56) including 5 centuries and 16 catches.

ROY PRONOB PANKAJ

India (born 1957) - A right-handed opening batsman, a patient and technically correct player and also a medium-fast bowler. He played for Bengal. In his first class career he made, 2,734 runs including 8 centuries and took 1 wicket.

Test Record - 2 Tests, 71 runs (Av. 33.50) and 1 catch.

RUBBER

Rubber-soled boots or shoes (colloquial).

RUMSEY FREDERICK EDWARD

England (born 1935) - A left-arm medium-fast bowler. He played for Worcestershire, Somerset and Derbyshire. In his first class career he made, 1,015 runs and took 580 wickets.

Test Record - 5 Tests, 30 runs (Av. 15.00) and 17 wickets (Av. 27.11).

RUN

The method of scoring (apart from the case of a wide or a no-ball, when a run is automatically added to the score). Runs are achieved when the batsman safely runs from one end of the pitch to the other or the ball reaches the boundary (a four) or clears in on the full (a six).

RUN THE BALL

In batting, to open the face of the bat and let the ball run from it down towards third man.

RUN THE BALL AWAY

In bowling, to make the ball move away from the batsman towards the slips.

RUN OUT

A mode of dismissal in which a batsman, while taking a run, does not reach his ground before the ball strikes the wickets.

RUNNER

The man, attired in full batting equipment, who comes out to do the running for an injured batsman.

M. SIMONS in Run Out Action

RUSSELL CHARLES ALBERT GEORGE

England (1887-1961) - A master of on-side strokes. He played for Essex. In his first class career he made, 27,546 runs including 71 centuries, took 285 wickets and 292 catches.

Test Record - 10 Tests, 910 runs (Av. 56.87) including 5 centuries and 8 catches.

RUSSELL WILLIAM ERIC

England (born 1936) - A right-handed batsman, off-side hitting off either foot. He played for Middlesex and Berkshire. In his first class career he made, 25,525 runs including 41 centuries, took 22 wickets and 304 catches.

Test Record - 10 Tests, 362 runs (Av. 21.29) and 4 catches.

RUTHERFORD KENNETH ROBERT

New Zealand (born 1965) - A right-handed batsman and a fine fielder. He played for Otago. In his first class career he made, 4,058 runs including 9 centuries and took 4 wickets.

Test Record - 16 Tests, 368 runs (Av. 15.33), 1 wicket (Av. 65.00) and 9 catches.

RYDER JOHN

Australia (1889-1977) - An attacking right-handed batsman and a medium-fast change-bowler. He played for Victoria. In his first class career he made, 10,499 runs including 24 centuries,and took 238 wickets and 132 catches.

Test Record - 20 Tests, 1,394 runs (Av. 51.62) including 3 centuries, 17 wickets (Av. 43.70) and 17 catches.

S

SACB

South African Cricket Board: The ruling body for non-white cricket in South Africa.

SACU

South African Cricket Union: The official body controlling cricket in South Africa.

SADIQ MOHAMMAD

Pakistan (born 1945) - A left-handed opening batsman and useful leg-spin bowler. He played for Karachi, United Bank,and Tasmania. In his first class career he made, 24,160 runs including 50 centuries, took 235 wickets and 326 catches.
Test Record - 41 Tests, 2,579 runs (Av. 35.81) including 5 centuries and 28 catches.

SAEED AHMED

Pakistan (born 1937) - A stroke-making right-handed batsman and a useful slow to medium off-break bowler. He was also an excellent fielder at cover. He played for Lahore and Pakistan International Airlines. In his first class career he made, 12,847 runs including 34 centuries, and took 332 wickets.
Test Record - 41 Tests, 2,991 runs (Av. 40.42) including 5 centuries, 22 wickets (Av. 36.45) and 13 catches.

SAGGERS RONALD ARTHUR

Australia (born 1917) - An accomplished second-string wicket-keeper and an attractive batsman. He played for New South Wales. In his first class career he made, 1,888 runs including 1 century and 221 dismissals.
Test Record - 6 Tests, 30 runs (Av. 10.00) and 24 dismissals (16ct, 8st).

SALAH-UD-DIN

Pakistan (born 1947) - A right-handed batsman, a useful slow off-break bowler and a good close fielder. He played for Karachi. In his first class career he made, 5,729 runs including 14 centuries and took 155 wickets.
Test Record - 5 Tests, 117 runs (Av. 19.50), 7 wickets (Av. 26.71) and 3 catches.

SALEEM ALTAF

Pakistan (born 1944) - A right-arm medium-fast bowler, using both in and out-swingers, and an uninhibited batsman. He played for Pakistan International Airlines. In his first class career he made, 3,067 runs including 1 century and took 334 wickets.
Test Record - 21 Tests, 276 runs (Av. 14.52), 46 wickets (Av. 37.17) and 3 catches.

SALEEM JAFFAR

Pakistan (born 1962) - A left-arm medium-fast bowler. He is one of three Pakistan's opening bowlers, but has yet to attain the heights of Hafeez and Wasim. His tall and bouncy left-arm style will put him in good stead during an Australian tour in 1988-89.
Test Record - 9 Tests, 22 runs (Av.3.66), 24 wickets (Av.34.70) and 1 catch.

SALEEM MALIK

SALEEM MALIK

SALEEM MALIK

Pakistan (born 1963) - A natural right-handed batsman with all the wristy strokes of the best Pakistan players and also a good close fielder. He plays for Lahore and Habib Bank. In his first class career he made, 7,911 runs including 25 centuries, and took 31 wickets.

Test Record - 52 Tests, 2,352 runs (Av. 39.20) including 6 centuries, 5 wickets (Av.19.80) and 42 catches.

SALEEM YOUSUF

SALEEM YOUSUF

Pakistan (born 1959) - An agile wicket-keeper and skilful hard-hitting right-handed batsman. He played for Sind, Karachi, Industrial Development Bank of Pakistan and Allied Bank. In his first class career he made, 3,035 runs including 7 centuries, took 1 wicket (Av. 16.00) and 198 dismissals.

Test Record - 24 Tests, 838 runs (Av.31.03) and 77 dismissals (66ct,11st).

SANDHAM ANDREW

England (1890-1982) - He was a right-handed opening batsman. He played for Surrey. In his first class career he made, 41,284 runs including 107 centuries, and took 18 wickets.

Test Record - 14 Tests, 879 runs (Av. 38.21) including 2 centuries and 4 catches.

BALWINDER SINGH SANDHU

SANDHU BALVINDER SINGH HARBANS SINGH

India (born 1956) - A left-arm opening medium-fast bowler and a right-handed tail-end batsman. He believes in hitting the ball hard and has played many spirited innings. He played for Bombay. In his first class career he made, 895 runs and took 153 wickets.

Test Record - 8 Tests, 214 runs (Av. 30.57), 10 wickets (Av. 55.70) and 1 catch.

SANDSHOE CRUSHER

Colloquial term for the yorker derived from the likelihood that a yorker aimed at the leg stump will hit the batsman on the foot.

SARDESAI DILIP NARAYAN

India (born 1940) - A right-handed batsman and a right-arm off-spin bowler. Test debut on December 1, 1961 against England at the age of 21 years and 114 days. Score on Test debut was 28 in the second Test at Kanpur. Last Test of the career played against England in December 1972. Scores on last appearance in Test were 12 and 10 in the first Test at New Delhi. Age at the time of retirement from Test cricket was 32 years and 137 days. He played for Bombay. In his first class career he made, 10,231 runs including 25 centuries.

Test Record - 30 Tests, 2,001 runs (Av. 39.23) including 5 centuries and 4 catches.

SARFRAZ NAWAZ

Pakistan (born 1948) - A medium-fast bowler of high class and was often extremely useful as a rugged, hard-hitting driving, late-order batsman. He played for Lahore, United Bank and Northamptonshire. In his first class career he made, 5,709 runs, took 1,005 wickets and 162 catches.

Test Record - 55 Tests, 1,045 runs (Av. 17.71), 177 wickets (Av. 32.75) and 26 catches.

SARWATE CHANDRASEKHAR TRIMBAK

India (born 1920) - A right-handed batsman and a right-arm leg-break googly bowler. Test debut on July 20, 1946 against England at the age of 26 years and 29 days. Scores on Test debut were 0 and 2 in the second Test at Manchester. Last Test of the career played against England in December 1951. Scores on last appearance in Test were 18 and 16 in the second Test at Bombay. Age at the time of retirement from Test cricket was 31 years and 178 days. He played for Central Provinces and Berar. In his first class career he made, 7,430 runs including 14 centuries and took 494 wickets.

Test Record - 9 Tests, 208 runs (Av. 13.00) and 3 wickets (Av. 124.66).

SAUNDERS JOHN VICTOR

Australia (1876-1927) - A left-arm medium-pace bowler. He played for Victoria and Wellington. In his first class career he made, 586 runs and took 553 wickets.

Test Record - 14 Tests, 39 runs (Av. 2.29), 79 wickets (Av. 22.74) and 5 catches.

SCARLETT REGINALD G.

West Indies (born 1934) - A useful right-handed batsman and an off-break bowler. He played for Jamaica. In his first class career he made, 477 runs and took 48 wickets.

Test Record - 3 Tests, 54 runs (Av. 18.00), 2 wickets (Av. 104.50) and 2 catches.

SCHWARZ REGINALD OSCAR

South Africa (1875-1918) - He was only a googly bowler without mixing in any leg-breaks and a useful batsman. He played for Oxfordshire and Transvaal. In his first class career he made, 3,798 runs including 1 century, took 398 wickets and 111 catches.

Test Record - 20 Tests, 374 runs (Av. 13.85), 55 wickets (Av. 25.76) and 18 catches.

SCOOP

Type of cricket bat with one or more scoops taken out of the back to better distribute the wood and weight throughout the blade.

SCORE

The state of the game, in terms of runs made and wickets lost, e.g., five wickets down for 242. Also the amount of runs made by an individual in an innings.

SCOREBOARD

A structure prominently placed outside the boundary but within the ground confines upon which the score is displayed prominently enough to be readable by those out in the middle.

SCOREBOOK

A specially designed book in which the details of a game are kept as play progresses.

SCORECARD

A card on which the names of the players on each side, in their batting order, are printed to enable the spectators to record dismissal details of each batsman.

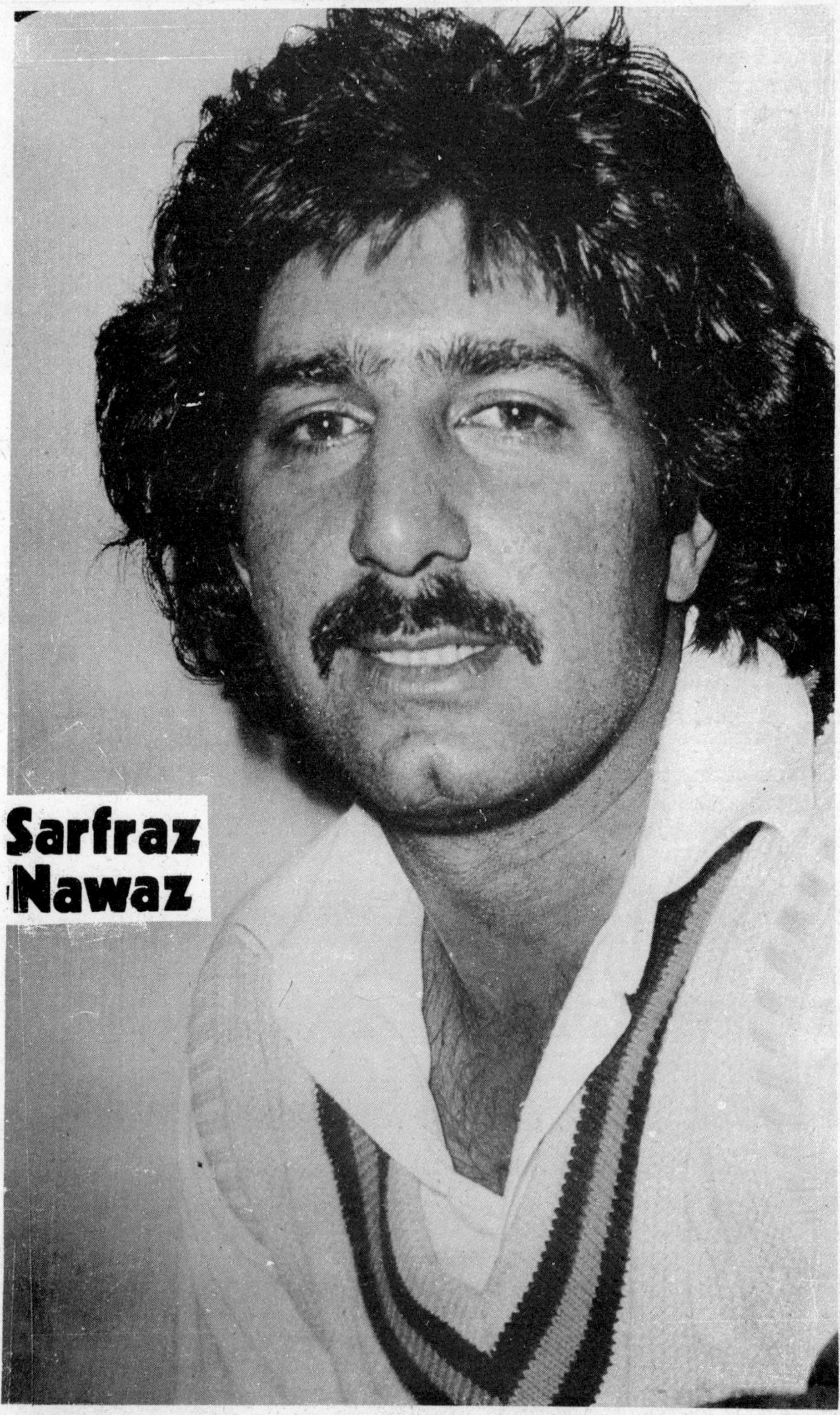
Sarfraz
Nawaz

SCORER
The person who keeps the score either in a book or on a board.

SCOTT DR.HENRY JAMES HERBERT
Australia (1858-1910) - A right-handed batsman. He played for Victoria. In his first class career he made, 2,863 runs including 4 centuries and took 18 wickets .
Test Record - 8 Tests, 359 runs (Av. 27.61) including 1 century and 8 catches.

SCOTT OSCAR CHARLES
West Indies (1893-1961) - A very useful right-handed batsman and a slow leg-break bowler. He played for Jamaica. In his first class career he made, 1,317 runs and took 182 wickets.
Test Record - 8 Tests, 171 runs (Av. 17.10) and 22 wickets (Av. 42.04).

SCOTT VERDUN JOHN
New Zealand (1916-1980) - A right-handed opening batsman and a good close fielder. He played for Auckland. In his first class career he made, 5,575 runs including 16 centuries.
Test Record - 10 Tests, 458 runs (Av. 28.62) and 7 catches.

SCOTTON WILLIAM HENRY
England (1856-1893) - He was a left-handed batsman and a good close fielder. He played for Nottinghamshire. In his first class career he made, 6,527 runs including 4 centuries, took 9 wickets and 120 catches.
Test Record - 15 Tests, 510 runs (Av. 22.17) and 4 catches.

SEALY JAMES EDWARD DEREK
West Indies (1912-1982) - A right-handed batsman with a strong defence and forcing strokes all round the wicket and also a reserve wicket-keeper. He played for Trinidad. In his first class career he made, 3,831 runs including 8 centuries, took 63 wickets, 67 catches and 13 stumpings.
Test Record - 11 Tests, 478 runs (Av. 28.11), 3 wickets (Av. 31.33), 6 catches and 1 stumping.

SEAM
The stitching that holds together the two halves of the outer covering of a cricket ball. It offers the bowlers something to grip when delivering the ball, and it helps the bowler make the ball spin or swing. Also, it determines the deviation of the ball to the left or right after it has landed on its seam. Both the bowler (who can achieve this movement off the wicket) and the type of delivery are known as 'seamers'.

SEAMER
Short for seambowler, a comparatively modern term for a bowler of medium pace or above who aims to make the ball deviate off the pitch by landing it on the seam.

SELBY JOHN
England (1849-1894) - A right-handed batsman. He played for Nottinghamshire. In his first class career he made, 6,215 runs including 4 centuries, 12 catches and 4 stumpings.
Test Record - 6 Tests, 256 runs (Av. 23.27) and 1 catch.

SELECTORS
Those appointed to choose cricket teams.

SELVEY MICHAEL WALTER WILLIAM
England (born 1948) - A strong medium-fast opening bowler. He played for Cambridge University and Orange Free State. In his first class career he made, 2,405 runs and took 772 wickets.
Test Record - 3 Tests, 15 runs (Av. 7.50), 6 wickets (Av. 57.16) and 1 catch.

SEN PROBIR
India (1926-1970) - A right-handed batsman and a useful wicket-keeper. Test debut on January 1, 1948 against Australia at the age of 21 years and 211 days. Scores on Test debut were 4 and 0 not out in the third Test at Melbourne. Last Test of the career played against Pakistan in December 1952. Score on last appearance in Test was 13 in the fifth Test at Calcutta. Age at the time of retirement from Test cricket was 26 years and 195

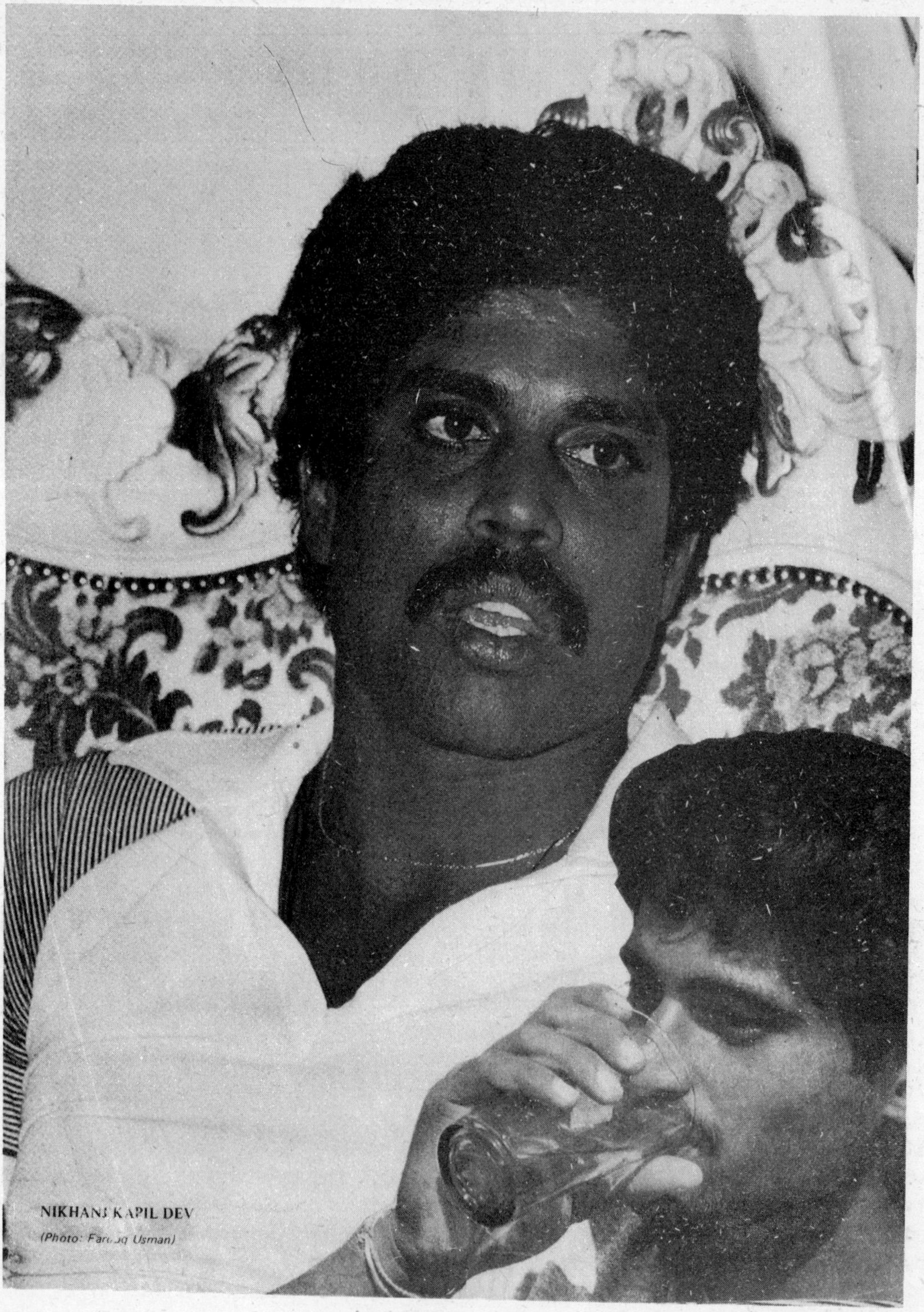

CHETAN SHARMA & KAPIL DEV

days. With four stumpings in an innings, in the fifth Test at Madras, he had set an Indian record and equalled the world record of the famous Australian Oldfield, who also had a hand in four stumpings against England at Melbourne in 1924-25. He played for Bengal. In his first class career he made, 2,580 runs including 3 centuries and 143 dismissals.
Test Record - 14 Tests, 165 runs (Av. 11.78) and 31 dismissals (20ct, 11st).

SEND BACK
To refuse, either by voice or signal, your partner's call for a run.

SERJEANT CRAIG STANTON
Australia (born 1951) - A right-handed batsman, a powerful hitter of the ball. He played for Western Australia. In his first class career he made, 4,030 runs including 9 centuries.
Test Record - 12 Tests, 522 runs (Av. 23.72) including 1 century, and 13 catches.

SESSION
A period of play in a cricket match, e.g., from partner's call for a run.

SEYMOUR DR.MICHAEL ARTHUR
South Africa (born 1936) - A right-arm off-break bowler. He played for Western Province. In his first class career he made, 569 runs and took 111 wickets.
Test Record - 7 Tests, 84 runs (Av. 12.00), 9 wickets (Av. 65.33) and 2 catches.

SHACKLETON DEREK
England (born 1924) - A right - arm leg spin bowler and a right-handed batsman. He played for Hampshire and Dorset. In his first class career he made, 9,561 runs, took 2,857 wickets and 223 catches.
Test Record - 7 Tests, 113 runs (Av. 18.83), 18 wickets (Av. 42.66) and 1 catch.

SHAFIQ AHMED
Pakistan (born 1949) - An attractive right-handed opening batsman and an occasional medium-pace bowler. He played for Punjab University and National Bank. In his first class career he made, 12,434 runs including 45 centuries, took 94 wickets and 175 catches.
Test Record - 6 Tests, 99 runs (Av. 11.00).

SHAFQAT RANA
Pakistan (born 1943) - A very good right-handed batsman and also an occasional off-break bowler. He played for Pakistan International Airlines. In his first class career he made, 4,947 runs including 9 centuries and took 16 wickets.
Test Record - 5 Tests, 221 runs (Av. 31.57) and 5 catches.

SHALDERS WILLIAM ALFRED
South Africa (1880-1917) - A right-handed opening batsman. He played for Griqualand and Transvaal. In his first class career he made, 3,351 runs including 2 centuries.
Test Record - 12 Tests, 355 runs (Av. 16.13), and 3 catches.

SHARMA CHETAN JAGATRAM
India (born 1966) - A five-foot-eight-inch right-arm medium-fast bowler. A right-handed batsman and also a fine fielder. He plays for Haryana. In his first class career he made, 1,024 runs and took 160 wickets.
Test Record - 23 Tests,396 runs (Av. 22.00), 61 wickets (Av. 35.45) and 7 catches.

SHARMA GOPAL
India (born 1960) - A slightly built off-spin bowler with nice flight and good control and also a right-handed late-order batsman. He played for Uttar Pradesh. In his first class career he made, 1,519 runs including 1 century and took 184 wickets.
Test Record - 4 Tests, 11 runs (Av. 5.50), 9 wickets (Av.39.22) and 1 catch.

SHARMA PARTHASARTHY
India (born 1948) - A right-handed batsman and a right-arm off-break bowler. Test debut on December 11, 1974 against West Indies at the age of 26

GOPAL SHARMA

years and 336 days. Scores on Test debut were 54 and 49 in the first Test at New Delhi. Last Test of the career played against England in January 1977. Scores on last appearance in Test were 9 and 20 in the second Test at Calcutta. Age at the time of retirement from Test cricket was 29 years and one day. He played for Rajasthan. In his first class career he made, 8,614 runs including 18 centuries and took 191 wickets and 146 dismissals.
Test Record - 5 Tests, 187 runs (Av. 18.70) and 1 catch.

SHARMA YASHPAL

India (born 1954) - A right-handed batsman. Test debut on August 2, 1979 against England at the age of 24 years and 352 days. Scores on Test debut were 11 and 5 * in the second Test at Lord's. First-ever Test century (100 not out) scored on October 14, 1979 against Australia in the fourth Test at New Delhi at the age of 25 years and 63 days. He played for Punjab and Haryana . In his first class career he made, 7,519 runs including 16 centuries and took 31 wickets.
Test Record - 37 Tests, 1,606 runs (Av. 33.45) including 2 centuries, 1 wicket (Av. 17.00) and 16 catches.

YASHPAL SHARMA

SHARP JOHN

England (1878-1938) - A right-handed batsman, a good medium-fast bowler and a good close fielder. He played for Lancashire. In his first class career he made, 22,715 runs including 38 centuries, took 440 wickets and 223 catches.
Test Record - 3 Tests, 188 runs (Av. 47.00) including 1 century, 3 wickets (Av. 37.00) and 1 catch.

SHARPE DUNCAN

Pakistan (born 1937) - A right-handed batsman and a useful wicket-keeper . He played for Quetta, Railways, Lahore and South Australia. In his first class career he made, 1,532 runs including 2 centuries.
Test Record - 3 Tests, 134 runs (Av. 22.33) and 2 catches.

SHARPE JOHN WILLIAM

England (1866-1936) - A right-arm medium-fast bowler and an excellent fielder. He played for Surrey. In his first class career he made, 657 runs and took 338 wickets.
Test Record - 3 Tests, 44 runs (Av. 22.00), 11 wickets (Av. 27.72) and 2 catches.

SHARPE PHILIP JOHN
England (born 1936) - A stocky right-handed batsman and also a good silp fielder. He played for Yorkshire and Derbyshire. In his first class career he made, 22,530 runs including 29 centuries and 616 catches.
Test Record - 12 Tests, 786 runs (Av. 46.23) including 1 century, and 17 catches.

SHASTRI RAVISHANKAR JAYADRITHA
India (born 1962) - Test debut on Feburary 21, 1981 against New Zealand at the age of 18 years and 262 days. Scores on Test debut were 3 not out and 19 in the first Test at Wellington. He also captured six wickets (3 for 54 in the first innings and 3 for 9 in the second innings) on debut. He played for Bombay. In his first class career he made, 6,711 runs including 16 centuries and took 348 wickets.
Test Record - 65 Tests, 2,872 runs (Av.34.60) including 8 centuries,139 wickets (Av.38.75) and 30 catches.

SHAW ALFRED
England (1842-1907) - A right-arm slow medium-pace bowler and a useful batsman. He played for Sussex. In his first class career he made,6,585 runs, took 2,021 wickets and 364 catches.
Test Record - 7 Tests, 111 runs (Av. 10.09), 12 wickets (Av. 23.75) and 4 catches.

SHEAHAN ANDREW PAUL
Australia (born 1946) - A right-handed batsman and a brilliant cover-point. He played for Victoria. In his first class career he made, 7,987 runs including 19 centuries.
Test Record - 31 Tests, 1,594 runs (Av. 33.91) including 2 centuries and 17 catches.

SHEFFIELD SHIELD
The trophy for which six States of Australia now compete in a home-and-away series of four-day games each season. The trophy was commissioned after the Earl of Sheffield had donated $1500 for the promotion of cricket in Australia. The competition began between New South Wales, Victoria and South Australia in the 1892 season. Queensland was admitted in 1926-27, Western Australia in 1947-48 and Tasmania in 1977-78.

WINNERS

1892-93	Victoria
1893-94	South Australia
1894-95	Victoria
1895-96	New South Wales
1896-97	New South Wales
1897-98	Victoria
1898-99	Victoria
1899-1900	New South Wales
1900-01	Victoria
1901-02	New South Wales
1902-03	New South Wales
1903-04	New South Wales
1904-05	New South Wales
1905-06	New South Wales
1906-07	New South Wales
1907-08	Victoria
1908-09	New South Wales
1909-10	South Australia
1910-11	New South Wales
1911-12	New South Wales
1912-13	South Australia
1913-14	New South Wales
1914-15	Victoria
1915-19	No competition
1919-20	New South Wales
1920-21	New South Wales
1921-22	Victoria
1922-23	New South Wales
1923-24	Victoria
1924-25	Victoria
1925-26	New South Wales
1926-27	South Australia
1927-28	Victoria
1928-29	New South Wales
1929-30	Victoria
930-31	Victoria
1931-32	New South Wales
1932-33	New South Wales
1933-34	Victoria
1934-35	Victoria
1935-36	South Australia
1936-37	Victoria
1937-38	New South Wales
1938-39	South Australia

RAVI SHASTRI

1939-40 New South Wales
1940-46 No Competition
1946-47 Victoria
1947-48 Western Australia
1948-49 New South Wales
1949-50 New South Wales
1950-51 Victoria
1951-52 New South Wales
1952-53 South Australia
1953-54 New South Wales
1954-55 New South Wales
1955-56 New South Wales
1956-57 New South Wales
1957-58 New South Wales
1958-59 New South Wales
1959-60 New South Wales
1960-61 New South Wales
1961-62 New South Wales
1962-63 Victoria
1963-64 South Australia
1964-65 New South Wales
1965-66 New South Wales
1966-67 Victoria
1967-68 Western Australia
1968-69 South Australia
1969-70 Victoria
1970-71 South Australia
1971-72 Western Australia
1972-73 Western Australia
1973-74 Victoria
1974-75 Western Australia
1975-76 South Australia
1976-77 Western Australia
1977-78 Western Australia
1978-79 Victoria
1979-80 Victoria
1980-81 Western Australia
1981-82 South Australia
1982-83 New South Wales
1983-84 Western Australia
1984-85 New South Wales
1985-86 New South Wales
1986-87 Western Australia
1987-88 Western Australia
1988-89 Western Australia

SHELL SHIELD AND RED STRIPE CUP WINNERS

The Shell Shield for Caribbean Regional Cricket Tournament was instituted in 1965-66 under the sponsorship of Shell.

The Shell Shield was replaced by the Red Stripe Cup after the 1986-87 season.

WINNERS

1965-66 Barbados
1966-67 Barbados
1967-68 No Competition
1968-69 Jamaica
1969-70 Trinidad
1970-71 Trinidad
1971-72 Barbados
1972-73 Guyana
1973-74 Barbados
1974-75 No Competition
1975-76 Trinidad, Barbados
1976-77 Barbados
1977-78 Barbados
1978-79 Barbados
1979-80 Barbados
1980-81 Combined Islands
1981-82 Barbados
1982-83 Guyana
1983-84 Barbados
1984-85 Trinidad and Tobago
1985-86 Barbados
1986-87 Guyana
1987-88 Jamaica
1988-89 Jamaica

SHELL TROPHY

New Zealand's major first-class competition.

WINNERS

1975-76 Canterbury
1976-77 Otago
1977-78 Auckland
1978-79 Otago
1979-80 Northern Districts
1980-81 Auckland
1981-82 Wellington
1982-83 Wellington
1983-84 Canterbury

1984-85 Wellington
1985-86 Otago
1986-87 Central Districts
1987-88 Otago
1988-89 Auckland

SHEPHERD BARRY KENNETH
Australia (born 1938) - A left-handed batsman. He played for Western Australia. In his first class career he made, 6,834 runs including 13 centuries.
Test Record - 9 Tests , 502 runs (Av. 41.83) and 2 catches.

SHEPHERD JOHN NEIL
West Indies (born 1943) - A right-arm medium-fast swing bowler and a very hard-hitting right-handed batsman. He played for Barbados, Kent and Gloucestershire. In his first class career he made, 13,353 runs including 10 centuries, took 1,155 wickets and 290 catches.,
Test Record - 5 Tests, 77 runs (Av. 9.62), 19 wickets (Av. 25.21) and 4 catches.

SHEPPARD RT.REV.DAVID STUART
England (born 1929) - A right-handed attacking batsman. He played for Cambridge University and Sussex. In his first class career he made, 15,838 runs including 45 centuries, and 195 catches.
Test Record - 22 Tests, 1,172 runs (Av. 37.80) including 3 centuries and 12 catches.

SHEPSTONE GEORGE HAROLD
South Africa (1876-1940) - A useful batsman. He played for Transvaal. In his first class career he made, 693 runs including 1 century and took 42 wickets.
Test Record - 2 Tests, 38 runs (Av. 9.50) and 2 catches.

SHERWELL PERCY WILLIAM
South Africa (1880-1948) - A good wicket-keeper especially adept at taking googly bowling and a good batsman in a crisis. He played for Cornwall and Transvaal. In his first class career he made, 1,808 runs including 3 centuries, and 119 dismissals.
Test Record - 13 Tests, 427 runs (Av. 23.72) including 1 century and 36 dismissals (20ct, 16st).

SHERWIN MORDECAI
England (1851-1910) - A very good wicket-keeper. He played for Nottinghamshire. In his first class career he made, 2,339 runs and 834 dismissals.
Test Record - 3 Tests, 30 runs (Av. 15.00) and 7 dismissals (5 ct, 2 st).

SHILLINGFORD GRAYSON CLEOPHAS
West Indies (born 1946) - A right-arm medium-fast bowler. He played for Windward Islands. In his first class career he made, 791 runs and took 217 wickets.
Test Record - 7 Tests, 57 runs (Av. 8.14), 15 wickets (Av. 35.80) and 2 catches.

SHILLINGFORD IRVINE THEODORE
West Indies (born 1944) - A right-handed batsman. He played for Windward Islands. In his first class career he made, 5,449 runs including 11 centuries and took 1 wicket.
Test Record - 4 Tests, 218 runs (Av. 31.14) including 1 century and 1 catch.

SHINDE SADASHIV GARPATRAO
India (1923-1955) - A right-handed batsman and a right-arm leg-break bowler. Test debut on June 22, 1946 against England at the age of 22 years and 304 days. Scores on Test debut were 10 and 4 not out in the first Test at Lord's. Last Test of the career played against England in June 1952. Scores on last appearance in Test were 5 and 14 in the second Test at Lord's. Age at the time of retirement from Test cricket was 28 years and 306 days. He played for Baroda and Bombay. In his first class career he made, 871 runs and took 230 wickets.
Test Record - 7 Tests, 85 runs (Av. 14.16) and 12 wickets (Av. 59.75).

SHINE
The amount of shine on the ball's surface, often enhanced by the illegal introduction of matter such as spit or face creams.

SHIVNARINE SEW
West Indies (born 1952) - A left-arm bowler and a right-handed batsman. He played for Guyana. In his first class career he made, 2,182 runs including 3 centuries and took 67 wickets.
Test Record - 8 Tests, 379 runs (Av. 29.15), and 6 catches.

SHOAIB MOHAMMAD
Pakistan (born 1962) - A right-handed opening batsman and an occasional off-spin bowler. He played for Karachi and Pakistan International Airlines. In his first class career he made, 5,319 runs including 18 centuries and took 10 wickets.
Test Record - 6 Tests, 213 runs (Av. 26.62) and 4 catches.

SHOAIB MOHAMMAD

SHODHAN ROSHAN HARSHADIAL
India (born 1928) - A left-handed batsman and left-arm medium-pace bowler. Test debut on December 12, 1952 against Pakistan at the age of 24 years and 55 days. Score on Test debut was 110 in the fifth Test at Calcutta, thus he became the second Indian batsman to make a century on Test debut on December 14, at the age of 24 years and 57 days. Only Lala Amarnath had achieved that feat before for India. Last Test of the career played against West Indies in March-April 1953. Score on last appearance in Test was 15 not out in the fifth Test at Kingston. Age at the time of retirement from Test cricket was 24 years and 166 days. His 110 on Test debut is the highest score by a batsman at No. 8 in the batting order for India. He played for Gujarat and Baroda. In his first class career he made, 1,821 runs including 4 centuries and took 73 wickets.
Test Record - 3 Tests, 181 runs (Av. 60.33) including 1 century and 1 catch.

SHOOTER
A ball that starts very low after hitting the pitch.

SHORT RUN
If a batsman fails to ground either his bat or part of his person behind the popping crease in turning

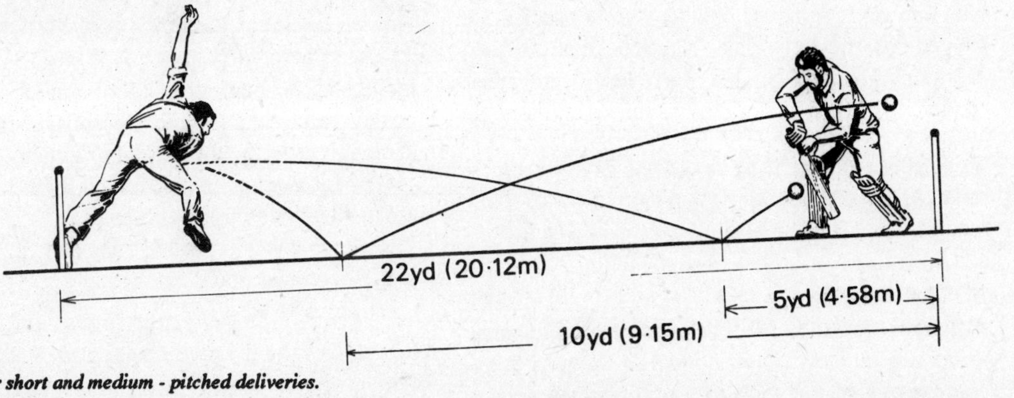

Lengths for short and medium - pitched deliveries.

for a further run, the umpire at that end must call and signal 'one short' when the ball becomes dead. If both batsmen run short in the same run, only one run is deducted; more than one run can be deducted only if more runs are attempted and a further infringement has been registered.

If a batsman takes his stance in front of the popping crease, he is entitled to run from that position without being penalised for one short run.

The occasion could arise when a recognised batsman is partnered by a lower order batsman and both run short deliberately to let the better batsman retain the strike. In that case, the umpire is justified in calling and signalling 'dead ball' and disallowing any runs.

SHORT-PITCHED

A delivery that hits the pitch well short of a good length. Usually related to fast bowling and often to intimidatory bowling.

SHOULDER

The top part of the bat where the cane handle is spliced into the willow blade.

SHREWSBURY ARTHUR

England (1856-1903) - A right-handed batsman and a fine fielder. He played for Nottinghamshire. In his first class career he made, 26,439 runs including 59 centuries, and 317 catches.

Test Record - 23 Tests, 1,277 runs (Av. 35.47) including 3 centuries and 29 catches.

SHRIMPTON MICHAEL JOHN FROUD

New Zealand (born 1940) - A right-handed batsman and an occasional leg-break bowler. He played for Hawke's Bay, Central Districts and Northern Districts. In his first class career he made, 5,812 runs including 7 centuries and took 81 wickets.

Test Record - 10 Tests, 265 runs (Av. 13.94), 5 wickets (Av. 31.60) and 2 catches.

SHUJA-UD-DIN

Pakistan (born 1930) - A right-handed batsman and a useful slow left-arm bowler of great stamina. He played for Services and Northern India. In his first class career he made, 3,342 runs including 6 centuries and took 298 wickets.

Test Record - 19 Tests, 395 runs (Av. 15.19), 20 wickets (Av. 40.05) and 8 catches.

SHUTTLEWORTH KENNETH

England (born 1944) - A very fine fast bowler and also a fine fielder. He played for Lancashire and Leicestershire. In his first class career he made, 2,589 runs, took 623 wickets and 128 catches.

Test Record - 5 Tests, 46 runs (Av. 7.66), 12 wickets (Av. 35.58) and 1 catch.

SIDHU NAVJOT SINGH

India (born 1963) - A right-handed opening batsman. He managed a top score of only 20 in four

NAVJOT SINGH SIDHU

innings in the beginning of his career and was not persevered with, though he subsequently toured Zimbabwe with the Young Indian Team. He played for Punjab. In his first class career he made, 2,616 runs including 7 centuries.

Test Record - 9 Tests,416 runs (Av.32.00) including 2 centuries and 2 catches.

SIEDLE IVAN JULIAN
South Africa (1903-1982) - A solid right-handed opening batsman. He played for Natal. In his first class career he made, 7,730 runs including 17 centuries.
Test Record - 18 Tests, 977 runs (Av. 28.73) including 1 century and 7 catches.

SIEVERS MORRIS WILLIAM
Australia (1912-1968) - A right-arm medium-fast bowler. He played for Victoria. In his first class career he made, 2,075 runs and took 116 wickets.
Test Record - 3 Tests, 67 runs (Av. 13.40), 9 wickets (Av. 17.88) and 4 catches.

SIDE
Team of eleven (XI).

SIDEGUARD
Now regarded by most as an essential part of the batsman's protective equipment. Brought into vogue in 1977 by Middlesex and England player Mike Brearley, who designed a fibreglass skull cap to fit under his ordinary headgear. Other players later came out into the open, first using motorcycle helmets in the World Series Cricket seasons of 1977-78 and 1978-79, and then helmets especially designed for cricket with full facial protection from a fitted visor or just temple protection from a sideguard. Also used by fieldsman standing close in. It is now not possible for a player to be caught out when the ball has skied off a fieldsman's helmet.

SIDE-ON
In batting, the copybook stance and position for the straight-bat shots with the batsman's chest aiming out towards point, the front elbow pointing at the bowler and the batsman looking at the bowler over his front shoulder. In bowling, a position most desirable for accuracy and swing (in the case of the right-armer, away from the right handed batsman). The bowler turns from a front-on run-up to a side-on position looking over his front shoulder at the batsman during the delivery stride. In fielding, a throw at the stumps from 'side-on' describes the extremely difficult task of trying to hit the stumps from side-on when only the closest stump is a visible target.

SIGHTSCREEN
A screen of white material used with the red ball in normal competition or of black material used with the white ball in night and some one-day cricket. It is situated behind the bowler's arm to improve the batsman's sight of the ball. Most such screens are mobile to enable alterations at the batsman's command, particularly when bowlers switch over and round the wicket or a left armer replaces a right armed bowler. A recent innovation is the development of mechanically powered screens controlled by radio from a handpiece held by the umpire.

SIKANDER BAKHT
Pakistan (born 1957) - A medium-fast bowler and a right-handed batsman. He played for United Bank, Public Works Department and Pakistan International Airlines. In his first class career he made, 1,427 runs and took 446 wickets.
Test Record - 26 Tests, 146 runs (Av. 6.34), 67 wickets (Av. 35.98) and 7 catches.

SILLY
Catching positions, other than the slips and gully, very close to the batsman.

SILVA SAMPATHWADUGE AMAL ROHITHA
Sri Lanka (born 1960) - A hard-hitting left-handed batsman and an agile wicket-keeper. He played for Nondescripts. In his first class career he made, 1,013 runs including 3 centuries, and 53 dismissals.
Test Record - 8 Tests, 336 runs (Av. 28.00) including 2 centuries and 31 dismissals (30ct, 1st).

SIMPSON REGINALD THOMAS
England (born 1920) - A right-handed batsman . He played for Sind and Nottinghamshire. In his first class career he made, 30,546 runs including 64 centuries, took 59 wickets and 189 catches.
Test Record - 27 Tests, 1,401 runs (Av. 33.35)

including 4 centuries, 2 wickets (Av. 11.00) and 5 catches.

SIMPSON ROBERT BADDELEY

Australia (born 1936) - A right-handed batsman, a good leg-spin and googly bowler and a fine silp fielder of all times. He played for New South Wales and Western Australia. In his first class career he made, 21,029 runs including 60 centuries, took 349 wickets and 383 catches.

Test Record - 62 Tests, 4,869 runs (Av. 46.81) including 10 centuries, 71 wickets (Av. 42.26) and 110 catches.

SIMPSON-HAYWARD GEORGE-HAYWARD THOMAS

England (1875-1936) - He was the most successful lob-bowlers to represent England. He played for Cambridge University. In his first class career he made, 5,582 runs including 3 centuries and took 510 wickets.

Test Record - 5 Tests, 105 runs (Av. 15.00), 23 wickets (Av. 18.26) and 1 catch.

SIMS JAMES MORTON

England (1903-1973) - A right-handed batsman and a right-arm leg-break bowler with a tricky googly. He played for Middlesex. In his first class career he made, 8,984 runs including 4 centuries, took 1,581 wickets and 253 catches.

Test Record - 4 Tests, 16 runs (Av. 4.00), 11 wickets (Av. 43.63) and 6 catches.

SINCLAIR BARRY WHITLEY

New Zealand (born 1936) - A right-handed batsman and an excellent fielder at cover. He played for Wellington. In his first class career he made, 6,114 runs including 6 centuries.

Test Record - 21 Tests, 1,148 runs (Av. 29.43) including 3 centuries, 2 wickets (Av. 16.00) and 8 catches.

SINCLAIR JAMES HUGH

South Africa (1876-1913) - A right-handed hard-hitting batsman and also a medium-fast bowler. He played for Transvaal. In his first class career he made, 4,483 runs including 6 centuries, and took 491 wickets.

Test Record - 25 Tests, 1,069 runs (Av. 23.23) including 3 centuries, 63 wickets (Av. 31.58) and 9 catches.

SINCOCK DAVID JOHN

Australia (born 1942) - A left-arm googly bowler. He played for South Australia. In his first class career he made, 838 runs and took 159 wickets.

Test Record - 3 Tests, 80 runs (Av. 26.66), 8 wickets (Av. 51.25) and 2 catches.

SINGH CHARRAN K.

West Indies (born 1938) - A left-arm slow-bowler. He played for Trinidad. In his first class career he made, 102 runs and took 48 wickets.

Test Record - 2 Tests, 11 runs (Av. 3.66), 5 wickets (Av. 33.20) and 2 catches.

SINGLE

One run.

SINGLE WICKET

A type of competition, quite popular in the 'sixties and seventies that pits one man against another at batting and bowling in normal match conditions and with a complement of 'neutral' fieldsman.

SITTER

A simple catch.

SIVARAMAKRISHNAN LAXMAN

India (born 1965) - An outstanding leg-spin bowler, fine fielder and also as a useful right-handed batsman. He played for Tamil Nadu. In his first class career he made, 912 runs including 1 century and took 133 wickets.

Test Record - 9 Tests, 130 runs (Av. 16.25), 26 wickets (Av. 44.03) and 9 catches.

SHIVARAMA KRISHNAN

SIX

A hit that clears the boundary without first touching the ground and is worth six runs.

SKIPPER

Team captain, a term particularly popular in English cricket.

SKITTLE

To comprehensively bowl out.

SKY

To hit the ball high in the air, to hit a 'skier'.

SLACK WILFRED NORRIS

England (1954 - 1989) - A sound determined left - handed opening batsman. He played for Middlesex and Windward Islands. In his first class career he made, 10,902 runs including 19 centuries, took 19 wickets and 142 catches.
Test Record - 3 Tests, 81 runs (Av. 13.50) and 2 catches.

SLASH

To flay with a half cross-bat motion at a ball outside the off stump sending the ball flying high over the off-side field, usually behind point.

SLEDGE

To use abusive words against an opponent (colloquial).

SLEEP PETER RAYMOND

Australia (born 1957) - A right-arm leg-spin bowler with a good action and also an attacking middle-order batsman. He played for South Australia. In his first class career he made, 4,488 runs including 9 centuries and took 212 wickets.
Test Record -12 Tests, 413 runs (Av. 22.94) and 24 wickets (Av. 51.16).

SLICE

Method of playing a delivery on or just outside the off stump with an open face of the bat with the aim of running it down behind point.

SLINGER

A type of pace bowler whose delivery arm describes a clean arc, slightly round-armed, as in the action of javelin thrower. A good example of a slinger, or a 'slingshot' action, is the great Australian Jeff Thomson.

SLIP FIELDERS

According to the type of bowler and the condition of the pitch, there may be one, two, three or even, very occasionally, four slips. Comparative immobility of foot, extraordinary quickness of eyes, arms, hands and fingers, and intense concentration are the main attributes of a first-class slip fielder. Literally every ball must be watched with extreme care, and it is of great mental strain to field for a long time at slip, concentrating as each ball is delivered and relaxing immediately afterwards. One hot summer afternoon at Bristol, W.R. Hammond stood for nearly four hours at slip without a ball going anywhere near him, and then, suddenly, a waist-high snick flashed off the bat, out shot Hammond's right hand and the catch was held.

So a good slip fielder watches every ball in the hope that a snick will come his way, and although he will naturally be disappointed time after time but when the occasion does come, he must be ready to seize his opportunity.

SLOG

A reckless attempt to thrash the bowling (colloquial).

SLOW BOWLER

Usually, a bowler who attempts to deceive the batsman with spin and flight.

SMALL GLADSTONE CLEOPHAS

SMALL GLADSTONE CLEOPHAS

England (born 1961) - A right-arm medium-fast bowler and a right-handed batsman. He played for Warwickshire and South Australia. In his first class career he made, 1,820 runs and took 399 wickets.

Test Record - 5 Tests, 61 runs (Av. 15.25), 20 wickets (Av. 22.70) and 1 catch.

SMALL JOSEPHA.

West Indies (1892-1958) - A medium-pace off-break bowler, a right-handed batsman. A fine close fielder for silp. He played for Trinidad. In his first class career he made, 3,063 runs including 3 centuries, and took 165 wickets.

Test Record - 3 Tests, 79 runs (Av.13.16), 3 wickets (Av.61.33) and 3 catches.

SMALL MILTON ASTER

West Indies (born 1964) - A medium-fast bowler. He played for Barbados. In his first class career he made, 19 runs and took 36 wickets.

Test Record - 2 Tests, 3 runs and 4 wickets (Av. 38.25).

SMITH ALAN CHRISTOPHER

England (born 1936) - A right-handed batsman, a right-arm medium-pace bowler and a very good wicket-keeper. He played for Oxford University and Warwickshire. In his first class career he made, 11,027 runs including 2 centuries, took 131 wickets and 776 dismissals.

Test Record - 6 Tests, 118 runs (Av. 29.50) and 20 dismissals (20ct).

SMITH CAMERON WILBERFORCE

West Indies (born 1933) - A right-handed opening batsman and a wicket-keeper. He played for Barbados. In his first class career he made, 2,277 runs including 5 centuries.

Test Record - 5 Tests, 222 runs (Av. 24.66) and 5 dismissals (4 ct, 1 st).

SMITH CEDRIC IVAN JAMES

England (1906-1979) - A right-arm bowler. He played for Wiltshire and Middlesex. In his first class career he made, 4,007 runs including 1 century and took 845 wickets.

Test Record - 5 Tests, 102 runs (Av. 10.20), 15 wickets (Av. 26.20) and 1 catch.

SMITH CHARLES JAMES EDWARD

South Africa (1872-1947) - A useful middle-order right-handed batsman. He played for Transvaal. In his first class career he made, 409

runs.
Test Record - 3 Tests, 106 runs (Av. 21.20) and 2 catches.

SMITH CHRISTOPHER LYALL
England (born 1958) - A right-handed opening batsman. He played for Natal, Glamorgan and Hampshire. In his first class career he made, 10,404 runs including 28 centuries and took 37 wickets.
Test Record - 8 Tests, 392 runs (Av. 30.15), 3 wickets (Av. 13.00) and 5 catches.

SMITH DAVID BERTRAM MILLER
Australia (1884-1963) - A fast-scoring right-handed batsman . He played for Victoria. In his first class career he made, 1,764 runs including 3 centuries.
Test Record - 2 Tests, 30 runs (Av. 15.00).

SMITH DAVID MARK
England (born 1956) - A left-handed batsman and also a medium-fast bowler. He played for Surrey and Worcestershire. In his first class career he made, 8,662 runs including 16 centuries, took 30 wickets and 129 catches.
Test Record - 2 Tests, 80 runs (Av. 20.00).

SMITH DAVID ROBERT
England (born 1934) - A right-arm medium-fast bowler with a very short run-up and also a useful batsman. He played for Gloucestershire. In his first class career he made, 4,970 runs, took 1,250 wickets and 290 catches.
Test Record - 5 Tests, 38 runs (Av. 9.50), 6 wickets (Av. 59.83) and 2 catches.

SMITH DENIS
England (1907-1979) - A left-handed batsman. He played for Derbyshire. In his first class career he made, 21,843 runs including 32 centuries, took 20 wickets, 378 catches and 5 stumpings.
Test Record - 2 Tests, 128 runs (Av. 32.00) and 1 catch.

SMITH DONALD VICTOR
England (born 1923) - A left-handed opening batsman and a useful left-arm medium-pace bowler. He played for Sussex. In his first class career he made, 16,960 runs including 9 centuries, took 340 wickets and 232 catches.
Test Record - 3 Tests, 25 runs (Av. 8.33).

SMITH ERNEST JAMES
England (1886-1979) - A right-handed opening batsman. He played for Warwickshire. In his first class career he made, 16,997 runs including 20 centuries and 878 dismissals.
Test Record - 11 Tests, 113 runs (Av. 8.69) and 20 dismissals (17ct, 3st).

SMITH FRANK BRUNTON
New Zealand (born 1922) - A right-handed batsman and an excellent fielder. He played for Canterbury. In his first class career he made, 2,588 runs including 4 centuries.
Test Record - 4 Tests, 237 runs (Av. 47.40) and 1 catch.

SMITH FREDERICK W.
South Africa - Details not known. A middle-order batsman. He played for Transvaal. In his first class career he made,140 runs.
Test Record - 3 Tests, 45 runs (Av. 9.00) and 2 catches.

SMITH IAN DAVID STOCKLEY
New Zealand (born 1957) - A right-handed batsman and a useful wicket-keeper. He played for Central Districts. In his first class career he made, 4,736 runs including 5 centuries, and 318 dismissals.
Test Record - 33 Tests, 808 runs (Av. 22.44) including 1 century and 98 dismissals (92ct, 6st).

SMITH MICHAEL JOHN KNIGHT
England (born 1933) - A right-handed batsman with great powers of improvisation and concentration. He played for Oxford University and Warwickshire. In his first class career he made, 39,832 runs including 69 centuries and 593 catches.

Test Record - 50 Tests, 2,278 runs (Av. 31.63) including 3 centuries and 53 catches.

SMITH O'NEIL GORDON

West Indies (1933-1959) - An off-break bowler and a right-handed batsman. He played for Jamaica. In his first class career he made, 4,031 runs including 10 centuries and took 121 wickets.
Test Record - 26 Tests, 1,331 runs (Av. 31.69) including 4 centuries, 48 wickets (Av. 33.85) and 9 catches.

SMITH STEPHEN BARRY

Australia (born 1961) - A right-handed opening batsman and a fine fielder. He played for New South Wales. In his first class career he made, 2,821 runs including 8 centuries.
Test Record - 3 Tests, 41 runs (Av. 8.20) and 1 catch.

SMITH THOMAS PETER BROMLEY

England (1908-1967) - A right-arm leg-break and googly bowler and a useful batsman. He played for Essex. In his first class career he made, 10,161 runs including 8 centuries, took 1,697 wickets and 359 catches.
Test Record - 4 Tests, 33 runs (Av. 6.60), 3 wickets (Av. 106.33) and 1 catch.

SMITH VIVIAN IAN

South Africa (born 1925) - A right-arm leg-break bowler without googly. He played for Natal. In his first class career he made, 547 runs and took 365 wickets.
Test Record - 9 Tests, 39 runs (Av.3.90), 12 wickets (Av. 64.08) and 3 catches.

SMITHSON GERALD ARTHUR

England (1926-1970) - A useful batsman. He played for Yorkshire. In his first class career he made, 6,940 runs including 8 centuries.
Test Record - 2 Tests, 70 runs (Av. 23.33).

SNEDDEN MARTIN COLIN

New Zealand (born 1958) - A right-arm medium-fast bowler and useful left-handed batsman. He played for Auckland. In his first class career he made, 1,870 runs and took 263 wickets.
Test Record - 11 Tests, 147 runs (Av. 14.70), 24 wickets (Av. 38.75) and 2 catches.

SNICK

When the ball just hits the edge of the bat on its way past the batsman.

SNOOKE SIBLEY JOHN

South Africa (1881-1966) - A right-handed stroke batsman. He played for Border. In his first class career he made, 4,821 runs including 7 centuries and took 120 wickets.
Test Record - 26 Tests, 1,008 runs (Av. 22.40) including 1 century, 35 wickets (Av. 20.05), and 24 catches.

JOHN SNOW

SNOW JOHN AUGUSTINE

England (born 1941) - A right-arm medium-fast bowler and a right-handed batsman. He played for Sussex and Warwickshire. In his first class career he made, 4,832 runs, took 1,174 wickets and 125 catches.
Test Record - 49 Tests, 772 runs (Av. 13.54), 202 wickets (Av. 26.66) and 16 catches.

SOBERS SIR GARFIELD ST AUBURN

SIR GARFIELD SOBERS with his wife

West Indies (born 1936) - A left-handed batsman. He was one of the greatest batsmen of all times. He was also a marvellous new-ball left-arm medium-fast over-the-wicket bowler, who was equally good as a slow left-arm orthodox bowler. As a fielder, he was brilliant, with feline reflexes close to the wicket, especially on the leg-side. He played for Barbados, South Australia and Nottinghamshire. He also trained the Sri Lankan team as a coach. In his first class career he made, 28,315 runs including 86 centuries, took 1,043 wickets and 407 catches.

Test Record - 93 Tests, 8,032 runs (Av. 57.78) including 26 centuries, 235 wickets (Av. 34.03) and 109 catches.

SOHONI SRIRANGA WASUDEO

India (born 1918) - A right-handed batsman and a right-arm medium-fast bowler. Test debut on July 20, 1946 against England at the age of 28 years and 135 days. Scores on Test debut were 3 and 11 not out in the second Test at Manchester. Last Test of the career played against England in December 1951. Scores on last appearance in Test were 6 and 28 in the second Test at Bombay. Age at the time of retirement from Test cricket was 33 years and 284 days. He played for Maharashtra, Baroda and Bombay. In his first class career he made, 4,245 runs including 8 centuries and took 232 wickets.

Test Record - 4 Tests, 83 runs (Av. 16.60), 2 wickets (Av. 101.00) and 2 catches.

SOLKAR EKNATH DHONDU

India (born 1948) - A left-handed batsman and a left-arm medium-pace and slow spin bowler. Test debut on October 15, 1969 against New Zealand at the age of 21 years and 208 days. Scores on Test debut were 0 and 13 not out in the third Test at Hyderabad. Last Test of the career played against England in January 1977. Scores on last appearance in Test were 2 and 3 in the second Test at Calcutta. Age at the time of retirement from Test cricket was 28 years and 289 days. Enjoys the unique distinction of being the only cricketer in Test history to be selected to play on the merits of fielding alone. Much of Indian spin quartet's (Bedi, Chandrasekhar, Prasanna, and Venkataghavan) success can be attributed to Solkar's phenomenal catching ability. His greatest triumph came in Victory Test at Port-of-Spain in 1971. Has held more catches for India in a Test series 12

EKNATH SOLKAR, PRASANNA

catches in the five - Test series against England in 1972-73. First-ever Test century 102 scored on January 27, 1975 against West Indies in the fifth Test at Bombay at the age of 26 years and 309 days. His 1,000 runs in Tests came in his 25th Test appearance (on January 27, 1975 in the fifth Test against West Indies at Bombay). Earned the distinction of being the first Indian fielder (excluding wicket-keeper) and the 23rd from all countires to held 50 or more catches in a Test cereer. He played for Bombay and Sussex. In his first class career he made, 6,851 runs including 8 centuries, took 276 wickets and 182 catches.

Test Record - 27 Tests, 1,068 runs (Av. 25.42) including 1 century, 18 wickets (Av. 59.44) and 53 catches.

SOLOMON JOSEPH STANISLAUS

West Indies (born 1930) - A right-handed batsman, a useful medium-pace leg-break change bowler and a fine close fielder. He played for British Guiana. In his first class career he made, 5,318 runs including 12 centuries and took 51 wickets.

Test Record - 27 Tests, 1,326 runs (Av. 34.00) including 1 century, 4 wickets (Av. 67.00) and 13 catches.

SOMERSET

Foundation of Present Club: August 18, 1875 in Sidmouth, Devon.
First First-Class Match: Lancashire v Somerset (Old Trafford) June 8, 9, 10 1882. The County was ranked as first-class 1886 to 1890 inclusive.
Present Principal Ground: County Ground, St. James's, St. Taunton.
County Championship: Best Seasons : 3rd in 1892, 1958, 1963, 1966, 1981.
JPL Champions: 1979.
B&H Cup: Winners in 1981 and 1982.
Nat West Trophy: Winners in 1979 and 1983.
Highest Team Total: 675-9 dec v Hampshire (Bath) 1924.
Lowest Team Total: 25 v Glos (Bristol) 1947.

SOUTHERTON JAMES

England (1827-1880) - A right-arm slow bowler and a good middle-order batsman. He played for Surrey and Hampshire. In his first class career he made, 3,159 runs, took 1,681 wickets and 218 dismissals.

Test Record - 2 Tests, 7 runs (Av. 3.50), 7 wickets (Av. 15.28) and 2 catches.

SPARLING JOHN TREVOR

New Zealand (born 1938) - A right-handed batsman, a small off-spin bowler and a very good fielder. He played for Auckland. In his first class career he made, 4,606 runs including 2 centuries and took 318 wickets.

Test Record - 11 Tests, 229 runs (Av. 12.72),5 wickets (Av. 65.40) and 3 catches.

SPINNER

A slow bowler whose main weapon is his ability to make the ball turn when it hits the wicket. He also uses flight and drift (or curve) through the air and obtains this either out of the front of the hand (in the case of the 'finger spinner') or the back of the hand (as with the 'wrist spinner').

SPOONER REGINALD HERBERT

England (1880-1961) - A useful right-handed batsman. He played for Lancashire. In his first class career he made, 13,681 runs including 31 centuries.

Test Record - 10 Tests, 481 runs (Av. 32.06) including 1 century and 4 catches.

SPOONER RICHARD THOMAS

England (born 1919) - A wicket-keeper and a left-handed opening batsman. He played for Durham and Warwickshire. In his first class career he made, 13,851 runs including 12 centuries, and 765 dismissals.

Test Record - 7 Tests, 354 runs (Av. 27.23) and 12 dismissals (10ct, 2st).

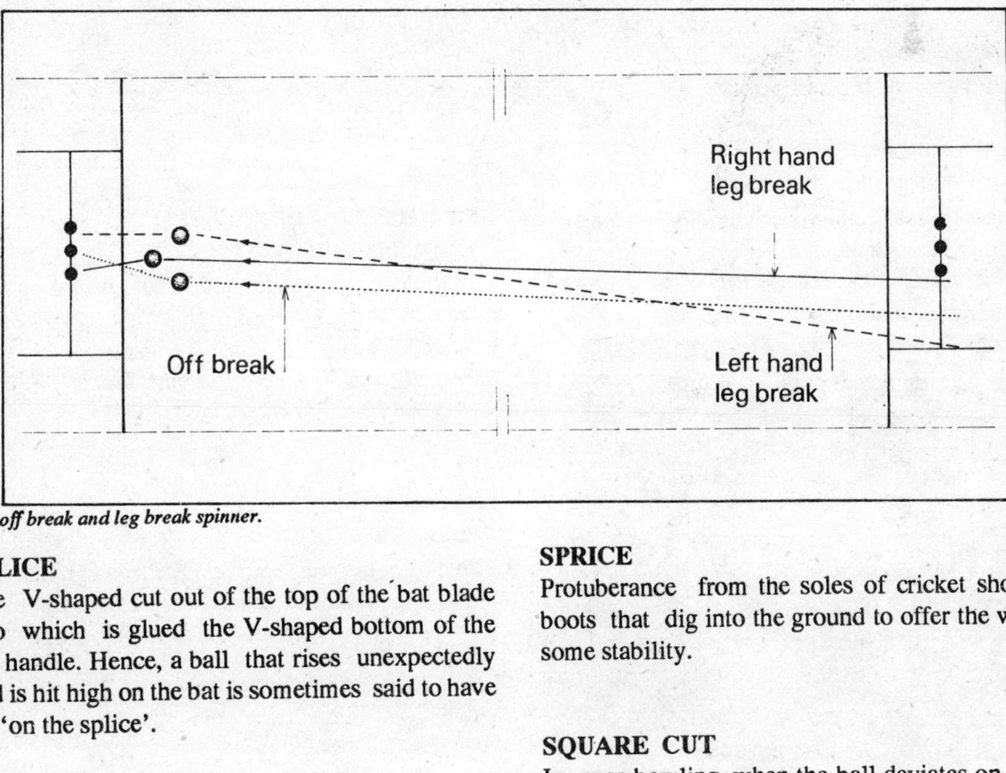

The off break and leg break spinner.

SPLICE

The V-shaped cut out of the top of the bat blade into which is glued the V-shaped bottom of the bat handle. Hence, a ball that rises unexpectedly and is hit high on the bat is sometimes said to have hit 'on the splice'.

SPOFFORTH FREDERICK ROBERT

Australia (1853-1926) - A famous medium-fast bowler. He played for New South Wales, Victoria and Derbyshire. In his first class career he made,1,928 runs and took 853 wickets.

Test Record - 18 Tests, 217 runs (Av. 9.43), 94 wickets (Av. 18.41) and 11 catches.

SPRICE

Protuberance from the soles of cricket shoes or boots that dig into the ground to offer the wearer some stability.

SQUARE CUT

In pace bowling, when the ball deviates on pitching because the bowler has imparted varying spins on it. More readily available on the softer wicket surface in England than in other parts of the cricketing world. In batting, the range of scoring strokes aimed from point to just wide of the wicket-keeper and played with a cross-bat motion to short-pitched deliveries outside the off stump. The 'square cut' is aimed at the point region, the 'back cut' fine of the gully, and the 'late cut' is played very late and with a chopping motion to angle the ball just wide of a single slip or the wicket-keeper.

SQUARE DRIVE

An attacking stroke off the front foot aimed at scoring through the point-cover point region. Two players famous for this stroke are the West Indian Learie Constantine and the Englishman Walter Hammond.

The Square Cut (start) The Square Cut (contact position)

SRIKKANTH KRISHNAMACHARI

India (born 1959) - A smiling cavalier of a right-handed batsman with a wide array of brilliant strokes, a useful fine fielder and also a useful right-arm bowler. He plays for Tamil Nadu. In his first class career he made, 7,002 runs including 15 centuries and took 13 wickets.

Test Record - 35 Tests, 1,830 runs (Av.33.88) including 2 centuries and 32 catches.

KRISHNAMACHARI SRIKKANTH

ST HILL EDWIN LLOYD

West Indies (1904-1957) - He was a right-arm medium-pace bowler and also a useful batsman. He played for Trinidad. In his first class career he made, 274 runs and took 64 wickets.

Test Record - 2 Tests, 18 runs (Av. 4.50) and 3 wickets (Av. 73.66).

ST HILL WILTON H.

West Indies (1893-1957) - He was a useful batsman. He played for Trinidad. In his first class career he made, 1,928 runs including 5 centuries.

Test Record - 3 Tests, 117 runs (Av. 19.50) and 1 catch.

STACKPOLE KEITH RAYMOND

Australia (born 1940) - A right-handed opening batsman and a useful leg-break bowler. He played for Victoria. In his first class career he made, 10,100 runs including 22 centuries, took 148 wickets and 166 catches.

Test Record - 43 Tests, 2,807 runs (Av. 37.42) including 7 centuries, 15 wickets (Av. 66.73) and 47 catches.

STANYFORTH LT-COL.RONALD THOMAS
England (1892-1964) - A useful wicket-keeper. He played for Yorkshire. In his first class career he made, 1,092 runs and 93 dismissals.
Test Record - 4 Tests, 13 runs (Av. 2.60) and 9 dismissals (7 ct, 2 st).

STAPLES SAMUEL JAMES
England (1892-1950) - A right-arm medium-pace bowler and a lower-order batsman. He played for Nottinghamshire. In his first class career he made, 6,470 runs including 1 century, took 1,331 wickets and 345 catches.
Test Record - 3 Tests, 65 runs (Av. 13.00) and 15 wickets (Av. 29.00).

STATHAM JOHN BRIAN
England (born 1930) - A right-arm great medium-fast bowler and a left-handed batsman. He played for Lancashire. In his first class career he made, 5,424 runs, took 2,260 wickets and 230 catches.
Test Record - 70 Tests, 675 runs (Av. 11.44), 252 wickets (Av. 24.82) and 28 catches.

STATISTICS
The summary or records of cricket covering team and individual figures. Recently fervent statisticians have developed this aspect of the game to its saturation point, despite the fact that the game's changing face has rendered comparisons of performances between yesteryear's and today's players almost worthless.

STAYERS SVEN CONRAD
West Indies (born 1937) - A good right-handed batsman and a medium-fast bowler. He played for British Guiana. In his first class career he made, 485 runs including 1 century and took 68 wickets.
Test Record - 4 Tests, 58 runs (Av. 19.33) and 9 wickets (Av. 40.44).

STEEL ALLAN GIBSON
England (1858 - 1914) - A right - arm slow bowler, quick-footed batsman and a superb driver on both sides of the wickets. He played for Cambridge University and Lancashire. In his first class career he made, 6,759 runs including 7 centuries and took 781 wickets.
Test Record - 13 Tests, 600 runs (Av. 35.29) including 2 centuries, 29 wickets (Av. 20.86) and 5 catches.

STEELE DAVID STANLEY
England (born 1941) - A right-handed batsman, a slow left-arm bowler and a fine close fielder. He played for Staffordshire and Northamptonshire. In his first class career he made, 22,346 runs including 30 centuries, took 623 wickets and 546 catches.
Test Record - 8 Tests, 673 runs (Av. 42.06) including 1 century, 2 wickets (Av. 19.50) and 7 catches.

STEVENS GAVIN BYRON
Australia (born 1932) - An opening batsman. He played for South Australia. In his first class career he made, 3,061 runs including 7 centuries.
Test Record - 4 Tests, 112 runs (Av. 16.00) and 2 catches.

STEVENS GREVILLE THOMAS SCOTT
England (1901-1970) - A leg-break and googly bowler, a right-handed batsman and a good close fielder. He played for Oxford University and Middlesex. In his first class career he made, 10,376 runs including 12 centuries, took 684 wickets and 216 catches.
Test Record - 10 Tests, 263 runs (Av. 15.47), 20 wickets (Av. 32.40) and 9 catches.

STEVENSON GRAHAM BARRY
England (born 1955) - A right-handed batsman and a medium-fast bowler. He played for Yorkshire. In his first class career he made, 3,963 runs including 2 centuries and took 486 wickets.
Test Record - 2 Tests, 28 runs (Av. 28.00) and 5 wickets (Av. 36.60).

STEWART MICHAEL JAMES
England (born 1932) - An opening batsman and a specialist short-leg fielder. He played for Surrey. In his first class career he made, 26,492 runs including 49 centuries and 634 catches.

Test Record - 8 Tests, 385 runs (Av. 35.00) and 6 catches.

STICKY WICKET

A wicket that has been seriously affected by rain and so made very difficult for batting.

STIRLING DEREK ANDREW

New Zealand (born 1961) - A medium-fast bowler. He played for Central Districts. In his first class career he made, 1,114 runs and took 163 wickets.

Test Record - 6 Tests, 180 runs (Av. 15.42), 11 wickets (Av. 50.27) and 1 catch.

STOCK BOWLER

One whose duty is to bowl tight and close up one end, while attacking bowlers either work at the other end or have a spell.

STOCK SINGLE

So - called because a run has been taken, not so much becuase it was an offer but because of the enterprise and daring of the runners.

STODDART ANDREW ERNEST

England (1863-1915) - He was a right-handed batsman with all the strokes, especially strong in driving and hitting to leg. He played for Middlesex. In his first class career he made, 16,738 runs including 26 centuries, took 278 wickets and 260 catches.

Test Record - 16 Tests, 996 runs (Av. 35.57) including 2 centuries, 2 wickets (Av. 47.00) and 6 catches.

STOLLMEYER JEFFREY BAXTER

West Indies (1921-1989) - A right-handed opening batsman, a useful leg-break bowler and also a fine close fielder. He played for Trinidad. In his first class career he made, 7,942 runs including 14 centuries and took 55 wickets.

Test Record - 32 Tests, 2,159 runs (Av. 42.33) including 4 centuries, 13 wickets (Av. 39.00) and 20 catches.

STONEWALLER

One who is consistently very slow at gathering one's runs.

STORER WILLIAM

England (1867-1912) - He was a useful change-bowler and also a useful wicket-keeper. He played for Derbyshire. In his first class career he made, 12,966 runs including 17 centuries, took 232 wickets and 431 dismissals.

Test Record - 6 Tests, 215 runs (Av. 19.54), 2 wickets (Av. 54.00) and 11 dismissals (11ct).

STRAIGHT DRIVE

This shot is played to a ball that pitches straight and is far enough up to let us get our left foot to the pitch. This half-volley is hit as it bounces, and the ball will then keep to the ground. The technique for this shot is relatively easy now that you can play the forward defensive. The left shoulder is over the left knee and the left foot is placed just beside the spot the ball has pitched. The left arm guides the face of the bat to the ball and the right hand with full grip produces the power to drive the ball as it pitches.

STRAIGHT BAT

When the bat is offered to the ball in a perpendicular pose, preferably with the handle forward of the toe to bring the ball to the ground soon after contact. Should be employed for the forward and backward defensive shots and drives from cover around to mid-wicket.

STREAKER

Colloquial name given to a person who runs naked on a cricket field. The first streaker in Test cricket interrupted the second Test between Australia and England at Lord's in 1975.

STRICKER LOUIS ANTHONY

South Africa (1884-1960) - A forcing right-handed opening batsman. He played for Transvaal. In his first class career he made, 2,105 runs including 2 centuries, and took 8 wickets.

Test Record - 13 Tests, 342 runs (Av. 14.25), and 3 catches.

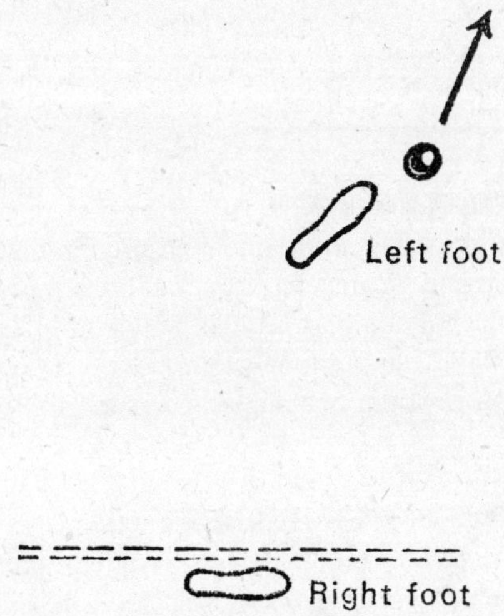

Forward straight drive

STRIKE
The batsman facing the bowler is said to be 'on strike'. Also, to hit the ball.

STRIKER
The man on strike.

STRIKING RATE
A player's batting rate measured in the number of runs he scores per hundred balls faced; in bowling, the number of balls bowled for each wicket taken. Can describe performance in one game, a competition, or a player's career.

STRUDWICK HERBERT
England (1880-1970) - A very good wicket-keeper. He played for Surrey. In his first class career he made, 6,445 runs and 1,495 dismissals.
Test Record - 28 Tests, 230 runs (Av. 7.93) and 72 dismissals (60 ct, 12 st).

STUDD CHARLES THOMAS
England (1860-1931) - A right-handed batsman and also a medium-fast bowler. He played for Cambridge University and Middlesex. In his first class career he made, 4,391 runs including 8 centuries and took 455 wickets.
Test Record - 5 Tests, 160 runs (Av. 20.00), 3 wickets (Av. 32.66) and 5 catches.

STUDD GEORGE BROWN
England (1859-1945) - He was a front-foot player and also a skilful and powerful driver. He played for Cambridge University and Middlesex. In his first class career he made, 2,892 runs including 3 centuries.
Test Record - 4 Tests, 31 runs (Av. 4.42) and 8 catches.

STUMPED
See section of the laws.

STUMPER
When a batsman, having received a delivery other than a no-ball, leaves his ground in an attempt to play a stroke and the wicket is broken by the wicket-keeper, the batsman has been stumped. The wicket-keeper is the only member of the fielding side who may effect a stumping and, in doing so, he may not take the ball in front of the stumps unless it has touched the bat or the striker's person.
However, once the batsman has left his ground in an attempt to run and the wicket keeper breaks the wicket the batsman is out, run out.

STUMPS
The three uprights, each twenty-eight inches high with bails atop, which comprise the wicket at each of the pitch. Also the call from the umpires to signal the close of play.

SUBBA ROW RAMAN
England (born 1932) - A left-handed batsman and also a good close fielder. He played for Cambridge University, Surrey and Northamptonshire. In his first class career he made, 14,182 runs including 30 centuries, took 87 wickets and 176 catches.
Test Record - 13 Tests, 984 runs (Av. 46.85) including 3 centuries, and 5 catches.

SUBRAMANYAM VENKATRAMAN
India (born 1936) - A right-handed batsman and a right-arm leg-break and googly bowler. Test debut in March 1963 against New Zealand at the age of 28 years and 243 days. Score on Test debut was 9 in the fourth Test at New Delhi. Last Test of the career played against New Zealand in March 1968. Score on last appearance in Test was 3 in the fourth Test at Auckland. Age at the time of retirement from Test cricket was 31 years and 237 days. He played for Mysore. In his first class career he made, 4,219 runs including 8 centuries and took 70 wickets.
Test Record - 9 Tests, 263 runs (Av. 18.78), 3 wickets (67.00) and 9 catches.

SUBSTITUTES
A substitute may be calleu upon either by the fielding side, when a fieldsman is incapacitated, or by

a batsman, when through illness or injury he is unable to do his own running.

The fieldsman substitute may not bat or bowl, but he may keep wickets with the consent of the batting captain. However, the batting captain has no other right, either about who is used as a substitute or where in the field he may be placed.

Should a bowler leave the field and be off the field for longer than fifteen minutes, then he shall not bowl again until he is back on the field for the same amount of time as he was absent.

In the case of the substitute runner, he must be wearing the same external protective equipment as that used by the injured batsman.

While the injured batsman is on strike, the substitute runner takes up a position near the square leg umpire and all normal laws of cricket apply to him. With regard to run-out and stumping decisions, the umpires will consider the popping crease to be continuous lines.

When the injured batsman is the nonstriker, he stands out near square leg and takes no part in the game.

SUGG FRANK HOWE

England (1862-1933) - A right-handed batsman . He played for Yorkshire, Derbyshire and Lancashire. In his first class career he made, 11,859 runs including 16 centuries, took 10 wickets, 167 catches and 1 stumping.

Test Record - 2 Tests, 55 runs (Av. 27.50).

SUNDERAM GUNDIBAIL RAMA

India (born 1930) - A competent right-arm medium-fast bowler and useful tail-end batsman. He played for Bombay. In his first class career he made, 558 runs and took 12 wickets.

Test Record - 2 Tests, 3 runs and 3 wickets (Av. 54.66).

SUNDRIES

Runs not scored off the bat, i.e. no-balls, byes, legbyes, and wides.

SURENDRANATH R.

India (born 1937) - A right-handed and a right-arm medium-fast bowler. Test debut on December 31, 1958 against West Indies at the age of 21 years and 357 days. Scores on Test debut were 8 and 3 in the third Test at Calcutta. Last Test of the career played against Pakistan in January 1961. Score on last appearance in Test was 6 in the fourth Test at Madras. Age at the time of retirement from Test cricket was 24 years and 14 days. He played for Services. In his first class career he made, 1,351 runs including 1 century and took 284 wickets.

Test Record - 11 Tests, 136 runs (Av. 10.46), 26 wickets (Av. 40.50) and 4 catches.

SURREY

Foundation of Present Club: August 21, 1845 at the Oval.

First First-Class Match: MCC v Surrey (Lord's) July 15, 1839. However, matches by Surrey from 1730 onwards were regarded as 'great'.

Present Principal Ground: Kennington Oval, London SE 11.

County Champions: 1864, 1888, 1889, 1891, 1892, 1894, 1895, 1899, 1914, 1950, 1952, 1954, 1955, 1956, 1957, 1958, 1971.

JPL Championship: Best Seasons: 5th in 1969 and 1980.

B&H Cup: Winners in 1974.

Nat West Trophy: Winners in 1982.

Highest Team Total: 811 v Somerset (Oval) 1899.

Lowest Team Total: 14 v Essex (Chelmsford) 1983.

SURTI RUSI FRAMROZ

India (born 1936) - A left-handed and left-arm medium-pace and slow-spin bowler. Test debut on December 2, 1960 against Pakistan at the age of 24 years and 188 days. Score on Test debut was 11 in the first Test at Bombay. Last Test of the career played against Australia in November 1969. Scores on last appearance in Test were 4 and 13 in the first Test at Bombay. Age at the time of retirement from Test cricket was 33 years and 164 days. He played for Gujarat, Rajasthan and Queensland. In his first class career he made, 8,066 runs including 6 centuries and took 285 wickets.

Test Record - 26 Tests, 1,263 runs (Av. 28.70), 42 wickets (Av. 46.71) and 26 catches.

SUSSEX

Foundation of Present Club: August 21, 1845 at The Oval

First First-Class Match: MCC v Sussex June 9, 1823. However, matches by Sussex from the 1730s onward were regarded as 'great'.

Present Principal Ground: County Ground, Eaton Road,Hove.

County Champions: Best Seasons: 2nd in 1902, 1932, 1933, 1934, 1953, 1981.

JPL Champions: 1982.

B&H Cup: Semi-finalists in 1982.

Nat West Trophy: Winners in 1963, and 1978.

Highest Team Total: 705-8 dec v Surrey (Hastings) 1902.

Lowest Team Total: 19 v Surrey (Godalming) 1830 and 19 v Notts (Hove) 1873.

SUSSKIND MANFRED JULIUS

South Africa (1891-1957) - A right-handed batsman and also an excellent fielder. He played for Middlesex, Cambridge University and Transvaal. In his first class career he made, 4,775 runs including 11 centuries.

Test Record - 5 Tests, 268 runs (Av. 33.50) and 1 catch.

SUTCLIFFE BERT

New Zealand (born 1923) - A left-handed opening batsman and left-arm slow bowler with a deceptive quicker ball. He was also rapid, clean and safe in the field. He played for Auckland, Otago and Northern Districts. In his first class career he made, 17,283 runs including 44 centuries, and took 86 wickets.

Test Record - 42 Tests, 2,727 runs (Av. 40.10) including 5 centuries, 4 wickets (Av. 86.00) and 20 catches.

SUTCLIFFE HERBERT

England (1894-1978) - He was an opening batsman, hitting the ball firmly off the front foot especially to the off-side. He played for Yorkshire. In his first class career he made, 50,138 runs including 149 centuries and 469 catches.

Test Record - 54 Tests, 4,555 runs (Av. 60.73) including 16 centuries, and 23 catches.

SWEEP

Cross-bat shot to a well-pitched delivery from a slow bowler when the batsman stretches forward and goes down on his back knee to swing the ball away square of the wicket on the one side.

THE SWEEP

The sweep is usually played to a ball of good length pitching outside leg stump (unless you're Alan Knott).

The head and shoulder lead to bring the pad onto the line of the ball.

The knee of the back leg bends. The arms are at full stretch as they bring the bat down.

A good finish, with the head over the front knee and not turning away too early.

SWERVE

Usually the craft of the pace bowler. It is the movement of the ball to left or right through the air during its flight. Caused by aerodynamics affected by the shine on the ball and the prominent seam that causes a drag on one side of the ball. Through reverse application of the principles and variations in body placements, the good swing bowler can make the ball move either way.

SWETMAN ROY

England (born 1933) - A useful batsman and a useful wicket-keeper. He played for Surrey, Nottinghamshire and Gloucestersire. In his first class career he made, 6,495 runs including 2 centuries and 597 dismissals.

Test Record - 11 Tests, 254 runs (Av. 16.93) and 26 dismissals (24 ct, 2 st).

SWING

See SWERVE.

SWING FROM THE BOOTLACES

Description given to a cross-bat swipe at a ball, a stroke taken anything but from the copybook.

T

TABER HEDLEY BRIAN

Australia (born 1940) - A very slow bowler and also a wicket-keeper. He played for New South Wales. In his first class career he made, 2,648 runs including 1 century and 395 dismissals.

Test Record - 16 Tests, 353 runs (Av. 16.04) and 60 dismissals (56ct, 4st).

TAHIR NAQQASH

Pakistan (born 1959) - A right-handed middle-order batsman and also a right-arm medium-fast bowler. He played for Punjab, Lahore and Muslim Commercial Bank. In his first class career he made, 988 runs, took 138 wickets and 14 catches.

Test Record - 15 Tests, 300 runs (Av. 21.42), 34 wickets (Av. 41.11) and 3 catches.

TAHIR NAQQASH

TAIL

The last three or four members of the batting line-up. Hence the terms 'tailender' and 'the tail wagged', the latter referring to a good return in the form of runs from the last three or four batsmen.

TAILENDER

Normally three or four batsmen at the end of batting order. They are not good batsmen but if a tailender makes good score, it is much appreciated.

TALAT ALI

Pakistan (born 1950) - A right-handed opening batsman and occasional medium-pace bowler. He played for Pakistan International Airlines. In his first class career he made, 7,296 runs including 14 centuries.

Test Record - 10 Tests, 370 runs (Av. 23.12), and 4 catches.

TALLON DONALD

Australia (1916-1984) - A quick and brilliant wicket-keeper. He played for Queensland. In his first class career he made, 6,034 runs including 9 centuries, and 432 dismissals.

Test Record - 21 Tests, 394 runs (Av. 17.13) and 58 dismissals (50ct, 8st).

TAMHANE NARENDRA SHANKER

India (born 1931) - A right-handed batsman and a wicket-keeper. Test debut on January 15, 1955 against Pakistan at the age of 23 years and 161 days. Scores on Test debut were 54 not out and 9 not out in the second Test at Bahawalpur. Last Test of the career played against Pakistan in December-January 1961. Score on last appearance in Test was 0 in the third Test at Calcutta. Age at the time of retirement from Test cricket was 29 years and 150 days. Shares with S.M.H. Kirmani the record of dismissing maximum batsmen behind the stumps in an innings (six - five catches and 1 stumping in the fifth Test against Pakistan at Karachi in 1954-55) and also in a series (19 catches and seven stumpings in five-Test series against Pakistan in 1954-55) for India. He had a lion's share in

the side which created a world record. Indian bowlers together with the wicket-keeper Tamhane, did not concede a single run by way of an 'extra' in Pakistan's total of 328 in the third Test at Lahore in 1954-55. This remains the world record total without any 'extra' conceded either by the wicket-keeper or any of the bowlers from India. He played for Bombay. In his first class career he made, 1,460 runs including 1 century and 253 dismissals.
Test Record - 21 Tests, 225 runs (Av. 10.22) and 51 dismissals (35ct, 16st).

TANCRED AUGUSTUS BERNARD
South Africa (1865-1911) - A useful batsman and also a fine fielder. He played for Kimberley and Transvaal. In his first class career he made, 708 runs including 1 century.
Test Record - 2 Tests, 87 runs (Av. 29.00) and 2 catches.

TANCRED LOUIS JOSEPH
South Africa (1876-1934) - An opening batsman. He played for Transvaal. In his first class career he made, 5,695 runs including 11 centuries.
Test Record - 14 Tests, 530 runs (Av. 21.20) and 3 catches.

TAPETTO
The pitch, so-called because cricket in Corfu is mostly played on matting. Like many Corfiot cricket terms it shows the strong Italian influence on the local language.

TAPSCOTT LIONEL ERIC
South Africa (1894-1934) - A right-handed batsman and a fine fielder. He played for Griqualand West. In his first class career he made, 1,759 runs including 2 centuries and took 34 wickets.
Test Record - 2 Tests, 58 runs (Av. 29.00).

TASLIM ARIF
Pakistan (born 1954) - A right-handed opening batsman, a useful wicket-keeper and a right-arm medium-pace bowler. He played for Karachi and Sind. In his first class career he made, 6,729 runs including 12 centuries, took 7 wickets and 311 dismissals.
Test Record - 6 Tests, 501 runs (Av. 62.62) including 1 century and 9 dismissals (6ct, 3st).

TATE MAURICE WILLIAM
England (1895-1956) - A right-handed batsman and also a right-arm slow off-break bowler. He played for Sussex. In his first class career he made, 21,717 runs including 23 centuries, took 2,784 wickets and 242 catches.
Test Record - 39 Tests, 1,198 runs (Av. 25.48) including 1 century, 155 wickets (Av. 26.13) and 11 catches.

TATTERSALL ROY
England (born 1922) - A right-arm off-break spin bowler. He played for Lancashire. In his first class career he made, 2,040 runs, took 1,369 wickets and 143 catches.
Test Record - 16 Tests, 50 runs (Av. 5.00), 58 wickets (Av. 26.08) and 8 catches.

TAUSEEF AHMED
Pakistan (born 1960) - A right-arm off-spin bowler. He played for Public Works Department and United Bank. In his first class career he made, 984 runs and took 438 wickets.
Test Record - 28 Tests,242 runs (Av. 17.28), 87 wickets (Av. 29.58) and 8 catches.

TAVARE CHRISTOPHER JAMES
England (born 1954) - A right-handed batsman, a right-arm bowler, a brilliant slip fielder and a man of nice temperament. He played for Oxford University. In his first class career he made, 15,952 runs including 30 centuries, took 4 wickets and 269 catches.
Test Record - 30 Tests, 1,753 runs (Av. 33.07) including 2 centuries and 20 catches.

TAYFIELD HUGH JOSEPH
South Africa (born 1928) - A right-arm off-spin bowler and a useful batsman. He played for Natal, Rhodesia and Transvaal. In his first class career he made, 3,668 runs, took 864 wickets and 149 catches.

CHRIS TAVARE Batting against India

Test Record - 37 Tests, 862 runs (Av. 16.90), 170 wickets (Av. 25.91) and 26 catches.

TAYLOR BRUCE RICHARD

New Zealand (born 1943) - A left-handed batsman and a right-arm medium-fast bowler. He played for Canterbury and Wellington. In his first class career he made, 4,579 runs including 4 centuries, and took 422 wickets.

Test Record - 30 Tests, 898 runs (Av. 20.40) including 2 centuries, 111 wickets (Av. 26.60) and 10 catches.

TAYLOR DANIEL

South Africa (1887-1957) - A sound batsman. He played for Natal. In his first class career he made, 394 runs.

Test Record - 2 Tests, 85 runs (Av. 21.25).

TAYLOR DONALD DOUGALD

New Zealand (1923-1980) - An attractive right-handed batsman, an occasional leg-break bowler and a useful fine fielder. He played for Auckland. In his first class career he made, 3,734 runs including 1 century and took 30 wickets.

Test Record - 3 Tests, 159 runs (Av. 31.80) and 2 catches.

TAYLOR HERBERT WILFERD

South Africa (1889-1973) - A right-handed opening batsman and a useful change bowler. He played for Natal, Transvaal and Western Province. In his first class career he made, 13,105 runs including 30 centuries and took 22 wickets.

Test Record - 42 Tests, 2,936 runs (Av. 40.77) including 7 centuries, 5 wickets (Av. 31.20) and 19 catches.

TAYLOR JASWICK OSSIE

West Indies (born 1932) - A right-arm medium-fast bowler. He played for Trinidad. In his first class career he made, 62 runs and took 50 wickets.

Test Record - 3 Tests, 4 runs (Av. 2.00) and 10 wickets (Av. 27.30).

TAYLOR JOHN MORRIS

Australia (1895-1971) - A right-handed batsman and a brilliant fielder. He played for New South Wales. In his first class career he made, 6,274 runs including 11 centuries.

Test Record - 20 Tests, 997 runs (Av. 35.60) including 1 century and 11 catches.

TAYLOR KENNETH

England (born 1935) - A right-handed opening batsman. He played for Yorkshire. In his first class career he made, 13,053 runs including 16

and a left-handed batsman. He played for Gloucestershire. In his first class career he made, 9,512 runs including 21 centuries, took 725 wickets and 193 catches.
Test Record - 2 Tests, 51 runs (Av. 17.00) and 3 wickets (Av. 25.00).

TOWNSEND DAVID CHARLES HUMPHERY
England (born 1912) - An opening batsman and a stroke-maker batsman. He played for Oxford University and Durham. In his first class career he made, 1,801 runs including 4 centuries and took 6 wickets.
Test Record - 3 Tests, 77 runs (Av. 12.83) and 1 catch.

TOWNSEND LESLIE FLETCHER
England (born 1903) - A right-handed batsman and also a right-arm medium-pace, off-spin bowler. He played for Derbyshire, Northumberland and Auckland. In his first class career he made, 19,555 runs including 22 centuries, took 1,088 wickets and 234 catches.
Test Record - 4 Tests, 97 runs (Av. 16.16), 6 wickets (Av. 34.16) and 2 catches.

TRACK
The particular line followed by a ball. The word track is also used with particular reference to the playing surface as it affects the play, e.g. hard track.

TRAICOS ATHANASIOS JOHN
South Africa (born 1947) - A right-arm off-break bowler of exceptional accuracy. He played for Rhodesia and Zimbabwe. In his first class career he made, 958 runs and took 222 wickets.
Test Record - 3 Tests, 8 runs (Av. 4.00), 4 wickets (Av. 51.75) and 4 catches.

TREMLETT MAURICE FLETCHER
England (1923-1984) - A right-arm medium-fast bowler. He played for Somerset and Central Districts. In his first class career he made, 16,038 runs including 16 centuries, took 351 wickets and 257 catches.
Test Record - 3 Tests, 20 runs (Av. 6.66) and 4 wickets (Av. 56.50).

TRENT BRIDGE
Trent Bridge,across the River Trent from the centre of Nottingham, is a ground with a great tradition of cricket, arising from the days when William Clarke, having married in 1837 the widow who owned the Trent Bridge Inn, developed the field attached to the Inn as a cricket ground.

TRIAL BALL
The ball delivered by a fresh bowler before the start of his spell. Maximum of two such balls were given but these were not counted. Now, the practice has been discontinued.

TRIBE GEORGE EDWARD
Australia (born 1920) - A left-handed batsman and a left-arm spin bowler. He played for Victoria and Northamptonshire. In his first class career he made, 10,177 runs including 7 centuries, took 1,378 wickets and 239 catches.
Test Record - 3 Tests, 35 runs (Av. 17.50) and 2 wickets (Av. 165.00).

TRIM JOHN
West Indies (1915-1960) - A right-arm medium-fast bowler. He played for British Guiana. In his first class career he made, 386 runs and took 96 wickets.
Test Record - 4 Tests, 21 runs (Av. 5.25), 18 wickets (Av. 16.16) and 2 catches.

TRIMBORN PATRICK HENRY JOSEPH
South Africa (born 1940) - A right-arm medium-fast bowler and fine close fielder. He played for Natal. In his first class career he made, 880 runs and took 314 wickets.
Test Record - 4 Tests, 13 runs (Av. 6.50), 11 wickets (Av. 23.36) and 7 catches.

TRIMMER
A fast ball of singular quality narrowly missing the stumps.

TROOT ALBERT EDWIN
Australia (1873-1914) - A right-arm bowler. He played for Victoria and Middlesex. In his first class career he made, 10,696 runs including 8 centuries, took 1,674 wickets and 449 catches.
Test Record - (Australia - 3): 205 runs (Av. 102.50) 9 wickets (Av. 21.33) and 4 catches (England - 2): 23 runs (Av. 5.75) and 17 wickets (Av. 11.64).

TROTT GEORGE HENRY STEPHENS
Australia (1866-1917) - A right-handed batsman and a right-arm leg-spin bowler. He played for Victoria. In his first class career he made, 8,804 runs including 9 centuries, took 386 wickets and 183 catches.
Test Record - 24 Tests, 921 runs (Av. 21.92) including 1 century, 29 wickets (Av. 35.13) and 21 catches.

TROUP GARY BERTRAM
New Zealand (born 1952) - A left-arm medium-fast bowler. He played for Auckland. In his first class career he made, 842 runs and took 266 wickets.
Tests Records - 15 Tests, 55 runs (Av. 4.58), 39 wickets (Av. 37.28) and 2 catches.

FRED TRUEMAN

TRUEMAN FREDERICK SEWARDS
England (born 1931) - A right-handed batsman, a useful right-arm bowler and a brilliant natural fielder. He played for Yorkshire. In his first class career he made, 9,231 runs including 3 centuries, took 2,304 wickets and 438 catches.
Test Record - 67 Tests, 981 runs (Av. 13.81), 307 wickets (Av. 21.57) and 64 catches.

TRUMBLE HUGH
Australia (1867-1938) - A right-arm medium-pace off-spin bowler. He played for Victoria. In his first class career he made, 5,395 runs including 3 centuries, took 929 wickets and 329 catches.
Test Record - 32 Tests, 851 runs (Av. 19.78), 141 wickets (Av. 21.78) and 45 catches.

TRUMBLE JOHN WILLIAM
Australia (1863-1944) - A useful all-rounder. He played for Victoria. In his first class career he made, 1,761 runs and took 109 wickets.
Test Record - 7 Tests, 243 runs (Av. 20.25), 10 wickets (Av. 22.20) and 3 catches.

TRUMPER VICTOR THOMAS
Australia (1877-1915) - A right-handed attacking batsman. He played for New South Wales. In his first class career he made, 16,939 runs including 42 centuries, took 64 wickets and 171 catches.
Test Record - 48 Tests, 3,163 runs (Av. 39.04) including 8 centuries, 8 wickets (Av. 37.62) and 31 catches.

TRUNDLE
(obsolete) to bowl.

TUCKETT LINDSAY
South Africa (born 1919) - A right-arm medium-fast bowler and also useful batsman. He played for Orange Free State. In his first class career he made, 1,496 runs including 1 century and took 225 wickets.
Test Record - 9 Tests,131 runs (Av. 11.90), 19 wickets (Av. 51.57) and 9 catches.

U

ULYETT GEORGE

England (1851-1898) - He was one of the best fast bowlers and a reliable fielder. He played for Yorkshire. In his first class career he made, 20,484 runs including 18 centuries, took 619 wickets and 367 catches.

Test Record - 25 Tests, 949 runs (Av. 24.33) including 1 century, 50 wickets (Av. 20.40) and 18 catches.

UMPIRE

One of the two officials appointed to control the game and give their decisions on the appeals made by the players, in accordance with the rules and regulations in force. One umpire stands behind the bowler's wicket. He is the main umpire. He counts the balls in an over, gives no ball, dead ball and wide, four runs, sixes, lbw and run out at the bowler's wicket. The other umpire stands in square-leg position at the batsman wicket. They adjudicate in regard to playing conditions, the weather, the light, fitness of the pitch and ball etc. They also consult each other whenever necessary. Their task has become all the more difficult due to electronic media which enables one to judge whether the decision taken by the umpire at the spin of the moment was right or wrong.

UMPIRES

Persons appointed to officiate a game.

UMRIGAR PAHLAN RATANJI

India (born 1926) - A right-handed batsman and a right-arm medium-pace and off-break bowler. Test debut on December 9, 1948 against West Indies at the age of 22 years and 252 days. Score on Test debut was 30 in the second Test at Bombay. Last Test of the career played against West Indies in April 1962. Scores on last appearance in Test were 32 and 60 in the fifth Test at Kingston. Age at the time of retirement from Test cricket was 36 years and 20 days. First-ever Test Century (130 not out) scored on February 9, 1952 in the fifth Test against England at the age of 25 years and 310 days. Made 41 consecutive appearances for India. One of the two Indians to score a century and capture five wickets in an innings in the same Test - scored 172 not out and took five wickets for 107 runs against West Indies at Port-of-Spain in the fourth Test in 1961-62. Earned the distinction of registering the first double-century (223 in the first Test against New Zealand at Hyderabad in 1955-56) for India. First Indian captain to win the first Test he captained. Held the record of highest score by an Indian, on tour - 252 not out against Cambridge University (England) in 1959 for a very long time. Also scored three double-centuries on his both tours to England (in 1952 and 1959), surpassed only by Sir Don Bradman of Australia. Only captain to win National Tournament five times, and that too in a row. Awarded the "Padma Shri " in 1962. Was the member of All-India Council of

Sports. His partnership of 238 runs with V.L. Manjrekar for the third wicket in the first Test against New Zealand at Hyderabad in 1955-56 is the highest for third wicket for India against West Indies. He is the first Indian to reach 3,000 run mark in Test career. He played for Bombay and Gujarat. In his first class career he made, 16,154 runs including 49 centuries, and took 326 wickets. *Test Record* - 59 Tests, 3,631 runs (Av. 42.22) including 12 centuries, 35 wickets (Av. 42.08) and 33 catches.

UNBEATEN

The score made by a batsman without loss of wicket.

UNDERARM

In bowling, to deliver the ball with the bowling arm coming through below the shoulder. Usually an acceptable mode of delivery, provided the batsman has been warned that the bowler intends to deliver in that style. In most one-day competitions, the practice has been extremely difficult to score off a ball rolled along the ground.

UNDEREDGE

A hit from the bottom edge of the bat.

UNDERWOOD DEREK LESLIE

England (born 1945) - A left-arm spin bowler and also a right-handed batsman. He played for Kent. In his first class career he made, 4,997 runs including 1 century, took 2,420 wickets and 258 catches. *Test Record* - 86 Tests, 937 runs (Av. 11.56), 297 wickets (Av. 25.83) and 44 catches.

UNFAIR PLAY

The umpire is the sole judge in regard to unfair play, contravention of rules and regulations, as damaging the pitch or ball, frequent bowling of bounces or seamers, obstructing the batsman, wasting time or refusing to accept decision of the umpires.

UNSIGHT

To enable the batsman to see the ball clearly as any movement in front of or near the screen.

UPPISH

Hitting the ball very high to enable an easy catch.

UPPISHLY

Sending an uppish stroke.

UPRIGHTS

See STUMPS (colloquial).

USE THE CREASE

In bowling, to vary the delivery position in relation to the stumps and the batting and return creases.

USEFUL

Expression of approval to any action or achievement.

V

VALENTINE ALFRED LEWIS

West Indies (born 1930) - He was left-arm slow-medium bowler. He played for Jamaica. In his first class career he made, 470 runs and took 475 wickets.

Test Record - 36 Tests, 141 runs (Av. 4.70), 139 wickets (Av. 30.32) and 13 catches.

VALENTINE BRYAN HERBERT

England (1908-1983) - A right-handed batsman, he was essentially an in-front-of-the-wicket player with a penchant for the leg-side. He played for Cambridge University and Kent .In his first class career he made,18,306 runs including 35 centuries, took 27 wickets and 309 catches.

Test Record - 7 Tests, 454 runs (Av.64.85) including 2 centuries and 2 catches.

VERITY HEDLEY

England (1905-1943) - He was the best left-arm spin bowler and also a lower-order batsman. He played for Yorkshire. In his first class career he made, 5,603 runs including 1 century, took 1,956 wickets and 244 catches.

Test Record - 40 Tests, 669 runs (Av. 20.90), 144 wickets (Av. 24.37) and 30 catches.

VENGSARKAR, DILIP BALWANT

India (born 1956)- A right-handed batsman and right-arm bowler. Test debut on January 24,1976 against New Zealand at the age of 19 years and 288 days. Scores on Test debut were 7 and 6 in the first Test at Auckland. First-ever Test century (157 not out) scored on January 2,1979 against West Indies in the third Test at Calcutta at the age of 22 years and 267 days. His unfinished partnership of 344 runs with S.M.Gavaskar for the second wicket in the third Test against West Indies at Calcutta in 1979-80 is the highest for second wicket for India against any country. He

DILIP VENGSARKAR

plays for Bombay. In his first class career he made,19,849 runs including 48 centuries.

Test Record - 98 Tests, 6,256 runs (Av.46.00) including 17 centuries.

VENKATRAGHAVAN, SRINIVASRAGHAVAN

India (born 1946)- Right-handed batsman and right-arm off-break bowler. Test debut on February 27,1965 against New Zealand at the age of 19 years and 306 days. Score on Test debut was 4 in the first Test at Madras. Last Test of the career played against Australia in October 1979. Scores on last appearance in Test were 1 and 4 not out in the third Test at Kanpur. Age at the time of retirement from Test cricket was 34 years and 167 days. Led Indian team for the first time at the age of 29 yers and 231days. In all captained Indian team five times out of which lost two and the remaining three Tests were drawn. Had an enviable crop of wickets and a commendable feat in the fourth Test at New Delhi against New Zealand in 1965. In bagging 12 wickets for 152 runs in the two innings, he had accounted for every New Zealand batsman. In the first innings he had Dowling, Jarvis, Morgan, Congdon, Sutcliffe, Pollard, Ward and Cameron. Those who "got away" Reid, Taylor, Collinge were trapped in the second innings. He played for Tamil Nadu. In his

VENKATRAGHAVAN Batting against England.

first class career he made 6,617 runs including 1 century, took 1,390 wickets and 318 catches.
Test Record - 57 Tests, 748 runs (Av.11.68), 156 wickets (Av.36.11) and 43 catches.

VERIVERS THOMAS ROBERT
Australia (born 1937) - A right-arm off-break bowler. He played for Queensland. In his first class career he made, 5,100 runs including 4 centuries and took 191 wickets.
Test Record - 21 Tests, 813 runs (Av. 31.26), 33 wickets (Av. 41.66) and 7 catches.

VILJOEN KENNETH GEORGE
South Africa (1910-1974) - A right-handed batsman and a brilliant fielder. He played for Orange Free State and Transvaal. In his first class career he made, 7,964 runs including 23 centuries, and took 29 wickets.
Test Record 27 Tests, 1,365 runs (Av. 28.43) including 2 centuries and 5 catches.

VINCENT CYRIL LEVERTON
South Africa (1902-1968) - A left-arm spin bowler and a competent batsman. He played for Transvaal. In his first class career he made,1,582 runs and took 293 wickets.
Test Record - 25 Tests,526 runs (Av.20.23),84 wickets (Av.31.32) and 27 catches.

VINCENT CHARLES HENRY
South Africa (1866-1943) - A left- handed batsman and a useful bowler. He played for Griqualand and Transvaal. In his first class career he made,119 runs and took 1 wicket.
Test Record - 3 Tests,27 runs (Av.4.50),4 wickets (Av.48.25) and 1 catch.

VINE JOSEPH
England (1875-1946) - A right-handed batsman and a slow leg-break bowler. He played for Sussex. In his first class career he made, 25,171 runs including 34 centuries, took 683 wickets (Av. 29.99) and 228 catches.
Test Record - 2 Tests, 46 runs (Av. 46.00).

VISOR
See HALMET.

VISWANATH GUNDAPPA RANGANATH
India (born 1949) - A right-handed batsman and a right-arm leg-break bowler. Brother-in-law of S.M.Gavaskar. Test debut on November 15, 1969 against Australia at the age of 20 years and 273 days. Scored a 'duck' and a century (137) on debut in the second Test at Kanpur, thus became the sixth Indian batsman to score a century on Test debut at the age of 20 years and 275 days. Has played in 87 Tests successively for India (from the third Test against West Indies at Georgetown in 1971 to sixth Test against Pakistan at Karachi in January - February1983) without a break of apearance. His career aggregate of 5,260 runs in 75 Tests runs next only to Gavaskar. He scored over 1,000 runs in a calendar year in 1979 (1,388 runs in 17 Tests). Also holds a record of playing most Test matches (75) and innings (132) as a batsman for India. His unbeaten knock of 161 in the second Test against Australia at Bangalore in 1979-80 at No. 5 in the batting order for India is the highest for any batsman at No.5. Took over the

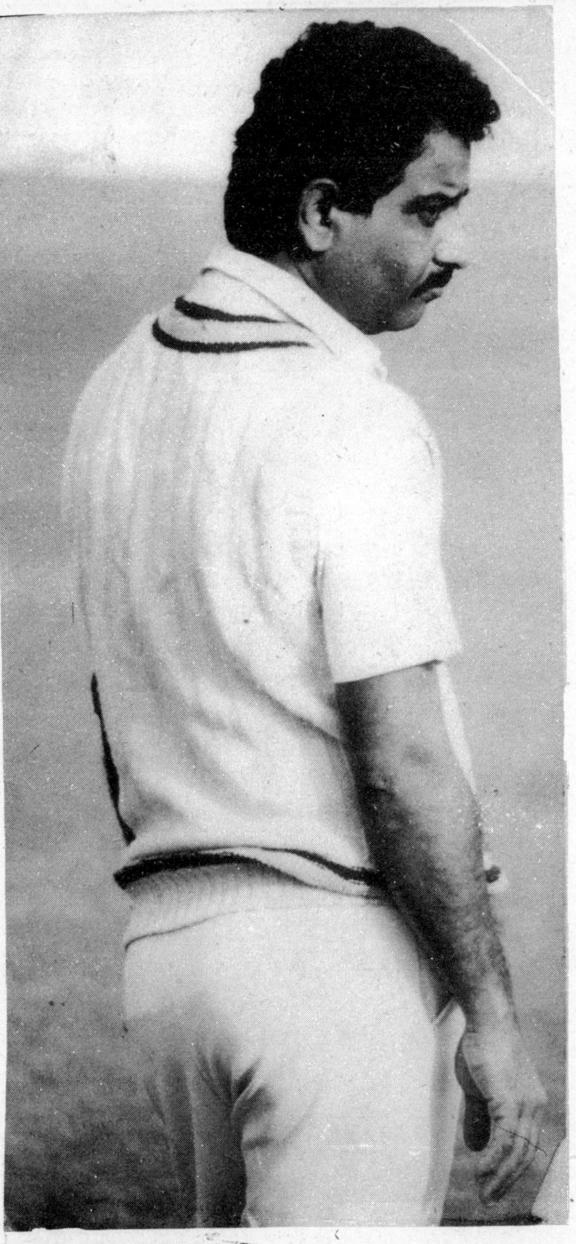

GUNDAPPA VISHWANATH

Indian captaincy from S.M.Gavaskar, when the latter decided to step down from the sixth Test against Pakistan at Calcutta in January 1980. Led India in two Tests only out of which one was drawn and the other (against England in 1980) lost. Became only the second player from India to cross 4,000 run mark in Test cricket, during the first Test between England and India at Edgbaston, on July 16, 1979. He reached the target with his 22nd run in the second innings. Viswanath took 53 Tests to achieve this feat. Became only the second Asian to complete a run aggregate of 5,000 in Tests against England in the "Jubilee Test" at Bombay. It was his 69th Test match. He played for Karnataka. In his first class career he made, 17,592 runs including 44 centuries, took 15 wickets and 221 catches.

Test Record - 91 Tests, 6,080 runs (Av. 41.93) including 14 centuries, 1 wicket (Av. 46.00) and 63 catches.

VISWANATH SADANAND

India (born 1962) - A sparkling and competitive wicket-keeper and useful right-handed batsman who some times opens. He played for Karnataka. In his first class career he made, 1,955 runs including 2 centuries and 121 dismissals.

Test Record - 3 Tests, 31 runs (Av. 6.20) and 11 catches.

SADANAND VISWANATH

VIVIAN GRAHAM ELLERY

New Zealand (born 1946) - A left-handed stroke-playing batsman, a superb deep fielder and a leg-spin and leg-break with a jerky action bowler. He played for Auckland. In his first class career he made, 3,259 runs including 3 centuries, and took 58 wickets.

Test Record - 5 Tests, 110 runs (Av. 18.33), and 3 catches.

VIVIAN HENRY GIFFORD

New Zealand (1912-1983) - A left-handed batsman, a left-arm leg-spin bowler and a very alert fielder. He played for Auckland. In his first class career he made, 4,443 runs including 6 centuries, and took 223 wickets.

Test Record - 7 Tests, 421 runs (Av. 42.10) including 1 century, 17 wickets (Av. 37.23) and 4 catches.

VIZIANAGRAM MAHARAJAH SIR VIAJAYA

India (1905-1965) - A right-handed batsman. Test debut on June 27, 1936 against England, as captain of the Indian team, at the age of 30 years and 179 days. Scores on Test debut were 19 and 6 in the first Test at Lord's. Last Test of the career played against England in August 1936. Scores on last appearance in Test were 1 and 1 in the third Test at the Oval. He played for United Provinces. In his first class career he made, 1,228 runs.

Test Record - 3 Tests, 33 runs (Av. 8.25) and 1 catch.

VOCE WILLIAM

England (1909-1984) - A left-arm slow, medium-fast over the wicket bowler. He played for Nottinghamshire. In his first class career he made, 7,583 runs including 4 centuries, took 1,558 wickets and 280 catches.

Test Record - 27 Tests, 308 runs (Av. 13.39), 98 wickets (Av. 27.88) and 15 catches.

VOGLER ALBERT EDWARD ERNEST

South Africa (1876-1946) - A right-arm leg-break and googly bowler and also a right-handed batsman. He played for Natal. In his first class career he made, 2,375 runs including 1 century, and took 393 wickets.

Test Record - 15 Tests, 340 runs (Av. 17.00), 64 wickets (Av. 22.73) and 20 catches.

AJIT WADEKAR

W

WADDINGTON ABRAHAM
England (1893-1959) - A left-arm medium-fast bowler and a tail-end batsman. He played for Yorkshire. In his first class career he made, 2,529 runs including 1 century, took 857 wickets and 217 catches.
Test Record - 2 Tests, 16 runs (Av. 4.00) and 1 catch.

WADE HERBERT FREDERICK
South Africa (1905-1980) - A right-handed batsman and captain. He played for Natal. In his first class career he made, 3,858 runs including 9 centuries.
Test Record - 10 Tests, 327 runs (Av. 20.43) and 4 catches.

WADE WALTER WAREHAM
South Africa (born 1914) - A very competent wicket-keeper and batsman. He played for Natal. In his first class career he made, 2,859 runs including 8 centuries.
Test Record - 11 Tests, 511 runs (Av. 28.38) including 1 century and 17 dismissals (15ct, 2st).

WADEKAR AJIT LAXMAN
India (born 1941) - A left-handed batsman and left-arm slow spin bowler. Test debut on December 13, 1966 against West Indies at the age of 25 years and 252 days. Scores on debut in Test were 8 and 4 in the First Test at Bombay. Last Test of the career played against England in July 1974. Scores on last appearance in Test were 36 and 5 in the third Test at Edgbaston. Age at the time of retirement from Test cricket was 33 years and 97 days. First and only Test century (143) scored on March 1, 1968 against New Zealand at the age of 26 years and 330 days. Earned the rare honour of winning three Test series successively (against West Indies in West Indies 1-0; England in England 1-0, both in 1971 and England in India 2-1 in 1972-73). He played for Bombay. In his first class career he made, 15,380 runs including 36 centuries, took 21 wickets and 270 catches.
Test Record - 37 Tests, 2,113 runs (Av. 31.07) including 1 century and 46 catches.

WADSWORTH KENNETH JOHN
New Zealand (1946-1976) - A right-handed batsman and a useful wicket-keeper. He played for Central Districts and Canterbury. In his first class career he made, 3,664 runs including 2 centuries and 282 dismissals.
Test Record - 33 Tests, 1,010 runs (Av. 21.48) and 96 dismissals (92ct, 4st).

WAINWRIGHT EDWARD
England (1865-1919) - A right-handed batsman and an off-break bowler. He played for Yorkshire. In his first class career he made, 12,485 runs including 19 centuries, took 1,062 wickets and 339 catches.
Test Record - 5 Tests, 132 runs (Av. 14.66) and 2 catches.

WAITE JOHN HENRY BICKFORD
South Africa (born 1930) - A right-handed batsman and a useful wicket-keeper. He played for Transvaal. In his first class career he made, 9,812 runs including 23 centuries, and 510 dismissals.
Test Record - 50 Tests, 2,405 runs (Av. 30.44) including 4 centuries and 141 dismissals (124ct, 17st).

WAITE MARVYN GEORGE
Australia (1911-1985) - An honest type of batsman and medium-pace bowler. He played for South Australia. In his first class career he made, 3,888 runs including 1 century and took 192 wickets.
Test Record - 2 Tests, 11 runs (Av. 3.66), and 1 catch.

WALCOTT CLYDE LEOPOLD
West Indies (born 1926) - A very useful medium-fast change-bowler, a right-handed bats-

man and one of the best wicket-keepers. He played for Barbados and British Guiana. In his first class career he made, 11,820 runs including 40 centuries, took 35 wickets and 208 dismissals.
Test Record - 44 Tests, 3,798 runs (Av. 56.68) including 15 centuries, 11 wickets (Av. 37.09) and 64 dismissals (53ct, 11st).

WALK
In batting, to give yourself out without waiting for the umpire's decision. In days gone by, particularly in English cricket, considered to be part of the unwritten code of ethics of the game. Not so popular in these days of more professional and competitive cricket.

WALKER MAXWELL HENRY NORMAN
Australia (born 1948) - A right-arm medium-pace bowler and a willing and determined batsman. He played for Victoria. In his first class career he made, 2,014 runs and took 499 wickets.
Test Record - 34 Tests, 586 runs (Av. 19.53), 138 wickets (Av. 27.47) and 12 catches.

WALKER PETER MICHAEL
England (born 1936) - A hard-hitting right-handed batsman and a brilliant specialist short-leg fieldsman. He played for Glamorgan and Western Province. In his first class career he made, 17,650 runs including 13 centuries, took 834 wickets and 697 catches.
Test Record - 3 Tests, 128 runs (Av. 32.00), and 5 catches.

WALLACE WALTER MERVYN
New Zealand (born 1916) - A right-handed attacking batsman. He played for Auckland. In his first class career he made, 7,609 runs including 16 centuries.
Test Record - 13 Tests, 439 runs (Av. 20.90) and 5 catches.

WALL THOMAS WELBOURNE
Australia (1904-981) - A right-arm medium-fast bowler. He played for South Australia. In his first class career he made, 1,063 runs and took 328 wickets.
Test Record - 18 Tests, 121 runs (Av. 6.36), 56 wickets (Av. 35.89) and 11 catches.

WALSH COURTNEY ANDREW
West Indies (born 1962) - A right-arm medium-fast bowler. He played for Jamaica and Gloucestershire. In his first class career he made, 814

COURTNEY WALSH

runs and took 388 wickets.
Test Record - 34 Tests, 277 runs (Av. 10.25), 122 wickets (Av. 24.24) and 4 catches.

WALTER KENNETH ALEXANDER
South Africa (born 1939) - A right-arm medium-fast bowler. He played for Transvaal. In his first class career he made, 594 runs and took 217 wickets.
Test Record - 2 Tests, 11 runs (Av. 3.66), 6 wickets (Av. 32.83) and 3 catches.

WALTERS CYRIL FREDERICK
England (born 1905) - A right-handed stroke-player batsman. He played for Glamorgan and

Worcestershire. In his first class career he made, 12,145 runs including 21 centuries.
Test Record - 11 Tests, 784 runs (Av. 52.26) including 1 century and 6 catches.

WALTERS KEVIN DOUGLAS
Australia (born 1945) - An all-rounder. He was a useful batsman and also a useful medium-pace swing bowler. He played for New South Wales. In his first class career he made, 16,180 runs including 45 centuries, took 190 wickets and 149 catches.
Test Record - 74 Tests, 5,357 runs (Av. 48.26) including 15 centuries, 49 wickets (Av. 29.08) and 43 catches.

WAQAR HUSSAN
Pakistan (born 1932) - An attractive right-handed batsman and a fine fielder. He played for Services and Karachi. In his first class career he made, 4,620 runs including 8 centuries.
Test Record - 21 Tests, 1,071 runs (Av. 31.50) including 1 century and 10 catches.

WARDLE JOHN HENRY
England (1923-1985) - A left-arm orthodox and googly bowler. He played for Yorkshire and Cambridgeshire. In his first class career he made, 7,333 runs, took 1,846 wickets and 257 catches.
Test Record - 28 Tests, 653 runs (Av. 19.78), 102 wickets (Av. 20.39) and 12 catches.

WARD ALAN
England (born 1947) - A right-arm medium-fast bowler and was also often useful as a tail-ender. He played for Border and Leicestershire. In his first class career he made, 928 runs and took 460 wickets.
Test Record - 5 Tests, 40 runs (Av. 8.00), 14 wickets (Av. 32.35) and 3 catches.

WARD ALBERT
England (1865-1939) - A right-handed opening batsman. He played for Yorkshire. In his first class career he made, 17,783 runs including 29 centuries, took 71 wickets and 159 catches.
Test Record - 7 Tests, 487 runs (Av. 37.46) including 1 century and 1 catch.

WARD FRANCIS ANTHONY
Australia (1909-1974) - A right-arm leg-break bowler. He played for South Australia. In his first class career he made, 871 runs and took 320 wickets.
Test Record - 4 Tests, 36 runs (Av. 6.00), 11 wickets (Av. 52.18) and 1 catch.

WARD JOHN THOMAS
New Zealand (born 1937) - A capable specialist wicket-keeper and a useful batsman. He played for Canterbury. In his first class career he made, 1,117 runs and 257 dismissals.
Test Record - 8 Tests, 75 runs (Av. 12.50) and 17 dismissals (16ct, 1st).

WARD THOMAS ALFRED
South Africa (1887-1936) - A wicket-keeper and a useful batsman. He played for Transvaal. In his first class career he made, 1,651 runs and 175 dismissals.
Test Record - 23 Tests, 459 runs (Av. 13.90) and 32 dismissals (19ct, 13st).

WARNAPURA BANDULA
Sri Lanka (born 1953) - A right-handed batsman. He played for Bloomfield. In his first class career he made, 2,280 runs including 2 centuries and took 13 wickets.
Test Record - 4 Tests, 96 runs (Av. 12.00), and 2 catches.

WARNER SIR PELHAM F RANCIS
England (1873-1963) - A right-handed batsman. He played for Oxford University and Middlesex. In his first class career he made, 29,028 runs including 60 centuries, took 15 wickets and 187 catches.
Test Record - 15 Tests, 622 runs (Av. 23.92) including 1 century and 3 catches.

WARR JOHN JAMES
England (born 1927) - A medium-fast bowler. He played for Cambridge University and Middlesex. In his first class career he made, 3,838 runs and took 956 wickets.
Test Record - 2 Tests, 4 runs (Av. 1.00).

WAR WICKSHIRE
Foundation of Present Club: April 8, 1882 in Coventry.
First First-Class Match: Notts v Warwickshire (Trent Bridge) May 3,4,5 1894.
Present Principal Ground: County Ground, Edgbaston, Birmingham.
County Champions: 1911, 1951, 1972.
JPL Champions: 1980.
B&H Cup: Losing finalists 1984.
Nat West Trophy: Winners 1966 and 1968.
Highest Team Total: 657-6 v Hampshire (Edgbaston).
Lowest Team Total: 16 v Kent (Tonbridge) 1913.

WASHBROOK CYRIL
England (born 1914) - A right-handed batsman. He played for Lancashire. In his first class career he made, 34,101 runs including 76 centuries, and 206 catches.
Test Record - 37 Tests, 2,569 runs (Av. 42.81) including 6 centuries, and 12 catches.

WASHER HAT
Wide-brimmed white hat popularly used to protect players from the sun in countries with a hot climate.

WASIM AKRAM
Pakistan (born 1966) - A left-arm medium-fast bowler. He plays for Lahore, and PACO. In his first class career he made, 1,184 runs and took 159 wickets.
Test Record - 20 Tests, 284 runs (Av. 14.94), 63 wickets (Av. 26.61) and 7 catches.

WASIM BARI
Pakistan (born 1948) - An outstanding natural wicket-keeper and also a late middle-order, right-

WASIM AKRAM

WASIM BARI

handed batsman. He played for Pakistan International Airlines and Sind. In his first class career he made, 5,749 runs including 2 centuries, took 1 wicket and 814 dismissals.
Test Record - 81 Tests, 1,366 runs (Av. 15.88) and 228 dismissals (201ct, 27st).

WASIM HASAN RAJA
Pakistan (born 1952) - A left-handed batsman and a right-arm leg-break top-spin bowler. He played

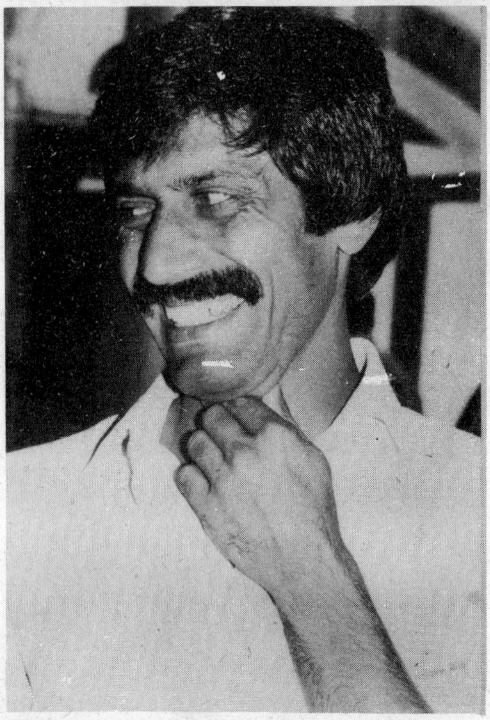

WASIM RAJA

for Lahore and Combined Universities. In his first class career he made, 11,403 runs including 17 centuries, took 558 wickets and 153 catches.
Test Record - 57 Tests, 2,821 runs (Av. 36.16) including 4 centuries, 51 wickets (Av. 35.80) and 20 catches.

WATCH
A term originally used for a fielder.

WATKINS ALLAN JOHN
England (born 1922) - A left-handed batsman and a left-arm medium-pace bowler. He played for Glamorgan. In his first class career he made, 20,362 runs including 32 centuries, took 833 wickets and 461 catches.
Test Record - 15 Tests, 810 runs (Av. 40.50) including 2 centuries, 11 wickets (Av. 50.36) and 17 catches.

WATKINS JOHN CECIL
South Africa (born 1923) - A right-handed batsman and a medium-pace bowler. He played for Natal. In his first class career he made, 2,158 runs including 2 centuries and took 96 wickets.
Test Record - 15 Tests, 612 runs (Av. 23.53), 29 wickets (Av. 28.13) and 12 catches.

WATSON CHESTER
West Indies (born 1939) - A right-arm medium-fast bowler. He played for Jamaica and Delhi. In his first class career he made, 197 runs and took 85 wickets.
Test Record - 7 Tests, 12 runs (Av. 2.40), 19 wickets (Av. 38.10) and 1 catch.

WATSON GRAEME DONALD
Australia (born 1945) - An attractive right-handed opening batsman. He played for Victoria. In his first class career he made, 4,674 runs including 7 centuries and took 186 wickets.
Test Record - 5 Tests, 97 runs (Av. 10.77), 6 wickets (Av. 42.33) and 1 catch.

WATSON WILLIAM
England (born 1920) - A natural left-handed batsman. He played for Yorkshire and Leicestershire. In his first class career he made, 25,670 runs including 55 centuries, and took 293 catches.
Test Record - 23 Tests, 879 runs (Av. 25.85) including 2 centuries, and 8 catches.

WATSON WILLIAM
New Zealand (born 1965) - A tall, athletic right-arm medium-fast bowler and also a right-handed batsman. He played for Auckland. In his first class career he made, 44 runs and took 58 wickets.
Test Record - 2 Tests, 9 runs (Av. 9.00), 4 wickets (Av. 49.00) and 2 catches.

WATSON WILLIAM JAMES

Australia (born 1931) - A sound right-handed opening batsman. He played for New South Wales. In his first class career he, made, 1,958 runs including 6 centuries.

Test Record - 4 Tests, 106 runs (Av. 17.66) and 2 catches.

WAUGH STEPHEN ROGER

Australia (born .965) - A right-handed batsman and a right-arm medium-fast bowler. He played for New South Wales. In his first class career he made, 755 runs including 2 centuries and took 16 wickets.

STEPHEN WAUGH

Test Record - 5 Tests, 113 runs (Av. 12.55), 7 wickets (Av. 21.71) and 2 catches.

WAZIR ALI SYED

India (1903-1950) - A right-handed batsman and a right-arm medium-fast bowler. Elder brother of S.Nazir Ali and father of Khalid Wazir of Pakistan. Test Debut on June 25, 1932 against England at the age of 28 years and 280 days. Scores on Test debut were 31 and 39 in the only Test played at Lord's. Last Test of the career played against England in August 1936. Scores on last appearance in Test were 2 and 1 in the third Test at The Oval. Age at the time of retirement from Test cricket was 32 years and 333 days.

He played for Southern Punjab. In his first class career he made, 6,906 runs including 20 centuries and took 33 wickets.

Test Record - 7 Tests, 237 runs (Av. 16.92) and 1 catch.

WAZIR MOHAMMAD

Pakistan (born 1929) - A right-handed middle-order batsman. He played for Bahawalpur and Karachi. In his first class career he made, 4,952 runs including 11 centuries.

Test Record - 20 Tests, 801 runs (Av. 27.62) including 2 centuries and 5 catches.

WCA

Women's Cricket Association.

WEBB MURRAY GEORGE

New Zealand (born 1947) - A right-arm medium-fast bowler. He played for Otago and Canterbury. In his first class career he made, 202 runs and took 133 wickets.

Test Record - 3 Tests, 12 runs (Av. 6.00) and 4 wickets (Av. 117.75).

WEBB PETER NEIL

New Zealand (born 1957) - A right-handed batsman and an occasional wicket-keeper. He played for Auckland. In his first class career he made, 3,196 runs including 5 centuries and took 4 wickets.

Test Record - 2 Tests, 11 runs (Av. 3.66) and 2 catches.

WEEKES EVERTON DE COURCRY

West Indies (born 1925) - A brilliant stroke-maker batsman. He played for Barbados. In his first class career he made, 12,010 runs including 36 centuries, 125 catches and 1 stumping.

Test Record - 48 Tests, 4,455 runs (Av. 58.61) including 15 centuries and 49 catches.

WEEKES KENNETH HUNNELL
West Indies (born 1912) - A stylish and fast-scoring left-handed batsman and also a good reserve wicket-keeper. He played for Jamaica. In his first class career he made, 1,731 runs including 3 centuries.
Test Record - 2 Tests, 173 runs (Av. 57.66) including 1 century.

WEIR GORDON LINDSAY
New Zealand (born 1908) - A right-handed batsman and a right-arm medium-pace change-bowler. He played for Auckland. In his first class career he made, 5,022 runs including 10 centuries and took 107 wickets.
Test Record - 11 Tests, 416 runs (Av. 29.71), 7 wickets (Av. 29.85) and 3 catches.

WELLARD ARTHUR WILLIAM
England (1902-1980) - A right-arm medium-fast bowler and a useful batsman. He played for Somerset. In his first class career he made, 12,515 runs including 2 centuries, took 1,614 wickets and 375 catches.
Test Record - 2 Tests, 47 runs (Av. 11.75), 7 wickets (Av. 33.85) and 2 catches.

WELLHAM DIRK MACDONALD
Australia (born 1959) - A compact right-handed batsman. He played for New South Wales. In his first class career he made, 4,833 runs including 11 centuries.
Test Record - 5 Tests, 239 runs (Av. 26.55) including 1 century, and 2 catches.

WELLINGTON
A unique history clings to this ground, for it was originally a lake which, it was intended should be made into an inner harbour. An earthquake in 1853 turned the lake into a swamp and the cricketers, who had lost their own ground, asked if they could make one out of the swamp. They were given permission and by 1868 were playing on it.

WESLEY COLIN
South Africa (born 1937) - A left-handed opening batsman and a brilliant fielder. He played for Natal. In his first class career he made, 1,892 runs including 3 centuries and took 15 wickets.
Test Record - 3 Tests, 49 runs (Av. 9.80) and 1 catch.

WESSELS KEPLER CHRISTOFFEL
Australia (born 1957) - A left-handed opening

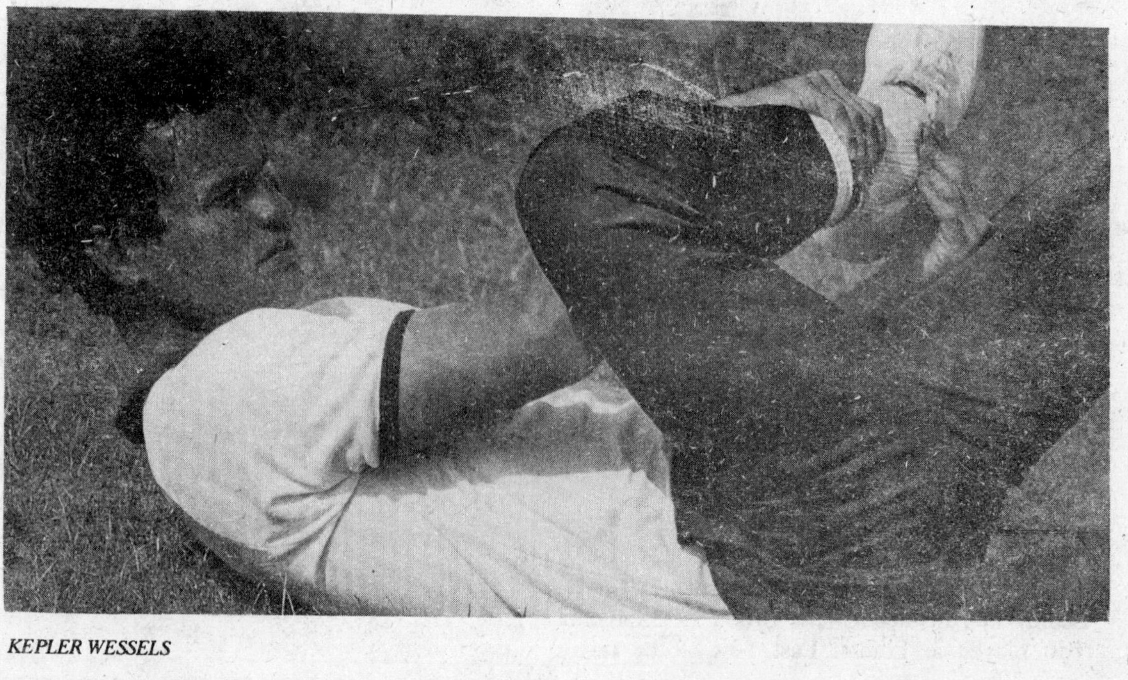

KEPLER WESSELS

batsman and a useful bowler. He played for Orange Free State and Sussex. In his first class career he made, 14,918 runs including 38 centuries, took 12 wickets and 131 catches.
Test Record - 24 Tests, 1,761 runs (Av. 42.95) including 4 centuries and 18 catches.

WESTCOTT RICHARD JOHN
South Africa (born 1927) - A right-handed opening batsman and a useful medium-pace bowler. He played for Western Province. In his first class career he made, 3,225 runs including 4 centuries and 10 wickets.
Test Record - 5 Tests, 166 runs (Av. 18.44).

WETTIMUNY SIDATH
Sri Lanka (born 1956) - A right-handed opening batsman. He played for Sinhalese. In his first class career he made, 2,523 runs including 5 centuries and took 2 wickets.
Test Record - 20 Tests, 1,112 runs (Av. 30.05) including 2 centuries and 9 catches.

WETTIMUNY MITHRA DE SILVA
Sri Lanka (born 1951) - A right-handed batsman. He played for Sinhalese. In his first class career he made, 268 runs.
Test Record - 2 Tests, 28 runs (Av. 7.00) and 2 catches.

WHATMORE DAVENELL FREDERICK
Australia (born 1954) - A compact and strong right-handed batsman. He played for Victoria. In his first class career he made, 4,087 runs including 6 centuries, took 3 wickets and 108 catches.
Test Record - 7 Tests, 293 runs (Av. 22.53) and 13 catches.

WHEEL
Bowling by slow bowlers for long duration.

WHIPPY
A movement by the bowler at the time of delivery.

WHITE GORDON CHARLES
South Africa (1882-1918) - A right-handed batsman and a leg-break and googly bowler. He played for Transvaal. In his first class career he made, 3,740 runs including 4 centuries, and took 155 wickets.
Test Record - 17 Tests, 872 runs (Av. 30.06) including 2 centuries, 9 wickets (Av. 33.44) and 10 catches.

WHITE JOHN CORNISH
England (1891-1961) - A left-arm bowler. He played for Somerset. In his first class career he made, 12,202 runs including 6 centuries, took 2,356 wickets and 6 catches.
Test Record - 15 Tests, 239 runs (Av. 18.38), 49 wickets (Av. 32.26) and 423 catches.

WHITE WINSTON ANTHONY
West Indies (born 1938) - A competent right-handed hard-hitting batsman and also a medium-pace and off-break bowler. He played for Barbados. In his first class career he made, 996 runs and took 95 wickets.
Test Record - 2 Tests, 71 runs (Av. 23.66), 3 wickets (Av. 50.66) and 1 catch.

WHITELAW PAUL ERSKINE
New Zealand (born 1910) - A sound and attractive right-handed opening batsman. He played for Auckland. In his first class career he made, 2,739 runs including 5 centuries.
Test Record - 2 Tests, 64 runs (Av. 32.00).

WHITNEY MICHAEL ROY
Australia (born 1959) - A very solid left-arm bowler and also right-handed tail-ender batsman. He played for New South Wales. In his first class career he made, 117 runs and took 134 wickets.
Test Record - 2 Tests, 4 runs (Av. 1.00) and 5 wickets (Av. 49.20).

WHITTY WILLIAM JAMES
Australia (1886-1974) - A left-arm medium-fast bowler. He played for New South Wales and South Australia. In his first class career he made,

Wicket-keeper's stance

TAKING ON THE OFF SIDE

The three illustrations above show the sequence of action for taking a ball at mid-height. The sequence below shows taking a higher, wider rising ball at shoulder height.

The right foot moves across to bring the head into line with the ball. The hands give as they take the ball.

The weight transfers to the inside leg as the ball is carried to the stumps.

1,465 runs and took 491 wickets.
Test Record - 14 Tests, 161 runs (Av. 13.41), 65 wickets (Av. 21.12) and 4 catches.

WHYSALL WILLIAM WILFIRD
England. (1887-1930) - A right-handed batsman. He played for Nottinghamshire. In his first class career he made, 21,592 runs including 51 centuries, 325 catches and 16 stumpings.
Test Record - 4 Tests, 209 runs (Av. 29.85), and 7 catches.

WICBC
West Indies Cricket Board of Control.

WICKET
Slightly confusing in the cricketing vocabulary. This word can mean the 22-yard playing surface (the pitch); one of the three uprights set at either end as the bowler's target (the stumps); and the dismissal of a batsman, as in the 'taking of the wicket'.

WICKET KEEPER
Also known by the abbreviated form of 'keeper', the man who stands behind the stumps, usually protected by leg pads and wearing gloves, with the job of taking the deliveries that pass the bat and of effecting catches and stumpings. Wicketkeepers place themselves in varying positions depending upon the speed and type of bowler in operation and the style of batsman on strike.

WICKET MAIDEN
An over in which the bowler has dismissed a batsman and not conceded a run.

WICKET IS DOWN
The wicket is 'down' if a bail falls from the top of the stumps, even if the bail lodges between the stumps and doesn't hit the ground. The wicket is not down if a bail merely has been disturbed, even if it moves out of its grooves and rests on top of one of the stumps.
For the purpose of a run-out or stumping, the wicket is considered to be 'made' even if only one bail is in place. If both bails have been dislodged, a fieldsman or the wicketkeeper may 'remake' the wicket by replacing one or both of the bails.
A fieldsman or the wicketkeeper attempting to make a run-out when both bails are off may do so by removing a stump from the ground with the ball in the hand or hands used.
A fieldsman or the wicketkeeper with the bail in his hand may break the wicket with that hand or that arm. In other words, it is not necessary that the ball actually touches the stumps when the wicket is being broken.
In conditions where strong winds may cause the bails to fall from their grooves, the umpires may remove the bails. In those circumstances it is for them to decide when the wicket is 'down'.

WIDE
A delivery which is far away or high up over a batsman that he is unable to play. The umpire signals it so and one run is added to the score as extra. If more than one run are made or ball goes to the boundary, these are also credited to the score as extra.

WIENER JULIEN MARK
Australia (born 1955) - A solid right-handed opening batsman. He played for Victoria. In his first class career he made, 3,609 runs including 7 centuries, and took 17 wickets.
Test Record - 6 Tests, 281 runs (Av. 25.24) and 4 catches.

WIGHT CLAUDE VIBART
West Indies (1902-Now reported dead) - A good right-handed batsman. He played for British Guiana. In his first class career he made, 1,547 runs including 3 centuries.
Test Record - 2 Tests, 67 runs (Av. 22.33).

WIJESURIYA ROGER GERRARD CHRISTOPHER EDIRIWEERA
Sri Lanka (born 1960) - A slow left-arm bowler and a right-handed batsman. He plays for Sinhalese. In his first class career he made, 109 runs

and took 34 wickets.
Test Record - 4 Tests, 22 runs (Av. 4.40), 1 wicket (Av. 294.00) and 1 catch.

WILKINSON LEONARD LITTON
England (born 1916) - A right-arm leg-break bowler with a lively action. He played for Lancashire. In his first class career he made, 321 runs and took 282 wickets.
Test Record - 3 Tests, 3 runs (Av. 3.00) and 7 wickets (Av. 38.71).

WILLETT ELQUEMEDO TONITO
West Indies (born 1953) - A steady left-arm orthodox spin bowler. He played for Leeward Islands. In his first class career he made, 933 runs and took 252 wickets.
Test Record - 5 Tests, 74 runs (Av. 14.80) and 11 wickets (Av. 43.81).

WILLEY PETER
England (born 1949) - A right-handed middle-order batsman and also a right-arm medium-pace off-spin bowler. He played for Northamptonshire and Eastern Province. In his first class career he made, 19,747 runs including 38 centuries, took 654 wickets and 187 catches.
Test Record - 26 Tests, 1,184 runs (Av. 26.90) including 2 centuries, 7 wickets (Av. 65.14) and 3 catches.

WILLIAMS ALVADON BASIL
West Indies (born 1949) - An attractive right-handed opening batsman. He played for Jamaica. In his first class career he made, 2,099 runs including 4 centuries.
Test Record - 7 Tests, 469 runs (Av. 39.08) including 2 centuries and 5 catches.

WILLIAMS EDWARD ALBERT VIVIAN
West Indies (born 1914) - A sound hard-hitting right-handed batsman with a powerful drive. He played for Barbados. In his first class career he made, 1,479 runs including 2 centuries and took 116 wickets.
Test Record - 4 Tests, 113 runs (Av. 18.83), 9 wickets (Av. 26.77) and 2 catches.

WILLIS ROBERT GEORGE DYLAN
England (born 1949) - A right-arm medium-fast bowler. He played for Surrey, Warwickshire and Northern Transvaal. In his first class career he made, 2,690 runs, took 899 wickets and 134 catches.
Test Record - 90 Tests, 840 runs (Av. 11.50), 325 wickets (Av. 25.20) and 39 catches.

WILSON DONALD
England (born 1937) - A slow left-arm bowler. He played for Yorkshire. In his first class career he made, 6,230 runs including 1 century, took 1,189 wickets and 250 catches.
Test Record - 6 Tests, 75 runs (Av. 12.50), 11 wickets (Av. 42.36) and 1 catch.

WILSON REV. CLEMENT EUSTACE MACROE
England (1875-1944) - A left-arm bowler. He played for Cambridge University and Yorkshire. In his first class career he made, 1,454 runs including 1 century, and took 121 wickets.
Test Record - 2 Tests, 42 runs (Av. 14.00).

WINSLOW PAUL LYNDHURST
South Africa (born 1929) - A hard-hitting right-handed batsman. He played for Sussex, Transvaal and Rhodesia. In his first class career he made, 2,755 runs including 2 centuries.
Test Record - 5 Tests, 186 runs (Av. 20.66) including 1 century, and 1 catch.

WOOD
Colloquial term for the ball, i.e. to 'get some wood on it' means to edge the ball or make some contact with the bat.

WOOD ARTHUR
England (1898-1973) - A competent right-handed batsman and a good wicket-keeper. He played for Yorkshire. In his first class career he made, 8,842 runs including 1 century and 878 dismissals.
Test Record - 4 Tests, 80 runs (Av. 20.00) and 11 dismissals (10ct, 1st).

WOOD BARRY

England (born 1942) - A correct and patient opening batsman, a fine gully fielder and also a useful slow-medium bowler. He played for Yorkshire and Eastern Province. In his first class career he made, 17,453 runs including 30 centuries, took 298 wickets and 283 catches.

Test Record - 12 Tests, 454 runs (Av. 21.61), and 6 catches.

WOOD GEORGE EDWARD CHARLES

England (1893-1971) - He was one of the best wicket-keepers. He played for Cambridge University and Kent. In his first class career he made, 2,773 runs and 170 dismissals.

Test Record - 3 Tests, 7 runs (Av. 3.50) and 6 dismissals (5ct, 1st).

WOOD GRAEME MALCOLM

Australia (born 1956) - A neat left-handed opening batsman. He played for Western Province. In his first class career he made, 9,428 runs including 23 centuries and 112 catches.

Test Record - 59 Tests, 3,374 runs (Av. 31.83) including 9 centuries and 41 catches.

WOOD HENRY

England (1854-1919) - A long-serving wicket-keeper and a useful batsman. He played for Kent and Surrey. In his first class career he made, 5,523 runs including 1 century, and 673 dismissals.

Test Record - 4 Tests, 204 runs (Av. 68.00) including 1 century and 3 dismissals (2ct, 1st).

WOODEN TRINITY

See STUMPS (colloquial).

WOODFULLL WILLIAM MADLON

Australia (1897-1965) - A right-handed opening batsman. He played for Victoria. In his first class career he made, 13,392 runs including 49 centuries.

Test Record - 35 Tests, 2,300 runs (Av. 46.00) including 7 centuries and 7 catches.

WOODS SAMUEL MOSES JAMES

Australia (1867-1931) - A right-arm bowler and a right-handed useful batsman. He played for Cambridge University and Somerset. In his first class career he made, 15,352 runs including 19 centuries, took 1,040 wickets and 282 catches.

Test Record - (Australia - 3): 32 runs (Av. 5.33), 5 wickets (Av. 24.20), and 1 catch. (England - 3): 122 runs (Av. 30.50), 5 wickets (Av. 25.80) and 4 catches.

WOOLLEY FRANK EDWARD

England (1887-1978) - A great all-rounder. He was a left-handed batsman and also a left-arm slow bowler. He played for Kent. In his first class career he made, 58,969 runs including 145 centuries, took 2,068 wickets and 1,018 catches.

Test Record - 64 Tests, 3,283 runs (Av. 36.07) including 5 centuries, 83 wickets (Av. 33.91) and 64 catches.

WOOLLEY ROGER DOUGLAS

Australia (born 1954) - A very useful wicket-keeper and a right-handed batsman. He played for Tasmania. In his first class career he made, 4,162 runs including 6 centuries, and 157 dismissals.

Test Record - 2 Tests, 21 runs (Av. 10.50) and 7 catches.

WOOLMER ROBERT ANDREW

England (born 1948) - A graceful right-handed batsman and a useful medium-fast bowler. He played for Kent, Natal and Western Province. In his first class career he made, 15,771 runs including 34 centuries, took 420 wickets and 239 dismissals.

Test Record - 19 Tests, 1,059 runs (Av. 33.09) including 3 centuries, 4 wickets (Av. 74.75) and 10 catches.

WORCESTERSHIRE

Foundation of Present Club: March 3, 1865.

First First-Class Match: Worcestershire v Yorkshire (Worcester) May 4,5,6 1899.

Present Principal Ground: County Ground, New Road, Worcester.

County Champions: 1971.

B&H Cup: Losing finalists in 1971 and 1976.
Nat West Trophy: Losing finalists in 1963 and 1966.
Highest Team Total: 633 v Warwicks (Worcester) 1906.
Lowest Team Total: 24 v Yorkshire (Huddersfield) 1903.

WORRALL JOHN

Australia (1863-1937) - A right-handed hard-hitting batsman. He played for Victoria. In his first class career he made, 4,660 runs including 7 centuries, took 105 wickets and 101 catches.
Test Record - 11 Tests, 478 runs (Av. 25.15), and 13 catches.

WORRELL SIR FRANK MORTIMORE MAGLINNE

West Indies (1924-1967) - A right-handed batsman. He commanded every orthodox stroke, was perfectly balanced and possessed quick judgment and footwork. He was also a left-arm bowler, who could be either a spinner or, more often, a medium-fast swing bowler with an easy, relaxed action. He played for Barbados and Jamaica. In his first class career he made, 15,025 runs including 39 centuries, took 349 wickets and 139 catches.
Test Record - 51 Tests, 3,860 runs (Av. 49.48) including 9 centuries, 69 wickets (Av. 38.73) and 43 catches.

WORTHINGTON THOMAS STANELY

England (1905-1973) - A right-arm medium-fast bowler and also a right-handed late-order batsman. He played for Derbyshire and Northumberland. In his first class career he made, 19,221 runs including 31 centuries, took 682 wickets and 340 catches.
Test Record - 9 Tests, 321 runs (Av. 29.18) including 1 century, 8 wickets (Av. 39.50) and 8 catches.

WRIGHT CHARLES WILLIAM

England (1863-1936) - A very steady batsman. He played for Cambridge University and Nottinghamshire. In his first class career he made, 6,976 runs including 2 centuries, took 183 catches and 41 stumpings.
Test Record - 3 Tests, 125 runs (Av. 31.25).

WRIGHT DOUGLAS VIVIAN PARSON

England (born 1914) - A leg-spin bowler, a useful tail-end batsman and also a good fielder. He played for Kent. In his first class career he made, 5,903 runs, took 2,056 wickets and 165 catches.
Test Record - 34 Tests, 289 runs (Av. 11.11), 108 wickets (Av. 39.11) and 10 catches.

WRIGHT JOHN GEOFFREY

New Zealand (born 1954) - A left-handed opening batsman and also a fine fielder. He played for Northern Districts and Derbyshire. In his first class career he made, 17,783 runs including 41 centuries, took 2 wickets and 158 catches.
Test Record - 63 Tests, 3,635 runs (Av. 33.34) including 7 centuries and 28 catches.

WRIGHT KEVIN JOHN

Australia (born 1956) - A wicket-keeper and a right-handed batsman. He played for Western Province and South Australia. In his first class career he made, 2,551 runs including 2 centuries, and 293 dismissals.
Test Record - 10 Tests, 219 runs (Av. 16.84) and 35 dismissals (31ct, 4st).

WRIST-SPIN

Spin is imparted to the ball by the movement of fingers or wrist at the time of delivery. When it is mainly imparted by movement of wrist it is termed as wrist-spin. The googly, the top-spin, the flipper and the china man are various forms of wrist-spin. It is not difficult than finger-spin for a bowler to bowl and a batsman to play.

WRIST-SPINNER

See SPIN.

WRISTY

Movement of wrists by a batsman or a spin bowler.

WRONG'UN

Named after the man said to have originated it on the 1903-04 MCC tour of Australia, England spinner BJT Bonsanquet. A delivery that appears to be a leg break to the right-handed batsman,but actually spins from off to leg.

WYATT ROBERT ELLIOTT STOREY

England (born 1901) - A right-handed batsman,a useful medium-pace swing bowler. He played for Warwickshire and Worcestershire. In his first class career he made, 39,404 runs including 85 centuries, took 901 wickets and 417 catches.
Test Record - 40 Tests, 1,839 runs (Av. 31.70) including 2 centuries, 18 wickets (Av. 35.66) and 16 catches.

WYNAYARD MAJOR EDWARD GEORGE

England (1861-1936) - A right-handed forcing batsman. He played for Army and Hampshire. In his first class career he made, 8,407 runs including 14 centuries, and took 66 wickets.
Test Record - 3 Tests, 72 runs (Av. 12.00).

WYNNE OWEN EDGAR

South Africa (1919-1975) - A solid right-handed opening batsman. He played for Transvaal and Western Province. In his first class career he made, 2,268 runs including 7 centuries.
Test Record - 6 Tests, 219 runs (Av. 18.25) and 3 catches.

Y

YADAV NANDLAL SHIVLAL
India (born 1957) - A right-handed batsman and a right-arm off-break bowler. Test debut on September 20, 1979 against Australia at the age of 22

SHIV LAL YADAV

years and 234 days. Played in the second Test at Bangalore on Test debut but did not bat. Took seven wickets for 81 runs (4 for 49 and 3 for 32)in the aforesaid Test on debut. He played for Hyderabad. In his first class career he made, 1,372 runs and took 247 wickets.
Test Record - 35 Tests, 403 runs (Av. 14.39), 102 wickets (Av. 35.09) and 10 catches.

YAJURVINDRA SINGH JASWANTSINGH
India (born 1952) - A right-handed batsman and a right-arm medium-pace and off-break bowler. Test debut on January 28, 1977 against England at the age of 24 years and 177 days. Scores on Test debut were 8 and 15 in the fourth Test at Bangalore. Shares with G.S. Chappell of Australia, the world record of holding most catches in a Test match, when he held seven catches (five in the first innings and two in the second innings) on debut. Last Test of the career played against Australia in September 1979. Score on last appearance in Test was 15 in the first Test at Madras. Age at the time of retirement from Test cricket was 27 years and 46 days. He played for Maharashtra and Saurashtra. In his first class career he made, 3,785 runs including 9 centuries and took 50 wickets.
Test Record - 3 Tests, 94 runs (Av. 18.80), and 10 catches.

YALLOP GRAHAM NEIL
Australia (born 1952) - A determined, vigorous and orthodox left-handed batsman, who hit the ball very hard. He played for Victoria. In his first class career he made, 11,063 runs including 29 centuries, took 11 wickets and 116 dismissals.
Test Record - 39 Tests, 2,756 runs (Av. 41.13) including 8 centuries and 23 catches.

YARDLE BRUCE
Australia (born 1947) - An all-rounder. He was a hard-hitting right-handed batsman and and off-spin bowler. He played for Western Province. In his first class career he made, 2,679 runs and took 334 wickets.
Test Record - 33 Tests, 978 runs (Av. 19.56), 126 wickets (Av. 31.63) and 31 catches.

YARDLEY NORMAN WALTER DRANSFIELD
England (born 1915) - A right-handed batsman and a right-arm medium-pace bowler. He played for Cambridge University and Yorkshire. In his first class career he made, 18,173 runs including 27 centuries, took 279 wickets and 320 catches.
Test Record - 20 Tests, 812 runs (Av. 25.37),21 wickets (Av. 33.46) and 14 catches.

YOGRAJ SINGH BHAGSINGH
India (born 1958) - A right-handed batsman and

a right-arm medium-fast bowler. Test debut on February 21, 1981 against New Zealand at the age of 22 years and 324 days. Scores on Test debut were 4 and 6 in the first Test at Wellington. He played for Haryana and Punjab. In his first class career he made, 398 runs and took 67 wickets.
Test Record - 1 Test, 10 runs (Av.5.00) and 1 wicket.

YORK
To dismiss a batsman by a yorker.

YORKER
In bowling, a delivery that passes under the bat, having pitched roughly on the length between a half-volley and a full toss.

YORKSHIRE
Foundation of Club: March 7, 1861 in Sheffield, but not truly representative of the whole county, until reorganised on December 10, 1891.

First First-Class Match: Surrey v Yorkshire (Oval) May 23,24, 1861. The Sheffield Club however had organised 'great' matches since 1927.
Present Principal Ground: Headingley, Leeds.
County Champions: 1867, 1869, 1870, 1893, 1896, 1898, 1900, 1901, 1902, 1905, 1908, 1912, 1919, 1922, 1923, 1924, 1925, 1931, 1933, 1935, 1937, 1938, 1939, 1946, 1949, 1959, 1960, 1962, 1963, 1966, 1967, 1968.
JPL Champions: 1983.
B&H Cup: Losing finalists in 1972.
Nat West Trophy: Winners in 1965 and 1969.
Highest Team Total: 887 v Warwickshire (Edgbaston) 1896.
Lowest Team Total: 23 v Hampshire (Middlesbrough) 1965.

YOUNG HARDING ISAAC
England (1876-1964) - A left-arm medium-pace bowler. He played for Essex. In his first class career he made, 2,328 runs and took 477 wickets.
Test Record - 2 Tests, 43 runs (Av. 21.50), 14 wickets (Av. 21.83) and 1 catch.

YOUNG JOHN ALBERT
England (born 1912) - A left-arm spin bowler. He played for Middlesex. In his first class career he made, 2,485 runs, took 1,361 wickets and 147 catches.
Test Record - 8 Tests, 28 runs (Av. 5.60), 17 wickets (Av. 44.52) and 5 catches.

YOUNG RICHARD ALFRED
England (1885-1968) - He was a useful batsman and one of the best wicket-keepers. He played for Cambridge University and Sussex. In his first class career he made, 6,502 runs including 6 centuries, and 105 dismissals.
Test Record - 2 Tests, 27 runs (Av. 6.75) and 6 dismissals (6ct).

YOUNIS AHMED MOHAMMAD
Pakistan (born 1947) - A left-handed batsman and also a left-arm slow spin-bowler. He played for Pakistan International Airways, Surrey and South Australia. In his first class career he made, 25,388 runs including 44 centuries, took 41 wickets and 239 catches.
Test Record - 4 Tests, 177 runs (Av. 29.50).

YUILE BRYAN WILLIAM
New Zealand (born 1941) - A left-arm slow-medium bowler and also a right-handed middle-order batsman. He played for Manawatu and Central Districts. In his first class career he made, 3,850 runs including 1 century and took 375 wickets.
Test Record - 17 Tests, 481 runs (Av. 17.81), 34 wickets (Av. 35.67) and 12 catches.

Z

ZAHEER ABBAS

Pakistan (born 1947) - A stylish and prolific right-handed middle-order batsman. He captained the Pakistani side for the first three Tests in 1983-84 in Australia. He played for Karachi and Gloucestershire. In his first class career he made, 34,289 runs including 107 centuries, took 28 wickets and 262 catches.

Test Record - 78 Tests, 5,062 runs (Av. 44.79) including 12 centuries, 3 wickets (Av. 44.00) and 34 catches.

ZAKIR KHAN

Pakistan (born 1963) - A tall and well-built right-arm seam bowler, with an aggressive streak. The bouncer is constant. He plays for Agricultural Development Bank. In his first class career he made, 1,577 runs including 3 centuries and took 245 wickets.

Test Record - 1 Test, 13 runs and 1 wicket.

ZOEHRER TIMOTHLY JOSEPH

Australia (born 1961) - A talented wicket-keeper. He played for Western Australia. In his first class career he made, 1,127 runs including 1 century, and 90 dismissals.

Test Record - 10 Tests, 246 runs (Av. 20.50) and 19 dismissals (18ct,1st).

ZULCH JOHN WILLIAM

South Africa (1886-1924) - A right-handed opening batsman with a wide range of strokes and sound defence, a very good fielder and a useful change-bowler. He played for Transvaal. In his first class career he made, 3,558 runs including 9 centuries.

Test Record - 16 Tests, 985 runs (Av. 32.83) including 2 centuries and 4 catches.

ZULFIQAR AHMED

Pakistan (born 1926) - A right-arm off-break bowler and also a reliable late-order batsman.

ZAHEER ABBAS

He played for Bahawalpur and Pakistan International Airlines. In his first class career he made, 973 runs and took 163 wickets.
Test Record - 9 Tests, 200 runs (Av. 33.33), 20 wickets (18.30) and 5 catches.

ZULQARNAIN
Pakistan (born 1962) - A useful wicket-keeper and also a right-handed batsman. He played for Pakistan Railways and Lahore. In his first class career he made, 539 runs and 190 dismissals.
Test Record - 3 Tests, 24 runs (Av. 6.00) and 10 dismissals (8ct, 2st).

TEST CRICKET RECORDS

TEAM RECORDS

Highest Innnings Totals

903-7d	England v Australia	The Oval	1938
849	England v West Indies	Kingston	1929-30
790-3d	West Indies v Pakistan	Kingston	1957-58
758-8d	Australia v West Indies	Kingston	1954-55
729-6d	Australia v England	Lord's	1930
708	Pakistan v England	The Oval	1987
701	Australia v England	The Oval	1934
695	Australia v England	The Oval	1930
687-8d	West Indies v England	The Oval	1976
681-8d	West Indies v England	Port-of-Spain	1953-54
676-7	India v Sri Lanka	Kanpur	1986-87
674-6	Pakistan v India	Faisalabad	1984-85
674	Australia v India	Adelaide	1947-48
668	Australia v West Indies	Bridgetown	1954-55
659-8d	Australia v England	Sydney	1946-47
658-8d	England v Austraila	Nottingham	1938
657-8d	Pakistan v West Indies	Bridgetown	1957-58
656-8d	Australia v England	Manchester	1964
654-5	England v South Africa	Durban	1938-39
652-7d	England v India	Madras	1984-85
652-8d	West Indies v England	Lord's	1973
652	Pakistan v India	Faisalabad	1982-83
650-6d	Austrialia v West Indies	Bridgetown	1964-65

The Highest Innings for other countries are:

622-9d	South Africa v Australia Durban	1969-70
553-7d	New Zealand v Austrialia Brisbane	1985-86
491-7d	Sri Lanka v England Lord's	1984

Lowest Innings Totals

26	New Zealand v England	Auckland	1954-55
30	South Africa v England	Port Elizabeth	1895-96
30	South Africa v England	Birmingham	1924
35	South Africa v England	Cape Town	1898-99
36	Australia v England	Birmingham	1902
36	South Africa v Australia	Melbourne	1931-32
42	Australia v England	Sydney	1887-88

42	New Zealand v Australia	Wellington	1945-46
42	India v England	Lord's	1974
43	South Africa v England	Cape Town	1888-89
44	Australia v England	The Oval	1896
45	England v Australia	Sydney	1886-87
45	South Africa v Australia	Melbourne	1931-32
47	South Africa v England	Cape Town	1888-89
47	New Zealand v England	Lord's	1958

Lowest Match Aggregates

Runs	Wickets		
234	29	Australia v South Africa (Melbourne)	1931-32
291	40	England v Australia (Lord's)	1888
295	28	New Zealand v Australia (Wellington)	1945-46

Most Runs in a Day (Both Sides)

588	England (396-6), India (190-0) at Manchester	(2nd day)1936
522	England (503-2), South Africa(19-0) at Lord's	(2nd day)1924
508	England (221-2), South Africa(287-6)at Oval	(3rd day)1935

Most Wickets in a day

27	England v Australia	Lord's (2nd day)	1888
25	Australia v England	Melbourne(1st day)	1901

BATTING RECORDS

Highest Individual Innings

365*	G. S. Sobers	WI v P	Kingston	1957-58
364	L. Hutton	E v P	The Oval	1938
337	Hanif Mohammad	P v WI	Bridgetown	1957-58
336*	W.R. Hammond	E v NZ	Auckland	1932-33
334	D.G. Bradman	A v E	Leeds	1930
325	A. Sandhan	E v WI	Kingston	1929-30
311	R.B.Simpson	A v E	Manchester	1964
310*	J.H. Edrich	E v NZ	Leeds	1965
307	R.M.Cowper	A v E	Melbourne	1965-66
304	D.G.Bradman	A v E	Leeds	1934
302	L.G. Rowe	WI v E	Bridgetown	1973-74
299*	D.G.Bradman	A v SA	Adelaide	1931-32
291	I.V.A.Richards	WI v E	The Oval	1976
287	R.E. Foster	E v A	Sydney	1903-04
285*	P.B.H. May	E v WI	Birmingham	1957
280*	Javed Miandad	P v I	Hyderabad	1982-83
278	D.C.S.Compton	E v P	Nottingham	1954

274	Zaheer Abbas	P v E	Birmingham	1971
274	R.G.Pollock	SA V A	Durban	1969-70
271	Javed Miandad	P v NZ	Auckland	1989
270*	G.A. Headley	WI v E	Kingston	1934-35
270	D.G.Bradman	A v E	Melbourne	1936-37
268	G.N.Yallop	A v P	Melbourne	1983-84
266	W.H.Ponsford	A v E	Melbourne	1934
262*	D.L.Amiss	E v WI	Kingston	1973-74
261	F.M.M.Worrel	WI v E	Nottingham	1950
260	C.C.Hunte	WI v P	Kingston	1957-58
260	Javed Miandad	P v E	The Oval	1987
259	G.M. Turner	NZ v WI	Georgetown	1971-72
258	T.W.Gravency	E v WI	Nottingham	1957
258	S.M. Nurse	WI v NZ	Christchurch	1968-69
256	R.B. Kanhai	WI v I	Calcutta	1958-59
256	K.F. Barrington	E v A	Manchester	1964
255*	D.J. McGlew	SA v NZ	Wellington	1952-53
254	D.G.Bradman	A V E	Lord's	1930
251	W.R. Hammond	E v A	Sydney	1928-29
250	K.D. Walters	A v NZ	Christchurch	1976-77
250	S.F.A.F. Bacchus	WI v I	Kanpur	1978-79

Most Hundreds

Total

34	Sunil Gavaskar	India
29	D.G.Bradman	Australia
26	G.S.Sobers	West Indies
24	G.S.Chappell	Australia
24	I.V.A.Richards	West Indies
23	A.R.Border	Australia
22	W.R.Hammond	England
22	M.C.Cowdrey	England
22	G.Boycott	England
21	R.N.Harvey	Australia
21	Javed Miandad	Pakistan
20	K.F. Barrington	England

Hundred on Test Debut

165*	C.Bannerman	A v E	Melbourne	1876-77
152	W.G.Grace	E v A	The Oval	1880
107	H. Graham	A v E	Lord's	1893
154*	K.S.Ranjitsinhji	E v A	Manchester	1896
132*	P.F.Warner	E v SA	Johannesburg	1898-99
104	R.A.Duff	A v E	Melbourne	1901-02
287	R.E.Foster	E v A	Sydney	1903-04
119	G.Gunn	E v A	Sydney	1907-08
116	R.J.Hartigan	A v E	Adelaide	1907-08

NAWAB PATAUDI

M. AZHARUDDIN

104	H.L.Collins	A v E	Sydney	1920-21
110	W.H.Ponsford	A v E	Sydney	1924-25
164	A.A.Jackson	A v E	Adelaide	1928-29
176	G.A.Headley	WI v E	Bridgetown	1929-30
117	J.E.Mills	NZ v E	Wellington	1929-30
102	Nawab Pataudi	E v A	Sydney	1932-33
136	B.H.Valentine	E v I	Bombay	1933-34
118	L.Amarnath	I v E	Bombay	1933-34
106	P.A.Gibb	E v SA	Johannesburg	1938-39
140	S.C.Griffith	E v WI	Port-of-Spain	1947-48
112	A.G.Ganteaume	WIv E	Port-of-Spain	1947-48
101*	J.W.Burke	A v E	Adelaide	1950-51
138	P.H.May	E v SA	Leeds	1951
110	R.H.Shodhan	I v P	Calcutta	1952-53
115	B.H.Pairaudeau	WIv I	Port-of-Spain	1952-53
104	O.G.Smith	WIv A	Kingston	1954-55
100*	A.G.Kripal Singh	I v NZ	Hyderabad	1955-56
142	C.C.Hunte	WIv P	Bridgetown	1957-58
104*	C.A.Milton	E v NZ	Leeds	1958-59
112	A.A.Baig	I v E	Manchester	1959-60
105	Hanumant Singh	I v E	Delhi	1963
166	Khalid Ibadulla	P v A	Karachi	1964-65
105	B.R.Taylor	NZv A	Calcutta	1965
155	K.D.Walters	A v E	Brisbane	1966
107	J.H.Hampshire	E v WI	Lord's	1968-69
137	G.R.Viswanath	I v A	Kanpur	1969-70
108	G.S.Chappell	A v E	Perth	1970-71

214,100*	L.G.Rowe	WI v NZ	Kingston	1971
100*	A.I.Kallicharan	WI v NZ	Georgetown	1971-72
107	R.E.Redmond	NZ v P	Auckland	1972-73
106*	F.C.Hayes	E v WI	The Oval	1973-74
107	C.G.Greenidge	WIv I	Bangalore	1974-75
105*	L.Baichan	WIv P	Lahore	1974-75
109	G.J.Cosier	A v WI	Melbourne	1975-76
124	S.Amarnath	I v NZ	Auckland	1976
163	Javed Miandad	P v NZ	Lahore	1976-77
100	A.B.Williams	WI v A	Georgetown	1978
103	L.M.Wellham	A v E	The Oval	1981
100*	Salim Malik	P v SL	Karachi	1981-82
162	K.C.Wessels	A v E	Brisbane	1982-83
159	W.B.Phillips	A v P	Perth	1983-84
110	M.Azharuddin	I v E	Calcutta	1984-85
201*	D.S.B.P.Kuruppu	SL v NZ	Colombo	1986-87
107*	J.Greatbatch	NZv E	Auckland	1987-88

Hundred and Double Hundreds in the Same Test

G.S. Chappell	Australia	247*and 133 v New Zealand
L.G.Rowe	West Indies	214 and 100* v New Zealand
S.M.Gavaskar	India	124 and 220 v West Indies
K.D.Walters	Australia	242 and 103 v West Indies

Highest Averages

D.G.Bradman	(Australia)	Av. 99.94
R.G. Pollock	(South Africa)	60.97
G.A.Headley	(West Indies)	60.83
H.Sutcliffe	(England)	60.73
E.Paynter	(England)	59.23
K.F.Barrington	(England)	58.67
E.D.Weekes	(West Indies)	58.61
W.R.Hammond	(England)	58.45
G.S.Sobers	(West Indies)	57.78
Javed Miandad	(Pakistan)	57.07
J.B.Hobbs	(England)	56.94
C.L.Walcott	(West Indies)	56.68
L.Hutton	(England)	56.67
E.Tyldesley	(England)	55.05

Most Runs in a Series

Runs		Series	M	I	NO	HS	Av.	100
974	D.G. Bradman(A v E)	1930	5	7	0	334	139.14	4
905	W.R. Hammond(E v P)	1928	5	9	1	251	113.12	4
839	M.Taylor (A v E)	1989	6	11	1	219	83.90	
2834	R.N.Harvey(A v SA)	1952	5	9	0	205	92.66	4
829	V.Richards (WI v E)	1976	4	7	0	291	118.42	3

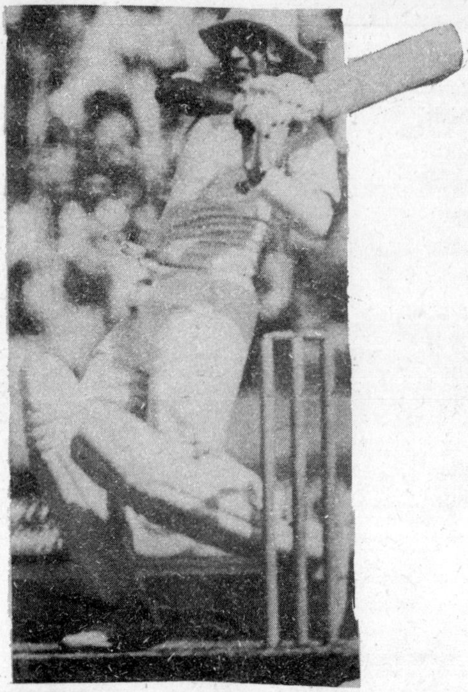

S.M. GAVASKAR

V. RICHARDS

827	C.L. Walcott(WI v A)	1954	5	10	0	155	82.70	5
824	G.Sobers (WI v P)	1957	5	8	2	365*	137.33	3
810	D.G. Bradman(A v E)	1936	5	9	0	270	90.00	3
806	D.G.Bradman(A v SA)	1931	5	5	1	299*	201.50	4
779	C. Weekes(WI v I)	1948	5	7	0	194	111.28	4
774	S.M. Gavaskar(Iv WI)	1970	4	8	3	220	201.50	4
761	Mudassar Nazar(P vI)	1982	6	8	2	231	126.83	4
758	D.G. Bradman(A v E)	1934	5	8	0	304	94.75	2
753	D.C.Compton(E v SA)	1947	5	8	0	208	94.12	4

Record Wickets Partnerships

1st	413	V.Mankand/Pankaj Roy	I v NZ	1955
2nd	451	W.H.Ponsford/D.G. Bradman	A v E	1934
3rd	451	Mudassar Nazar/Javed Miandad	P v I	1982
4th	411	P.B.H.May/M.C.Cowdrey	E v WI	1957
5th	405	S.G.Barnes/D.G.Bradman	A v E	1946
6th	346	J.H.W. Fingleton/D.G.Bradman	A v E	1936
7th	347	D.St E.Atkinson/C.C.Depeiza	WI v A	1954
8th	246	L.E.G. Ames/G.O. B.Alen	E v NZ	1931
9th	190	Asif Iqbal/Intikhab Alam	P v E	1967
10th	151	B.F.Hastings/ R.O. Collinge	NZ v P	1972

Wickets Partnership of Over 400

451	2nd	W.H.Ponsford/D.G.Bradman	A v E	1934
451	3rd	Mudassar Nazar/Javed Miandad	P v I	1982

446	2nd	C.C.Hunte/G.St. A. Sobers	WI v P	1957
413	1st	V.Mankad/ Pankaj Roy	I v NZ	1955
411	4th	P.B.H.May/M.C.Cowdrey	E v WI	1957
405	5th	S.G.Barnes/D.G.Bradman	A v E	1946

5000 Runs in Tests

Runs		M	I	HS	Av.	100	50
10122	S.M.Gavaskar	125	214	236*	51.12	34	45
8272	A.R.Border	108	188	205	53.34	23	48
8114	G.Boycott	108	193	246*	47.72	22	42
8032	G.St.A.Sobers	93	160	365*	57.78	26	30
7849	I.V.A.Richard	108	161	291	51.97	24	42
7624	M.C.Cowdrey	114	188	182	44.06	22	38
7515	C.H.Lloyd	110	175	242*	46.67	19	39
7422	Javed Miandad	97	148	280*	57.09	21	38
7249	W.R.Hammond	85	140	336*	58.45	22	24
7110	G.S.Chappell	87	151	247*	53.86	24	31
7000	D.I.Gower	100	172	215	44.02	14	32
6996	D.G.Bradman	52	80	334	99.94	29	13
6971	L.Hutton	79	138	364	56.67	19	33
6826	C.G.Greenidge	96	163	223	46.15	17	36
6806	K.F.Barrington	82	131	256	58.67	20	35
6498	D.B.Vengsarkar	105	168	166	44.50	17	32
6227	R.B.Kanhai	79	137	256	47.53	15	28
6149	R.N.Harvey	79	137	205	48.41	21	24
6080	G. R. Vishwanath	91	155	222	41.93	14	35
5807	D.C.S.Compton	78	131	278	50.06	17	28
5410	J.B.Hobbs	61	102	211	56.94	15	28
5357	K.D.Walters	74	125	250	48.26	15	33
5345	I.M.Chappell	75	136	196	42.42	14	26

A. R. BORDER

D.VENGSARKAR

DAVID GOWER

5234	W.M.Lawry	67	123	210	47.15	13	27
5138	J.H.Edrich	77	127	310*	43.54	12	24
5062	Zaheer Abbas	78	124	274	44.79	12	20
5057	I.T.Botham	94	150	208	34.87	14	22

Most Sixes in an Innings

10	W.R.Hammond (336*)	E v NZ	1932
7	B.Sutcliffe (80*)	NZ v SA	1953
6	J.H.Sinclair (104)	SA v A	1902
6	I.V.A.Richards (192*)	WI v I	1974
6	Haroon Rashid (108)	P v E	1977
6	I.T.Botham (118)	E v A	1981

Most Sixes off consecutive balls

3	W.R.Hammond (336*) off J.Newman	E v NZ	1932
3	S.T.Clarke (107) off Mohammad Nazir	WI v P	1980

Most Fours off consecutive balls

5	D.T.Lindsay (60) off J.W.Gleeson	SA v A	1969
5	R.E.Redmond (107) off Majid Khan	NZ v P	1972
5	D.W.Hookes (56) off A.W.Greig	A v E	1976

ZAHEER ABBAS

Most Runs off one over

8 Balls	25	B.Sutcliffe and R.W.Blair	NZ v SA	1953
6 Balls	24	A.M.E.Roberts	WI v E	1980
6 Balls	24	S.M.Patil	I v E	1982

Fastest Fifties

Minutes			
28	J.T.Brown	E v A	1894
29	S.A. Durani	I v E	1963
30	E.A.V.Williams	WI v E	1947
30	B.R.Taylor	NZ v WI	1968
33	C.A.Roach	WI v E	1933
34	C.R.R.Browne	WI v E	1929

The Fastest Fifties in terms of balls received (where recorded) are:

Balls			
30	Kapil Dev	I v P	1982
32	I.T.Botham	E v NZ	1986
33	R.C. Fredericks	WI v A	1975
33	Kapil Dev	I v E	1982
33	I.V.A.Richards	WI v E	1985

Fastest Hundred

Minutes			
70	J.M.Gregory	A v SA	1921
75	G.L.Jessop	E v E	1902
78	R.Benaud	A v WI	1954
80	J.H.Sinclair	SA v A	1902
81	I.V.A.Richards	WI v E	1985
86	B.R.Taylor	NZ v WI	1968

The Fastest Hundred in terms of balls received (where recorded) are:

Balls			
56	I.V.A. Richards	WI v E	1985
67	J.M.Gregory	A v SA	1921
71	R.C.Fredericks	WI v A	1975
74	Kapil Dev	I v SL	1986
76	G.L.Jessop	E v A	1902
77	Majid Khan	P v NZ	1976

Fastest Double-Hundred

Minutes			
214	D.G.Bradman	A v E	1930
223	S.J.McCabe	A v E	1938
226	V.T.Trumper	A v SA	1910
234	D.G.Bradman	A v E	1930

240	W.R.Hammond	E v NZ	1932
241	S.E.Gregory	A v E	1894
245	D.C.S.Compton	E v P	1954

The fastest Double-Hundred in terms of balls received (where recorded) are:

Balls			
219	I.T.Botham	E v I	1982
233	C.G.Greenidge	WI v E	1984
240	C.H.Lloyd	WI v I	1974
241	Zaheer Abbas	P v I	1982
242	D.G.Bradman	A v E	1934
242	I.V.A.Richards	WI v A	1984

Fastest Triple-Hundred

Minutes			
288	W.R.Hammond	E v NZ	1932
336	D.G.Bradman	A v E	1930

Most runs in a day by a Batsman

309	D.G.Bradman	A v E	1930
295	W.R.Hammond	E v NZ	1932
273	D.C.S.Compton	E v P	1954
271	D.G.Bradman	A v E	1934

Slowest Individual Batting

2*	in 80 Minutes	C.E.H.Croft	WI v A	1979
3*	in 100 Minutes	J.T.Murray	E v A	1962
5	in 102 Minutes	Nawab Pataudi jun.	I v E	1972
7	in 123 Minutes	G. Miller	E v A	1978
9	in 125 Minutes	T.W.Jarvis	NZ v I	1964
10*	in 133 Minutes	T.G.Evans	E v A	1946
16	in 188 Minutes	G.M.Ritchie	A v NZ	1985
18	in 194 Minutes	W.R.Playle	NZ v E	1958
19	in 217 Minutes	M.D.Crowe	NZ v SL	1983
28*	in 250 Minutes	J.W.Burke	A v E	1958
31	in 264 Minutes	K.D.Mackay	A v E	1956
34*	in 271 Minutes	Younis Ahmed	P v I	1981
35	in 332 Minutes	C.J.Tavare	E v I	1981
55	in 336 Minutes	B.A.Edgar	NZ v A	1981
57	in 346 Minutes	G.S.Camacho	WI v E	1967
58	in 367 Minutes	Ijaz Butt	P v A	1959
60	in 390 Minutes	D.N.Sardesai	I v WI	1961
62	in 408 Minutes	Ramiz Raja	P v WI	1986
68	in 458 Minutes	T.E.Bailey	E v A	1958
99	in 505 Minutes	M.L.Jaisimha	I v P	1960
105	in 575Minutes	D.J.McGlew	SA v A	1957
114	in 591 Minutes	Mudassar Nazar	P v E	1977
120*	in 609 Minutes	J.J.Crowe	NZ v SL	1986
158	in 648 Minutes	C.T.Radley	E v NZ	1977

163	in 720 Minutes	Shoaib Mohammad	P v NZ	1978
172	in 708 Minutes	S.M. Gavaskar	I v E	1981
337	in 970 Minutes	Hanif Mohammad	P v WI	1957

Slowest Hundreds

Minutes			
557	Mudassar Nazar	P v E	1977
545	D.J.McGlew	SA v A	1957
515	J.J.Crowe	NZ v SL	1986
488	P.E.Richardson	E v SA	1956

BOWLING RECORDS

Most Wickets in an Innings

10-53	J.C.Laker	E v A	Manchester	1956
9-28	G.A.Lohmann	E v SA	Johannesburg	1895
9-37	J.C.Laker	E v A	Manchester	1956
9-52	R.J.Hadlee	NZ v A	Brisbane	1985
9-56	Abdul Qadir	P v E	Lahore	1987
9-69	J.M.Patel	I V A	Kanpur	1959
9-83	Kapil Dev	I v WI	Ahmedabad	1983
9-86	Sarfraz Nawaz	P v A	Melbourne	1978
9-95	J.M.Noreiga	WI v I	Port-of-Spain	1970
9-102	S.P.Gupte	I v WI	Kanpur	1958
9-103	S.F.Barnes	E v SA	Johannesburg	1913
9-113	H.J.Tayfield	SA v E	Johannesburg	1956
9-121	A.A.Mailey	A v E	Melbourne	1920

Most Wickets in a Series

Wkts			M	Balls	Runs	5wI	10WM
49	S.F.Barnes	E v SA	4	1356	536	7	3
46	J.C.Laker	E v A	5	1703	442	4	2
44	C.V.Grimmett	A v SA	5	2077	642	5	3
42	T.M.Alderman	A v E	6	1950	893	4	-
41	R.M.Hogg	A v E	6	1740	527	5	2
41	T.M.Alderman	A v E	6	1616	712	6	1
40	Imran Khan	P v I	6	1339	558	4	2
39	A.V.Bedser	E v A	5	1591	682	5	1
39	D.K.Lillee	A v E	6	1870	870	2	1
38	M.W.Tate	E v A	5	2528	881	5	1
37	W.J.Whitty	A v SA	5	1395	632	2	-
37	H.J.Tayfield	SA v E	5	2280	636	4	1
36	A.E.E.Vogler	SA v E	5	1349	783	4	1
36	A.A. Mailey	A v E	5	1465	946	4	2
35	G.A.Lohrmann	E v SA	3	520	203	4	2
35	B.S.Chandrasekhar	I v E	5	1747	662	4	-
35	M.Marshall	WI v E	5	1433	443	4	1

250 Wickets in Tests

Wickets			M	Balls	Runs	5wI
396	R.J.Hadlee	NZ	79	20232	8799	34
373	I.T.Botham	E	94	20801	10392	27
355	D.K.Lillee	A	70	18467	8493	23
347	Kapil Dev	I	99	20670	10072	21
341	Imran Khan	P	75	17757	7519	23
326	M.D.Marshall	WI	66	14868	6698	22
325	R.G.D.Willis	E	90	17357	8190	16
309	L.R.Gibbs	WI	79	27115	8989	18
307	F.S.Trueman	E	67	15178	6625	17
297	D. L. Underwood	E	86	21862	7674	17
266	B.S.Bedi	I	67	21364	7637	14
259	J.Garner	WI	58	13169	5433	7
252	J.B.Statham	E	70	16056	6261	9

Hat-Tricks

F.R.Spofforth	A v E	Melbourne	1878-79
W.Bates	E v A	Melbourne	1882-83
J.Briggs	E v A	Sydney	1891-92
G.A.Lohmann	E v SA	Port Elizabeth	1895-96
J.T.Hearne	E v A	Leeds	1899
H.Turmble	A v E	Melbourne	1901-02
H.Turmble	A v E	Melbourne	1903-04
T.J.Matthews(2)*	A v SA	Manchester	1912
M.J.C.Allom+	E v NZ	Christchurch	1929-30
T.W.J.Goddard	E v SA	Johannesburg	1938-39
P.J.Loader	E v WI	Leeds	1957
L.F.Kline	A v SA	CapeTown	1957-58
W.W.Hall	WI v P	Lahore	1958-59
G.M.Griffin	SA v E	Lord's	1960
L.R.Gibbs	WI v A	Adelaide	1960-61
P.J.Petherick	NZ v P	Lahore	1976-77
C.A.Walsh	WI v A	Brisbane	1988-89
M.G.Hughes	A v WI	Perth	1988-89

WICKET-KEEPING RECORDS

Most Dismissals in an Innings

7	Wasim Bari	P v NZ	Auckland	1978-79
7	R.W.Taylor	E v I	Bombay	1979-80
6	A.T.W.Grout	A v SA	Johannesburg	1957-58
6	D.T.Lindsay	SA v A	Johannesburg	1966-67
6	J.T.Murray	E v I	Lord's	1967
6	S.M.H.Kirmani	I v NZ	Christchurch	1975-76
6	R.W.Marsh	A v E	Brisbane	1982-83
6	S.A.R. Silva	SL v I	Colombo	1985-86

Most Stumpings in an Innings

5	K.S.More	I v WI	Madras	1987-88

Most Dismissals in a Test

10	R.W.Taylor	E v I	Bombay	1979-80
9	G.R.A.Langley	A v E	Lord's	1956
9	D.A.Murray	WI v A	Melbourne	1981-82
9	R.W.Marsh	A v E	Brisbane	1982-83
9	S.A.R.Silva	SL v I	Colombo	1985-86
9	S.A.R.Silva	SL v I	Colombo	1985-86

Most Dismissals in a Series

28	R.W.Marsh	A v E	1982-83
26 inc 3st	J.H.B.Waite	SA v NZ	1961-62
26	R.W.Marsh	A v WI	1975-76
24 inc 2st	D.L.Murrary	WI v E	1963
24	D.T.Lindsay	SA v A	1966-67
24 inc 3st	A.P.Knott	E v A	1970-71

Above 170 Dismissals in Tests

Total			Tests	Ct.	St.
355	R.W.Marsh	Australia	96	343	12
269	A.P.E.Knott	England	95	250	19
228	Wasim Bari	Pakistan	81	201	27
219	T.G.Evans	England	91	173	46
208	P.J.L.Dujon	West Indies	64	203	5
198	S.M.H.Kirmani	India	88	160	38
189	D.L.Murray	West Indies	62	181	8
187	A.T.W.Grout	Australia	51	163	24
174	R.W. Taylor	England	57	167	7

FIELDING RECORDS

Most Catches in an Innings

5	V.Y. Richardson	Australia v South Africa	1935
5	Yajurvindra Singh	India v England	1976-77

Most Catches in a Test

7	G.S.Chappell	Australia v England	1974-75
7	Yajurvindra Singh	India v England	1976-77

Most Catches in a Series

15	J.M. Gregory	Australia v England	1920-21

Wasim
Bari

100 Catches in Tests

Total	Tests		
122	87	G.S.Chappell	Australia
120	114	M.C.Cowdrey	England
118	108	A.R.Border	Australia
112	97	I.T.Botham	England
110	107	I.V.A.Richards	West Indies
110	62	R.B.Simpson	Australia
110	85	W.R.Hammond	England
109	93	G.St.A.Sobers	West Indies
108	125	S.M. Gavaskar	India
105	75	I.M.Chappell	Australia

OTHER RECORDS

Youngest Test Players

	Years	Days			
Mushtaq Mohammad	15	124	P v W I	(Lahore)	1958-59
Aaqib Javed	16	189	P v NZ	(Wellington)	1988-89
Aftab Baloch	16	191	P v N.Z	(Dacca)	1969-70
Nasi-ul-Ghani	16	248	P v W.I	(Bridgetown)	1957-58
Khalid Hassan	16	352	P v E	(Nottingham)	1954-55
L.Sivaramakrishnan	17	118	I v W I	(St.John's)	1982-83

Oldest Test Players

	Years	Days			
W.Rhodes	52	165	E v W I	(Kingston)	1929-30
H.Ironmonger	50	327	A v E	(Sydney)	1932-33
W.G.Grace	50	320	E v A	(Nottingham)	1899
G.Gunn	50	303	E v W I	.(Kingston)	1929-30

Oldest Players on Test Debut

	Years	Days			
J. Southerton	49	119	E v A	(Melbourne)	1876-77
Miran Box	47	284	P v I	(Lahore)	1954-55
D.D.Blackie	46	253	A v E	(Sydney)	1928-29
H. Ironmonger	46	237	A v E	(Brisbane)	1928-29

Most Test Appearances

S.M. Gavaskar	125	India
Javed Miandad	97	Pakistan
M.C.Cowdrey	114	England
R.W. Marsh	96	Australia
A.Border	108	Australia

J.H.B. Waite	50	S.Africa
C.H. Lloyd	110	West Indies
R.J.Hadlee	79	New Zealand

Most Consecutive Test Appearances

106	S.M.Gavaskar	India	(1974-1987)
105	A.R.Border	Australia	(1978-1988)
87	G.R.Vishwanath	India	(1970-1983)
85	G.S. Sobers	West Indies	(1954-1972)
72	D.L. Haynes	West Indies	(1979-1988)
71	I.M.Chappell	Australia	(1965-1976)
66	Kapil Dev	India	(1978-1985)

ENGLAND V AUSTRALIA

Captains

Season	England	Australia	T	E	A	D
1876	James Lilly White	D.W.Gregory	2	1	1	0
1878	Lord Harris	D.W.Gregory	1	0	1	0
1880	Lord Harris	W.L.Murdoch	1	1	0	0
1881	A. Shaw	W.L.Murdoch	4	0	2	2
1882	A.N.Hornby	W.L.Murdoch	1	0	1	0
1882	Hon.Ivo Bligh	W.L.Murdoch	4	2	2	0
1884	Lord Harris	W.L.Murdoch	3	1	0	2
1884	A. Shrewsbury	T.Horan	5	3	2	0
1886	A.G.Steel	H.J.H.Scott	3	3	0	0
1886	A. Shrewsbury	P.S.McDonnell	2	2	0	0
1887	W.W.Read	P.S.McDonnell	1	1	0	0

VISHWANATH Out against Pakistan

1888	W.G.Grace	P.S.McDonnell	3	2	0	0
1890	W.G.Grace	W.L.Murdoch	2	2	0	0
1891	W.G.Grace	J.McC.Blackham	3	1	2	0
1893	W.G.Grace	J.McC.Blackham	3	1	0	2
1894	A.E.Stoddart	G.Giffen	5	3	2	0
1896	W.G.Grace	G.H.S.Trott	3	2	1	0
1897	A.E.Maclaren	G.H.S.Trott	5	1	4	0
1899	A.C.Maclaren	J.Darling	5	0	1	4
1901	A.C.MacLaren	J.Darling	5	1	4	0
1902	A.C.MacLaren	J.Darling	5	1	2	2
1903	P.F.Warner	M.A.Noble	5	3	2	0
1905	Hon. F.S.Jackson	J.Darling	5	2	0	3
1907	A.O.Jones	M.A.Noble	5	1	4	0
1909	A.C.MacLaren	M.A.Noble	5	1	2	2
1911	J.W.H.T.Douglas	C.Hill	5	4	1	0
1912	C.B.Fry	S.E.Gregory	3	1	0	2
1920	J.W.T.H.Douglas	W.W.Armstrong	5	0	5	0
1921	Hon.L.H.Tenyson	W.W.Armstrong	5	0	3	2
1924	A.F.R.Gilligan	H.L.Collins	5	1	4	0
1926	A.W.Carr	H.L.Collins	5	1	0	4
1928	A.P.E.Chapman	J.Ryder	5	4	1	0
1930	A.P.E.Chapman	W.M.Woodfull	5	1	2	2
1932	D.R.Jardine	W.M.Woodfull	5	4	1	0
1934	R.E.S.Wyatt	W.M.Woodfull	5	1	2	2
1936	G.O.Allen	D.G.Bradman	5	2	3	0
1938	W.R.Hammond	D.G.Bradman	5	0	4	1
1946	W.R.Hammond	D.G.Bradman	5	0	3	2
1948	N.W.D.Yardley	D.G.Bradman	5	0	4	1
1950	F.R.Brown	A.L.Hassett	5	1	4	0
1953	L.Hutton	A.L.Hassett	5	1	0	4
1954	L. Hutton	I.W.Joshnson	5	3	1	1
1956	P.B.H.May	I.W.Joshnson	5	2	1	2
1958	P.B.H.May	R.Benaud	5	0	4	1
1961	P.B.H.May	R.Benaud	5	1	2	2
1962	E.R.Dexter	R.Benaud	5	1	1	3
1964	E.P.Dezter	R.B.Simpson	5	0	1	4
1965	M.J.K.Smith	R.B.Simpson	5	1	1	3
1968	M.C.Cowdrey	W.M.Lawry	5	1	1	3
1970	R.Illingworth	W.M.Lawry	6	2	0	4
1972	R.Illingworth	I.M.Chappell	5	2	2	1
1974	M.H.Denness	I.M.Chappell	6	1	4	1
1975	A.W.Greig	I.M.Chappell	4	1	0	3
1976	A.W.Greig	G.S.Chappell	1	0	1	0
1977	J.M.Brearley	G.S.Chappell	5	3	0	2
1978	J.M.Brearley	G.N.Yallop	6	5	1	0
1979	J.M.Brearley	G.S.Chappell	3	0	3	0
1980	I.T.Botham	G.S.Chappell	1	0	0	1
1981	J.M.Brearley	K.J.Hughes	6	3	1	2
1982	R.G.D.Willis	G.S.Chappell	5	1	2	2
1985	D.I.Gower	A.R.Border	6	3	1	2
1986	M.W.Gatting	A.R.Border	5	2	1	2

1987	M.W.Gatting	A.R.Border	1 0 0 1
1989	D.I.Gower	A.R.Border	6 0 4 2
In Australia			140 51 67 22
In England			129 37 34 58
Total			269 88 101 80

HIGHEST INNINGS TOTALS

For England in England : 903 -7 dec. at the Oval	1938
in Australia: 636 at Sydney	1928
For Australia in England: 729 -6 dec. at Lord's	1930
in Australia: 659-8 dec. at Sydney	1947

LOWEST INNINGS TOTALS

For England in England : 52 at The Oval	1948
in Australia: 45 at Sydney	1886
For Australia in England: 36 at Birmingham	1902
in Australia: 42 at Sydney	1887

MOST RUNS IN A SERIES

England in England	D.I.Gower	732 (Av.81.33)	1985
England in Australia	W.R.Hammond	905 (Av.113.12)	1928
Australia in England	D.G.Bradman	974 (Av.139.14)	1930
Australia in Australia	D.G.Bradman	810 (Av.90.00)	1936-37

MOST WICKETS IN A SERIES

England in England	J.C.Laker	46(Av.9.60)	1956
England in Australia	M.W.Tate	38(Av.23.18)	1924-25
Australia in England	T.M.Alderman	42(Av.21.18)	1981
Australia in Australia	R.M.Hogg	41 (Av.12.85)	1978-79

INDIVIDUAL HUNDREDS (England)

1	Abel R.	132*	Sydney	1891-92
1	Ames L.E.G.	120	Lords	1934
1	Border R.W.	185	Sydney	1965-66
1	Barnes W	134	Adelaide	1984-85
2	Barnett C.J.	129	Adelaide	1936-37
		126	Nottingham	1938
5	Barrington K.F.	132*	Adelaide	1962-63
		101	Sydney	1962-63
		256	Manchester	1964
		102	Adelaide	1965-66
		115	Melbourne	1965-66
4	Botham I.T.	119*	Melbourne	1979-80
		149*	Leeds	1981

		118	Manchester	1981
		138	Brisbane	1986-87
7	Boycott G.	113	The Oval	1964
		142*	Sydney	1970-71
		119*	Adelaide	1970-71
		107	Nottingham	1977
		191	Leeds	1977
		128*	Lord's	1980
		137	The Oval	1981
2	Braund L.C.	103*	Adelaide	1901-02
		102	Sydney	1903-04
1	Briggs J.	121	Melbourne	1984-85
4	Broad B.C.	162	Perth	1986-87
		116	Adelaide	1986-87
		112	Melbourne	1986-87
		139	Sydney	1987-88
1	Brown J.T.	140	Melbourne	1894-95
1	Capman A.P.F.	121	Lord's	1930
5	Compton D.C.S.	102	Nottingham	1938
		147	Adelaide	1946-47
		103*	Adelaide	1946-47
		184	Nottingham	1948
		145*	Manchester	1948
5	Cowdrey M.C.	102	Melbourne	1954-55
		100*	Sydney	1958-59
		113	Melbourne	1962-63
		104	Melbourne	1965-66
		104	Birmingham	1968
1	Denness M.H.	188	Melbourne	1974-75
2	Dexter E.R.	180	Birmingham	1961-62
		173	Manchester	1964
2	D'Oliveira B.L.	158	The Oval	1968
		117	Melbourne	1970
1	Duleepsinhji K.S.	173	Lord's	1930
7	Edrich J.H.	120	Lord's	1964
		109	Melbourne	1965-66
		103	Sydney	1965-66
		164	The Oval	1968
		115*	Perth	1970-71
		130	Adelaide	1970-71
		175	Lord's	1975
2	Edrich W.J.	119	Sydney	1946-47
		111	Leeds	1948
1	Fletcher K.W.R.	146	Melbourne	1974-75
1	Foster R.E.	287	Sydney	1903-04
1	Fry C.B.	144	The Oval	1905
3	Gatting M.W.	160	Manchester	1985
		100	Birmingham	1985
		100*	Adelaide	1986-87
1	Gooch G.A.	196	The Oval	1985
7	Gower D.I.	102	Perth	1978-79

		114	Adelaide	1982-83
		166	Nottingham	1985
		215	Birmingham	1985
		157	The Oval	1985
		136	Perth	1986-87
		106	Lord's	1989
2	W.G.Grace	152	The Oval	1880
		170	The Oval	1886
1	Graveney T.W.	111	Sydney	1954-55
1	Greig A.W.	110	Brisbane	1974-75
2	Gunn G.	119	Sydney	1907-08
		122*	Sydney	1907-08
1	Gunn W.	102*	Manchester	1893
9	Hammond W.R.	251	Sydney	1928-29
		200	Melbourne	1928-29
		119*	Adelaide	1928-29
		177	Adelaide	1929
		113	Leeds	1930
		112	Sydney	1932-33
		101	Sydney	1932-33
		231*	Sydney	1936-37
		240	Lord's	1938
1	Hardstaff jun.	169*	The Oval	1938-39
2	Hayward T.W.	130	Manchester	1899
		137	The Oval	1899
1	Hearne J.W.	114	Melbourne	1911-12
3	Hendren E.H.	127*	Lord's	1926
		169	Brisbane	1928
		132	Manchester	1934
12	Hobbs J.B.	126*	Melbourne	1911
		187	Adelaide	1911-12
		178	Melbourne	1911-12
		107	Lord's	1912
		122	Melbourne	1920-21
		123	Adelaide	1920-21
		115	Sydney	1924-25
		154	Melbourne	1925
		119	Lord's	1926
		100	The Oval	1926
		142	Melbourne	1928-29
1	Hutchings K.L.	126	Melbourne	1907-08
5	Hutton L.	100	Nottingham	1938
		364	The Oval	1938
		122*	Sydney	1946
		156*	Adelaide	1950
		145	Lord's	1953
5	Jackson F.S.	103	The Oval	1893-94
		118	The Oval	1899
		128	Manchester	1902
		144*	Leeds	1905
		113	Manchester	1905-06

ALLEN BORDER

1	Jessop G.L.	104	The Oval	1902
2	Knott A.P.E.	106*	Adelaide	1974
		135	Nottingham	1977
1	Lamb A.J.	125	Leeds	1989
7	Leyland M.	137	Melbourne	1928-29
		109	Lord's	1934-35
		153	Manchester	1934
		110	The Oval	1934
		126	Brisbane	1936-37
		111*	Melbourne	1937
		187	The Oval	1938
2	Luckhurst B.W.	131	Perth	1970
		109	Melbourne	1970-71
5	Maclaren A.C.	120	Melbourne	1894-95
		109	Sydney	1897-98
		124	Adelaide	1897-98
		116	Sydney	1901-02
		140	Nottingham	1905
1	Makepeace J.W.H.	117	Melbourne	1920-21
3	May P.B.H.	104	Sydney	1954-55
		101	Leeds	1956-57
		113	Melbourne	1958
1	Mead C.P.	182*	The Oval	1921
1	Nawab Pataudi sen.	102	Sydney	1932-33
1	Paynter E.	216	Nottingham	1938
3	Randall D.W.	174	Melbourne	1976-77
		150	Sydney	1978-79
		115	Perth	1982-83
2	Ranjitsinhji K.S.	154*	Manchester	1896
		175	Sydney	1897-98
1	Read W.W.	117	The Oval	1884
1	Rhodes W.	179	Melbourne	1911-12
1	Richards C.J.	133	Perth	1986-87
1	Richardson P.E.	104	Manchester	1956
2	Robinson R.T.	175	Leeds	1985
		148	Birmingham	1985
3	Russell A.C.	135*	Adelaide	1920-21
		101	Manchester	1921
		102*	The Oval	1921
1	Russell R.C.	128*	Manchester	1989
1	Sharp J.	105	The Oval	1909
2	Sheppard D.S.	113	Manchester	1956
		113	Melbourne	1962-63
3	Shrewsbury	105*	Melbourne	1884-85
		164	Lord's	1886
		106	Lord's	1893
1	Simpson R.T.	156*	Melbourne	1950-51
2	Smith R.A.	143	Manchester	1989
		101	Nottingham	1989
2	Steel A.G.	135*	Sydney	1882-83
		148	Lord's	1884

2	Stoddart A.E.	134	Adelaide	1891-92
		173	Melbourne	1894-95
2	Subba Row R.	112	Birmingham	1961
		137	The Oval	1961
8	Sutcliffe H.	115	Sydney	1924-25
		176	Melbourne	1924-25
		127	Melbourne	1924-25
		143	Melbourne	1924-25
		161	The Oval	1926
		135	Melbourne	1928-29
		161	The Oval	1930
		194	Sydney	1932-33
3	Tyldesley J.T.	138	Birmingham	1902
		100	Leeds	1905
		112*	The Oval	1905
1	Ulyett G.	149	Melbourne	1881-82
1	Ward A.	117	Sydney	1894-95
2	Washbrook	112	Melbourne	1946-47
		143	Leeds	1948
1	Watson W.	109	Lord's	1953
2	Woolley F.E.	133*	Sydney	1911-12
		123	Sydney	1924-25
3	Woolmer R.A.	149	The Oval	1975
		120	Lord's	1977
		137	Manchester	1977

(Australia)

4	Armstrong W.W.	133*	Melbourne	1907-08
		158	Sydney	1920-21
		121	Adelaide	1920-21
		123*	Melbourne	1920-21
1	Badcock C.L.	118	Melbourne	1936-37
1	Bannerman C.	165*	Melbourne	1876-77
3	Bardsley W.	136	The Oval	1909
		130	The Oval	1909
		193*	Lord's	1926
2	Barnes S.G.	234	Sydney	1946-47
		141	Lord's	1948
1	Bonnor G.J.	128	Sydney	1884-85
2	Boon D.C.	103	Adelaide	1986-87
		184*	Sydney	1987-88
2	Booth B.C.	112	Brisbane	1962-63
		103	Melbourne	1962-63
7	Border A.R.	115	Perth	1979-80
		123*	Manchester	1981
		106*	The Oval	1981
		196	Lord's	1985
		146*	Manchester	1985
		125	Perth	1986-87
		100*	Adelaide	1986-87

19	Bradman D.G.	112	Melbourne	1928-29
		123	Melbourne	1928-29
		131	Nottingham	1930
		254	Lord's	1930
		334	Leeds	1930
		232	The Oval	1930
		103*	Melbourne	1932-33
		304	Leeds	1934
		244	The Oval	1934
		270	Melbourne	1936-37
		212	Adelaide	1936-37
		169	Melbourne	1936-37
		144*	Nottingham	1938
		102*	Lord's	1938
		103	Leeds	1938
		187	Brisbane	1946-47
		234	Sydney	1946-47
		138	Nottingham	1948
		173*	Leeds	1948
3	Brown W.A.	105	Lord's	1934
		133	Nottingham	1938
		206*	Lord's	1938
4	Burge P.J.	181	The Oval	1961
		103	Sydney	1962-63
		160	Leeds	1964
		120	Melbourne	1965-66
1	Burke J.W.	101*	Adelaide	1950-51
6	Chappell G.S.	108	Perth	1970-71
		131	Lord's	1972
		112	Manchester	1977
		114	Melbourne	1979-80
		117	Perth	1982-83
		115	Adelaide	1982-83
4	Chappell I.M.	111	Melbourne	1970-71
		104	Adelaide	1970-71
		118	The Oval	1972
		192	The Oval	1975
3	Collins H.L.	104	Sydney	1920-21
		162	Adelaide	1920-21
		114	Sydney	1924-25
1	Cowper R.M.	307	Melbourne	1965-66
3	Darling J.	101	Sydney	1897-98
		178	Adelaide	1897-98
		160	Sydney	1897-98
2	Duff R.A.	104	Melbourne	1901-02
		146	The Oval	1905
1	Dyson J.	102	Leeds	1981
2	Edwards R.	170*	Nottingham	1972
		115	Perth	1974-75
2	Fingleton J.H.	100	Brisbane	1936-37
		136	Melbourne	1936-37

1	Giffen G.	161	Sydney	1894-95
2	Graham H.	107	Lord's	1893
		105	Sydney	1894-95
1	Gregory J.M.	100	Melbourne	1920-21
4	Gregory S.E.	201	Sydney	1894-95
		103	Lord's	1896
		117	The Oval	1899
		112	Adelaide	1903-04
1	Hartigan R.J.	116	Adelaide	1907-08
6	Harvey R.N.	112	Leeds	1948-49
		122	Manchester	1953
		162	Brisbane	1954-55
		167	Melbourne	1958-59
		114	Birmingham	1961
		154	Adelaide	1962
4	Hassett A.L.	128	Brisbane	1946-47
		137	Nottingham	1948
		115	Nottingham	1953
		104	Lord's	1953
1	Hendry H.S.T.L	112	Sydney	1928-29
1	Hilditch	119	Leeds	1985
4	Hill C.	188	Melbourne	1897-98
		135	Lord's	1899
		119	Sheffield	1902
		160	Adelaide	1907-08
1	Horan T.P.	124	Melbourne	1881
3	Hughes K.J.	129	Brisbane	1978-79
		117	Lord's	1980
		137	Sydney	1982-83
2	Iredale F.A.	140	Adelaide	1894-95
		108	Manchester	1896
1	Jackson A.A.	164	Adelaide	1894-95
3	Jones D.M.	184*	Sydney	1986-87
		157	Birmingham	1989
		122	The Oval	1989
1	Kelleway C.	147	Adelaide	1920-21
1	Kippax A.F.	100	Melbourne	1928-29
7	Lawry W.M.	130	Lord's	1961
		102	Manchester	1961
		106	Manchester	1964-65
		166	Brisbane	1965-66
		119	Adelaide	1966
		108	Melbourne	1966
		135	The Oval	1968
1	Lindwall R.R.	100	Melbourne	1946-47
1	Lyons J.J.	134	Sydney	1891-92
5	Macartney C.G.	170	Sydney	1920-21
		115	Leeds	1920-21
		133*	Lord's	1926
		151	Leeds	1926
		109	Manchester	1926

4	McCabe S.J.	187*	Sydney	1932-33
		137	Manchester	1934
		112	Melbourne	1936-37
		232	Nottingham	1938
1	McCool C.L.	104*	Melbourne	1946-47
2	McCosker R.B.	127	The Oval	1975
		107	Nottingham	1977
2	McDonald C.C.	170	Adelaide	1958-59
		133	Melbourne	1958-59
3	McDonnel P.S.	147	Sydney	1981-82
		103	The Oval	1884
		124	Adelaide	1884-85
1	McLeod C.E.	112	Melbourne	1897-98
2	Marsh G.R.	110	Brisbane	1986-87
		138	Nottingham	1989
1	Marsh R.W.	110*	Melbourne	1976
3	Miller K.R.	141*	Adelaide	1946-47
		145*	Sydney	1950-51
		109	Lord's	1953
8	Morris A.R.	155	Melbourne	1946-47
		122	Adelaide	1946-47
		124*	Adelaide	1946-47
		105	Lord's	1948
		182	Leeds	1948
		196	The Oval	1948-49
		206	Adelaide	1950-51
		153	Brisbane	1954-55
2	Murdoch W.L.	153*	The Oval	1880
		211	The Oval	1884
1	Noble M.A.	133	Sydney	1903-04
2	O'Neill N.C.	117	The Oval	1961
		100	Adelaide	1962-63
2	Pellew C.E.	116	Melbourne	1920-21
		104	Adelaide	1920-21
5	Ponsford W.H.	110	Sydney	1924-25
		128	Melbourne	1924-25
		110	The Oval	1930-31
		181	Leeds	1934
		266	The Oval	1934
1	Ransford V.S.	143*	Lord's	1909
2	Redpath I.R.	171	Perth	1970-71
		105	Sydney	1974-75
1	Richardson A.J.	100	Leeds	1926
1	Richardson V.Y.	138	Melbourne	1924
1	Ritchie G.M.	146	Nottingham	1985
2	Ryder J.	201*	Adelaide	1924-25
		112	Melbourne	1928-29
1	Scott H.J.H.	102	The Oval	1884
2	Simpson R.B.	311	Manchester	1964
		225	Adelaide	1965-66
3	Stackpole K.R.	207	Brisbane	1970-71

		136	Adelaide	1970-71
		114	Nottingham	1972
1	Taylor J.M.	108	Sydney	1924-25
2	Taylor M.A.	136	Leeds	1989
		219	Nottingham	1989
1	Trott G.H.S.	143	Lord's	1896
6	Trumper V.T.	135*	Lord's	1899
		104	Manchester	1902
		185*	Sydney	1903-04
		113	Adelaide	1904
		166	Sydney	1907-08
		113	Sydney	1911-12
4	Walters K.D.	155	Brisbane	1965-66
		115	Melbourne	1966
		112	Brisbane	1970-71
		103	Perth	1974-75
2	Waugh S.R.	177*	Leeds	1989
		152*	Lord's	1989
1	Welham D.M.	103	The Oval	1981
1	Wessels K.C.	162	Brisbane	1982-83
3	Wood G.M.	100	Melbourne	1978-79
		112	Lord's	1980
		172	Nottingham	1985-86
6	Woodfull W.M.	141	Leeds	1916
		117	Manchester	1926
		111	Sydney	1928-29
		107	Melbourne	1928-29
		102	Melbourne	1929
		155	Lord's	1930
3	Yallop G.N.	102	Brisbane	1978-79
		121	Sydney	1978-79
		114	Manchester	1981

ENGLAND V SOUTH AFRICA

	Captains					
Season	**England**	**South Africa**	**T**	**E**	**SA**	**D**
1888	C.A.Smith	O.R.Dunell	2	2	0	0
1891	W.W.Read	W.H.Miton	1	1	0	0
1895	Lord Hawke	E.A.Halliwell	3	3	0	0
1898	Lord Hawke	M.Bisset	2	2	0	0
1905	P.F.Warner	P.W.Sherwell	5	1	4	0
1907	R.E.Foster	P.W.Sherwell	3	1	0	2
1909	H.D.Leveson	S.J.Snooke	5	2	3	0
1912	C.B.Fry	F.Mitchell	3	3	0	0
1913	J.W.Douglas	H.W.Taylor	5	4	0	1
1922	F.T.Mann	H.W.Taylor	5	2	1	2
1924	A.E.Gilligan	H.W.Taylor	5	3	0	2
1927	R.T.Stanyforth	H.G.Deane	5	2	1	1

1929	J.C.White	H.G.Deane	5	2	0	3
1931	A.P.Chapman	H.G.Deane	5	0	1	4
1935	R.E.Wyatt	H.F.Wade	5	0	1	4
1938	W.R.Hammond	A.Melville	5	1	0	4
1947	N.W.Yardley	A.Melville	5	3	0	2
1948	F.G.Mann	A.D.Nourse	5	2	0	3
1951	F.R.Brown	A.D.Nourse	5	3	1	1
1955	P.B.H.May	J.E.Cheetham	5	3	2	0
1957	P.B.H.May	C.B.Ryneveld	5	2	2	1
1960	M.C.Cowdrey	D.J.McGlew	5	3	0	2
1965	M.J.K.Smith	T.L.Goddard	5	1	0	4
1965	M.J.K.Smith	P.L.Merwe	3	0	1	2

In South Africa	58	25	13	20
In England	44	21	05	18
Total	102	46	18	38

HIGHEST INNINGS TOTALS

For England in England: 554-8 dec. at Lord's	1947
in South Africa: 654-5 at Durban	1938-39
For South Africa in England: 538 at Leeds	1951
in South Africa:530 at Durban	1938-39

LOWEST INNINGS TOTALS

For England in England:76 at Leeds	1907
in South Africa:92 at Cape Town	1898-99
For South Africa in England :30 at Birmingham	1924
in South Africa: 30 at Port Elizabeth	1895-96

MOST RUNS IN A SERIES

England in England	D.C.S.Compton	753(Av.94.12)	1947
England in South Africa	E.Paynter	653(Av.81.62)	1938
South Africa in England	A.D.Nourse	621(Av.69.00)	1947
South Africa in South Africa	H.Taylor	582(Av.64.66)	1922

MOST WICKETS IN A SERIES

England in England	S.F.Barnes	34(Av.8.29)	1912
England in South Africa	S.F.Barnes	49(Av.10.93)	1913
South Africa in England	H.J.Tayfield	26(Av.21.84)	1955
	N.A.T.Adcock	26(Av.22.57)	1960
South Africa in South Africa	H.J.Tayfield	37(Av.17.18)	1956

INDIVIDUAL HUNDREDS (England)

1	Abel R.	120	Cape Town	1988-89
2	Ames L.E.G.	148*	The Oval	1935

		115	Cape Town	1938-39
2	Barrington K.F.	148*	Durban	1964-65
		121	Johannesburg	1964-65
1	Boycott G.	117	Pt.Elizabeth	1965
1	Braund L.C.	104	Lord's	1907
7	Compton D.C.S.	163	Nottingham	1947
		208	Lord's	1947
		115	Manchester	1947
		113	The Oval	1947-48
		114	Johannesburg	1948-49
		112	Nottingham	1951
		158	Manchester	1955-56
3	Cowdrey M.C.	101	Cape Town	1956-57
		155	The Oval	1960
		105	Nottingham	1965
1	Denton D.	104	Johannesburg	1909-10
1	Dexter E.R.	172	Johannesburg	1964-65
1	Douglas J.W.H.T.	119	Durban	1938-39
3	Edrich W.J.	219	Durban	1938-39
		189	Lord's	1947
		191	Manchester	1947
1	Fane F.L.	143	Johannesburg	1905-06
1	Fry C.B.	129	The Oval	1907
2	Gibb P.A.	106	Johannesburg	1938-39
		120	Durban	1938-39
6	Hammond W.R.	138*	Birmingham	1929
		101*	The Oval	1929
		136*	Durban	1930
		181	Cape Town	1938-39
		120	Durban	1938-39
		140	Durban	1938-39
1	Hayward T.W.	122	Johannesburg	1895-96
2	Hendren E.H.	132	Leeds	1924
		142	The Oval	1924
1	Hill A.J.L.	124	Cape Town	1895-96
2	Hobbs J.B.	187	Cape Town	1909
		211	Lord's	1924
4	Hutton L.	100	Leeds	1947
		158	Johannesburg	1948-49
		123	Johannesburg	1948-49
		100	Leeds	1951
1	Insole D.J.	110*	Durban	1956
2	Leyland M.	102	Lord's	1929
		161	The Oval	1935
1	Mann F.G.	136*	Pt.Elizabeth	1948-49
3	May P.B.H.	138	Leeds	1951-52
		112	Lord's	1955
		117	Manchester	1955
3	Mead C.P.	102	Johannesburg	1913-14
		117	Pt.Elizabeth	1913-14
		181	Durban	1922

1	Parfitt P.H.	122*	Johannesburg	1964-65
1	Parks J.M.	108*	Durban	1964-65
3	Paynter E.	117	Johannesburg	1938-39
		100	Johannesburg	1938-39
		242	Durban	1938-39
1	Pullar G.	175	The Oval	1960-61
1	Rhodes W.	152	Johannesburg	1913
1	Richardson P.E.	117	Johannesburg	1956-57
1	Robins R.W.V.	108	Manchester	1935
2	Russell A.C.	140	Durban	1922-23
		111	Durban	1922-23
1	Simpson R.T.	137	Nottingham	1951
1	Smith M.J.K.	121	Cape Town	1964-65
1	Spooner R.H.	119	Lord's	1912
6	Sutcliffe H.	122	Lord's	1924
		102	Johannesburg	1927
		114	Birmingham	1929-30
		100	Lord's	1929-30
		104	The Oval	1929-30
		109*	The Oval	1929-30
1	Tate M.W.	100*	Lord's	1929-30
2	Tyldesley E.	122	Johannesburg	1927
		100	Durban	1927
1	Tyldesley J.T.	112	Cape Town	1898-99
1	Valentine B.H.	112	Cape Town	1938-39
1	Warner P.F.	132*	Johannesburg	1898-99
1	Washbrook C.	195	Johannesburg	1948-49
1	Watkins A.J.	111	Johannesburg	1948-49
1	Wood H.	134*	Cape Town	1891-92
3	Wooley F.E.	115*	Johannesburg	1922
		134*	Lord's	1924
		154	Manchester	1929
2	Wyatt R.E.S.	113	Manchester	1929
		149	Nottingham	1935

(South Africa)

1	Barlow E.J.	138	Cape Town	1964-65
2	Bland K.C.	144*	Johannesburg	1964
		127	The Oval	1965
3	Catterall R.H.	120	Birmingham	1924
		120	Lord's	1924
		119	Durban	1927
2	Dalton E.L.	117	The Oval	1935
		102	Johannesburg	1938-39
1	Endean W.R.	116*	Leeds	1955
1	Faulkner G.A.	123	Johannesburg	1909
1	Goddard T.L.	112	Johannesburg	1964-65
1	Hathorn C.M.H.	102	Johannesburg	1905
2	McGlew D.J.	104*	Manchester	1955-56
		133	Leeds	1955-56

3	McLean R.A.	142	Lord's	1955
		100	Durban	1956-57
		109	Manchester	1960
4	Melville A.	103	Durban	1938-39
		189	Nottingham	1947
		104*	Nottingham	1947
		117	Lord's	1947
7	Mitchell B.	123	Cape Town	1930
		164*	Lord's	1935
		128	The Oval	1935
		109	Durban	1938
		120	The Oval	1947
		189*	The Oval	1947
		120	Cape Town	1948-49
7	Nourse A.D.	120	Cape Town	1938
		103	Durban	1938
		149	Nottingham	1947
		115	Manchester	1947
		129*	Johannesburg	1948-49
		112	Cape Town	1948-49
		208	Nottingham	1951-52
1	Owen-Smith H.G.	129	Leeds	1929
1	Pithey A.J.	154	Cape Town	1964-65
2	Pollock R.G.	137	Pt.Elizabeth	1964-65
		125	Nottingham	1965
2	Rowan E.A.B.	156*	Johannesburg	1948-49
		236	Leeds	1951
1	Sherwell P.W.	115	Lord's	1907
1	Siedle I.J.	141	Cape Town	1930-31
1	Sinclair J.H.	106	Cape Town	1898-99
7	Taylor H.W.	109	Durban	1913
		176	Johannesburg	1922-23
		101	Johannesburg	1922-23
		102	Durban	1922-23
		101	Johannesburg	1927
		121	The Oval	1929
		117	Cape Town	1930-31
1	Vander Biji P.G.	125	Durban	1938
1	Viljoen K.G.	124	Manchester	1935
1	Wade W.W.	125	Pt.Elizabeth	1948
1	Waite J.H.B.	113	Manchester	1955
2	White G.C.	147	Johannesburg	1905-06
		118	Durban	1909-10
1	Winslow P.L.	108	Manchester	1955

ENGLAND V WEST INDIES

Season	Captains England	Captains West Indies	T	E	WI	D
1928	A.P.F.Chapman	R.K.Nunes	3	3	0	0
1929	F.S.Calthorpe	E.L.G.Hoad	4	1	1	2
1933	D.R.Jardine	G.C.Grant	3	2	0	1
1934	R.E.S.Wyatt	G.C.Grant	4	1	2	1
1939	W.R.Hammond	R.S.Grant	3	1	0	2
1948	G.O.Allen	J.D.Goddard	4	0	2	2
1950	N.W.D.Yardley	J.D.Goddard	4	1	3	0
1953	L.Hutton	J.B.Stollmeyer	5	2	2	1
1957	P.B.H.May	J.D.C.Goddard	5	3	0	2
1959	P.B.H.May	F.C.C.Alexander	5	1	0	4
1963	E.R.Dexter	F.M.Worrell	5	1	3	1
1966	M.C.Cowdrey	G.S.Sobers	5	1	3	1
1968	M.C.Cowdrey	G.S.Sobers	5	1	0	4
1969	R.Illingworth	G.S.Sobers	3	2	0	1
1973	R.Illingworth	R.B.Kanhai	3	0	2	1
1974	M.H.Denness	R.B.Kanhai	5	1	1	3
1976	A.W.Greig	C.H.Lloyd	5	0	3	2
1980	I.T.Botham	C.H.Lloyd	5	0	1	4
1981	I.T.Botham	C.H.Lloyd	4	0	2	2
1984	D.I.Gover	C.H.Lloyd	5	0	5	0
1985	D.I.Gover	I.V.A.Richards	5	0	5	0
1988	J.E.Emburey	I.V.A.Richards	5	0	4	1
In England			54	14	24	16
In West Indies			41	7	15	9
Total			95	21	39	35

HIGHEST INNINGS TOTALS

For England in England : 619-6 dec.at Nottingham 1957
in West Indies:849 at Kingston 1929-30
For West Indies in England :687-8 dec. at The Oval 1976
in West Indies:681-8 dec.at Port-of-Spain 1953

LOWEST INNINGS TOTALS

For England in England :71 at Manchester 1976
in West Indies:103 at Kingston 1934-35
For West Indies in England : 86 at The Oval 1957
in West Indies:102 at Bridgetown 1934-35

INDIVIDUAL HUNDREDS (England)

3	Ames L.E.G.	105	Port-of-Spain	1929
		149	Kingston	1929

		126	Kingston	1934-35
4	Amiss D.L.	174	Port-of-Spain	1973
		262*	Kingston	1973
		118	Georgetown	1973
		203	The Oval	1976
1	Bakewell A.H.	107	The Oval	1933-34
3	Barrington K.F.	128	Bridgetown	1959-60
		121	Port-of-Spain	1959-60
		143	Port-of-Spain	1967
5	Boycott G.	116	Georgetown	1967-68
		128	Manchester	1969
		106	Lord's	1969
		112	Port-of-Spain	1973
		104	St John's	1980
2	Compton D.C.S.	120	Lord's	1939
		133	Port-of-Spain	1953
6	Cowdrey M.C.	154	Birmingham	1957
		152	Lord's	1957
		114	Kingston	1959-60
		119	Port-of-Spain	1959-60
		101	Kingston	1967-68
		148	Port-of-Spain	1967-68
2	Dexter E.R.	136*	Bridgetown	1959-60
		110	Georgetown	1959-60
1	Edrich J.H.	146	Bridgetown	1967-68
1	Evans T.G.	104	Manchester	1950
1	Fletcher K.W.R.	129*	Bridgetown	1973-74
1	Fowler G.	106	Lord's	1984
4	Gooch G.A.	123	Lord's	1980
		116	Bridgetown	1980-81
		153	Kingston	1980-81
		146	Nottingham	1988
1	Gower D.I.	154*	Kingston	1980-81
5	Graveney T.W.	258	Nottingham	1957
		164	The Oval	1957
		109	Nottingham	1966
		165	The Oval	1966
		118	Port-of-Spain	1967-68
3	Greig A.W.	148	Bridgetown	1973-74
		121	Georgetown	1973-74
		116	Leeds	1976
1	Griffith S.C.	140	Port-of-Spain	1947-48
1	Hammond W.R.	138	The Oval	1939
1	Hampshire J.H.	107	Lord's	1969
1	Hayes F.C.	106*	The Oval	1973
2	Hendren E.H.	205*	Port-of-Spain	1929-30
		123	Georgetown	1929-30
1	Hobbs J.B.	159	The Oval	1928
5	Hutton L.	196	Lord's	1939
		165*	The Oval	1939
		202*	The Oval	1950

ALLAN LAMB

		169	Georgetown	1953-54
		205	Kingston	1953-54
1	Illingworth R.	113	Lord's	1969
1	Jardine D.R.	127	Manchester	1933
1	Knott A.P.E.	116	Leeds	1976
4	Lamb A.J.	110	Lord's	1984
		100	Leeds	1984
		100*	Manchester	1984
		113	Lord's	1988
3	May P.B.H.	135	Port-of-Spain	1953
		285*	Birmingham	1957
		104	Nottingham	1957
1	Milburn C.	126*	Lord's	1966
1	Murray J.T.	112	The Oval	1966
1	Paarks J.M.	101	Port-of-Spain	1959-60
1	Place W.	107	Kingston	1947-48
2	Richardson P.E.	126	Nottingham	1957
		107	The Oval	1957
1	Robertson J.D.	133	Port-of-Spain	1947
2	Sandham A.	152	Bridgetown	1929
		325	Kingston	1929
1	Smith M.J.K.	108	Port-of-Spain	1959
1	Steele D.S.	106	Nottingham	1976
1	Subba Row R.	100	Georgetown	1959
1	Tyldesley E.	122	Lord's	1928
2	Washbrook C.	114	Lord's	1950
		102	Nottingham	1950
1	Watson W.	116	Kingston	1953
2	Willey P.	100*	The Oval	1980
		102*	St. John's	1980-81

(West Indies)

1	Barrow I.	105	Manchester	1933
2	Butcher B.F.	133	Lord's	1963
		209*	Nottingham	1966
1	Carew G.M.	107	Port-of-Spain	1947-48
1	Davis C.A.	103	Lord's	1969
1	Dujon P.J.L.	101	Manchester	1984
3	Fredericks R.C.	150	Birmingham	1973
		138	Lord's	1976
		109	Leeds	1976
1	Ganteaume A.G.	112	Port-of-Spain	1947
2	Gomes H.A.	143	Birmingham	1984
		104*	Leeds	1984
6	Greenidge C.G.	134	Manchester	1976
		101	Manchester	1976
		115	Leeds	1976
		214*	Lord's	1984
		223	Manchester	1984
		103	Lord's	1988

3	Haynes D.L.	184	Lord's	1980
		125	The Oval	1984
		131	St. John's	1985
8	Headley G.A.	176	Bridgetown	1929
		114	Georgetown	1929
		112	Georgetown	1929
		223	Kingston	1929
		169*	Manchester	1933
		270*	Kingston	1934-35
		106	Lord's	1939
		107	Lord's	1939
1	Holford D.A.J.	105	Lord's	1966
1	Holt J.K.	166	Bridgetown	1953-54
3	Hunte C.C.	182	Manchester	1963
		108*	The Oval	1963
		135	Manchester	1966
1	Jullien B.D.	121	Lord's	1973
2	Kallicharan A.I.	158	Port-of-Spain	1973
		119	Bridgetown	1973
5	Kanhai R.B.	110	Port-of-Spain	1959-60
		104	The Oval	1966
		153	Port-of-Spain	1967
		150	Georgetown	1967
		157	Lord's	1973
5	Lloyd C.H.	118	Port-of-Spain	1967
		113*	Bridgetown	1967
		132	The Oval	1973
		101	Manchester	1980
		100	Bridgetown	1980
2	Nurse S.M.	137	Leeds	1966
		136	Port-of-Spain	1967
2	Rae A.F.	106	Lord's	1950
		109	The Oval	1950
8	Richards I.V.A.	232	Nottingham	1976
		135	Manchester	1976
		291	The Oval	1976
		145	Lord's	1980
		182*	Bridgetown	1980-81
		114	St. John's	1980-81
		117	Birmingham	1984
		110*	St. John's	1985
2	Richardson R.B.	102	Port-of-Spain	1985
		160	Bridgetown	1985
2	Roach C.A.	122	Bridgetown	1929
		209	Georgetown	1929
3	Rowe L.G.	120	Kingston	1973-74
		302	Bridgetown	1973-74
		123	Port-of-Spain	1973-74
2	Smith O.G.	161	Birmingham	1957
		168	Nottingham	1957
10	Sobers G.S.	226	Bridgetown	1959

RICH RICHARDSON *G. GREENIDGE*

		147	Kingston	1959
		145	Georgetown	1959
		102	Leeds	1963
		161	Manchester	1966
		163*	Lord's	1966
		174	Leeds	1966
		113*	Kingston	1967
		152	Georgetown	1967
		150*	Lord's	1973
4	Walcott C.L.	168*	Lord's	1950
		220	Bridgetown	1953-54
		124	Port-of-Spain	1953-54
		116	Kingston	1953-54
3	Weekes E.D.	141	Kingston	1947-48
		129	Nottingham	1950
		206	Port-of-Spain	1953-54
1	Weekes K.H.	137	The Oval	1939
6	Worrell F.M.M.	131*	Georgetown	1947-48
		261	Nottingham	1950
		138	The Oval	1950
		167	Port-of-Spain	1953
		191*	Nottingham	1957
		197*	Bridgetown	1959-60

ENGLAND V PAKISTAN

Captains

Season	England	Pakistan	T	E	P	D
1954	L.Hutton	A.H. Kardar	4	1	1	2
1961-62	E.R.Dexter	Imtiaz Ahmed	3	1	0	2
1962	E.R.Dexter	Javed Burki	5	4	0	1
1967	D.B.Close	Hanif Mohammad	3	2	0	1
1968-69	M.C.Cowdrey	Saeed Ahmed	3	0	0	3
1971	R. Illingworth	Intikhab Alam	3	1	0	2
1972-73	A.R.Lewis	Majid Khan	3	0	0	3
1974	M.H.Denness	Intikhab Alam	3	0	0	3
1977-78	J.M.Brearley	Wasim Bari	3	0	0	3
1978	J.M.Brearley	Wasim Bari	3	2	0	1
1982	R.G.D.Willis	Imran Khan	3	2	1	0
1983-84	R.G.D.Willis	Zaheer Abbas	3	0	1	2
1987	M.W.Gatting	Imran Khan	5	0	1	4
1987-88	M.W.Gatting	Javed Miandad	3	0	1	2
In England			29	12	3	14
In Pakistan			18	1	2	15

Total 47 13 5 29

HIGHEST INNINGS TOTALS

For England in England : 558 -6 dec. at Nottingham 1954
in Pakistan : 546 -8 dec. at Faisalabad 1983-84
For Pakistan in England : 708 at The Oval 1987
in Pakistan : 569 -9 dec. at Hyderabad 1972-73

LOWEST INNINGS TOTALS

For England in England : 130 at The Oval 1954
in Pakistan : 130 at Lahore 1987-88
For Pakistan in England : 87 at Lord's 1954
in Pakistan : 191 at Faisalabad 1987-88

INDIVIDUAL HUNDREDS (For England)

3	Amiss D.L.	112	Lahore	1972
		158	Hyderabad	1972-73
		183	The Oval	1974
1	Athey C.W.J.	123	Lord's	1987
4	Barrington K.F.	139	Lahore	1961
		148	Lord's	1967
		109*	Nottingham	1967
		142	The Oval	1967
2	Botham I.T.	100	Birmingham	1978
		108	Lord's	1978
3	Boycott G.	121	Lord's	1971

		112	Leeds	1971
		100*	Hyderabad	1977-78
1	Broad B.C.	116	Faisalabad	1987
1	Compton D.C.S.	278	Nottingham	1954
3	Cowdrey M.C.	159	Birmingham	1962-63
		182	The Oval	1962-63
		100	Lahore	1968
2	Dexter E.R.	205	Karachi	1961
		172	The Oval	1962
1	D'Oliveira B.L.	114*	Dacca	1968
1	Fletcher K.W.R.	122	The Oval	1974
2	Gatting M.W.	124	Birmingham	1987
		150*	The Oval	1987
2	Gower D.I.	152	Faisalabad	1983
		173*	Lahore	1983
3	Graveney T.W.	153	Lord's	1962
		114	Nottingham	1962
		105	Karachi	1968
1	Knott A.P.E.	116	Birmingham	1971
1	Luckhurst B.W.	108*	Birmingham	1971
1	Milburn C.	139	Karachi	1961
4	Parfitt P.H.	111	Karachi	1961
		101*	Birmingham	1962
		119	Leeds	1962
		101*	Nottingham	1962
1	Pullar G.	165	Dacca	1961
1	Radley C.T.	106	Birmingham	1978
1	Randall D.W.	105	Birmingham	1982
1	Robinson R.T.	166	Manchester	1987
1	Simpson R.T.	101	Nottingham	1954

(For Pakistan)

1	Alim-ud-Din	109	Karachi	1961
3	Asif Iqbal	146	The Oval	1967
		104*	Birmingham	1971
		102	Lahore	1972
3	Hanif Mohammad	111	Dacca	1961
		104	Dacca	1961
		187*	Lord's	1967
2	Haroon Rashid	122	Lahore	1977-78
		108	Hyderabad	1977-78
1	Imran Khan	118	The Oval	1987
1	Intikhab Alam	138	Hyderabad	1972
3	Javed Burki	138	Lahore	1961
		140	Dacca	1961
		101	Lord's	1962
1	Javed Miandad	260	The Oval	1987
2	Mohsin Khan	200	Lord's	1982
		104	Lahore	1983
3	Mudassar Nazar	114	Lahore	1977-78

		124	Birmingham	1987
		120	Lahore	1987
3	Mushtaq Mohammad	100	Nottingham	1962
		100	Birmingham	1971
		157	Hyderabad	1972
1	Nasim-ul Ghani	101	Lord's	1962
1	Sadiq Mohammad	119	Lahore	1972
2	Salim Malik	116	Faisalabad	1983-84
		102	The Oval	1987
1	Wasim Raja	112	Faisalabad	1983
2	Zaheer Abbas	274	Birmingham	1971
		240	The Oval	1974

ZAHEER ABBAS

MOHSIN KHAN

ENGLAND V NEW ZEALAND

Season	Captains England	New Zealand	T	E	NZ	D
1929-30	A.H.H.Gilligan	T.C.Lowry	4	1	0	3
1931	D.R.Jardine	T.C.Lowry	3	1	0	2
1932-33	D.R.Jardine	M.L.Page	2	0	0	2
1937	R.W.V.Robins	M.L.Page	3	1	0	1
1946-47	W.R.Hammond	W.A.Hadlee	1	0	0	1
1949	F.G.Mann	W.A.Hadlee	4	0	0	4
1950-51	F.R.Brown	W.A.Hadlee	2	1	0	1
1954-55	L.Hutton	G.O.Rabone	2	2	0	0
1958	P.B.H.May	J.R.Reid	5	4	0	1
1958-59	P.B.H.May	J.R.Reid	2	1	0	1
1962-63	E.R.Dexter	J.R.Reid	3	3	0	0
1965	M.J.K.Smith	J.R.Reid	3	3	0	0
1965-66	M.J.K.Smith	B.W.Sinclair	3	0	0	3
1969	R.Illingworth	G.T.Dowling	3	2	0	1
1970-71	R.Illingworth	G.T.Dowling	2	1	0	1
1973	R.Illingworth	B.E.Congdon	3	2	0	1
1974-75	M.H.Denness	B.E.Congdon	2	1	0	1
1977-78	G.Boycott	M.G.Burgess	3	1	1	1
1978	J.M.Brearley	M.G.Burgess	3	3	0	0
1983	R.G.D.Willis	G.P.Howarth	4	3	1	0
1983-84	R.G.D.Willis	G.P.Howarth	3	0	1	2
1986	M.W.Gatting	J.V.Coney	3	0	1	2
1987-88	M.V.Gatting	J.J.Crowe	3	0	0	3
In New Zealand			32	11	2	19
In England			34	19	2	13
Total			66	30	4	32

HIGHEST INNINGS TOTALS

For Englad in England : 546-4 dec. at Leeds 1965
in New Zealand :593-6 dec.at Auckland 1975
For New Zealand in England : 551-9 dec.at Lord's 1973
in New Zealand : 537 at Wellington 1983-84

LOWEST INNINGS TOTALS

For England in England :187 at Manchester 1937
in New Zealand : 64 at Wellington 1977-78
For New Zealand in England : 47 at Lord's 1958
in New Zealnd: 26. at Auckland 1954-55

INDIVIDUAL HUNDREDS (For England)

1	Allen G.O.B.	122	Lord's	1931
2	Ames L.E.G.	137	Lord's	1931

		103	Christchurch	1932-33
2	Amiss D.L.	138*	Nottingham	1973
		164*	Christchurch	1974
1	Bailey T.E.	134*	Christchurch	1950
3	Barrington K.F.	126	Auckland	1962-63
		137	Birmingham	1965
		163	Leeds	1965
3	Botham I.T.	103	Christchurch	1977
		103	Nottingham	1983
		138	Wellington	1983-84
1	Bowley E.H.	109	Auckland	1929-30
2	Boycott G.	115	Leeds	1973
		131	Nottingham	1978
1	Broad B.C.	114	Christchurch	1987-88
2	Compton D.C.S.	114	Leeds	1949
		116	Lord's	1949
2	Cowdrey M.C.	128*	Wellington	1962-63
		119	Lord's	1965
1	Denness M.H.	181	Auckland	1974-75
1	Dexter E.R.	141	Christchurch	1958-59
1	D'Oliveira B.L.	100	Christchurch	1970-71
2	Duleepsinhji K.S.	117	Auckland	1929
		109	The Oval	1931
3	Edrich J.H.	310	Leeds	1965
		155	Lord's	1969
		115	Nottingham	1969
1	Edrich W.J.	100	The Oval	1949
2	Fletcher K.W.R.	178	Lord's	1973
		216	Auckland	1974-75
1	Fowler G.	105	The Oval	1983
1	Gatting M.W.	121	The Oval	1986
1	Gooch G.A.	183	Lord's	1986
4	Gower D.I.	111	The Oval	1978
		112*	Leeds	1983
		108	Lord's	1983
		131	The Oval	1986
1	Greig A.W.	139	Nottingham	1973
4	Hammond W.R.	100*	The Oval	1931
		227	Christchurch	1932-33
		336*	Auckland	1932-33
		140	Lord's	1937
2	Hardstaff jun. J.	114	Lord's	1937
		103	The Oval	1937
3	Hutton L.	100	Manchester	1937
		101	Leeds	1949
		206	The Oval	1949
1	Knight B.R.	125	Auckland	1962-63
1	Knott A.P.E.	101	Auckland	1970
2	Lamb A.J.	102*	The Oval	1983
		137*	Nottingham	1983
1	Legge G.B.	196	Auckland	1929

3	May P.B.H.	113*	Leeds	1958
		101	Manchester	1958
		124*	Auckland	1958-59
1	Milton C.A.	104*	Leeds	1958
1	Parfitt P.H.	131*	Auckland	1962
1	Radley C.T.	158	Auckland	1977
2	Randall D.W.	164	Wellington	1983
		104	Auckland	1983
1	Richardson P.E.	100	Birmingham	1958
1	Robertson J.D.	121	Lord's	1949
1	Sharpe P.J.	111	Nottingham	1969
1	Simpson R.T.	103	Manchester	1949
2	Sutcliffe H.	117	The Oval	1931
		109	Manchester	1931
1	Tavare C.J.	109	The Oval	1983
1	Washbrook C.	103*	Leeds	1949

(For New Zealand)

1	Bracewell J.G.	110	Nottingham	1986
2	Burgess M.G.	104	Auckland	1970-71
		105	Lord's	1973
1	Coney J.V.	174*	Wellington	1983-84
3	Congdon B.E.	104	Christchurch	1965-66
		176	Nottingham	1973
		175	Lord's	1973
1	Crowe J.J.	128	Auckland	1983-84
3	Crowe M.D.	100	Wellington	1983-84
		106	Lord's	1986
		143	Wellington	1987-88
2	Dempster C.S.	136	Wellington	1929-30
		120	Lord's	1931
1	Donnelly M.P.	206	Lord's	1949
1	Greatbatch M.J.	107*	Auckland	1987-88
1	Hadlee W.A.	116	Christchurch	1946-47
3	Howarth G.P.	122	Auckland	1977-78
		102	Auckland	1977-78
		123	Lord's	1978
1	Mills J.E.	117	Wellington	1929-30
1	Page M.L.	104	Lord's	1931
1	Parker J.M.	121	Auckland	1974-75
2	Pollard V.	116	Nottingham	1973
		105*	Lord's	1973
1	Reid J.R.	100	Christchurch	1962-63
1	Rutherford K.R.	107*	Wellington	1987-88
1	Sinclair B.W.	114	Auckland	1965-66
1	Smith I.D.S.	113*	Auckland	1983-84
2	Sutcliffe B.	101	Manchester	1949
		116	Christchurch	1950-51
3	Wright J.G.	130	Auckland	1983-84
		119	The Oval	1986
		103	Auckland	1987-88

Indian Team

ENGLAND V INDIA

Captains

Season	England	India	T	E	I	D
1932	D.R.Jardine	C.K.Nayudu	1	1	0	0
1933-34	D.R.Jardine	C.K.Nayudu	3	2	0	1
1936	G.O.Allen	Pataudi sen.	3	1	0	2
1946	W.R.Hammond	Pataudi sen.	3	1	0	2
1951-52	N.D.Howard	V.S.Hazare	5	1	1	3
1952	L.Hutton	V.S.Hazare	4	3	0	1
1959	P.B.H. May	D.K.Gaekwad	5	5	0	0
1961-62	E.R.Dexter	N.J.Contractor	5	0	2	3
1963-64	M.J.K.Smith	Pataudi jun.	5	0	0	5
1967	D.B.Close	Pataudi jun.	3	3	0	0
1971	R Illingworth	A.L.Wadekar	3	0	1	2
1972-73	A.R.Lewis	A.L.Wadekar	5	1	2	2
1974	M.H.Denness	A.L.Wadekar	3	3	0	0
1976-77	A.W.Greig	B.S.Bedi	5	3	1	1
1979	J.M.Brearley	S.Venkataraghavan	4	1	0	3
1979-80	J.M.Brearley	G. R. Vishwanath	1	1	0	0
1981-82	K.W.R.Fletcher	S.M.Gavaskar	6	0	1	5
1982	R.G.D.Willis	S.M.Gavaskar	3	1	0	2
1984-85	D.I.Gover	S.M.Gavaskar	5	2	1	2
1986	M.W.Gatting	Kapil Dev	3	0	2	1
In England			35	20	3	12
In India			40	10	8	22
Total			75	30	11	34

HIGHEST INNINGS TOTALS

For England in England: 633 -5 dec.at Birmingham 1979
in India : 652-7 dec. at Madras 1984-85
For India in England : 510 at Leeds 1967
in India: 553-8 dec. at Kanpur 1984-85

LOWEST INNINGS TOTALS

For England in England : 101 at The Oval 1971
in India : 102 at Bombay 1981-82
For India in England : 42 at Lord's 1974
in India : 83 at Madras 1976-77

INDIVIDUAL HUNDREDS (For England)

2	Amiss D.L.	188	Lord's	1974
		179	Delhi	1976
3	Barrington K.F.	151*	Bombay	1961-62
		172	Kanpur	1961-62
		173*	Delhi	1961-62
5	Botham I.T.	137	Leeds	1979
		114	Bombay	1979
		142	Kanpur	1981
		128	Manchester	1982
		208	The Oval	1982
4	Boycott G.	246*	Leeds	1967
		155	Birmingham	1979
		125	The Oval	1979
		105	Delhi	1981
3	Cowdrey M.C.	160	Leeds	1959
		107	Calcutta	1963
		151	Delhi	1981-82
2	Denness M.H.	118	Lord's	1974
		100	Birmingham	1974
1	Dexter E.R.	126*	Kanpur	1961
1	D'Oliveira B.L.	109	Leeds	1967
1	Edrich J.H.	100*	Manchester	1974
1	Evans T.G.	104	Lord's	1952
2	Fletcher K.W.R.	113	Bombay	1972-73
		123*	Manchester	1974
1	Fowler G.	201	Madras	1984-85
3	Gatting M.G.	136	Bombay	1984
		207	Madras	1984
		183*	Birmingham	1986
2	Gooch G.A.	129	Madras	1981
		114	Lord's	1986
1	Gower D.I.	200*	Birmingham	1979
2	Graveney T.W.	175	Bombay	1951
		151	Lord's	1967
3	Greig A.W.	148	Bombay	1972
		106	Lord's	1974

		103	Calcutta	1976
2	Hammond W.R.	167	Manchester	1936
		217	The Oval	1936
1	Hardstaff jun. J.	205*	Lord's	1946
2	Hutton L.	150	Lord's	1952
		104	Manchester	1952
1	Illingworth R.	107	Manchester	1971
1	Knight B.R.	127	Kanpur	1963
1	Lamb A.J.	107	The Oval	1982
1	Lewis A.R.	125	Kanpur	1972-73
1	Lloyd D.	214*	Birmingham	1974
1	Luckhurst B.W.	101	Manchester	1971
1	May P.B.H.	106	Nottingham	1959
1	Parfitt P.H.	121	Kanpur	1963-64
2	Pullar G.	131	Manchester	1959
		119	Kanpur	1961-62
1	Randall D.W.	126	Lord's	1982
1	Robinson R.T.	160	Delhi	1984
1	Sheppard D.S.	119	The Oval	1952
1	Smith M.J.K.	100	Manchester	1959
1	Tavare C.J.	149	Delhi	1981
1	Valentine B.H.	136	Bombay	1933-34
1	Walters C.F.	102	Madras	1933-34
1	Watkins A.J.	137	Delhi	1951
1	Worthington T.S.	128	The Oval	1936

(For India)

1	Amarnath L.	118	Bombay	1933
3	Azharuddin M.	110	Calcutta	1984-85
		105	Madras	1984-85
		122	Kanpur	1984-85
1	Baig A.A.	112	Manchester	1959
1	Engineer F.M.	121	Bombay	1972-73
4	Gavaskar S.M.	101	Manchester	1974
		108	Bombay	1976-77
		221	The Oval	1979
		172	Bangalore	1981-82
1	Hanumant Singh	105	Delhi	1963-64
2	Hazare V.S.	164*	Delhi	1951-52
		155	Bombay	1951-52
2	Jaisimha M.L.	127	Delhi	1961-62
		129	Calcutta	1963-64
1	Kapil Dev	116	Kanpur	1981-82
1	Kirmani S.M.H.	102	Bombay	1984-85
2	Kunderan B.K.	192	Madras	1963-64
		100	Delhi	1963-64
3	Manjrekar V.L.	133	Leeds	1952
		189*	Delhi	1961-62
		108	Madras	1963-64
1	Mankad V.	184	Lord's	1952

3	Merchant V.M.	114	Manchester	1936
		128	The Oval	1946
		154	Delhi	1951-52
1	Mushtaq Ali	112	Manchester	1936
1	Nadkarni R.G.	122*	Kanpur	1963-64
3	Nawab Pataudi jun.	103	Madras	1961-62
		203*	Delhi	1963-64
		148	Leeds	1967
1	Patil S.M.	129*	Manchester	1982
1	Phadkar D.G.	115	Calcutta	1951-52
2	Pankaj Roy	140	Bombay	1951-52
		111	Madras	1951-52
2	Shastri R.J.	142	Bombay	1984-85
		111	Calcutta	1984-85
3	Umrigar P.R.	130*	Madras	1951-52
		118	Manchester	1959
		147*	Kanpur	1961-62
5	Vengsarkar D.B.	103	Lord's	1979
		157	Lord's	1982
		137	Kanpur	1984-85
		126*	Lord's	1986
		102*	Leeds	1986
4	Vishwanath G.R.	113	Bombay	1972-73
		113	Lord's	1979
		107	Delhi	1981-82
		222	Madras	1981-82
1	Yashpal Sharma	140	Madras	1981-82

ENGLAND V SRI LANKA

	Captains					
Season	**England**	**Sri Lanka**	**T**	**E**	**SL**	**D**
1981-82	K.W.R.Fletcher	B.Warnapura	1	1	0	0
1984	D.I.Gower	L.R.D.Mendis	1	0	0	1
1988	G.A.Gooch	R.S.Madugalle	1	1	0	0
In England			2	1	0	1
In Sri Lanka			1	1	0	0
Total			3	2	0	1

Highest innings total for England :429 at Lord's 1988
for Sri Lanka : 491 -7 dec. at Lord's 1984
Lowest innings total for England : 233 at Colombo 1981-82
for Sri Lanka : 175 at Colombo 1981-82

INDIVIDUAL HUNDREDS (For England)

1	Lamb A.J.	107	Lord's	1984

(For Sri Lanka)

1	Mendis L.R.D.	111	Lord's	1984
1	Silva S.A.R.	102*	Lord's	1984
1	Wettimuny S.	190	Lord's	1984

AUSTRALIA V SOUTH AFRICA

	Captains					
Season	Australia	South Africa	T	A	SA	D
1902-03	J Darling	H.M.Taberer	3	2	0	1
1910-11	C.Hill	P.W.Sherwell	5	4	1	0
1912	S.E.Gregory	F.Mitchell	3	2	0	1
1921-22	H.L.Collins	H.W.Taylor	3	1	0	2
1931-32	W.M.Woodfull	H.B.Cameron	5	5	0	0
1935-36	V.Y.Richardson	H.F.Wade	5	4	0	1
1949-50	A.L.Hassett	A.D.Nourse	5	4	0	1
1952-53	A.L.Hassett	J.E.Cheetham	5	2	2	1
1957-58	I.D.Craig	C.B.Ryneveld	5	3	0	2
1963-64	R.B.Simpson	T.L.Goddard	5	1	1	3
1966-67	R.B.Simpson	P.L.Merwe	5	1	3	1
1969-70	W.M.Lawry	A.Bacher	4	0	4	0
In South Africa			30	15	7	8
In Australia			20	12	4	4
In England			3	2	0	1
Total			53	29	11	13

HIGHEST INNINGS TOTALS

For Australia in Australia : 578 at Melbourne	1910-11
in South Africa:549-7 dec.at Pt.Elizabeth	1950
For South Africa in Australia : 595 at Adelaide	1963-64
in South Africa: 622-9 dec. at Durban	1969-70

LOWEST INNINGS TOTALS

For Australia in Australia: 153 at Melbourne	1931-32
in South Africa: 75 at Durban	1949-50
For South Africa in Australia: 36 at Melbourne	1931-32
in South Africa: 85 at Johannesburg	1902-03

INDIVIDUAL HUNDREDS (For Australia)

2	Armstrong W.W.	159*	Johannesburg	1902-03
		132	Melbourne	1910-11
3	Bardsley	132	Sydney	1910-11
		121	Manchester	1912
		164	Lord's	1912
2	Benaud R.	122	Johannesburg	1957
		100	Johannesburg	1957
2	Booth B.C.	169	Brisbane	1963
		102*	Sydney	1963
4	Bradman D.G.	226	Brisbane	1931
		112	Sydney	1931
		167	Melbourne	1931
		299*	Adelaide	1931
1	Brown W.A.	121	Cape Town	1935
1	Burke J.W.	189	Cape Town	1957
1	Chipperfield A.G.	109	Durban	1935
1	Collins H.L.	203	Johannesburg	1921
3	Fingleton J.H.	112	Cape Town	1935
		108	Johannesburg	1935
		118	Durban	1935
1	Gregory J.M.	119	Johannesburg	1921
8	Harvey R.N.	178	Cape Town	1949
		151*	Durban	1949
		100	Johannesburg	1949
		116	Pt. Elizabeth	1949
		109	Brisbane	1952
		190	Sydney	1952
		116	Adelaide	1952
		205	Melbourne	1952
3	Hassett A.L.	112	Johannesburg	1949
		167	Pt. Elizabeth	1949
		163	Adelaide	1952
3	Hill C.	142	Johannesburg	1902-03
		191	Sydney	1910-11
		100	Melbourne	1910-11
2	Kelleway	114	Manchester	1912
		102	Lord's	1912
1	Lawry W.M.	157	Melbourne	1963
1	Loxton S.J.E.	101	Johannesburg	1949
2	Macartney C.G.	137	Sydney	1910-11
		116	Durban	1921
2	McCabe S.J.	149	Durban	1935
		189*	Johannesburg	1935
1	McDonald C.C.	154	Adelaide	1952
2	Moroney J.	118	Johannesburg	1949
		101*	Johannesburg	1949
2	Morris A.R.	111	Johannesburg	1949
		157	Pt. Elizabeth	1949
1	Rigg K.E.	127	Sydney	1931
1	Ryder J.	142	Cape Town	1921

1	Simpson R.B.	153	Cape Town	1966
1	Stackpole K.R.	134	Cape Town	1966
2	Trumper V.T.	159	Melbourne	1910-11
		214*	Adelaide	1910-11
1	Woodfull W.M.	161	Melbourne	1931

For South Africa

5	Barlow E.J.	114	Brisbane	1963
		109	Melbourne	1963
		201	Adelaide	1963
		127	Cape Town	1969
		110	Johannesburg	1969
1	Bland K.C.	126	Sydney	1963
1	Endean W.R.	162*	Melbourne	1952
3	Faulkner G.A.	204	Melbourne	1910-11
		115	Adelaide	1910-11
		122*	Manchester	1912
1	Frank C.N.	152	Johannesburg	1921
1	Irvine B.L.	102	Pt. Elizabeth	1969
3	Lindsay D.T.	182	Johannesburg	1966
		137	Durban	1966
		131	Johannesburg	1966
2	McGlew D.J.	108	Johannesburg	1957
		105	Durban	1957
2	Nourse A.D.	231	Johannesburg	1935
		114	Cape Town	1949
1	Nourse A.W.	111	Johannesburg	1921
5	Pollock R.G.	122	Sydney	1963
		175	Adelaide	1963
		209	Cape Town	1966
		105	Pt. Elizabeth	1966
		274	Durban	1969
2	Richards B.A.	140	Durban	1969
		126	Pt. Elizabeth	1969
1	Rowan E.A.B.	143	Durban	1949
2	Sinclair J.H.	101	Johannesburg	1902
		104	Cape Town	1902
1	Snooke S.J.	103	Adelaide	1910-11
1	Viljoen K.G.	111	Melbourne	1931
2	Waite J.H.B.	115	Johannesburg	1957
		134	Durban	1957
2	Zulch J.W.	105	Adelaide	1910
		150	Sydney	1910

AUSTRALIA V WEST INDIES

	Captains					
Season	Australia	West Indies	T	A	WI	D
1930-31	W.M.Woodfull	G.C.Grant	5	4	1	0
1951-52	A.L.Hassett	J.D.C.Goddard	5	4	1	0
1954-55	I.W.Johnson	D.S.Atkinson	5	3	0	2
1960-61	R.Benaud	F.M.M.Worrell	5	2	1	2
1964-65	R.B.Simpson	G.S.Sobers	5	1	2	2
1968-69	W.M.Lawry	G.S.Sobers	5	3	1	1
1972-73	I.M.Chappell	R.B.Kanhai	5	2	0	3
1975-76	G.S.Chappell	C.H.Lloyd	6	5	1	0
1977-78	R.B.Simpson	A.I.Kallicharan	5	1	3	1
1979-80	G.S.Chappell	C.H. Lloyd	3	0	2	1
1981-82	G.S.Chappell	C.H.Lloyd	3	1	1	1
1983-84	K.J.Hughes	C.H.Lloyd	5	0	3	2
1984-85	A.R.Border	C.H.Lloyd	5	1	3	1
1988-89	A.R.Border	I.V.A.Richards	5	1	3	1
In Australia			42	21	14	7
In West Indies			25	7	8	10
Total			67	28	22	17

HIGHEST INNINGS TOTALS

For Australia in Australia: 619 at Sydney	1968-69
in West Indies 758-8 dec. at Kingston	1954-55
For West Indies in Australia : 616 at Adelaide	1968-69
in West Indies : 573 at Bridgetown	1964-65

LOWEST INNINGS TOTALS

For Australia in Australia: 76 at Perth	1984-85
in West Indies : 90 at Port-of-Spain	1977-78
For West Indies in Australia:78 at Sydney	1951-52
in West Indies: 109 at Georgetown	1972-73

INDIVIDUAL HUNDREDS (For Australia)

1	Archer R.G.	128	Kingston	1954-55
1	Benaud R.	121	Kingston	1954-55
1	Boon D.C.	149	Sydney	1988-89
1	Booth B.C.	117	Port-of-Spain	1964
2	Border A.R.	126	Adelaide	1981
		100*	Port-of-Spain	1983
2	Bradman D.G.	223	Brisbane	1930-31
		152	Melbourne	1930-31
5	Chappell G.S.	106	Bridgetown	1972
		223	Brisbane	1975
		109*	Brisbane	1975

The 1878 Australia[n]
cricket team.

		182*	Sydney	1975
		124	Brisbane	1979
5	Chappell I.M.	117	Brisbane	1968
		165	Melbourne	1968
		106*	Bridgetown	1972
		109	Georgetown	1972
		156	Perth	1975-76
1	Cosier G.J.	109	Melbourne	1975-76
2	Cowper R.M.	143	Port-of-Spain	1964-65
		102	Bridgetown	1964-65
1	Dyson J.	127*	Sydney	1981
3	Harvey R.N.	133	Kingston	1954
		133	Port-of-Spain	1954-55
		204	Kingston	1954-55
2	Hassett A.L.	132	Sydney	1951
		102	Melbourne	1951
1	Hilditch A.M.J.	113	Melbourne	1984
2	Hughes K.J.	130*	Brisbane	1979
		100*	Melbourne	1981-82
1	Jones D.M.	216	Adelaide	1930
1	Kippax A.F.	146	Adelaide	1930
4	Lawry W.M.	210	Bridgetown	1964
		105	Brisbane	1968
		205	Melbourne	1968
		151	Sydney	1968
1	Lindwall R.R.	118	Bridgetown	1954
1	McCosker R.B.	109*	Melbourne	1975
2	McDonald C.C.	110	Port-of-Spain	1954-55
		127	Kingston	1954-55
4	Miller K.R.	129	Sydney	1951
		147	Kingston	1954
		137	Bridgetown	1954
		109	Kingston	1954
1	Morris A.R.	111	Port-of-Spain	1954
1	O'Neill N.C.	181	Brisbane	1960-61
1	Phillips W.B.	120	Bridgetown	1983
2	Ponsford W.H.	183	Sydney	1930-31
		109	Brisbane	1930-31
4	Redpath I.R.	132	Sydney	1968
		102	Melbourne	1975
		103	Adelaide	1975
		101	Melbourne	1975
1	Serjeant C.S.	124	Georgetown	1977-78
1	Simpson R.B.	201	Bridgetown	1964
1	Stackpole K.R.	142	Kingston	1972
1	Toohey P.M.	122	Kingston	1977-78
1	Turner A.	136	Adelaide	1975
6	Walters K.D.	118	Sydney	1968
		110	Adelaide	1968
		242	Sydney	1968
		103	Sydney	1968

CLIVE LLOYD

		102*	Bridgetown	1972-73
		112	Port-of-Spain	1972-73
1	Wessels K.C.	173	Sydney	1984-85
2	Wood G.M.	126	Georgetown	1977-78
		111	Perth	1988

(For West Indies)

1	Alexander F.C.M.	108	Sydney	1960
1	Atkinson D.S.E.	219	Bridgetown	1954
3	Butcher B.F.	117	Port-of-Spain	1964-65
		101	Sydney	1968
		118	Adelaide	1968
1	Depeiza C.C.	122	Bridgetown	1954
2	Dujon P.J.L.	130	Port-of-Spain	1983-84
		139	Perth	1984
1	Foster M.L.C.	125	Kingston	1972
1	Fredericks R.C.	169	Perth	1975
6	Gomes H.A.	101	Georgetown	1977-78
		115	Kingston	1977-78
		126	Sydney	1981
		124	Adelaide	1981
		127	Perth	1984
		120*	Adelaide	1984
3	Greenidge C.G.	120*	Georgetown	1983
		127	Kingston	1983
		104	Adelaide	1988
4	Haynes D.L.	103*	Georgetown	1983
		145	Bridgetown	1983
		100	Perth	1988
		143	Sydney	1988
2	Headley G.A.	102*	Brisbane	1930-31
		105	Sydney	1930-31
1	Hunte C.C.	110	Melbourne	1960
4	Kallicharan A.I.	101	Brisbane	1975
		127	Port-of-Spain	1977
		126	Kingston	1977
		106	Adelaide	1979-80
5	Kanhai R.B.	117	Adelaide	1960
		115	Adelaide	1960
		129	Bridgetown	1964
		121	Port-of-Spain	1964
		105	Bridgetown	1972
6	Lloyd C.H.	129	Brisbane	1968
		178	Georgetown	1972
		149	Perth	1975
		102	Melbourne	1975
		121	Adelaide	1979-80
		114	Brisbane	1984
1	Martin F.R.	123*	Sydney	1930-31
2	Nurse S.M.	201	Bridgetown	1964

		137	Sydney	1968-69
5	Richards I.V.A.	101	Adelaide	1975
		140	Brisbane	1979-80
		178	St. John's	1983
		208	Melbourne	1984
		146	Perth	1988
5	Richardson R.B.	131*	Bridgetown	1983
		154	St. John's	1983
		138	Brisbane	1984
		122	Melbourne	1988
		106	Adelaide	1988
1	Rowe L.G.	107	Brisbane	1975
1	Smith O.G.	104	Kingston	1954-55
4	Sobers G.S.	132	Brisbane	1960
		168	Sydney	1960
		110	Adelaide	1968-69
		113	Sydney	1968-69
1	Stollmeyer J.B.	104	Sydney	1951
5	Walcott C.L.	108	Kingston	1954
		126	Port-of-Spain	1954
		110	Port-of-Spain	1954
		155	Kingston	1954
		110	Kingston	1954
1	Weekes E.D.	139	Port-of-Spain	1954
1	Williams A.B.	100	Georgetown	1977-78
1	Worrell F.M.M.	108	Melbourne	1951

AUSTRALIA V NEW ZEALAND

Captains

Season	Australia	New Zealand	T	A	NZ	D
1945-46	W.A.Brown	W.A.Hadlee	1	1	0	0
1973-74	I.M.Chappell	B.E.Congdon	3	2	0	1
1973-74	I.M.Chappell	B.E.Congdon	3	1	1	1
1976-77	G.S.Chappell	G.M.Turner	2	1	0	1
1980-81	G.S.Chappell	G.P.Howarth	3	2	0	1
1981-82	G.S.Chappell	G.P.Howarth	3	1	1	1
1985-86	A.R.Border	J.V.Coney	3	1	2	0
1985-86	A.R.Border	J.V.Coney	3	0	1	2
1987-88	A.R.Border	J.J.Crowe	3	1	0	2
In Australia			12	6	2	4
In New Zealand			12	4	3	5
Total			24	10	5	9

HIGHEST INNINGS TOTALS

For Australia in Australia : 496 at Adelaide 1987-88
in New Zealand : 552 at Christchurch 1976-77
For New Zealand in Australia: 553-7dec. at Brisbane 1985-86
in New Zealand : 484 at Wellington 1973-74

LOWEST INNINGS TOTALS

For Australia in Australia : 162 at Sydney 1973-74
in New Zealand : 103 at Auckland 1985-86
For New Zealand in Australia: 121 at Perth 1980-81
in New Zealand : 42 at Wellington 1945-46

INDIVIDUAL HUNDREDS (For Australia)

1	Boon D.C.	143	Brisbane	1987-88
4	Border A.R.	152*	Brisbane	1985
		140	Christchurch	1985
		114*	Christchurch	1985
		205	Adelaide	1987-88
3	Chappell G.S.	247*	Wellington	1973
		133	Wellington	1973
		176	Christchurch	1981
2	Chappel I.M.	145	Wellington	1973
		121	Wellington	1973
1	Gilmour G.J.	101	Christchurch	1976
1	Marsh G.R.	118	Auckland	1985
1	Marsh R.W.	132	Adelaide	1973
2	Matthews G.R.J.	115	Brisbane	1985
		130	Wellington	1985
1	Redpath I.R.	159*	Auckland	1973
1	Stackpole K.R.	122	Melbourne	1973-74
3	Walters K.D.	104*	Auckland	1973-74
		250	Christchurch	1976
		107	Melbourne	1980
2	Wood G.M.	111	Brisbane	1980
		100	Auckland	1981

(For New Zealand)

1	Coney J.V.	101*	Wellington	1985
2	Congdon B.E.	132	Wellington	1973
		107*	Christchurch	1976
3	Crowe M.D.	188	Brisbane	1985-86
		137	Christchurch	1985-86
		137	Adelaide	1987
1	Edgar B.A.	161	Auckland	1981
1	Hastings B.F.	101	Wellington	1973
1	Jones A.H.	150	Adelaide	1987
1	Morrison J.F.M.	117	Sydney	1973-74
1	Parker J.M.	108	Sydney	1973-74

1	Reid J.F.	108	Brisbane	1985
2	Turner G.M.	101	Christchurch	1973-74
		110*	Christchurch	1973-74
1	Wright J.G.	141	Christchurch	1981

AUSTRALIA V INDIA

Captains

Season	Australia	India	T	A	I	D
1947-48	D.G.Bradman	L.Amarnath	5	4	0	1
1956-57	I.W.Johnson	P.R.Umrigar	3	2	0	1
1959-60	R.Benaud	G.S.Ramchand	5	2	1	2
1964-65	R.B.Simpson	Pataudi jun.	3	1	1	1
1967-68	R.B.Simpson	Pataudi jun.	4	4	0	0
1969-70	W.M.Lawry	Pataudi jun.	5	3	1	1
1977-78	R.B.Simpson	B.S.Bedi	5	3	2	0
1979-80	K.J.Hughes	S.M.Gavaskar	6	0	2	4
1980-81	G.S.Chappell	S. M. Gavaskar	3	1	1	1
1985-86	A.R.Border	Kapil Dev	3	0	0	3
1986-87	A.R.Border	Kapil Dev	3	0	0	3
In Australia			20	12	3	5
In India			25	8	5	12
Total			45	20	8	17

HIGHEST INNINGS TOTALS

For Australia in Australia : 674 at Adelaide	1947-48
in India : 574-7 dec. at Madras	1986-87
For India in Australia: 600-4 dec. at Sydney	1985-86
in India 517-5 dec. at Bombay	1986-87

LOWEST INNINGS TOTALS

For Australia in Australia:83 at Melbourne	1980-81
in India:105 at Kanpur	1959-60
For India in Australia: 58 at Brisbane	1947-48
in India : 135 at Delhi	1959-60

INDIVIDUAL HUNDREDS (For Australia)

1	Barnes S.G.	112	Adelaide	1947
3	Boon D.C.	123	Adelaide	1985
		131	Sydney	1985
		122	Madras	1986-87
4	Border A.R.	162	Madras	1979
		124	Melbourne	1980
		163	Melbourne	1985

		106	Madras	1986-87
4	Bradman D.G.	185	Brisbane	1947
		127*	Melbourne	1947
		132	Melbourne	1947
		201	Adelaide	1947
1	Burke J.W.	161	Bombay	1956
1	Chappell G.S.	204	Sydney	1980
2	Chappell I.M.	151	Melbourne	1967-68
		138	Delhi	1969
2	Cowper R.M.	108	Adelaide	1967
		165	Sydney	1967
1	Favell L.E.	101	Madras	1959
4	Harvey R.N.	153	Melbourne	1947
		140	Bombay	1956
		114	Delhi	1959
		102	Bombay	1959
1	Hassett A.L.	198*	Adelaide	1947
2	Hughes K.J.	100	Madras	1979
		213	Adelaide	1980
1	Jones D.M.	210	Madras	1986-87
1	Lawry W.M.	100	Melbourne	1967
1	Mann A.L.	105	Perth	1977
1	Marsh G.R.	101	Bombay	1986-87
1	Matthews G.R.J.	100*	Melbourne	1985
1	Morris A.R.	100*	Melbourne	1947
2	O'Neill N.C.	163	Bombay	1959
		113	Calcutta	1959
1	Ritchie G.M.	128	Adelaide	1985-86
1	Sheahan A.P.	114	Kanpur	1969
4	Simpson R.B.	103	Adelaide	1967
		109	Melbourne	1967
		176	Perth	1977
		100	Adelaide	1977
1	Stackpole K.R.	103	Bombay	1969
1	Walters K.D.	102	Madras	1969
1	Wood G.M.	125	Adelaide	1981
2	Yallop G.N.	121	Adelaide	1977
		167	Calcutta	1979

(For India)

2	Amarnath M.	100	Perth	1977
		138	Sydney	1985
1	Contractor N.J.	108	Bombay	1959-60
8	Gavaskar S.M.	113	Brisbane	1977
		127	Perth	1977
		118	Melbourne	1977
		115	Delhi	1979
		123	Bombay	1979-80
		166*	Adelaide	1985
		172	Sydney	1985

Yashpal Sharma

YASHPAL SHARMA

		103	Bombay	1986-87
2	Hazare V.S.	116	Adelaide	1947
		145	Adelaide	1947
1	Jaisimha M.L.	101	Brisbane	1967
1	Kapil Dev	119	Madras	1986-87
1	Kirmani S.M.H.	101*	Bombay	1978
2	Mankad V.	116	Melbourne	1947
		111	Melbourne	1947
1	Nawab Pataudi jun.	128*	Madras	1964
1	Patil S.M.	174	Adelaide	1980-81
1	Phadkar D.G.	123	Adelaide	1947
1	Ramchand G.S.	109	Bombay	1956-57
1	Shastri R.J.	121*	Bombay	1986-87
1	Srikkant K.	116	Sydney	1985
2	Vengsarkar D.B.	112	Bangalore	1979
		164*	Bombay	1986-87
4	Vishwanath G.R.	137	Kanpur	1969
		161*	Bangalore	1979
		131	Delhi	1979
		114	Melbourne	1980
1	Yashpal Sharma	100*	Delhi	1979

AUSTRALIA V PAKISTAN

	Captains					
Season	Australia	Pakistan	T	A	P	D
1956-57	I.W.Johnson	A.H.Kardar	1	0	1	0
1959-60	R.Benaud	Fazal Mahmood	3	2	0	1
1964-65	R.B.Simpson	Hanif Mohammad	1	0	0	1
1964-65	R.B.Simpson	Hanif Mohammad	1	0	0	1
1972-73	I.M.Chappell	Intikhab Alam	3	3	0	0
1976-77	G.S.Chappell	M. Mohammad	3	1	1	1
1978-79	G.N.Yallop	M. Mohammad	2	1	1	0
1979-80	G.S.Chappell	Javed Miandad	3	0	1	2
1981-82	G.S.Chappell	Javed Miandad	3	2	1	0
1982-83	K.J.Hughes	Imran Khan	3	0	3	0
1983-84	K.J.Hughes	Imran Khan	5	2	0	3
1988-89	A.R.Border	Javed Miandad	3	0	1	2
In Pakistan			14	2	6	6
In Australia			17	9	3	5
Total			31	11	9	11

HIGHEST INNINGS TOTALS

For Australia in Australia : 585 at Adelaide	1972-73
in Pakistan: 617 at Faisalabad	1979-80
For Pakistan in Australia: 624 at Adelaide	1983-84
in Pakistan: 521-6 dec at Faisalabad	1982-83

LOWEST INNINGS TOTALS

For Australia in Australia :125 at Melbourne	1981-82
in Pakistan : 80 at Karachi	1956-57
For Pakistan in Australia : 62 at Perth	1981-82
In Pakistan : 134 at Dacca	1959-60

INDIVIDUAL HUNDREDS (For Australia)

1	Benaud J.	142	Melbourne	1972
6	Border A.R.	105	Melbourne	1978
		150*	Lahore	1979
		153	Lahore	1979
		118	Brisbane	1983-84
		117*	Adelaide	1983-84
		113*	Faisalabad	1988
6	Chappell G.S.	116*	Melbourne	1972
		121	Melbourne	1976
		235	Faisalabad	1979
		201	Brisbane	1981
		150*	Brisbane	1983
		182	Sydney	1983
1	Chappell I.M.	196	Adelaide	1972
1	Cosier G.J.	168	Melbourne	1976
1	Davis I.C.	105	Adelaide	1976
2	Hughes K.J.	106	Perth	1981
		106	Adelaide	1983
1	McCosker R.B.	105	Melbourne	1976
1	Marsh R.W.	118	Adelaide	1972
1	O'Neill N.C.	134	Lahore	1959-60
1	Phillips W.B.	159	Perth	1983
1	Redpath I.R.	135	Melbourne	1972
1	Ritchie G.M.	106*	Faisalabad	1982
1	Sheanhan A.P.	127	Melbourne	1972
2	Simpson R.B.	153	Karachi	1964
		115	Karachi	1964
1	Walters K.D.	107	Adelaide	1983
1	Wessels K.C.	179	Adelaide	1983
1	Wood G.M.	100	Melbourne	1981
3	Yallop G.N.	172	Faisalabad	1979
		141	Perth	1983
		268	Melbourne	1983

(For Pakistan)

3	Asif Iqbal	152*	Adelaide	1976
		120	Sydney	1976
		134*	Perth	1978
2	Hanif Mohammad	101*	Karachi	1959
		104	Melbourne	1964
1	Ijaz Ahmed	122	Faisalabad	1988-89
6	Javed Miandad	129*	Perth	1978

		106*	Faisalabad	1979
		138	Lahore	1982
		131	Adelaide	1983
		211	Karachi	1988-89
		107	Faisalabad	1988-89
1	Khalid Ibadulla	166	Karachi	1964
3	Majid Khan	158	Melbourne	1972
		108	Melbourne	1978
		110*	Lahore	1979
1	Mansoor Akhtar	111	Faisalabad	1982
3	Mohsin Khan	135	Lahore	1982
		149	Adelaide	1983
		152	Melbourne	1983
1	Mushtaq Mohamd.	121	Sydney	1972
1	Qasim Omar	113	Adelaide	1983
2	Sadiq Mohammad	137	Melbourne	1972
		105	Melbourne	1976
1	Saeed Ahmed	166	Lahore	1959
1	Taslim Arif	210*	Faisalabad	1979
2	Zaheer Abbas	101	Adelaide	1976
		126	Faisalabad	1982

AUSTRALIA V SRI LANKA

	Captains					
Season	**Australia**	**Sri Lanka**	**T**	**A**	**LS**	**D**
1982-83	G.S.Chappell	L.R.D.Mendis	1	1	0	0
1987-88	A.R.Border	R.S.Madugalle	1	1	0	0
Total			2	2	0	0.

INDIVIDUAL HUNDREDS (For Australia)

1	Hookes D.W.	143*	Kandy	1982
1	Jones D.M.	102	Perth	1987-88
1	Wessels K.C.	141	Kandy	1982

SOUTH AFRICA V NEW ZEALAND

	Captains					
Season	**South Africa**	**New Zealand**	**T**	**SA**	**NZ**	**D**
1931-32	H.B. Cameron	M.L.Page	2	2	0	0
1952-53	J.E.Cheetham	W.M. Wallace	2	1	0	1
1953-54	J.E.Cheetham	G.O.Rabone	5	4	0	1
1961-62	D.J.McGlew	J.R.Reid	5	2	2	1
1963-64	T.L.Goddard	J.R.Reid	3	0	0	3

QASIM OMAR

In New Zealand	7	3	0	4
In South Africa	10	6	2	2
Total	17	9	2	6

HIGHEST INNINGS TOTALS

For South Africa in South Africa: 464 at Johannesburg	1961
in New Zealand : 524 at Wellington	1952-53
For New Zealand in South Africa : 505 at Cape Town	1953-54
in New Zealand: 364 at Wellington	1931-32

LOWEST INNINGS TOTALS

For South Africa in South Africa: 148 at Johannesburg	1954
in New Zealand : 223 at Dunedin	1963-64
For New Zealand in South Africa: 79 at Johannesburg	1953-54
in New Zealand : 138 at Dunedin	1963-64

INDIVIDUAL HUNDREDS (For South Africa)

1	Balaskas X.C.	122*	Wellington	1931
1	Christy J.A.J.	103	Christchurch	1931
1	Endean W.R.	116	Auckland	1952
3	McGlew D.J.	255*	Wellington	1952
		127*	Durban	1961-62
		120	Johannesburg	1961-62
2	McLean R.A.	101	Durban	1953
		113	Cape Town	1961-62
1	Mitchell B.	113	Christchurch	1931
1	Murray A.R.A.	109	Wellington	1952
1	Waite J.H.B.	101	Johannesburg	1961-62

(For New Zealand)

1	Barton P.T.	109	Pt. Elizabeth	1961-62
1	Harris P.G.Z.	101	Cape Town	1961-62
1	Rabone G.O.	107	Durban	1953
2	Reid J.R.	135	Cape Town	1953
		142	Johannesburg	1961-62
1	Sinclair B.W.	138	Auckland	1963
1	Vivian H.G.	100	Wellington	1931

WEST INDIES V NEW ZEALAND

	Captains					
Season	West Indies	New Zealand	T	WI	NZ	D
1951-52	J.D.C. Goddard	B. Sutcliffe	2	1	0	1
1955-56	D.ST. E. Atkinson	J.R.Reid	4	3	1	0
1968-69	G.S Sobers	G.T.Dowling	3	1	1	1
1971-72	G.S.Sobers	G.T.Dowling	5	0	0	5
1979-80	C.H.Lloyd	G.P.Howarth	3	0	1	2
1984-85	I.V.A.Richards	G.P.Howarth	4	2	0	2
1986-87	I.V.A.Richards	J.V.Coney	3	1	1	1
In West Indies			9	2	0	7
In New Zealand			15	6	4	5
Total			24	8	4	12

HIGHEST INNINGS TOTALS

For West Indies in West Indies: 564-8 at Bridgetown	1972
in New Zealand :546-6 dec. at Auckland	1952
For New Zealand in West Indies:543-3dec.at Georgetown	1972
in New Zealand : 460 at Christchurch	1979-80

LOWEST INNINGS TOTALS

For West Indies in West Indies: 133 at Bridgetown	1971-72
in New Zealand: 77 at Auckland	1955-56
For New Zealand in West Indies: 94 at Bridgetown	1984-85
in New Zealand : 74 at Dunedin	1955-56

INDIVIDUAL HUNDREDS (By West Indies)

1	Carew M.C.	109	Auckland	1968
1	Davis C.A.	183	Bridgetown	1971-72
1	Fredericks	163	Kingston	1971-72
2	Greenidge C.G.	100	Port-of-Spain	1984
		213	Auckland	1986
3	Haynes D.L.	105	Dunedin	1979
		122	Christchurch	1979
		121	Wellington	1986
2	Kallicharan A.I.	100*	Georgetown	1971-72
		101	Port-of-Spain	1971-72
1	King C.L.	100*	Christchurch	1979
2	Nurse S.M.	168	Auckland	1968
		258	Christchurch	1968
1	Richards I.V.A.	105	Bridgetown	1984
1	Richardson R.B.	185	Georgetown	1984
3	Rowe L.G.	214	Kingston	1971-72
		100*	Kingston	1971-72
		100	Christchurch	1979

1	Sobers G.S.	142	Bridgetown	1971
1	Stollmeyer	152	Auckland	1951
1	Walcott C.L.	115	Auckland	1951
3	Weekes E.D.	123	Dunedin	1955
		103	Christchurch	1955
		156	Wellington	1955
1	Worrell F.M.M.	100	Auckland	1951

(By New Zealand)

1	Burgess M.G.	101	Kingston	1971-72
2	Congdon B.E.	166*	Port-of-Spain	1971-72
		126	Bridgetown	1971-72
1	Crowe J.J.	112	Kingston	1984
3	Crowe M.D.	188	Georgetown	1984
		119	Wellington	1986
		104	Auckland	1986
1	Edger B.A.	127	Auckland	1979
1	Hadlee R.J.	103	Christchurch	1979
2	Hastings B.F.	117*	Christchurch	1968
		105	Bridgetown	1971-72
1	Howarth G.P.	147	Christchurch	1979
1	Jarvis T.W.	182	Georgetown	1971-72
1	Taylor B.R.	124	Auckland	1968
2	Turner G.M.	223*	Kingston	1971-72
		259	Georgetown	1971-72
1	Wright J.G.	138	Wellington	1986

WEST INDIES V PAKISTAN

	Captains					
Season	**West Indies**	**Pakistan**	**T**	**WI**	**P**	**D**
1957-58	P.C.Alexander	A.H.Kardar	5	3	1	1
1958-59	F.C.M.Alexander	Fazal Mahmood	3	1	2	0
1974-75	C.H.Lloyd	Intikhab Alam	2	0	0	2
1976-77	C.H.Lloyd	M. Mohammad	5	2	1	2
1980-81	C.H.Lloyd	Javed Miandad	4	1	0	3
1986-87	I.V.A.Richards	Imran Khan	3	1	1	1
1987-88	I.V.A.Richards	Imran Khan	3	1	1	1
In West Indies			13	6	3	4
In Pakistan			12	3	3	6
Total			25	9	6	10

HIGHEST INNINGS TOTALS

For West Indies in West Indies: 790-3dec. at Kingston 1957
in Pakistan: 493 at Karachi 1974-75
For Pakistan in West Indies: 657-8 dec. at Bridgetown 1957

LOWEST INNINGS TOTALS

For West Indies in West Indies: 154 at Port-of-Spain	1977
in Pakistan: 53 at Faisalabad	1986-87
For Pakistan in West Indies: 106 at Bridgetown	1957-58
in Pakistan: 77 at Lahore	1986-87

INDIVIDUAL HUNDREDS (For West Indies)

1	Baichan L.	105*	Lahore	1974-75
1	Dujon P.J.L.	106*	Port-of-Spain	1987-88
1	Fredericks	120	Port-of-Spain	1976
1	Greenidge C.G.	100	Kingston	1976-77
3	Hunte C.C.	142	Bridgetown	1957
		260	Kingston	1957
		114	Georgetown	1957
1	Julien B.D.	101	Karachi	1974
1	Kallicharan A.I.	115	Karachi	1974
1	Kanhai R.B.	217	Lahore	1958
1	Lloyd C.H.	157	Bridgetown	1976
2	Richards I.V.A.	120*	Multan	1980
		123	Port-of-Spain	1987-88
1	Shillingford I.T.	120	Georgetown	1976
3	Sobers G.S.	365*	Kingston	1957
		125	Georgetown	1957
		109*	Georgetown	1957
1	Walcott C.L.	145	Georgetown	1957
1	Weekes E.D.	197	Bridgetown	1957

(For Pakistan)

1	Asif Iqbal	135	Kingston	1976
2	Hanif Mohammad	337	Bridgetown	1957
		103	Karachi	1958
1	Imtiaz Ahmed	122	Kingston	1957
1	Imran Khan	123	Lahore	1980-81
2	Javed Miandad	114	Georgetown	1987-88
		102	Port-of-Spain	1987-88
2	Majid Khan	100	Karachi	1974
		167	Georgetown	1976
2	M.Mohammad	123	Lahore	1974
		121	Port-of-Spain	1976
1	Saeed Ahmed	150	Georgetown	1957
2	Wasim Raja	107*	Karachi	1974
		117*	Bridgetown	1976
2	Wazir Mohammad	106	Kingston	1957
		189	Port-of-Spain	1957

S. M. GAVASKAR

WEST INDIES V INDIA

Season	Captains West Indies	India	T	WI	I	D
1948-49	J.D.C.Goddard	L.Amarnath	5	1	0	4
1952-53	J.B Stollmeyer	V.S.Hazare	5	1	0	4
1958-59	F.C.M.Alexander	Ghulam Ahmed	5	3	0	2
1961-62	F.M.M.Worrell	N.J.Contractor	5	5	0	0
1966-67	G.S.Sobers	Pataudi jun.	3	2	0	1
1970-71	G.S.Sobers	A.L.Wadekar	5	0	1	4
1974-75	C.H.Lloyd	Pataudi jun.	5	3	2	0
1975-76	C.H.Lloyd	B.S.Bedi	4	2	1	1
1978-79	A.I.Kallicharan	S.M.Gavaskar	6	0	1	5
1982-83	C.H.Lloyd	Kapil Dev	5	2	0	3
1983-84	C.H.Lloyd	Kapil Dev	6	3	0	3
1987-88	I.V.A.Richards	D.B.Vengsarkar	4	1	1	2
1988-89	I.V.A.Richards	D.B.Vengsarkar	4	3	0	1
In India			34	13	4	17
In West Indies			28	13	2	13
Total			62	26	6	30

HIGHEST INNINGS TOTALS

For West Indies in West Indies: 631-8 dec. at Kingston	1961
in India: 644-8 dec. at Delhi	1958-59
For India in West Indies: 469-7 at Port-of-Spain	1982-83
in India: 644 -7 dec. at Kanpur	1978-79

LOWEST INNINGS TOTALS

For West Indies in West Indies : 214 at Port-of-Spain	1970
in India : 127 at Delhi	1987-88
For India in West Indies: 97 at Kingston	1975-76
in India : 75 at Delhi	1987-88

INDIVIDUAL HUNDREDS (For West Indies)

1	Bacchus S.F.A.F.	250	Kanpur	1978
2	Butcher B.F.	103	Calcutta	1958
		142	Madras	1958
1	Christiani R.J.	107	Delhi	1948
2	Davis C.A.	125*	Georgetown	1970
		105	Port-of-Spain	1970
1	Dujon P.J.L.	110	St. John's	1982-83
2	Fredericks R.C.	100	Calcutta	1974
		104	Bombay	1974
1	Gomes H.A.	123	Port-of-Spain	1982-83
1	Gomez G.E.	101	Delhi	1948
5	Greenidge C.G.	107	Bangalore	1974

LOGIE & GOMES

		154*	St. John's	1982
		194	Kanpur	1983
		141	Calcutta	1987-88
		117	Bridgetown	1988-89
2	Haynes D.L.	136	St. John's	1982-83
		112*	Bridgetown	1988-89
1	Holt J.K.	123	Delhi	1958
1	Hooper C.L.	100*	Calcutta	1987-88
1	Hunte C.C.	101	Bombay	1966
3	Kallicharan A.I.	124	Bangalore	1974
		103*	Port-of-Spain	1975
		187	Bombay	1978
4	Kanhai R.B.	256	Calcutta	1958
		138	Kingston	1961
		139	Port-of-Spain	1961
		158*	Kingston	1970
7	Lloyd C.H.	163	Bangalore	1974
		242*	Bombay	1974
		102	Bridgetown	1975
		143	Port-of-Spain	1982
		106	St. John's	1982
		103	Delhi	1983
		161*	Calcutta	1983
2	Logie A.L.	130	Bridgetown	1982
		101	Calcutta	1987-88
1	McMorris E.D.A.	125	Kingston	1961
1	Pairaudeau B.H.	115	Port-of-Spain	1952
2	Rae A.F.	104	Bombay	1948
		109	Madras	1948
8	Richards I.V.A.	192*	Delhi	1974
		142	Bridgetown	1975
		130	Port-of-Spain	1975
		177	Port-of-Spain	1975
		109	Georgetown	1982
		120	Bombay	1982
		109*	Delhi	1987-88
		110	Kingston	1988-89
2	Richardson R.B.	194	Georgetown	1988-89
		156	Kingston	1988-89
1	Smith O.G.	100	Delhi	1958
8	Sobers G.S.	142	Bombay	1958
		198	Kanpur	1958
		106*	Calcutta	1958
		153	Kingston	1961
		104	Kingston	1961
		108*	Georgetown	1970
		178*	Bridgetown	1970
		132	Port-of-Spain	1970
1	Solomon J.S.	100*	Delhi	1958
2	Stollmeyer J.B.	160	Madras	1948
		104*	Port-of-Spain	1952

4	Walcott C.L.	152	Delhi	1948
		108	Calcutta	1948
		125	Georgetown	1952
		118	Kingston	1952
7	Weekes E.D.	128	Delhi	1948
		194	Bombay	1948
		162	Calcutta	1948
		101	Calcutta	1948
		207	Port-of-Spain	1952
		161	Port-of-Spain	1952
		109	Kingston	1952
1	Williams A.B.	111	Calcutta	1978
1	Worrell F.M.M.	237	Kingston	1952

(For India)

1	Adhikari H.R.	114*	Delhi	1948
3	Amarnath M.	101*	Kanpur	1978
		117	Port-of-Spain	1982
		116	St. John's	1982
1	Apte M.L.	163*	Port-of-Spain	1952

GAVASKAR & SRIKKANT

MOHINDER AMARNATH

3	Borde C.G.	109	Delhi	1958
		121	Bombay	1966
		125	Madras	1966
1	Durani S.A.	104	Port-of-Spain	1966
1	Engineer F.M.	109	Madras	1966
1	Gaekwad A.D.	102	Kanpur	1978
13	Gavaskar S.M.	116	Georgetown	1970
		117*	Bridgetown	1970
		124	Port-of-Spain	1970
		220	Port-of-Spain	1970
		156	Port-of-Spain	1975
		102	Port-of-Spain	1975
		205	Bombay	1978
		107	Calcutta	1978
		182*	Calcutta	1978
		120	Delhi	1978
		147*	Georgetown	1982
		121	Delhi	1983
		236*	Madras	1983
2	Hazare V.S.	134*	Bombay	1948
		122	Bombay	1948
3	Kapil Dev	126*	Delhi	1978
		100*	Port-of-Spain	1983
		109	Madras	1987-88
1	Manjrekar S.V.	108	Bridgetown	1988-89
1	Modi R.S.	112	Bombay	1948
1	Mushtaq Ali	106	Calcutta	1948
1	Patel B.P.	115*	Port-of-Spain	1975
1	Roy P.	150	Kingston	1952
3	Sardesai D.N.	212	Kingston	1970
		112	Port-of-Spain	1970
		150	Bridgetown	1970
2	Shastri R.J.	102	St. John's	1982
		107	Bridgetown	1988-89
1	Sidhu N.S.	116	Kingston	1988-89
1	Solkar E.D.	102	Bombay	1974
3	Umrigar P.R.	130	Port-of-Spain	1952
		117	Kingston	1952
		172*	Port-of-Spain	1961
6	Vengsarkar D.B.	157*	Calcutta	1978
		109	Delhi	1978
		159	Delhi	1983
		100	Bombay	1983
		102	Delhi	1987-88
		102*	Calcutta	1987-88
4	Vishwanath G.R.	139	Calcutta	1974
		112	Port-of-Spain	1975
		124	Madras	1978
		179	Kanpur	1978

NEW ZEALAND V INDIA

Season	New Zealand	India	T	NZ	I	D
	Captains					
1955-56	H.B.Cave	P.R.Umrigar	5	0	2	3
1964-65	J.R.Reid	Pataudi jun.	4	0	1	3
1967-68	G.T.Dowling	Pataudi jun.	4	1	3	0
1969-70	G.T.Dowling	Pataudi jun.	3	1	1	1
1975-76	G.M.Turner	B.S.Bedi	3	1	1	1
1976-77	G.M.Turner	B.S.Bedi	3	0	2	1
1980-81	G.P.Howarth	S.M.Gavaskar	3	1	0	2
1988-89	J.G.Wright	D.B.Vengsarkar	3	1	2	0
In New Zealand			10	3	4	3
In India			18	2	8	8
Total			28	5	12	11

HIGHEST INNINGS TOTALS

For New Zealand in New Zealand : 502 at Christchurch	1967
in India 462-9dec. at Calcutta	1964-65
For India in New Zealand : 414 at Auckland	1975-76
in India : 537-3dec. at Madras	1955-56

LOWEST INNINGS TOTALS

For New Zealand in New Zealand : 100 at Wellington	1980-81
in India: 124 at Hyderabad	1988-89
For India in New Zealand: 81 at Wellington	1975-76
in India: 88 at Bombay	1964-65

INDIVIDUAL HUNDREDS (For New Zealand)

3	Dowling G.T.	120	Bombay	1964
		143	Dunedin	1967
		239	Christchurch	1967
1	Guy J.W.	102	Hyderabad	1955
1	Howarth G.P.	137*	Wellington	1980
1	Parker J.M.	104	Bombay	1976
1	Reid J.F.	123*	Christchurch	1980
2	Reid J.R.	119*	Delhi	1955
		120	Calcutta	1955
3	Sutcliffe B.	137*	Hyderabad	1955
		230*	Delhi	1955
		151*	Calcutta	1964
1	Taylor B.R.	105	Calcutta	1964
2	Turner G.M.	117	Christchurch	1975
		113	Kanpur	1976
1	Wright J.G.	110	Auckland	1980

(For India)

1	Amarnath S.	124	Auckland	1975
1	Borde C.G.	109	Bombay	1964
2	Gavaskar S.M.	116	Auckland	1975
		119	Bombay	1976
1	Kripal Singh A.G	100*	Hyderabad	1955
3	Manjrekar V.L.	118	Hyderabad	1955
		177	Delhi	1955
		102*	Madras	1964
2	Mankad V.	223	Bombay	1955
		231	Madras	1955
2	Nawab Pataudi jun.	153	Calcutta	1964
		113	Delhi	1964
1	Ramchand G.S.	106*	Calcutta	1955
2	Pankaj Roy	100	Calcutta	1955
		173	Madras	1955
2	Sardesai D.N.	200*	Bombay	1964
		106	Delhi	1964
1	Sidhu N.S.	116	Bangalore	1988-89
1	Umrigar P.R.	223	Hyderabad	1955
1	Vishwanath G.R.	103*	Kanpur	1976
1	Wadekar A.L.	143	Wellington	1967

NEW ZEALAND V SRI LANKA

Captains

Season	New Zealand	Sri Lanka	T	NZ	SL	D
1982-83	G.P.Howarth	D.S.de Silva	2	2	0	0
1983-84	G.P.Howarth	L.R.D.Mendis	3	2	0	1
1986-87	J.J.Crowe	L.R.D.Mendis	1	0	0	1
Totals			6	4	0	2

HIGHEST INNINGS TOTALS

For New Zealand :459 at Colombo 1983-84
For Sri Lanka : 397-9dec. at Colombo 1986-87

LOWEST INNINGS TOTALS

For New Zealand : 198 at Colombo 1983-84
For Sri Lanka : 93 at Wellington 1982-83

INDIVIDUAL HUNDREDS (For New Zealand)

1	Crowe J.J.	120*	Colombo	1986
1	Hadlee R.J.	151*	Colombo	1986
1	Reid J.F.	180	Colombo	1983

(For Sri Lanka)

1	Dias R.L.	108	Colombo	1983
1	Kuruppu D.S.B.P.	201	Colombo	1986

NEW ZEALAND V PAKISTAN

	Captains					
Season	**New Zealand**	**Pakistan**	**T**	**NZ**	**P**	**D**
1955-56	H.B.Cave	A.H.Kardar	3	0	2	1
1964-65	J.R.Reid	Hanif Mohammad	3	0	0	3
1964-65	J.R.Reid	Hanif Mohammad	3	0	2	1
1969-70	G.T.Dowling	Intikhab Alam	3	1	0	2
1972-73	B.E.Congdon	Intikhab Alam	3	0	1	2
1976-77	G.M.Turner	M. Mohammad	3	0	2	1
1978-79	M.G.Burgess	M. Mohammad	3	0	1	2
1984-85	J.V.Coney	Zaheer Abbas	3	0	2	1
1984-85	G.P.Howarth	Javed Miandad	3	2	0	1
1988-89	J.G.Wright	Imran Khan	2	0	0	2
In New Zealand			14	2	2	10
In Pakistan			15	1	8	6
Total			29	3	10	16

HIGHEST INNINGS TOTALS

For New Zealand in New Zealand : 492 at Wellington	1984
in Pakistan : 482-6 dec. at Lahore	1964-65
For Pakistan in New Zealand : 616-5dec. at Auckland	1989
in Pakistan : 565-9dec. at Karachi	1976-77

LOWEST INNINGS TOTALS

For New Zealand in New Zealand: 156 at Dunedin	1972-73
in Pakistan: 70 at Dacca	1955-56
For Pakistan in New Zealand: 169 at Auckland	1984-85
in Pakistan: 114 at Lahore	1969-70

INDIVIDUAL HUNDREDS (For New Zealand)

2	Burgess M.G.	119*	Dacca	1969
		111	Lahore	1976
1	Coney J.V.	111*	Dunedin	1984
1	Crowe M.D.	174	Wellington	1988-89
1	Edger B.A.	129	Christchurch	1978
1	Hastings B.F.	110	Auckland	1972
1	Howarth G.P.	114	Napier	1978
1	Lees W.K.	152	Karachi	1976

1	McGregor S.N.	111	Lahore	1955
1	Redmond R.E.	107	Auckland	1972
3	Reid J.F.	106	Hyderabad	1984
		148	Wellington	1984
		158*	Auckland	1984
1	Reid J.R.	128	Karachi	1964
1	Sinclair B.W.	130	Lahore	1964
1	Turner G.M.	110	Dacca	1969
1	Wright J.G.	107	Karachi	1984

(For Pakistan)

3	Asif Iqbal	175	Dunedin	1972
		166	Lahore	1976
		104	Napier	1978
3	Hanif Mohamd.	103	Dacca	1955
		100*	Christchurch	1964
		203*	Lahore	1964
1	Imtiaz Ahmed	209	Lahore	1955
7	Javed Miandad	163	Lahore	1976
		206	Karachi	1976
		160*	Christchurch	1978
		104	Hyderabad	1984
		103*	Hyderabad	1984
		118	Wellington	1988
		271	Auckland	1988
3	Majid Khan	110	Auckland	1972
		112	Karachi	1976
		119*	Napier	1978
1	Mohammad Ilyas	126	Karachi	1964
1	Mudassar Nazar	106	Hyderabad	1984
3	Mushtaq Mohamd.	201	Dunedin	1972
		101	Hyderabad	1976
		107	Karachi	1976
2	Sadiq Mohamd.	166	Wellington	1972
		103*	Hyderabad	1976
1	Saeed Ahmed	172	Karachi	1964
1	Salim Malik	119*	Karachi	1964
2	Shoaib Mohamd.	163	Wellington	1988
		112	Auckland	1988
1	Waqar Hassan	189	Lahore	1955
1	Zaheer Abbas	135	Auckland	1978

INDIA V PAKISTAN

Captains

Season	India	Pakistan	T	I	P	D
1952-53	L.Amarnath	A.H.Kardar	5	2	1	2
1954-55	V.Mankad	A.H.Kardar	5	0	0	5

IMRAN KHAN

1960-61	N.J.Contractor	Fazal Mahmood	5	0	0	5
1978-79	B.S.Bedi	M. Mohammad	3	0	2	1
1979-80	S.M.Gavaskar	Asif Iqbal	6	2	0	4
1982-83	S.M.Gavaskar	Imran Khan	6	0	3	3
1983-84	Kapil Dev	Zaheer Abbas	3	0	0	3
1984-85	S.M.Gavaskar	Zaheer Abbas	2	0	0	2
1986-87	Kapil Dev	Imran Khan	5	0	1	4
In India			24	4	2	18
In Pakistan			16	0	5	11
Total			40	4	7	29

HIGHEST INNINGS TOTALS

For India in India: 539-9 dec. at Madras	1960-61
in Pakistan : 500 at Faisalabad	1984-85
For Pakistan in India: 487-9 dec. at Madras	1986-87
in Pakistan : 674-6 at Faisalabad	1984-85

LOWEST INNINGS TOTALS

For India in India: 106 at Lucknow	1952-53
in Pakistan: 145 at Karachi	1954-55
For Pakistan in India: 116 at Bangalore	1986-87
in Pakistan: 158 at Dacca	1954-55

INDIVIDUAL HUNDREDS (For India)

4	Amarnath M.	109*	Lahore	1982-83
		120	Lahore	1982-83
		103*	Karachi	1982-83
		101*	Lahore	1984
2	Azharuddin M.	141	Calcutta	1986
		110	Jaipur	1986
1	Borde C.G.	177*	Madras	1960
1	Gaekwad A.D.	201	Jullundur	1983
5	Gavaskar S.M.	111	Karachi	1978
		137	Karachi	1978
		166	Madras	1979
		127*	Faisalabad	1982-83
		103*	Bangalore	1983
1	Hazare V.S.	146*	Bombay	1952
1	Patil S.M.	127	Faisalabad	1984
3	Shastri R.J.	128	Karachi	1982-83
		139	Faisalabad	1984
		125	Jaipur	1986
1	Shodhan R.H.	110	Calcutta	1952
1	Srikkant K.	123	Madras	1986
5	Umrigar P.R.	102	Bombay	1952

		108	Peshawar	1954
		115	Kanpur	1960
		117	Madras	1960
		112	Delhi	1960
2	Vengsarkar D.B.	146*	Delhi	1979
		109	Ahmedabad	1986
1	Vishwanath G.R.	145	Faisalabad	1978

(For Pakistan)

1	Alim-ud-Din	103*	Karachi	1954
1	Asif Iqbal	104	Faisalabad	1978
2	Hanif Mohammad	142	Bahawalpur	1954
		160	Bombay	1960
1	Ijaj Faqih	105	Ahmedabad	1986
1	Imtiaz Ahmed	135	Madras	1960
2	Imran Khan	117	Faisalabad	1982-83
		135*	Madras	1986
4	Javed Miandad	154*	Faisalabad	1978
		100	Karachi	1978
		126	Faisalabad	1982-83
		280*	Hyderabad	1982-83
1	Mohsin Khan	101*	Lahore	1982-83
6	Mudassar Nazar	126	Bangalore	1979
		119	Karachi	1982-83
		231	Hyderabad	1982-83
		152*	Lahore	1982-83
		152	Karachi	1982-83
		199	Faisalabad	1984
1	Mushtaq Mohamd.	101	Delhi	1960
1	Nazar Mohamd.	124*	Lucknow	1952
1	Qasim Omar	210	Faisalabad	1984
1	Ramiz Raja	114	Jaipur	1986
2	Saeed Ahmed	121	Bombay	1960
		103	Madras	1960
2	Salim Malik	107	Faisalabad	1982-83
		102*	Faisalabad	1984
1	Shoaib Mohamd.	101	Madras	1986
1	Wasim Raja	125	Jullundur	1983
6	Zaheer Abbas	176	Faisalabad	1978
		235*	Lahore	1978
		215	Lahore	1982-83
		186	Karachi	1982-83
		168	Faisalabad	1982-83
		168*	Lahore	1984

PAKISTAN V SRI LANKA

Captains

Season	Pakistan	Sri Lanka	T	P	SL	D
1981-82	Javed Miandad	B.Warnapura	3	2	0	1
1985-86	Javed Miandad	L.R.D.Mendis	3	2	0	1
1985-86	Imran Khan	L.R.D.Mendis	3	1	1	1
Total			9	5	1	3

HIGHEST INNINGS TOTALS

For Pakistan : 555-3 at Faisalabad 1985-86
For Sri Lanka: 479 at Faisalabad 1985-86

LOWEST INNINGS TOTALS

For Pakistan : 132 at Colombo 1985-86
For Sri Lanka: 101 at Kandy 1985-86

INDIVIDUAL HUNDREDS (For Pakistan)

1	Haroon Rashid	153	Karachi	1981
1	Javed Miandad	203*	Faisalabad	1985
1	Mohsin Khan	129	Lahore	1981
1	Qasim Omar	206	Faisalabad	1985-86
1	Ramiz Raja	122	Colombo	1985-86
1	Salim Malik	100*	Karachi	1981
1	Zaheer Abbas	134	Lahore	1981

(For Sri Lanka)

2	De Silva P.A.	122	Faisalabad	1985-86
		105	Karachi	1985-86
1	Dias R.L.	109	Lahore	1981
1	Gurusinha A.P.	116*	Colombo	1985-86
1	Ranatunga A.	135*	Colombo	1985-86
1	Wettimuny S.	157	Faisalabad	1981

INDIA V SRI LANKA

Captains

Season	India	Sri Lanka	T	I	SL	D
1982-83	S.M.Gavaskar	B.Warnapura	1	0	0	1
1985-86	Kapil Dev	L.R.D.Mendis	3	0	1	2
1986-87	Kapil Dev	L.R.D.Mendis	3	2	0	1
Total			7	2	1	4

HIGHEST INNINGS TOTALS

For India: 676 - 7 dec. at Kanpur	1986-87
For Sri Lanka 420 at Kanpur	1986-87

LOWEST INNINGS TOTALS

For India : 198 at Colombo	1985-86
For Sri Lanka: 141 at Nagpur	1986-87

INDIVIDUAL HUNDREDS (For India)

2	Amarnath M.	116*	Kandy	1985
		131	Nagpur	1986-87
1	Azharuddin M.	199	Kanpur	1986-87
2	Gavaskar S.M.	155	Madras	1982
		176	Kanpur	1986-87
1	Kapil Dev	163	Kanpur	1986-87
1	Patil S.M.	114	Madras	1982
2	Vengsarkar D.B.	153	Nagpur	1986
		166	Cuttuck	1986

(For Sri Lanka)

1	Dias R.L.	106	Kandy	1985
1	Madugalle R.S.	103	Colombo	1985
3	Mendis L.R.D.	105	Madras	1982
		105	Madras	1982
		124	Kandy	1985
1	Ranatunga A.	111	Colombo	1985
1	Silva S.A.R.	111	Colombo	1985

INDIA IN ONE DAY INTERNATIONALS

SUMMARY OF RESULTS

Season	Against	M	W	L	Abd
1974	England	2	-	2	-
1975	England	1	-	1	-
	East Africa	1	1	-	-
	New Zealand	1	-	1	-
1975-76	New Zealand	2	-	2	-
1978-79	Pakistan	3	1	2	-
1979	West Indies	1	-	1	-
	New Zealand	1	-	1	-
	Sri Lanka	1	-	1	-
1980-81	Australia	5	1	4	-
	New Zealand	5	2	3	-
1980-81	New Zealand	2	-	2	-
1981-82	England	3	2	1	-
1982	England	3	2	1	-
1982-83	Sri Lanka	3	3	-	-
	Pakistan	4	1	3	-
	West Indies	3	1	2	-
1983	West Indies	3	2	1	-
	Zimbabwe	2	2	-	-
	Australia	2	1	1	-
	England	1	1	-	-
1983-84	Pakistan	2	2	-	-
	West Indies	5	-	5	-
	Sri Lanka	1	1	-	-
	Pakistan	1	1	-	-
1984-85	Australia	5	-	3	2
	Pakistan	2	-	1	1
	England	5	1	4	-
	Pakistan	2	2	-	-
	England	1	1	-	-
	Australia	1	1	-	-
	New Zealand	1	1	-	-
1984-85	Pakistan	1	1	-	-
	Australia	1	1	-	-
1985-86	Sri Lanka	3	1	1	1
	West Indies	1	-	1	-
	Pakistan	1	-	1	-
	Australia	7	2	5	-
	New Zealand	5	3	2	-
	New Zealand	1	1	-	-
	Sri Lanka	1	1	-	-
	Pakistan	1	-	1	-
1986	England	2	1	1	-

1986-87	Australia	6	3	2	1
	Sri Lanka	1	1	-	-
	West Indies	1	-	1	-
	Pakistan	1	-	1	-
	Sri Lanka	5	4	1	-
	Pakistan	6	1	5	-
	England	1	1	-	-
	Australia	1	1	-	-
	Pakistan	1	-	1	-
1987-88	Australia	2	1	1	-
	New Zealand	2	2	-	-
	Zimbabwe	2	2	-	-
	England	1	-	1	-
1987-88	West Indies	8	1	7	-
	New Zealand	2	2	-	-
	Sri Lanka	1	1	-	-
1988-89	West Indies	2	1	1	-
	Pakistan	1	-	1	-
	Sri Lanka	2	1	1	-
	Pakistan	1	1	-	-
	Bangladesh	1	1	-	-
	New Zealand	4	4	-	-
	West Indies	5	-	5	-
1989	Pakistan	2	-	2	-
	West Indies	2	1	1	-

TEAM RECORDS

HIGHEST TOTALS BY A TEAM

By India

299-4 in 40 overs v Sri Lanka	1986-87
289-6 in 50 overs v Australia	1987-88
282 -5 in 47 overs v West Indies	1982-83
282-8 in 47.1 overs v New Zealand	1988-89
281-4 in 40.5 overs v Sri Lanka	1982-83

Against India

334-4 in 60 overs by England	1975
334-4 in 60 overs by West Indies	1983-84
320-9 in 60 overs by Australia	1983
292-6 in 50 overs by Australia	1985-86
289-7 in 40 overs by Sri Lanka	1986-87
286-6 in 44 overs by Pakistan	1986-87
282-9 in 60 overs by West Indies	1983

LOWEST TOTALS BY A TEAM

By India

63 in 25.5 overs v Australia	1980-81
78 in 24.1 overs v Sri Lanka	1986-87
79 in 34.2 overs v Pakistan	1978-79
112-9 in 34.2 overs v New Zealand	1980-81
113 in 44.2 overs v New Zealand	1985-86
120-9 in 42.4 overs v Pakistan	1986-87
125 in 42.4 overs v Pakistan	1984-85

Against India

87 in 32.5 overs by Pakistan	1984-85
96 in 41 overs by Sri Lanka	1983-84
99-8 in 45 overs by Bangladesh	1988-89
120 in 55.3 overs by East Africa	1975
129 in 38.2 overs by Australia	1983

HIGHEST MATCH AGGREGATES

588-11 in 80 overs , India (299),Sri Lanka(289)	1986-87
562-13 in 90 overs West Indies (333), India (229)	1983
560-11 in 97.1 overs, New Zealand (278),India (282)	1988
558-12 in 90.5 overs,Sri Lanka (277),India (281)	1982-83
539-16 in 99.5 overs, Australia (270), India (269)	1987-88
537-14 in 94 overs ,India (282), West Indies(255)	1982-83
531-16 in 105 overs,India (265), England (266)	1974
531-15 in 88 overs,Pakistan(286), India (245)	1986-87

LOWEST MATCH AGGREGATES

127-11in 46.5 overs, India (63), Australia (64)	1981-82
162-12 in 51.1 overs India(79),Pakistan (83)	1978-79
193-10 in 62.4 overs, Sri Lanka (96),India (97)	1983-84
199-10 in 71 overs,Bangladesh (99), India (100)	1988-89

LARGEST MARGINS OF VICTORY

For India

10 wkts v East Africa	1975
10 wkts v Sri Lanka	1983-84
9 wkts v New Zealand	1987-88

Against India

10 wkts by New Zealand	1980-81
9 wkts by New Zealand	1975-76
9 wkts by West Indies	1979
9 wkts by Australia	1980-81
9 wkts by Australia	1980-81
9 wkts by England	1982
9 wkts by West Indies	1987-88

NARROWEST MARGINS OF VICTORY

By India

2 wkts v Sri Lanka	1985-86
2 wkts v New Zealand	1988-89
4 runs v Pakistan	1978-79

Against India

1 run by Australia	1987-88
2 runs by West Indies	1987-88
7 runs by England	1984-85
10 runs by West Indies	1987-88
1 wkt by Pakistan	1985-86
2 wkts by Pakistan	1986-87

INDIVIDUAL RECORDS - BATTING

HUNDREDS

For India

Kapil Dev	175*	v Zimbabwe	1983
R.Shastri	102	v Australia	1984-85
	102	v England	1984-85
D.Vengsarkar	105	v England	1984-85
K.Srikkant	102	v Australia	1986-87
	123	v Pakistan	1986-87
	101	v West Indies	1987-88
	112	v West Indies	1988-89
R.Lamba	102	v Australia	1986-87
M.Azharuddin	108*	v Sri Lanka	1986-87
	108*	v New Zealand	1988-89
M.Prabhakar	106	v Pakistan	1986-87
S.M.Gavaskar	103*	v New Zealand	1987-88
M.Amarnath	100*	v West Indies	1987-88
	102*	v New Zealand	1987-88
Chetan Sharma	101	v England	1989

Against India

For England (3)

D.L.Amiss	127	1975
M.W.Gatting	115*	1984-85
G.A.Gooch	115	1987-88

For Australia (7)

A.R.Border	105	1980-81
T.M.Chappell	110	1983
K.C.Wessels	107	1984-85
G.R.Marsh	123	1985-86
	104	1986-87

	110	1987-88
D.C.Boon	111	1986-87

For West Indies

I.V.A.Richards	119	1983
	149	1983-84
	110	1987-88
G.Greenidge	106*	1979
	115	1983-84
C.L.Hooper	113*	1987-88
P.V.Simmons	104*	1987-88
D.L.Haynes	117*	1988-89
	152*	1988-89
G.Greenidge	117	1988-89

For Pakistan

Zaheer Abbas	118	1982-83
	105	1982-83
	113	1982-83
Javed Miandad	106*	1982-83
	119*	1982-83
	116*	1985-86
Mohsin Khan	117*	1982-83
Salim Malik	101	1988-89

SRIKKANT & KAPIL DEV

D. VENGSARKAR

RICHARD HADLEE

For New Zealand

G.Turner	114*	1975

For Sri Lanka

R.L.Dias	121	1982-83
	102	1982-83

BOWLING

FIVE OR MORE WICKETS IN A MATCH

For India

5-43	Kapil Dev	v Australia	1983
5-26	S.K.Sharma	v West Indies	1988-89
5-21	Arshad Ayub	v Pakistan	1988-89
5-27	K.Srikkant	v New Zealand	1988-89
5-32	K.Srikkant	v New Zealand	1988-89

Against India

6-14	Imran Khan	for Pakistan	1984-85
6-39	K.H.MacLeay	for Australia	1983
6-29	B.P.Patterson	for West Indies	1987
5-23	R.O.Collinge	for New Zealand	1975
5-15	G.S.Chappell	for Australia	1980-81
5-32	R.J.Hadlee	for New Zealand	1980
5-53	B.A.Reid	for Australia	1985
5-57	G.F.Labrooy	for Sri Lanka	1986-87

MOST ECONOMICAL BOWLING

For India

O	M	R	W			
6	3	7	0	Kapil Dev	v New Zealand	1985-86
7	4	4	0	Kapil Dev	v West Indies	1988-89
8	2	11	1	Madan Lal	v Sri Lanka	1983-84
9	6	9	3	Maninder Singh	v Bangladesh	1988-89
12	8	6	1	B.S.Bedi	v East Africa	1975

Against India

5	2	3	1	D.K.Lillee	for Australia	1980-81
7.2	4	4	2	Wasim Akram	for Pakistan	1986-87
8	4	7	3	C.G.Rackemann	for Australia	1984-85
9	4	11	2	J.Garner	for West Indies	1985-86

MADAN LAL

INDIVIDUAL RECORDS - WICKET KEEPING

MOST DISMISSALS BY A WICKET-KEEPER IN A MATCH

For India

5 (5ct)	S.M.H.Kirmani	v Zimbabwe	1983
5(3ct+2st)	S.Vishwanath	v England	1984-85
5(3ct +2st)	K.S.More	v New Zealand	1987
4 (2ct+2st)	C.S.Pandit	v Australia	1986-87
4 (2ct+2st)	K.S.More	v Zimbabwe	1987-88

Against India

4 (4ct)	R.W.Marsh	for Australia	1980-81
4 (4ct)	T.W.Taylor	for England	1982
4 (4ct)	D.L.Houghton	for Zimbabwe	1983
4(3ct+4st)	W.B.Phillips	for Australia	1984-85
4(3ct+1st)	P.J.Dujon	for West Indies	1987-88

FIELDING

MOST CATCHES BY A FIELDSMAN IN A MATCH

For India

4	S.M.Gavaskar	v Pakistan	Leeds	1984-85
3	D.B.Vengsarkar	v New Zealand	Perth	1980-81
3	D.B.Vengsarkar	v New Zealand	Hamilton	1980-81
3	L.Sivaramakrishnan	v Pakistan	Melbourne	1984-85
3	S.M.Gavaskar	v New Zealand	Perth	1985-86
3	M.A.Azharuddin	v England	The Oval	1986
3	Kapil Dev	v England	The Oval	1986

Against India

3	J.M.Parker	for New Zealand	1980-81
3	I.V.A.Richards	for West Indies	1982-83
3	A.R.Border	for Australia	1985-86

LIMITED OVERS INTERNATIONAL RECORDS

3000 OR MORE RUNS

		M	I	NO	R	HI	100s	Av.
I.V.A.Richards	(West Indies)	165	148	23	6200	189*	49.60	11
D.L.Haynes	(West Indies)	158	157	20	5883	152*	42.94	14
Javed Miandad	(Pakistan)	145	140	31	5060	119*	46.42	6
A.R.Border	(Australia)	182	171	23	4572	127*	30.89	3
C.G.Greenidge	(West Indies)	116	115	11	4868	133*	46.80	11
S.M.Gavaskar	(India)	107	102	14	3092	133*	35.13	1

Leading run scores for other countries

J.G.Wright	(New Zealand)	119	118	1	3180	101	27.17	1
D.I.Gower	(England)	105	102	8	3030	158	32.23	7
A.Ranatunge	(Sri Lanka)	71	68	11	1642	86*	28.8	-
D.B.Vengsarkar	(India)	114	108	18	3287	105	36.52	1

HIGHEST INDIVIDUAL SCORES

189*	I.V.A.Richards	West Indies v England	1984
181	I.V.A.Richards	West Indies v Sri Lanka	1987
175*	Kapil Dev	India v Zimbabwe	1983
171*	G.M.Turner	New Zealand v East Africa	1975
158	D.I.Gower	England v New Zealand	1982-83

SEVEN OR MORE HUNDREDS

Total		
11	I.V.A. Richards	(West Indies)
14	D.L.Haynes	(West Indies)
11	C.G.Greenidge	(West Indies)
7	D.I.Gower	(England)
7	Zaheer Abbas	(Pakistan)

HIGHEST PARTNERSHIP FOR EACH WICKET

212	for 1st	G.R.Marsh (104)	and D.C.Boon (111),Australia v India	1986-87
221	for 2nd	C.G.Greenidge (115)	and I.V.A.Richards (149),West Indies v India	1983-84
224*	for 3rd	D.M.Jones (99*)	and A.R.Border (118*),Australia v Sri Lanka	1984-85
173	for 4th	D.M.Jones (121)	and S.R.Waugh (82),Australia v Pakistan	1986-87
152	for 5th	I.V.A.Richards (98)	and C.H.Lloyd (89*),West Indies v Sri Lanka	1984-85
144	for 6th	Imran Khan (102*)	and Shahid Mahboob (77),Pakistan v Sri Lanka	1983
115	for 7th	P.J.L.Dujon (57*)	and M.D.Marshall (66),West Indies v Pakistan	1986-87
117	for 8th	D.L.Houghton (141)	and I.P.Butchart (54),Zimbabwe v New Zealand	1987
126*	for 9th	Kapil Dev (175*)	and S.M.H.Kirmani (24*),India v Zimbabwe	1983
106	for 10th	I.V.A.Richards (189*)	and M.A.Holding (12*),West Indies v England	1984

100 OR MORE WICKETS

	M	Balls	R	W	Av.
J.Garner (West Indies)	98	5,330	2,752	146	18.84
Kapil Dev (India)	137	6,954	4,297	160	26.85
R.J.Hadlee (New Zealand)	108	5,777	3,167	148	21.39
M.A.Holding (West Indies)	102	5,473	3,034	142	21.36
E.J.Chatfield (New Zealand)	113	6,023	3,600	136	26.47
Imran Khan (Pakistan)	121	5,238	3,317	140	23.69
I.T.Botham (England)	95	5,076	3,398	116	29.29
M.D.Marshall (West Indies)	100	5,315	2,979	127	23.45
Mudassar Nazar (Pakistan)	121	4,855	3,432	111	30.91
D.K.Lillee (Australia)	63	3,593	2,145	103	20.82
R.J.Shastri (India)	109	5,192	3,599	103	34.94

BEST BOWLING FOR EACH COUNTRY

7-15 W.W.Davis West Indies v Australia	1983
6-14 G.J.Gilmour Australia v England	1975
6-14 Imran Khan Pakistan v India	1984-85
5-20 V.J.Marks England v New Zealand	1983-84
5-23 R.O.Collinge New Zealand v India	1975-76
5-26 U.S.H.Karnain Sri Lanka v New Zealand	1983-84
5-27 K.Srikkanth India v New Zealand	1988-89

HAT-TRICKS

Jalal-ud-Din Pakistan v Australia	1982-83
B.A.Reid Australia v New Zealand	1985-86
Chetan Sharma India v New Zealand	1987-88

MOST DISMISSALS IN A MATCH

5 (all ct.) R.W.Marsh Australia v England	1981
5 (all ct.) R.G.Dealwis Sri Lanka v Australia	1982-83
5 (all ct.) S.M.H.Kirmani India v Zimbabwe	1983
5 (3ct,2st) S.Vishwanath India v England	1984-85
5 (3ct,2st) K.S.More India v New Zealand	1987-88

MOST CATCHES IN A MATCH

4 Salim Malik Pakistan v New Zealand at Sialkot	1984-85
4 S.M.Gavaskar India v Pakistan at Sharjah	1984-85

ALL-ROUND

1,000 Runs and 100 Wickets

		M	R	W
I.T.Botham	(England)	95	1,693	116
R.J.Hadlee	(New Zealand)	108	1,601	148
Imran Khan	(Pakistan)	121	2,329	140
Kapil Dev	(India)	137	2808	160
Mudassar Nazar	(Pakistan)	121	2,607	111
R.J.Shastri	(India)	109	2,235	103

1,000 Runs and 100 Dismissals

		M	R	D
P.J.L.Dujon	(West Indies)	138	1,546	168
R.W.Marsh	(Australia)	91	1,220	123

HIGHEST INNINGS TOTAL

360-4 (50 overs)	West Indies v Sri Lanka	1987-88
338-5 (60 overs)	Pakistan v Sri Lanka	1983
334-4 (60 overs)	England v India	1975
333-8 (45 overs)	West Indies v India	1983-84
333-9 (60 overs)	England v Sri Lanka	1983
330-6 (60 overs)	Pakistan v Sri Lanka	1975
328-5 (60 overs)	Australia v Sri Lanka	1975

323-2 (50 overs)	Australia v Sri Lanka	1984-85
322-6 (60 overs)	England v New Zealand	1983
320-8 (55 overs)	England v Australia	1980
320-9 (60 overs)	Australia v India	1983

LOWEST INNINGS TOTALS

45 (40.3 overs)	Canada v England	1979
55 (28.3 overs)	Sri Lanka v West Indies	1986-87
63 (25.5 overs)	India v Australia	1980-81
64 (35.5 overs)	New Zealand v Pakistan	1985-86
70 (25.2 overs)	Australia v England	1977
70 (26.3 overs)	Australia v New Zealand	1985-86
74 (29 overs)	New Zealand v Australia	1981-82
78 (24.1 overs)	India v Sri Lanka	1986-87
79 (34.2 overs)	India v Pakistan	1978-79

FIRST WORLD CUP

Prudential 1975 : Results and Records

DAY	WINNER	LOSER	MARGIN	VENUE	MAN OF THE MATCH
June 7	England	India	202 runs	Lord's	Dennis Amiss
June 7	New Zealand	East Africa	181 runs	Edgbaston	Glen Turner
June 7	West Indies	Sri Lanka	9 wkts	Old Trafford	Bernard Julien
June 7	Australia	Pakistan	73 runs	Headingley	Dennis Lillee
June 11	India	East Africa	10 wkts	Headingley	Farokh Engineer
June 11	England	New Zealand	80 runs	Trent Bridge	Keith Fletcher
June 11	West Indies	Pakistan	1 wkt	Edgbaston	Sarfaraz Nawaz
June 11	Australia	Sri Lanka	52 runs	The Oval	Alan Turner
June 14	New Zealand	India	4 wkts	Old Trafford	Glenn Turner
June 14	England	East Africa	196 runs	Edgbaston	John Snow
June 14	West Indies	Australia	7 wkts	The Oval	Alvin Kallicharan
June 14	Pakistan	Sri Lanka	4 wkts	Trent Bridge	Zaheer Abbas
June 18	Australia	England	4 wkts	Headingley	Gary Gilmour
June 18	West Indies	New Zealand	5 wkts	The Oval	Alvin Kallicharan
June 21	West Indies	Australia	17 runs	Lord's	Clive Lloyd

HIGHEST TOTAL: 334 for 4 England v India (Lord's)
LOWEST TOTAL : 86 Sri Lanka v West Indies (Old Trafford)
TOP SCORE : 171 not out Glenn Turner for New Zealand v East Africa (Edgbaston)
BEST STAND : 182 (Ist wicket) McCosker and Alan Turner for Australia v Sri Lanka (The Oval)
BEST BOWLING : 6 for 14 Gary Gilmour for Australia v England (Headingley)

Prudential 1975 : The Leading Batting Averages

		M	I	N.O.	Runs	Highest	Av.
Glenn Turner	(NewZealand)	4	4	2	333	171 *	166.50
Sunil Gavaskar	(India)	3	3	2	113	65 *	113.00
Deryck Murry	(West Indies)	5	3	2	105	61 *	105.00
Majid Khan	(Pakistan)	3	3	-	209	84	69.66
Keith Fletcher	(England)	4	3	-	207	131	69.00
Dennis Amiss	(England)	4	4	-	243	137	60.75
Mike Denness	(England)	4	4	2	113	37 *	56.50
Ross Edwards	(Australia)	5	4	1	166	80 *	55.20
Rohan Kanhai	(West Indies)	5	4	2	109	55	54.50
Clive Lloyd	(West Indies)	5	3	-	158	102	52.66
Alvin Kallicharan	(West Indies)	5	5	1	197	78	49.25
Zaheer Abbas	(Pakistan)	3	3	-	136	97	40.33
Alan Turner	(Australia)	5	5	-	201	101	40.20

DENNIS LILLEE

THE LEADING BOWLING AVERAGES (Qualification :Minimum 5 wickets)

		Overs	Maidens	Runs	Wickets	Best	Average
Gary Gilmour	(Australia)	24	8	62	11	6 for 14	5.63
John Snow	(England)	36	8	65	6	4 for 11	10.82
Imran Khan	(Pakistan)	17.1	3	59	5	3 for 15	11.80
Chris Old	(England)	32.3	8	86	7	3 for 29	12.28
Tony Greig	(England)	31	2	89	6	4 for 45	14.83
Bernard Julien	(West Indies)	60	11	177	10	4 for 20	17.70
Peter Lever	(England)	36	3	92	5	3 for 32	18.40
Keith Boyce	(West Indies)	52	3	185	10	4 for 50	18.50
Abid Ali	(India)	36	7	115	6	2 for 22	19.16
Naseer Malik	(Pakistan)	30	5	98	5	2 for 37	19.60
Dayle Hadlee	(New Zealand)	46	5	162	8	3 for 21	20.25
Andy Roberts	(West Indies)	56.4	11	165	8	3 for 39	21.00
Sarfraz Nawaz	(Pakistan)	24	1	107	5	4 for 44	21.40
Richard Collinge	(New Zealand)	48	13	137	6	3 for 28	22.83
Dennis Lillee	(Australia)	53	7	223	8	5 for 34	27.87
Madan Lal	(India)	33.2	4	141	5	3 for 15	28.20
Hadley Howarth	(New Zealand)	40	5	148	5	3 for 29	29.60
Max Walker	(Australia)	57.2	10	210	6	3 for 22	35.00
Vanburn Holder	(West Indies)	43.2	4	184	5	3 for 30	36.80

Prudential 1975: Scoring Pattern

In 15 matches contested by eight countries in the 1975 Prudential World Cup Tournament,6,162 runs were scored off 1,573.2 overs for the loss of 208 wickets--an average of 29.62 runs per wicket and 3.91 runs per over.The countrywise break-up:

	Runs scored	Overs faced	Wickets lost	Runs per over	Runs per wicket
West Indies	999	226.31	26	4.41	38.42
Australia	1,166	261	38	4.46	30.68
England	983	216.2	25	4.54	39.32
New Zealand	886	231.1	31	3.83	28.58
Pakistan	801	173	23	4.63	34.82
India	485	149.5	13	3.23	37.30
Sri Lanka	500	147.3	24	3.38	20.83
East Africa	342	168	28	2.03	12.21
Total	6,162	1,573.2	208	3.91	29.62

MAJOR REFERENCE WORKS

WISDEN BOOK OF COUNTY CRICKET

WISDEN BOOK OF TEST CRICKET

WISDEN BOOK OF ONE DAY CRICKET

WISDEN ILLUSTRATED HISTORY OF CRICKET

VIV.RICHARD'S MASTER CLASS:VIV RICHARDS

BENSION & HEDGES WORLD SERIES CRICKET

BENSON & HEDGES CRICKET YEAR

SKILLS & RULES OF CRICKET : VIVEK THANI

CRICKET QUIZ : LOKESH THANI

YOUNG CRICKETER YEAR BOOK

BARRY RICHARD'S STORY

SANDY STORM: SANDEEP PATIL

THE STORY OF RELIANCE CUP

THE JOY OF CRICKET : J.BRIGHT

FROM BRADMAN TO BOYCOTT

THE WORLD OF ONE DAY CRICKET

HOW TO WIN AT CRICKET

CRICKET COLOURED ALBUM

WEST INDIES HISTORY OF CRICKET

SPORTS WEEK BOOK OF RELIANCE CUP

IAN BOTHAM: DON MOSEY

FIFTY YEARS IN CRICKET: LEN HUTTON

CRICKETERS WHO'S WHO 1988

BY GOD'S DECREE: KAPIL DEV

THE TEMPESTUOUS YEAR: RAY ILLINGWORTH

IDOLS : SUNIL GAVASKAR

CRICKET YEAR BOOK 1986

ONE DAY INTERNATIONAL CRICKET RECORDS

THE INDEPENDENT WORLD CUP CRICKET 1987